Foundations of

# Research Methods

*— for —*

# Social Workers

## A Critical Thinking Approach

Richard M. Grinnell, Jr

**Field Guide     Road Map     Workbook     Survival Guide**

Printed and bound in the United States of America by Pair Bond Publications LLC
© 2021 Pair Bond Publications, LLC.
ISBN: 978-0-9815100-9-5

Credits appear on pages 570–572 and represent an extension of the copyright page.

# Preface

Today's topic:

How to write a preface

"I'd like to preface my excuse of why I can't hand in my paper with a proclamation that I didn't pay attention and take notes in class, I didn't read the assigned chapters in my research book, and my social media apps are down."

**T**his book is for beginning social work students as their first introduction to basic social work research methodology. Our philosophy is to provide a very inexpensive, easily accessible, straightforward, "student-friendly" book that promotes the use of the scientific method of inquiry process to create knowledge for our profession—the most commonly used framework to generate relevant, valid, and reliable social work knowledge. We use a conversational style of writing in an effort to provide simple, reader-friendly content. Hopefully this will help students engage with the book in a relaxed, stress-free manner.

In a nutshell, our book is a primer, an introduction, a beginning. Our aim is to skim the surface of the research enterprise—to put a toe in the water, so to speak—and to give beginning social work students a taste of what it might be like to swim. Within this spirit, we have two goals, one major and one minor.

## MAJOR GOAL

**O**ur major goal is to provide basic social work research methodology. With the book's audience and philosophy in mind, we follow the traditional progression of the generic scientific method of inquiry process from beginning to end: finding a meaningful problem area to study, developing ethically and culturally sensitive research questions and hypotheses, measuring variables, selecting samples, constructing research designs, collecting and analyzing data, and writing reports.

We want students to understand and appreciate how the entire scientific method of inquiry process generates relevant knowledge for our profession, and how this knowledge helps them to become more effective social work practitioners.

## MINOR GOAL

**O**ur **minor goal** is to introduce students to the basic critical thinking process. To assist students in achieving our main goal we've integrated critical thinking concepts into all the chapters. That is, they are introduced at the end of Chapter 1 and subsequently are woven into the remaining chapters. As you know, and on a very basic level, the critical thinking process contains three fundamental steps:

**Step 1**  Ask questions

**Step 2**  Answer questions by reasoning them out

**Step 3**  Believe the results of the reasoning process

### THE APPENDIXES

Students can use the three appendixes (A, B, and C) at the back of this book to ask potential questions about what they read, see, and hear (Step 1 above). More specifically,

- **Appendixes A and B** provide a few basic "evaluative-type" questions students can ask to assess the overall credibility and usefulness of all kinds of "evidence" or "facts," or "knowledge" that are created by all five ways of knowing (see pages 11–17 and Figure P.1 on the following page). This knowledge can come from a worker's past experiences, agency traditions, a worker's intuition, various authority figures, and last but not least, from findings derived via research studies that used the scientific method of inquiry process (the main focus of this book).

  As we know, when evidence (in the form of findings or recommendations) is generated from research studies, more often than not they are practice/policy recommendations derived from quantitative studies (chapter 8 and appendix A), qualitative studies (chapter 9 and appendix B), or mixed-method studies (chapter 10 and appendixes A and B).

- **Appendix C** helps students gauge the authenticity and believability of any given website's author in addition to the information provided within the site itself.

> Instructions on how to use the three appendixes can be found on pages 468–473.

Thus, students will not only increase their knowledge of the social work research process (major goal) but will also begin to become comfortable with the very first step of the critical thinking process: asking questions about everything (minor goal)—a twofer, so to speak.

In the simplest of terms, our overall ambition is for students to understand and appreciate basic social work research methodology through a beginning critical thinking lens. Admittedly, this is a framework at best, but it does mark the beginning path to becoming a critical thinker.

## ENHANCING PROFESSIONAL JUDGMENTS

**A**s discussed on pages 20–27, the numerous professional judgments our graduates will make when they are in actual practice situations will be significantly enhanced by their critical thinking abilities. So a simple hypothesis could be formulated:

**Our Hypothesis**

Social workers' overall assessment of the trustworthiness and usefulness of any piece of "evidence" they come across (that was derived from any one of the five ways of knowing) increases the likelihood of the workers making good professional client-centered judgments—which in turn leads to good client outcomes.

We strongly believe that the only way a social worker can assess the trustworthiness and usefulness of any piece of evidence (practice/policy recommendation) is through the use of critical thinking skills. See Figure P.1 below for an oversimplified graphic display of our hypothesis.

## PRACTICALITY AND REALITY PREVAIL

**U**nnecessary information overload is avoided at all costs. Given our ever-changing student population, you as a social work research instructor could rightfully ask: What basic research concepts can I realistically teach within a one-semester social work research methods course where my students will fully grasp, digest, and appreciate the course's content in relation to how this content directly relates to their future practices? We believe the answer to this question is contained within the pages that follow.

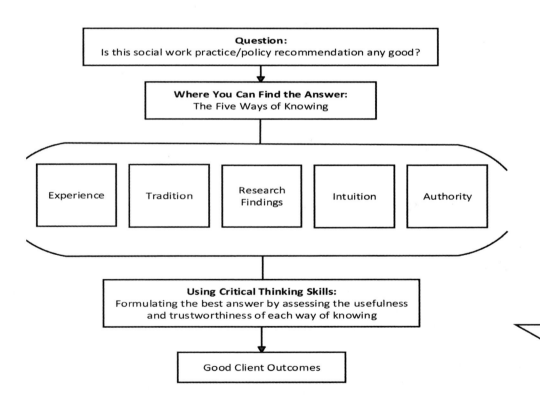

**Figure P.1**

The Book's Philosophy in a Nutshell

## STUDENT LEARNING OBJECTIVES

**I**n order to meet our major and minor goals we've formulated a few learning objectives students should be able to master by the end of their research course. These objectives are broken down into two of our non-mutually exclusive goals: research methodology (objectives 1–9) and critical thinking (objectives 10–12).

## MAJOR GOAL: RESEARCH METHODOLOGY

**1  Students will understand and appreciate the need to become accountable social work practitioners.**

**2  Students will understand and appreciate how using research findings—or "evidence," if you will—in their daily practice activities enhances their overall effectiveness as social work practitioners, which in turn will improve our profession's overall accountability.**

Where does this basic "evidence-based" content come from? The answer is simple: It's mostly obtained from social work research methods courses and books such as the one you're holding in your hands. On a side note, and more important, this evidence-based model of practice we're hearing so much about nowadays must be reinforced throughout all the courses within the entire social work curriculum, not just in the mandatory "research courses" that students are required (read *forced*) to take.

**3  Students will understand basic social work research methodology and how to do simple research studies using the scientific method of inquiry process.**

Students need to know the typical components that make up a research study. A study is only as good as the quality of its components, such as problem formulation, ethical and cultural considerations, measurement techniques, sampling methods, research design, data collection and analysis, and so forth. On a general level, most of the components included in basic research studies are the chapters in this book.

No matter how you slice it, dice it, peel it, cut it, chop it, break it, split it, squeeze it, crush it, or squash it, students need to know how valid and reliable evidence is created in the first place if they are to become successful *evidence-based* practitioners, *evidence-informed* practitioners, or practitioners who are implementing *evidence-based programs.*

**4  Students will understand and appreciate that evidence comes from many sources in all shapes, sizes, and forms.**

As can be seen in Figure P.1 on the previous page, we believe that social workers should strive to make professional client-related decisions that utilize all five ways of knowing. However, and at the present time, there has not been much discussion on how we can meaningfully integrate all the ways of knowing to form the "right practice decision."

We've spent the past four decades looking for a good framework (or rubric) of some kind that can effectively assess and integrate the trustworthiness of the evidence generated by each of the five ways of knowing when they are applied to simple, client-centered outcome variables that we, as social workers, wish to change (such as client depression, self-esteem, and anxiety levels, to name a few).

We anticipated that this five-prong "amalgamation of knowledge" approach would produce better evidence than simply using evidence from only one way of knowing. And here's the product of our efforts: We're still looking. Perhaps in another lifetime we'll find the answer. This book encourages students to ask and answer six basic

> We define "evidence" as anything that you see, experience, read, or are told that causes you to believe that something is true or has really happened.

| Box P.1 | Kellyanne Conway States the White House Has Its Own "Alternative Facts" |
|---------|--------------------------------------------------------------------------|

1  **Who said it?**
   Someone you know? Someone in a position of authority or power? Does it matter who told you this?

2  **What did they say?**
   Did they give facts or opinions? Did they provide all the facts? Did they leave anything out?

3  **Where did they say it?**
   Was it in public or in private? Did other people have a chance to respond and provide an alternative account?

4  **When did they say it?**
   Was it before, during, or after an important event? Is timing important?

5  **Why did they say it?**
   Did they explain the reasoning behind their opinion? Were they trying to make someone look good or bad? Would they benefit from the "fact"?

6  **How did they say it?**
   Were they happy or sad, angry or indifferent? Did they write it or say it? Could you understand what was said?

**NOTE:** Title of box taken from a phrase used by U.S. Counselor to the President Kellyanne Conway during a *Meet the Press* interview on January 22, 2017, in which she defended White House Press Secretary Sean Spicer's false statement about the attendance numbers of Donald Trump's inauguration as President of the United States.

generic questions about all the "facts" they will come across in their professional careers. Box P.1 above lists the six questions they should ask about any "fact" they come across. We stress that there is not such a thing as "alternative facts."

5  **Students will understand and appreciate how the three non-mutually exclusive research approaches (i.e., quantitative, qualitative, mixed-methods) can produce useful evidence for contemporary social work practice.**

We believe that students must thoroughly comprehend and appreciate, regardless of their professional interests, how the three complementary research approaches to knowledge generation produce evidence that helps them to become effective evidence-based practitioners. Thus, research in social work is presented as more than just a way to solve human problems, or to add to our existing knowledge base, or to guide evidence-based practice—although it's all of these.

6  **Students will be prepared to engage in three research roles after they graduate and become social work practitioners.**

Students will quickly realize that they will have a solid foundation of what they need to know when they:

- Actually implement research studies after graduation (knowledge creator and disseminator)
- Incorporate research findings within their daily practices (research consumer)
- Participate in research studies (research partner)

These three research roles are emphasized throughout the entire book. As contained in all the chapter openings, this book stresses that for students to become successful evidence-based practitioners, who make rational professional judgments, they have an ethical obligation to integrate at least one of the three research roles into their daily practice activities—especially the research consumer role. This is what evidence-based practice is all about. Evidence-based practitioners (or research consumers, if you will) incorporate evidence—only after they have evaluated its trustworthiness and usefulness, of course—into their daily practices when appropriate.

**7  Students will be prepared for advanced research courses and texts.**

Many beginning research courses first cover basic research methodology and then apply this content to more advanced research courses that specialize in single-subject designs or program evaluation. Accordingly, this book is designed to provide students with the basic methodological foundation they will need in order to obtain the advanced knowledge and skills presented in these two specialized advanced research courses.

**8  Students will fully understand and appreciate three of the Council on Social Work Education's 2015 EPAS main "research-type" competencies:**

**Competency 1**  Demonstrate Ethical and Professional Behavior

**Competency 4**  Engage in Practice-Informed Research and Research-Informed Practice

**Competency 9**  Evaluate Practice with Individuals, Families, Groups, Organizations, and Communities

**9  Students will know relevant material to successfully pass the "research content" contained within the various licensing exams after they graduate and become practitioners.**

## MINOR GOAL: CRITICAL THINKING

**10  Students will understand and appreciate how the beginning critical thinking process works and how to apply this process to help assess all types of evidence they may come across in their professional careers.**

Expanding on Number 4, various proclamations (aka "I've got the correct answers or facts") can spring up from a variety of sources such as social work supervisors, television news broadcasts, television commercials, clients, professors, Trump's tweets, books, fliers/brochures, magazines, neighbors next door, the Internet, social media, and, last but not least, from the results (or findings) of peer-reviewed research studies that are published in professional social work journals. As John Wodarski and Laura Hopson (2014) persuasively point out:

> In social work practice, critical thinking includes analyzing the state of the research evidence. When evaluating the quality of research findings, practitioners can focus on guiding questions for invoking critical thinking when examining various theories of practice:
>
> • What is the issue or claim being made, stated in simple and direct language?
>
> • Are there any ambiguities or a lack of clarity in the claim?
>
> • What are the underlying value and theory assumptions?
>
> • Is there indication of any misleading beliefs or faulty reasoning?
>
> • How good is the evidence presented?
>
> • Is any important information missing?

Students are taught that their use of critical thinking skills will increase the quality of their professional judgments, which in turn will increase the chances of their clients having successful outcomes.

- Is consideration given to alternative explanations?
- Are the conclusions reasonable?

To provide answers for these critical thinking questions, students have no other alternative but to learn what's involved in doing a typical research study.

**11 Students will understand and appreciate how to evaluate each component of a research study.**

Expanding on Number 3, students need to know how to assess the quality of all components of research studies by asking relevant and meaningful questions. Knowing what questions to ask will assist them to better assess the overall trustworthiness of a "research finding" or "evidence" they will hear and/or read about after graduation—particularly when it comes to the effectiveness of social work treatments or interventions. Some of the various questions they can ask are contained in the three appendixes.

**12 Students will understand and appreciate that they should not haphazardly incorporate any "evidence" into their daily practices without first questioning the overall credibility, practicality, and trustworthiness of that evidence.**

Expanding on Number 2, students will understand and appreciate that all evidence isn't created equal. We stress that they should never take any piece of evidence they come across as gospel—they have to evaluate what they find by using their critical thinking skills.

This book encourages students to use all five ways of knowing when making decisions of any kind, taking into account that the evidence produced by all five ways of knowing is only as good as the overall trustworthiness of the data, philosophies, rationales, and political and social motivations that generated these respective pieces of evidence in the first place (i.e., Box P.1 on page vii). They will learn that all five ways of knowing produce some form of evidence or proclamations. Each way of knowing just uses different methods to produce this respective evidence—some methods are good, some are bad, and some are just plain awful.

## ADDITIONAL HIGHLIGHTS

**This book:**

- Is the least expensive social work research methods book on the market today.
- Is written in conversational language in an effort not to intimidate students who may have a bit of anxiety about taking a research methods course for the first time.
- Provides a user-friendly, straightforward, unintimidating introduction to social work research methods, couched within the scientific method of inquiry—the most commonly used framework to generate relevant social work knowledge.
- Is easy to teach with and from.
- Constantly repeats concepts throughout the entire book. Instructors who have taught research courses for several years are acutely aware of the need to keep reemphasizing basic research concepts throughout the entire semester, such as validity and reliability, constants and variables, directional and nondirectional hypotheses, randomization and random assignment, internal and external validly, and conceptualization and operationalization, in addition to standardized and nonstandardized measuring instruments. Thus, major concepts have been carefully tied together not only within the chapters but across the chapters as well. The only

way students can really understand fundamental research concepts is for them to come across these concepts throughout the entire semester—via the chapters contained in this book.

- Discusses numerous ethical (chapter 5) and cultural (chapter 6) issues that can crop up when doing a research study.

- Includes human diversity content throughout all chapters. Many of the examples center around women and minorities, in recognition of the need for social workers to be knowledgeable about their special needs and problems.

- Contains numerous real-life social work examples throughout the entire book that demonstrate how research studies are done using the generalist practice framework in mind. These examples emphasize the link between practice and research in actual social work settings.

- Clearly illustrates throughout the entire book how social work research does not take place in a vacuum, and alerts students to the fact that their own ethnocentric perspectives might influence how they will do research studies, participate in research studies, or consume the findings of published research studies.

- Links the latest relevant 2015 CSWE EPAS Core Competencies within all chapters (see all the chapter openings). Every chapter addresses three of the competencies:

**Competency 1**   Demonstrate Ethical and Professional Behavior

**Competency 4**   Engage in Practice-Informed Research and Research-Informed Practice

**Competency 9**   Evaluate Practice with Individuals, Families, Groups, Organizations, and Communities

- Makes available to instructors numerous resources within the book's website (www. PairBondPublications.com).

## ORGANIZATION

**T**his book is neither a brief primer in social work research nor intended for use as a reference manual. It is organized in a way that makes good logical sense in teaching introductory research methods. Many other sequences that could be followed would make just as much sense, however. The chapters are consciously planned to be independent of one another. They can be read out of the order in which they are presented, or they can be selectively omitted. Its creative use is highly encouraged.

### PART I   THE CONTEXTS OF SOCIAL WORK RESEARCH

The main purpose of Part I is to introduce students to the contexts in which social work research studies take place. **Chapter 1** describes the place of research in social work and presents the various ways we obtain our knowledge base. It presents the research enterprise as a problem-solving process. **Chapter 2** then goes on to discuss how social work research problems and questions are formulated in the first place. It simply addresses the question, "Where do research questions and hypotheses come from?"

Now that students understand the place of research in social work and know how to formulate meaningful and useful research questions, **Chapter 3** introduces students to the concept of evidence-based practice and the three research roles the students will engage in after they graduate. **Chapter 4** discusses how literature reviews are used in formulating research questions and in the evidence-based practice process.

Students also need to understand how to actually perform a research study in an ethically and culturally sensitive manner. Thus, Part I contains **Chapter 5** on how to do a social work research study in an ethical manner and **Chapter 6** on how to work with minority and disadvantaged groups.

## PART II    APPROACHES TO KNOWLEDGE DEVELOPMENT

With the research question in hand, the following chapters present different research approaches that can be used to answer research questions or to test hypotheses that were generated in Chapter 2. This part starts off with **Chapter 7** on discussing what the scientific method of discovery is all about and how it's used to generate objective research findings. The next three chapters discuss the three different research approaches to knowledge development: the quantitative research approach (**chapter 8**), the qualitative research approach (**chapter 9**), and the mixed-method research approach (**chapter 10**).

## PART III    MEASUREMENT

**Chapter 11** discusses measurement validity and reliability, and **Chapter 12** describes how to find and evaluate the validity and reliability of the various standardized measuring instruments that are most often used in social work research and practice situations alike.

## PART IV    SAMPLING AND RESEARCH DESIGNS

Now that students know how to measure variables via the two chapters in the preceding part, the purpose of Part IV is to introduce them to two of the nuts and bolts of the scientific method of inquiry process: sampling and research designs. The next three chapters in this part focus on *sampling—* probability and nonprobability (**chapter 13**); *single-subject designs—* exploratory, descriptive, and explanatory (**chapter 14**); and *group research designs—*exploratory, descriptive, and explanatory (**chapter 15**).

## PART V    COLLECTING AND ANALYZING DATA

The purpose of Part V is to provide students with a basic understanding of how to collect data for either a single-subject design or a group design. Once the data are collected via the guidelines presented in **Chapters 16** and **17,** it's time to analyze them. So Part V consists of two introductory data analysis chapters: *analysis of quantitative data—*descriptive and inferential statistics (**chapter 18**); and *analysis of qualitative data—*first- and second-level coding. Then we look for meaningful relationships (**chapter 19**).

## PART VI    RESEARCH PROPOSALS AND REPORTS

The final two chapters discuss how to write quantitative research proposals and reports (**chapter 20**) and qualitative research proposals and reports (**chapter 21**)—the first (proposal) and last (report) steps of the research process.

## APPENDIXES    ASKING QUESTIONS

In relation to Step 1 of the critical thinking process, Appendixes A and B contain potential questions students can ask about any given research finding they come across. More specifically, **Appendix A** lists a few questions for evaluating *quantitative* studies, and **Appendix B** lists questions for evaluating *qualitative* ones. Students can also use **Appendix C** to gauge the authenticity, legitimacy, and overall believability of the content found within any given website in addition to the author's credibility.

## A FINAL WORD

**I**t is hoped that the apparent levity with which we've treated basic research methodology is accepted in the same spirit as it was intended (yes, cartoons and all). Our goal was not to diminish research but to present the scientific method of inquiry process (major goal) and critical thinking process (minor goal) with warmth and humanness so that our students' first experience with it will be a positive one. After all, if wetting their big toes scares them, they will never learn to swim.

The field of research in our profession is continuing to grow and develop. We believe this book will contribute to that growth. We are anticipating a second edition, and suggestions for it are more than welcome. Please e-mail your comments directly to: rick.grinnell@wmich.edu.

Richard M. Grinnell, Jr.

# Contents in Brief

"This one holds all your music, digital photos, movies, and the entire contents of your brain."

**PART I** Contexts of Social Work Research  1

1  Toward Accountability  2
2  Research Questions  30
3  Toward Evidence-Based Practice  56
4  Literature Reviews  76
5  Research Ethics  92
6  Culturally Competent Research  118

**PART II** Knowledge Development  137

7  The Scientific Method of Inquiry  138
8  The Quantitative Research Approach  160
9  The Qualitative Research Approach  184
10  The Mixed-Methods Research Approach  210

**PART III** Measuring Variables  209

11  Measurement  210
12  Measuring Instruments  234

**PART IV** Sampling and Research Designs  249

13  Sampling  250
14  Single-Subject Designs  268
15  Group Designs  292

**PART V** Collecting and Analyzing Data  329

16  Collecting Data  330
17  Selecting a Data-Collection Method  366
18  Analyzing Quantitative Data  382
19  Analyzing Qualitative Data  404

**PART VI** Research Proposals and Reports  425

20  Quantitative Proposals and Reports  426
21  Qualitative Proposals and Reports  446

**APPENDIXES** Asking Questions  467

How to Use the Appendixes  468
A  Evaluating Quantitative Studies  474
B  Evaluating Qualitative Studies  495
C  Evaluating Internet Resources  511

Glossary  523
Credits  570
References and Further Readings  573
Index  582

# Contents in Detail

"How can I possibly provide more details about your grade when your report doesn't have any content?"

**PART I   CONTEXTS OF SOCIAL WORK RESEARCH  1**

**Chapter 1   Toward Accountability  2**
RESEARCH AND ACCOUNTABILITY  5
   Council on Social Work Education  6
   National Association of Social Workers  7
THIS BOOK'S OBJECTIVES  7
   This Book's Philosophy  8
THE PURPOSES OF RESEARCH IN SOCIAL WORK  8
PURE AND APPLIED RESEARCH STUDIES  9
   Pure Research Studies  9
   Applied Research Studies  10
WAYS OF KNOWING  11
   Authority  12
      *Where Does "Credible Evidence" Come From?  13*
   Tradition  14
      *That's the Way It's Done Around Here  14*
      *The Need to "Fit In"  15*
   Experience  15
   Beliefs and Intuition  16
      *Professional Ethical Concerns  16*
   Research Findings  17

*A Toothy Dilemma  17*

THE PROCESS OF THE SCIENTIFIC METHOD  18
  Is Everything Observable and Measurable?  19
  Nothing Is Absolutely Certain Forever  19
  Example of the Scientific Inquiry Process  19
    *Phase 1: Observing and/or Measuring  19*
    *Phase 2: Assuming  20*
    *Phase 3: Testing  20*
    *Phase 4: Revising  21*
FORMING PROFESSIONAL JUDGMENTS  21
  Having a Solid Knowledge and Skills Base  21
  Using Critical Thinking Skills  21
    *Definition of Critical thinking  22*
    *Beginning Steps of the Critical Thinking Process  23*
    *What Activities Does a Critical Thinker Do?  24*
    *Hints to Help You to Become a Critical Thinker  25*
  Using the Three Appendixes  25
    *Get Acquainted with the Three Appendixes  27*
    *Don't Get Intimidated  27*
    *Is There a Standard Evaluation Rubric?  27*
CHAPTER RECAP  27  /  REVIEW EXERCISES  28

**Chapter 2  Research Questions  30**
RESEARCH QUESTIONS AND ACCOUNTABILITY  33
  Social Problems Must Be Changeable  34
FACTORS AFFECTING RESEARCH QUESTIONS  34
  The Social Work Program  34
  The Researcher  35
    *Value Systems of the Researchers  37*
  Ethical and Cultural Considerations  38
  Political and Social Considerations  38
THE KNOWLEDGE-LEVEL CONTINUUM  39
  Exploratory Research Studies  41
  Descriptive Research Studies  42
  Explanatory Research Studies  43
EVIDENCE-BASED HIERARCHY  44
CLASSIFICATIONS OF QUESTIONS  47
  Existence Questions  47
  Composition Questions  49
  Relationship Questions  49
  Descriptive-Comparative Questions  49
  Causality Questions  49
  Causality-Comparative Questions  49
  Causality-Comparative Interaction Questions  50

CRITERIA FOR GOOD QUESTIONS  50
    Relevant  52
    Researchable  52
    Feasible  52
    Ethical and Culturally Sensitive  53
EVALUATING A STUDY'S RESEARCH QUESTION  53
    Use the Appendixes  53
        *Tasks  53*
CHAPTER RECAP  54  /  REVIEW EXERCISES  54

**Chapter 3   Toward Evidence-Based Practice  56**
ARE THESE RESEARCH FINDINGS FOR REAL?  59
    What's Up with These Research Findings?  60
        *Dilemma Solved  60*
DO YOU HAVE WHAT IT TAKES?  61
    Are You Aware of Your Values?  61
    Are You Skeptical?  61
    Do You Share Your Stuff with Others?  62
    Are You Honest?  62
    Got Attitude?  62
        *Using the Internet Café  63*
        *Thinking Logically, Completely, and Fairly  63*
THREE RESEARCH ROLES  63
    The Research Consumer  64
    The Creator and Disseminator of Research  65
    The Contributing Partner  65
INTEGRATING THE THREE RESEARCH ROLES  66
RESEARCH AND PRACTICE  67
EVIDENCE-BASED PRACTICE  68
DEFINITION OF SOCIAL WORK RESEARCH  72
COMMITTING TO LIFELONG LEARNING  72
CHAPTER RECAP  73  /  REVIEW EXERCISES  73

**Chapter 4   Literature Reviews  76**
WHAT'S A LITERATURE REVIEW?  79
THE LOGIC OF DOING LITERATURE REVIEWS  81
    Brings Clarity and Focus to the Question  81
    Identifies Gaps in the Literature  82
    Prevents the Duplication of Knowledge  82
    Broadens Our Knowledge Base  82
    Contextualizes the Research Project  82
    Improves a Study's Methodology  83
    Assists in Identifying Opposing Views  83
WHERE AND HOW TO SEARCH FOR INFORMATION  83
    The Internet  84

STORING AND MANAGING INFORMATION 84
READING FOR A LITERATURE REVIEW 84
    Preview 85
    Overview 85
    Inview 85
DEVELOPING A THEORETICAL FRAMEWORK 86
WRITING AND ORGANIZING A LITERATURE REVIEW 87
CRITERIA OF A GOOD LITERATURE REVIEW 89
    Evaluating a Literature Review 90
        *Use the Appendixes 90*
CHAPTER RECAP 90 / REVIEW EXERCISES 90

**Chapter 5 Research Ethics 92**
WHY ARE RESEARCH ETHICS IMPORTANT? 95
USING CLIENTS AS RESEARCH PARTICIPANTS 95
OBTAINING INFORMED CONSENT 96
    Bribery and Deception 97
    Elements of an Informed Consent Form 98
        *Consent versus Assent Forms 98*
ANONYMITY VERSUS CONFIDENTIALITY 99
    Ensuring Confidentiality 99
DESIGNING A STUDY IN AN ETHICAL MANNER 99
    Step 1: Develop the Research Question 100
        *Refine the Research Question 100*
        *Evaluate the Literature 101*
    Step 2: Select a Research Approach 102
    Step 3: Measurement of Variables 102
        *Be Aware of Cultural Issues 102*
    Step 4: Select a Sample 103
        *Recruitment 104*
    Step 5: Select a Research Design 105
        *Beneficence 106*
        *Equipoise, or the Uncertainty Principle 106*
        *Deception 106*
    Step 6: Select a Data-Collection Method 108
        *How Data Are Collected 108*
        *Who's Going to Collect the Data? 109*
        *Frequency and Timing of Data Collection 109*
    Step 7: Analyze the Data 109
    Step 8: Disseminate the Research Report 110
ETHICS AND OUR SOCIAL SERVICE PROGRAMS 111
    Misuses of Research Results112
        *Justifying Decisions Already Made 112*
        *Safeguarding Public Relations 113*
        *Appraising Staff Performance 113*

*Fulfilling Funding Requirements  113*
EVALUATING A STUDY'S ETHICAL CONDUCT  114
   Use the Appendixes  114
      *Tasks  114*
CHAPTER RECAP  114  /  REVIEW EXERCISES  115

**Chapter 6   Culturally Competent Research   116**
OUR VILLAGE  119
   Working with Stakeholders/Research Teams  120
THE IMPACT OF CULTURE  121
BRIDGING THE CULTURE GAP122
   Cultural Awareness  122
      *Ethnocentrism  123*
      *Enculturation  123*
   Intercultural Communication  123
      *Nonverbal Communication  124*
      *Verbal Communication  124*
CRITICAL THINKING AND THE CULTURE GAP  125
CULTURAL FRAMEWORKS  126
   Orientation to Data  126
   Decision Making  127
   Individualism  127
   Tradition  128
   Pace of Life  129
CULTURALLY COMPETENT RESEARCHERS  129
   Cultural Awareness  130
   Intercultural Communication Skills  131
   Specific Knowledge about the Culture  131
   Appropriately Adapting Research Studies  132
      *Working with Stakeholders  132*
      *Adapting Processes  133*
      *Providing Meaningful Products  134*
EVALUATING A RESEARCH STUDY'S ADHERENCE TO CULTURAL COMPETENCY ISSUES  134
   Use the Appendixes  134
CHAPTER RECAP  135  /  REVIEW EXERCISES  135

**PART II**  APPROACHES TO KNOWLEDGE DEVELOPMENT  137

**Chapter 7   The Scientific Method of Inquiry   138**
WHICH RESEARCH APPROACH IS BEST?  141
   Selecting a Research Approach  142
THE QUANTITATIVE RESEARCH APPROACH  145
   What Is the Positivistic Way of Thinking?  146
      *Striving toward Measurability  146*
      *Striving toward Objectivity  147*
      *Striving toward Duplication  147*

*Striving toward the Use of Standardized Procedures 148*
THE QUALITATIVE RESEARCH APPROACH 149
What Is the Interpretive Way of Thinking? 149
*One Reality versus Many 150*
*Subjects versus Research Participants 150*
*Researchers' Values 151*
*Commonalities of All Qualitative Research Studies 151*
THE MIXED-METHODS RESEARCH APPROACH 153
USING BOTH APPROACHES IN A SINGLE STUDY 155
What Do You Really Want to Know? 155
*Example 156*
EVALUATING A RESEARCH STUDY 156
Use the Appendixes 158
*Let's Get Reacquainted 158*
CHAPTER RECAP 158 / REVIEW EXERCISES 158

**Chapter 8   The Quantitative Research Approach   160**
STEPS OF THE QUANTITATIVE RESEARCH APPROACH 163
STEP 1: IDENTIFYING THE RESEARCH PROBLEM 163
STEP 2: SELECTING SPECIFIC VARIABLES 164
Substep 2a: What Have Others Found? 164
Substep 2b: Refining the General Problem Area 165
Substep 2c: Developing Concepts 165
*Concepts 165*
Substep 2d: Identifying Variables 166
Substep 2e: Defining Attributes of Variables 166
Substep 2f: Defining Variables 169
*No Independent or Dependent Variables 169*
Substep 2g: Constructing a Hypothesis 170
*Nondirectional Hypotheses 170*
*Directional Hypotheses 170*
Substep 2h: Evaluating the Hypothesis 171
*Relevance 171*
*Completeness 171*
*Specificity 172*
*Potential for Testing 172*
*Ethically and Culturally Sensitive 172*
STEP 3: DESIGNING THE STUDY 172
Substep 3a: Measuring Variables 173
Substep 3b: Sample and Research Design 173
Substep 3c: Ethical and Cultural Issues 173
STEP 4: COLLECTING THE DATA 173
STEP 5: ANALYZING THE DATA 174
Descriptive Statistics 174
Inferential Statistics 175

STEP 6: INTERPRETING THE FINDINGS  175

    Substep 6a: Comparing Results  176

    Substep 6b: Study's Limitations  176

STEP 7: DISSEMINATING THE STUDY'S FINDINGS  176

AN EXTENDED EXAMPLE  176

    What's the Problem?  176

    Formulating Initial Impressions  177

    Determining What Others Have Found  177

    Refining the General Problem Area  177

    Measuring the Variables  178

    Selecting a Sample  178

    Addressing Ethical and Cultural Issues  179

    Collecting the Data  179

    Analyzing the Data  179

    Interpreting the Data  180

    Comparing Results  180

    Specifying the Study's Limitations  180

    Disseminating the Study's Results  181

EVALUATING QUANTITATIVE RESEARCH STUDIES  181

    Use Appendix A  181

CHAPTER RECAP  181  /  REVIEW EXERCISES  182-

**Chapter 9   The Qualitative Research Approach   184**

QUANTITATIVE VERSES QUALITATIVE APPROACHES  187

PHASES OF THE QUALITATIVE RESEARCH APPROACH  188

    Phases 1 & 2: Problem Identification and Question Formulation  188

    Phase 3a: Designing the Research Study  189

    Phase 3b: Collecting the Data  189

    Phases 3c & 3d: Analyzing and Interpreting Data  190

        *Numbers versus Words  190*

        *Data ≠ Information  190*

    Phases 4 & 5: Presentation and Dissemination of Findings  191

COMPARING RESEARCH APPROACHES  191

ADVANTAGES AND DISADVANTAGES  192

EVALUATING QUALITATIVE RESEARCH STUDIES  193

    Use Appendix B  194

CHAPTER RECAP  194  /  REVIEW EXERCISES  194

**Chapter 10   The Mixed-Methods Research Approach   196**

POPULARITY OF THE APPROACH  199

    An Intuitive Research Method  200

    An Accessible Approach to Scientific Inquiry  200

RESEARCH PROBLEMS AND MIXED METHODS  200

    One Data Source May Be Insufficient  201

        *Example  201*

Explain a Study's Initial Results  202
  *Example  202*
Generalize Exploratory Findings  202
  *Example  202*
Enhance a Study  203
  *Example  203*
Employ a Theoretical Stance  203
  *Example  203*
Understand a Research Objective  203
  *Example  204*
ADVANTAGES  204
CHALLENGES  205
Skills of the Researcher  205
  *Quantitative Skills  205*
  *Qualitative Skills  206*
  *Solid Grounding in Mixed-Methods Research  206*
Time and Resources  206
CONVINCING OTHERS  207
FINDING MIXED-METHODS RESEARCH STUDIES  207
CHAPTER RECAP  208  /  REVIEW EXERCISES  208

**PART III**  MEASURING VARIABLES  209

**Chapter 11  Measurement  209**
LEVELS OF MEASUREMENT  213
Nominal Measurement  214
Ordinal Measurement  214
Interval Measurement  215
Ratio Measurement  215
DESCRIBING VARIABLES BY MEASURING THEM  216
Correspondence  217
Standardization  217
Quantification  217
Duplication  217
CRITERIA FOR SELECTING AN INSTRUMENT  219
Utility  219
Sensitivity to Small Changes  220
Nonreactivity  220
Reliability  221
  *Test-Retest Method  221*
  *Alternate-Form Method  222*
  *Split-Half Method  223*
  *Observer Reliability  223*
Validity  224
  *Content Validity  224*

          *Criterion Validity   224*
               Concurrent   225
               Predictive   225
          *Face Validity   225*
          *Construct Validity   225*
RELIABILITY AND VALIDITY REVISITED   227
MEASUREMENT ERRORS   227
     Constant Errors   227
     Random Errors   228
IMPROVING VALIDITY AND RELIABILITY   230
EVALUATING THE MEASUREMENT OF VARIABLES   231
     Use Appendix A   231
CHAPTER RECAP   231  /  REVIEW EXERCISES   231

**Chapter 12   Measuring Instruments   234**
QUESTIONS TO ASK BEFORE MEASURING   237
     Why Do We Want to Make the Measurement?   238
     What Do We Want to Measure?   238
     Who Will Make the Measurement?   239
     What Format Do We Require?   239
     Where Will the Measurement Be Made?   240
     When Will the Measurement Be Made?   240
TYPES OF MEASURING INSTRUMENTS   242
     Journals or Diaries   242
     Logs   243
     Inventories   243
     Checklists   243
     Summative Instruments   244
STANDARDIZED MEASURING INSTRUMENTS   244
     Advantages and Disadvantages   245
     Locating Measuring Instruments   246
          *Commercial or Professional Publishers   246*
          *Professional Books and Journals   246*
EVALUATING MEASURING INSTRUMENTS   247
CHAPTER RECAP   247  /  REVIEW QUESTIONS   248

**PART IV**  SAMPLING AND RESEARCH DESIGNS   249

**Chapter 13   Sampling   250**
POPULATIONS AND SAMPLING FRAMES   254
     Sampling Frames   254
SAMPLING PROCEDURES   254
     Probability Sampling   255
          *Simple Random Sampling   255*
          *Systematic Random Sampling   256*
          *Stratified Random Sampling   257*

*Cluster Random Sampling  258*

Nonprobability Sampling  259

*Availability Sampling  260*

*Purposive Sampling  260*

*Quota Sampling  260*

*Snowball Sampling  261*

SAMPLE SIZE  262

Lessons about Sample Quality  263

ADVANTAGES AND DISADVANTAGES  264

EVALUATING RESEARCH SETTINGS AND SAMPLES  265

Research Settings  265

Samples  266

CHAPTER RECAP  266  /  REVIEW EXERCISES  266

## Chapter 14   Single-Subject Designs   268

WHAT ARE SINGLE-SUBJECT DESIGNS?  271

THE RESEARCH PROCESS  272

UNIT OF ANALYSIS  273

REQUIREMENTS  273

Setting Measurable Client Objectives  274

*Target Problems  274*

Selecting Outcome Measures  275

Graphically Displaying the Data  276

EXPLORATORY DESIGNS  276

*A* Design  278

*B* Design  279

*BB$_1$* Design  281

*BC* Design  281

DESCRIPTIVE DESIGNS  282

*AB* Design  282

*ABC* and *ABCD* Designs  283

EXPLANATORY DESIGNS  284

Reversal Designs  284

ABA *and* ABAB *Designs  284*

BAB *Design  285*

BCBC *Design  286*

Multiple-Baseline Designs  286

*More Than One Case  286*

*More Than One Setting  289*

*More Than One Problem  289*

RETROSPECTIVE BASELINES  289

CHAPTER RECAP  291  /  REVIEW EXERCISES  291

**Chapter 15  Group Designs  292**
KNOWLEDGE LEVELS  295
CHARACTERISTICS OF "IDEAL" EXPERIMENTS  296
　　Controlling the Time Order of Variables  296
　　Manipulating the Independent Variable  297
　　Establishing Relationships between Variables  297
　　Controlling Rival Hypotheses  297
　　Holding Extraneous Variables Constant  298
　　　　*Using Correlated Variation  299*
　　　　*Using Analysis of Covariance  299*
　　　　*Using a Control Group  299*
　　Randomly Assigning Participants to Groups  300
　　　　*Matched-Pairs Method  300*
CLASSIFYING GROUP RESEARCH DESIGNS  301
ONE-GROUP DESIGNS  302
　　One-Group Posttest-Only Design  302
　　Cross-Sectional Survey Design  304
　　Longitudinal Designs  305
　　　　*Trend Studies  305*
　　　　*Cohort Studies  307*
　　　　*Panel Studies  308*
　　One-Group Pretest-Posttest Design  311
INTERNAL VALIDITY  312
　　History  313
　　Maturation  314
　　Testing Effects  315
　　Instrumentation Error  315
　　Statistical Regression  315
　　Differential Selection of Participants  316
　　Mortality  316
　　Reactive Effects of Research Participants  317
　　Interaction Effects  317
　　Relations between Groups  318
　　　　*Diffusion of Treatments  318*
　　　　*Compensatory Equalization  318*
　　　　*Compensatory Rivalry  318*
　　　　*Demoralization  318*
TWO-GROUP DESIGNS  319
　　Comparison Group Pretest-Posttest Design  319
　　Comparison Group Posttest-Only Design  320
　　Classical Experimental Design  321
　　Randomized Posttest-Only Control Group Design  322
EXTERNAL VALIDITY  323
　　Selection-Treatment Interaction  323

Specificity of Variables  323

Multiple-Treatment Interference  324

Researcher Bias  324

EVALUATING RESEARCH DESIGNS  324

Use the Appendixes  325

CHAPTER RECAP  325  /  REVIEW EXERCISES  325

**PART V**  COLLECTING AND ANALYZING DATA  329

**Chapter 16   Collecting Data   330**

DATA COLLECTION METHODS AND SOURCES  333

TYPES OF DATA  333

Firsthand Data versus Secondhand Data  324

Original Data versus Existing Data  324

Quantitative Data versus Qualitative Data  334

QUANTITATIVE DATA-COLLECTION METHODS  335

Survey Questionnaires  335

*Establishing Data Collection Procedures  337*

*Recording Survey Data  337*

*Establishing Reliability and Validity  338*

Structured Observations  341

*Establishing Data Collection Procedures  342*

*Recording Structured Observational Data  343*

*Establishing Reliability and Validity  343*

*Advantages and Disadvantages  344*

Secondary Data  346

*Establishing Data Collection Procedures  346*

*Recording Secondary Data  347*

*Establishing Reliability and Validity  347*

*Advantages and Disadvantages  348*

Existing Statistics  350

*Example of Using Existing Statistics  350*

*Establishing Data Collection Procedures  351*

*Recording Existing Statistical Data  351*

*Establishing Reliability and Validity  351*

*Advantages and Disadvantages  352*

QUALITATIVE DATA-COLLECTION METHODS  352

Narrative interviewing  353

*Establishing Data Collection Procedures  353*

*Recording Narrative Data  354*

*Trustworthiness and Truth-Value of Narrative Data  355*

*Advantages and Disadvantages  356*

Participant Observation  356

*Establishing Procedures to Collect Data  356*

*Recording Participant Observational Data  357*

*Trustworthiness and Truth-Value  358*

*Advantages and Disadvantages  358*

Secondary Content Data  358

*Establishing Procedures  359*

*Recording  359*

*Establishing the Trustworthiness and Truth-Value  359*

*Advantages and Disadvantages  359*

Historical Data  359

*Establishing Procedures to Collect Data  360*

*Recording  360*

*Establishing the Trustworthiness and Truth-Value  361*

*Advantages and Disadvantages  361*

Mixed-Method Data-Collection Methods  361

EVALUATING A DATA COLLECTION PLAN  362

Use the Appendixes  362

CHAPTER RECAP  362  /  REVIEW EXERCISES  363


**Chapter 17   Selecting a Data-Collection Method   366**

DATA COLLECTION VIA THE RESEARCH PROCESS  369

Selecting a Topic and Research Question  369

Designing the Study and Collecting Data  370

Analyzing and Interpreting the Data  371

*Example  372*

Presentation and Dissemination of Findings  372

SELECTING A DATA-COLLECTION METHOD  372

Size  373

Scope  373

Program Participation  374

Worker Cooperation  374

Intrusion into Research Participants' Lives  375

Resources  375

Time  376

Data-Collection Methods Used in Previous Studies  376

EXAMPLE: SELECTING A DATA-COLLECTION METHOD  376

TRYING OUT THE METHOD  377

IMPLEMENTATION AND EVALUATION  380

Implementation  380

Evaluation  380

CHAPTER RECAP  381  /  REVIEW EXERCISES  381


**Chapter 18   Analyzing Quantitative Data   382**

ENTERING DATA INTO COMPUTERS  385

DESCRIPTIVE STATISTICS  386

Frequency Distributions  388

Measures of Central Tendency  390

*Mode  391*

*Median  392*

*Mean  392*

Measures of Variability  392

*Range  392*

*Standard Deviation  392*

INFERENTIAL STATISTICS  395

Statistics That Determine Associations  395

*Chi-Square  396*

*Correlation  397*

Statistics That Determine Differences  398

*Dependent t-Tests  398*

*Independent t-Tests  399*

*Analysis of Variance  400*

EVALUATING A QUANTITATIVE ANALYSIS  401

CHAPTER RECAP  401  /  REVIEW EXERCISES  401

**Chapter 19   Analyzing Qualitative Data  404**

PURPOSE OF QUALITATIVE DATA ANALYSIS  407

Checking Your Biases at the Door  408

PHASE 1: PLANNING THE ANALYSIS  409

Step 1: Transcribe the Data  409

*Task 1a: Select a Computer Program  409*

*Task 1b: Transcribe the Data  409*

Step 2: Establishing Rules for the Analysis  410

*Task 2a: Preview the Data  411*

*Task 2b: Keep a Journal  411*

PHASE 2: DOING THE ANALYSIS  412

Step 3: Doing First-Level Coding  412

*Task 3a: Identify Meaning Units  412*

*Task 3b: Create Categories  412*

*Task 3c: Assign Codes to Categories  413*

*Task 3d: Refine Categories  414*

Step 4: Doing Second-Level Coding  

*Task 4a: Comparing Categories  415*

PHASE 3: LOOKING FOR MEANING  415

Step 5: Interpreting Data and Building Theory  416

*Task 5a: Developing Conceptual Classifications Systems  416*

*Task 5b: Presenting Themes or Theory  417*

Step 6: Assessing the Results  418

*Task 6a: Establishing Our Own Credibility  418*

*Task 6b: Establishing the Dependability of the Data  418*

*Task 6c: Establishing Our Control of Biases  419*

EVALUATING YOUR DATA ANALYSIS PLAN  420

EVALUATING A QUALITATIVE ANALYSIS  423

CHAPTER RECAP  423  /  REVIEW EXERCISES  424

**PART VI**  RESEARCH PROPOSALS AND REPORTS  425

**Chapter 20   Quantitative Proposals and Reports   426**
WRITING QUANTITATIVE RESEARCH PROPOSALS  429
    Part 1: Research Topic  430
    Part 2: Literature Review  431
    Part 3: Conceptual Framework  431
    Part 4: Research Question or Hypothesis  432
    Part 5: Methodology  432
        *Part 5a: Research Design  432*
        *Part 5b: Operational Definitions  433*
        *Part 5c: Population and Sample  435*
        *Part 5d: Data Collection  436*
        *Part 5e: Data Analysis  436*
    Part 6: Limitations  436
    Part 7: Administration  437
WRITING QUANTITATIVE RESEARCH REPORTS  437
    Part 1: Problem  438
    Part 2: Method  439
    Part 3: Findings  440
    Part 4: Discussion  442
        *Limitations  442*
CHAPTER RECAP  443  /  REVIEW EXERCISES  443

**Chapter 21   Qualitative Proposals and Reports   446**
WRITING QUALITATIVE RESEARCH PROPOSALS  449
    Purpose of Writing a Proposal  449
    Intended Audience  450
    Content and Writing Style  451
ORGANIZING THE RESEARCH PROPOSAL  451
    Part 1: Research Topic  451
    Part 2: Literature Review  451
    Part 3: Conceptual Framework  452
    Part 4: Questions and Hypotheses  453
    Part 5: Operational Definitions  453
    Part 6: Research Design  455
    Part 7: Population and Sample  456
    Part 8: Data Collection  458
    Part 9: Data Analysis  459
    Part 10: Limitations  460
    Part 11: Administration  462
WRITING QUALITATIVE RESEARCH REPORTS  462
    Abstract  463
    Introduction  463

Method  464

Analysis and Findings  464

Discussion  465

References  466

CHAPTER RECAP  466  /  REVIEW EXERCISES  466

**APPENDIXES  476**

How to Use the Three Appendixes  468

**A**  Evaluating Quantitative Studies  474

**B**  Evaluating Qualitative Studies  495

**C**  Evaluating Internet Resources  511


Glossary  523

Credits  570

References and Further Readings  573

Index  582

# CONTEXTS OF SOCIAL WORK RESEARCH

**CHAPTER 1:** Toward Accountability    **2**

**CHAPTER 2:** Research Questions    **30**

**CHAPTER 3:** Toward Evidence-Based Practice    **56**

**CHAPTER 4:** Literature Reviews    **76**

**CHAPTER 5:** Research Ethics    **92**

**CHAPTER 6:** Culturally Competent Research    **116**

# 1
CHAPTER

## 2015 EPAS COMPETENCIES

| COMPETENCY 1 | Demonstrate Ethical and Professional Behavior |
|---|---|

You will learn that in order to be a successful evidence-based practitioner you have an ethical obligation to integrate three research roles into your daily practice activities as discussed in Chapter 3: (1) research consumer, (2) research partner—either as a co-researcher or research participant, and (3) creator and disseminator of research (or knowledge).

    This entire chapter pertains to these three professional roles in that you'll learn that one of the best ways to help you become an ethical and professional evidence-based social work practitioner is knowing how our profession's knowledge base is best generated through "objective" research studies; that is, you have an ethical obligation to fully understand and appreciate how objective social work research studies can produce reliable and valid "practice implications" for our profession.

| COMPETENCY 4 | Engage in Practice-Informed Research and Research-Informed Practice |
|---|---|

Competency 4 also pertains to the entire chapter because you have to:

1   Evaluate the degree of objectivity that a social work research study has obtained, given the needs of the study's specific population or research participants (**research consumer**—research-informed practice);

2   Participate in a research study—either as a co-researcher or research participant (**research partner**—practice-informed research). See 1 above and 3 below; and

3   Know how to design a research study that is as objective as possible before you actually start the study (**creator and disseminator of research**—practice-informed research).

    You also need to utilize evidence-based practice recommendations whenever possible; that is, you need to integrate (1) the best available research-based evidence with (2) your clinical expertise and (3) your client's values.

    All of the above implies you'll need to know how objective a research study actually was that produced the research-based evidence. In short, you need to ask and then answer a simple question: How seriously should I take the findings of any specific research study given the level of its objectivity?

| COMPETENCY 9 | Evaluate Practice with Individuals, Families, Groups, Organizations, & Communities |
|---|---|

You will learn that the only way you can legitimately evaluate the effectiveness of your day-to-day practice activities (in addition to the social work program where you work) is by knowing how the entire research process unfolds and, more important, how the "research" process is the same as the social work "practice" process.

# Toward Accountability

| CHAPTERS 1 & 3 | Step 1. Understanding the Research Process |
| CHAPTER 2 | Step 2. Formulating Research Questions |
| CHAPTER 4<br>APPENDIXES A–C | Step 3. Reviewing the Literature<br>Evaluating the Literature |
| CHAPTERS 5 & 6 | Step 4. Being Aware of Ethical and Cultural Issues |
| CHAPTERS 7–10 | Step 5. Selecting a Research Approach |
| CHAPTERS 11 & 12 | Step 6. Specifying How Variables Are Measured |
| CHAPTER 13 | Step 7. Selecting a Sample |
| CHAPTERS 14 & 15 | Step 8. Selecting a Research Design |
| CHAPTERS 16 & 17 | Step 9. Selecting a Data-Collection Method |
| CHAPTERS 18 & 19 | Step 10. Analyzing the Data |
| CHAPTERS 20 & 21 | Step 11. Writing the Research Report |

# Toward Accountability

CHAPTER

1

CHAPTER OUTLINE

"The trouble with this agency is nobody is willing to be held accountable for anything. But don't tell anyone I said that."

RESEARCH AND ACCOUNTABILITY

    Council on Social Work Education

    National Association of Social Workers

THIS BOOK'S OBJECTIVES

    This Book's Philosophy

THE PURPOSES OF RESEARCH IN SOCIAL WORK

PURE AND APPLIED RESEARCH STUDIES

    Pure Research Studies

    Applied Research Studies

WAYS OF KNOWING

    Authority

    Tradition

    Experience

    Beliefs and Intuition

    Research Findings

THE PROCESS OF THE SCIENTIFIC METHOD

    Is Everything Observable and Measurable?

    Nothing Is Absolutely Certain Forever

Example of the Scientific Inquiry Process

    *Phase 1: Observing and/or Measuring*

    *Phase 2: Assuming*

    *Phase 3: Testing*

    *Phase 4: Revising*

FORMING PROFESSIONAL JUDGMENTS

    Having a Solid Knowledge and Skills Base

    Using Critical Thinking Skills

    *Definition of Critical thinking*

    *Beginning Steps of the Critical Thinking Process*

    *What Activities Does a Critical Thinker Do?*

    *Hints to Help You to Become a Critical Thinker*

    Using the Three Appendixes

    *Get Acquainted with the Three Appendixes*

    *Don't Get Intimidated*

    *Is There a Standard Evaluation Rubric?*

CHAPTER RECAP

REVIEW EXERCISES

| SCENARIO 1.1 | And once upon a time there was an astrologer . . . |
|---|---|

During the customary tradition of your never-ending quest of searching Facebook, Snapchat, Instagram, and WhatsApp, you accidently click on a website containing an advertisement that reads:

**Astrological Consultant**

See me, Madame Cleo, for better insights into love, business, health, sex, grades in your research methods class, and relationships. I will help you to achieve a more fulfilling and gratifying life. Call (800) FOR-SCAM (367-7226), or go to: www.bigfraud.com.

"HA!" YOU THINK, "I bet she can't do this for me! I bet she's just out for the money! But if she could only tell me . . . How do I know if she's for real or I'm just getting taken for a ride?"

There's a parallel here between the clients who receive social services and you, the future social worker. Most of the people we help—in common with all those people who are never seen by social workers—would like more fulfilling and rewarding lives.

## RESEARCH AND ACCOUNTABILITY

Like Madame Cleo's naïve clientele, who get hoodwinked into calling her on the phone, many of our clients also have personal issues, money issues, relationship issues, or health issues. Unlike Madame Cleo, however, who only has to be accountable to her bank balance, we as professionals are required to be accountable to society and must be able to provide reasonable answers to four basic accountability questions:

1  How *do I know* if I have helped my clients?
2  How *do my clients know* I have helped them?
3  How does *our profession know* that we, as a collective group of social workers, have helped our clients?

5

**4** How do *the funding bodies* that support our programs (which employ us) know how effectively their dollars are being spent?

What's the role that research plays in answering the previous four accountability questions? A significant one! That's the position of both the Council on Social Work Education (CSWE) and the National Association of Social Workers (NASW).

The jurisdiction of these two prestigious national organizations includes determining what required curriculum content is taught in all accredited social work programs in the United States (CSWE) and how students practice their craft once they have graduated (NASW). Let's now take a closer look at what CSWE and NASW are all about.

## COUNCIL ON SOCIAL WORK EDUCATION

The CSWE is the official educational organization that sets minimum curriculum standards for bachelor of social work (BSW) and master of social work (MSW) programs throughout the United States. This accreditation organization firmly believes that all social work students should know the basic principles of research methodology (the topic of this book)—and so do your professors.

More specifically, the current 2015 version of the CSWE's *Educational Policy and Accreditation Standards* contains three very general "research-type" of policy competency statements that all social work students must follow.

| | |
|---|---|
| **Competency 1** | **Demonstrate ethical and professional behavior.** Given Competency 1, you will be expected to: Make ethical decisions by applying the standards of the NASW *Code of Ethics,* relevant laws and regulations, models for ethical decision-making, ethical conduct of research, and additional codes of ethics as appropriate to context. |
| **Competency 4** | **Engage in practice-informed research and research-informed practice.** Given Competency 4, you will be expected to: (a) Use practice experience and theory to inform scientific inquiry and research; (b) Apply critical thinking to engage in analysis of quantitative and qualitative research methods and research findings; and (c) Use and translate research evidence to inform and improve practice, policy, and service delivery. |
| **Competency 9** | **Evaluate practice with individuals, families, groups, organizations, and communities.** Given Competency 9, you will be expected to: (a) Select and use appropriate methods for evaluation of outcomes; (b) Apply knowledge of human behavior and the social environment, person-in-environment, and other multidisciplinary theoretical frameworks in the evaluation of outcomes; and (c) Critically analyze, monitor, and evaluate intervention and program processes and outcomes; and apply evaluation findings to improve practice effectiveness at the micro, mezzo, and macro levels. |

> As a current social work student you are accountable to the Council on Social Work Education.

To comply with the above three research competency statements requires basic research methodology and critical thinking skills. That is, it would be extremely difficult—if not impossible—for you to fulfill the CSWE's three policy statements unless you understand the contents of this book. Now that you know what the CSWE has to say about "student-orientated research competencies," let's turn our attention to the second professional organization that you will be accountable to after graduation—the NASW.

## NATIONAL ASSOCIATION OF SOCIAL WORKERS

Just like the CSWE, the NASW is a parallel practice organization that works to enhance the professional growth and development of social workers. Like the CSWE for social work students, the NASW (2017) also believes that practicing social workers should know the basic ethical principles of research and evaluation:

> 1　Social workers should monitor and evaluate policies, the implementation of programs, and practice interventions.
>
> 2　Social workers should promote and facilitate evaluation and research to contribute to the development of knowledge.
>
> 3　Social workers should critically examine and keep current with emerging knowledge relevant to social work and fully use evaluation and research evidence in their professional practice.
>
> 4　Social workers should report evaluation and research findings accurately. They should not fabricate or falsify results and should take steps to correct any errors later found in published data using standard publication methods.
>
> 5　Social workers engaged in evaluation or research should be alert to and avoid conflicts of interest and dual relationships with participants, should inform participants when a real or potential conflict of interest arises, and should take steps to resolve the issue in a manner that makes participants' interests primary.
>
> 6　Social workers should educate themselves, their students, and their colleagues about responsible research practices.

As a future social work practitioner you will be accountable to the National Association of Social Workers.

Do the other nonresearch social work courses that you're taking, or will take, address any of these principles? Do you think Madam Cleo, mentioned at the beginning of this chapter, has to abide by practice principles for astrologers as she practices her trade?

## THIS BOOK'S OBJECTIVES

**T**his book provides you with the basic research methodology and beginning critical thinking skills you'll need to comply with the research standards set out by the CSWE and NASW. Briefly stated, we take you through the entire research process from problem formulation to writing up and disseminating your study's results.

To enhance your critical thinking skills, we provide basic questions you can ask for each step of the research process. Thus, this book will not only increase your knowledge of the social work research process but will also sharpen a few of your critical thinking skills—a twofer, so to speak. So our four objectives for you are:

All facts derived from research studies need to be questioned and never taken for granted and assumed to be true.

> 1　**Given the preceding discussion:** To understand and appreciate the need for you to become more accountable to our society, our profession, our clients, and yourself.
>
> 2　**Given number 1 above:** To know and appreciate how the use of "research findings" in your daily practice activities can enhance your overall effectiveness as a social work practitioner, which in turn will improve our overall accountability.
>
> 3　**Given number 2 above:** To know and appreciate the limitations of haphazardly incorporating research findings (aka: "facts") into your daily social work practices without first questioning the overall credibility and practicality of the "facts". All "research findings" have limitations.
>
> 4　**Given number 3 above:** To know and appreciate how the critical thinking process works and how to apply beginning critical thinking skills (and attitudes) to assess all "research findings"—or any form of "facts"—you come across.

## THIS BOOK'S PHILOSOPHY

First and foremost, we want you to know basic research methodology. Second, we begin to lay the fundamental groundwork for sharpening your critical thinking skills by suggesting various questions you can ask in relation to the generation of knowledge via the scientific method of inquiry.

In a nutshell, we want you to know how the scientific method of inquiry process works inside out, backwards, and forwards. Then we want you to feel comfortable in asking questions about the results or findings (aka: "facts") that the process produces.

Asking questions about all facts is the first step (of three) in becoming a critical thinker. So, in essence, we provide you with a beginning springboard for asking questions about the astonishing amount of "facts" you will come across on your journey toward becoming a first-rate practitioner who possesses beginning critical thinking skills.

> It's okay to ask questions about what you read, hear, and see.

## THE PURPOSES OF RESEARCH IN SOCIAL WORK

**N**ow that you know you have some "research-related" accountability tasks ahead of you, you're in an excellent position to ask a simple question: What kind of research studies can we do that will increase our accountability? Allan Rubin and Earl Babbie (2017) have beautifully outlined four non-mutually exclusive purposes for doing social work research/evaluation studies. You need to remember that not all social work research studies will fall neatly into one of the four categories and most studies have more than one purpose.

1  **Exploration.** Much of social work research is conducted to explore a topic—to provide initial familiarity with it. This purpose is typical when a researcher is examining a new interest, when the subject of interest is relatively new or unstudied, or when a researcher wants to test the feasibility of undertaking a more carefully planned-out study. For example, suppose your first job as a social worker is to develop services for frail, older adults in a predominantly ethnic minority community about which you know very little.

   To start, you'll want to conduct a community-wide survey to assess the precise extent of the need for and likely utilization of the alternative services that you are contemplating developing. However, before you mount a large-scale study to produce conclusive findings, you'd be well advised to begin with a smaller, more flexible exploratory study to help you plan your larger, more careful study in a culturally sensitive manner.

2  **Description.** Many social work studies have a second purpose: to describe situations and events. The researcher observes and then describes what was observed. Because scientific observations are careful and deliberate, they're typically more accurate and precise than casual descriptions. For example, a researcher might assess the needs of a community by conducting a survey of community residents.

3  **Explanation.** The third general purpose of social work research is to explain things. Reporting why some cities have higher child abuse rates than others is a case of explanation; simply reporting the different child abuse rates is description. Researchers have an explanatory purpose if they wish to know why battered women repeatedly return to live with their batterers rather than simply describing how often they do.

4  **Evaluation.** A fourth purpose of social work research is to evaluate social policies, programs, and interventions. The evaluative purpose of social work

> The main purpose of doing research in social work is to advance our knowledge base, which in turn increases our overall accountability.

research actually encompasses all three of the preceding purposes: exploration, description, and explanation. Evaluation is simply finding out whether a particular policy, program, or intervention is effective and efficient.

## PURE AND APPLIED RESEARCH STUDIES

**N**ot only can research studies be classified into four non-mutually exclusive purposes, they can also be classified into pure and applied research studies. There are many ways to classify research studies, and there is not a "correct" classification system. The most important thing to remember when doing any research study is to put the research question you are trying to answer first and foremost—the classification of it comes second (see chapter 2, pages 47–50). Let's now turn our attention to discussing how pure and applied research studies enhance our profession's knowledge base.

### PURE RESEARCH STUDIES

Pure research studies are motivated primarily by a researcher's curiosity. The questions they address are considered important because they can produce results that improve our ability to describe or explain phenomena. Successfully answering a pure research question advances theory (Grinnell, Rothery, & Thomlison, 1993).

Social workers with a sociology background may be interested, for example, in the organizational patterns that evolve in a social system such as John Wilson Elementary School when an intruder threatens the children (see Box 1.1 below). A few pure research questions that could be formulated from Box 1.1 could be:

1 What are the specific processes whereby the teachers articulate a coherent response to the threat?

2 How are parents, who are often relatively marginal members of the school community, drawn into more central positions and made effective partners in the effort to maintain a defense?

3 What differentiates this school, where the children reportedly cope with danger while maintaining good morale, from other schools where similar stressors would have more debilitating effects?

| Box 1.1 | Another Kidnapping Has Parents Nervous |
|---|---|

**Innisfail**—Anxious parents are uniting to protect their kids after the fifth child abduction incident since June in this normally peaceful town.

And teachers are on red alert for strangers.

Drastic precautions have been forced on them by the latest kidnap bid—the attempted abduction last Friday of a seven-year-old girl inside the town's only elementary school.

As John Wilson Elementary School ended its day Tuesday, the parking lot was jammed with parents, big brothers, big sisters, friends, and neighbors.

"Now, everybody's coming to the school to pick up their kids—or other people's kids. Even parents that never used to come and get their kids are walking them to school every day now," said Jeanette Clark, waiting for her daughter.

"We have to make sure every child gets home safely now.

"This last abduction was really serious because the guy went right into the school," she said.

The culprit, described as a 50-year-old white male with brown hair and a moustache, walked into the school, grabbed the girl, who was just coming out of the bathroom, and demanded, "Come with me."

But the girl bit his arm and ran for help.

Laurie Moore, mother of a Grade 3 girl, said she and her friends with children are emphasizing "stay away from strangers" warnings.

"I tell my daughter not to talk to anyone, and if anyone comes near her she has to scream and run. It really is sad that we all have to go through this," she said.

School Principal Bill Hoppins has created a volunteer program where parents can help each other by supervising kids on the playground during the morning.

Tim Belbin, whose daughter attends Grade 2, said he's willing to offer his time to watch his and other children.

"I find this all really disturbing . . . really scary."

The abduction attempt has also prompted teachers to supervise all the students in their classes as they leave the school grounds and make sure they can identify all adults in the area.

"If we don't know them, we have to go up and ask them, even if they don't like it," said Hoppins.

And Hoppins said that when students are absent without a parental notification, their homes are called immediately. "There have been a number of precautions taken here since the last abduction attempt. And we are working together with the parents."

Social workers with a psychology background also would be interested in responses to stress, but from a different perspective. If their focus is on the development of personality, they may attempt to identify the traits that allow some children to cope more effectively with danger than others. If they focus on the perpetrators, they may try to learn what drives such people to behave in ways that others find disgusting.

All these potential research questions are motivated by a desire to increase or improve the knowledge base of our profession. The questions have a theoretical relevance, and the purpose in seeking to answer them is to advance our basic knowledge about how social systems organize themselves or how personality develops.

## Applied Research Studies

The advantage of applied research over pure research can be found in Sherlock Holmes's defense of "useful" rather than "useless" facts to his companion, Dr. Watson, in Arthur Conan Doyle's classic story *A Study in Scarlet* (1901):

"You see," he explained, "I consider that a man's brain originally is like a little empty attic, and you have to stock it with such furniture as you choose. . . . It's a mistake to think that the little room has elastic walls and can distend to any extent.

. . . There comes a time when for every addition of knowledge, you forget something that you knew before. It's of the highest importance, therefore, not to have useless facts elbowing out the useful ones."

"But the Solar System!" I protested.

"What the deuce is it to me?" he interrupted impatiently: "You say that we go around the sun. If we went around the moon it would not make a pennyworth of difference to me or to my work." (11)

A social worker with professional responsibilities for knowing how to be helpful in circumstances like those at Innisfail's elementary school may have some sympathy for Holmes's position. Theory about the dynamics of social organizations or the development of personality is fine—for those who have time to invest in such issues.

For an applied researcher there's reason to be interested in the young girl who bit her assailant and ran for help, for example. How did she know so clearly what to do that she could handle the attack with such competence? Can anything be learned from her history that would help parents or teachers prepare other children to be equally effective should the need arise?

> The distinction between theoretical results and practical results marks the principal difference between pure and applied research studies.

A researcher could also be interested in how the principal of the school handled the situation. Can generalizable guidelines be extracted from the principal's approach to mobilizing teachers and parents? Should other professionals be informed about what the principal did to enable the children to keep their spirits up while at the same time alerting them to the danger?

Many social workers would be interested in the long-term effects of this kind of experience on the children. Some children will certainly be more deeply affected than others, and it's important to know how they are affected and what kinds of attention to their emotional needs will help them cope adaptively with the experience and its aftermath. These questions are motivated by curiosity, as pure research questions are, but there is another need operating as well, and that is mastery.

In sum, the goal of pure research studies is to develop theory and expand our profession's knowledge base, and the goal of applied research studies is to develop solutions for problems and applications in practice.

## WAYS OF KNOWING

**W**e have previously discussed our need to become more accountable to our various stakeholder groups and introduced the notion that social work research studies, and their corresponding research questions, can help us in this effort. In addition to being either pure or applied we also know that our research studies can have four or more purposes.

Nevertheless, all four purposes of doing a research study—whether pure or applied—have one common overlapping goal: to produce a solid knowledge base for our profession. And it's going to be you who is doing all the producing. You now need to ask the question, How is this knowledge base formed anyhow? That is, how does knowledge get into our so-called knowledge base? The answer is quite simple: Knowledge is fed into our knowledge base by social work researchers, practitioners, and students like yourself. We use five highly interrelated knowledge-generating approaches collectively known as "the ways of knowing." You can know something through:

1 Authority
2 Tradition
3 Experience
4 Beliefs and intuition
5 Research findings (obtained through the scientific method of inquiry process)

All five of these ways of knowing heavily overlap with one another, but it greatly simplifies things to discuss them separately. Let's start our discussion on the ways of knowing by reading about your first client named Joline, as depicted in Scenario 1.2 on the following page.

| SCENARIO 1.2 | Your First Job after You Graduate |

**Pretend for the moment** you're a newly employed social worker in a university's student counseling center. A first-generation first-year ethnic minority student named Joline comes into your office where she tells you she feels depressed, lonely, and isolated, is receiving poor grades, and is thinking of dropping out of school and going home.

You readily identify with Joline because you were once a first-generation first-year ethnic minority student and you've been down that road before. You know exactly what to do with Joline because you've done it yourself. You feel you have the best intervention package known to personkind: (1) Have Joline enroll in a student support group. (2) Encourage her to participate in extracurricular social activities. (3) Urge her family to come to campus more often to visit with her, as she has a good relationship with her parents. (4) Persuade her to move into a dormitory with a roommate rather than continuing to live alone in an apartment. (5) Do a bit of weekly group–cognitive behavioral therapy sessions to lessen her depression levels. (6) Encourage her to go to the university's writing center to get help with her studying habits. (7) Perhaps also work on a few needed socialization and assertiveness skills.

This basic intervention package, containing seven components, worked for you, so it's just got to work for Joline, too. Right? Well . . . at best maybe, or probably.

After Joline has agreed to your plan, you ask your supervisor for support to implement your seven-prong intervention package. She tells you that it's not a good idea. She then tells you that she knows what intervention package is best for Joline—the one the counseling center has been using for years: (1) Drop out of school, and save some tuition bucks to boot. (2) Return home. (3) Mature a bit more. (4) Re-enroll when she's actually ready, willing, and able to positively engage in her studies. Your supervisor says that she knows that this is best for Joline because she's seen numerous situations like Joline's in her 10 years at the university's counseling center.

However, after rereading the research book you're holding in your hands, you see that there are five ways to know something. And how did your supervisor come up with her knowledge (her intervention package) in the first place? Your "knowledge" seems to differ from her "knowledge." How can this be? Could you both be viewing the world differently? And, more important, who's right? And is there a "right"? Also, what does Joline want to do? What's Joline's "right"?

## AUTHORITY

The first way you "know" something is that someone in an authority position—like your supervisor in Scenario 1.2 above—told you so. That is, some things you know because someone in authority told you they were true. Had you lived in Galileo's time, for example, you would have "known" that there were seven heavenly bodies: the sun, the moon, and five planets. Since seven was a sacred number in the seventeenth century, the correctness of this belief was self-evident and was proclaimed by professors of philosophy.

Let's not forget that the earth was also flat at the time, and it was the center of the universe! After Galileo peeked through his telescope in 1610 and saw four satellites circling Jupiter, it was still absolutely clear to those in authority that Galileo was wrong. Not only was he wrong, he had blasphemed against the accepted order. They denounced Galileo and his telescope and continued to comfortably believe in the sacredness of the number seven. But the authorities could have looked through Galileo's telescope! They could have seen for themselves that the number of heavenly bodies had risen to eleven! In fact, they refused to look because it wasn't worth their while to look: They "knew" they were right.

They had to be right because, in Galileo's time, the primary source of "how you know something" was by authority—not by reason, and certainly not by observation. Today, this may seem a bit strange, and we may feel a trifle smug about the fact that in our time we rely on our own observations *in addition* to authority.

So, in Scenario 1.2, if you take the easy way out and unquestioningly implement your supervisor's recommended intervention package with Joline, you have attained your "knowledge" of how to help students like Joline from an authority figure. You might also wonder in the back of your mind if your supervisor could indeed be wrong, and you might believe that your own seven-prong intervention package would be better. But then again, it's difficult to question the authority of your immediate supervisor.

You need to decide for yourself which good "facts," or treatment/policy recommendations you will clutch to your heart and use to help your future clients, and which recommendations you will disregard because they were spawned from dubious or debatable "authority type" of sources (e.g., scenario 1.1 on page 5). You must remember that every recommendation a *not* a good one. Also remember that there are many good ones that we can use with our clients. Good treatment/policy recommendations will have *credible evidence* to substantiate their effectiveness. Period. Full stop.

### WHERE DOES "CREDIBLE EVIDENCE" COME FROM?

We always need to ask, "Where did the evidence (or data, or facts) come from that was used to substantiate the social work practice or policy recommendation in the first place?" The kind of evidence on which any recommendation is based must always be evaluated in terms of the overall quality of the source that produced it. For example, we obtain knowledge by watching television shows and movies in addition to reading newspapers, journals, and magazine articles. These forms of communication provide rich information (both right and wrong) about the social life of individuals and society in general.

> We must be able to distinguish good practice/policy recommendations from the bad and awful ones.

Television media (especially Faux News) as a data source always has questionable value. Most people who have had no contact with criminals learn about crime by these forms of communication—and as we know all too well the media can easily perpetuate the myths of any given culture (Neuman & Robson, 2018):

> The media show that most people who receive welfare are African American (most are actually non-African American), that most people who are mentally ill are violent and dangerous (only a small percentage actually are), and that most people who are elderly are senile and in nursing homes (a tiny minority are).

> Television repeatedly shows low-income, inner-city African American youth using illegal drugs. Eventually, most people "know" that urban African Americans use illegal drugs at a much higher rate than other groups in the United States, even though this notion is false.

Bruce Thyer and Monica Pignotti (2015) have beautifully assembled a list of additional myths to those Lilenfeld, Lynn, Ruscio, and Beyerstein (2010) outlined in their book *50 Great Myths of Popular Psychology* (2010):

- Old age is typically associated with increased dissatisfaction and senility.
- When dying, people pass through a universal series of psychological stages.
- Human memory works like a tape recorder or video camera, and accurately records the events we've experienced.
- Most students learn best when teaching styles are matched to their learning styles.
- Low self-esteem is a major cause of psychological problems.
- Most people who were sexually abused in childhood develop severe personality

disturbances in adulthood.

- Psychiatric labels cause harm by stigmatizing people.
- Only deeply depressed people commit suicide.
- Adult children of alcoholics display a distinctive pattern of symptoms.
- There has recently been a massive epidemic of infantile autism.
- Expert judgment and intuition are the best means of making clinical decisions.
- Abstinence is the only realistic goal for alcoholics.
- All effective psychotherapies force people to confront the "root" causes of their problems in childhood.

## TRADITION

The second way of adding to our knowledge base is simply through tradition. Obviously, authority and tradition are highly related to one another. For example, some things you "know" because your mother "knew" them and her mother before her, and they are a part of your cultural tradition. Your mother was also an authority figure who learned her bits and pieces through tradition and authority.

More often than not, people tend to accept cultural beliefs without much question. They may doubt some of them and test others for themselves, but for the most part they behave and believe as tradition dictates. To be sure, such conformity is useful, as our society could not function if each and every custom and belief was reexamined by each individual in every generation.

> The unquestioning acceptance of traditional principles can easily lead to stagnation and to the perpetuation of wrongs.

It would be unfortunate, for example, if women were never allowed to vote because women had never traditionally voted, or if racial segregation and slavery were perpetuated because traditionally that's just the way it was. And let's not forget that interracial marriage was at one time illegal. Some traditional beliefs are based on the dictates of authority carried on through time, such as opposition to same-sex marriages and abortions. The origins of other beliefs are lost in history.

### THAT'S THE WAY IT'S DONE AROUND HERE

Even in our social service programs, whose history is relatively brief, things tend to be done in certain ways because they have always been done in those ways. When you first enter a social service program as a practicum student, for example, your colleagues will show you how the program runs.

You may be given a manual detailing your program's policies and procedures, which contains everything from staff holidays and locking up client files at night, to standard interviewing techniques with children who have been physically and emotionally abused. Informally, you will be told other things such as how much it costs to join the coffee club, whom to ask when you want a favor, whom to phone for certain kinds of information, what form to complete to be put on the waiting list for a parking space, and what form to fill out to order more forms.

In addition to this practical information, you may also receive advice about how to help your future clients. Your colleagues may offer you a few of their opinions about the most effective treatment intervention strategies that are used in your practicum setting. If your practicum setting is a child sexual abuse treatment program, for example, it may be suggested to you that the nonoffending mother of a child who has been sexually abused herself does not need to address her own sexual abuse history in therapy in order to empathize with and protect her daughter. Such a view would support the belief that the best interventive approach is a learning one, perhaps helping the mother learn better communication skills with her daughter.

Conversely, the suggestion may be that the mother's personal exploration into her psyche (whatever that is) is essential, so the intervention should be of a psychodynamic nature. Whatever the suggestion, it's likely that you, as a beginning social work student, will accept it, along with the information about the coffee club.

### THE NEED TO "FIT IN"

To be sure, you will want to fit in and become a valued member of the team. We all want to fit in somewhere. If the nonoffending mother is the first client you have really been responsible for, you may also be privately relieved that the intervention decision has been made for you. You may believe that your colleagues have more professional experience than you and surely should know best.

In all likelihood, they probably do know best. However, they also were once beginning social work students like yourself, and they probably formed their professional opinions in the same way you are currently forming yours. They too once trusted their supervisors' knowledge bases and their experiences (to be discussed below). In other words, much of what you will initially be told is based upon the way your practicum site has traditionally worked. This should not come as a surprise to you.

> We must fully realize that we have no business intervening in other people's lives simply on the assumption that our good intentions will lead to good client outcomes.

This might be a good moment to use your newfound library skills to explore the literature on the best way to intervene with children who have been sexually abused. But if you actually happen to find a different and more effective intervention, you may quickly discover that your colleagues are unreceptive or even hostile. They "know" what they do already works with their clients—they "know it works" because it has traditionally worked for years.

Thus, on the one hand, tradition as a way of knowing is extremely useful in that it simply allows you to learn from the achievements and mistakes of those who have done your job before you. You don't have to reinvent the wheel; you've been given a head start. On the other hand, tradition can become way too comfortable. It can blind you to better ways of doing things. And tradition dies hard, very hard indeed.

## EXPERIENCE

The third way of acquiring your knowledge base is through plain old-fashioned experience. You "know" how buttered bread falls when you drop it—buttered side down, of course. You "know" that knives cut and fire burns. You "know," as you gain experience in social work, that certain interventional approaches tend to work better than others with certain types of clients in certain types of situations. Such experience is of enormous benefit to your clients.

Experience is a great way to "know" things. Use it when you can. However, as with anything else, experience has its advantages and disadvantages. Experience in one area, for example, can blind you to the issues in another. Health planners from mental health backgrounds, for example, may see mental illness as the most compelling community health problem simply because of their experiences with the mentally ill.

Mental health issues may therefore command more dollars and attention than other public health issues that are equally deserving such as homelessness, high student tuition rates, poverty, and child abuse. Being aware of your own biases will allow you to make the most of your own experience while taking due account of the experiences of others.

## BELIEFS AND INTUITION

At this point, it's useful to differentiate among knowledge, beliefs, and intuition. Like everything else in life, they heavily interact with each other. Knowledge is an accepted body of facts or ideas mainly acquired through the use of the scientific method. We now know that the earth is round, for example, because we have been into space and observed it from above.

A few centuries ago, we would have known that the earth is flat because someone in authority said it is or because tradition had always held it to be flat—very flat indeed. Thus, knowledge is never final or certain. It's always changing as new facts come to our attention and new theories explaining the facts are developed, tested, and accepted or rejected.

Beliefs (or faith), on the other hand, are a body of ideas that are acquired mainly through the reliance on tradition and/or authority. Beliefs represent a way of thinking about something that has not been proven by the scientific method, and thus they are unscientific opinions, or ideas, at best.

Belief systems have remarkable staying power. Various beliefs about life after death, for example, have been held since the beginning of time by large numbers of people, and they will doubtless continue to be held, without much change, because there's nothing to change them. More recently, the belief that one acquires worth through hard work has become strongly held in North American society. This belief holds that the harder you work, the more virtue you acquire. At the same time, it's believed that people will avoid work if at all possible—presumably because they value ease over virtue—so many of the social service programs we have in place today are designed to punish our clients' "idleness" and reward their "productivity."

Intuition is a feeling that guides a person to act a certain way without fully understanding why. It can be described in a number of ways: revelation through insight, conviction without reason, or immediate apprehension without rational thought. In short, you "know" something without having a clue of how you know it. It has been suggested that intuition springs from a rational process at the subconscious level.

With the preceding discussion in mind, professional ethical concerns dictate that we should never rely solely on our beliefs and intuition when working with clients. Take careful note of the word *solely*. Unfortunately, like tradition, beliefs and intuition also die hard (Grinnell, 1981, 1985, 1995; Grinnell & Siegel, 1988; Grinnell & Stothers, 1988; Grinnell & Unrau, 2018).

### Professional Ethical Concerns

Let's use an example to illustrate a professional ethical concern about using beliefs and intuition in your daily practices. Suppose one day Jane goes to her family physician for a medical checkup because she has been feeling tired and depressed. After talking with her for a few minutes, the physician says, "My intuition tells me that you have high blood pressure," and then proceeds to give Jane hypertension medication. Following the physician's advice, she takes the medication for a few months and begins to feel better. Because she's now feeling better, Jane phones the physician and asks if it's okay to stop taking the medication. The physician says yes.

At no time did the physician take Jane's blood pressure, either to confirm the initial diagnostic intuitive hunch or to determine the effects of the medication later. Hence, it was entirely possible that she was taking a drug for which she had no need, or a drug that could actually harm her; alternatively, she may be stopping a medication that has indeed been helping her. The point here is that the physician made crucial decisions about beginning and ending an intervention without gathering and evaluating all the necessary data.

### Moral and Ethical Obligations

Ethical social workers do not treat clients the way this physician did. Just as the wrong medication has the potential to harm, so does the wrong social work intervention. In the past, some studies have shown that the recipients of social work services have fared worse

---

Authority, tradition, and experience, when it comes to ways of knowing, are highly related to one another.

- **Knowledge** is an accepted body of facts or ideas mainly you acquired through the use of the scientific method.
- **Beliefs** (or faith) are a body of ideas that you acquired mainly through the reliance on tradition and/or authority.
- **Intuition** is a feeling that guides you to act a certain way without fully understanding why.

or no better than those who did not receive our services. Thus, we always have a responsibility to evaluate the effect of our interventions. Although we may mean well, our good intentions alone do not ensure that we really "help" our clients.

Truly professional social workers never rely solely on their good intentions, intuitions, experiences, uninformed opinions, and subjective judgments. They also use the results of research findings that were derived from good research studies to guide their interventions. And, more important, these findings must have been derived from the use of the scientific method of inquiry, which now brings our discussion to the fifth and final way of knowing—research results (or findings), generated by the scientific method of inquiry.

## RESEARCH FINDINGS

We now come to the fifth and final way of knowing. This way of acquiring knowledge is through the use of research findings that were derived via the scientific method—sometimes called the *problem-solving process*, the *research method*, or the *research process*. The scientific method is the newest way of knowing when compared with the other four.

The scientific method is a way of knowing that demands the knowledge it produces be based on observable and/or measurable facts and objectivity. In practice, it's a method of knowing that can be shared and objectively critiqued by others. It's the use of careful thought and the systematic use of sound data-gathering and analytical procedures that makes the findings derived via a research study more easily verifiable by other researchers than the other four ways of knowing (Maschi & Youdin, 2012).

### A TOOTHY DILEMMA

Aristotle believed that women had fewer teeth than men. Although he was twice married and the number of teeth possessed by women and men was a contentious issue in his day (believe it or not), it never occurred to him to ask either of his two wives to open their mouths so he could observe and count the number of teeth each had.

Aristotle didn't use the scientific method to determine if woman had fewer teeth than men: he never simply compared the number of teeth each of his wives had with the number of teeth he had. This is a solution that would easily occur to anyone born in the twenty-first century because we're accustomed to evaluating our assumptions in the light of our observations. The social work profession—and modern society to boot—is enamored with knowledge development through the use of the scientific method. Acquiring knowledge through the use of research findings that were derived from this method of knowing is the most objective way of knowing something. Lawrence Neuman and Karen Robson (2018) nicely sum up what it's all about:

> The scientific method arises from a loose consensus within the community of scientists. It includes a way of looking at the world that places a high value on professionalism, craftsmanship, ethical integrity, creativity, rigorous standards, and diligence. It also includes strong professional norms such as honesty and uprightness in doing a research study, great candor and openness about how one conducted a study, and a focus on the merits of the research study itself and not on any characteristics of individuals who conducted the study.

## THE PROCESS OF THE SCIENTIFIC METHOD

One of the most objective ways of obtaining any kind of knowledge is through the use of the scientific method of inquiry. It's a process that contains four phases. On a very general level, and in the simplest of terms, the scientific method is a process as illustrated in Figure 1.1 on the following page.

We have a moral obligation to use solid research findings—even more so when clients have not asked for our services.

Research findings that produce practice/policy recommendations are only as good as the overall credibility of the research study that created them.

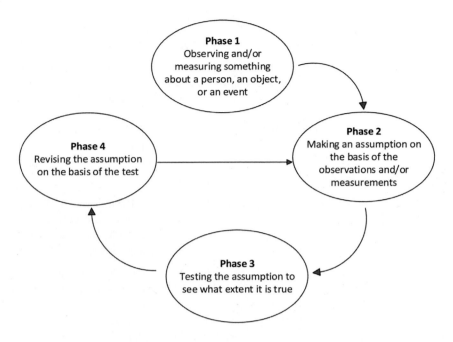

**Figure 1.1**

Phases of the Scientific Method of Inquiry

It begins with the first phase: some kind of an observation and/or measurement. Suppose, for example, we find in the garage an unidentified bag of seeds, and we don't know what kind of seeds they are. We plant a random seed from the bag into the ground, and it grows into a petunia. This might be a coincidence, but if we plant thirty-seven more seeds from the same bag, and all of them grow into petunias, we might assume that all the seeds in our bag have something to do with the petunias. We have now reached the second phase in the scientific method: We have made an assumption based on our observations.

The third phase is to test our assumption. This is done by planting yet another seed (the thirty-eighth) in the same way as before. If it too, becomes a petunia, we will be more certain that all the seeds in our bag will grow into petunias. On the other hand, if the thirty-eighth seed grows into a cabbage, we will begin to wonder if our original assumption—that the bag contains *all* petunia seeds—was wrong, which is the fourth phase of the scientific method. It's possible, of course, that we are quite mad and we only imagined those petunias in the first place. We would be more certain of the real existence of those petunias if someone else had seen them as well. The more people who observed them, the surer we would become.

> Knowledge is an accepted body of facts or ideas mainly acquired through the use of the scientific method of inquiry.

## Is Everything Observable and Measurable?

The scientific inquiry process holds that, in most cases, something exists only if we can observe and/or measure it. To guard against objects that are "seen" without existing, such as cool pools of water observed by people dying of thirst in deserts, the scientific method has taken the premise one step farther: A thing exists if, and only if, we can measure it. The cool pools of water that we observed, for example, probably could not be measured by a thermometer or a depth gauge. The wind cannot be seen but it can be easily measured.

## NOTHING IS ABSOLUTELY CERTAIN FOREVER

Things that have always occurred in sequence, such as summer and fall, probably will continue to occur in sequence. In all likelihood, rivers will continue to flow downhill, water will freeze at zero degrees centigrade, and crops will grow if planted in the spring. But nothing is certain; nothing is absolute.

It's a matter of slowly acquiring knowledge by making observations and measurements, deriving assumptions from those observations and measurements, and testing the assumptions by making more observations and measurements. Even the best-tested assumption is held to be true only until another observation comes along to disprove it.

> The scientific method is a way of knowing that demands the knowledge it produces be based on observable and/or measurable facts and objectivity.

Let's say you have lived your whole life all alone in a log cabin in the middle of a large forest. You have never ventured as far as a hundred yards from your cabin and have had no access to the outside world whatsoever—yup, no Internet either, gasp! You have observed for your entire life that all the ducks that flew over your land were white. You have never seen a differently colored duck. Thus, you assume, and rightfully so, that all ducks are white. You would only have to see one nonwhite duck to disprove your white-duck assumption. Nothing is certain, no matter how long you "objectively observed" it.

## EXAMPLE OF THE SCIENTIFIC INQUIRY PROCESS

Suppose, for a moment, you're interested in determining whether the strength of a child's attachment to his or her mother affects the child's social skills. In order to test your assumption (hypothesis, if you will), you must now decide on what you mean by "child" (say, under 6 years of age), and you obviously need to find some young children and mothers.

### PHASE 1: OBSERVING AND/OR MEASURING

Next, you need to decide what you mean by "attachment," and you need to observe how attached the children are to their mothers. Because you need to measure your observations, you will also need to come up with some system whereby certain observed behaviors mean "strong attachment," other behaviors mean "medium attachment," and still other behaviors mean "weak attachment."

> One of the most objective ways of obtaining any kind of knowledge is through the use of the scientific method of inquiry.

Then you need to decide what you mean by "social skills," and you now need to observe and measure the children's social skills. All of these definitions, observations, and measurements constitute Phase 1 of the scientific inquiry process (see Figure 1.1 on the previous page).

### PHASE 2: ASSUMING

On the basis of your Phase 1 data, you might formulate an assumption, hunch, or hypothesis to the effect (for instance) that children who have higher attachments to their mothers will have higher social skills than children who have lower attachments to their mothers. This is Phase 2 of the scientific inquiry process and involves inductive logic (see Figure 1.2 on the following page). When using inductive logic, you simply begin with detailed observations and/or measurements of the world obtained in Phase 1 and move toward more abstract generalizations and ideas.

If your assumption is correct, you can use it to predict that a particular child with a strong attachment to her mother will also demonstrate strong social skills. This is an example of deductive logic—you are deducing from the general to the particular.

### PHASE 3: TESTING

In Phase 3, you set about testing your assumption, observing and measuring the attachment levels and social skills of as many other children as you can manage. Data from this phase may confirm or cast doubt upon your assumption. The data might also cause

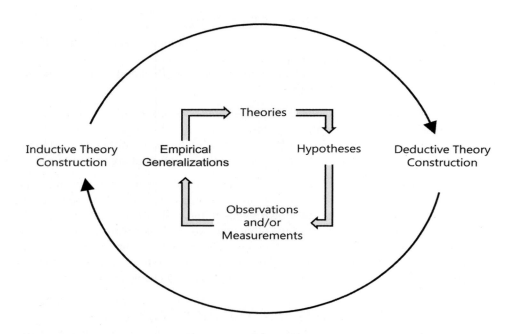

**Figure 1.2**

Inductive/Deductive Cycle of Theory Construction

you to realize that "attachment" is not as simple a concept as you had first imagined. It's not just a matter of the strength of the attachment; rather, the type of the attachment is also a factor (such as secure, insecure, or disorganized).

If you have tested enough children from diverse cultural backgrounds, you might also wonder if your assumption holds up better in some cultures than it does in others. Is it more relevant, say, for children raised in nuclear families than for children raised in a more communal environment such as a First Nations reserve or an Israeli kibbutz?

### PHASE 4: REVISING

These considerations in Phase 3 will lead you to Phase 4, in which you revise your conjecture in the light of your observations (inductive logic) and begin to test your revised hunch all over again (deductive logic). Hopefully, this will not be a lonely effort on your part. Other researchers interested in attachment will also examine your assumption and the evidence you formulated it from, and conduct their own studies to see how right you really were. This combined work, conducted with honesty, skepticism, sharing, and freedom from entrenched beliefs, simply allows our knowledge base in the area of attachment to increase.

> Inductive reasoning allows us to generate new knowledge and theories.

> Deductive reasoning allows us to test existing theories and reasoning.

## FORMING PROFESSIONAL JUDGMENTS

**G**iven what you've read so far, we now come to professional judgments. A professional judgment is a conscious process whereby facts, as far as they are known, are supplemented with the knowledge derived from all five ways of knowing to form the basis for rational decisions. In this eminently reasonable process, you know what facts you have and how reliable they are, you know what facts are missing, and you know what experiences you're using to fill in the gaps.

You, and you alone, are in a position to gauge whether your professional judgment is almost certainly right (you have all the facts), probably right (you have most of the facts), or simply out to lunch (you know you're almost entirely guessing). You can significantly improve your professional judgments by:

1 Having a solid professional knowledge and skill base
2 Using your critical thinking skills
3 Using the three appendixes at the end of this book

## HAVING A SOLID KNOWLEDGE AND SKILLS BASE

Unlike Madame Cleo (see scenario 1.1 on page 5), social work students and practitioners alike are expected to have a solid knowledge base to guide and support their interventions. This knowledge base is generally derived from your social work education.

> Your opinions are not professional judgments. They're just opinions and everyone has them.

Of course, we, as a profession, tend to have more credibility than astrological consultants like Madame Cleo. We have graduated from accredited social work programs (CSWE) and have solid, recognized practice qualifications (NASW). You are expected to have not only good intentions but also the knowledge and skills to convert your good intentions into desired practical results that will help your clients.

It all boils down to the fact that we have to be accountable to society. Being accountable means that we must acquire the knowledge and skills to help our clients in an effective and efficient manner. Much of this knowledge comes from the results of research studies that are disseminated through our professional literature. Where do you think Madam Cleo's knowledge base comes from?

## USING CRITICAL THINKING SKILLS

You can increase the accuracy of your professional judgments by simply digging out and using your critical thinking skills. Critical thinking is a way of thinking about whatever is presently occupying your mind so that you come to the best possible conclusion.

The word "critical" can mean different things in different contexts. For example, it can refer to the importance of something, or it can mean pointing out the negative aspects of something (i.e., to criticize something). It's also about not accepting what you read or hear at face value, but always questioning the facts, ideas, and arguments you come across. For example, you can ask a lot of questions about Madam Cleo's proclamations (scenario 1.1 on page 5).

### DEFINITIONS OF CRITICAL THINKING

> A reasoned professional judgment on your part that uses all five ways of knowing, no matter how uncertain you may be, is far more beneficial to your clients than using only one of the ways of knowing.

There are an abundant number of definitions of critical thinking floating around in our professional literature (Paul & Elder, 2016; studylib.net, 2019). We have listed just a few of them in the order of their wordiness; that is, the longer definitions (number 1) come first and the shorter ones are last (numbers 14–17):

1 Critical thinking includes the ability to respond to material by distinguishing between facts and opinions or personal feelings, judgments and inferences, inductive and deductive arguments, and the objective and subjective. It also includes the ability to generate questions, construct, and recognize the structure of arguments, and adequately support arguments; define, analyze, and devise solutions for problems and issues; sort, organize, classify, correlate, and analyze materials and data; integrate information and see relationships; evaluate information, materials, and data by drawing inferences, arriving at reasonable and informed conclusions, applying understanding and knowledge to new and different problems, developing rational and reasonable interpretations, suspending beliefs and remaining open to new information, methods, cultural systems, values and beliefs and by assimilating information.

2   Critical thinking is the use of those cognitive skills or strategies that increase the probability of a desirable outcome. It is used to describe thinking that is purposeful, reasoned, and goal directed—the kind of thinking involved in solving problems, formulating inferences, calculating likelihoods, and making decisions when the thinker is using skills that are thoughtful and effective for the particular context and type of thinking task.

3   Critical thinking is concerned with reason, intellectual honesty, and open-mindedness, as opposed to emotionalism, intellectual laziness, and closed-mindedness. Thus, critical thinking involves following evidence where it leads; considering all possibilities; relying on reason rather than emotion; being precise; considering a variety of possible viewpoints and explanations; weighing the effects of motives and biases; being concerned more with finding the truth than with being right; not rejecting unpopular views out of hand; and being aware of one's own prejudices and biases, and not allowing them to sway one's judgment.

> Critical thinkers think outside the box and ask questions—lots of them.

4   Critical thinking is careful and deliberate determination of whether to accept, reject, or suspend judgment. The purpose of critical thinking is, therefore, to achieve understanding, evaluate view points, and solve problems. Since all three areas involve the asking of questions, we can say that critical thinking is the questioning or inquiry we engage in when we seek to understand, evaluate, or resolve.

5   Critical thinking is a self-directed, self-disciplined, self-monitored, and self-correcting process. It requires rigorous standards of excellence and mindful command of their use. It entails effective communication and problem-solving abilities and a commitment to overcoming our native egocentrism and sociocentrism.

6   Critical thinking involves evaluating the thinking process—the reasoning that went into the conclusion we've arrived at and the kinds of factors considered in making a decision.

7   Critical thinking is the art of thinking about your thinking while you are thinking in order to make your thinking better: clearer, more accurate, or more defensible.

8   Critical thinkers distinguish between fact and opinion, ask questions, make detailed observations, uncover assumptions and define their terms, and make assertions based on sound logic and solid evidence.

> Facts are verifiable, opinions are not. And all people are entitled to their own opinions, but not to their own facts.

9   Critical thinking is a process that stresses an attitude of suspended judgment, incorporates logical inquiry and problem solving, and leads to an evaluative decision or action.

10   Critical thinking is understanding the meaning of a statement, judging ambiguity, judging whether an inductive conclusion is warranted, and judging whether statements made by authorities are acceptable.

11   Critical thinking is sometimes called directed thinking because it focuses on a desired outcome.

12   Critical thinking is the examination and testing of suggested solutions to see whether they will work.

13   Critical thinking is the art of analyzing and evaluating thinking with a view to improving it.

14   Critical thinking is the formation of logical inferences.

15   Critical thinking is the development of cohesive and logical reasoning patterns.

16   Critical thinking is reasonably and reflectively deciding what to believe or do.

17   Critical thinking is deciding rationally what to or what not to believe.

As can be seen, there are as many definitions of critical thinking as there are people willing to provide one. Can you spot what they all have in common? Let's now turn our attention to the steps you need to go through to think critically.

### BEGINNING STEPS OF THE CRITICAL THINKING PROCESS

Regardless of which definition of critical thinking you decide to hang your hat on, they all contain three generic steps that critical thinkers follow (Nosich, 2009):

**Step 1**  **It involves asking questions.** It involves asking questions that need to be asked, asking good questions, questions that go to the heart of the matter. It involves noticing that there are questions that need to be asked.

> **Note**: Step 1 of the critical thinking process is presented throughout the entire book using Appendixes A–C. This book does not discuss Steps 2 and 3 since they are covered in detail in books that are specifically devoted to critical thinking. In any event, let's see what the two remaining steps are all about.

> To see what Steps 2 and 3 are all about, we strongly suggest you obtain a copy of Eileen Gambrill's fantastic book titled, *Critical Thinking and the Process of Evidence-Based Practice* (2019).

**Step 2**  **It involves trying to answer those questions by reasoning them out.** Reasoning out answers to questions is different from other ways of answering questions. It's different from giving an answer you have always taken for granted but never thought about. It's different from answering impressionistically ("That reminds me of . . ."), or answering simply according to the way you were raised, or answering in accordance with your personality. It's also different from answering by saying the first thing that comes into your mind, and then using all your power of reasoning to defend your initial premature answer.

**Step 3**  **It involves believing the results of your reasoning.** Critical thinking is different from just engaging in a mental exercise. When you think through an issue critically, you internalize the results. You don't give merely verbal agreement: you actually believe the results because you have done your best to reason the issue out and you know that reasoning things out is the best way to get reliable answers. Furthermore, when you think critically through a decision about what to do in a situation, then what follows your reasoning is not just your belief, but action: Unless something unforeseen occurs, you end up taking the action you concluded was most reasonable.

### WHAT ACTIVITIES DOES A CRITICAL THINKER DO?

Now that you know your professional judgments are enhanced by thinking critically, what exactly does a critical thinker actually do? What does a critical thinker look like? Given all the various definitions of critical thinking previously mentioned, we can extract common "critical thinking type" activities (or skills, if you will) you will need to possess as a critical thinker (studylib.net, 2019). You may already have some of the skills securely stored in your professional toolkit.

Others you may have to work on as your social work courses proceed. Don't worry if you don't believe you have them right now—you'll have them by the end of your social work program, or soon afterward when you're practicing your craft:

1  A critical thinker asks pertinent questions independently and thinks outside the box.

2  A critical thinker reasons, analyzes, and weighs statements and arguments.

3 A critical thinker has a sense of curiosity and wonder, in addition to being interested in finding out new information or solutions.

4 A critical thinker defines criteria for analyzing ideas and problems.

5 A critical thinker is willing to examine beliefs, challenge assumptions and opinions, and weigh them against facts (distinguishing between fact, opinion, bias, and prejudice).

6 A critical thinker listens with an open mind, respectfully and carefully, to others even when they have opposing points of view in order to provide feedback, and also welcomes criticisms of beliefs and assumptions.

7 A critical thinker suspends judgment until all facts have been gathered and considered.

8 A critical thinker looks for evidence to support personal preconceived assumptions and beliefs.

9 A critical thinker is able and flexible enough to adjust personal opinions when new facts are found.

10 A critical thinker examines problems closely and looks for proof.

11 A critical thinker has the courage to consider ideas that may challenge personal positions or beliefs.

12 A critical thinker is able to identify and reject information that is incorrect or irrelevant.

13 A critical thinker can think independently and is not afraid to disagree with the "group" opinion.

14 A critical thinker makes assertions based on sound logic and solid evidence.

15 A critical thinker bases personal views on facts and evidence rather than on self-interest.

16 A critical thinker is able to admit a lack of understanding or information.

17 A critical thinker is in love with the truth and is curious about a wide range of issues.

18 A critical thinker recognizes that critical thinking is a lifelong process of self-assessment and development.

### HINTS TO HELP YOU TO BECOME A CRITICAL THINKER

Critical thinking is a fundamental skill for university students, but it should also be a lifelong pursuit. Laura Lucas (2017) has suggested six strategies to help you develop your critical thinking skills that you can use in your social work courses and in everyday life:

1 **Reflect and practice.** Always reflect on what you've learned. Is it true all the time? How did you arrive at your conclusions?

2 **Use wasted time.** It's certainly important to make time for relaxing, but if you find you are indulging in too much of a good thing, think about using your time more constructively. Determine when you do your best thinking and try to learn something new during that part of the day.

3 **Redefine the way you see things.** It can be very uninteresting to always think the same way. Challenge yourself to see familiar things in new ways. Put yourself in someone else's shoes and consider things from a different angle or perspective. If you're trying to solve a problem, list all your concerns: what you need in order to solve it, who can help, and what some possible barriers might be. It's often possible to reframe a problem as an opportunity. Try to find a solution where there seems to be none.

4 **Analyze the influences on your thinking and in your life.** Why do you think or feel the way you do? Analyze your influences. Think about who in your life influences you. Do you feel or react a certain way because of social convention or because you believe it is what is expected of you? Try to break out of any molds that may be constricting you.

5 **Express yourself.** Critical thinking also involves being able to express yourself clearly. Most important in expressing yourself clearly is stating one point at a time. You might be inclined to argue every thought, but you might have greater impact if you focus just on your main arguments. This will help others to follow your thinking clearly. For more abstract ideas, assume that your audience may not understand.

6 **Enhance your wellness.** It's easier to think critically when you take care of your mental and physical health. Try taking activity breaks throughout the day to reach 30 to 60 minutes of physical activity each day. Scheduling physical activity into your day can help lower stress and increase mental alertness. Also, do your most difficult work when you have the most energy. Think about the time of day you are most effective and have the most energy. Plan to do your most difficult work during these times. And be sure to reach out for help if you feel you need assistance with your mental or physical health. For a bit of Zen time, relax and read Box A on pages 471–473.

## USING THE THREE APPENDIXES

Remember the three steps of the critical thinking process mentioned on page 23? Well, the first step is to ask questions. So, when someone like Madam Cleo spouts off a "fact" (or you read something) such as "all news is fake" you'll automatically—consciously or unconsciously—try to determine the overall credibility of the facts you've been told (or read). It's only natural to do so.

However, before you start to judge the overall integrity of what you've been told, heard, or read (aka: "facts"), we encourage you to ask questions about the credibility of the very source that provided you with the "facts" in the first place. For example, Appendix C (pages 511–522) contains an evaluation grid that includes a number of questions you can ask about an Internet author in addition to the actual content provided by the author. More specifically, you can ask:

1 Potential questions about an *Internet author* (i.e., 1. Authority/Author—questions 461–477 on pages 514–515); poor author credibility can lead to poor "facts."

2 Potential questions about the *website's content* provided by the author (i.e., 2. Purpose/Coverage; 3. Accuracy; 4. Reasonableness; 5. Support; 6, Currency; 7. Objectivity; and 8. Ease of Use/Navigation—questions 478–583 on pages 515–522); poor trustworthiness of a webpage's content can lead to poor "facts."

Facts are verifiable, opinions are not. Thus, if a "fact" can't be verified, then it's an opinion—simple as that.

Thus, you must not only evaluate the overall believability of the source who provided you with the facts, you also must assess the overall trustworthiness of the facts themselves in either oral, visual, or written forms. For example, in reference to Scenario 1.1 on page 5 you can assess Madam Cleo's overall professionalism as an astrologer and the facts she yammers off such as, "You'll have better insights into love, business, health, sex, *grades in your research methods class*, and relationships." Box 1.2 on the following page illustrates just a few of the questions you could ask to assess the credibility of Madam Cleo and the facts she spouts off. Can you think of any more questions you can ask?

| Box 1.2 | Kellyanne Conway States the White House Has Its Own "Alternative Facts" |
|---|---|

**1  Who said it?**
Someone you know? Someone in a position of authority or power? Does it matter who told you this?

**2  What did they say?**
Did they give facts or opinions? Did they provide all the facts? Did they leave anything out?

**3  Where did they say it?**
Was it in public or in private? Did other people have a chance to respond and provide an alternative account?

**4  When did they say it?**
Was it before, during, or after an important event? Is timing important?

**5  Why did they say it?**
Did they explain the reasoning behind their opinion? Were they trying to make someone look good or bad?

**6  How did they say it?**
Were they happy or sad, angry or indifferent? Did they write it or say it? Could you understand what was said?

**NOTE:** Title of box taken from a phrase used by U.S. Counselor to the President Kellyanne Conway during a *Meet the Press* interview on January 22, 2017, in which she defended White House Press Secretary Sean Spicer's false statement about the attendance numbers of Donald Trump's inauguration as President of the United States.

> Your evaluation of any "fact" is only as good as the questions you ask and answer about the "fact".

## GET ACQUAINTED WITH THE THREE APPENDIXES

This is the perfect time for you to become familiar with how to use the three appendixes at the end of this book (i.e., Appendixes A–C).

- First, read over the general structure of the appendixes and the directions on how to use them on pages 468–473. This is very important.
- Second, glance over the potential questions you can ask about any "facts" you come across from:

  — Reading *quantitative* research studies (Appendix A)

  — Reading *qualitative* research studies (Appendix B)

  — Reading *mixed-methods* research studies (Appendixes A and B)

  — Finding information on the *Inter*net (Appendix C)

## DON'T GET INTIMIDATED

At this point, it's extremely important for you not to become intimidated by the sheer number of questions you can ask about any information or "facts" that you come across. We only provide you with a few potential questions since you have to know what questions to ask before you can answer them. And yes, that also means you have a responsibility to assess the creditability of facts that were derived from our current "gold standard" of knowing something: facts derived via the scientific method of inquiry—the most objective way of knowing.

### IS THERE A STANDARD EVALUATION RUBRIC?

Answer: There isn't one! Unfortunately, there's not a simple standardized grid, manual, template, rulebook, rubric, cheat sheet, assessment instrument, worksheet, checklist, or magic wand that can help you evaluate the overall credibility of Internet sources by coming up with a magic score of some kind.

In short, two people can evaluate the same information's source (such as Madam Cleo in scenario 1.1 on page 5) and come up with two different opinions on the overall credibility of Madam Cleo. The same is true for the actual content such as Madam Cleo's statement, "You'll have better insights into love, business, health, sex, grades in your research methods class, and relationships."

## CHAPTER RECAP

- We have to be accountable to ourselves, our clients, our profession, and our funders.

- There are "research-type" competencies that are expected of you while you are a student (CSWE) and after you graduate (NASW).

- Doing research studies helps our profession to become more accountable.

- There are four non-mutually exclusive purposes of social work research.

- Social work research studies can be pure or applied.

- There are five ways to "know" something.

- The five ways to know something are highly related to each other.

- Facts are verifiable, opinions are not.

- All people are entitled to their own opinions, but not to their own facts.

- Critical thinking is about questioning and thinking outside the box.

- Inductive reasoning allows us to generate new knowledge and theories.

- Deductive reasoning allows us to test existing theories and reasoning.

- Findings generated from research studies that used the scientific method of inquiry are the most objective way of knowing something.

- Professional judgments are based on using all five ways of knowing.

- Critical thinking enhances the accuracy of professional judgments.

- Critical thinking is logical and reflective thinking focused on deciding what to believe or do.

- A reasoned professional judgment on your part that uses all five ways of knowing, no matter how uncertain you may be, is far more beneficial to your clients than using only one of the ways of knowing.

- Critical thinking involves questioning and evaluating facts. Critical and creative thinking both contribute to our ability to solve problems in a variety of contexts.

- Evaluating facts, information, and opinions is a complex, but an essential task.

## REVIEW EXERCISES

1   In your own words, list—and fully discuss—the seven main "research-related" competencies that the CSWE expects you to have upon graduation in addition to the six that the NASW expects you to have after your graduate.

- Let's say you have just graduated from your social work program. What skills to you think you have, at this time, that would demonstrate that you are competent in each of the thirteen combined areas as identified by the CSWE and NASW? In a nutshell, what skill sets do you believe you have mastered? Not mastered?

- Now discuss how you plan to integrate each competency into your daily social work practice activities after you have graduated and become a professional social worker. You need to formulate a plan for how you're going to do this. Provide as many examples as you can to justify your position.

2   There are four purposes for doing research in social work, and any single social problem area can be studied under each

one of the four purposes. Choose a social problem area of your choice such as homelessness, bullying, school shootings, secondary trauma, abused children, unemployment, post-traumatic stress disorder, human trafficking, immigration, student tuition rates, or food insecurity.

- Now given with what you know so far, describe how you think your selected social problem area could be studied under each one of the four purposes.
- What specific research question do you think could be asked for each purpose given your problem area?
- Provide a hypothetical finding that each purpose could produce, given your social problem area; that is, you should have four hypothetical findings—one for each purpose.

3   Social work research studies can loosely be classified into pure and applied. Like Exercise 2, choose a social problem area of your choice.

- Write a "pure" research question you think could be asked and an "applied" research question.
- Provide a hypothetical finding that each type of research study could produce, given your social problem area.

4   List the five ways we obtain our knowledge base. Now discuss how you plan to use each one after you have graduated and become a professional social worker.

5   What are the main differences among knowledge, experience, tradition, beliefs, and intuition? Provide social work examples to justify your response.

6   What is the *scientific method* all about? Provide as many social work examples as you can to justify your response.

7   What is a *professional judgment*? Provide as many social work examples as you can to justify your response.

8   Discuss why a professional judgment on your part, no matter how uncertain you may be, is far more beneficial to your clients than just using only one way of knowing. Provide a social work example to illustrate your main points.

9   Discuss how you can enhance your professional judgments by using critical thinking skills. Provide examples in your discussion.

10  Take a look at Figure 1.1 on page 18 and describe the phases of the scientific inquiry process in your own words using one common social work example throughout your discussion.

11  Take a look at Figure 1.2 on page 20. What is inductive logic? What is deductive logic? Compare the two forms of logic using one social work research example of your choice. When would you use each of them? Provide as many examples as you can to justify your response.

**Time to think critically**

12  Now, given the knowledge you gained from this book so far, click on an excellent article by Gary Holden and Kathleen Barker:

> Holden, G., & Barker (2018). Should social workers be engaged in these practices? *Journal of Evidence-Informed Social Work, 15*, 1–13.
> DOI: 10.1080/23761407.2017.1422075

At the end of the article there are hundreds of honest-to-goodness websites that are sponsored by real MSW-level social workers (Table 1). Find four sites that interest you and answer all seventeen questions in Appendix C (i.e., questions 461–477 listed on pages 514–515) about each site's author. What did you learn from this exercise? And yes, these websites are for real. No kidding.

13  Reread pages 25–27 in addition to "How to Use the Three Appendixes" on pages 468–473. In your own words, discuss:

- How you can use Appendixes A and B to evaluate any practice/policy recommendation that was derived from a research study.
- How you can use Appendix C to evaluate the credibility and trustworthiness of the information you find on the Internet.

14  Take a look at the list of 18 generic critical thinking skills you'll need when you graduate on pages 23–24. In your opinion, what critical thinking skills do you currently possess? Provide examples that would demonstrate you have each skill. Now, which ones don't you have? Where, when, and how do you plan on obtaining them?

15  In reference to Madam Cleo's assertions as depicted in Scenario 1.1 on page 5, what do you believe her website would have to contain to satisfy each one of the seventeen questions in Appendix C (i.e., numbers 461–477 on pages 514–515) contained in the section titled, "1. Authority/Author"? That is, what would

she have had to provide for you to check "Yes" to each question?

16 Pick any one of the seventeen questions from question 15. Discuss where, when, and how you would obtain the necessary data to rate your chosen question as either "Yes" or "No".

17 Let's say you're a beginning social work student. Discuss who you believe knows more about the problems beginning social work students face—you as a student, or your research professor who has been teaching social work students for 30 years—and has three daughters who have graduated with social work degrees? Justify your opinions.

**Looking ahead by looking back**

18 At this point in your research methods course, how comfortable are you with discussing the place of research in social work with your field instructor, with your practice instructor, with your research instructor, with your supervisor at work, with the director of your social work program, or with your classmates.

# 2
CHAPTER

## 2015 EPAS COMPETENCIES

| COMPETENCY 1 | Demonstrate Ethical and Professional Behavior |
| --- | --- |

You will learn that in order to be a successful evidence-based practitioner you have an ethical obligation to integrate three research roles into your daily practice activities as will be discussed in Chapter 3: (1) research consumer, (2) research partner—either as a co-researcher or research participant, and (3) creator and disseminator of research (or knowledge).

This entire chapter pertains to these three professional roles as you'll learn that one of the best ways to become an ethical and professional evidence-based social work practitioner is knowing how to apply basic criteria in the assessment of a research question (or hypothesis) for relevancy, practicality, and usefulness to real-life social work practice, education, or policy.

| COMPETENCY 4 | Engage in Practice-Informed Research and Research-Informed Practice |
| --- | --- |

Competency 4 also pertains to the entire chapter because you have to:

1   Evaluate the degree to which a research study adhered to the basic principles of formulating social work research questions (or hypotheses), given the study's specific population or research participants. You will learn that the only way you can legitimately evaluate the effectiveness of your day-to-day practice activities (in addition to the social work program where you work) is not only knowing how research questions (or hypotheses) are formulated in the first place, but also becoming fully aware of what they are trying to accomplish: to explore, to describe, or to explain (**research consumer**—research-informed practice);

2   Participate in a research study—either as a co-researcher or research participant (**research partner**—practice-informed research). See 1 above and 3 below; and

3   Know how to formulate meaningful, relevant, and useful research questions (or hypotheses) before you actually begin a research study (**creator and disseminator of research**—practice-informed research).

You'll also need to utilize evidence-based practice recommendations whenever possible; that is, you'll need to integrate (1) the best available research-based evidence with (2) your clinical expertise and (3) your client's values.

All of the above implies you'll need to know how a research study formulated its final research question (or hypothesis) that produced the research-based evidence. In short, you need to ask and then answer a simple question: How seriously should I take the findings of any specific research study given the overall creditability and usefulness of its research question (or hypothesis)?

| COMPETENCY 9 | Evaluate Practice with Individuals, Families, Groups, Organizations, & Communities |
| --- | --- |

See Competencies 1 and 4.

**2**

# Research Questions

| | | |
|---|---|---|
| CHAPTERS 1 & 3 | Step 1. | Understanding the Research Process |
| CHAPTER 2 | Step 2. | Formulating Research Questions |
| CHAPTER 4<br>APPENDIXES A–C | Step 3. | Reviewing the Literature<br>Evaluating the Literature |
| CHAPTERS 5 & 6 | Step 4. | Being Aware of Ethical and Cultural Issues |
| CHAPTERS 7–10 | Step 5. | Selecting a Research Approach |
| CHAPTERS 11 & 12 | Step 6. | Specifying How Variables Are Measured |
| CHAPTER 13 | Step 7. | Selecting a Sample |
| CHAPTERS 14 & 15 | Step 8. | Selecting a Research Design |
| CHAPTERS 16 & 17 | Step 9. | Selecting a Data-Collection Method |
| CHAPTERS 18 & 19 | Step 10. | Analyzing the Data |
| CHAPTERS 20 & 21 | Step 11. | Writing the Research Report |

# Research Questions

Test today on how to formulate research questions

"Professor, I'm afraid I've got way more meaningless questions than meaningful answers."

RESEARCH QUESTIONS AND ACCOUNTABILITY
    Social Problems Must Be Changeable
FACTORS AFFECTING RESEARCH QUESTIONS
    The Social Work Program
    The Researcher
       *Value Systems of the Researchers*
    Ethical and Cultural Considerations
    Political and Social Considerations
THE KNOWLEDGE-LEVEL CONTINUUM
    Exploratory Research Studies
    Descriptive Research Studies
    Explanatory Research Studies
EVIDENCE-BASED HIERARCHY
CLASSIFICATIONS OF QUESTIONS
    Existence Questions
    Composition Questions

    Relationship Questions
    Descriptive-Comparative Questions
    Causality Questions
    Causality-Comparative Questions
    Causality-Comparative Interaction Questions
CRITERIA FOR GOOD QUESTIONS
    Relevant
    Researchable
    Feasible
    Ethical and Culturally Sensitive
EVALUATING A STUDY'S RESEARCH QUESTION
    Use the Appendixes
       *Tasks*
CHAPTER RECAP
REVIEW EXERCISES

THE PREVIOUS CHAPTER discussed how our profession can become more accountable to society by undertaking research studies that can answer meaningful and useful social work research questions in addition to testing hypotheses. The most important thing to remember about any research study is that it's only as good as the research question it's trying to answer, or the hypothesis it's trying to test. Poor question/hypothesis = poor study.

Given the above, this chapter is a logical extension of the previous one in that we present how you can formulate research questions that can be answered through the use of the scientific method of inquiry—one of the five ways of knowing.

## RESEARCH QUESTIONS AND ACCOUNTABILITY

Our profession welcomes with open arms pure and applied research questions that are geared toward increasing our profession's knowledge base. It seems only reasonable that the knowledge specific to our field should be obtained by social workers who formulate their own research questions and conduct subsequent research studies that answer them in their particular areas of expertise.

As we have established, if we are to remain involved in the well-being of our clients, we must become more active in assessing the effectiveness and efficiency of our interventions. The social problem of domestic violence, for example, will not be solved by indiscriminate funding of emergency shelters for women who have been battered, by treatment for men who have been abusive toward their partners, by services for children who have been victimized, or by higher education for all and sundry. In short, good research questions are needed both to determine the most effective ways of helping people and to evaluate the usefulness of our social service programs currently being funded.

It would benefit both social workers and their clients alike if we were to take more responsibility for formulating research questions and conducting subsequent research studies that answer them on our own programs. This would provide us with the authority to advocate for clients, to be heard by other professionals with regard to our clients, to maintain control over programs serving our clients, and to bring about needed change. In this present age of accountability, there is no doubt that a profession that strives for status must be accountable.

> Social work research topics—and the research questions and hypotheses they generate—deal with social problems that our profession is trying to eradicate.

The way to achieve accountability is by answering well-formulated and well-thought-out research questions. However, we must never forget that accountability is not all a facade. As we know, the scientific method—as one of the five ways of knowing—is not just a path to authority and status. It also allows us to determine how best to serve our clients, how to determine the effectiveness of our services, and how to improve the services.

## SOCIAL PROBLEMS MUST BE CHANGEABLE

We strongly invite research questions that will solve social problems. However, the social problems we would like to solve must be in fact changeable—and have a solution to boot. We have already talked about what motivates social workers to do research studies in the last chapter. Your supervisor may want you to, or you might have to for the sake of your clients, or you could be just interested in something. Sometimes the research question is mostly already there, and it only remains for you to word it more precisely so that it can become researchable.

Perhaps, for example, your social service program provides substance abuse treatment to First Nations adolescents, and it wants to know whether the spirituality component it has recently introduced makes the intervention package more effective. At other times, you begin more generally with a broad topic area—poverty, for example—and then you will need to decide what particular aspects of your general topic area you want to address before you can formulate a sound and crystal-clear research question.

Simply put, social work research topics—and the research questions they generate— deal with social problems. A social problem is something we wish we didn't have. This may not sound particularly profound, but consider for a moment what it is that causes some social circumstances and not others to be defined as "problems." In our day, for example, poverty is seen as a social problem. In earlier times, however, poverty certainly existed, but it was not considered a problem in the sense that we felt we ought to do something about it. The attitude was very much that the poor are always with us and that's just the way it is.

> We do not define a social problem in the first place unless we believe that change both ought to and probably can occur.

## FACTORS AFFECTING RESEARCH QUESTIONS

**T**he following main factors affect how a research question is finally formulated. They all highly overlap with one another, and it's just about impossible to discuss them separately, but we'll give it a try. The four factors are:

1   The social work program
2   The researcher
3   Ethical and cultural considerations
4   Political and social considerations

> Today, funders want "objective data" derived from research studies that determine if the agency's goals are being met at the least possible cost.

## THE SOCIAL WORK PROGRAM

Most of us are employed by a social work program housed within an agency. A child protection agency, for example, may run an investigation program whose sole purpose is to investigate alleged cases of child abuse and neglect. The same agency may provide in-home support services to families who have abused or neglected their children—a second program. The agency may run a survivor-witness program for children and nonoffending parents who have to appear in court—a third program.

Research studies that answer research questions are usually conducted within the confines of a program. The word "confines" is used advisedly because no study can be undertaken without the support, or at least the toleration, of the program's director. Some program directors are supportive of research studies, while others shiver at the merest mention, but all of them have some things in common. The first of these is that they all worry about money.

Directors of social work agencies have very little money. They worry that in the coming year they may have even less money—that their funding will be cut or even terminated, their clients will suffer, and their staff will be unemployed. They worry that all these disasters will follow in the wake of an evaluative research study. People doing research studies often have access to client files and to clients.

We sometimes talk to staff and examine agency procedures. We are in an excellent position to embarrass everyone by breaching client confidentiality, making inappropriate statements at the wrong times to the wrong people, and writing reports that comment on the program's weaknesses but disregard its strengths.

All programs, like all people, have flaws. Few are efficient in the business sense, and most are open to doubt concerning their effectiveness. Program directors know this. They work to improve programs, serving their clients as best they can with limited resources and knowledge that is patchy at best—because the knowledge has not been gained and the research studies necessary to gain it have not been undertaken.

It's not surprising, then, that agency directors find themselves torn with regard to the place of the research enterprise in our profession. They understand that increased knowledge, via answering research questions, is necessary in order to serve clients better, but sometimes they wish that the knowledge could be gathered somewhere else: not through their programs, not with their client files, not using their scarce resources, and not taking up the time of their staff. They correctly argue that resources given to research studies are resources taken away from client services.

They may think, privately, that research reports are useful only to those engaged in the studies in the first place. There is an upside to all of this gloom, however. It's possible that the research report might reflect the program in a good light, delighting its funders and improving its standing in the public eye. In addition, the study might reveal a genuinely practical way in which the program could improve its services to its clients or do what it does more efficiently.

Many program directors will therefore give permission for research studies to be conducted, provided that the person(s) doing the study is of good standing in the social work community, the proposed study meets the staff's approval, and agreements are entered into concerning confidentiality and the use of the program's staff and financial resources.

## THE RESEARCHER

The second factor that affects the formulation of research questions is the person actually doing the study—you, the researcher. To illustrate how social work researchers are motivated to come up with specific research questions, two articles from Canadian newspapers will be used as examples (Grinnell, Rothery, & Thomlison, 1993).

As you know, the article reproduced in Box 1.1 in Chapter 1 on pages 9–10 is concerned with the attempted abduction of a child in an elementary school at Innisfail, Alberta, and the article in Box 2.1 in this chapter (on the following page) remarks on the unusual lack of stereotyping of Native Canadians in a Canadian television program. The two articles can easily be applied equally to the problems of child abuse and racism throughout the world. What motivates social workers to pose research questions? One way to answer this question is by examining possible reactions to the articles contained in Boxes 1.1 and 2.1.

> The opinions and attitudes of social workers in regard to research practices play a vital part in the formulation of research questions.

> A researcher's positive relationships with program staff cannot be overemphasized.

| Box 2.1 | Show Ignores Native Stereotypes |

**Gibsons, B.C. (CP)**—Native actress Marianne Jones had to fight to keep from laughing when a script once called for her to utter the line: "Him shot six times."

"It was really a difficult thing to say," recalls Jones, who now plays Laurel on CBC's Beachcombers.

That, she says, is typical of the way natives are portrayed on TV and films.

And that, she says, is what's different about Beachcombers.

"It's one of the only shows that portrays native people on a day-to-day basis," says Jones.

"No other series has that sort of exposure. When you think of how many native people there are in the country, it's amazing that there isn't more."

Television's portrayal of natives touches a nerve in Jones.

The striking actress with shoulder-length raven hair cherishes her Haida heritage. She identifies her birthplace as "Haida Gwaii—that's the Queen Charlotte Islands, the real name."

The four natives in Beachcombers are depicted as people rather than stereotypes.

"I've done a lot of other shows and they sort of want to put you in a slot: You're a noble savage, you know, the Hollywood stereotypes that have been perpetuated forever."

She admits that natives are struggling with their identity these days; wrestling with tradition and the attractions of the 21st century.

"We're all weighing the traditional life, the spirituality, against being human . . . We're living today."

"Everybody has a fridge, so to speak," she adds with a raspy laugh.

Jones is doing her part by venturing into video production, starting with a documentary on a Haida artist.

"For a long time, native people have not been allowed or able to define their own images."

"We need to take control to get rid of those Hollywood stereotypes, and to change native people on television to real people."

In reference to the first article (Box 1.1), parents of young children, for example, may feel fear and anxiety about the safety of their children because they may be reminded that in their communities there are those who could harm them. They and others may experience anger toward those who victimize children and a desire to see them caught, restrained, or punished. They may feel concern for the abducted seven-year-old, mixed with feelings of relief that she was returned to her family.

An adult who was victimized as a child, for example, may be likely to have more complex and strong emotional reactions than a person who was not victimized as a child. Teachers, social workers, and police officers whose jobs entail responsibility for such situations may experience professional curiosity.

With the second article (Box 2.1), a reader may react with admiration for Marianne Jones, who has overcome the barriers imposed by racism to establish herself in a difficult career. Those of you who are members of a minority group may well applaud more enthusiastically than those of you who are not; you may even share her success in some way.

An administrator in a school system that serves minority students may sense an opportunity—a chance to answer a meaningful research question into what images of minorities are perpetuated through the educational system and what impact this has on the students. Some readers may have little or no reaction, however. If nothing in their past history or current involvements is linked to the issues of child abuse (Box 1.1) or racism (Box 2.1), they may merely glance at the articles and pass them over quickly.

A great variety of responses to these two news items is possible, each shaped by the reader's personal history, experiences, and circumstances. It is in reactions such as these that research questions are born. We may be drawn into research projects simply because they are there—support is available to conduct a particular study, or our careers will benefit from seizing the opportunities. Potential researchers begin with the sense (often vaguely formulated) that there is more to be known about a problem area; a question exists that is important enough to justify investing time and other resources in the search for an answer.

The most important thing to peruse before doing any research study is to clearly specify the potential implications the study's findings might have on advancing the knowledge base of social work practice, and/or education, and/or policy.

### VALUE SYSTEMS OF THE RESEARCHERS

At every stage in the research process, there are decisions to be made based on the knowledge and value systems of the person formulating the research question and conducting the research study. If we are investigating poverty, for example, and believe that poverty results from character flaws in the poor, we might study treatment interventions designed to overcome those flaws. On the other hand, if we believe that ghettos are a factor, we might prefer to focus on environmental causes. In short, the research questions we finally select are determined by our own value systems as well as by the social and political realities of the hour.

Another factor in our study of poverty is how the researcher defines "poor." What annual income should a person earn in order to be categorized as poor? We may decide that "poor", in the context of our study, means an annual income of less than $20,000, and that we do not need to talk to anyone who earns more than that. If we decide that the upper limit should be $30,000, we are automatically including many more people as potential participants for our study. Thus, the data collected about "the poor" will depend largely on who the researcher defines as "poor".

Our final report will probably include recommendations for change based on our study's findings—which is based on our research question of course. These recommendations, too, will depend on our personal value systems, modified by social, political, and economic realities.

> If you don't possess sound social skills you'll never be given permission to do a research study within a social work agency.

It may be our private opinion, for example, that welfare recipients should be given only the absolute minimum of resources necessary to sustain life in order to motivate them to find work. On the other hand, we may believe that a decent standard of living is every human being's birthright. Whatever our opinion, it's likely that we will clothe it in suitable phraseology and incorporate it somehow into our recommendations.

Personal value systems are particularly evident in program evaluations. Our programs are often labeled as ineffective, not as a result of poor goal achievement, but because there is disagreement about the goal itself. Is a drug prevention program "successful" if it reduces drug use among its clients, or must clients abstain altogether before success can be claimed? Then there is the question of how much success constitutes "success."

Is a job placement program worth funding if it finds jobs for only 50 percent of its clients? Should an in-home support program be continued if the child is removed from the home in 30 percent of the cases?

Next, there is the matter of what types of clients are the most deserving. Should limited resources be used to counsel people dying of cancer, or would the money be better spent on those who are newly diagnosed? Is it worthwhile to provide long-term treatment for one family whose potential for change is small, while other families with more potential linger on the waiting list? These types of value-based questions are endless.

## ETHICAL AND CULTURAL CONSIDERATIONS

Another important factor affecting the formulation of social work research questions is ethical and cultural considerations. Physical scientists are by no means exempt from ethical considerations. Consider Robert Oppenheimer and other atomic scientists, who learned too late that their scientific findings about splitting the atom were used to create an atomic bomb—a purpose the scientists themselves opposed.

A physical scientist who wishes to run tests on water samples, for example, does not have to consider the feelings of the water samples or worry about harming them. No large dilemma is presented if one of the water samples must be sacrificed to the cause of knowledge building.

For people engaged in social work research studies, however, the ethical issues are far more pervasive and complex. A fundamental principle of formulating a social work research question is that any increase in our knowledge base, while much desired, must never be obtained at the expense of human beings. Since many of our research questions revolve directly around human beings, safeguards must be put in place to ensure that our research participants are never harmed, either physically or psychologically.

An American committee known as the National Commission for the Protection of Human Subjects of Biomedical and Behavioral Research is only one of several professional organizations and lay groups that focus on protecting the rights of research participants. Most research participants, however, have never heard of any of them. It's therefore incumbent upon all of us to be familiar with ethical principles so that our clients' trust will never be betrayed.

Essentially, there are three precautionary ethical measures that must be taken before beginning any research study and will be covered extensively in Chapter 5 on ethics:

1   Obtaining the participant's informed consent
2   Designing the study in an ethical manner
3   Ensuring that others will be properly told about the study's findings

## POLITICAL AND SOCIAL CONSIDERATIONS

The final factor that affects social work research questions is political and social considerations. Ethics and politics are interrelated, but a useful distinction exists in that ethics has to do with the methods employed in answering the research question, whereas politics is concerned with the practical costs and uses of the study's findings.

Consider, for example, the area of race relations. Most social researchers in the 1960s supported the cause of African American equality in America. In 1969, Arthur Jensen, a Harvard psychologist, examined data on racial differences in IQ test results and concluded that genetic differences between African Americans and Caucasians accounted for the lower IQ scores of African Americans. Jensen was labeled a racist, and such was the furor surrounding his study that other people were reluctant to pursue any line of inquiry involving comparisons between Caucasians and African Americans.

Consequently, a needed investigation into the higher rate of mortality seen in African American women with breast cancer compared to similarly afflicted Caucasian women

Clients participating in research studies do not put their trust in committees; they trust the individual practitioners who involve them in the studies.

was not conducted. The study may have revealed racial differences in genetic predispositions to breast tumors, and the National Cancer Institute, at that time, was understandably reluctant to use the word "genetic" in connection with African Americans. It's not infrequently the case that sensitivity about vulnerable populations leads to avoidance of research studies that might benefit those groups.

Politics plays an important role not only in what research studies are funded or conducted but also in what findings are published. Contrary opinions or unpopular opinions are no longer punished, as they were in Galileo's day, by the Inquisitional Tribunal or the rack, but they are still punished. Punishment may be delivered in the form of articles and books that are never published, invitations to present research papers that are never offered, academic appointments that are never given—and research proposals that are never funded.

Finding the answer to a research question can be an extremely expensive endeavor. If a funding body cannot be found to support the research project, the study may never be conducted. Funding bodies tend either to be governments or to be influenced by government policies and a person doing a research study is as interested as anyone else in money, recognition, and professional advancement. It's therefore often the case that funded studies follow directions consistent with the prevailing political climate.

Studies under one administration may inquire into ways of improving social services and discovering better designs for public housing. Under another administration, attention may shift to the efficiency of existing programs, as measured through program evaluations. It's important to remember, though, that not all research studies are expensive, and many can be conducted without the aid of government money. No large amounts of extra funding are needed to integrate evaluation into the normal routine of clinical practice. Program evaluations do not cost large amounts of money when conducted by program staff themselves.

In sum, social work research questions are affected not only by the personal biases of the person conducting the study to answer the questions, but also by prevailing beliefs on such sensitive issues as race, gender, poverty, disability, sexual orientation, violence, gerrymandering, and so forth. Government positions both shape and are shaped by these beliefs, leading to support of some research questions but not others. Legitimate inquiry is sometimes restricted by fear that data uncovered on one of these sensitive issues will be misinterpreted or misused, thereby bringing harm to vulnerable client groups.

> Politics has to do with the practical costs and uses of the study's findings.

> Ethics has to do with the methods employed in answering a research question.

## THE KNOWLEDGE-LEVEL CONTINUUM

**G**iven that your final research question has been seriously influenced by the previous discussion, it now has to be answered via the scientific method of inquiry. All research questions, and their resulting studies, fall anywhere along a knowledge-level continuum depending on how much is already known about the research question under investigation. There are three complementary research approaches within the scientific method of inquiry that can answer research questions. They are:

**1** The *quantitative* (positivistic) research approach

**2** The *qualitative* (interpretive) research approach

**3** The *mixed-methods* research approach (combines quantitative and qualitative approaches into one study)

Which approach is to be taken is determined by the research question (or hypothesis) and/or by the philosophical inclination of the researcher. All three approaches complement each other and are equally important in the generation and testing of social work knowledge. They all strive to generate valid and reliable research findings that are relevant to our profession. All three generally follow the four phases of the scientific method as outlined in Figures 7.1 (page 145) and 7.2 (page 149) but they do so in their own particular way.

1  **Quantitative research studies.** They rely on the quantification of collecting and analyzing numeric data and sometimes use statistics to test hypotheses established prior to actually carrying out the study (i.e., Figure 7.1 on page 145). The quantitative research approach will be thoroughly discussed in Chapters 7 and 8.

2  **Qualitative research studies.** They rely on qualitative and descriptive methods of data collection and generate hypotheses and generalizations during the research study (i.e., Figure 7.2 on page 149). The qualitative research approach will be thoroughly discussed in Chapters 7 and 9.

3  **Mixed-methods research studies.** They gather quantitative and qualitative data within a single study. They then purposively and systematically integrate the two types of data in an effort to strengthen the studies' overall findings. The mixed-methods approach will be thoroughly discussed in Chapters 7 and 10.

The mixed-method research approach can easily be used at all three knowledge levels—especially at the exploratory and descriptive levels. However, at the explanatory level, the findings from a quantitative study are given first priority and then can be supplemented with qualitative data that provide meaning to the quantitative findings.

How much is known about the research question determines the purpose of the study. If you don't know anything, for example, you will merely want to explore the research area, gathering basic data. Studies like this, conducted for the purpose of exploration, are known, logically enough, as *exploratory studies* and fall at the bottom of the knowledge-level continuum as can be seen in Figure 2.1 on the following page.

Exploratory research questions usually adopt a qualitative, or interpretive, research approach. However, they can also adopt a quantitative, or positivistic, approach as well, in which case they would be classified as mixed-methods—assuming of course that the findings from both approaches are truly *integrated* into the study's overall research design. One again, note the word *integrated.*

When you have gained some knowledge of the research topic area through exploratory studies, the next task is to describe a specific aspect of the topic area in greater detail using words (qualitative) and/or numbers (quantitative). These studies, whose purpose is description, are known as *descriptive studies* and fall in the middle of the knowledge-level continuum as presented in Figure 2.1 on the following page.

Descriptive studies can adopt a quantitative and/or qualitative research approach. After descriptive studies have provided a substantial knowledge base in the research topic area, you will be in a position to ask very specific and more complex research questions—causality questions. These kinds of studies are known as *explanatory studies.*

The division of the knowledge continuum into three parts—exploratory, descriptive, and explanatory—is a useful way of categorizing research studies in terms of their purpose, the kinds of questions they can answer, and the research approach(es) they can take in answering the questions.

However, as in all categorization systems, the three divisions are totally arbitrary, and some social work research studies simply defy categorization at all costs, falling nastily somewhere between exploratory and descriptive, or between descriptive and explanatory. This defiance is only to be expected since the knowledge-level continuum is essentially that—a continuum, not a neat collection of mutually exclusive categories.

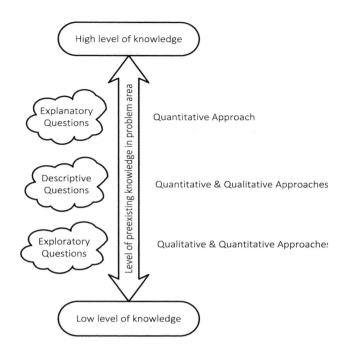

**Figure 2.1**

The Knowledge-Level Continuum (arrow), Predominate Approaches to the
Scientific Method (right), and Types of Questions Answered (left)

## EXPLORATORY RESEARCH STUDIES

Exploratory studies are most useful when the research topic area is relatively new. In the United States during the 1970s, for example, the development of new drugs to control the symptoms of mental illness, together with new federal funding for small, community-based mental health centers, resulted in a massive discharge of people from large state-based mental health institutions.

Some folks applauded this move as restoring the civil liberties of the mentally ill. Others were concerned that current community facilities would prove inadequate to meet the needs of the people being discharged and their families. Social workers active in the 1970s were eager to explore the situation, both with an eye on influencing social policy and in order to develop programs to meet the perceived needs of this group of people.

> How much is known about the research question determines the purpose of the study.

The topic area here is very broad. What are the consequences of a massive discharge of people who are psychiatrically challenged and were recently institutionalized? Many different questions pertaining to the topic can be asked. Where are these people living now? Alone? In halfway houses? With their families? On the street? Are they receiving proper medication and nutrition? What income do they have? How do they spend their time? What stresses do they suffer? What impact have they had on their family members and the communities in which they now reside? What services are available to them? How do they feel about being discharged?

No single study can answer all these questions. It's a matter of devising a sieve-like procedure where the first sieve with the biggest holes identifies general themes. Each general theme is then put through successively finer sieves until more specific research questions can be asked.

Let's take a look at Figure 2.2 on the following page for a minute. You might begin to explore the consequences of the massive discharge by gathering together a group of these discharged people and asking them a basic qualitatively oriented exploratory question: What have been your experiences since you were discharged? (What are the components that make up the discharge experience?) The question will be answered using qualitative data. Individual answers via words—not numbers—will generate common themes.

At this point, you might feel a need for numbers. How many of them are living where? How many times have they moved on average? What percentage of those who moved in with their families stayed there? These are quantitatively oriented descriptive questions, aimed at describing or providing an accurate profile of this group of people.

You are now moving up the knowledge continuum in Figure 2.1 from the exploratory to the descriptive category, but before we go there let's summarize the general goals of exploratory research studies (Neuman & Robson, 2018):

> Exploratory research studies are also called nonexperimental research studies.

- Become familiar with the basic facts, people, and concerns involved
- Develop a well-grounded mental picture of what is occurring
- Generate many ideas and develop tentative theories and conjectures
- Determine the feasibility of doing additional research
- Formulate questions and refine issues for more systematic inquiry
- Develop techniques and a sense of direction for future research

## DESCRIPTIVE RESEARCH STUDIES

At the descriptive level, suppose you have decided to focus your research questions on those people who moved in with their families. You have an idea, based on your previous qualitatively oriented exploratory study, that there might be a relationship between the length of time spent in the institution and whether or not this group of people moved in with their families after discharge.

You would like to confirm or refute this relationship by using a much larger group of respondents than you used in your exploratory study (Figure 2.2). Another important tentative relationship that emerged at the exploratory level was the relationship between staying in the family home and the level of acceptance shown by the family.

> Descriptive research studies are also called quasi-experimental research studies.

You would like to know if this relationship holds with a larger group. You would also like to know if there is a real difference between accepting and rejecting families: Is Group A different from Group B? And what factors contribute to acceptance or rejection of the discharged family member? Eventually, you would like to know if there is anything social workers can do to facilitate acceptance, but you don't have enough data yet to be able to usefully ask that question. In general, the goals of descriptive research studies are as follows (Neuman & Robson, 2018):

- Provide an accurate profile of a group
- Describe a process, mechanism, or relationship
- Give a verbal or numerical picture (e.g., percentages)
- Find information to stimulate new explanations
- Create a set of categories or classify types

## EXPLANATORY RESEARCH STUDIES

Suppose you have learned from your descriptive studies that there are real differences between accepting and rejecting families and that these differences seem to have a major

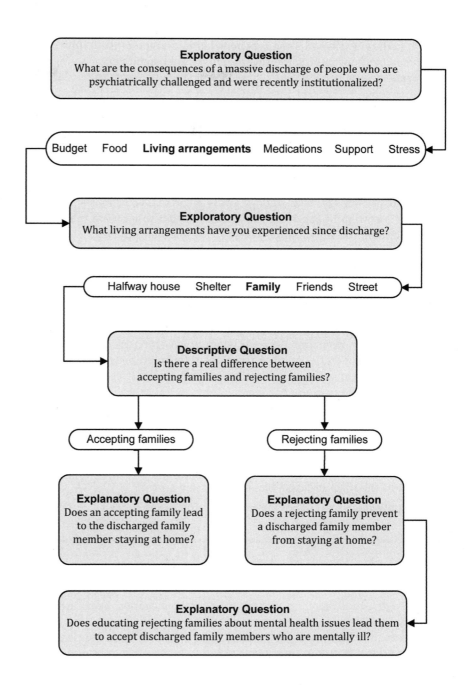

**Figure 2.2**

Example of a Simple Sieving Procedure

impact on whether or not the discharged person stays at home. Now you would like to ask two related explanatory, or causality, questions:

**Explanatory research questions**
- Does an accepting family lead to a discharged family member staying at home?
- Does a rejecting family prevent a discharged family member from staying at home?

In both cases, the answers will probably be yes, to some extent. Perhaps 30 percent of staying at home is explained by an accepting family and the other 70 percent remains to be explained by other factors: the severity of the discharged person's symptoms, for example, or the degree of acceptance shown by community members outside the family.

Now you might want to know whether acceptance on the part of the family carries more weight in the staying-at-home decision than acceptance on the part of the community. The answer to this question will provide a direction for possible intervention strategies. You will know whether to focus your attention on individual families or on entire communities.

Suppose you decide, for example, on the basis of your own and other explanatory studies, to focus on the families, and the intervention that you choose for increasing their acceptance is education about mental illness. In order to evaluate the effectiveness of your intervention, you will eventually need to ask another explanatory question:

### Explanatory research question
Does educating rejecting families about mental health issues lead them to accept discharged family members who are mentally ill?

> Explanatory research studies are also called experimental research studies.

With the answer to this question, you have concluded your sieving procedures, as outlined in Figure 2.2, moving from a broad exploratory question about discharge experiences to a tested intervention designed to serve the discharged people and their families. In general, these are the goals of explanatory research studies (Neuman & Robson, 2018):

- Determine the accuracy of a principle or theory
- Find out which competing explanation is better
- Link different issues or topics under a common general statement
- Build and elaborate a theory so it becomes more complete
- Extend a theory or principle into new areas or issues
- Provide evidence to support or refute an explanation

## EVIDENCE-BASED HIERARCHY

So far, we discussed how research studies can answer research questions on a knowledge-level continuum that contains three categories: exploratory, descriptive, and explanatory. They can also be arranged on a six-level evidence hierarchy as illustrated in Box 2.2 on the following pages Because most of the methods are described in detail elsewhere in this text, Box 2.2 presents a simple overview of the six levels:

**Level 1**   Systematic Reviews and Meta-Analyses
**Level 2**   Evidence-Based Guidelines
**Level 3**   Experimental Research
**Level 4**   Quasi-Experimental Research
**Level 5**   Nonexperimental Research
**Level 6**   Clinical Experience and Reports from Experts or Committees

**Box
2.2**    The Evidence-Based Hierarchy

**There are six classification categories,** or levels, that research studies can be classified under. In a nutshell, and in the simplest of terms, the degree of a research study's overall "objectivity" and "rigor" determines its category. The more rigor and objectivity, the higher up on the hierarchy it goes.

**Level 1: Systematic Reviews & Meta-Analyses**
A systematic review is a comprehensive review of a body of data, or a series of studies, that uses explicit methods to locate primary studies of the "gold standard" of evidence (i.e., RCTs: randomized control trials), appraise them, and then summarize them according to a standard methodology (Higgins & Green, 2005). Systematic reviews can be conducted quantitatively by using meta-analysis techniques or qualitatively by summarizing the results in narrative form.

A meta-analysis is a statistical technique that combines or integrates the results of several independent RCTs that are similar enough statistically that the results can be combined and analyzed as if they were one study. Systematic reviews and meta-analyses provide an efficient way to obtain evidence on a particular topic across multiple research studies.

However, these reviews should still be used with caution. In addition to the same problems encountered in the literature for individual studies (i.e., poor design/methods), meta-analyses that do not account for variation across treatments, samples, measuring instruments, and analyses could lead to misleading conclusions (Bigby, 1998). For additional information about reading and evaluating systematic reviews and meta-analyses, we recommend reading Higgins and Green (2005).

**Level 2: Evidence-Based Guidelines**
Evidence-based guidelines, sometimes referred to as *practice guidelines*, are systematically compiled and organized statements of empirically tested knowledge and procedures that help social workers select and implement interventions that are most effective and appropriate for attaining the desired outcomes (Rosen & Proctor, 2003). Most often, expert scholars in a particular area compile such guidelines based on standard review procedures.

When drawing upon this body of literature, it's important to understand how the evidence base was reviewed (systematic versus expert opinion) in order to compile a compendium of evidence, as well as the methods used in the original primary research study. For example, a compendium of evidence on child abuse prevention programs, which was derived from expert opinion, case studies, and/or observational studies, might be less reliable than evidence from primarily well-designed RCTs or quasi-experimental studies. Again, it depends on the quality of the original study's research methodology. For evaluating quantitative studies, see Appendix A; for evaluating qualitative ones, see Appendix B.

### Level 3: Experimental Research

Bias and design flaws are two primary reasons that studies conclude that an intervention is effective when really it may not be, and vice versa. However, well-controlled experimental research designs are powerful methods to address these flaws. In a well-controlled RCT, participants are randomly assigned to either a treatment group (which is the treatment or intervention under investigation) or a control group (which receives nothing or the current standard of care). Because Chapter 15 provides a comprehensive discussion of experimental designs, we will only briefly review a few of the major strengths and limitations of this methodology.

As you will see in Chapters 13 and 15 the use of random selection from a population and random assignment to groups in experimental research studies is a powerful method to reduce bias, which is any factor that causes the results to exaggerate or underestimate the effects of an intervention or treatment (Jadad, 1998). If random selection and assignment are carried out correctly, there is an increased probability that differences between, or among, groups can be attributed to the treatment alone.

For example, if you are searching for evidence on a school violence prevention program, you would first look for RCTs and then would search for other types of studies only if you do not find any.

Obviously, RCTs are not the appropriate method to use for all research questions. As we will see in Chapter 5 on research ethics, to assess the effects of alcohol on health, for example, and for ethical reasons alone, you would not randomly assign some individuals to a group that drinks alcohol daily and the others to a second group that abstains.

RCTs are not without limitations. If an RCT is not methodologically sound, its results are not necessarily any better than the results derived from a quasi-experimental study. Thus, when assessing the quality of evidence, it's important to look beyond the hierarchy of categories (Petticrew & Roberts, 2003). In addition, as mentioned above, various research designs and methods are necessary to answer different types of research questions. To answer your research question adequately and appropriately, you might need to seek out additional types of evidence.

### Level 4: Quasi-Experimental Research

The next level of evidence is the quasi-experimental design. Unlike true experimental designs, quasi-experimental designs do not randomly assign research participants to groups. These designs usually have comparison groups rather than control groups. They do, however, tend to provide more causal support for the intervention under investigation than descriptive studies without comparison groups. Evidence generated from quasi-experimental research designs can be very informative for your research study.

Although quasi-experimental designs attempt to achieve the internal validity of experimental designs, their evidence in terms of cause-and-effect relationships should be interpreted with caution. Evidence from these types of designs is generally less reliable than that from well-controlled randomized trials, since the two groups may differ in ways other than the treatment under investigation. In other words, the effects of the treatment may be due to other factors that were not controlled for by using random assignment. Nevertheless, quasi-experimental designs might be the most appropriate method to use to obtain evidence about a particular topic.

### Level 5: Nonexperimental Research

A less preferred method for obtaining evidence is through observational studies, which may range from cross-sectional surveys to case studies (or case reports). Observational studies are exploratory or descriptive and are far less powerful than experimental and quasi-experimental designs primarily because they lack control groups or comparison groups.

Because data are collected in an uncontrolled or unsystematic environment, evidence from nonexperimental research designs cannot be generalizable to the larger population; thus, it's relegated to a lower level of evidence on the hierarchy. However, evidence from nonexperimental studies may be the most feasible to use under certain circumstances and may also provide information that cannot be derived from higher research designs. For example, results from a nonexperimental study using client charts could reveal additional information that will help you to understand a client's symptoms or diagnosis that could not be obtained from other types of research designs.

**Level 6: Clinical Experience and Reports from Experts or Committees**
Knowledge from a practitioner's clinical experience and/or the opinions of experts or committees is usually considered the lowest level of evidence. However, this should not negate the value of this kind of evidence. It can help you understand the process of implementing an intervention, the barriers and facilitators to implementation, and unexpected adverse effects related to the intervention.

## CLASSIFICATIONS OF QUESTIONS

Figures 2.1–2.3 show how research questions can be placed on a continuum from simple (exploratory studies) to complex (explanatory studies). Not surprisingly we need to ask simple questions first. When we have the answers to these simple questions, we then proceed to ask more complex ones. We are thus moving from "little knowledge about our research question" to "more knowledge about our research question."

Figure 2.3 presents the knowledge continuum (from high to low—middle arrow), seven general classifications that research questions can take (left side), and the research approach (right side) that is most appropriate to answer each question classification. Once again, the mixed-method approach can be used at all seven levels depending on the research questions. As can be seen in Figure 2.3, there are seven classifications of questions that social work research studies can answer:

1  Existence
2  Composition
3  Relationship
4  Descriptive-comparative
5  Causality
6  Causality-comparative
7  Causality-comparative interaction

## EXISTENCE QUESTIONS

Suppose for a moment you have an assumption that there is an association between low self-esteem in women and spousal abuse. You are going to study this topic—over number of studies—starting at the beginning. The beginning, at the bottom of the knowledge continuum, is an existence question. In fact, it is two existence questions since your assumption involves two concepts: self-esteem and spousal abuse.

First, knowing nothing whatsoever about either self-esteem or spouse abuse, let alone whether there is an association between them, you want to know if self-esteem and

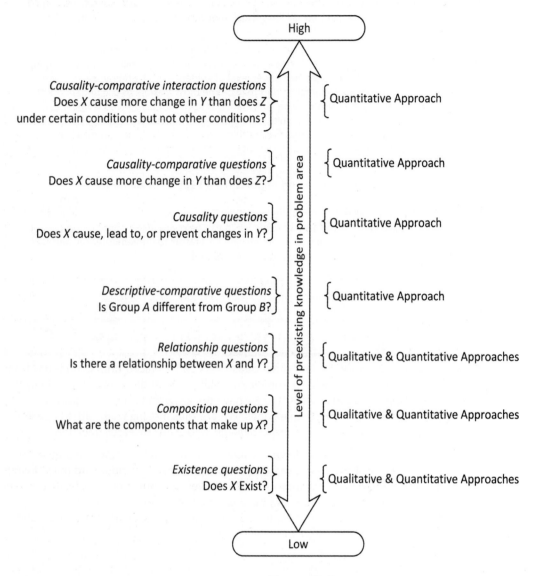

*Causality-comparative interaction questions*
Does *X* cause more change in *Y* than does *Z*
under certain conditions but not other conditions?

{ Quantitative Approach

*Causality-comparative questions*
Does *X* cause more change in *Y* than does *Z*?

{ Quantitative Approach

*Causality questions*
Does *X* cause, lead to, or prevent changes in *Y*?

{ Quantitative Approach

*Descriptive-comparative questions*
Is Group *A* different from Group *B*?

{ Quantitative Approach

*Relationship questions*
Is there a relationship between *X* and *Y*?

{ Qualitative & Quantitative Approaches

*Composition questions*
What are the components that make up *X*?

{ Qualitative & Quantitative Approaches

*Existence questions*
Does *X* Exist?

{ Qualitative & Quantitative Approaches

Level of preexisting knowledge in problem area

High

Low

**Figure 2.3**

Types of Research Questions (left column) and PREDOMINATE Research
Approaches That Answer the Research Questions (right column)

spousal abuse actually exist in the first place. Self-esteem and spouse abuse are concepts—they are nothing more than ideas, human inventions if you like—that have become
very familiar to social workers, and it's tempting just to say, "Of course they exist! But
there must have been a time when self-esteem was no more than a vague idea among
students of human nature that some people seem to feel better about themselves than
other people do. It would then have been just a matter of contacting Ms. Smith—and Ms.
Jones, and Ms. Tasmania—and asking them, "Do you feel good about yourself?"

This qualitative study, sometimes referred to as *interpretive*—and many others like it,
conducted by different researchers over time—would have provided an indication that
yes indeed, some people do feel better about themselves than other people do. Self-esteem, if that is what you want to call (or label) the feeling, does in fact exist. The same

Concepts are ideas.

process can be done to determine if spouse abuse exists. However, spouse abuse can be more easily observed and measured than self-esteem.

## COMPOSITION QUESTIONS

The second question—"What is it that makes you feel good about yourself?"—is a simple attempt to find out what particular personal attributes contribute to self-esteem. That is, it answers the composition question next on the knowledge continuum. Qualitative studies exploring this dimension may have discovered that people who feel good about themselves in general also specifically feel that they are liked by others; that they are competent, intelligent, caring, and physically attractive; and that they have a host of other attributes that together make up the concept "self-esteem."

Thus, qualitative studies provide descriptive or qualitative data indicating that self-esteem exists and what it is. Similarly, they indicate that women are in fact sometimes abused by their partners and what particular forms such abuse can take.

## RELATIONSHIP QUESTIONS

Going up one more notch on the list, you next come to relationship questions. What, if any, is the relationship between women's self-esteem and spousal abuse? Here, you might begin with another qualitative study, trying to determine, on an individual basis, whether there seems to be any connection between having low self-esteem and being abused.

If there does seem to be enough evidence to theorize that such a relationship may exist, you might then use the quantitative research approach to see if the relationship holds for a larger number of women rather than just the small number you interviewed in your qualitative study.

## DESCRIPTIVE-COMPARATIVE QUESTIONS

Next on the continuum you come to descriptive-comparative questions: Is Group A different from Group B? Here you might go in a number of different directions. You might wonder, for example, whether there is any difference in self-esteem levels between women in heterosexual relationships and women in lesbian relationships.

Does self-esteem differ between First Nations women and non–First Nations women? Do women with different sexual orientations or from different cultural groups also differ in how often they are abused, or how severely, or in what particular way? Because you are asking about differences between social groups, which involve large numbers of people, you will need quantitative methods to address these questions. These will be discussed in Chapters 7 and 8.

## CAUSALITY QUESTIONS

Third from the top of the continuum are the causality questions. Does low self-esteem actually cause women to be abused? Or, for that matter, does being abused cause low self-esteem? Most complex behaviors don't have single causes. Being abused might certainly contribute to having low self-esteem, but it's unlikely to be the sole cause.

Similarly, it's unlikely that having low self-esteem leads inevitably to being abused. Positivistic studies here, with their use of impressive statistics, can tell us what percentage of the abuse can be explained by low self-esteem and what percentage remains to be explained by other factors.

## CAUSALITY-COMPARATIVE QUESTIONS

If factors other than low self-esteem cause abuse, it would be nice to know what they are and how much weight they have. Perhaps heavy drinking on the part of the abuser is a factor. Perhaps poverty is, or the battering suffered by the abuser as a child. Once these

possible factors have been explored, using the same process you used in your exploration of self-esteem and spousal abuse, quantitative methods can again tell us what percentage of abuse is explained by each factor.

If low self-esteem accounts for only 2 percent, say, and heavy drinking accounts for 8 percent, you will have answered the causality-comparative question. You will know, on the average, that heavy drinking on the abuser's part has more effect on spousal abuse than does the woman's self-esteem level.

## CAUSALITY-COMPARATIVE INTERACTION QUESTIONS

At the tip-top of the continuum are the causality-comparative interaction questions. They ask whether your research findings only hold up under certain conditions. For example, if it's true that heavy drinking contributes more to spousal abuse than does the woman's level of self-esteem, perhaps that is only true for couples who are living in poverty. Or it's only true for couples with children, or it's only true if the abuser was himself abused.

This final type of question, again answered through quantitative methods, reflects the highest aim of social work research: explanation. If we are to give our clients the best possible service, we need to know about causes and effects. What action or attribute on the part of whom causes how much of what effect, and under what conditions? What type of treatment will cause the most change in a particular type of client in a particular situation?

## CRITERIA FOR GOOD QUESTIONS

**L**et's review for a moment. So far, we know that our profession engages in research studies to become more accountable to society, to our funders, to our clients, and to ourselves. And the questions we finally want to answer are influenced by numerous factors.

On a general level, our questions and the resulting answers (findings) can be placed on a three-category knowledge-level continuum (e.g., Figure 2.1) and can be classified into seven different categories (e.g., Figure 2.3). In addition, research studies and the questions they answer can be categorized into one of six levels within the evidence hierarchy, as illustrated in Box 2.2 on pages 45–47.

Thus, you know from the preceding discussion how research questions spring to life and how they can be classified. Your research question now needs to be evaluated. Every research question must be:

1 Relevant
2 Researchable
3 Feasible
4 Ethical and culturally sensitive
5 Thought provoking
6 Related to the study's overall objectives
7 Short
8 Unambiguous and straightforward
9 Comprehensive
10 Expressed in common vocabulary
11 Stated clearly and precisely (see Box 2.3 on the following page)

| Box 2.3 | Two Critical Thinking Standards to Consider When Formulating Research Questions: *Clarity* and *Precision* |
|---|---|

### Clarity

Before we can effectively evaluate a person's argument or claim, we need to understand clearly what he or she is saying. Unfortunately, that can be difficult because people often fail to express themselves clearly. Sometimes this lack of clarity is due to laziness, carelessness, or a lack of skill. At other times it results from a misguided effort to appear clever, learned, or profound. Consider the following passage from philosopher Martin Heidegger's (1927) influential but notoriously obscure book *Being and Time*:

> Temporality makes possible the unity of existence, facticity, and falling, and in this way constitutes primordially the totality of the structure of care. The items of care have not been pieced together cumulatively any more than temporality itself has been put together "in the course of time" ["mit der Zeit"] out of the future, the having been, and the Present. Temporality "is" not an entity at all. It is not, but it temporalizes itself. . . . Temporality temporalizes, and indeed it temporalizes possible ways of itself. These make possible the multiplicity of Dasein's modes of Being, and especially the basic possibility of authentic or inauthentic existence.

The above gibberish may be profound, or it may be nonsense, or it may be both. Whatever exactly it is, it is quite needlessly obscure. As William Strunk Jr. and E. B. White remark in their 1979 classic, *The Elements of Style,*

> Muddiness is not merely a disturber of prose, it is also a destroyer of life, of hope: death on the highway caused by a badly worded road sign, heartbreak among lovers caused by a misplaced phrase in a well-intentioned letter.

Only by paying careful attention to language can we avoid such needless miscommunications and disappointments. Critical thinkers not only strive for clarity of language but also seek maximum clarity of thought. As self-help books constantly remind us, to achieve our personal goals in life we need a clear conception of our goals and priorities, a realistic grasp of our abilities, and a clear understanding of the problems and opportunities we face. Such self-understanding can be achieved only if we value and pursue clarity of thought.

### Precision

Detective stories contain some of the most interesting examples of critical thinking in fiction. The most famous fictional sleuth is, of course, Sherlock Holmes, the immortal creation of British writer Sir Arthur Conan Doyle. In Doyle's stories Holmes is often able to solve complex mysteries when the bungling detectives from Scotland Yard haven't so much as a clue. What is the secret of his success? An extraordinary commitment to precision. First, by careful and highly trained observation, Holmes is able to discover clues that others have overlooked. Then, by a process of precise logical inference, he is able to reason from those clues to discover the solution to the mystery.

Everyone recognizes the importance of precision in specialized fields such as medicine, mathematics, architecture, and engineering. Critical thinkers also understand the importance of precise thinking in daily life. They understand that to cut through the confusions and uncertainties that surround many everyday problems and issues, it is often necessary to insist on precise answers to precise questions: What exactly is the problem we're facing? What exactly are the alternatives? What exactly are the advantages and disadvantages of each alternative? Only when we habitually seek such precision are we truly critical thinkers.

If your research question doesn't pass muster on all eleven criteria, it's worthless and must be discarded like an old pair of sneakers or your iPhone 11. This section explores only the first four of the eleven criteria as they are the most important to consider when evaluating a research question or hypothesis.

1   Relevancy.
2   Researchability.
3   Feasibility.
4   Ethical and cultural sensitivity.

## RELEVANT

Relevance is one of those things, like efficiency, that is never absolute: The same research question may be less or more relevant depending on who is defining what is meant by "relevant" in what particular context. A research question about Chinese pottery, for example, might be relevant to researchers who are interested in Chinese potters or to archaeologists but may be less relevant to social workers. The degree of relevance of any particular study is usually decided by the organization that funds it, the program that houses it, and the research team who undertakes it.

## RESEARCHABLE

Some very interesting questions cannot be answered through the research process, either because of the nature of the question or because of the difficulties inherent in collecting the necessary data. For example, research studies cannot answer the question "Does God exist"? or "Is abortion wrong"? With respect to the latter, we may be able to collect evidence related to the effects of experiencing or being denied an abortion, but we cannot answer the underlying moral question.

Then there is the matter of technical difficulties inherent in the research question itself. For example, Aristotle believed that children would be healthier if conceived when the wind was from the north. We are as interested in the health of children as Aristotle was, but even supposing that we accepted the direction of the wind at conception as a possible contributing factor to healthier children, the question would not be researchable because of the practical difficulties associated with determining the direction of the wind at conception in a large enough number of cases.

Researchability, then, has to do with whether the research question is appropriate for scientific inquiry and whether it's possible to collect valid and reliable data that would be needed to answer the question.

## FEASIBLE

Feasibility carries the "collection of the necessary data" issue one step farther in that your research study has to be feasible. Feasibility means just that—whether your research project is feasible to carry out. Perhaps it's possible to collect data about the direction of the wind at conception (windsocks attached to every home combined with careful record-keeping), but it's not possible for you to do it, given your limited resources and your inability to influence homebuilding and protection of privacy standards.

The question about the relationship between the wind and the health of children might therefore be researchable, but it's not feasible as far as you are concerned. Your available resources have a profound effect on the scope of the research study you are able to mount and thus on the questions you are able to answer. In other words, given all these things, could you practically do what you have planned?

> Relevant and researchable questions are those whose answers will have an impact on our social policies, and/or theories, and/or practices, and/or educational content.

## ETHICAL AND CULTURALLY SENSITIVE

There is a potential for harm not just in the way the study is conducted but in the way the research question is phrased. Researchers are in a wonderful position to offend just about everyone if they fail to pay attention to the cultural, gender, and sexual orientation aspects of their research questions. Not only might they offend people, but they might cause harm, not just to research participants but to entire groups of people.

We will discuss ethics in depth in Chapter 5, and in Chapter 6 we will address the cultural sensitivities that must be considered when doing research studies. For now, just remember that your research question must be ethical and culturally sensitive in addition to being relevant, researchable, and feasible.

## EVALUATING A STUDY'S RESEARCH QUESTION

**M**ost published research studies contain some form of information (also called findings) that, more often than not, is nothing more than answers to research questions. All research studies are only as good as the research questions (or hypotheses) they try to answer. Poor questions/hypotheses can lead to poor studies which can lead to questionable findings.

There are a few highly interweaved and non-mutually exclusive questions you can ask as you try to evaluate the overall practicality, thoroughness, clarity, and ethical and cultural sensitivity of a study's research question or hypothesis. These questions are contained in the three appendixes located in the back of this book. Let's now use them.

## USE THE APPENDIXES

Appendix A lists numerous questions you can ask (when you put on your "critical thinking" hat) for each step of the *quantitative* research process and Appendix B lists questions you can ask about each phase of the *qualitative* research process. On a general level, both research approaches answer research questions—and you, as a critical thinker, can ask some questions about the research questions they are trying to answer.

More specifically, you can find numerous questions in Appendix A that you can ask about research questions that were formulated for *quantitative* studies (i.e., questions 35–52 on pages 477–478) and Appendix B for *qualitative* ones (i.e., questions 310–370 on pages 498–502). It's important to note that many of the questions we can ask for quantitative studies can also be asked for qualitative ones as well. And vice versa.

### TASKS

This is the perfect time for you to become reacquainted with how to use the three appendixes at the end of this book (i.e., Appendixes A–C).

- First, and most important, read over the overall structure of the appendixes and the directions on how to use them on pages 468–473.
- Second, glance over the potential questions you can ask about any research question a study is trying to answer from:
  — Reading *quantitative* research studies (Appendix A)
  — Reading *qualitative* research studies (Appendix B)
  — Reading *mixed-methods* research studies (Appendixes A and B)
  — Finding information on the *Internet* (Appendix C)

---

Many of the questions we can ask about quantitative studies can also be asked for qualitative ones as well. And vice versa.

---

Two people can assess the same research question and come up with two different opinions in reference to its overall credibility, integrity, and usefulness to our profession.

How to assess the overall creditability and usefulness of a research question is totally up to you—and only you. You're the one who must ask and answer the questions contained in the appendixes. More importantly, you need to have a rationale for why you're asking each question in the first place. You just can't ask questions without knowing why you're asking them. You also must have some kind of an idea of what you're going to do with your answer to each question.

In reference to the assessment of a research question contained within a *quantitative* study, for example, question 47 on page 477 asks, "Is the research question thought provoking?" Let's say your answer was "no". What are you going to do with your answer? That is, how are you going to use your assessment of this specific question when formulating your *overall research question's credibility* score on page 478? Now what about if your answer was "yes"? Don't look for a magic rubric to appear. There isn't one. This is the time to put on your critical thinking hat.

In reference to the assessment of a research question contained within a *qualitative* study, for example, question 328 on page 499 asks, "Does the study have research questions? If so, were they clearly stated?" Let's say your answer was "no". What are you going to do with your answer? That is, how are you going to use your assessment of this specific question when formulating your *overall research question's credibility* score on page 502? Now what about if your answer was "yes"?

## CHAPTER RECAP

- A social work research study is only as good as the quality and meaningfulness of the research question it attempts to answer or the hypothesis it tests.

- There are numerous factors that affect how social work research questions are formulated.

- All research questions can be answered via the scientific method of inquiry.

- The scientific method of inquiry contains three complementary research approaches.

- Research questions, and their resulting studies, can be placed on a knowledge-level continuum that contains three non-mutually exclusive groupings.

- Research questions, and their resulting studies, can be placed on an evidence hierarchy that contains six levels.

- Research questions, and their resulting studies, can be classified into one of seven categories.

- Research questions can be evaluated by eleven criteria.

## REVIEW EXERCISES

1   Before you entered your social work program and before you read this chapter, how did you think our profession formulated research questions? Provide as many examples as you can to justify your response.

2   List the factors that affect social work research studies. Discuss how they are highly related to one another using one common social work example throughout your discussion.

3   What social work research question would you like answered? Why? Discuss how it was influenced by each one of the factors presented in the book.

4   Discuss what the knowledge-level continuum is all about. Provide specific social work examples for each one of the three levels.

5   Select a social work problem area such as homelessness, depression, anxiety, domestic violence, child abuse, or truancy. Now formulate a research question within your problem area for each one of the three knowledge levels: exploratory, descriptive, and explanatory.

6   With Question 5 in mind, list all three research questions. Then list and discuss how each of your three research questions will have been influenced by each of the factors that affect the formulation of research questions/problems.

7 With Questions 5 and 6 in mind, evaluate each of your three research questions with the criteria contained in the book.

8 With Questions 5, 6, and 7 in mind, formulate a social work research question for each of the seven classifications that research studies can fall under (figure 2.3 on page 48). Be sure to use your general problem area as you did with Questions 5, 6, and 7.

9 What is the sieving procedure all about, as illustrated in Figure 2.2 on page 43? Provide a social work example throughout your discussion to illustrate your main points.

10 Locate any published social work research article that contains a social work problem area or population that you're interested in. Be sure the study tried to answer a research question of some kind.

   • What was the study's research question?

   • What was the knowledge level of the research question?

   • Where on Figures 2.1 and 2.3 did the research question fall? Provide a rationale for your selection.

   • Using the contents within this chapter, discuss all of the factors that must have affected the researcher's formulation of the final research question. Provide hypothetical examples throughout your discussion.

   • Evaluate the study's research question on all of the criteria presented in this chapter.

11 Research questions social workers formulate to study can be evaluated on eleven criteria. Like Exercise 5, choose a social problem area of your choice.

   • Write a simple research question and discuss how it meets the eleven criteria. Provide a rationale for each criterion.

   • Write a research question that violates all of the evaluative criteria. Discuss how your research question does not meet each one of the criteria. Be very specific.

**Time to think critically**

12 **Scenario 1:** Make an argument that to be an effective evidence-based social work practitioner *you need to know* how to formulate relevant, useful, and ethical social work research questions. Provide a clear and explicit practice-related social work example to illustrate your main points.

13 **Scenario 2:** Make an argument that *you do not need to know* how to formulate relevant, useful, and ethical social work research questions to be an effective evidence-based social work practitioner. Provide a clear and explicit practice-related social work example to illustrate your main points.

14 **Time to choose:** Which of the preceding two scenarios (i.e., 12 or 13) do you feel is more consistent with the concept of the contemporary evidence-based social work practice process as illustrated on pages 68–72? Why? Provide relevant social work examples to illustrate your main points.

**Looking ahead by looking back**

15 At this point in your research methods course, how comfortable are you with discussing the place of research in social work with your field instructor, with your practice instructor, with your research instructor, with your supervisor at work, with the director of your social work program, or with your classmates.

## 2015 EPAS COMPETENCIES

| COMPETENCY 1 | Demonstrate Ethical and Professional Behavior |
|---|---|

You will learn that in order to be a successful evidence-based practitioner you have an ethical obligation to integrate three research roles into your daily practice activities as discussed in this chapter: (1) research consumer, (2) research partner—either as a co-researcher or research participant, and (3) creator and disseminator of research (or knowledge).

This entire chapter pertains to these three professional roles as you'll learn that one of the best ways to become an ethical and professional evidence-based social work practitioner is knowing the steps of the evidence-based practice process. In addition, you'll fully appreciate that the process of social work practice mirrors the process of the scientific method of inquiry.

| COMPETENCY 4 | Engage in Practice-Informed Research and Research-Informed Practice |
|---|---|

Competency 4 also pertains to the entire chapter because you have to:

1   Understand the three major research-related roles you will undertake when you graduate from your social work program: research consumer, research partner, and creator and disseminator of research.

2   Understand the five essential characteristics that you have to have in order to be a good social work researcher. And, more important, these five characteristics are exactly the same you need to become a good social work evidence-based practitioner (**research consumer**—research-informed practice);

3   Understand you will participate in research studies—either as a co-researcher or research participant (**research partner**—practice-informed research). See 1 above and 3 below; and

4   Understand that you will actually do research studies as a professional evidence-based practitioner (**creator and disseminator of research**—practice-informed research).

You'll also utilize evidence-based practice recommendations whenever possible; that is, you'll need to integrate (1) the best available research-based evidence with (2) your clinical expertise and (3) your client's values.

All of the above implies you'll need to become a lifelong learner which suggests that your critical thinking skills increase over time.

| COMPETENCY 9 | Evaluate Practice with Individuals, Families, Groups, Organizations, & Communities |
|---|---|

See Competencies 1 and 4.

# 3

# Toward Evidence-Based Practice

| | | |
|---|---|---|
| CHAPTERS 1 & 3 | Step 1. | Understanding the Research Process |
| CHAPTER 2 | Step 2. | Formulating Research Questions |
| CHAPTER 4 APPENDIXES A–C | Step 3. | Reviewing the Literature Evaluating the Literature |
| CHAPTERS 5 & 6 | Step 4. | Being Aware of Ethical and Cultural Issues |
| CHAPTERS 7–10 | Step 5. | Selecting a Research Approach |
| CHAPTERS 11 & 12 | Step 6. | Specifying How Variables Are Measured |
| CHAPTER 13 | Step 7. | Selecting a Sample |
| CHAPTERS 14 & 15 | Step 8. | Selecting a Research Design |
| CHAPTERS 16 & 17 | Step 9. | Selecting a Data-Collection Method |
| CHAPTERS 18 & 19 | Step 10. | Analyzing the Data |
| CHAPTERS 20 & 21 | Step 11. | Writing the Research Report |

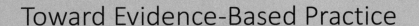

# Toward Evidence-Based Practice

"Are you telling me that the grade you received in your Evidence-Based Practice Course is because the course wasn't evidence-based? Seriously?"

CHAPTER

# 3

CHAPTER OUTLINE

ARE THESE RESEARCH FINDINGS FOR REAL?

    What's Up with These Research Findings?

        *Dilemma Solved*

DO YOU HAVE WHAT IT TAKES?

    Are You Aware of Your Values?

    Are You Skeptical?

    Do You Share Your Stuff with Others?

    Are You Honest?

    Got Attitude?

        *Using the Internet Café*

        *Thinking Logically, Completely, and Fairly*

THREE RESEARCH ROLES

    The Research Consumer

    The Creator and Disseminator of Research

    The Contributing Partner

INTEGRATING THE THREE RESEARCH ROLES

RESEARCH AND PRACTICE

EVIDENCE-BASED PRACTICE

DEFINITION OF SOCIAL WORK RESEARCH

COMMITTING TO LIFELONG LEARNING

CHAPTER RECAP

REVIEW EXERCISES

**By now it should be obvious** to you that our profession has to be accountable to a number of stakeholder groups, and doing research studies that can increase our knowledge base helps us to become more accountable. Researchers, practitioners, and students alike can contribute to this knowledge base by using five different, non-mutually exclusive "ways of knowing," as briefly discussed in Chapter 1.

As covered in the previous two chapters, when we're working with our various client systems we need to use our professional judgments whenever possible—a process whereby facts, as far as they are known, are supplemented with the knowledge derived from *all* five ways of knowing to form the basis for rational decisions (see figure P.1 on page *v*). Thus, this chapter builds upon the two previous ones by describing how you can use the research process and your critical thinking skills to form professional judgments.

## ARE THESE RESEARCH FINDINGS FOR REAL?

**S**it back and relax for a moment. Let's pretend you recently obtained your MSW and were promoted to a supervisory position in your children and family services agency. You are now totally responsible for hiring a new family preservation worker who has a BSW and/or an MSW degree from a CSWE accredited school of social work. Now pretend that you've just hauled yourself out of bed, where you were dreaming about interviewing the applicants.

Obviously, and as usual, your first instinctive task after getting out of bed and before your first cup of coffee is to check your social media feeds to see what happened last night while you were in dreamland. You come across the below News Flash 3.1 in a tweet on Twitter, and it's a bit intellectually stimulating and thought provoking.

---

**News Flash 3.1**
BSW Students' Research Project at a Local University Determines That BSW-Level
Social Workers Are More Effective Than MSW-Level Social Workers

---

Something's amiss in paradise! "Wow," you say, "how can this be? A BSW is more effective than me, a true-to-the-bone MSW?" It just doesn't make sense, and you ask yourself, "Why did I go to graduate school?" Luckily then you remember from your previous research methods courses that all research studies—yes, all—have limitations and that you, as a professional MSW-level social worker, need to ask a bunch of questions about these researchers' pronouncements to assess their overall truthfulness and relevance. You say to yourself, "This may be fake news."

## WHAT'S UP WITH THESE RESEARCH FINDINGS?

Should you automatically offer the position to a BSW applicant rather than a MSW applicant because "research findings" state BSWs are more effective than their graduate-level counterparts? Wouldn't this be the ethical thing to do, since you want to hire the most effective person?

However, you also remember that you should never automatically and uncritically accept as "true" any statement you see on television or read in the papers or professional journals without asking a horde of questions about the statements. It's so easy—in fact, it's way too easy—to relegate a statement to the "fake" category when you simply disagree with it.

For example, let's say you have been led to believe that the earth is only 5,000 years old. Then you see a bunch of expert geologists, geographers, astrophysicists, and astronomers being interviewed on television who claim that their research findings have calculated the earth to be $4.54 \pm 0.05$ billion years old. Your belief in 5,000 years is not even close to congruent with these experts. It would be extremely easy to dismiss their claim as "fake news" and proceed to go about your business as usual, thinking nothing about what you have done.

### DILEMMA SOLVED

Now you have remembered that the questions that need to be asked about any research study's findings form the headings and subheadings contained in this textbook. Very convenient! So before you make any hiring decisions for your agency's family preservation position, you decide to yank this textbook off your bookshelf and use it as a guide in asking questions about the overall credibility of the research study you read about on Twitter—paying particular attention to the process that generated the "facts" or "findings."

Even more important, you have just remembered discussing fake news in your research methods courses. As Dave Lazer and his colleagues (2018) eloquently pointed out,

> "Fake news" is fabricated information that mimics news media content in form but not in organizational process or intent. Fake-news outlets, in turn, lack the news media's editorial norms and processes for ensuring the accuracy and credibility of information. Fake news overlaps with other information disorders, such as *misinformation* (false or misleading information) and *disinformation* (false information that is purposely spread to deceive people).

"Fake news" is not news you disagree with. In fact, it's not news at all.

After that, you spot News Flash 3.2 on Twitter. Seven MSW students at the university where you just graduated also don't believe BSWs are "more effective" than MSWs. They want to prove that the research findings mentioned in News Flash 3.1 are wrong. So these students approach you for help in doing another study to see whether they obtain the same results—this is technically called *replication* in the research world.

---

**News Flash 3.2**
MSW Students at Local University to Study the Differential
Effectiveness of BSW and MSW Social Workers

---

However, they, like you, soon realize they don't even know what "more effective" means. Is it more effective at getting jobs or funding? Or does it mean more effective apartment cleaners, dog walkers, client interviewers, moms and dads, brothers and sisters, slackers, coffee baristas, or procrastinators? More effective at what?

So you agree to help your comrades. But you know full well that they, like you, should ideally possess five specific characteristics before you all can undertake any research study—including the proposed study in News Flash 3.2. We're now going to discuss these highly intertwined, comingled five characteristics by putting you, along with your co-researchers, in the driver's seat.

## DO YOU HAVE WHAT IT TAKES?

**R**emember, social work researchers are people too! They are the ones producing the research findings, so you'll need to know a bit more about the common characteristics most of them share before you start your own research project (Grinnell, 1997a, 1997b). Spoiler alert: You more than likely have most of these characteristics yourself. More specifically, folks who do research studies:

1   Are aware of their own values
2   Are skeptics
3   Share their findings with others
4   Are honest
5   Have good research attitudes

### ARE YOU AWARE OF YOUR VALUES?

Like a judge (and not a TV reality-type of judge!), you must be aware of and be able to set aside your values when you do a research study. Value awareness means that you must know your own values and your research study must not be affected by them. You must be unbiased and impartial to the highest possible degree.

If your personal value system dictates, for example, that health care should be publicly funded and equally available to everyone, you should still be able to acquire and evaluate knowledge about the advantages and disadvantages of a privatized system. If the evidence (or data) from your own or someone else's study shows that privatized health care is superior in some respects to the system you believe is best, you should be able to weigh this evidence objectively, even though it conflicts with your personal value system.

### ARE YOU SKEPTICAL?

Now that you have your values under control, you must also become insatiably curious. You found out in the previous two chapters that knowledge we acquire is never certain. Scientific "truth" remains true only until new evidence comes along to show that it's not true or only partly true. Wherever possible, new studies should be conducted by different researchers to see if the same results are obtained again. In other words, research studies (whenever possible) should be replicated.

Replication of the same study, with the same results, by another researcher makes it less likely that the results of the first study were affected by bias, dishonesty, or just plain error. Replicated findings are more likely to be "true" in the sense that they are more likely to reflect a reality external to the researchers. We will come back to this business of external reality later on. For now, it's enough to say that the continual replication of research studies is a routine practice in the physical sciences, but it's far rarer in the social sciences, especially in the social work profession, for two main reasons:

> Value awareness means that you should be able to put aside your personal values both when you are conducting research studies and when you are evaluating the results obtained by other researchers.

> Skeptical curiosity means that all research findings must be questioned.

1  It's much more difficult to replicate a study of people than a study of physical objects

2  Unfortunately, researchers in the social sciences, such as social work, have a harder time finding money to do research studies than researchers in the physical sciences

## DO YOU SHARE YOUR STUFF WITH OTHERS?

You more than likely have been told, "You must share your stuff with others." It's worth noting that sharing findings from a research study is a modern value. After all, it wasn't that long ago that illiteracy among peasants and women was valued by those who were neither. Knowledge has always been a weapon as well as a tool. Those who know little may be less likely to question the wisdom and authority of those who are above them in the social hierarchy. Public education is thus an enormously powerful social force that allows people to access and question the evidence or data that their leaders use to make decisions on their behalf.

## ARE YOU HONEST?

Not only must you share your stuff with others, you must also be honest in what you share. This may sound fairly straightforward, but keep in mind that the results of research studies are rarely as clear-cut as we would like them to be. Quite often, even in the most respectable of social work research centers and institutes, social policies are formulated on the basis of whether one wiggle on a graph is slightly longer than the corresponding woggle.

If dishonesty means a deliberate intention to deceive, then probably very few researchers are dishonest. But if it means that researchers allow their value systems and their preconceived ideas to influence their data-collection methods, their data analyses, or their interpretations of the data, then there are probably a few guilty ones among us. In this sense, the term honesty includes an obligation, on the part of researchers, to be explicit about what their values and ideas are.

Researchers need to be sufficiently self-aware in both identifying their value systems and perceiving the effects of these on their own work. Then they need to be sufficiently honest to make an explicit statement about where they stand so that others can evaluate the conclusions they have drawn from their research studies.

## GOT ATTITUDE?

You're a social work student so no doubt you've got attitude or you wouldn't be studying social work. But is it the research attitude? As you saw in the previous two chapters, the scientific method of inquiry refers to the many ideas, rules, techniques, and approaches that the research community use. The research attitude, on the other hand, is simply a way of viewing the world. It's an attitude that highly values craftsmanship, with pride in creativity, high-quality standards, and hard work (Grinnell, 1992).

Most people learn about the "scientific method" rather than about the scientific attitude. The scientific method is an ideal construct, but the scientific attitude is a way people have of looking at the world. Doing science includes many methods; what makes the scientific is their acceptance by the scientific collective. When you've got the right attitude, you will,

1  Use the Internet Café

2  Think logically, completely, and fairly

Sharing means that the results of your research study and the methods used to conduct it must be available to everyone so that your study's findings can be critiqued and the study replicated.

Honesty means that you are not supposed to fiddle with the results obtained from your study.

### USING THE INTERNET CAFÉ

Now that you are value free, a skeptic, have a curious nature, share your research findings with others, are honest in what you share, and have a good attitude about research and science, you must also be willing to use the Internet Café, when appropriate of course (Harris, 2018).

Simply put, folks who have a good research attitude use the Internet CAFÉ—Challenge, Adapt, File, and Evaluate—whenever possible. The Internet Café helps you to assess the world of information, disinformation, and misinformation that will come to you at lighting speeds. So just take all this stuff to the Café and use this approach to assess research findings and help you to become a better critical thinker which in turn will help you to become a better social work practitioner.

> Using the Internet Café approach to assessing a research finding will help you to become a better critical thinker.

**C** **Challenge information and demand accountability.** Stand right up to the information and ask questions. Who says so? Why do they say so? Why was this information created? Why should I believe it? Why should I trust this source? How is it known to be true? Is it the whole truth? Is the argument reasonable? Who supports it? (see box 1.2 on page 26)

**A** **Adapt your skepticism and requirements for quality to fit the importance of the information and what is being claimed.** Require more credibility and evidence for stronger claims. You are right to be a little skeptical of dramatic information or information that conflicts with commonly accepted ideas. The new information may be true, but you should require a robust amount of evidence from highly credible sources.

**F** **File new information in your mind rather than immediately believing or disbelieving it.** Avoid premature closure. Do not jump to a conclusion or come to a decision too quickly. It is fine simply to remember that someone claims XYZ to be the case. You need not worry about believing or disbelieving the claim right away. Wait until more information comes in, you have time to think about the issue, and you gain more general knowledge.

**É** **Evaluate and re-evaluate regularly.** New information or changing circumstances will affect the accuracy and hence your evaluation of previous information. Recognize the dynamic, fluid nature of information. The saying "Change is the only constant" applies to much information, especially in technology, science, medicine, and business.

### THINKING LOGICALLY, COMPLETELY, AND FAIRLY

If you have a scientific attitude you have no other alternative but to think logically, completely, and fairly. In fact these are three key ingredients of what makes up a critical thinker, as outlined in Box 3.1 on the following page.

## THREE RESEARCH ROLES

**W**hether you like it or not, you will engage in research when you graduate. Period. Full stop. No way around it. In fact, you even have an ethical obligation to do so. The CSWE requires you to demonstrate ethical and professional behaviors before you can post your degree on your office wall. Remember, you have an ethical obligation to integrate at least one of the three research roles into your daily practice activities:

**1** Research consumer

**2** Creator and disseminator of research (or knowledge)

**3** Research partner—either as a co-researcher or research participant

| Box 3.1 | Three Critical Thinking Standards to Help Enrich your Scientific Attitude: *Logicalness, Completeness,* and *Fairness* |

**Logical Correctness**

To think logically is to reason correctly—that is, to draw well-founded conclusions from the beliefs we hold. To think critically we need accurate and well-supported beliefs. But, just as important, we need to be able to reason from those beliefs to conclusions that logically follow from them.

Unfortunately, illogical thinking is all too common in human affairs. Bertrand Russell, in his classic 1950 essay, *An Outline of Intellectual Rubbish,* provides an amusing example:

I am sometimes shocked by the blasphemies of those who think themselves pious—for instance, the nuns who never take a bath without wearing a bathrobe all the time. When asked why, since no man can see them, they reply: "Oh, but you forget the good God." Apparently they conceive of the deity as a Peeping Tom, whose omnipotence enables Him to see through bathroom walls, but who is foiled by bathrobes. This view strikes me as curious. (255)

As Russell observes, from the proposition,

   **1** God sees everything.

the pious nuns correctly drew the conclusion

   **2** God sees through bathroom walls.

However, they failed to draw the equally obvious conclusion that

   **3** God sees through bathrobes.

Such illogic is, indeed, curious—but not, alas, uncommon.

**Completeness**

In most contexts, we rightly prefer deep and complete thinking to shallow and superficial thinking. Thus, we justly condemn slipshod criminal investigations, hasty jury deliberations, superficial news stories, sketchy driving directions, and snap medical diagnoses. Of course, there are times when it is impossible or inappropriate to discuss an issue in depth; no one would expect, for example, a thorough and wide-ranging discussion of the ethics of human genetic research in a short newspaper editorial. Generally speaking, however, thinking is better when it is deep rather than shallow, thorough rather than superficial.

**Fairness**

Finally, critical thinking demands that our thinking be fair—that is, openminded, impartial, and free of distorting biases and preconceptions. That can be very difficult to achieve. Even the most superficial acquaintance with history and the social sciences tells us that people are often strongly disposed to resist unfamiliar ideas, to prejudge issues, to stereotype outsiders, and to identify truth with their own self-interest or the interests of their nation or group.

It is probably unrealistic to suppose that our thinking could ever be completely free of biases; to some extent we all perceive reality in ways that are powerfully shaped by our individual life experiences and cultural backgrounds. But as difficult as it may be to achieve, basic fair-mindedness is an essential attribute of a critical thinker.

# THE RESEARCH CONSUMER

The first social work research role you can take is that of the research consumer. If you go to your doctor to discuss your arthritis, for example, you would surely expect the doctor to be aware of the most recent advances in the management and treatment of arthritis. All professionals, in all disciplines, are expected by their clients to keep up with the latest developments in their fields.

They do this by attending conferences, reading books and journals, and paying attention to the results derived from research studies. In other words, these professionals—which includes you as a social worker—are research consumers, and, as previously noted, they need to know enough about research methods—the topic of this book—to consume research studies wisely, separating the nutritious wheat from the dubious chaff.

## THE CREATOR AND DISSEMINATOR OF RESEARCH

You may be certain that you will never yourself conduct a research study. "Never ever!" you say—but then you find that you are the only staff person in a small voluntary social service program that desperately requires a needs assessment if the program is to serve its clients and keep its funding base. You look up "needs assessment" in forgotten research texts, and you sweat and stumble through them because someone has to do the study and there's no one there but you. You will now take the role of creator and disseminator of knowledge—which means you'll be doing a research study.

> The research consumer is what the evidence-based practice model is all about.

This may seem like an unlikely scenario, but in fact many social service programs are very small and are run on a wing and a prayer by a few poorly paid staff and a large volunteer contingent. They rise and flourish for a time and die, and death is often hastened along by their inability to demonstrate, in "objective" research terms, how much good they are doing on their clients' behalf, how little it's costing, and what the dreadful social consequences would be if they weren't there to do it.

You may escape being the sole social worker in a program that needs research know-how. But even if you are a mere cog in an immense machine of interlocking social workers, the time may come when you want to try a new intervention. Most social workers implement interventions in some way or another, but more often than not, many of them don't:

1  Carry out their interventions in any meaningful structured way
2  Write down exactly what the interventions were (perhaps an intervention for raising Jody's self-esteem)
3  Provide a rationale as to why they needed them in the first place (Nothing else was working with Jody)
4  Specify how they evaluated them (Jody's self-esteem was measured before and after implementing the intervention)
5  Communicate to others how effective the interventions actually were (Jody's self-esteem score rose significantly from $X$ to $Y$ and was still at its higher level three months later)

They simply don't tell anyone else they did it, except for a few murmurs, rapidly forgotten, to a colleague over coffee. One consequence of this is that other Jody-types, who might benefit from the same intervention, never have the opportunity to do so because their social workers didn't know that it existed. Another consequence is that the social service program cannot use this newfound intervention as evidence of its effectiveness to place before its funders such as the United Way or local foundations.

## THE CONTRIBUTING PARTNER

In reality, many social service programs conduct some kind of research studies from time to time, particularly evaluative studies. Many more agree to host studies conducted by researchers external to the program such as university professors and graduate students.

You'll become a contributing partner in a research study when you agree to participate in the endeavor in one way or another.

Social work research studies rarely take place in a laboratory, but instead they're usually conducted in field settings. Data may be taken from the program's clients and/or their case files and may be collected in the program or in the clients' homes. Since social workers are usually employed by social service programs, they are often drawn into the program's research activities by default.

Such activities are normally conducted by a team, consisting of researchers and program staff members. The solitary social work researcher, like the solitary mad scientist, is very much a thing of the past. Staff members who contribute to research studies may have specific skills to offer that they never imagined were related to "research."

One worker, for example, may be particularly acute and accurate when it comes to observing client behaviors. A second may work well as a liaison between the clients and the researcher or between one program and another. Some social workers are cooperative in research endeavors and others are less so, depending on their attitudes toward knowledge development through the use of the scientific method.

Those of us who know the most about scientific methods tend to be the most cooperative and also the most useful. Hence, the greater the number of social workers who understand research principles, the more likely it is that relevant studies will be successfully completed and that our knowledge base will be increased.

> You will more than likely participate in several research studies during your professional social work career. Thus, you will be a contributing partner to knowledge development.

## INTEGRATING THE THREE RESEARCH ROLES

**Just about everything in life** is interdependent on everything else. Chaos theory comes readily to mind concerning the idea of interdependence. The same holds true with the three research roles noted earlier—they are not independent of one another. They must be integrated if research is to accomplish its main goal of increasing our profession's knowledge base and improving the effectiveness of our interventions with clients.

The issue is not whether we should consume research findings, produce and disseminate research results, or become contributing partners in research studies. Rather, it's whether we can engage the full spectrum of available knowledge and skills in the continual improvement of our practices. Social workers who adopt only one or two of the three research roles are shortchanging themselves and their clients (Reid & Smith, 1989):

> If research is to be used to full advantage to advance the goals of social work, the profession needs to develop a climate in which both doing and consuming research are normal professional activities. By this we do not mean that all social workers should necessarily do research or that all practice should be based on the results of research, but rather that an ability to carry out studies at some level and the facility in using scientifically based knowledge should be an integral part of the skills that social workers have and use. (17)

There are economic as well as ethical reasons for integrating the three research roles into our daily activities. For example, it was once believed that throwing money haphazardly at social problems would solve them. This simply didn't work then and it doesn't work now. Today, funding sources demand valid and reliable data or evidence that social service programs are accomplishing their intended goals and objectives. In the competitive scramble of social service programs for limited funds, the programs that can demonstrate their effectiveness and efficiency will prevail. Hence, learning how to integrate the three research roles into our daily practices is a matter of survival in our profession.

Anecdotal case studies alone are lame if they are not accompanied by valid and reliable data of the program's effectiveness.

Expanding our research/practice base is also a way of enabling our profession to assert its place in the community of human service professionals. It's a way of carving out a niche of respectability, of challenging the insidious stereotype that, although social workers have their hearts in the right place, they're uninformed and ineffective in addition to being overly optimistic.

Any profession (and especially ours) that bases its credibility on faith or ideology alone will have a hard time surviving. Although a research base in our profession will not guarantee us public acceptance, the absence of such a base and the lack of vigorous research efforts to expand it will—in the long run—undoubtedly erode our credibility (Grinnell & Siegel, 1988).

## RESEARCH AND PRACTICE

**B**elieve it or not, social work research and practice have much in common. In fact, they have more commonalities than differences in that they are both problem-solving processes. As can be seen in Figure 3.1 below, there are parallels among the general problem-solving approach, social work research, and social work practice (Duehn, 1985).

All social work activities, both practice and research, are organized around one central assumption: There is a preferred order of thinking and action that, when rigorously followed, will increase the likelihood of achieving our objectives. Social work practitioners and researchers base their conclusions on careful observation, systematic trial, and intelligent analysis. Both observe, reflect, conclude, try, monitor results, and continuously re-apply the same problem-solving process until the problem at hand is addressed.

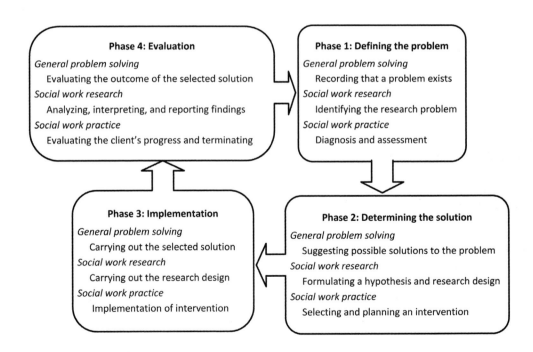

**Phase 4: Evaluation**

*General problem solving*
Evaluating the outcome of the selected solution
*Social work research*
Analyzing, interpreting, and reporting findings
*Social work practice*
Evaluating the client's progress and terminating

**Phase 1: Defining the problem**

*General problem solving*
Recording that a problem exists
*Social work research*
Identifying the research problem
*Social work practice*
Diagnosis and assessment

**Phase 3: Implementation**

*General problem solving*
Carrying out the selected solution
*Social work research*
Carrying out the research design
*Social work practice*
Implementation of intervention

**Phase 2: Determining the solution**

*General problem solving*
Suggesting possible solutions to the problem
*Social work research*
Formulating a hypothesis and research design
*Social work practice*
Selecting and planning an intervention

**Figure 3.1**

Parallels among General Problem Solving, Research, and Practice

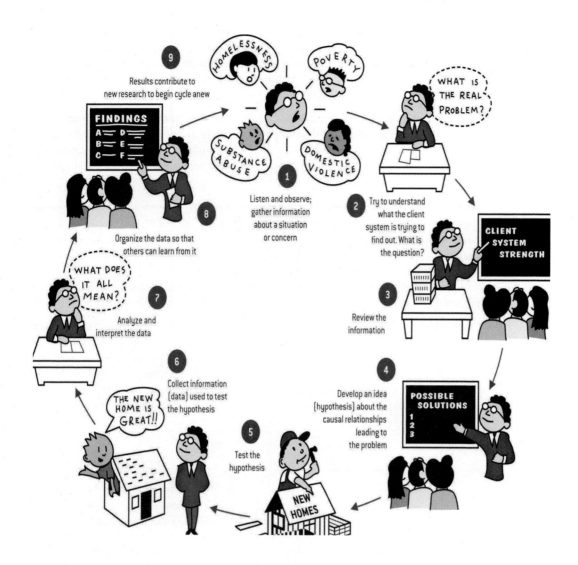

**Figure 3.2**

Research as a Problem-Solving Process
(an expansion of figure 3.1 on the previous page)

Bruce Friedmann (2007), via Figure 3.2 above, provides us with a very simple pictorial example of how the research process is nothing more than the application of the problem-solving model that you learned in your introductory social work practice courses.

## EVIDENCE-BASED PRACTICE

**E**vidence-based practice is often described as a process in which practitioners integrate information about client needs and values with knowledge of research findings on effective interventions (Gambrill, 2003, 2006, 2019; Sackett, Straus, Richardson, Rosenberg, & Haynes, 2000).

Eileen Gambrill (2006) outlines the following five-step process in conducting evidence-based practice, which was originally articulated by David Sackett and colleagues (2000) and eloquently stated by John Wodarski and Laura Hopson (2012):

1 **Construct well-structured answerable questions that will guide practice decisions.** Creating specific questions based on information provided during the assessment process will help practitioners and clients define the primary presenting problem and choose an appropriate intervention strategy. An example of a well-structured answerable question is:

> Will my client's anxiety symptoms be reduced by participation in weekly cognitive behavioral therapy sessions?

2 **Find the best available evidence with which to answer these questions.** Clinicians have access to a number of online resources for finding information on evidence-based practices. Many federal funders of social service programs provide a list of the interventions they consider to be evidence based. Such lists are available through the National Registry of Effective Programs and Practices, the National Institute of Drug Abuse, the Office of Juvenile Justice and Delinquency Prevention, the Centers for Disease Control and Prevention, and other federal organizations. University libraries typically provide online access to current research articles for students, but practitioners who are not affiliated with a university are unlikely to have access to these resources.

3 **Apply critical thinking in analyzing the evidence for its validity, impact on client outcomes, and applicability for practice settings.** Although practitioners are limited in the amount of time they can devote to reading research articles, it's important to examine studies for the size of the effect on client outcomes. Practitioners also need the skills to evaluate whether something other than the intervention evaluated may be responsible for their outcomes. This information is invaluable in determining whether the researcher's conclusions are justified and the intervention is likely to be helpful to your client.

4 **Use this critical analysis of the research to guide practice decisions.** This includes deciding whether the intervention is relevant for your clients and their presenting problems given the existing research support and considering your clients' values and preferences.

5 **Evaluate the effectiveness of the intervention with your unique clients within your practice settings.** Even interventions with solid research support need to be evaluated with your clients. The client populations, settings, and clinicians participating in research studies may differ from those in your setting, and the intervention may affect your clients differently. Therefore, systematically measuring your clients' progress toward achieving their desired outcomes is important even when the intervention has been shown to be effective with other clients.

Ed Mullen, Jennifer Bellamy, and Sarah Bledsoe (2018), among others, believe that the evidence-based practice framework will help social workers to operate efficiently and effectively by using the technology recently developed within our new global information age. This age has already empowered us to make more rational and informed decisions about the service options we have at our disposal. It can enhance our ability, for example, to successfully navigate the mass of information that is now readily available through the Internet and other forms of media in an attempt to make our intervention choices mindfully without being overwhelmed or misled (Wodarski & Hopson, 2012).

Evidence-based practice improves the flow of information back and forth from researchers, practitioners, and clients alike. This makes social workers better equipped to help a client system to make informed choices in the selection of the final interventions utilized. Within this framework, social work practitioners join with their clients and provide them with both empirical and practical knowledge about various treatment options. Although the final treatment decisions are made in the context of the best available evidence, clients' values and preferences ultimately drive the process.

In short, what evidence is found is then integrated with client circumstances and preferences—again drawing on clinical expertise to integrate data from the various sources. In essence, research evidence supports and guides—*but does not drive*—the evidence-based process.

A few good examples (via box 3.2) of how you can use the evidence-based practice process when you graduate from your social work program are nicely summed up by Bonnie Yegidis, Bob Weinbach, and Laura Myers (2018).

| Box 3.2 | Steps of the Evidence-Based Practice Process |
|---|---|

The **five-step process of evidence-based practice** (EBP) is briefly illustrated below (Straus et al., 2005):

**Step 1**  Convert your need for information about the causes of the problem, and for possible interventions, into an answerable question;

**Step 2**  Track down the best evidence with which to answer that question;

**Step 3**  Critically appraise that evidence for its validity, impact, and applicability;

**Step 4**  Integrate the critical appraisal with your clinical expertise and the client's unique values and circumstances; and

**Step 5**  Evaluate your effectiveness and efficiency in carrying out Steps 1 to 4 and seek ways to improve your practice. (pp. 3–4)

A considerable amount of literature, both within and outside the field of social work, is available that focuses on each of these five steps. An excellent resource for understanding EBP is the Social Workers' Desk Reference (Corcoran & Roberts, 2015). Gambrill and Gibbs (2009) describe effective ways to develop well-structured questions (related to Step 1 of EBP). These questions typically contain four parts:

**P**  (the population of clients),

**I**  (the intervention of concern),

**C**  (what the intervention may be compared to), and

**O**  (hoped for outcomes).

Three simple examples of PICO questions include:

**1**  How do persons with obsessive-compulsive disorder fare after being treated with exposure therapy and response prevention, compared to similar clients who are not treated at all?

**2**  How do clients receiving Temporary Assistance for Needy Families (TANF) benefits who also receive a job-finding club intervention fare compared with TANF recipients who did not receive this intervention?

**3**  Are people with alcoholism who regularly attend Alcoholics Anonymous (AA) meetings more abstinent than similar individuals who do not attend AA meetings?

**Step 1: Ask an Answerable Question**
The idea is when a social worker meets a client with a problem, one of the outcomes of the assessment process will be to formulate one or more answerable questions, which might have a bearing on what intervention(s) options are presented to that particular client. However, not all answerable questions bear on the topic of choosing interventions. Similar questions may be created to evaluate assessment methods, as in the following two questions:

- Do children who are assessed for potential sexual abuse through the use of anatomically correct dolls more accurately report actual episodes of abuse

Evidence-based practitioners always use their professional judgments and critical thinking skills when selecting the best treatment intervention(s) to use with specific client populations and problems.

compared with similar children who are assessed without the use of such dolls?

- Does the use of the genogram to assess clients result in a more accurate understanding of the client's background than standard clinical interviews?

Other questions may be focused on issues such as the etiology of certain conditions, the cost benefits of certain interventions, or questions related to the potentially harmful effects of a possible treatment intervention(s) such as rebirthing therapy or facilitated communication.

### Step 2: Track Down Evidence to Answer the Question in Step 1

Once one or more answerable questions have been formulated, the next step is to track down credible information that may help answer the question. This process is addressed by Allen Rubin and Danielle Parrish (2009) and may involve searching electronic databases, locating credible practice guidelines, or finding systematic reviews bearing on the relevant topic.

Among the higher or more credible forms of evidence that EBP particularly seeks to locate are randomized controlled trials (see Montgomery & Mayo-Wilson, 2009), meta-analyses (Corcoran & Littell, 2009), systematic reviews (Littell & Corcoran, 2009), and practice guidelines (Howard, Perron, & Vaughn, 2009).

### Step 3: Appraise Evidence Found in Step 2

The third step, critically appraising studies for EBP, is the focus of Bronson's (2009) study. Here, social workers bring to bear their skills in reading and appraising research, paying attention to issues of internal and external validity, relevance, sampling, statistical analysis, and so forth.

### Step 4: Integrate Evidence Found in Step 3

The fourth step in EBP is integrating the information found from diverse sources with your clinical expertise and the client's unique values and preferences. Of course, your professional ethical standards are also a crucial consideration, as are available resources. This important topic is discussed by Gambrill (2009, 2019).

### Step 5: Evaluate Your Own Effectiveness and Efficiency

The fifth step involves self-evaluating your own effectiveness and efficiency. This requires your ability to not only conduct EBP but also evaluate the outcomes with your client, which is actually the point of the entire exercise. Thyer and Myers's works (2007, 2009) are good resources to use in this regard. Portions of the preceding description of EBP are based on Thyer and Myers (2010).

In the twenty-first century there remain obstacles to the use of—and objections to—EBP (Rosen, 2003). However, most of the obstacles can be overcome, and many of the objections reflect a misunderstanding of EBP. EBP is not intended to dictate to social workers what decisions they should make, only to get them to use all of the available data (including their practice expertise, professional values, and their knowledge of individual clients and their values and preferences) in making them.

While EBP can result in cost savings for health insurance providers and other third parties alike, that's not its purpose—its purpose is to offer services and programs with the greatest potential for client success. Besides, what's wrong with cost cutting so long as our clients are the ultimate beneficiaries?

While there are still problems for which effective interventions have not been identified through research, these gaps do not negate the need for social work practitioners to know how to conduct research studies, locate and critically evaluate the research findings of others, and—when available—to use these findings as important components of their practice decision making.

Describing how the evidence-based practice process works is way beyond the scope of this introductory research methods book. Nevertheless, you need to know the contents in this book in order for you to have a meaningful appreciation of its applicability and relevance to contemporary social work practice.

At this point, the most important thing to remember is that the social work practice/helping/problem-solving/research/evaluation processes are practically identical to each other and they all require you to have basic critical thinking skills as outlined at the end of Chapter 1. This would be an excellent time to expand your knowledge of evidence-based practice by obtaining a copy of Eileen Gambrill's book titled, *Critical Thinking and the Process of Evidence-Based Practice* (2019).

## DEFINITION OF SOCIAL WORK RESEARCH

**S**o far, we have discussed the various ways of obtaining knowledge and briefly looked at the characteristics and phases of the scientific method along with what evidence-based practice is all about. Armed with this knowledge, we now need a definition of research, which is composed of two syllables, *re* and *search.*

Dictionaries define the former syllable as a prefix meaning "again, anew, or over again," and the latter as a verb meaning "to examine closely and carefully, to test and try, or to probe" (Duehn, 1985). Together, these syllables form a noun that describes a careful and systematic study in some field of knowledge, undertaken to establish facts or principles. Social work research therefore can be defined as follows:

> Social work research is a systematic and objective inquiry that utilizes the scientific method of inquiry to solve human problems and creates new knowledge that is generally applicable to the social work profession.

We obtain much of our knowledge base from the findings derived from research studies that utilize the scientific method. However, all research studies have built-in biases and limitations that create errors and keep us from being absolutely certain about the studies' outcomes.

This book helps you to understand these limitations and to take them into account in the interpretation of research findings, and helps you to avoid making errors or obtaining wrong answers. One of the principal products of a research study is obtaining systematic and objective data—via the scientific method—about reality as it genuinely is, unbiased and error-free.

## COMMITTING TO LIFELONG LEARNING

**A**s you know by now, a research base within our profession will not guarantee its public acceptance, but there is no doubt that the absence of such a base and the lack of vigorous research efforts to expand it will, in the long run, erode our credibility and be harmful to our clients. To be sure that this doesn't happen, you'll need to a become lifelong learner after your graduate with your social work degree.

Lifelong learning is nothing more than for you to continue to learn new and exciting stuff after your graduate—it means that your learning doesn't stop when you walk across the stage at graduation. Judy Krysik (2018) provides some fantastic tips on how to become a lifelong learner. The expectations for producing and using research in professional social work practice are clear; the question that remains is, How?

> Entry-level social work jobs can be demanding, leaving little time for consultation, research, or even reflection. A social worker is more likely to use research if the

employing agency or organization has a culture that supports it and if the worker is committed to making it happen. Will you commit yourself to a career of lifelong learning? If so, your very first step is to develop an action plan to make it happen. Below are a few ideas that you might consider adopting.

1  Join the National Association of Social Workers

2  Choose a professional social work conference that is relevant to your practice area, and make a commitment to attend every year

3  Ask your manager or supervisor to subscribe to a professional journal(s)

4  Join a Listserv dedicated to critiquing knowledge in your area of practice

5  Join your local library, and spend at least one day a month in professional development reading about the latest research in your area

6  Initiate a brown-bag lunch session at your workplace at which you and your colleagues discuss research

7  Attend research-based training and workshops whenever possible

8  Continue your formal education by taking courses online or at a university or college

9  Make a presentation to share your research findings at a conference

10  Evaluate your day-to-day practices; that is, evaluate if you are effective with your clients

11  Collaborate with others to evaluate the services provided by your agency or organization

12  Seek employment in agencies and organizations whose culture supports using research and evaluating practice

## CHAPTER RECAP

- "Fake news" is not news you disagree with. In fact, it's not news at all.

- Most social work researchers and practitioners share common characteristics.

- Evidence-based practitioners use the Information Café.

- Social workers can perform three research roles within their agencies.

- Social workers can easily integrate three research roles into their daily practices.

- The process of problem solving, research, and practice are identical.

- Evidence-based practitioners use a five-step process when selecting the best intervention to use with a specific client system.

- Social work practitioners make a lifelong commitment to learning.

- A professional social worker uses evidence-based practice models when appropriate.

## REVIEW EXERCISES

1  List and discuss the characteristics that social work researchers must possess. Identify one characteristic that you think you may have trouble with as a future social work researcher and delineate the ways you could grow in this area.

2  In reference to Question 1, what additional characteristics do you feel social work researchers should have? Are there any of those listed that you feel social work

researchers should not have?

3  In reference to Question 1, do you feel that line-level social work practitioners should also possess these four characteristics? If so, which ones?

4  What is the *Information Café*? How would it be helpful to you as an evidence-based practitioner? Provide a social work example throughout your discussion to illustrate your main points.

5   List the three research roles you can take as a professional social work practitioner. Now discuss how you could be in each role as a social worker upon graduation. Use specific social work examples throughout your discussion.

6   Why is making a commitment to lifelong learning so important? Provide examples as you can to justify your response.

7   Quickly skim through the rest of the chapters in this book. At this point do you see any chapters that may be helpful to you when you become an evidence-based practitioner? If so, which chapters stick out the most to you, and why? Which ones don't, and why?

8   **Practice:** Pretend for the moment you're employed as a social worker in your university's student counseling center. A first-generation ethnic minority student comes into your office where she tells you she feels lonely and isolated and wants to go home and drop out of school.

- Using this chapter as a guide—and in particular Figures 3.1 and 3.2—describe the steps you would go through to help your client with her problems. Be specific and back up all your statements with specific examples.

9   **Research:** Let's suppose that now you want to do a research study that tries to find out what factors are involved that make first-generation ethnic minority students at your university feel lonely and isolated.

- Using this chapter as a guide—and in particular Figures 3.1 and 3.2—describe the steps you would go through to answer your research question: Why do first-generation ethnic minority students feel isolated? Be specific and back up all your statements with specific examples.

10   Review the evidence-based practice process on pages 68–72.

- At this point in your research course discuss what knowledge and skills you think you'll need to carry out all five steps embedded within the evidence-based process.

- Where do you plan on obtaining the knowledge and skill set you have just identified above to become an evidence-based practitioner?

- Quickly skim through the rest of the chapters in this book. At this point do you see any chapters that may be helpful to you when you become an evidence-based practitioner? If so, which chapters stick out the most to you, and why? Which ones don't, and why?

11   Review Figures 3.1 (page 67) and 3.2 (page 68) for a moment. In your own words describe how the social work research process is the same as the social work practice process. Use a social work example throughout your discussion. Also discuss how you think the two processes are not the same.

12   Background: Review our definition of social work research on page 72.

- After reading Chapter 3, formulate your own definition of social work research.

- Use Google to find five other definitions of social work research.

- Compare and contrast the ones you found with your own.

- What are their commonalities? What are their differences?

- Now the hard part: Revise your own definition of social work research by integrating our definition of social work research and the 5 definitions you found on the Internet. Don't be shy, go for it!

- Present your revised definition to the rest of the class. What were their comments?

- Did they help you refine your revised definition even further?

13   Review the three social work research-related roles you can take when you graduate—CSWE Competency 1 at the beginning of this chapter (page 56) and on pages 63–67. Thoroughly discuss how you feel this chapter will help you to perform one or more research-related roles when you graduate. Which one of the three roles do you believe this chapter helped you with the most? Why? Discuss in detail and provide an example to illustrate your main points.

14   Review CSWE Competency 4 at the beginning of this chapter (page 56). Thoroughly discuss how you feel this chapter will help you to become a practice-informed researcher and a research-informed practitioner. Discuss in detail and provide an example to illustrate your main points.

**The scientific method and the practitioner**

15   **Scenario 1:** Make an argument that to be an effective evidence-based social work practitioner *you need to know* how the scientific method of inquiry process advances our profession's knowledge

base. Provide clear and explicit practice-related social work examples to illustrate your main points.

16 **Scenario 2:** Make an argument that *you do not need to know* how the scientific method of inquiry process advances our profession's knowledge base to be an effective evidence-based social work practitioner. Provide clear and explicit practice-related social work examples to illustrate your main points.

17 **Time to choose:** Which one of the above two scenarios (i.e., 15 or 16) do you feel is more consistent with the concept of the contemporary evidence-based social work practice process as illustrated in this chapter. Why? Provide relevant social work examples to illustrate your main points.

### The scientific method and the researcher

18 **Scenario 1:** Make an argument that to be a competent social work researcher *you need to know* how the scientific method of inquiry process advances our profession's knowledge base. Provide clear and explicit research-related social work examples to illustrate your main points.

19 **Scenario 2:** Make an argument that *you do not need to know* how the scientific method of inquiry process advances our profession's knowledge base to be a competent social work researcher. Provide clear and explicit research-related social work examples to illustrate your main points.

20 **Time to choose:** Which one of the above two scenarios (i.e., 18 or 19) do you feel is more consistent with the place of research in social work? Why? Discuss in detail and provide an example to illustrate your main points.

### Looking ahead by looking back

21 At this point in your research methods course, how comfortable are you with discussing the place of research in social work with your field instructor, with your practice instructor, with your research instructor, with your supervisor at work, with the director of your social work program, or with your classmates.

# 4

CHAPTER

# 2015 EPAS COMPETENCIES

| COMPETENCY 1 | Demonstrate Ethical and Professional Behavior |
|---|---|

You will learn that in order to be a successful evidence-based practitioner you have an ethical obligation to integrate three research roles into your daily practice activities as discussed in Chapter 3: (1) research consumer, (2) research partner—either as a co-researcher or research participant, and (3) creator and disseminator of research (or knowledge).

This entire chapter pertains to these three professional roles as you'll learn that one of the best ways to become an ethical and professional evidence-based social work practitioner is knowing how the existing literature is utilized to formulate relevant, useful, and meaningful research and practice questions. More importantly, you'll learn that you must use the existing literature in every step of the research process and practice process as well (see figure 3.1 on page 67 and figure 3.2 on page 68).

| COMPETENCY 4 | Engage in Practice-Informed Research and Research-Informed Practice |
|---|---|

Competency 4 also pertains to the entire chapter because you have to:

1  Evaluate the degree to which a social work research study appropriately utilized the literature in reference to the formulation of the study's research question or hypothesis (**research consumer**—research-informed practice);

2  Participate in a research study—either as a co-researcher or research participant (**research partner**—practice-informed research). See 1 above and 3 below; and

3  Know how to actually find, evaluate, and use the literature when formulating a meaningful, relevant, and useful research question (or hypothesis) before you actually do a research study (**creator and disseminator of research**—practice-informed research).

You also need to utilize evidence-based practice recommendations whenever possible; that is, you need to integrate (1) the best available research-based evidence with (2) your clinical expertise and (3) your client's values.

All of the above implies you'll need to evaluate the degree to which a research study used the literature to formulate its research question (or hypothesis) that led to its research-based evidence. In short, you need to ask and then answer a simple question: How seriously should I take the findings of any specific research study given its overall creditability in relation to how well it utilized the existing literature within every step of the research process?

| COMPETENCY 9 | Evaluate Practice with Individuals, Families, Groups, Organizations, & Communities |
|---|---|

See Competencies 1 and 4.

# Literature Reviews

| | | |
|---|---|---|
| CHAPTERS 1 & 3 | Step 1. | Understanding the Research Process |
| CHAPTER 2 | Step 2. | Formulating Research Questions |
| CHAPTER 4 APPENDIXES A–C | Step 3. | Reviewing the Literature Evaluating the Literature |
| CHAPTERS 5 & 6 | Step 4. | Being Aware of Ethical and Cultural Issues |
| CHAPTERS 7–10 | Step 5. | Selecting a Research Approach |
| CHAPTERS 11 & 12 | Step 6. | Specifying How Variables Are Measured |
| CHAPTER 13 | Step 7. | Selecting a Sample |
| CHAPTERS 14 & 15 | Step 8. | Selecting a Research Design |
| CHAPTERS 16 & 17 | Step 9. | Selecting a Data-Collection Method |
| CHAPTERS 18 & 19 | Step 10. | Analyzing the Data |
| CHAPTERS 20 & 21 | Step 11. | Writing the Research Report |

# Literature Reviews

TOPIC FOR THIS WEEK:
Learning how to do literature reviews

"Look, I don't care what topic your literature review is on, just write on something you know anything about. That should leave you with a lot of free time."

CHAPTER

4

CHAPTER OUTLINE

WHAT'S A LITERATURE REVIEW?
THE LOGIC OF DOING LITERATURE REVIEWS
    Brings Clarity and Focus to the Question
    Identifies Gaps in the Literature
    Prevents the Duplication of Knowledge
    Broadens Our Knowledge Base
    Contextualizes the Research Project
    Improves a Study's Methodology
    Assists in Identifying Opposing Views
WHERE AND HOW TO SEARCH FOR INFORMATION
    The Internet
STORING AND MANAGING INFORMATION
READING FOR A LITERATURE REVIEW
    Preview
    Overview
    Inview
DEVELOPING A THEORETICAL FRAMEWORK
WRITING AND ORGANIZING A LITERATURE REVIEW
CRITERIA OF A GOOD LITERATURE REVIEW
    Evaluating a Literature Review
      *Use the Appendixes*
CHAPTER RECAP
REVIEW EXERCISES

**ALL SOCIAL WORK RESEARCH studies** must draw upon the literature in just about every step of the research process. Your research study will be no exception. A literature review is an essential early step in refining your research question or writing a research proposal. This chapter demystifies the literature review process by focusing on what it is, how it's perceived by social work students, why you are required to undertake a literature review when doing a research study (or writing a research proposal), how to go about doing a literature review, and finally what the characteristics of a good literature review look like.

## WHAT'S A LITERATURE REVIEW?

**D**oing a research study can be seen as an entry into an academic conversation that has been going on in professional social work journals and books. Just as you would do when joining any other conversation, you'll first listen to what the conversation is about, figure out what the main issues of debate are, and determine who is responding to whom—and in what way.

The literature review section of your research study is a way of reporting to your reader on the academic conversation in which you are planning to participate. In the simplest of forms, a literature review generally involves the search for and documentation of primary (original) sources of scholarship, rather than secondary sources, which are reports of other people's work. Cooper and Hedges (1994) describe the literature review as,

> A literature review reports on primary or original scholarship. The primary reports used in a literature review may be verbal, but in the vast majority of cases they are written documents. The types of scholarship may be empirical, theoretical, critical/analytical, or methodological in nature. Second, a literature review seeks to describe, summarize, evaluate, clarify, and/or integrate the content of primary reports. (13)

This should give you some idea of what a literature review may involve. Reviewing the literature is a continuous process. It begins before a specific research question has been finalized, and it continues until the final report is finished. To summarize:

1  The literature review draws mainly on primary sources

2  It can have a variety of purposes:

— to help you identify a suitable topic for study

— to help you identify relevant literature for your study

— to help you get an idea of what the main debates are on your topic area

— to help you understand the issues involved

— to help inform your own ideas about your research problem area

— to gain familiarity with the accepted research approaches and methods in our profession

— to become a critical co-conversant in the "academic conversation"

**3** It's a continuous process, which begins before a research question is finalized and continues to the end

**4** It's a well-written, coherent product, appropriate to the purpose for which you need it

---

| **Box 4.1** | Literature Review Tips |
|---|---|

**One of the most important** early steps in a research project is conducting the literature review. This is also one of the most humbling experiences you're likely to have. Why? Because you're likely to find out that just about any worthwhile idea you will have has been thought of before, at least to some degree. Every time I teach a research methods course, I have at least one student come to me complaining that they couldn't find anything in the literature that was related to their topic. And nearly every time they have said that, I was able to show them that was only true because they had looked for articles that were exactly the same as their research topic.

A literature review is designed to identify related research, to set the current research project within a conceptual and theoretical context. When looked at that way, there is almost no topic that is so new or unique that we can't locate relevant and informative related research. Below are tips for conducting the literature review.

**Tip 1**    **Concentrate your efforts on the scientific literature.** Try to determine what the most credible research journals are in your topic area and start with those. Put the greatest emphasis on research journals that use a blind review system. In a blind review, authors submit potential articles to a journal editor, who in turn asks several reviewers to provide a critical review of the paper. The paper is sent to these reviewers with no identification of the author so that there will be no personal bias (either for or against the author). Based on the reviewers' recommendations, the editor can accept the article for publication, reject it, or recommend that the author revise and resubmit it. Articles in journals with blind review processes can be expected to have a fairly high level of credibility.

**Tip 2**    **Do your review early in the research process.** You are likely to learn a lot during the literature review that will help you in making the trade-offs you'll need to face. After all, previous researchers also had to face trade-off decisions.

**What should you look for in the literature review?**

- You might be able to find a study that is quite similar to the one you are thinking of doing. Because all credible research studies have to review the literature themselves, you can check their literature review to get a quick-start on your own.

- Prior research will help ensure that you have included all the major relevant constructs in your study. You may find that other, similar studies have routinely looked at an outcome that you might not have included. If you did your study without that construct, it would not be judged credible because it ignored a major construct.

- The literature review will help you to find and select appropriate measuring instruments. You will readily see what measurement instruments researchers have been using in contexts similar to yours.
- The review will help you to anticipate common problems in your research context. You can use the prior experiences of others to avoid common pitfalls.

Now that you have some idea of what a literature review is, the question that must be looked at more closely concerns the reasons for engaging in a literature review: Why is it regarded as an essential part of your research study?

# THE LOGIC OF DOING LITERATURE REVIEWS

A **literature review** is based on the assumption that doing a research study is not something that happens in isolation. It's something that is done and developed by a community of academic researchers. (Think of the academic conversation analogy: You can't have a conversation all on your own!) This means that knowledge development is seen to be a cumulative activity, and you can learn from what other researchers and writers have done before you.

What you are researching in the present must be built upon the knowledge of what has been researched in the past. Researchers read previous studies to compare, replicate, or criticize the findings of other writers. When you are participating in the academic conversation—by doing a research study or writing a research proposal—you are responding to issues raised, drawing links between what various authors have said, showing where there might be some contradictions, or raising some considerations that haven't been addressed before.

But you can do this only if you know what the conversation has been and is about, so you must know what the past and current debates are in the literature. Ranjit Kumar (1994) has put together a useful list of seven overlapping purposes of a literature review:

1. It helps to bring clarity and focus to the research question
2. It helps to identify gaps
3. It prevents the duplication of knowledge
4. It helps to broaden the knowledge base
5. It helps to contextualize the research project
6. It helps to improve a study's methodology
7. It assists in identifying opposing views

## BRINGS CLARITY & FOCUS TO THE RESEARCH QUESTION

You cannot undertake a literature review unless you know what you want to find out. On the other hand, a literature review is also necessary in helping you to shape and narrow your research question. This is because reviewing the literature helps you to better understand your subject area, and thus helps you to conceptualize your research question much more clearly and precisely.

A literature review helps you to understand the relationship between your research question and the body of existing knowledge in that area. In other words, the literature contributes to your understanding of why your research question is a problem. When you do a literature review, you can identify more information and ideas that might be directly relevant to your study.

## IDENTIFIES GAPS IN THE LITERATURE

To identify the obvious gaps in your general problem area, you have to know the literature. In doing a literature review, you become aware of what has already been done and what remains to be done in your study's area. Be careful of claiming that there are gaps in the knowledge when you have not done a thorough review of the literature.

## PREVENTS THE DUPLICATION OF KNOWLEDGE

You may feel excited about a particular idea—your research question that was derived from a general problem area—and believe that you are the only person to have had this idea. More often than not, after you read the existing literature, you will quickly discover that your research question has indeed been thought of before.

A good literature review helps you to avoid reinventing the wheel. In other words, it can keep you from merely answering research questions that were previously answered by other researchers before you. Of course, planning to replicate studies (a legitimate form of research) or aiming to study an issue for which there is no definitive answer (e.g., the link between mind and brain) is not merely duplicating research studies. You are contributing to the body of knowledge by either validating previous studies or contributing some new insights on a long-standing issue. Very few research studies produce a definitive answer to a research question.

A literature review is also useful to get to know what has worked—and what has not—in terms of scientific methodology so that you can avoid making the same mistakes as others may have made.

> Don't think because your research question has been previously written about that the final answer also has been discovered.

## BROADENS OUR KNOWLEDGE BASE

You should read widely in the subject area in which you intend to conduct your research study. It's important that you know what other researchers have found, who the authors considered to be movers and shakers are, what the seminal works are in your research study's problem area, what the key issues and crucial questions are, and what theories have been put forward in the relevant body of knowledge.

You will also be able to see how others have defined concepts that you will be using, and what the widely accepted definitions (or interpretations) are. You will be in a better position to work out interpretations of your key concepts that suit your study's purposes from this existing knowledge base.

Our profession has, over the years, developed basic research practices and conventions. Consult the literature to familiarize yourself with the acceptable research conventions and approaches adopted in the research literature. When you undertake a degree in social work, you are supposed to be an expert in your concentration area, or at least an apprentice who demonstrates mastery in your area of study. The more you know, the better the position you are in to study your topic.

## CONTEXTUALIZES THE RESEARCH PROJECT

You must provide a signpost to let your readers know where your research question and your methodological research approach that will answer the question are coming from. This signposting allows readers to see which theories and principles have been influential in shaping your approach to your research study or research proposal. As has already been indicated, the literature review enables you to build a platform based on existing knowledge from which you can carry on and explain what your contribution will be to the field when your research study is finished.

The literature review can put your study into historical and other perspectives, and can provide an intellectual context for your work. This enables you to position your study in relation to what others have written. Context reviews help you to (1) place your project in the larger picture, (2) establish links between your topic and the existing body of knowledge, (3) establish the relevance and significance of your research question, and (4) establish the possible implications of your position.

## IMPROVES A STUDY'S METHODOLOGY

Going through the existing literature helps you to acquaint yourself with the various scientific methodologies that others have used to answer research questions similar to those you are investigating. You can see what has worked and what has not worked for others who were using similar procedures and methods, and what problems they faced.

In learning about the scientific methodologies that others have used, you will be better able to select a methodology that is capable of giving you reliable and valid answers to your research question and that is appropriate for the problem area in which you are studying (Kumar, 1994).

## ASSISTS IN IDENTIFYING OPPOSING VIEWS

A literature review helps identify differences between your study and previous studies. The idea that your research study builds on earlier work does not necessarily imply that it extends, flows from, or approves of earlier work found in the literature. Indeed, your work might be highly critical of earlier work and even seek to discredit it.

However, even if you are critical of a particular theory or methods of conducting a research study, you will still need to review the literature to argue the weaknesses of the previous studies and the benefits of the alternative approach that you have chosen. In a nutshell, you cannot justifiably reject or criticize something if you don't clearly understand (and demonstrate to your readers that you clearly understand) what it is you are rejecting or criticizing.

## WHERE AND HOW TO SEARCH FOR INFORMATION

**Y**ou need to know how to use the computers in your university or college library and how to use indexes and abstracts. You can organize searches based on subjects, themes, or keywords. Find out who your subject librarians are and make friends with them. Interlibrary loans are extremely useful and provide an efficient service.

When searching electronic databases and the shelves of the library, it's important to establish the credibility of the source you find. Is it an academically acknowledged database? Are the entries still relevant? The date of the publication is important. For empirical studies, you should concentrate on the latest publications and work backward from these as they become outdated.

Remember, researchers build on the work of those who have gone before them (just as you need to do in your own study). With theoretical articles, it's not as important to have the most current articles as you might be drawing on classic texts that are more dated. The quickest way of getting an overview of the trends in the debates is to look at the professional journals in your problem area. You will eventually get an idea of what will make a successful study in your study's problem area.

You can compare the studies you find and any publications that come from them with what you intend to do in your study. More important authors tend to be quoted more frequently, and you will be able to tell who the highly regarded authors are in your study's problem area simply by perusing the literature.

## The Internet

The Internet is a terrific tool for obtaining information. However, you need to know your way around it if you want to avoid drawing on inappropriate sites. Most professional journals are now available in electronic form online, and you should check which of these are available at your university or college. Although some journals are available in this form, it should not be seen as an alternative to searching the print versions of journals and books in your university or college library. This is because some of the literature is still only available in printed form.

The Internet is also useful for "gray material," which is information such as government policy documents, speeches, press releases, and so forth. The advantage of the Internet is its immediacy of access, and the information is often very recent. But you must be careful of what you find on the Internet because anyone can write anything there—so unless you know that a site is an academically acknowledged one, you can't be sure of the credibility of information you find there.

## STORING AND MANAGING INFORMATION

In searching the literature, it's important to develop some sort of filing system—either as hard copy or on a computer. Remember to store all details so that you don't have to go back to the original sources. This can be a very annoying task, but outstanding or incomplete references must be tracked down when you write your final research report or develop your research proposal. Details on the following should be kept and arranged alphabetically:

- Author(s) (surname and initial)
- Title of the book (if a chapter in an edited collection is used, note the chapter title as well) and publisher
- Journal title (and title of article)
- Relevant pages
- Journal volume
- Year and month of publication
- Library where the information is found
- How the item relates to your research project

It's important to keep these sources accurately and consistently. You can either write the details of each reference separately on a blank index card (on sale in any stationery store), which you will file alphabetically, or you can use one of the many inexpensive software programs such as EndNote (www. endnote.com) to enter your references.

## READING FOR A LITERATURE REVIEW

There is no shortcut to doing a good research study. You must read—period, full stop. There is simply no way around it. But there are different ways of reading. The process of reading has three different aspects:

1  **Preview,** in which you do a broad and superficial sweep of the literature
2  **Overview,** in which you slightly engage with the material
3  **Inview,** in which you read very carefully for understanding of the material

# PREVIEW

Lots of information from books, journals, and the Internet is available to you as a university or college student. You can waste hundreds of hours reading irrelevant information and, in this way, procrastinate about getting down to writing. You need to become skilled at selecting the right sources for your purposes.

To do so, you need to be able to *preview* books and journal articles quickly by looking at the title, date of publication, author, organization responsible for publication, and the table of contents:

> You should read broadly and deeply in your field of study before beginning to write a literature review.

- **The title.** From the title, you can predict whether some of the information for your research question may be covered.
- **Date of publication.** Is the book or journal article fairly current and up to date?
- **Author(s)/organization/publisher.** Are they reputable? Have you heard of them before? Is there any information on them? Are they attached to a credible institution?
- **Table of contents/subheadings.** Will some of the necessary information for your research question be covered? Will it be directly relevant to your topic, or will it just give you a broad overview? Which chapters or sections of the book look relevant to your research study?

In the preview stage, to locate literature it helps if you jot down your research question, what you know about it, what you would like to know about it, any questions you have about it, and the value it may have for your literature review.

# OVERVIEW

Once you have selected a book or journal article you want to read, the best way to begin to understand it is to get a sense of how the whole book or journal article (or sections of it) is structured. You can do this by *overviewing* the work. This will give you a sense of its whole framework (or structure) so that when you read it in detail you will be able to fit what you read into the whole context of the work.

Not only will the overview help you to find information quickly, it will assist your understanding as you read. In doing a survey or overview, you should concentrate on headings, subheadings, introductions, conclusions, the opening and closing sentences of sections, graphs, tables, and any summaries that the piece provides.

# INVIEW

The *inview* involves a detailed and careful reading of the subject matter, ensuring that you understand the concepts and follow the argument. Take clear and detailed notes of everything you read. Keep your research question in mind, and don't record pages of information that aren't directly relevant to your study's research question.

You could keep summaries of your readings in a particular file or in a software program. Don't forget, at the same time, to record all the necessary details of the reference. In your summaries, you might include what the main issues and arguments are, a critical comment, and how the content relates to your proposed research study.

You should read broadly and deeply in your field of study before beginning to write a literature review. This helps you to locate your study in a wider theoretical landscape. Then read deeply in the narrower field of your research question so that you have a detailed account of the existing literature as it relates to your study's problem area. After reading in an intensive way, you need to make notes of your own, draw a conceptual map, and respond—this is how you begin to prepare an argument for your literature review. Select a suitable structure in terms of which to organize the literature, and use subheadings.

You could begin your inview of the literature by finding an introductory book or key articles that introduce the main concepts and theoretical language in the problem area that you are going to study. Try to identify the concepts that you don't understand, and discuss these with your fellow students and instructor.

You should develop a conceptual map and try to fit new readings into this map. Pull together themes and issues that belong together. Once you have developed a map, a rough structure of your draft framework, keep slotting in information under the headings and subheadings that you develop. Ranjit Kumar (1994) suggests the following four points:

1   Note the theories put forward, the criticisms of these and their basis, and the methodologies adopted (e.g., study design, sample size and its characteristics, measurement procedures) and the criticisms of them

2   Examine to what extent the findings can be generalized to other situations

3   Notice where significant differences of opinion exist among researchers, and give your view about the validity of these differences

4   Ascertain the areas in which little or nothing is known—the gaps that exist in the body of knowledge

## DEVELOPING A THEORETICAL FRAMEWORK

Students struggle with developing theoretical frameworks. A possible reason for this is that no correct and clear-cut theoretical framework exists. The question about which framework in your subject area is most appropriate is itself a question of debate within the literature.

Nevertheless, the theoretical framework is where you highlight the main thrust of the academic conversation you are entering. Note the similarities and differences between themes and theories, agreements and disagreements among authors, and the bearing that these have on your research topic. Use these as a basis for developing the theoretical framework that is best suited to the purpose of your study.

A theoretical framework sets up key concepts, interpretations, approaches, claims, foundations, principles, and other items that will influence the design of your structure, and how you will sort the information and analyze the findings of your study. Unless you review the literature in relation to this framework, you won't be able to develop a focus in your literature search. In other words, the theoretical framework provides you with a guide as you read (Kumar, 1994).

You must first go through the literature to develop this framework, and then have the framework in hand while you go through the literature. A good idea is to go through some of the literature to develop this framework, then use this skeleton framework to guide your readings further. As you read more, you may change the framework, but if you don't have some structure, you will be bogged down in a lot of unnecessary readings and note taking that aren't directly relevant to your study.

The theoretical framework is the basis of your research problem. Of course, competing theoretical frameworks are put forward to explain the issue you will be researching, so you will need to discuss—based on the arguments put forward by other authors—why this particular framework is appropriate for your purposes.

## WRITING AND ORGANIZING A LITERATURE REVIEW

**Y**our writing should be signposted at every point; that is, you should say what you are going to do, then do it, then say what you have done. You will need to do and redo things—the process of research and writing is messy and doubles back on itself. Only in the end does it appear as seamless and linear.

Coherence only emerges over time. Unfortunately, there are no shortcuts. In the literature review, you should present an exposition (a clear and coherent summary with a particular purpose) of the issue you are studying, which you then use as the basis for an argument. Rather than just stating facts, use an argument to convince the reader that your particular interpretation is true.

You can use the findings of other authors to support your claims. You should have a central argument (the main point you want to put forward), then use each paragraph to develop a part of the main argument. You must state the argument early on and sum it up in the conclusion. All your points should link to your main argument. You can organize your literature review in one of the following four ways:

> Even the best authors have reworked their text many, many times before it was finally printed.

1  **By date of study.** Here, you would start with older studies and work toward the latest. This is the least ordered of the literature reviews.

2  **By school of thought/theory.** This is a review of the theoretical positions of scholars. You could organize it from oldest to most recent, or you could start with approaches or definitions that you feel to be inappropriate or that have been discredited by recent scholarship. You would follow this with a discussion of those points that would form the frame of reference for your study.

3  **By themes that have emerged from the literature.** The headings and subheadings should be based on the literature and should be precise, should be descriptive of the contents, and should follow a logical progression. Substantiations and contradictions should be clearly referenced. Your arguments should be conceptually clear, highlighting the reasons for and against and referring to the main findings, gaps, and issues.

4  **By research approach.** You can, for example, compare past positivistic approaches (chapter 8), interpretive approaches (chapter 9), and mixed-methods approaches (chapter 10) in your study's problem area and show how they produced different results, if any.

**Try to answer the following five questions:**

1  What do you consider to be the most important theories and perspectives to arise from the literature? How have these affected your understanding of your topic?

2  How does your research question link with the state of knowledge as reflected in the literature?

3  What questions are raised by the literature that your research study addresses?

4  Has anyone ever done this before? What partial answers to your research question have been found before? How did previous researchers go about asking such questions? What methodological issues are raised by the literature in question?

5  In what way is your topic valid, important, and doable? How will your research study add to the literature?

If you're still undecided on how to construct your literature review, here's a suggestion on how to get started. Go back to your research proposal and list the ten keywords (or phrases) you have noted as capturing the main concepts of your study. Jot them down in a column. Then, for each concept jotted down, ask yourself, "What does the literature say about this?"

| **Box 4.2** | A Critical Thinking Standard to Consider When Answering the Preceding Five Questions: *Reasoning* |
| --- | --- |

**Although asking questions is necessary** to begin critical thinking, merely asking the questions is not enough; the questions need to be answered (or at least addressed). Often we raise questions only to worry about them, or to torment ourselves, or even to put off action instead of trying to answer them by thinking them through.

For example, a significant number of students have difficulty in math-related fields. They sometimes ask the question, "Why am I so bad at math?" They then use this question to make negative judgments about themselves ("I'm just hopeless at math, and I always will be") or about the field ("I don't need to know math to be a good social worker"), or they answer it with unhelpful generalities ("I'm no good at it because of the way I was taught").

Reasoning it out, however, requires approaching the question in a different way and with a different spirit. It is the spirit of genuinely wanting to figure out a clear, accurate answer to a question that is important to you. Reasoning it out might begin with rethinking the question and then reformulating it in a more neutral and productive way: "What are the main causes of my problems with math, and what are some good ways to begin dealing with them?"

You might then read a little about what causes problems in learning math and apply the information to your own case. You could talk to counselors about alternative approaches that have helped other students, take seriously what the counselors say, and note any resistance you feel to the new approaches. Reasoning it out may not "solve" the problem, but it does provide a significantly better way of addressing the problem than not reasoning it out at all.

In contrast, there are many uncritical ways to try to answer questions, ones that do not involve much reasoning. You can:

1  Ask someone (and simply accept the answers uncritically).
2  Answer according to the way you have been raised (and accept that without examining whether it was a healthy way to be raised).
3  Answer without looking for information, even if it's readily available—the topic of this chapter.
4  Answer in accordance with your personality (without examining the extent to which your "personality" helps or hinders you in this kind of situation).
5  Answer with what first comes into your head.

It is easy to misunderstand questions about reasoning. Thus you might interpret the second item listed as implying that critical thinking is opposed to the way you were raised, but that is not what it means. What critical thinking is opposed to is acting in the way you were raised without examining it. For example, someone raised in a family where violence and abuse were taught, or where blind obedience to authority was taken for granted, should not simply follow those values.

The two greatest difficulties in reasoning are not what you might expect. It isn't that people aren't good at reasoning, or that they make mistakes. Everyone is good at it in some areas and not so good in others; everyone makes mistakes; everyone can improve. But these are not the most crucial difficulties. They go deeper. The first is that, when presented with a problem, people often don't think to reason in the first place.

It's just not the usual human reaction to a problem. This is partly because societies do not encourage reasoning as an approach to important questions. The second difficulty is that people often do not know the difference between reasoning through something and other ways of responding. As a result, people respond with what seems to be reasoning, but isn't.

For example, a discussion is not automatically an example of critical thinking. Often in discussions each participant says what he or she believes, and that's the end of the matter. In a reasoned discussion, however, listening is as important as speaking. Participants try to understand the reasons behind other people's beliefs, and they try to identify both the strong and weak points of the views expressed. The whole spirit is different.

So "reasoning things out" really means reasoning them out well. What does it mean, then, to reason through something well? Reasoning itself is drawing conclusions on the basis of reasons. Good reasoning, therefore, is drawing conclusions on the basis of reasons and giving due weight to all relevant factors. Relevant factors include the implications of drawing those conclusions, the assumptions on which the reasoning is based, the accuracy of the reasons used, the alternatives available, and a number of other elements and standards.

Although it's not difficult to define good reasoning in an open-ended way, the challenge is to spell it out in a way that is usable by you, one that lays a foundation so your ability to reason well can improve and deepen during the rest of your life.

Next to each one, identify three or four readings that address this concept. Make clear and honest summaries of each reading. Then critically engage with your summaries, noting the trends, similarities, differences, gaps, and implications.

Rewrite this draft into flowing text. Do this for each listed concept (the concept can be a subheading), and you'll have the first draft of your literature review. You should keep a log or a journal of information that you gathered during your whole writing process. You need to ignore references that aren't relevant anymore and pare the references down if needed.

## CRITERIA OF A GOOD LITERATURE REVIEW

**Y**our literature review must cover the main aspects of your study and be fair in its treatment of authors. The literature review should do justice to an author's arguments before critiquing them. (You can't agree or disagree with something if you don't have a clear idea of what it is you're agreeing or disagreeing with!) It should be topical.

The review shouldn't exclusively be confined to Internet sources. It should be well organized around your research questions and key concepts rather than just a summary of what you have read. Take note of the authority of authors and the reliability and validity of the research methods they used to answer their research questions.

There's a delicate balance between discussing what others have said and found, and developing your own voice. You are neither just listing what others have said, nor are you merely "telling your own story." You need to demonstrate that you have an informed voice. So don't quote too many studies or begin with "Smith (20xx) found that . . ." because it shifts the focus of your own argument onto that of others. It's better to develop a theme and then cite the work of relevant authors to reinforce your argument.

Don't be tempted to report everything you know—be selective about what you report. Every reference you use must build on the evidence you are presenting to support your case. Using your own words to describe difficult concepts will help convince yourself and others that you really understand the material.

Many of the questions we can ask about the literature reviews found in quantitative studies can also be asked for qualitative ones as well. And vice versa.

## EVALUATING A LITERATURE REVIEW

Assessing the overall usefulness and credibility of a literature review can be a formidable task. All research studies are only as good as the literature reviews they contain. It's just like the research problems we discussed in Chapter 2—poorly thought-out research problems lead to poor studies; poorly conducted literature reviews lead to poor studies.

By now we hope you have come to the conclusion that to be an accountable (chapter 1), evidence-based (chapter 3) practitioner you should only integrate research findings into your daily practices that were derived from research studies that answered useful and practical research questions (chapter 2) which were derived from comprehensive literature reviews (this chapter).

There are a few highly interweaved and non-mutually exclusive questions you can ask as you try to evaluate the overall practicality, thoroughness, clarity, and ethical and cultural sensitivity of a study's literature review. A lot of these questions are contained in the appendixes at the end of this book.

> Two people can assess the same literature review and come up with two different opinions in reference to its overall credibility, integrity, and usefulness to our profession.

### USE THE APPENDIXES

As you know, Appendix A lists numerous evaluative-type of questions you can ask (when you put on your "critical thinking" hat) for each step of the *quantitative* research process, and Appendix B lists questions for each phase of the *qualitative* research process.

In reference to the assessment of the quality of a literature review contained within a *quantitative* study, for example, question 72 on page 479 asks, "Is the literature review organized logically?" Let's say your answer was "no". What are you going to do with your answer? That is, how are you going to use your assessment of this specific question when calculating the literature review's *overall credibility* found on page 481? Now what about if your answer was "yes"? Don't look for a magic rubric to appear. There isn't one. This is the time to put on your critical thinking hat.

In reference to the assessment of the quality of a literature review contained within a *qualitative* study, for example, question 315 on page 498 asks, "Is there evidence the literature was researched iteratively?" Let's say your answer was "no". Once again, what are you going to do with your answer? That is, how are you going to use your assessment of this specific question when formulating your *overall credibility* score for a qualitative research study found on page 502? Now what about if your answer was "yes"?

## CHAPTER RECAP

- A literature review draws mainly on primary sources.
- A literature review is a well-written, coherent product.
- A literature review helps to bring clarity and focus to the research question.
- A literature review helps to identify gaps in the literature.
- A literature review is a continuous process, which begins before a research question is finalized and continues to the end of the research study.
- A literature review prevents the duplication of knowledge.
- A literature review helps to broaden our knowledge base.
- A literature review helps to contextualize the research project.
- A literature review helps to improve a research study's methodology.
- A literature review helps identify opposing views.

## REVIEW EXERCISES

1   Discuss how a literature review can be thought of as an academic conversation.

2   What are *primary sources* of scholarship? Provide a social work example. What are *secondary sources* of scholarship? Provide examples to illustrate your main points.

3   Discuss why a literature review should use primary sources of scholarship rather than secondary ones. Provide examples.

4   List the main purposes of literature reviews. Provide a social work example for each purpose.

5   Discuss in detail how a literature review can help you to bring clarity and focus to your research question. Provide an example in your discussion.

6   Discuss in detail how a literature review can help you to identify gaps in the literature. Provide an example in your discussion.

7   Discuss in detail how a literature review can help you to avoid doing a research study that has already been done before. Provide an example in your discussion.

8   Discuss in detail how a literature review can help you to broaden your knowledge base. Provide an examples.

9   Discuss in detail how a literature review can help you to put your research project into context. Provide an example in your discussion.

10   Discuss in detail how a literature review can help you to improve your research study's methodology. Provide an example in your discussion.

11   Discuss in detail how a literature review can help you to identify both opposing views and any differences between your proposed study and previous studies. Provide an example in your discussion.

12   Discuss how you plan to file what you find in the literature; that is, what information are you going to collect about each source you find and how are you going to catalog what you find?

13   What is a *preview*. Discuss how you would go about previewing the literature for a social work topic of your choice.

14   Given your topic on number 13 above, discuss how you would go about *overviewing* the literature.

15   Given your topic on number 13, discuss how you would go about *inviewing* the literature.

16   What is a theoretical framework? How is it useful to you as a social work researcher? As a social work practitioner? Provide an example in your discussion.

17   List and then discuss each of the four ways a literature review can be organized. Provide one common social work example throughout your discussion.

18   List the common mistakes you can make when doing a literature view. Now discuss in detail how you plan to avoid making each mistake.

19   Locate any published social work research article that contains a social work problem area or population that you're interested in. Be sure the study tried to answer a research question of some kind.

   •   How was the literature review organized: by date of study, by school of thought/theory, or by themes that have emerged from the literature?

   •   Did the research study develop a theoretical framework? If so, what was it?

   •   How did the study's literature review help bring clarity and focus to the research question? Provide specific examples from the article.

   •   How did the study's literature review help identify any gaps in the existing literature? Provide specific examples from the article.

   •   How did the study's literature review prevent the duplication of knowledge? Provide specific examples from the article.

   •   How did the study's literature review help to broaden our profession's knowledge base? Provide specific examples from the article.

   •   How did the study's literature review help to contextualize the entire research project? Provide specific examples from the article.

# 2015 EPAS COMPETENCIES

| COMPETENCY 1 | Demonstrate Ethical and Professional Behavior |
|---|---|

You will learn that in order to be a successful evidence-based practitioner you have an ethical obligation to integrate three research roles into your daily practice activities as discussed in Chapter 3: (1) research consumer, (2) research partner—either as a co-researcher or research participant, and (3) creator and disseminator of research (or knowledge).

This entire chapter pertains to these three professional roles when it comes to becoming an ethically sensitive social work practitioner (research consumer) and an ethically sensitive social work researcher (research partner and creator and disseminator of research).

| COMPETENCY 4 | Engage in Practice-Informed Research and Research-Informed Practice |
|---|---|

Competency 4 also pertains to the entire chapter because you have to:

1   Evaluate the degree to which a social work research study was ethically sensitive, given the needs of the study's specific population or research participants (**research consumer**—research-informed practice);

2   Participate in a research study—either as a co-researcher or research participant (**research partner**—practice-informed research). See 1 above and 3 below; and

3   Know how to become an ethically sensitive social work researcher before you actually do a research study (**creator and disseminator of research**—practice-informed research).

You also need to utilize evidence-based practice recommendations whenever possible; that is, you need to integrate (1) the best available research-based evidence with (2) your clinical expertise and (3) your client's values.

All of the above implies you'll need to know how a research study addressed the various ethical issues that produced its ethically-sensitive research-based evidence. In short, you need to ask and then answer a simple question: How seriously should I take the findings of any specific research study given how well it addressed the various ethical issues throughout the entire research process?

| COMPETENCY 9 | Evaluate Practice with Individuals, Families, Groups, Organizations, & Communities |
|---|---|

See Competencies 1 and 4.

# Research Ethics

| CHAPTERS 1 & 3 | Step 1. | Understanding the Research Process |
| CHAPTER 2 | Step 2. | Formulating Research Questions |
| CHAPTER 4 APPENDIXES A–C | Step 3. | Reviewing the Literature Evaluating the Literature |
| CHAPTERS 5 & 6 | Step 4. | Being Aware of Ethical and Cultural Issues |
| CHAPTERS 7–10 | Step 5. | Selecting a Research Approach |
| CHAPTERS 11 & 12 | Step 6. | Specifying How Variables Are Measured |
| CHAPTER 13 | Step 7. | Selecting a Sample |
| CHAPTERS 14 & 15 | Step 8. | Selecting a Research Design |
| CHAPTERS 16 & 17 | Step 9. | Selecting a Data-Collection Method |
| CHAPTERS 18 & 19 | Step 10. | Analyzing the Data |
| CHAPTERS 20 & 21 | Step 11. | Writing the Research Report |

# Research Ethics

"The way I see it, unethical ethics are better than no ethics at all."

CHAPTER

# 5

CHAPTER OUTLINE

WHY ARE RESEARCH ETHICS IMPORTANT?
USING CLIENTS AS RESEARCH PARTICIPANTS
OBTAINING INFORMED CONSENT
    Bribery and Deception
    Elements of an Informed Consent Form
    Consent versus Assent Forms
ANONYMITY VERSUS CONFIDENTIALITY
    Ensuring Confidentiality
DESIGNING A STUDY IN AN ETHICAL MANNER
    Step 1: Develop the Research Question
        *Refine the Research Question*
        *Evaluate the Literature*
    Step 2: Select a Research Approach
    Step 3: Measurement of Variables
        *Be Aware of Cultural Issues*
    Step 4: Select a Sample
        *Recruitment*
    Step 5: Select a Research Design
        *Beneficence*
        *Equipoise*

Step 6: Select a Data-Collection Method
    *How Data Are Collected*
    *Who's Going to Collect the Data?*
    *Frequency and Timing of Data Collection*
Step 7: Analyze the Data
Step 8: Disseminate the Research Report
ETHICS AND OUR SOCIAL SERVICE PROGRAMS
    Misuses of Research Results
        *Justifying Decisions Already Made*
        *Safeguarding Public Relations*
        *Appraising Staff Performance*
        *Fulfilling Funding Requirements*
EVALUATING A STUDY'S ETHICAL CONDUCT
    Use the Appendixes
    *Tasks*
CHAPTER RECAP
REVIEW EXERCISES

THE FIRST CHAPTER OF THIS BOOK discussed the five ways of acquiring knowledge and stressed how you should obtain your knowledge from findings that were derived from the scientific method whenever possible. Chapter 2 presented how to formulate social work research questions that can be answered by using the scientific method. As you know, we presented four criteria on page 52 that you must apply when evaluating any question you want to research—and one of the four criteria was ethics, the purpose of this chapter.

## WHY ARE RESEARCH ETHICS IMPORTANT?

**R**esearch ethics are extremely important. The ethical guidelines presented in this chapter must be followed very closely if your research project is going to have any credibility whatsoever (Resnick, 2015). The below list presents five reasons why research ethics are important.

1  They promote the aims of research, such as expanding knowledge

2  They support the values required for collaborative work, such as mutual respect and fairness. This is essential because scientific research depends on collaboration between researchers and groups

3  They mean that researchers can be held accountable for their actions. Many researchers are supported by public money, and regulations on conflicts of interest, misconduct, and research involving humans or animals are necessary to ensure that money is spent appropriately

4  They ensure that the public can trust research. For people to support and fund research, they have to have confidence in it

5  They support important social and moral values, such as the principle of doing no harm to others

## USING CLIENTS AS RESEARCH PARTICIPANTS

**M**any social work research studies use clients as *research participants*, sometimes inappropriately called *subjects*. When using clients within our research studies, we need to be extremely careful not to violate any of their ethical rights. Sounds simple, you say. Well, read on.

Consider Aristotle, for example. He believed that horses would become severely ill if they were bitten by pregnant shrewmice. He never tested his belief via the scientific method. If he wanted to he could have done a simple research study that arranged for a group of horses to be bitten by pregnant shrewmice (experimental group) and a group of horses that would not be bitten (control group). He then could have compared the illness rate of the horses in the experimental group (i.e., the bitten horses) to the illness rate of those in the control group (i.e., the nonbitten horses).

If he did this simple study, however, he would have had to solve the resulting ethical dilemma: Was he justified in subjecting a few horses to the discomfort of being bitten by pregnant shrewmice just to gain enough knowledge to help all horses in the future? Now suppose the horses were people. To social workers, the answer is apparent: No, we are not justified! Increasing the sum of knowledge is a worthy aim, but the client, or research participant, must not be harmed in the process. We are not in the business of committing lesser evils for the sake of greater goods.

> The responsibility of not hurting any of your research participants is squarely on your shoulders.

Not harming our clients, by commission or omission, is a cardinal rule of the research process and imposes a major limitation. There are a number of bodies devoted to ensuring that harm does not occur. All universities, for example, have ethics committees or institutional review boards (IRBs), and many large social service programs do as well.

There are also various professional associations and lay groups that focus on protecting research participants. However, it's likely that the participants in your research study will never have heard of any of these bodies. They will do what you ask them to do either because they trust you or because they think they have no other choice but to participate.

We will now turn our attention to obtaining the informed consent of your clients to participate in your research study, with an eye to doing no harm to them whatsoever. You must always remember that their safety comes first, and your research project second.

## OBTAINING INFORMED CONSENT

**B**efore you involve any human being in your study, you must obtain the person's informed consent. The key word here is *informed*. The word "informed" means that all of your potential research participants must fully understand what is going to happen in the course of your study, why it's going to happen, and what its effect will be on them.

If the person is psychiatrically challenged, mentally delayed, or in any other way incapable of full understanding, your study must be fully and adequately explained to someone else—perhaps a parent, guardian, social worker, spouse, or someone to whom the participant's welfare is important.

All written communications must be couched in simple language that all potential participants will understand. Some researchers, particularly academics, tend to confuse obscurity with profundity. They use technical terms so firmly embedded in convoluted sentence structures that the meaning falters and disappears altogether at the second comma (see box 2.3 on page 51 for examples).

It's clear that no research participant may be bribed, threatened, deceived, or in any way coerced into participating in your study. Questions must be encouraged, both initially and throughout the course of the study. People who believe they understand may have misinterpreted your explanation or understood it only in part.

They may say they understand when they do not, in an effort to avoid appearing foolish. They may even sign documents they do not understand to confirm their supposed understanding, and it's your responsibility to ensure that their understanding is real and complete. They may decide at any time to withdraw from the study without penalty, without so much as a reproachful glance. When completed, the study's results must also be made available to them.

## BRIBERY AND DECEPTION

It goes without saying that consent must never be obtained through bribery, threats, deception, or any form of coercion. You may feel insulted that such a possibility would even be mentioned in a text addressed to social workers, but consider what constitutes bribery. For example, if you offer $100 to the chief executive officer of an agency to persuade her to take part in your study, this is bribery.

> It's extremely important for potential participants to know that they are not signing away their rights when they sign a consent form.

If you want to know how your research participants really behave when no one else is looking, you will have to deceive them into believing that they are not being watched. You might think you can do this using an interview room with a one-way mirror, or you might pretend to be an ordinary member of a group when you are, in fact, a glint-eyed observer. Neither of these behaviors is ethically acceptable.

The only conditions under which deception *might* be tolerated—and it's a very large might—are when the data to be obtained are vitally important and there is no other way to get them. If you can persuade the various ethics committees that review your research proposal that both these conditions exist, you might be given permission to carry out the study.

Even then, you would have to be sure that the deception was thoroughly explained to all the participants when the study was over and that arrangements had been made—free counseling, for example—to counter any harm your research participants might have suffered. If your proposed research study includes deceiving your research participants, your university's IRB will require you to include the following 10 points in the research proposal you submit for their approval *before* you can proceed with your study:

1 Confirmation that the study design meets all the criteria for a waiver of consent

2 Justification for the deception

3 A description of the manner of deception and how the deception will take place

4 An explanation of why deception is necessary to this protocol

5 A description of whether the deception results in any increased risk to participants

6 An indication of whether the deception may affect a subject's willingness to participate in the research study

7 A description of the post-study debriefing that includes offering the participant the option to withdraw their data from the study

8 A review by the full IRB board if an exception to the requirement for a debriefing is requested

9 A description of any previous use of deception in similar research and a summary of any actual harms or reactions from participants to the use of deception

10 A description of the alternatives to deception that were considered and an explanation of why these alternatives were rejected

Last, but not least, there are threats. No researcher would ever persuade potential participants to cooperate by threatening that, if they do not, worse things will befall them. But a perceived threat, even if not intended, can have the same effect. For example, a woman awaiting an abortion may agree to provide private information about herself and her partner because she believes that, if she does not, she will be denied the abortion. It's of no use to tell her that this is not true; she may simply feel she is not in a position to take any chances.

There are captive populations in prisons, schools, and institutions who may agree out of sheer boredom to take part in a research study. Or they may participate in return for certain privileges or because they fear some reprisal. There may be people who agree because family members pressure them into it, or they want to please their social workers, or they need some service or payment that they believe depends on their cooperation. Often, situations like these cannot be changed, but at least you can be aware of them and do your best to deal with them in an ethical and straightforward manner.

## ELEMENTS OF AN INFORMED CONSENT FORM

A written consent form should be only part of the process of informing research participants of their role in the study and their rights as volunteers. As we have said before, the form must give the potential participants a basic description of the purpose of the study, the study's procedures, and their rights as voluntary participants. A consent form must provide in plain and simple straightforward language sixteen key ingredients:

1   That participants are being asked to participate in a research study

2   That their participation is voluntary, and that they may discontinue participation at any time without penalty or loss of benefits to which they are otherwise entitled (e.g., in their standing as a patient, student, or employee)

3   The names of the investigators and their affiliations

4   The purposes of the research study, simply explained

5   What the study's procedures will be

6   The expected duration of their participation

7   Any reasonably foreseeable risks or discomforts

8   Any safeguards to minimize the risks

9   Any benefits to the participants or to others that may reasonably be expected from the research study. (In most cases, the study is not being performed for the benefit of the participants but for the potential benefit of others. This broader social benefit to the public should be made explicit.)

> Consent must never be obtained through bribery, threats, deception, or any form of coercion.

10   In cases where an incentive is offered, a description of the incentive and of how and under what conditions it is to be obtained

11   Appropriate alternative procedures or courses of treatment, if applicable

12   The extent, if any, to which confidentiality of records identifying the participants will be maintained (not an issue unless participants can be identified)

13   Any restrictions on confidentiality. (For example, if any of the information gained during the study might have to be disclosed as required by law, as in instances of child abuse, absolute confidentiality cannot be ensured.)

14   What monetary compensation or medical or psychological treatment will be provided for any research-related injury (if more than minimal risk)

15   Contact information for questions about the study (name, office address, and phone contacts for the researcher, faculty advisor, and IRB staff—do not include home phone numbers)

16   That the researcher will keep one copy of the signed consent form and give another signed copy to the participants

### CONSENT VERSUS ASSENT FORMS

Consent forms need to be signed by adults or legal guardians, and assent forms must be signed by nonadults—children and adolescents. If your study is going to use children or adolescents as research participants, you will have to obtain the consent of at least one of their parents or legal guardians (via consent forms) in addition to your research participants' consent (via assent forms). In this case you will have to write two forms, one for the adolescents' legal guardians (consent form) and one for the adolescents (assent form). Writing consent and assent forms takes an astronomical amount of time—never underestimate the time factor.

## ANONYMITY VERSUS CONFIDENTIALITY

**A** **promise of particular concern** to many research participants is that of anonymity. A current illegal drug user may be afraid of being identified. Folks receiving social services may be concerned about whether anyone else might learn that they are receiving them. Also, there is often some confusion between the terms "anonymity" and "confidentiality."

> Sometimes complete confidentiality cannot be guaranteed.

Some research studies are designed so that no one, not even the person doing the study, knows which research participant gave what response. An example is a mailed survey form bearing no identifying marks whatsoever and asking the respondent not to provide a name. In a study like this, the respondent is *anonymous*. It's more often the case, however, that we do in fact know how a particular participant responded and have agreed not to divulge the information to anyone else. In such cases, the information is considered *confidential*. Part of our explanation to a potential research participant must include a clear statement of what information will be shared and with whom it will be shared.

### ENSURING CONFIDENTIALITY

The first step in the process for ensuring confidentiality is often to assign a code number to each participant. For instance, the researcher may assign Ms. Smith the number 132. All data concerning participant 132 are then combined with data from all the other participants to produce summary aggregated results that do not identify participant 132 in any way. No one reading the final research report or any publication stemming from it will know that Ms. Smith took part in the study at all.

Sometimes, however, complete confidentiality cannot be guaranteed. In a study undertaken in a small community, for example, direct quotes from an interview with "a" social worker may narrow the field to three because there are only three social workers there. Then the flavor of the quote may narrow it again to Mr. Jones, who said the same thing in church last Sunday. If there is any risk that Mr. Jones might be recognized as the source of the quote, this possibility must be clearly acknowledged in the letter of consent that Mr. Jones is asked to sign.

Although the ideal is to obtain written consent from the potential participant before the study begins, it's not always possible to obtain the consent in writing. In a telephone interview, for example, the information that would have been contained in a letter of consent is usually read to the participant, and oral consent is obtained.

If a number of participants are to be interviewed by telephone, the same information, set out in exactly the same way, must be read to them all. A mailed questionnaire is sent out with an accompanying introductory letter. This letter contains a statement that filling out the questionnaire and sending it back constitutes consent.

## DESIGNING A STUDY IN AN ETHICAL MANNER

**O**nce you have obtained informed consent from your research participants, you then need to actually carry out your research study in an ethical manner. During every step in any proposed social work research study, you will be called upon to make numerous ethical decisions. There are eight overlapping steps that we need to take when conducting any research study.

This section covers various steps of the research process and discusses the ethical issues we need to address for each one. Each step overlaps with the other steps. Thus, it's totally impractical to discuss ethical issues that need to be addressed within each step in a complete vacuum, isolated from the other steps; that is, all steps are influenced by the ethical decisions made in the other steps (contained as chapters in this book):

**Step 1**   Develop the research question (Chapter 2)

**Step 2**   Select a research approach (Chapters 7–10)

**Step 3**   Specify how variables are measured (Chapters 11 and 12)

**Step 4**   Select a sample (Chapter 13)

**Step 5**   Select a research design (Chapters 14 and 15)

**Step 6**   Select a data-collection method (Chapters 16 and 17)

**Step 7**   Analyze the data (Chapters 18 and 19)

**Step 8**   Write and disseminate the research report (Chapters 20 and 21)

## STEP 1: DEVELOP THE RESEARCH QUESTION

As we know from Chapter 2, we must address a simple question: What is the purpose of our research study in the first place? Will it increase our understanding of the problem we are investigating? Is it likely to benefit individuals (or groups) in need? Sometimes a research study can *directly benefit* those who participate in it—that is, the research participants themselves. In addition, it may *indirectly benefit* others who share the same or a similar condition or problem but are not actually participating in the study; that is, they are not directly involved in the study as research participants.

If the study does not directly or indirectly benefit its participants, then it must contribute to our professional social work knowledge base. If the research question posed already has been answered, however, what's the argument for answering it again? The researcher may believe it's important to replicate clinical findings and/or generalize the study's findings to other populations, or to simply replicate the study using a more rigorous and creditable research design, which in turn would produce more trustworthy findings.

Research training is another acceptable reason for conducting a research study that may not directly benefit its participants. In many universities and research institutions alike, providing opportunities for students to learn how to conduct research studies is an important function. The National Association of Social Worker's *Code of Ethics* (2017) also contains an ethical standard that requires students to be educated in research methodology. In cases where there may be little direct or indirect benefit to the research participants, the level of risk posed by their participation in research studies should be minimal; that is, there should be little to no chance that their participation in the research studies could harm them in any way.

> The National Association of Social *Worker's Code of Ethics* (2017) contains an ethical standard that requires social work students to be educated in research methodology.

### REFINE THE RESEARCH QUESTION THROUGH THE LITERATURE

After identifying a general research question, the next goal is to refine it further by surveying the relevant literature, as discussed in the previous chapter. This involves a thorough review of the theory and other research studies related to the research question. It's important to base any research inquiry on a solid understanding of what came before: "What do we already know about the potential research question under investigation?" Critical to refining the initial research question is asking an answerable question. For example,

**Research question**
What social work intervention(s) will decrease gang-related graffiti on public school grounds?

As we know from Chapter 2, once we have a question that can be answered, such as the one above, we can then refine it a bit more. This part of the research process is roughly analogous to the assessment phase in clinical social work practice. Once the client's presenting problem (the research question) is posed, we then proceed to identify the parameters of the problem and explore its impact on the client's functioning.

As newer and more specific client information is drawn out during the assessment phase of social work practice, we then refine and increase the clarity and precision of the original problem statement. This process in clinical assessment is called *targeting*. Basing our choice of intervention on conclusions drawn quickly and imprecisely about the target problem compromises ethical practice.

### EVALUATE THE LITERATURE

What is acceptable knowledge? Is all information found on Google "good"? Is one search engine or bibliographic resource superior to another in the value of the information it generates? And what impact do the answers to these questions have on the services we provide to our clients? Even many elementary schools now inform their students that Wikipedia is not an acceptable reference source to be used in an academic paper.

Using search engines to find treatments for depression, for example, yields numerous links to psychotropic medication before psychosocial treatments are even cited. Indeed, information on how to commit suicide exists side by side with scholarly papers on factors related to preventing suicide!

> It's important to base any research inquiry on a solid understanding of what came before.

Evaluating sources of knowledge was much easier (however inefficient) before the advent of the Internet. Professional journals and books, along with professional consensus, were considered the building blocks of our profession's knowledge base. These were available by subscription and in bookstores; most of us had to go to libraries or buy books to access this information. The Internet has broadened and extended our information sources beyond expectation and, at the same time, has made it much more difficult to critically assess the information found there.

Today, credible sources of practice information are available on the Internet, such as the Cochrane Collaboration (www.cochrane.org) and the Campbell Collaboration (www.campbellcollaboration.org). These organizations' websites include both systematic reviews and meta-analyses covering the assessment and treatment of health, mental health, and social welfare problems.

Evidence-based practice guidelines represent the best of scholarly consensus and are available for mental health, substance abuse, and other areas of social work practice. What's the best kind of evidence to inform our day-to-day practice? An evidence credibility hierarchy continuum exists that stretches from lowest to highest (see box 2.2 on pages 45–47). It starts with clinical experiences and reports from experts or committees (lowest) and moves up to systematic reviews and meta analyses (highest). This hierarchy is helpful in guiding our choice of what intervention to use in solving a client's problem. The most robust type of evidence to support a particular intervention for a particular client problem is the most ethical one to use.

## STEP 2: SELECT A RESEARCH APPROACH

As we refine our research question in Step 1, the research approach finally used will become much clearer. Figure 2.3 on page 48 provides a diagram of how research questions are refined. Certain questions can be better answered by a quantitative (positivistic) approach, a qualitative (interpretive) approach, or a mixed-methods approach. All three of these interconnected approaches are discussed in Chapters 7–10.

Our literature review, discussed in Chapter 4, will probably suggest what approach may be the most appropriate for our particular topic area and the intended population (research participants) we wish to explore. Sometimes our own biases about research approaches or the biases of the larger research community influence us as we select a research approach.

For example, some researchers do not have a high regard for qualitative approaches, whereas others have a strong preference for them. As we know from the preceding chapters, a research approach should not be dictated by this kind of sophomoric thinking. As we noted at the outset of this section, our selected research approach—and the ethical issues contained within it—should strive to reduce, not introduce, bias.

All too often, a randomized clinical trial is held up as the gold standard of scientific inquiry. In certain fields of inquiry, a rich history of research and development exists, and a social work intervention might be ready for a randomized experimental study like those discussed in Chapter 15.

But what about an intervention that has not yet been described as a detailed proceduralized or manualized treatment? In this case, it's unethical to choose a randomized control research design because the intervention is clearly not ready to be tested. We have a responsibility to our research participants—as well as to the larger professional community—to select a research approach that will produce useful findings.

> We have a responsibility to our research participants to select a research approach that will produce useful, reliable, and valid findings.

## STEP 3: SPECIFY HOW VARIABLES ARE MEASURED

Many of the guidelines for specifying the measurement of variables (covered in chapters 11 and 12) are helpful in avoiding the potential ethical pitfalls in Step 3. If we are studying the sexual habits of men and women, for example, the language of the questions we formulate should not assume that all the research participants are heterosexual.

In fact, our *Code of Ethics* stresses the need for us to understand and respect the full extent of social diversity found within our client systems. This understanding and respect for individual differences must be reflected in the selection and measurement of the variables we wish to study. In selecting the variables to study, we also need to base our selection on the literature and not conduct a fishing expedition in which every variable imaginable is included in the study in an effort to search for something of significance.

Having specific research questions and hypotheses guiding each phase of the study is not just good research practice, it's also good ethical practice. In a nutshell, research participants should not be asked to provide a wealth of information that may or may not address the central question(s) of the research study.

> We must strive to explain our study's procedures in terms that can be easily understood by prospective participants.

### BE AWARE OF CULTURAL ISSUES

As we will see in the next chapter, a study that fails to take into account cultural issues is unlikely to produce valid and reliable findings. Cultural issues must be considered at every step of the research process, from developing the research question to disseminating the study's findings. As we know from our social work practice classes, perceptions and definitions of child sexual abuse are socially constructed and are shaped by specific cultural, social, and historical perspectives.

Thus, we must take into account how our potential study's participants perceive and understand child sexual abuse, in addition to the cultural customs about discussing such a sensitive topic. These cultural contexts influence how the research questions are asked, how study participants are recruited, and how data are collected and finally analyzed. We may find that little or no information is available on the social problem being addressed in the culture of the population in which we are interested. In this case, we need to consult representatives from the group we are studying for advice and guidance.

Focus groups with these individuals will help to clarify many potential issues. Pilot testing the measuring procedures using people from the group of interest is absolutely essential in an effort to avoid any misunderstandings, the possibility of offending our study's participants, and, ultimately, the production of data that are not reliable and valid.

> We need to avoid measurement methods and instruments with obvious biases, such as the biases related to gender, age, sexual orientation, and culture.

**EXAMPLES OF CULTURAL ISSUE AWARENESS.** A proposed research study of the experiences of political refugees to the United States from former Soviet Bloc countries may be a relatively novel area of inquiry, with limited advice available in the professional literature. Thus, in designing a research questionnaire, we would likely find that talking to the immigrants and the social service staff who works with refugees will be the most helpful in understanding the challenges faced by this particular population.

Another example of an extremely important topic under the general area of cultural issues is that of language. If the data collection method(s), such as those discussed in Chapter 16, involve gathering data directly from our research participants, then we need to be sensitive to issues related to language. When doing research studies with adolescents or Millennials, for example, you have to consider the trade-off between using Standard English, slang, web speak, or other types of communication they commonly use.

As we know from earlier in this chapter, when obtaining informed consent from potential research participants, we must strive to explain our study's procedures in terms that can be easily understood by prospective participants. Our *Code of Ethics* and the next chapter clearly address the importance of considering cultural issues when designing a research study. We are reminded to respect the cultural and ethnic backgrounds of the people with whom we work.

This includes recognizing the strengths that exist in all cultures—which is critical when designing research questions and hypotheses, selecting variables to be studied, and conducting all other steps of the research process itself. Thus, the above-mentioned study of political refugees needs to consider their strengths as well as their challenges and difficulties.

## STEP 4: SELECT A SAMPLE

How we select research participants for potential participation in our research studies is a very important ingredient of the research process. Although sampling methods are primarily driven by the study's purpose, sampling decisions also are influenced by our own personal values and sometimes by convenience. Ethical concerns include whether the potential research participants are representative of the target population we really want to study.

In other words, is this the group most affected by the problem we are trying to answer via the research study? As we will see in Chapter 13 on sampling, it's important to ask whether the group is diverse enough to represent those who are affected by the problem.

Research studies with samples lacking in cultural diversity may limit generalization to the broader population under study, and they also compromise social work ethical tenets that address social justice and increased inclusion. Intentionally or inadvertently excluding certain individuals or groups from participating in a research study can markedly affect the data gathered and the conclusions drawn about the phenomena under study.

For instance, a research study of immigrants that excludes non–English-speaking individuals, nonreaders, and agency clients who come in before or after regular hours for the convenience of the researchers introduces several types of sampling biases that will directly affect the generalizability of the study's results. This example also ignores the mandate that all social workers must engage in culturally competent practice and research that respects client diversity.

## RECRUITMENT

How potential research participants are recruited also requires an ethical lens. Assessing all possible ways that a potential research participant might feel undue influence to participate—such as a personal appeal, a financial incentive, the status of being part of a special group, other tangible or intangible benefits, or just plain-old fear of repercussions—can be a daunting task, to say the least.

Who is actually recruiting the participants? Does the gatekeeper—or the process of the recruitment effort itself—exert pressure, subtle or direct, to participate or not to participate? Social workers hold an ethical obligation to examine the fairness or equity of recruitment strategies within target populations and the representativeness (or diversity) of the sample finally selected to be included in the study.

As we know from earlier portions of this chapter, our *Code of Ethics* includes standards that mandate that we obtain potential research participants without threatening to penalize anyone who refuses to participate—and without offering inappropriate rewards for their participation. Just as clients have the right to self-determination in social work practice, so too do participants who volunteer for research projects. And speaking of ethical recruitment, take a peek at Box 5.1 below.

> When collecting data from research participants who speak the same language as the social worker, we must be sensitive to regional dialects, the age of the respondents, and the like.

| Box 5.1 | How Not To Recruit Research Participants: Heart's in the Right Place but Head Isn't |
|---|---|

**Let's begin our venture into** recruiting research participants from an ethical perspective with a short vignette that illustrates how a beginning graduate-level social work student, Margaret, wanted to recruit clients (research participants) for a research study. In her field practicum, Margaret is helping her professor recruit families for a research study that is aimed at providing an intervention to improve the parenting skills of pregnant and parenting teenagers. She recruits potential research participants at the local public social services office (her practicum setting), where the pregnant teenagers meet weekly with their child protection workers.

According to the research study's recruitment protocol, recruitment takes place via colorful flyers handed out to clients by the receptionist as they enter the agency. The clients are asked by the receptionist to talk with Margaret to get further information on an "important" study in which they may wish to participate.

One day, Margaret notices a young pregnant teenager crying in the waiting room and asks her if she can do anything to help. Listening to her story, Margaret unwittingly finds herself strongly encouraging the teenager to participate in the research project (a new intervention, yet to be tested) by telling her how much the intervention would improve her parenting skills.

She also suggests that her participation in the research study would reflect favorably on the child protection worker's evaluation of the teen. At this point, do you see anything wrong with Margaret's behaviors? Margaret responded to the client's sad story with encouragement that she believed to be in the client's best interests—participating in the research study. Margaret increases the client's motivation to participate by telling her it will improve her parenting skills.

> Just as clients have the right to self-determination in social work practice, so too do participants who volunteer for research projects.

In addition, Margaret asserts that the client's participation would favorably impact the child protection worker's assessment of the teen. Although Margaret's intentions may be understandable to the novice, she has in fact violated the ethical principles of both practice and research in one brief three-minute conversation. More specifically, and in no particular order, Margaret:

- Assumed she understood the client's problem without conducting an adequate assessment
- Did not fully disclose the purpose of the research study
- Exerted coercive influence over the client to participate by telling her the intervention will work for her without actually knowing if it would
- Suggested that the client's participation in the study would favorably affect the agency's perception of her
- Did not realize that the young woman may have felt that she had to participate in the research study to receive the services she was asking for by coming in to the agency in the first place
- Did not tell the client that she may be randomly assigned to a control group (those who do not receive the treatment) and, thus, may receive no intervention whatsoever (at this time, that is)
- Did not obtain the consent of the teen's parents or legal guardian

## STEP 5: SELECT A RESEARCH DESIGN

The research design that is finally chosen also warrants examination from an ethical perspective. In intervention or evaluation research, in which participants are randomized to either an intervention (experimental) group or a control group, concerns often arise about withholding treatment or providing a less potent intervention for control group members.

This decision, however, must be weighed against the reality of the participant's life or problem situation. Clients can be randomly assigned to two groups: one group receives the intervention (experimental group), and the other group does not receive it (control group). If the experimental group does better than the control group after the study is completed, the control group would then receive the same intervention that the experimental group received earlier. Because the control group receives the intervention at a later date (if, and only if, it was successful), there are no ethical violations present in this particular research design when implemented correctly. However, a delay must always be weighed against the benefit, as some delays may be detrimental or even fatal.

> The ability to randomly assign research participants to groups significantly strengthens arguments about whether a particular intervention is responsible for the change (if any) that has occurred for the individuals in the intervention group.

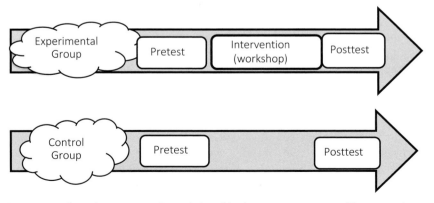

One important fact that we may lose sight of is that a new, untested intervention may not necessarily be better than no treatment at all. It is, as they say, an "empirical question" and deserves testing. What is clear is that individuals applying for social work services have the right to receive the best-known evidence-based interventions at that time.

In other words, it's unethical to withhold an intervention that has already been demonstrated to be effective. Protecting clients from deprivation of services and ensuring that they have access to the best interventions is also a mandate of our *Code of Ethics.* Individuals applying for experimental or innovative services of any type have the right to know of the availability of alternative forms of interventions and the risks and benefits of each intervention. Exploring the use of different kinds of control conditions and determining which is best, both for the clients and for answering the research question, is an important ethical task.

### BENEFICENCE

Central to the consideration of the ethical issues in experimental designs is the question of beneficence. Researchers and the IRBs that guide them must consider how to maximize the benefit and minimize harm to participants when considering how best to test the effectiveness of a social work intervention.

The possibility of other viable treatment methods must be considered as well, as opposed to offering no treatment. Again, our *Code of Ethics* mandates that we must protect both clients and research participants from deprivation of access to services that have been proven to be successful.

### EQUIPOISE, OR THE UNCERTAINTY PRINCIPLE

Highly related to providing the most effective services as possible is the concept of equipoise, also called the *uncertainty principle*. This principle maintains that research studies that randomize their research participants to different treatment groups should be conducted only if there is a true uncertainty about which of the treatment alternatives is most likely to benefit them. Some questions are easy to answer, but some pose serious dilemmas to the researcher.

For instance, if an intervention being tested is known to be superior to an alternative inferior intervention, it's unethical to assign individuals to the inferior intervention. Similarly, an experimental research study that contains two interventions is unethical if a third intervention exists that is known to be more effective, unless the researchers have questions about the efficacy of the effective intervention for a particular subgroup of clients.

All too often, however, beneficence and equipoise raise challenging questions for social work researchers, especially those working in fields where there are relatively few data to support the effectiveness of alternative interventions. Moreover, if the usual intervention (sometimes called "treatment as usual", or TAU) has little or no evidence to support its effectiveness, can it be considered an appropriate comparison treatment?

### DECEPTION

Deception is another aspect of a study's research design that requires ethical forethought. Let's consider an example to illustrate this point. José wanted to study racial/ethnic bias in employment practices in family service agencies in Chicago. He mailed numerous fake application letters to all family service agencies in Chicago that had current openings for full-time clinicians. Each letter contained the exact same qualifications, but he would change his name to reflect four different groups of people: African American, Latinx, Asian, or Irish heritage. In short, everything was the same except his name. José planned to simply count the number of interview requests he received, broken down by each group. Sounds harmless, you say? Read on.

In no way in his cover letter for employment did José indicate he was conducting a research study. To José's surprise, all of Chicago's executive directors of family service agencies met at a local conference and started talking about good job candidates they were going to follow up on. José's name came up several times in the conversation. The

Beneficence means refraining from maltreatment and maximizing potential benefits to clients while minimizing potential harm.

It's unethical to withhold an intervention that has already been demonstrated to be effective.

executive directors soon became angry when they found out they had been duped by José. Several of them had not interviewed other qualified individuals because they were holding slots open to interview José when time permitted.

José, his school, his dean, and the federal government all became involved in addressing the consequences of his unethical use of deception. José's actions ignored a key concept of our *Code of Ethics*: Whether acting as a practitioner or a researcher, social workers are mandated to act with integrity and in a trustworthy manner.

Although it sounds reasonable to say that good social work researchers should never lie to their potential research participants or provide them with less than a full disclosure about the methods of their studies, in reality this is not always desirable. For example, a social worker assessing bias toward developmentally delayed clients by staff employed at correctional institutions understandably initially might not want to disclose the entire purpose of the study because it might affect how the custodial staff responds.

We need to ask the ethical question: Is deception absolutely necessary to carry out the study? In other words, is deception necessary to prevent participants from trying to respond in a contrived and/or socially desirable manner?

Next, we need to ask whether there is a possibility that the deception will harm our research participants, in either the short or long term. If the deception causes or encourages participants to react in ways they might not otherwise, or allows them to make choices at odds with their personal views of themselves (e.g., a decision-making study that allows a participant to lie, cheat, or steal), learning later about their behavior might be psychologically distressing.

> Generally, it's good practice to avoid deception whenever possible.

Our *Code of Ethics* mandates not only that we protect our research participants from mental distress but also that we protect our clients from all harm to the fullest extent possible. The majority of deception that is approved in research studies is of minimal risk to research participants and is far less dramatic than José's study of racial/ethnic bias in hiring practices.

For example, Jennifer would have been wiser if she had used more deception in her study that monitored children's seat belt use on school buses. Climbing onto a school bus after the young children had boarded, she announced, "I am doing a research study for your principal, and I'm counting the number of safe and smart children on this bus who buckle up!"

In this one simple very honest sentence she immediately gave away the purpose of her study, which resulted in an immediate flurry of seat belt buckling—thus defeating her ability to get an accurate and realistic count of those children who would not have buckled up if it weren't for her disclosure of the study. On another topic, do you think Jennifer needed permission from the children's parents to do her simple head count? Why or why not? After all, the children were minors.

**DEBRIEFING.** One of the ways in which we can appropriately counteract the use of deception is by using debriefing procedures after the study is over. Debriefing involves explaining the true purpose of the research study to the participants after the study is completed, along with why the deception was necessary in the first place. If there is a concern about psychological distress as a result of having been deceived by the study, for example, then participants must be offered adequate means of addressing this distress.

In some cases of minimal-risk research involving deception, debriefing participants about the true nature of the study and their responses may cause greater distress than not fully understanding their actions in the study. Also, experienced mental health professionals and IRBs might disagree on whether distressing self-knowledge can be mitigated effectively and how this should best be done, or even whether a study should be conducted in view of the psychological risks to potential participants. One possible way that our *Code of Ethics* offers to mitigate the situation is to offer participants "appropriate supportive services" after the study.

## STEP 6: SELECT A DATA-COLLECTION METHOD

Step 6 of the research process, data collection, contains the following three ethical issues that surround the data-collection process.

1   How data are collected
2   Who's going to collect the data
3   Frequency and timing of data collection

### HOW DATA ARE COLLECTED

As we will see in Chapter 17, a researcher's choice of how to collect the data that best answer the research question can introduce unintended bias, coercing some and potentially excluding other desired participants. Awareness is the key to understanding the ethical implications of data collection.

**EXAMPLE 1.** Aiesha wants to do a follow-up study with juveniles released from custody in her state's detention facilities. She conducts a phone survey during the hours she's at work (standard business hours) and calls the youths' "home" phone numbers. She is unaware that she is missing the youths who (1) do not have phones, (2) have phones but simply do not answer them, (3) do not hang out at home during the day, and (4) operate primarily from cell phones. Also, (5) she is possibly inadvertently informing housemates who answer that the person being called was formerly detained.

**EXAMPLE 2.** One of Aiesha's colleagues, Barbara, is using an "anonymous" Internet-based survey to examine the educational aspirations of high-risk young adults. As part of her study, she asks participants about their recreational drug use and about any knowledge they might have about their parents' recreational use of illegal substances.

Although she does not ask for names or other identifying information, it's possible to trace respondents by their computers' Internet protocol (IP) addresses. Barbara forgot that all researchers must protect their participants' identities, just as practitioners must protect clients' privacy, according to our *Code of Ethics.* Further, although the youths have consented to participate via completion of the Internet survey itself, Barbara also was gathering data about the youths' parents. The parents have not consented to have their children give Barbara data about them.

Collecting data about parental substance abuse via their children without the parents' consent is not a good idea to say the least. A situation similar to this one resulted in the temporary shutdown of all federal research at one eastern university after a very irate parent contacted the U.S. DHHS's Office for Human Research Protection.

### WHO'S GOING TO COLLECT THE DATA?

Who is actually going to collect the data that will answer the research question constitutes yet another ethical decision to be made. Anyone in a position of power or authority over the participant, such as teachers, social workers, health-care officials, administrators—anyone who can either supply or deny the resources that research participants need—introduces the potential for undue influence.

Coercion can easily result in less-than-willing participation. It also may influence the quality of the data collected because the participants may respond differently than they normally would if they believe that individuals who have authority over them may see their responses.

Paper and pencil surveys about anger and urges to act impulsively that are completed by clients arrested for interpersonal violence are an example. Our *Code of Ethics* also asserts that the presence of coercion violates the tenets of voluntary participation in both practice and research activities.

### FREQUENCY AND TIMING OF DATA COLLECTION

Finally, the choice we make about the frequency and timing of data-collection activities also may raise privacy issues. Some research designs call for collecting data at additional intervals after the main part of the study has been completed with all research participants. In situations such as these, the consent and/or assent letter(s) must inform potential research participants that they will be contacted in the future.

## STEP 7: ANALYZE THE DATA

Data analysis and drawing conclusions from the data, unfortunately, represent one step in the research process that many social workers most often wish to outsource or turn over to others. Those of us who are not research oriented are often unfamiliar with data analysis beyond basic statistics and may avoid reading the results section of journal articles, skipping ahead to the discussion section and assuming that the author will review what is most important.

We rely heavily on the peer review process in professional publications for assurance that appropriate methods of data analysis are used. However, does this excuse us from not knowing statistics? Some have suggested that ethical data analysis begins with our moral responsibility to understand the analyses that data undergo before we make use of the research results.

Ethical problems in data analysis are rooted, broadly speaking, in the research environment. Don't be more invested in supporting your theories than in testing them! The researcher's personal attachment to specific theories and the importance of obtaining statistical significance so that the research results can be published or receive other indicators of peer approval are real parts of the research environment.

Our common understanding of research "success" is based on the outcomes of the study—that is, whether the study's findings support the researcher's hypotheses. Hearing a researcher say the project did not "turn out", generally means that the results did not support the researcher's theories. The following are guidelines related to data analysis:

1　Present research findings and results openly and honestly. Do not omit contradictory findings

2　Untrue or deceptive statements should be avoided in research reports

3　Clearly delineate the limits and boundaries of inference used. This may include subjects sampled for participation or levels of experimental variables

4　Provide complete and clear documentation, including how the data were gleaned (edited), the statistical procedures used, and the assumptions made about the data

5　The role of data analyst ideally is neutral so that statistical procedures may be applied without concern for a favorable outcome

Social workers wishing to employ ethical analysis strategies should incorporate these five principles into their work. Much more will be said about analyzing quantitative data in Chapter 18 and qualitative data in Chapter 19.

## Step 8: Disseminate the Research Report

The final step, writing and disseminating the research report, is fraught with potential ethical dilemmas. To begin, all too often we neglect to write a report and disseminate the findings of our research studies. Somehow we get caught up in our busy schedules and the need to move on to the next project, and we fail to attend to this crucial last step. Not reporting findings is a disservice to everyone who participated in and funded the study.

Moreover, our *Code of Ethics* calls for us to facilitate informed participation in the general community for shaping public social policy and human service institutions, as well as to engage in social and political action ourselves. Depending on the nature of the research study, the findings might be important in advocating for social justice for our constituents, such as providing equal access to benefits and resources that will meet their basic needs and allow them to realize their full potential.

In addition to reporting to the community at large, we have a responsibility to report our findings to our research participants and our community that is supposed to benefit from our study's findings. In particular, if our recruitment process involved promising to make a report available to potential study participants, it's critical that we share our findings with them in clear, understandable language.

There are a host of methods for disseminating research findings, including research summaries, journal articles, books, press releases, flyers, posters, brochures, letters of thanks to study participants, study newsletters, local conferences, and seminars. Social workers need to consider the goal of the reporting and the needs of the target audience in selecting a distribution method.

For a broader audience, we need to find ways to make the content comprehensible and interesting. We need to be good storytellers when communicating research findings while taking care not to distort them. As we will see in the following chapter, we must also find culturally sensitive ways to report our study's findings to both our research participants and communities, when appropriate.

Our *Code of Ethics* also provides a thorough discussion of the importance of protecting clients' right to privacy. To illustrate, our research participants may have been in domestic violence shelters, mental health institutions, or juvenile justice placements and then were returned home or released to more open settings. Simply obtaining a current address is often difficult, but even when the address is obtained, involuntary clients often do not want others to know that they have received social services.

> Providing feedback to our participants while still maintaining their confidentiality can be challenging in certain situations.

Hence, participants may not wish to receive research reports, which in some way labels them as affiliated with a particular agency or service. For example, a cover letter thanking a woman for her involvement in an interpersonal violence study can "out" her and may even create a dangerous situation. Incarcerated youth, who were once eager to see the results of a study they participated in, may feel awkward and embarrassed 18 months later when the report arrives mailed to their homes.

Another ethical dilemma that we sometimes face arises when there's a conflict between the participants' agency, policymakers, advocacy groups, and/or the group that funded the study and the researcher. If stakeholders are displeased with certain findings, or with the way in which the researcher has interpreted them, this can seriously complicate the dissemination of the findings. Our *Code of Ethics* highlights our responsibility to report accurately our evaluation and research findings—and, it should go without saying, not to fabricate the results.

To the extent possible, we should come to some general agreement in the early stages of planning our research study about how these issues will be resolved. In fact, our *Code of Ethics* cautions us to identify potential conflicts of interest, inform the participants when a real or potential conflict of interest develops, and place primary importance on the participants' interests in resolving any conflicts of interest.

Often, the sharing of findings will be a delicate matter. Agency staff may be reluctant to hear, for example, that their program may be less effective than they had thought. If they were not engaged in the research process in the first place and they know little about the research methods, they may be tempted to dismiss the findings and block any attempt on the part of the researcher to discuss recommendations for improvement.

Practitioners wrestle every day with a similar problem. Mr. Yen might not want to be told that his daughter is still threatening to run away despite all those parenting classes and family therapy sessions he attended. His daughter might not want him to know. His wife might not want him to know either, in case this bit of data spurs him to take inappropriate disciplinary steps. The social worker must decide whom to tell, as well as how, when, and how much. The same holds true when doing research studies.

> Our findings must be presented carefully, to the right people, in the right order, and at the right time.

## ETHICS AND OUR SOCIAL SERVICE PROGRAMS

We noted in Chapter 1 that one thing all agency administrators have in common is worry. They worry about how effectively they are serving their clients and how they can demonstrate their effectiveness to funders. They worry about offending people. They worry about whether they will be seen to be doing the right thing, with the right people, in the right place, and at the right time. All these worries have ethical and political overtones.

Take effective service to clients, for example. There is nothing absolute about effectiveness. The same service may be deemed to be effective or ineffective depending on how effectiveness is defined and who does the defining. For instance, the aim of a drug rehabilitation program might be to ensure that every client who comes through its doors will absolutely and positively abstain 100% from using any type of drug forevermore.

This aim, though worthy, is probably impossible to achieve. The program's actual achievement—in terms of the percentage of clients who completely abstained, partially abstained, or did not abstain from using a particular drug over a particular period—will be seen as successful or not depending on the political climate.

If marijuana is currently viewed as a gateway to hell, for example, the program's lack of success in curtailing its use will be judged more harshly than in a more tolerant climate. If a more immediate concern is gasoline sniffing among First Nations children, the program is likely to be judged on how well it's dealing with solvent abuse. Effectiveness thus tends to be defined and evaluated with respect to the external political/social issues of the hour.

There are also the internal politics of the program to be considered. Staff members will each have their individual views about which of the many issues facing the program should be given priority, how scarce resources should be used, which treatment modality is best, what the reporting structure ought to be, and, in general, who ought to do what, where, how, and when. These tensions affect the research climate within the program.

Most social service programs will be less or more receptive to research endeavors at different times, depending on their internal political situations and their current level of staff morale. When staff are feeling overworked, underpaid, and unappreciated, they will be less inclined to cooperate with research efforts, but, at the same time, this is the moment when they might benefit most from an evaluative study designed to improve client service delivery or to optimize the organizational structure.

Conversely, when morale is low due to conflicts with administrators, an evaluative study might just serve to exacerbate the conflicts. Researchers, like all social workers, have the potential to help or to harm. If they are to help, they must be sensitive to internal and external political considerations so that they can conduct a useful study in the right way, in the right place, at the right time.

## MISUSES OF RESEARCH RESULTS

It might be worthwhile here to consider the misuses of research results. A study that sets out to be useful can turn out to be harmful if the results are used in an unethical way. There are four primary ways in which research results may be misused within social service programs:

1 To justify decisions already made
2 To safeguard public relations
3 To appraise the performance of staff
4 To fulfill funding requirements

> Researchers need to be sensitive to the political currents both within and outside the agency setting.

### JUSTIFYING DECISIONS ALREADY MADE

We said earlier that a common aim among agency administrators is to avoid offending people. In our opinion, there is no one on earth who is more politically correct than an agency's executive director. Indeed, in the present political climate where services to clients are increasingly community based, programs make it a priority to establish and maintain good relationships with community stakeholders. There are usually a large number of stakeholder groups, each with its own agenda, so maintaining good relationships with all of them requires a great deal of tact.

For example, mindful of the needs of its client group, the agency might propose to build a hospice for AIDS patients in a nearby residential area. The homeowners in the area object. In company with other public-spirited citizens, they approve of hospices for AIDS patients—and rehabilitation programs for young offenders, and homes for pregnant adolescents—but they don't want them in their own backyards. Sound familiar?

The agency, trapped between its duty to its clients and its duty to its neighbors, will go through the normal processes of convening meetings, establishing committees, collecting comments, and issuing reports. It's also quite likely that a research study will be commissioned to look into the advisability of building the hospice as proposed. Probably some stakeholders have already decided that they want the hospice built and are looking to the research report to confirm this opinion.

Other stakeholders will not want the hospice built in their neighborhood and also expect that the research report will support their position. Trapped like the agency between a rock and a hard place, the researchers will need to consider very carefully the uses that are likely to be made of their research results.

If the results will be used solely to justify a decision that has already been made on other grounds, then it's unethical to undertake the study. On the other hand, if it's possible that an objective, bias-free appraisal of the advantages and disadvantages of building the hospice will actually sway the decision, then the study should be done. The researchers must decide whether to undertake the study based on their judgment of the ethical and political factors involved.

### SAFEGUARDING PUBLIC RELATIONS

Another of the worries shared by agency administrators is negative publicity. Perhaps a worker in a group home has been indicted for the sexual abuse of residents, or a foster parent has abused a child. These kinds of incidents inevitably attract intense media scrutiny, and it's tempting for administrators to immediately commission an evaluative study to investigate the problem, declining to comment until the research results become available.

Now, there's nothing wrong with an evaluative study. It may, indeed, be the best way to determine why the problem occurred and what can be done to prevent it from occurring again in the future. But if the sole purpose of the study is to delay comment until the furor has died down, then it's simply not ethical for a researcher to undertake the study. Neither is it ethical if there is an unspoken expectation that the researcher will discover only what the foster care program wants.

If parts of the report are taken out of context in order to show the program in a good light, or if the results are distorted to avoid public embarrassment, then the integrity of the study will obviously be compromised. In such a situation, the researcher will be at fault as well. It used to be the case that researchers were not held responsible for the uses made of their study results and recommendations. Their jobs were merely to produce them. Now, however, it's considered essential for researchers to do the best they can to ensure that results are used in an ethical way.

### APPRAISING STAFF PERFORMANCE

The third possible misuse of research results is for performance appraisals. Again, there is nothing wrong with a performance appraisal. Most workers are required to undergo an annual evaluation of how well they performed during the previous year. However, a performance appraisal and a research study are two separate things.

For example, consider a research study designed to document overall client progress within a program by aggregating (or adding up) the progress made by the clients of each individual social worker. Before they are aggregated, the study results have the potential to demonstrate that the clients of one social worker made more progress overall than the clients of another. And this, in turn, may be taken to indicate that one social worker is more competent than the other.

In a study of this kind, it's unethical for researchers to release results before they have been aggregated—that is, before they are in a form that will protect the confidentiality of the social workers that participated in the study. In the event that they are prematurely released, it's certainly not ethical for administrators to use the information to appraise a particular social worker. Nevertheless, there have been instances when research results have been used for political purposes, to promote or undermine a specific worker or program, so researchers need to be wary of this.

### FULFILLING FUNDING REQUIREMENTS

Most evaluation studies are used, at least in part, to demonstrate accountability to funders. Indeed, almost all social service programs, particularly new or pilot projects, are funded with the stipulation that they should be evaluated. It's not unethical, therefore, to use evaluation research to fulfill funding requirements. But it is unethical to use evaluation research solely to fulfill funding requirements without any real intention of using the information gathered to improve the program.

## EVALUATING A STUDY'S ETHICAL CONDUCT

**D**etermining the degree that a researcher adhered to good ethical conduct is extremely hard to do since most researchers who publish research reports do not address how they abided by the ethical principles covered in this chapter. There's simply not enough room in a research report to do so.

Thus, if researchers follow the ethical protocols as contained in their research proposals that have been officially approved by their respective IRBs, then we have no other choice but to assume that their studies were ethically conducted. We simply have to trust the integrity of how IRB's determine ethical standards and safeguards for the research proposals they review. Nevertheless, you can still ask a couple of questions (contained in the appendixes) that you might be able to answer from simply reading a published research study.

## Use the Appendixes

All three research approaches (i.e., quantitative, qualitative, mixed-methods) must abide by the ethical principles as outlined in this chapter—and you, as a critical thinker, can ask some questions about the ethical conduct (or *ethical sensitivity*, if you will) of any given research study.

More specifically, you can find numerous "ethical sensitivity" type of questions in Appendix A for *quantitative* studies (questions 99–107 on page 481) and Appendix B for *qualitative* ones (questions 371–379 on page 502). Obviously, mixed-methods studies need to address the questions, or potential issues, contained in both Appendixes A and B.

> On a general level, most researchers receive permission to do their studies from their respective IRBs before they can even begin.

### Tasks

This is the perfect time for you to become reacquainted with how to use the three appendices at the end of this book (i.e., Appendixes A–C on pages 468–522).

- First, and most important, read over the overall structure of the appendixes and the directions on how to use them on pages 468–473.

- Second, glance over the potential questions you can ask about a research study's overall adherence to its ethical conduct from:

  — Reading q*uantitative* research studies (Appendix A, questions 99–107 on page 481). Note: Same questions contained in qualitative reports.

  — Reading *qualitative* research studies (Appendix B, questions 371–379 on page 502). Note: Same questions contained in quantitative reports.

  — Reading *mixed-methods* research studies (see questions for Appendixes A & B).

> Many of the ethical type of questions we can ask about quantitative studies can also be asked for qualitative ones as well. And vice versa.

In reference to evaluating the ethical conduct all research studies, for example, question 99 on page 481 asks, "Does the author use appropriate consent forms?" Let's say your answer was "no". What are you going to do with your answer? That is, how are you going to use your assessment of this specific question when calculating the study's *overall credibility score for ethical sensitivity* found on page 481? Now what about if your answer was "yes"? Once again, don't look for that magic rubric to appear. There isn't one. This is the time to put on your critical thinking hat.

## Chapter Recap

- All consent and assent forms must contain sixteen key elements.

- Researchers should never bribe or deceive research participants in any manner.

- You, and only you, are totally responsible for the ethical conduct of your research study. Your research participants are trusting that you have followed the guidelines presented in this chapter.

- Research studies should never be done merely to justify decisions already made, safeguard public relations, appraise the performance of staff, or only to fulfill funding requirement.

- All researchers must ensure that the confidentiality of the research participants be maintained at all costs.

- All research studies must be designed in an ethical manner in relation to all steps of the research process.
- All researchers must obtain informed consent and assent (if appropriate) forms from perspective research participants.
- Most published research studies do not include how the studies adhered to ethical research standards since there is not enough space in research reports to include them.

## REVIEW EXERCISES

1   What is *informed consent*? Discuss why this is important in a research study. Provide examples.

2   What are *consent forms*? Why are consent forms necessary when conducting a research study? What are their ingredients? Provide as many examples as you can to justify your response. Are there any other topics that you think should be included in a consent form that this chapter didn't cover? If so, what are they?

3   What are *assent forms*? Why are assent forms necessary when conducting a research study? What are their ingredients? Provide as many examples as you can to justify your response. Are there any other topics that you think should be included in an assent form that this chapter didn't cover? If so, what are they?

4   What are *bribery* and *deception*? When can you ethically bribe or deceive a research participant? Provide examples to illustrate your points.

5   What is the difference between *anonymity* and *confidentiality?* Provide social work examples to fully justify your response.

6   Discuss the ethical issues that may arise in all steps of the research process as presented in this chapter. Discuss them in detail and apply a social work example throughout.

7   Discuss the ethical issues that surround the misuse of research results in relation to justifying decisions already made.

Provide a social work example throughout your discussion.

8   Discuss the ethical issues that surround the misuse of research results in relation to public relations. Provide a social work example throughout your discussion.

9   Discuss the ethical issues that surround the misuse of research results in relation to performance appraisals. Provide a social work example throughout your discussion.

10  Discuss the ethical issues that surround the misuse of research results in relation to fulfilling funding requirements. Provide a social work example throughout your discussion.

11  Now, given the ethical knowledge you gained from this chapter, click on an excellent article by Gary Holden and Kathleen Barker:

> Holden, G., & Barker (2018). Should social workers be engaged in these practices? *Journal of Evidence-Informed Social Work, 15*, 1–13.
> DOI: 10.1080/23761407.2017.1422075

At the end of the article there are hundreds of honest-to-goodness websites that are sponsored by real MSW-level social workers (table 1). Find four sites that interest you and discuss the ethical issues of offering these interventions to potential clients. And yes, these websites are for real. No kidding.

# 6

**CHAPTER**

## 2015 EPAS COMPETENCIES

| COMPETENCY 1 | Demonstrate Ethical and Professional Behavior |
|---|---|

You will learn that in order to be a successful evidence-based practitioner you have an ethical obligation to integrate three research roles into your daily practice activities as discussed in Chapter 3: (1) research consumer, (2) research partner—either as a co-researcher or research participant, and (3) creator and disseminator of research (or knowledge).

This entire chapter pertains to these three professional roles when it comes to becoming a culturally competent practitioner (research consumer) and a culturally competent researcher (research partner and creator and disseminator of research).

| COMPETENCY 4 | Engage in Practice-Informed Research and Research-Informed Practice |
|---|---|

Competency 4 also pertains to the entire chapter because you have to:

1   Evaluate the overall degree to which a social work research study was culturally sensitive, given the needs of the study's specific population or research participants (**research consumer**—research-informed practice);

2   Participate in a research study—either as a co-researcher or research participant (**research partner**—practice-informed research). See 1 above and 3 below; and

3   Know how to become a culturally competent social work researcher before you actually do a research study (**creator and disseminator of research**—practice-informed research).

You also need to utilize evidence-based practice recommendations whenever possible; that is, you need to integrate (1) the best available research-based evidence with (2) your clinical expertise and (3) your client's values.

All of the above implies you'll need to know how to assess the overall cultural competency level of a research study that produced its culturally competent research-based evidence. In short, you'll need to ask and then answer a simple question: How seriously should I take the findings of any specific research study given how well it addressed the various cultural competency issues throughout the entire research process?

| COMPETENCY 9 | Evaluate Practice with Individuals, Families, Groups, Organizations, & Communities |
|---|---|

See Competencies 1 and 4.

# Culturally Competent Research

CHAPTERS 1 & 3        Step 1.  Understanding the Research Process

CHAPTER 2          Step 2.  Formulating Research Questions

CHAPTER 4          Step 3.  Reviewing the Literature
APPENDIXES A–C              Evaluating the Literature

CHAPTERS 5 & 6        Step 4.  Being Aware of Ethical and Cultural Issues

CHAPTERS 7–10        Step 5.  Selecting a Research Approach

CHAPTERS 11 & 12       Step 6.  Specifying How Variables Are Measured

CHAPTER 13         Step 7.  Selecting a Sample

CHAPTERS 14 & 15       Step 8.  Selecting a Research Design

CHAPTERS 16 & 17       Step 9.  Selecting a Data-Collection Method

CHAPTERS 18 & 19      Step 10.  Analyzing the Data

CHAPTERS 20 & 21      Step 11.  Writing the Research Report

# Culturally Competent Research

"Can't live without coffee. Right? So, since our office coffee machine makes 50 different flavors then that counts as workplace diversity, doesn't it?"

CHAPTER

# 6

CHAPTER OUTLINE

OUR VILLAGE
    Working with Stakeholders/Research Teams
THE IMPACT OF CULTURE
BRIDGING THE CULTURE GAP
    Cultural Awareness
        *Ethnocentrism*
        *Enculturation*
    Intercultural Communication
        *Nonverbal Communication*
        *Verbal Communication*
CRITICAL THINKING AND THE CULTURE GAP
CULTURAL FRAMEWORKS
    Orientation to Data
    Decision Making
    Individualism

    Tradition
    Pace of Life
CULTURALLY COMPETENT RESEARCHERS
    Cultural Awareness
    Intercultural Communication Skills
    Specific Knowledge about the Culture
    Appropriately Adapting Research Studies
        *Working with Stakeholders*
        *Adapting Processes*
        *Providing Meaningful Products*
EVALUATING A RESEARCH STUDY'S ADHERENCE TO CULTURAL COMPETENCY ISSUES
    Use the Appendixes
CHAPTER RECAP
REVIEW EXERCISES

THIS CHAPTER EXPLORES basic culture issues that need to be taken into account when doing a social work research study. As you know from reading the previous chapter on ethics, many cultural and ethical issues are highly intertwined. Thus, this chapter is a logical extension of the previous one in that we provide an overview of culture and cultural competence, followed by a discussion of key issues in culturally competent research practices.

As the issues are discussed, we make use of examples of worldview perceptions, communications, and behaviors that may be characteristic of particular cultures. These are intended only as examples of cultural patterns and not to suggest that any characteristics describe all members of the group. Before we begin our discussion on how to become a culturally-competent social work researcher, let's review four terms:

- **Cultural knowledge** means that you know about some cultural characteristics, history, values, beliefs, and behaviors of another ethnic or cultural group.
- **Cultural awareness** is the next stage of understanding other groups—being open to the idea of changing cultural attitudes.
- **Cultural sensitivity** is knowing that differences exist between cultures, but not assigning values to the differences (better or worse, right or wrong).
- **Cultural competence** brings together the previous three stages—and adds operational effectiveness.

We fully recognize that cultures are not monolithic and that a variety of cultural patterns may exist within broadly defined cultural groups. The descriptions provided within this chapter are for illustrative purposes only and are not meant to be stereotypical of the members of any culture. We also know that each individual is unique, and we recognize that within any culture a wide range of individual perceptions, communications, and behaviors may exist. In social work research, as in any other human interactive process, there is no substitute for meeting each person with acceptance, regardless of background.

## OUR VILLAGE

Our village has grown to encompass the world. Faster means of transportation (e.g., air travel) and communication (e.g., Internet, social media), the expansion of trade, and the human desire to seek a better life have created societies that no longer find their roots in one cultural tradition or their voice in one common language. Rather, migration trends and globalization activities have laid the foundations for complex, culturally diverse societies with representation from several racial, ethnic, and cultural groups.

Diversity is reflected throughout our society: in schools, in the workplace, and within all types of formal and informal organizations. Social service organizations are no exception; there is increasing diversity both among staff and also among service recipients. Of course, diversity also has an impact on social work research; the challenge for researchers is to work effectively in culturally diverse settings.

## WORKING WITH STAKEHOLDERS/RESEARCH TEAMS

As is made clear throughout this book, doing a research study is more than the technical practice of formulating research questions, organizing and implementing data collection activities, analyzing data, and reporting findings. Although these are important research activities, researchers also need to work effectively with a variety of stakeholders or research teams in a wide range of organizations. The tasks include working with research teams to clarify expectations, identify interests, and win cooperation.

When working with different cultural groups or in different cultural settings, you must be culturally competent and also have the ability to adapt the technical aspects of the research procedures so that they are appropriate for your specific research setting and research participants alike. To achieve community involvement with a lens toward culturally sensitivity, the following questions should be considered when forming a research team that will guide you through your study:

- What history (e.g., prior practice and research, knowledge of group and/or community) does the research team have with the racial/ethnic group members included in your study?

- What efforts have been made to ensure the inclusion of the perspective of racial/ethnic group members in the design, conduct, and analysis of the study?

- What is the race/ethnicity of the research team, including the principal investigator, consultants, data collectors, and coders?

- Have potential biases of research team members been recognized?

- What efforts have been made to counter potential biases of the research team in working with racial/ethnic minority groups?

> You must be adept at establishing interpersonal and working relationships in addition to bringing technical expertise to the research process.

| Box 6.1 | Some Important Concepts to Consider When Doing Cross-Cultural Research |
| --- | --- |

- How ethnic and cultural groups are defined has been a source of confusion and, often, inaccurate representation of cultural and ethnic groups in research.

- Many factors have adversely influenced cultural research. These include racism, homophobia, and gender bias. Research with cultural groups tends to be pathology-based as a result of the cultural biases toward some groups.

- The monolithic perspective—the assumption that cultural groups are homogenous—has hampered research with cultural groups. Overgeneralizations related to the monolithic perspective have led to increased stigma and stereotyping of some ethnic groups.

- Ethnic research should have, as its primary concern, an agenda of improving the social, political, emotional, and economic conditions for members of ethnic communities. To improve the lives of ethnic groups, research must address the social, political, and economic factors that create and maintain disadvantage for some ethnic groups.

- Within- and between-group comparisons are difficult when examining ethnic groups. Inadequate definitions of populations render much of what we consider ethnic research marginally useful.

- The role of socioeconomic factors and ethnic group functioning has not received sufficient attention in research. Members of ethnic and cultural groups experience more economic and social disadvantage than European Americans.

- Obtaining adequate samples remains problematic in cultural and ethnic research. Mistrust of investigators, lack of meaningful incentives for participants, fear of negative reception by researchers, and economic hardship create participant barriers in cultural and ethnic research.

- Faulty research methodology and design has further blurred the perception of ethnic groups. Research methods emphasizing the strengths of ethnic groups are rare.

- The use of standardized measuring instruments when evaluating diverse groups is also problematic. Sometimes findings are invalid because the measurement instruments have not been normed for use (validated) with ethnic and cultural groups.

- Publication in mainstream journals can be difficult. Research that challenges widely held views of cultural groups may be rejected by major journals. Much of the best cultural research is published in second- and third-tier journals. This limits the dissemination of important works.

- Academic institutions need to refine cultural education. While there have been some advances, the language used to describe cultural groups and the scope of educational material require expansion and refinement.

- Ethical considerations are also important. Participant rights, such as confidentiality and informed consent, are vital if we are to increase ethnic participation in research. The introduction of Internet technology to research also requires strict adherence to ethical guidelines.

- Increasing ethnic participation in research is a continuing struggle. However, when a strengths-based approach is used, there is a greater likelihood that members of ethnic groups will participate.

## THE IMPACT OF CULTURE

**C**ulture is many things: a set of customs, traditions, and beliefs, and a worldview. It's socially defined and passed on from generation to generation (Porter & Samovar, 2006; Thomas & Inkson, 2009). Culture is manifested in the perceptions through which we view our surroundings and the patterns of language and behavior through which we interact with others. Culture exists at two levels:

1 **Micro-level culture** is found with individuals and is reflected in their personal values, beliefs, communication styles, and behaviors.

2 **Macro-level culture** exists within organizations, institutions, and communities; it's manifested in mandates, policies, and practices.

Fundamentally, culture acts as a filter through which people view, perceive, and evaluate the world around them. At the same time, it also provides a framework within which people process information, think, communicate, and behave. Because different cultures establish different frameworks for perceiving and judging as well as for thinking and acting, misperceptions, miscommunications, and conflicts are not only possible but also likely. Where people are unaware of how culture filters thinking, actions, perceptions, and judgments, the likelihood for misunderstanding is even greater.

The Japanese, for example, have traditionally used bowing as a form of greeting, but in North America handshakes are prevalent; in certain European countries, hugging and kissing are customary. It's easy to see that what is meant as a friendly gesture in one culture may be viewed as an intrusion in another. In a meeting, for example, a statement that is meant as a hypothetical example in one culture may be viewed as a firm commitment in another.

Unless you sit at the table and know the rules the group operates by, you could develop a research study that misses the point. You need to start off with a model that is culturally informed in order to come up with data and meaningful recommendations that will be helpful and relevant to the community you are working in.

In North America, for example, there is considerable emphasis on the "bottom line," which may translate to outcomes in a positivistic research study. Thus, social work evaluations are often concerned with assessing the outcomes of a social service program. In some cultures, however, the fact that a program has been created and now operates and provides employment for community members may be viewed as at least as important as the actual results of the social services it delivers.

> In social work research, as in any other human interactive process, there is no substitute for meeting each person with openness and acceptance, regardless of cultural background.

## BRIDGING THE CULTURE GAP

**U** nder the principle "respect for people," researchers are expected to be aware of— and respect differences among—people and to be mindful of the implications of cultural differences on the research or evaluation processes. Social work researchers need:

1   A clear understanding of the impact of culture on human and social processes generally and on evaluation processes specifically (cultural awareness).

2   Skills in cross-cultural communication to ensure that they can effectively interact with people from diverse backgrounds (intercultural communication).

## CULTURAL AWARENESS

As the previous discussion makes clear, culture provides a powerful organizing framework that filters perceptions and communications and also shapes behaviors and interactions. To practice effectively in different cultural settings, researchers need a general awareness of the role that culture plays in shaping our perceptions, ideas, and behaviors.

Further, we need fundamental attitudes of respect for difference, a willingness to learn about other cultures, and a genuine belief that cultural differences are a source of strength and enrichment rather than an obstacle to be overcome. In particular, social work researchers need cultural awareness: they need to be on guard that their perceptions, communications, and actions are not unduly influenced by ethnocentrism, enculturation, and stereotyping—processes that act as barriers to effective communication and relationships. The term cultural awareness contains two overlapping concepts:

1   Ethnocentrism

2   Enculturation

### ETHNOCENTRISM

Because our own history is inevitably based in our own culture, and because we generally continue to be immersed in that culture, a natural human tendency is to judge others and other cultures by the standards of our own beliefs and values. This is known as ethnocentrism, and it leads to defining the world in our own terms. Thus, we might tend to view as normal that which is typical in our own culture; the different practices, structures, or patterns that may be typical in other cultures are likely then to be viewed as "abnormal" or even problematic.

Among some social groups, for example, child rearing is viewed as a community responsibility, with extended family and other community members taking an active role when necessary. This is seldom typical in urban North American culture, where high mobility often places families in communities without extended family or other support networks.

Thus, in a large urban setting, an appropriate outcome for family support programs may be that the family remains intact, but in communities located in rural or remote areas or on Native American reservations, a more appropriate outcome might be that suitable caregiving arrangements are identified within the family's kinship or community network. An ethnocentric researcher might unwittingly apply mainstream North American values to a Native American family support program, which would clearly result in a distortion in the evaluation process.

### ENCULTURATION

Enculturation is a close cousin to ethnocentrism. It's a related process, which refers to the fact that, as children, we learn to behave in ways that are appropriate to our culture. We also come to adopt a variety of core beliefs about human nature, human experience, and human behavior.

This process teaches us how to behave, interact, and even think. Of course, other cultural groups will have different ways of thinking, behaving, and interacting. In some Asian cultures, for example, people value discussion, negotiation, and relationship, whereas in North America, people tend to be more direct and task-oriented (Hall, 1983). Similarly, some cultures such as the Swiss and Germans emphasize promptness, whereas in some Southern U.S. cultures, a meeting is seldom expected to start at the appointed time, but only after everyone has arrived (Lewis, 1997).

The differences in behavior patterns and interactions are real; however, it's important for researchers to recognize that others' patterns are as legitimate and appropriate as their own. When we are unable to do this, stereotyping may occur, resulting in misunderstanding and misjudgment.

For example, a social work researcher may become frustrated because it's difficult to start meetings on time in a community or because it's not possible to keep to a tight schedule, and she may begin to stereotype the group she is working with as uninterested, uncooperative, and disorganized. Obviously, such stereotypes will have the effect of creating additional barriers to communications and interactions and will hinder the research process.

## INTERCULTURAL COMMUNICATION

Awareness of the impact of culture is important, but effective relationships depend on the actual communications. Because social work research is as much a relationship process as a technical matter, effective communication is always important, particularly so in communication across cultures.

There are many models of intercultural communication. One of the more useful ones is offered by Richard Porter and Larry Samovar (2006). In this model, perceptions are regarded as the gateway to communication; they are the means by which people select, evaluate, and organize information about the world around them.

---

Ethnocentrism is defining the world in our own terms.

---

Enculturation refers to the fact that, as children, we learn to behave in ways that are appropriate to our culture.

Perceptions, of course, depend in large part upon an individual's worldview, which is, in part, formed as a result of his or her cultural experiences. Perceptions help us select, organize, and interpret a variety of external stimuli, including the communications that others direct toward us. After we process the communications that are directed toward us, we usually respond.

Different cultures support different communication patterns and styles, and thus our response is also shaped and formed, at least in part, by our cultural background. Communications, then, are inextricably bound with culture. The opportunity for misunderstanding, ever present in any communication, is even greater when individuals from different cultural backgrounds interact.

Intercultural communication takes place at both the nonverbal and verbal levels. Anyone who interacts with members of another culture needs an understanding of both nonverbal and verbal communication patterns typical in that culture. We will briefly look at communication at each of these levels:

1   Nonverbal communication
2   Verbal communication

### Nonverbal Communication
An important part of human communication takes place nonverbally. Facial expressions, time, use of space, and gestures convey much information and are deeply based in culture. Without an understanding of the meaning of nonverbal communication symbols used by a culture, it's all too easy to misinterpret signs. For example, the OK sign, widely used in North America, is a circle formed by the thumb and the first finger; this sign is considered to be offensive and unacceptable in Brazil, and to mean money in Japan.

One's physical position in relation to another person may result in an inadvertent message of disinterest or aggression. North Americans usually feel comfortable standing at a distance of about two and a half to four feet from others. However, members of some cultures, among them Arabic societies, prefer to stand much closer when engaged in conversations (Hall, 1983). Researchers who position themselves at a North American distance may be perceived as cold, aloof, and uninterested by members of such cultures.

Similarly, the use of eye contact carries culturally specific meaning. In European-based cultures, eye contact is used extensively to demonstrate interest and to confirm that one is listening. Many other cultures, however, do not use eye contact extensively and may perceive it as disrespectful and even threatening. For example, prolonged eye contact in Japanese is considered to be rude (Samovar, Porter, & Stefani, 1998).

### Verbal Communication
On the verbal level, words also derive much of their meaning through culture. As language is the primary means through which a culture communicates its values and beliefs, the same words may have different meanings within different cultures.

For example, the Japanese use the word hai, meaning "yes," to indicate that they have heard what was said and are thinking about a response. Because, in many circumstances, it's considered impolite to openly express disagreement, hai is used even when the listener actually disagrees with what is being said (Koyama, 1992). Thus, the meaning assigned to "yes" is quite different than that commonly understood by North Americans, who consider "yes" to mean that the listener agrees. It's vital that verbal communications be accurate and effective. Without an understanding of intercultural communication generally and an ability to understand the specific patterns used by the group with whom the researcher is dealing, communication problems may arise and derail the research process.

The social work research process uses an extensive transmission of information through communications.

A hand gesture that has virtually no meaning in one culture can easily be a vulgar symbol in another culture.

# CRITICAL THINKING AND THE CULTURE GAP

**H**ow does critical thinking help us close the culture gap? Well, let's take a look at one of the most popular definitions of critical thinking by Richard Paul and Linda Elder (2016), which we mentioned in Chapter 1:

> Critical thinking is a self-directed, self-disciplined, self-monitored, and self-correcting process. It requires rigorous standards of excellence and mindful command of their use. It entails effective communication and problem-solving abilities and a commitment to overcoming our native egocentrism and sociocentrism (see box 6.2 below).

| Box 6.2 | Two Critical Thinking Standards to Consider When Overcoming a Cultural Gap: *Egocentric Thinking* and *Sociocentric Thinking* |
|---|---|

**Egocentric thinking** results from the unfortunate fact that humans do not naturally consider the rights and needs of others. We do not naturally appreciate the point of view of others or the limitations in our own point of view. We become explicitly aware of our egocentric thinking only if trained to do so. We do not naturally recognize our egocentric assumptions, the egocentric way we use information, the egocentric way we interpret data, the source of our egocentric concepts and ideas, or the implications of our egocentric thought. We do not naturally recognize our self-serving perspective.

As humans we live with the unrealistic but confident sense that we have fundamentally figured out the way things actually are, and that we have done this objectively. We naturally believe our intuitive perceptions—however inaccurate. Instead of using intellectual standards in thinking, we often use self-centered psychological standards to determine what to believe and what to reject. Below are the most commonly used psychological standards in human thinking:

1  **It's true because I believe it.** Innate egocentrism: I assume that what I believe is true even though I have never questioned the basis for many of my beliefs.

2  **It's true because we believe it.** Innate sociocentrism: I assume that the dominant beliefs of the groups to which I belong are true even though I have never questioned the basis for those beliefs.

3  **It's true because I want to believe it.** Innate wish fulfillment: I believe in whatever puts me (or the groups to which I belong) in a positive light. I believe what "feels good," what does not require me to change my thinking in any significant way, and what does not require me to admit I have been wrong.

4  **It's true because I have always believed it.** Innate self-validation: I have a strong desire to maintain beliefs that I have long held, even though I have not seriously considered the extent to which those beliefs are justified by evidence.

5  **It's true because it is in my selfish interest to believe it.** Innate selfishness: I believe whatever justifies my getting more power, money, or personal advantage even though these beliefs are not grounded in sound reasoning or evidence.

**Sociocentric thinking** is when people do not understand the degree to which they have uncritically internalized the dominant prejudices of their society or culture. Sociologists and anthropologists identify this as the state of being "cultured bound." This phenomenon is caused by sociocentric thinking, which includes:

1   The uncritical tendency to place one's culture, nation, religion, above all others.

2   The uncritical tendency to select self-serving positive descriptions of ourselves and negative descriptions of those who think differently from us.

3   The uncritical tendency to internalize group norms and beliefs, take on group identities, and act as we are expected to act—without the least sense that what we are doing might reasonably be questioned.

4   The tendency to blindly conform to group restrictions (many of which are arbitrary or coercive).

5   The failure to think beyond the traditional prejudices of one's culture.

6   The failure to study and internalize the insights of other cultures (improving thereby the breadth and depth of one's thinking).

7   The failure to distinguish universal ethics from relativistic cultural requirements and taboos.

8   The failure to realize that mass media in every culture shapes the news from the point to view of that culture.

9   The failure to think historically and anthropologically (and hence to be trapped in current ways of thinking).

10  The failure to see sociocentric thinking as a significant impediment to intellectual development.

Sociocentric thinking is a hallmark of an uncritical society. It can be diminished only when replaced by cross-cultural, fair-minded thinking—critical thinking in the strong sense.

## CULTURAL FRAMEWORKS

As we have seen, culture often defines a group's values and beliefs, and creates its communication patterns. In addition, culture also provides frameworks for other complex structures and processes. Different cultural groups have different methods of gathering data and of making decisions. An understanding of these patterns is essential to ensure that data collection and analytical processes are appropriate and final research reports are practical and relevant. We will now discuss the following five cultural frameworks:

1   Orientation to data

2   Decision making

3   Individualism

4   Tradition

5   Pace of life (and concepts of time)

## ORIENTATION TO DATA

Some cultures thrive on "hard data" and greatly value processes, such as research studies, that produce data that can then be considered and acted upon (Lewis, 1997; Thomas & Inkson, 2009). These cultures, which include the North American mainstream culture, are considered data oriented.

On the other hand, some cultures such as Middle Eastern and Latin American cultures are viewed as "dialogue oriented," in that they pay more attention to relationships and process than to data (Lewis, 1997). These groups tend to view statistics and data with some suspicion and regard them as only part of a picture. Such cultures consider relationships and context to be more important than numbers.

## DECISION MAKING

In many Western cultures, logic and rationality are highly valued and used extensively in making decisions about important matters (Lewis, 1997). The quantitative (positivistic) research approach (chapter 8) is an example of this style of "scientific" thinking. However, some cultures are less impressed by "hard science" and prefer a softer, more personal approach to knowledge development, often called the qualitative (interpretive) research approach (chapter 9).

When researchers prepare a report for people whose culture supports a scientific orientation to thinking, quantitative data with statistical analyses are quite appropriate; however, if the users are people who come from a culture that prefers more subjective and intuitive approaches to decision making, a report organized around the presentation of strictly quantitative results can easily become useless and/or incomprehensible.

## INDIVIDUALISM

Although most cultures support both individualistic and collectivistic tendencies, there is in every culture a bias toward one or the other. In individualistic cultures, such as the mainstream North American culture, people work toward individual goals and achievements.

In collectivistic cultures, people are group oriented; loyalty, relationships, and overall community development are valued while individual goals are downplayed. In such cultures, the family, organizations with which people are affiliated (including the workplace), and the community are particularly important.

---

| **Box 6.3** | Guiding Principles for Multicultural Evaluation |
| --- | --- |

**Inclusion in Design and Implementation**
- Multicultural evaluation is not imposed on diverse communities; communities understand and support the rationale for the research and agree with the methods used to answer key evaluation questions.
- Diverse beneficiary stakeholders are actively involved in all phases of the evaluation, including problem definition, development of research questions, methods chosen, data collection, analysis, and reporting.
- To the extent possible, multicultural evaluation empowers diverse communities to do self-evaluation through intentional capacity building in evaluation.

**Acknowledgment/Infusion of Multiple Worldviews**
- Evaluators in multicultural evaluations have a genuine respect for the communities being studied and seek a deep understanding of different cultural contexts, practices, and paradigms of thinking.
- "Expert" knowledge does not exclusively reside with the evaluator; the grantee and/or community being studied is assumed to know best their issues, strengths, and challenges.
- The diversity of communities studied is represented in multicultural evaluation staffing and expertise whenever possible.

**Appropriate Measures of Success**
- Measures of success in multicultural evaluations are discussed and/or

collaboratively developed with those being evaluated.

- Data-collection instruments and outcome measures are tested for multicultural validity across populations who may not speak English, may be less literate, or may be from a different culture.

- Multicultural evaluation data-collection methods and instruments accommodate different cultural contexts and consider alternative or nontraditional ways of collecting data.

**Cultural and Systems Analysis**

- Multicultural evaluations take into account how historical and current social systems, institutions, and societal norms contribute to power and outcome disparities across different racial and ethnic communities.

- Multicultural evaluations incorporate and trace the impacts of factors related to racial, cultural, gender, religious, economic, and other differences.

- Multicultural evaluation questions take a multiple-level approach to understanding root causes and impacts at the individual, interpersonal, institutional, cultural, system, and policy levels rather than focusing the analysis solely on individual behavior.

**Relevance to Diverse Communities**

- Multicultural evaluations inform community decision-making and program design.

- Findings from multicultural evaluations are co-owned with diverse communities and shared in culturally appropriate ways.

Keeping in perspective an organization's cultural view on individualism versus collectivism is important in understanding the behaviors, interactions, work processes, and structures that may be found in the course of a research or evaluation study. What may appear from an individualistic perspective to be an unwieldy work process involving too many people may, in fact, be explained by a culture-based desire not to leave anyone out and to create as wide a network of involvement as possible.

## TRADITION

Some cultures are more traditional and value the status quo and conformity while others encourage innovation and view change as necessary if progress is to be made. Change-oriented cultures such as mainstream North American society encourage experimentation, risk taking, and innovation. They consider change to be an opportunity to improve.

In other cultures, such as some traditional Asian cultures, values are centered on tradition and continuity. The young are expected to give way to the wishes of the older generation, and new ideas are not encouraged because they might disrupt the structure of society. You should readily recognize that the research process, as a change- and improvement-oriented activity, is grounded in Western cultural values. After all, research and evaluations are concerned with identifying areas for improvement, which therefore implies change, but traditional cultures value stability and continuity.

> The concept of "research" itself may seem alien to those steeped in more traditional cultures.

Inevitably, social work researchers will sometimes work with organizations that are based in a tradition-oriented culture. In such circumstances, we need to be sensitive to the fact that there may not exist a common understanding even about the basic premises of the research processes.

## PACE OF LIFE

In North America, especially in larger cities, we live our lives at an accelerated pace. Our schedules are jammed with many activities, our agendas are overloaded, and there is an expectation that everything is a priority and must be done immediately. Time is viewed as linear and rigid; we live with the sense that if we miss an event it's forever gone. In such cultures, which are called monochronic, people tend to organize their lives by the clock (Hall, 1983).

Clearly, in such cultures it's important to be on time for meetings, to meet deadlines, and to stay on schedule (Cooper, Calloway-Thomas, & Simonds, 2007; Samovar, Porter, & Stefani, 1998). In a sense, time is so central that members of the culture are hardly aware of its importance, but all things, including personal relationships, take second place to successful time management.

On the other hand, in polychronic cultures life is lived at a slower pace; activities grind to a halt on weekends, during rest times, and during festivals and important celebrations. Slower-paced cultures—for example, those in Latin America, the Middle East, and Indonesia—tend to be less aware of time and hold less of a concept of it as a commodity that must be managed.

Time may be seen as circular and flexible; the Indonesians even refer to it as "rubber time" (Harris & Moran, 1996). In polychronic cultures, time is not nearly as important an organizing force in people's lives as it is in monochronic cultures; if the scheduled start time passes without the event taking place, people are not unduly disturbed as another appropriate start time can be set.

"Time is money" could not have arisen as a central idea in these cultures, which focus on relationships and interactions. Time management and business come second in such cultures (Hall, 1983); rather, it's vital to establish a personal relationship before conducting business. Obviously, researchers need to have a good understanding of the concept of time that is held within the setting where they conduct their work. Tight schedules that provide few opportunities for cementing working relationships and that disregard widely observed rest periods, holidays, and celebrations are obviously unrealistic and will be unsuitable in polychronic cultures. Attempting to impose such a schedule will be regarded as thoughtless and will impede rather than facilitate the research process.

Further, in assessing the achievement of milestones and other accomplishments, we need to consider the concept of time and the pace of life prevalent in the particular culture. In setting up a new social service program, for example, planning, procedure, policy development, initial staffing, and other preparatory activities may be accomplished in a much briefer period of time in one setting than in another. Both the concepts of time and the pace of life might be, in fact, equally appropriate when the cultural orientation toward time is considered.

> Inevitably, researchers will bring their own culturally based beliefs, values, and perspectives as well as their culturally based toolkit to their work.

> The methods of social work research are, to a large degree, based in a Western or North American cultural tradition.

## CULTURALLY COMPETENT RESEARCHERS

Although some researchers come from minority backgrounds, many do bring a mainstream North American cultural orientation to their work. This orientation will result in part from their own cultural background and in part from their formation and education as researchers.

More and more research studies are conducted in settings that are culturally different from mainstream North American culture. Research studies are conducted on reservations, at women's shelters, in organizations serving immigrants, and at agencies that grew from the needs and aspirations of minority communities and reflect the cultures of those communities.

Those of us who undertake a research study in a culturally different setting or among people from different cultural backgrounds require the skills to effectively conduct the work and to make the research process more meaningful within those settings. The essential competencies for a researcher to be culturally sensitive are:

1  Cultural awareness
2  Intercultural communication skills
3  Specific knowledge about the culture in which we hope to work
4  An ability to appropriately adapt evaluation methods and processes

## CULTURAL AWARENESS

To be effective in intercultural work, social work researchers need a degree of cultural awareness that provides them with an understanding of the impact of culture on all human values, attitudes, and behaviors as well as interactions and processes. They need to understand how culture filters communications and how the research process itself is a culture-based activity. Further, we should understand concepts such as ethnocentrism, enculturation, and stereotyping—all of which may subtly, or not so subtly, raise barriers to effective communication and relationships.

In addition, we need to bring attitudes of openness and acceptance to our work as well as a genuine belief that cultural differences need not pose barriers but rather can strengthen and enrich the research process. Researchers who wish to practice in diverse settings also need a high degree of self-awareness as well as an understanding of their own cultural values and experiences, and the impact of these values and experiences on their communication patterns, relationships, and professional work.

> Cultural awareness increases through contact with other cultures and through experiencing differences.

| Box 6.4 | A Critical Thinking Standard to Consider When Determining Your Cultural Awareness: *Assumptions* |
|---|---|

**An assumption is something** we take for granted, something we believe to be true without any proof or conclusive evidence. Almost everything we think and do is based on assumptions. If the weather report calls for rain, we take an umbrella because we assume that the meteorologist is not lying, that the report is based on a scientific analysis of weather patterns, that the instruments are accurate, and so forth. There may be no proof that any of this is true, but we realize that it is wiser to take the umbrella than to insist that the weather bureau provide exhaustive evidence to justify its prediction.

Although we often hear the injunction "Don't assume," it would be impossible to get through a day without making assumptions; in fact, many of our daily actions are based on assumptions we have drawn from the patterns in our experience. You go to class at the scheduled time because you assume that class is being held at its normal hour and in its same place. You don't call the professor each day to ask if class is being held; you just assume that it is.

Such assumptions are warranted, which means that we have good reason to hold them. When you see a driver coming toward you with the turn signal on, you have good reason to believe that the driver intends to turn. You may be incorrect, and it might be safer to withhold action until you are certain, but your assumption is not unreasonable.

**Unwarranted Assumptions**
Unwarranted assumptions, however, are unreasonable. An unwarranted assumption is something taken for granted without good reason. Such assumptions often prevent our seeing things clearly. For example, our attraction for someone might cause us to assume that he or she feels the same way and thus to interpret that person's actions incorrectly.

One of the most common types of unwarranted assumptions is a *stereotype*. The word "stereotype" comes from the printing press era, when plates, or stereotypes, were used to produce identical copies of one page. Similarly, when we stereotype, as the word is now used, we assume that individual people have all been stamped from one plate, so all politicians are alike, or Muslims, or African Americans, professors, women, and so forth.

When we form an opinion of someone that is based not on his or her individual qualities but on his or her membership in a particular group, we are assuming that all or virtually all members of that group are alike. Because people are not identical, no matter what race or other similarities they share, stereotypical conceptions will often be false or misleading.

Typically, stereotypes are arrived at through a process known as hasty generalization, in which one draws a conclusion about a large class of things (in this case, people) from a small sample. If we meet one South Bergian who is rude, we might jump to the conclusion that all South Bergians are rude. Or we might generalize from what we have heard from a few friends or read in a single news story. Often the media—advertisements, the news, movies, and so forth—encourage stereotyping by the way they portray groups of people.

The assumptions we need to become most conscious of are not the ones that lead to our routine behaviors, such as carrying an umbrella or going to class, but the ones on which we base our more important attitudes, actions, and decisions. If we are conscious of our tendency to stereotype, we can take measures to end it.

## INTERCULTURAL COMMUNICATION SKILLS

The ability to approach others with openness and acceptance is foundational to effective communication, regardless of setting; in intercultural communication, it's particularly important. However, effective intercultural communication also requires specific knowledge of the other culture and its communication symbols. As we now know, the meaning of nonverbal or verbal symbols is culturally defined. It's therefore important to know the meaning of common nonverbal and verbal communication symbols to ensure accuracy in both the transmission and the reception of messages.

Social work researchers can prepare for their work by reading novels set in the culture, watching high-quality movies, and perusing books and guides that describe prevailing communication patterns. The use of cultural guides, discussed in the following section, is also helpful in learning to understand the meaning of common communication symbols.

## SPECIFIC KNOWLEDGE ABOUT THE CULTURE

In the previous section, the importance of developing specific understandings about prevailing communication patterns in a specific culture was discussed. However, a researcher who wishes to be effective in a culturally different setting must understand more than communication patterns. Specific knowledge about various details of the culture is important to ensure that effective relationships can be established, that the work is planned in a realistic manner, and that the resulting products will have utility.

On Native American reservations, for example, the history of oppression and dislocation is vitally important and has framed their values, attitudes, and beliefs. Among certain immigrant groups, escape from oppression is a dominant theme, and an emphasis on newly found freedoms and opportunities frames these individualistic and achievement-oriented cultures.

Beyond history, the specific values, beliefs, and perspectives that shape individuals' and groups' perceptions and communications are vital to understand, as are the cultural structures, processes, and frameworks that are characteristic of the group. For example, in working with Native American groups on reservations, it's customary to include elders on advisory committees and to listen with respect to the ideas and opinions that they express.

Concepts of time have been discussed previously; it's sufficient to say that the scheduled starting time for meetings may or may not be firmly fixed, depending on the setting. Meetings on reservations may begin with a prayer to the Creator rather than a review of the agenda as is the case in most Western-oriented institutions.

There are numerous other details about a culture that are important to understand if we wish work successfully in any research setting. For example, one of the authors of this book conducted an evaluation on a reservation and had the opportunity to observe restorative justice circles in action. The program had been conceived carefully with extensive use of traditional symbols. One of these symbols was the circle itself, which symbolized a teepee; a convention had developed over time that participants entered and left the circle in one particular place, which symbolized the entry to the teepee.

Entering or leaving the circle in any other place was regarded as the equivalent of walking through the walls of the teepee. Of course, a social work researcher coming from the outside would not have been aware of this and would inevitably have committed a cultural faux pas. Happily, the researcher's team included a member from the community itself, who served as a cultural guide and briefed the researcher on the meaning of the cultural symbols involved as well as the appropriate behaviors.

In general, specific cultural knowledge can be obtained through the same methods as suggested for understanding the specifics of communication patterns: travel, reading guidebooks and histories by writers from the culture, and watching movies. Engaging collaborators from within the cultural group, even if not from within the organization itself, is perhaps the most effective way of learning about values, beliefs, traditions, behavior patterns, and the detailed texture of another culture.

> Traveling, working in culturally different settings, and living in diverse communities are ways that you can develop your awareness and attitudes.

## APPROPRIATELY ADAPTING RESEARCH STUDIES

Developing cultural awareness, intercultural communication skills, and specific knowledge of the culture of the group with which researchers are involved is foundational to conducting effective research studies. The final set of skills involves adapting the research process so that it will be appropriate and meaningful within the culture of the organization where the study is being conducted. Adapting research studies involves:

1  Working with stakeholders
2  Ensuring that the work processes are appropriate
3  Ensuring that the products are meaningful

### WORKING WITH STAKEHOLDERS

As discussed throughout this book, a variety of groups—including funders, staff members, program participants, and community members—may have an interest in how a social work research study is done and, consequently, in the final results. Different groups of stakeholders are likely to have different interests, and this will particularly be true in the case of conducting evaluations in settings with culturally different stakeholders.

Generally, funders represent powerful institutions such as governments and foundations within mainstream society. They will therefore articulate their interests from a North American or Western cultural perspective. For example, funders for a social service program will likely be interested in data that shed light on the extent to which the program is delivering the services that had been contracted and with what effect. Further, they will prefer to have the data packaged as a formal report, replete with quantitative data and statistics as well as specific recommendations for improvement.

> It's important to have some sense of the history of the group who comprise the culture in which the research study will be conducted.

On the other hand, if the setting is based in a different culture, staff members, service recipients, and community members may be more interested in understanding the role that the program is playing within the community. If they come from a dialogue-oriented culture, they may be interested in descriptions of the service process and the service recipients' stories about their experiences with the service and its impact on their families.

They will be looking not so much to receive data for the purpose of making changes but rather to develop a broader and deeper understanding of the program and its place in the community. Researchers need to work at understanding each stakeholder group's perspectives, expectations, and interests and to realize that these may be fundamentally different from one another.

### ADAPTING PROCESSES

> A culturally competent researcher must be committed to accommodating the different perspectives and interests of the diverse stakeholders within the research process.

A program evaluation, for example, always involves obtaining the cooperation of staff members and other stakeholder groups in carrying out the required research procedures—particularly for the data collection system. The effectiveness of such a system depends on staff members carrying out their assigned roles in the research process in a knowledgeable and consistent manner. It's therefore very important that the work processes be designed so that they are congruent with the culture within the organization.

For example, we need to take into account the cultural meaning of time in the organization. If the organization is polychronic and operates at a relatively relaxed pace, the scheduling of research activities such as data collection must take this into account. A schedule that is appropriate in an organization that operates from a monochronic cultural perspective may be totally unfeasible within a polychronic culture. Attempting to impose such a schedule will likely create tensions and stresses. At best, it may result in an inconsistent implementation of the research activities; at worst, the entire research study may be discredited and collapse.

It's thus important that we design work processes in a manner that is congruent with the cultural meaning of time. Scheduling should take into account the concept of time and orientation to time so as not to impose a burden that would be regarded by the culture as unduly stressful or inappropriate. The process should ensure that holidays, community celebrations, and festivals are taken into account when setting schedules.

> Data collection activities need to consider the cultural orientation of both the staff members who are likely to collect the data and the research recipients who are likely to provide the data.

In dialogue-oriented cultures, the collection of highly quantitative data involving the use of standardized measures, rating scales, and structured surveys may be inappropriate and result in inconsistent data collection at best. At worst, research participants and staff members will go through the motions of providing and collecting data without really understanding why the data are needed or how they are to be used. The reliability and validity of such data, of course, are likely to be low, compromising the entire research effort.

Data collection protocols and procedures need to take into account whether research participants are oriented to "data" or "dialogue" and should be designed to be as meaningful and culturally appropriate as possible. In dialogue-oriented cultures, it may not be entirely possible or advisable to avoid the collection of quantitative data, but such data collection methods should be used sparingly. Ample explanations and support should also be provided to research participants so that they can find meaning in these tasks and carry them out effectively.

### PROVIDING MEANINGFUL PRODUCTS

Ultimately, research studies are undertaken to generate information products that stakeholders will find useful. It's particularly important that the final products be appropriate to the culture of stakeholders. As discussed earlier, funders are likely to find reports useful when they address the extent to which the social service program meets its contractual obligations for providing services and describe the outcomes of those services.

Further, funders will look for quantitative data and statistical analyses that support the findings of the report. Managers who regularly deal with funders may also favor reports of this type.

However, other stakeholder groups may not find such products useful or understandable. This will be especially the case if stakeholders come from cultural backgrounds that are dialogue oriented. Reports with descriptions, stories, illustrations, and even pictures are likely to prove more meaningful to such stakeholders. Culturally competent researchers should accommodate all stakeholder groups who have a legitimate interest in the results derived from a research study.

> The final products from a research study should support the efforts of managers and staff to develop the social work program by providing data that are meaningful, practical, and useful.

Tailoring final reports to funders' needs alone is a poor practice and is unlikely to result in meaningful program change. Program development necessarily comes from the inside and is based primarily on the initiative of the managers and staff.

It's usually the case that positivistic (chapter 8) and interpretive (chapter 9) approaches can be combined within a single study (chapter 10). Although matters that interest funders are likely to be more suited to quantitative data collection and analyses, increased understanding can result from including descriptively oriented material that focuses on contextual matters.

Statistics describing the demographic makeup of clients, for example, can be supplemented by providing more detailed descriptions of a few selected clients. Often this can be accomplished by providing people with the opportunity to tell their stories in their words.

## EVALUATING A RESEARCH STUDY'S ADHERENCE TO CULTURAL COMPETENCY ISSUES

**D**etermining the overall degree of a research study's cultural competency is extremely hard to do since most authors who publish research reports do not address how they adhered to the cultural competency principles covered in this chapter. There's simply not enough room in a research report to do so. However, you can still ask a couple of questions that you might be able to find answers to within the research report.

> Many of the cultural sensitivity type of questions we can ask about quantitative studies can also be asked for qualitative ones as well. And vice versa.

On a general level, most researchers receive permission to do their studies from their respective IRBs before they can even begin. Thus, if researchers follow the ethical (last chapter) and cultural (this chapter) protocols as contained in their research proposals that have been approved by their respective IRBs, then we can safely assume that their studies were *ethically* (last chapter) and *culturally* (this chapter) sensitive.

### USE THE APPENDIXES

As with the "ethical sensitivity" type questions contained in the last chapter, you also need to ask several "cultural sensitivity" type of questions, which you might be able to answer from simply reading a published research study. Both research approaches must abide by the culturally competent principles as outlined in this chapter—and you, as a critical thinker, can ask some questions about the cultural sensitivity of any given research study. More specifically, you can find numerous "cultural sensitivity" questions in Appendix A for *quantitative* studies (questions 108–116 on page 482), and Appendix B for *qualitative* ones (questions 448–457 on pages 508–509).

How to assess the overall creditability of a research study is totally up to you—and only you. You're the one who must ask and answer the questions contained in the appendixes. More importantly, you need to address the following task.

**A VERY VERY VERY VERY DIFFICULT TASK.** There's a lot of "varies" here. You must have a rationale for why you're asking each question in the first place. You just can't ask questions without knowing why you're asking them. You also must have some kind of an idea of what you're going to do with your answer to each question.

In reference to evaluating a *quantitative* research study's adherence to cultural competent issues, for example, question 116 on page 482 asks, "Do you feel the author was respectful to people with other perspectives throughout the study?" Let's say your answer was "no". What are you going to do with your answer? That is, how are you going to use your assessment of this specific question when formulating your *overall credibility score for cultural sensitivity* on page 482? Now what about if your answer was "yes"? Don't look for a magic rubric to appear.

In reference to evaluating a *qualitative* research study's adherence to cultural competent issues, for example, question 457 on page 509 asks, "Is the author's role and status within the research site explicitly described?" Let's say your answer was "no". What are you going to do with your answer? That is, how are you going to use your assessment of this specific question when formulating your *overall credibility score for cultural sensitivity* on page 509? Now what about if your answer was "yes"? Remember, don't look for some kind of rubric to help you out. There isn't any.

## CHAPTER RECAP

- Researchers should form a culturally-competent research team (stakeholders) at the very beginning of a research study.
- Researchers must be aware of the micro-level and macro-level cultures that pertain to their research studies.
- Researchers must fully understand the concepts of ethnocentrism and enculturation before they begin any research study.
- Researchers need to address the concept of intercultural communication.
- Researchers need to be aware of all nonverbal and verbal communication patterns within their research studies.
- Researchers need to understand and be fully aware of how the five cultural frameworks can affect all research studies.

## REVIEW EXERCISES

1  Before you entered your social work program and before you read this chapter, how knowledgeable were you about the various issues that need to be addressed when using minorities and disadvantaged groups as research participants? Discuss fully.

2  Discuss in detail why it's important to know the cultural makeup of the stakeholders who are on your research team. How does this affect the research process? Provide as many examples as you can to justify your response.

3  List and discuss the specific "social work" skills you think you will need when working with your stakeholders or research group. Provide examples to illustrate your points.

4  Discuss how social work research can be affected by culture at both the micro-level (e.g., research participants, researchers) and at the macro-level (e.g., your organization, institutions, the greater community). What cultural barriers exist at these levels and how would you work through them.

5  Discuss how your biases as a social work researcher can affect the research process in relation to *ethnocentrism*. Provide as many examples as you can.

6  Discuss how your biases as a social work researcher can affect the research process in relation to *enculturation*. Provide as many examples as you can to justify your response.

7   List and discuss in detail the issues you will need to consider to become a culturally competent social work researcher. In your own words, define a culturally competent researcher. Use a common social work example throughout your discussion.

8   When doing a social work research study, discuss the practical strategies we can use to produce an accurate portrayal and understanding of minorities and disadvantaged groups. Use a common social work example throughout your discussion.

9   Discuss in detail how you will become a competent social work researcher in relation to "intercultural communication skills." Use a common social work example throughout your discussion.

10   Discuss in detail how you will become a competent social work researcher in relation to "specific knowledge about the culture in which you hope to study." Use a common social work example throughout your discussion.

11   Discuss in detail how you will become a competent social work researcher in relation to "your ability to appropriately adapt evaluation methods and processes." Use a common social work example throughout your discussion.

12   Discuss how you will go about developing specific cultural knowledge about your research participants. Provide as many examples as you can to illustrate your points.

13   Discuss how you will go about explicitly examining the theoretical framework that is the foundation of your research study with a cultural lens. Provide as many examples as you can to illustrate your points.

14   Discuss how you will go about defining and measuring "ethnicity" in a meaningful manner. Why is this important? Provide as many examples as you can to illustrate your points.

15   Discuss how you will go about choosing measuring instruments that are appropriate for all the ethnic groups in your study. Why is this important?

16   Discuss how you will go about making sure that you will interpret your study's results to accurately reflect the lives of your research participants. Why is this important? Provide as many examples as you can to illustrate your points.

17   Discuss how you will precisely define the population of your research participants. Why is this important? Provide as many examples as you can to illustrate your points.

18   Discuss how you will go about developing meaningful collaborations with your research participants. Why is this important? Provide as many examples as you can to illustrate your points.

19   Discuss how you will go about encouraging buy-in with all of your stakeholders. Why is this important? Provide as many examples as you can to illustrate your points.

20   Discuss how you will go about providing timely feedback of your study's results in a clear and useful format conveyed through culturally appropriate methods. Why is this important? Provide as many examples as you can to illustrate your points.

21   Take a look at Box 6.2. Provide a social work example for each one of the five problems of *egocentric thinking*. Now discuss how you plan to avoid and/or solve each problem so it doesn't affect your professional social work practice and research activities.

22   Take a look at Box 6.2. Provide a social work example for each one of the ten problems of *sociocentric thinking*. Now discuss how important it is for you to be aware of the issues and how they can affect your professional social work practice and research activities.

23   Take a look at Box 6.3. After reading all the bullet points, describe how you can use each one when planning a social work research study using ethnic minorities as research participants.

24   Take a look at Box 6.4. Discuss how easily it is to assume something. Discuss what unwarranted assumptions are all about and discuss how they can creep into a research study. Discuss how you will avoid using unwarranted assumptions when doing a culturally competent research study.

# PART II

# APPROACHES TO KNOWLEDGE DEVELOPMENT

CHAPTER 7:  The Scientific Method of Inquiry  138

CHAPTER 8:  The Quantitative Research Approach  160

CHAPTER 9:  The Qualitative Research Approach  184

CHAPTER 10:  The Mixed-Methods Research Approach  210

# 7

## 2015 EPAS COMPETENCIES

| COMPETENCY 1 | Demonstrate Ethical and Professional Behavior |
|---|---|

You will learn that in order to be a successful evidence-based practitioner you have an ethical obligation to integrate three research roles into your daily practice activities as will be discussed in Chapter 3: (1) research consumer, (2) research partner—either as a co-researcher or research participant, and (3) creator and disseminator of research (or knowledge).

This entire chapter pertains to these three professional roles as you'll learn that one of the best ways to become an ethical and professional evidence-based social work practitioner is knowing how the scientific method of inquiry produces the most objective data that can be integrated into our daily social work practices. You'll also learn the advantages and disadvantages of each of the three research approaches couched within the scientific method of inquiry process (i.e., quantitative, qualitative, mixed-methods).

| COMPETENCY 4 | Engage in Practice-Informed Research and Research-Informed Practice |
|---|---|

Competency 4 also pertains to the entire chapter because you have to:

1   Evaluate the degree to which a research study adhered to the basic principles the scientific method of inquiry. To do this you need to be fully aware of what a particular research study is trying to accomplish: to explore, to describe, or to explain (**research consumer**—research-informed practice);

2   Participate in a research study—either as a co-researcher or research participant (**research partner**—practice-informed research). See 1 above and 3 below; and

3   Know how the three approaches to the generation of knowledge (i.e., quantitative, qualitative, mixed-methods) can be used to produce meaningful, relevant, and useful research findings for our profession (**creator and disseminator of research**—practice-informed research).

You'll also need to utilize evidence-based practice recommendations whenever possible; that is, you'll need to integrate (1) the best available research-based evidence with (2) your clinical expertise and (3) your client's values.

All of the above implies you'll need to know how the scientific method of inquiry process generates useful research findings. In short, you need to ask and then answer a simple question: How seriously should I take the findings of any specific research study given how closely the study followed the scientific method of discovery process, regardless of research approach used (i.e., quantitative, qualitative, mixed-methods)?

| COMPETENCY 9 | Evaluate Practice with Individuals, Families, Groups, Organizations, & Communities |
|---|---|

See Competencies 1 and 4.

# The Scientific Method of Inquiry

CHAPTERS 1 & 3    Step 1.  Understanding the Research Process

CHAPTER 2    Step 2.  Formulating Research Questions

CHAPTER 4    Step 3.  Reviewing the Literature
APPENDIXES A–C           Evaluating the Literature

CHAPTERS 5 & 6    Step 4.  Being Aware of Ethical and Cultural Issues

CHAPTERS 7–10    Step 5.  Selecting a Research Approach

CHAPTERS 11 & 12    Step 6.  Specifying How Variables Are Measured

CHAPTER 13    Step 7.  Selecting a Sample

CHAPTERS 14 & 15    Step 8.  Selecting a Research Design

CHAPTERS 16 & 17    Step 9.  Selecting a Data-Collection Method

CHAPTERS 18 & 19    Step 10.  Analyzing the Data

CHAPTERS 20 & 21    Step 11.  Writing the Research Report

# The Scientific Method of Inquiry

TODAY'S TOPIC:
The Scientific Method

The real purpose of the scientific method is to make
sure nature hasn't misled you into thinking you
know something you actually don't know."

WHICH RESEARCH APPROACH IS BEST?
    Selecting a Research Approach
THE QUANTITATIVE RESEARCH APPROACH
    What Is the Positivistic Way of Thinking?
        *Striving toward Measurability*
        *Striving toward Objectivity*
        *Striving toward Duplication*
        *Striving toward the Use of Standardized Procedures*
THE QUALITATIVE RESEARCH APPROACH
    What Is the Interpretive Way of Thinking?
        *One Reality versus Many*
        *Subjects versus Research Participants*
        *Researchers' Values*
        *Commonalities of All Research Studies*
THE MIXED-METHODS RESEARCH APPROACH
USING BOTH APPROACHES IN A SINGLE STUDS
    What Do You Really Want to Know?
        *Example*
EVALUATING A RESEARCH STUDY
    Use the Appendixes
        *Let's Get Reacquainted*
CHAPTER RECAP / REVIEW EXERCISES

140

THE PREVIOUS SIX CHAPTERS have provided a solid foundation for understanding and appreciating how the scientific method of inquiry process not only can guide our research studies but also can help us in our professional practices. We now turn our attention to the three complementary research approaches the scientific method of inquiry contains. It's important to note that all three are geared toward increasing the knowledge base of our profession. The three approaches are:

1  The *quantitative (*positivistic) research approach
2  The *qualitative* (interpretive) research approach
3  The *mixed-methods* research approach (combines quantitative and qualitative approaches into one study)

## WHICH RESEARCH APPROACH IS BEST?

**W**hich approach is best? The answer: None! The approach is to be taken is determined by the research question or hypothesis, and by the philosophical inclination of the researcher. All three approaches complement each other, and all are equally important in the generation and testing of social work knowledge.

All three research approaches strive to generate valid and reliable research findings (aka "facts") that are relevant to our profession. All three contain the four phases of the scientific method as outlined in Figure 1.1 on page 18, but they do so in their own particular, idiosyncratic, and distinctive way; that is,

- **Quantitative research studies** rely on the quantification of collecting and analyzing data and sometimes use statistics to test hypotheses established *before* actually carrying out the study.

- **Qualitative research studies** rely on qualitative and descriptive methods of data collection and generate hypotheses and generalizations *during* the research study.

- **Mixed-methods research studies** gather quantitative *and* qualitative data within a single study. They then purposively and systematically integrate the two types of data in an effort to strengthen the studies' overall findings. Notice the words *purposively* and *systematically* integrate.

## SELECTING A RESEARCH APPROACH

Keith Punch (2014) suggests you ask yourself a series of questions before finally selecting on one of the three research approaches to answer your research question:

1. What exactly am I trying to find out? Different research questions require different methods to answer them.

2. What kind of focus on my topic do I want to achieve? Do I want to study this phenomenon or situation in detail? Or am I mainly interested in making standardized and systematic comparisons and in accounting for variance?

3. How have other researchers dealt with this topic? To what extent do I wish to align my research project with the existing literature?

4. What practical considerations should sway my choice? For instance, how long might my study take, and do I have the resources to study it this way? Can I get access to the single case I want to study in depth? Are samples and data readily available?

5. Will I learn more about this topic using a quantitative, a qualitative, or a mixed-methods research approach? What will be the knowledge payoff of each research approach?

6. What seems to work best for me? Am I committed to a particular research approach, which implies a particular methodology? Do I know what good quantitative, qualitative, and mixed-methods research studies look like?

Before we start to discuss the three research approaches contained within the scientific method of inquiry, it may be useful to briefly compare and contract them on 12 concepts listed in the left-hand column in Table 7.1 that follows.

**Table 7.1**
The Three Complementary Research Approaches
within the Scientific Method of Inquiry

| Differences with respect to: | Three Research Approaches to the Scientific Method of Inquiry | | |
|---|---|---|---|
| | *Quantitative Approach* | *Qualitative Approach* | *Mixed-Methods Approach* |
| **Approaches to reality** | One objective reality is unchanged during the course of the study. | Many subjective "realities" are changed during the course of the study and are clearly acknowledged within the final research report. | The differences between unchanged and changed realities during the study are acknowledged and embraced. Integrates how two different views of reality mesh with each other to strengthen the study's findings. |
| **Underpinning philosophy** | Rationalism: We acquire knowledge because of our capacity to reason. | Empiricism: We acquire knowledge from our sensory experiences. | We gain knowledge through our capacity to reason and from our sensory experiences. |

| Differences with respect to: | Three Research Approaches to the Scientific Method of Inquiry | | |
| --- | --- | --- | --- |
| | *Quantitative Approach* | *Qualitative Approach* | *Mixed-Methods Approach* |
| **Main purpose** | Quantifies the extent of variation in a phenomenon, situation, or issue. Seeks to explain, predict, or test existing hypotheses. | Describes a variation within a phenomenon, situation, or issue. Provides a deeper meaning of particular human experiences and generates deeper observations that are not easily quantifiable. May seek to generate future hypotheses. | Integrates both quantitative and qualitative data into a single study in an effort to increase our understanding of the phenomenon being studied. |
| **Approach to inquiry** | Structured, rigid, predetermined methodology. Deductive logic is usually applied. | Subjective, unstructured, flexible, open methodology. Inductive logic is usually applied. | Structured, unstructured, or both methodologies. Integrates results generated from the deductive portion of the study with the inductive portion when feasible. |
| **Researcher's dominant value base** | Researcher puts aside own values. Reliability and objectivity (value-free) are paramount. | Researcher recognizes own values and does not claim to be value-free. | Dominant value of one or both. |
| **Role of research subject** | Passive (as research subject). | Active (as research participant). | Recognizes, embraces, and integrates the quantitative and qualitative findings that are generated via the research participants. |
| **Sample size** | Many research participants are involved, with an emphasis on greater sample sizes whenever possible. | Few research participants are involved. | A larger sample size for some aspects of the study and smaller for other aspects may be involved, depending on the study's overall purpose. |

| Differences with respect to: | Three Research Approaches to the Scientific Method of Inquiry | | |
| --- | --- | --- | --- |
| | *Quantitative Approach* | *Qualitative Approach* | *Mixed-Methods Approach* |
| **Cost** | Generally the least expensive of the three research approaches. | More expensive than a quantitative approach but cheaper than a mixed-methods approach. | Generally the most expensive of the three research approaches. |
| **Measurement of variables** | Data are obtained by structured observations and measurements with an emphasis on using standardized measuring instruments whenever possible. | Data are obtained by observations and asking questions with an emphasis on describing the variables studied. The researcher is the measuring instrument. | Acknowledges and clearly describes how the study's quantitative and qualitative variables are measured. Provides a qualitative meaning behind quantitative findings. |
| **Analysis of data** | Data are quantitative in nature. Uses statistical procedures depending on the study's purpose. | Data are qualitative in nature. Research participants' responses, narratives, or observational data are used to identify and describe main themes within the data obtained. | Acknowledges how the study's quantitative and qualitative variables are analyzed. |
| **Communication of findings** | Organization is usually analytical in nature, drawing inferences and conclusions, and testing the magnitude and strength of the relationships between and among variables. | Organization is usually descriptive and narrative in nature. | Organization is similar to a quantitative or qualitative research report. However, generally speaking, qualitative and mixed-methods research reports are much longer than quantitative reports. |
| **Generalizability of findings** | High. | Limited. | Appreciates and clearly delineates the strengths and limitations of a study's findings when it comes to generalizing its results to a larger population. |

# THE QUANTITATIVE RESEARCH APPROACH

**T**he garden-variety quantitative research study follows the general steps of the scientific method in a more-or-less straightforward manner, as outlined in Figure 7.1 below:

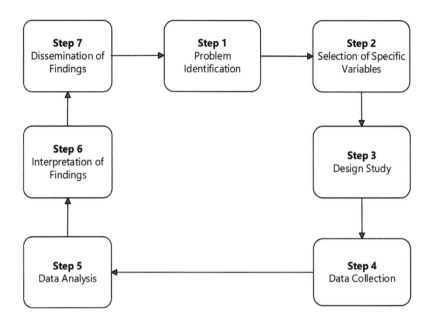

**Figure 7.1**

Steps of the Quantitative (Positivistic) Research Approach

**Step 1**    A problem area is chosen and a relevant researchable question or specific hypothesis is specified.

**Step 2**    Relevant variables within the research question or hypothesis are delineated.

**Step 3**    An overall plan is developed for implementing Steps 4–7.

**Step 4**    Relevant data are collected from the research participants for each variable specified within step 2.

**Step 5**    Data collected are then analyzed to determine what they mean.

**Step 6**    On the basis of the data generated, conclusions and interpretations are drawn regarding the research question or hypothesis.

**Step 7**    A report is written giving the study's findings, conclusions, and recommendations.

The study may then be evaluated by others and perhaps duplicated (or repeated) to support or repudiate the application of the study's findings. In general, quantitative research studies are usually deductive in nature (see figure 1.2 on page 20) and attempt to draw large and representative samples of people so that the findings can be generalized to larger populations (Engel & Schutt, 2016).

In order for you to fully understand and appreciate the quantitative research approach, however, you'll need to see how it's embedded within the positivist way of thinking.

## WHAT IS THE POSITIVISTIC WAY OF THINKING?

Our discussion on how positivists think has been adapted and modified from work by Rick Grinnell and Margaret Williams (1990), Judy Krysik and Rick Grinnell (1997), Margaret Williams, Leslie Tutty, and Rick Grinnell (1995), and Margaret Williams, Yvonne Unrau, and Rick Grinnell (1998). In a nutshell, the positivist way of thinking strives to reduce uncertainty. However, since all observations and/or measurements in the social sciences are made by human beings, personal bias cannot be entirely eliminated. There's always the possibility that an observation or measurement is in error, no matter how many people agree about what they saw or measured.

There is also the possibility that the conclusions drawn from even an accurate observation or measurement will be wrong. A huge number of people may agree, for example, that an object in the sky is a UFO when in fact it's really a meteor. Even if they agree that it's a meteor, they may conclude—probably erroneously—that the meteor is a warning from angry extraterrestrials.

In the twentieth century, most people do not believe that natural phenomena have any-thing to do with extraterrestrial beings. They prefer the explanations that modern researchers have proposed. Nevertheless, no researcher would say—or at least be quoted as saying—that meteors and extraterrestrial beings are not related for certain.

Even the best-tested theory is only tentative and accepted as true until newly discovered evidence shows it to be untrue or only partly true. All knowledge gained through the scientific method is thus provisional. Everything currently accepted as true is true only with varying degrees of probability.

> When utilizing the scientific method of knowledge development, nothing is certain.

To rule out as much uncertainty as possible in research studies, the positivist research approach:

1  Strives for the measurability of variables
2  Strives for total objectivity
3  Strives for the duplication of research studies
4  Strives for the use of standardized procedures

### STRIVING TOWARD MEASURABILITY

The positivist way of thinking tries to study only those things that can be objectively measured. That is, knowledge gained through this belief is based on objective measurements of the real world, not on someone's opinions, beliefs, hunches, intuitions, or past experiences.

Conversely, and as you know from Chapter 1, knowledge gained through tradition or authority may rely more on people's experiences, opinions, and beliefs than on the use of the scientific method of inquiry, which as you know relies heavily on the measurement of variables. Concepts that cannot be measured or even seen—such as the id, ego, or superego—are not amenable to a positivistic-oriented research study but rather rely on tradition and authority.

> A major positivistic principle is that the things you believe to exist must be able to be measured.

However, at this point in our discussion, it's useful to remember that researchers doing studies within a positivistic framework believe that practically everything in life is measurable. In fact, some say that a thing—or a variable, if you will—doesn't exist unless it can be measured. What's your opinion on this statement?

### STRIVING TOWARD OBJECTIVITY

The second ideal of the positivistic belief is that research studies must be as objective as possible. The variables that are being observed and/or measured must not be affected in any way by the person doing the observing or measuring. Physical scientists have observed inanimate matter for centuries, confident in the belief that objects do not change as a result of being observed.

In the subatomic world, however, physicists are beginning to learn what social workers have always known: Things do change when they are observed. People think, feel, and behave very differently as a result of being observed. Not only do they change, they change in different ways depending on who's doing the observing and/or measuring.

There is yet another problem. Some observed behaviors, for example, are open to interpretation by the folks doing the observing. To illustrate this point, let's take a simple example of a client you are seeing, named Ron, who is severely withdrawn. He may behave in one way in your office in individual treatment sessions and in quite another way when his mother joins the interviews.

You may think that Ron is unduly silent, while his mother remarks on how much he's talking. If his mother wants him to talk, perhaps as a sign that he is emerging from his withdrawal, she may perceive him to be talking more than he really is.

All folks doing research studies with the positivistic framework go to great lengths to ensure that their own hopes, fears, beliefs, and biases do not affect their research results, and that the biases of others do not affect them either. Nevertheless, as discussed in later chapters, complete objectivity is rarely possible in social work research despite the many strategies that have been developed over the years to achieve it.

Suppose, for example, that a social worker is trying to help a mother interact more positively with her child. The worker, together with a colleague, may first observe the child and mother in a playroom setting, recording how many times the mother makes eye contact with the child, hugs the child, criticizes the child, makes encouraging comments, and so forth on a 3-point scale: discouraging, neutral, or encouraging. The social worker may perceive a remark that the mother has made to the child as "neutral," while the colleague thinks it was "encouraging."

As you will see throughout this book, in such a situation it's impossible to resolve the disagreement. If there were six objective observers, for example, five opting for neutral and only one for encouraging, the sole "encouraging observer" is more likely to be wrong than the other five, so it's very likely that the mother's remark was neutral.

As should be obvious by now, objectivity is largely a matter of agreement. There are some things, usually physical phenomena, about which most people agree. Most people agree, for example, that objects fall when dropped, water turns to steam at a certain temperature, and seawater contains salt.

However, there are other things—mostly to do with values, attitudes, and feelings—about which agreement is far rarer. An argument about whether Beethoven is a better composer than Willie Nelson or Taylor Swift, for example, cannot be objectively resolved. Neither can a dispute about the rightness of capital punishment, euthanasia, same-sex marriages, or abortion. It's not surprising, therefore, that physical researchers, who work with physical phenomena, are able to be more objective than social work researchers who, more often than not, work with human beings.

> As more people agree on what they have observed, the less likely it becomes that the observation was distorted by bias, and the more likely it is that the agreement reached is "objectively true."

### STRIVING TOWARD DUPLICATION

Suppose, for a moment, you're running a twelve-week intervention program to help fathers who have abused their children to manage their anger without resorting to physical violence. You have put a great deal of effort into designing your program, and you believe that your intervention (the program) is more effective than other interventions that are geared toward anger management.

You develop a method of measuring the degree to which the fathers in your group have learned to dissipate their anger in nondamaging ways, and you find that, indeed, the group of fathers shows marked improvement. Improvement shown by one group of fathers, however, is not convincing evidence for the effectiveness of your intervention.

Perhaps your measurements were in error, and the improvement was not as great as you hoped for. Perhaps the improvement was a coincidence, and the fathers' behaviors changed because they had joined health clubs and each had vented his fury on a punching bag. To be more certain, you duplicate your intervention and measuring procedures with a second group of fathers. In other words, you duplicate your study.

After you have used the same procedures with a number of groups and obtained similar results each time, you might expect that other social workers will eagerly adopt your anger-management intervention. But, as presented in the previous chapters, tradition dies hard. Other social workers have a vested interest in their interventions, and they may suggest that you found the results you did only because you wanted to find them.

To counter any suggestion of bias, you ask another, independent social worker to use your same anger-management intervention and measuring methods with other groups of fathers. If the results are the same as before, your colleagues in the field of anger management may choose to adopt your intervention method.

Whatever your colleagues decide, you are excited about your newfound intervention. You wonder if your methods would work as well with women as they do with men, with adolescents as well as with adults, with Native Americans, Asians, or African Americans as well as with Caucasians, with mixed groups, larger groups, or groups in different settings. In fact, you have identified a lifetime project, since you will have to apply your intervention and measuring procedures repeatedly to all these different groups of people.

> Positivistic researchers try to do research studies in such a way that their studies can be duplicated by other researchers.

### STRIVING TOWARD THE USE OF STANDARDIZED PROCEDURES

Finally, a true-to-the-bone positivistic researcher tries to use well-accepted "research-type" standardized procedures. For a positivistic-oriented research study to be creditable and before others can accept its results, others must be satisfied that your study was conducted according to accepted scientific standardized procedures. The allegation that your work lacks objectivity is only one of the criticisms they might bring.

In addition, they might suggest that the group of fathers you worked with was not typical of abusive fathers in general, and that your results are not therefore applicable to other groups of abusive fathers. It might be alleged that you did not make proper measurements, or you measured the wrong variables, or you did not take enough measurements, or you did not analyze your data correctly, and so on.

To negate these kinds of criticisms, over the years social work researchers have agreed on a set of standard procedures and techniques that are thought most likely to produce "true and unbiased" knowledge—which is what this book is all about. Certain steps must be performed in a certain order. Foreseeable errors must be guarded against.

Ethical behavior with research participants and colleagues must be maintained, as discussed in detail in Chapter 5. These procedures must be followed if your study is both to generate usable results and to be accepted as useful by other social workers.

## THE QUALITATIVE RESEARCH APPROACH

**M**eaningful problem areas also drive qualitative research studies. However, their direct relationship to the scientific method is somewhat different than in the quantitative approach. In a quantitative study, conceptual clarity about the research question (or hypothesis) more often than not *precedes* the collection and analysis of data.

In contrast to the quantitative approach, researchers doing qualitative studies do not use the data-collection and analysis process simply to answer questions (or to test hypotheses). It's used first to discover what the most important questions are, and then to refine and answer questions (or test hypotheses) that are increasingly more specific. The process involves moving back and forth between data and their interpretation, between answers and questions and the development of social work theory.

Using an inductive process (see figure 1.2 on page 20), qualitative methods generate narrative data from information-rich cases. Qualitative inductive methods emphasize the deeper meanings of the research participants' experiences.

Note that the quantitative research approach has steps (figure 7.1) and the qualitative approach, as illustrated in Figure 7.2 below, has phases. Figure 7.2 shows how the qualitative research approach unfolds. Note how Phases 3a–d heavily interact with one another (see the dashed arrows among the four phases).

> Using a holistic attitude, the qualitative research approach explores the richness, depth, and complexity of phenomena being studied.

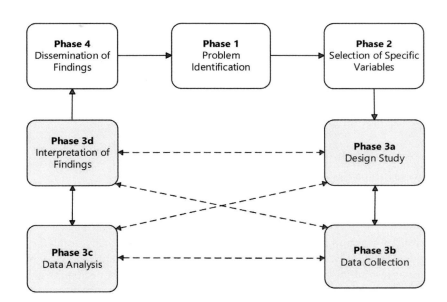

**Figure 7.2**

Phases of the Qualitative (Interpretive) Research Approach

## WHAT IS THE INTERPRETIVE WAY OF THINKING?

As we know, the quantitative approach to knowledge development is embedded within the positivistic way of thinking about or viewing the world. In direct contrast to the quantitative approach, the qualitative approach to knowledge development is embedded within the interpretive way of thinking about or viewing the world. It basically discards the quantitative notion that there is only one "external reality" waiting to be "objectively" discovered. Instead, it's based on the interpretive perspective that takes the position that "reality" is defined by the research participants' interpretations of their own realities. In sum, subjective reality is studied via the qualitative research approach rather than an objective one studied by the quantitative approach.

As you will see later in this book, the differences between the philosophy of the quantitative and qualitative research approaches naturally lead to different data collection methods and analyses. Subjective reality, for example, cannot be easily explored through quantitatively oriented data-collection methods such as mailed surveys, structured observations, and analyses of existing statistics. However, there are a few good qualitatively oriented ways we can use to determine our research participant's subjective reality: interviewing, participant observations, secondary text data, and historical data.

### One Reality versus Many

From the quantitative standpoint, if you do not accept the idea of a single reality—which is not changed by being observed and/or measured, and from which you, the researcher, are "detached" from the study—then you are not a "real researcher" doing a "real research study." Thus, your study's findings are not considered to be of much use by those who strictly follow the positivistic approach.

But many of these researchers whose views were considered invalid were women or came from diverse minority groups. Some feminists, for example, have argued that there is not only one reality—there are many realities. They contend that men and women experience the world differently, so they both exist in different realities, constructed by them from their own perceptions.

**Changing Realities.** People from various cultural groups view their "world" from their individual perspectives, beliefs, and traditions, which means they will experience their own realities. As for the idea that reality is not changed by being observed and/or measured, some feminists have argued that a relationship of some kind is always formed between the researcher and the research participant (subject), resulting in yet another mutual reality constructed between the two of them. In any study involving human research participants, there will thus be at least three realities:

1  The researcher's reality
2  The research participant's reality
3  The mutual reality they (researcher and research participant) both create and share

The quantitative notion of a single unchanged and unchanging reality, some feminists have argued, was typically a male idea, probably due to the fact that men view human relationships as less important than do women. This is a low blow that will quite properly be resented by the many men who do in fact ascribe importance to relationships. But, that aside, perhaps the problem lies less with *phenomenalism* (a single unchanged reality as opposed to multiple changing realities) than it does with *scientism* (the idea that the physical and social sciences can be approached in the same way).

### Subjects versus Research Participants

Having dealt with what data are (don't ever write "data is"), let's go back to the implications of collecting data about people's subjective realities. Because it's the research participant's reality you want to explore, the participant is a very important data source.

The quantitative approach may seem like it tends to relegate the research participant to the status of an object or subject. In a study of cesarean births at a hospital during a certain period, for example, the quantitative approach to knowledge development does not view Ms. Smith as an individual, only as the seventeenth woman who experienced

The differences between the philosophy of the quantitative and qualitative research approaches naturally lead to different data collection methods and analyses.

All three realities are constantly changing as the study proceeds and as further interactions occur.

such a birth during that period. Details of her medical history can be gathered without any reference to her as a separate person with her own hopes, fears, failings, and strengths.

Conversely, a qualitative lens to cesarean births will focus on Ms. Smith's individual experiences. What was her experience? What did it mean to her? How did she interpret it in the context of her own reality? Compared with the quantitative approach where research participants (subjects) are more passive than active, the qualitative approach actively engages the research participants to vigorously engage and guide the studies as they go along.

### RESEARCHERS' VALUES

In order to discover the truth of Ms. Smith's reality, however, you must be clear about the nature of your own reality. In Chapter 3 we talked about value awareness as one of the characteristics that you must have if you're going to do a quantitatively oriented research study; that is, you need to put aside your own values when you are conducting a study or when you are evaluating the results obtained by other researchers. This is sometimes called *disinterestedness*.

Researchers who are disinterested are those who are able to accept evidence or data that run counter to their own values. From a hardline positivistic perspective, this putting aside of values seems more akin to sweeping them under the carpet and pretending they don't exist. Researchers engaged in quantitative studies will deny that their own values are important. They claim their values have nothing to do with the study. In a nutshell, their values cease to exist.

Qualitative researchers take a very different view. Their values are not only a part of their own realities, they are a part of the mutual reality that is constructed through their interactions with their research participants. Qualitative researchers must therefore acknowledge and thoroughly explore their values so that the mutual shaping of realities resulting from the interaction with their research participants may be more completely and honestly understood.

The term *value awareness*, while important to both research approaches, is thus understood in different ways. To quantitative researchers, it means putting values aside so they don't affect the study. To qualitative researchers, it means an immersion in values so that their inevitable effect is understood and their research participants' realities emerge more clearly.

### COMMONALITIES OF ALL QUALITATIVE RESEARCH STUDIES

There are five characteristics that most qualitative research studies have in common (Tutty, Rothery, & Grinnell, 1996):

1 They are conducted primarily in the natural settings where the research participants carry out their daily business in a "non-research" atmosphere.

2 Variables cannot be controlled and experimentally manipulated (though changes in variables and their effect on other variables can certainly be observed).

3 The questions to be asked are not always completely conceptualized at the outset of the study (although they can be).

4 The data collected are heavily influenced by the experiences and priorities of the research participants, rather than being collected by predetermined and/or highly structured and/or standardized measurement instruments.

5 Meanings are drawn from the data (and presented to others) using processes that are more natural and familiar than those used within the quantitative method. The data need not be reduced to numbers and statistically analyzed although counting and statistics can be employed if they are thought useful.

---

The quantitative research approach gathers numbers from passive subjects whereas the qualitative research approach gathers words from active research participants.

---

Qualitative researchers are not only a part of their own realities; they are a part of the mutual reality that is constructed through their interactions with their research participants.

**Table 7.2**

Philosophical Differences between the Quantitative and Qualitative Research Approaches Investigating an Identical Problem Area—Racial Discrimination within the Public Social Service System

| Philosophical Concept | Research Approach | |
| --- | --- | --- |
| | *Quantitative (Positivistic)* | *Qualitative (Interpretive)* |
| **Perceptions of Reality** | Ethnic minorities share similar experiences within the public social service system. These experiences can be described objectively; that is, a single reality exists outside any one person. | Individual and ethnic group experiences within the public social service system are unique. Their experiences can only be described subjectively; that is, a single and unique reality exists within each person. |
| **Ways of "Knowing"** | The experience of ethnic minorities within public social services can be revealed by closely examining specific parts of their experiences. Scientific principles, rules, and tests of sound reasoning are used to guide the research process. | The experience of ethnic minorities within public social services is revealed by capturing the whole experiences of a few cases. Parts of their experiences are considered only in relation to the whole of them. Sources of knowledge are stories, diagrams, and pictures that are shared by the people with their unique life experiences. |
| **Value Bases** | The researchers suspend all their values related to ethnic minorities and social services from the steps taken within the research study. The research participant "deposits" data, which are screened, organized, and analyzed by the researchers who do not attribute any personal meaning to the participants or to the data they provide. | The researcher is the research process, and any personal values, beliefs, and experiences of the researcher will influence the research process. The researcher learns from the research participants, and their interaction is mutual. |
| **Applications** | Research results are generalized to the population from which the sample was drawn (e.g., other minority groups, other social service programs). The research findings tell us the average experience that ethnic minorities have within the public social service system. | Research results tell a story of a few individuals' or one group's experience within the public social service system. The research findings provide an in-depth understanding of a few people. The life context of each research participant is key to understanding the stories he/she tells. |

Table 7.2 on the previous page presents a simple example of the philosophical differences between the quantitative and qualitative research approaches while investigating an identical social problem area—racial discrimination within the public social service system.

## THE MIXED-METHODS RESEARCH APPROACH

**W**ith a little forethought you can integrate both quantitative and qualitative data in a single study. When this is done, a new "third research approach" naturally emerges—not surprisingly called the *mixed-methods research approach*. It capitalizes on the advantages that both quantitative and qualitative research approaches bring to the research enterprise. The best way to describe what the mixed methods research approach is all about is by looking at how John Creswell and Vicki Plano Clark (2017, 282–284) have defined it via the six core characteristics it contains:

1   **Collects, analyzes, and justifies the use of both quantitative and qualitative data (based on the research question, of course).**

    *Example:* A researcher collects quantitative data via standardized measuring instruments and qualitative data via interviews with focus groups to see if the two types of data show similar results but from different perspectives. See the study on developing a health-promotion perspective for older driver safety in the occupational science area by Sherrilene Classen and colleagues (2007).

2   **Mixes, integrates, or links quantitative and qualitative data by (1) combining or merging them, (2) having one build on the other, or (3) embedding one within the other.**

    *Example:* A researcher collects data using a quantitative-type experimental procedure then follows up with qualitative-type interviews with a few individuals who participated in the research study to help explain their scores on the experimental outcomes. See the study of college students' copy-and-paste note-taking by L. Brent Igo, Kenneth Kiewra, and Roger Bruning (2008).

3   **Gives priority to one or both forms of data.**

    *Example:* A researcher explores how individuals describe a topic by starting with face-to-face qualitative interviews, analyzing the qualitative data, and using the findings to develop a mailed survey instrument. This instrument is then administered to a sample from a population to see if the findings can be generalized to a larger population. See the study of lifestyle behaviors among Japanese college women by Junko Tashiro (2002) and the psychological study of the tendency to perceive the self as significant to others in young adults' romantic relationships by Leanne Mak and Sheila Marshall (2004).

4   **Uses these procedures in a single study or in multiple phases of a program of study.**

    *Example:* A researcher conducts an experiment in which quantitatively oriented measuring instruments are used to assess the impact of a treatment intervention on an outcome variable. Before the experiment begins, however, the researcher collects qualitative data to help design the treatment intervention itself or to design better strategies to recruit participant to the study. See the study of physical activity and diet for families in one community by John Brett and colleagues (2002).

5  **Frames these procedures within philosophical worldviews and theoretical lenses.**

*Example:* A researcher seeks to change our understanding of some issues facing women. The researcher gathers data through a qualitatively oriented focus group to explore the meaning of the issues for women. The larger framework of change guides the researcher and informs all aspects of the study, including the issues being studied, data collection, and the call for reform at the end of the study. See the study exploring student-athlete culture and understanding specific rape myths by Sarah McMahon (2007).

6  **Combines the procedures into specific research designs that direct the plan for conducting the study.**

*Example:* A researcher seeks to evaluate a social service program that has been implemented in the community. The first step is to collect and analyze qualitative data via face-to-face interviews to determine what questions need to be addressed. Then a measuring instrument is designed to measure the impact of the program. This instrument is then used to compare certain outcomes both before and after the program has been implemented. From this comparison, follow-up individual face-to-face interviews are conducted to determine why the program did or did not work. This multiphase mixed-methods study is often found in long-term evaluation projects. See the study of the long-term impacts of qualitative programs at a historical site by James Farmer and Doug Knapp (2008).

Box 7.1 below provides a simple example of how the mixed-methods approach can be used in a single study on domestic violence.

---

| **Box 7.1** | Example: The Mixed-Methods Research Approach to Understanding Domestic Violence |

**Suppose you're interested** in studying domestic violence and want to conduct a research study with the following six subobjectives:

1  To determine the prevalence of domestic violence in your community.

2  To understand the nature and extent of domestic violence in your community.

3  To find out what it means for a woman and a man to live in a household with domestic violence.

4  To understand why, in spite of domestic violence, some victims—men as well as women—continue to live in the relationship.

5  To describe the types of social work services that are available to victims of domestic violence in your community.

6  To establish the socioeconomic demographic profile of people who are consumers of your services.

To achieve the subobjectives, your overall study needs to be carried out by using the quantitative and qualitative research approaches at the same time. For example:

1  **Subobjective 1** may be best studied through data-collection methods that are usually associated with the quantitative (positivistic) research approach—that is, counting the number of households with domestic violence episodes using a predetermined and accepted set of criteria. This approach will provide numerical data.

2  For **subobjective 2,** you will need to use data-collection and analysis methods from both research approaches. The nature of domestic violence can best be

explored through traditional qualitative (interpretive) data-collection methods such as in-depth personal interviews, focus groups, narratives, participant observation, and oral histories. The extent of domestic violence is probably best answered through traditional quantitative (positivistic) data-collection methods such as mailed and telephone surveys and analyses of agency records.

3 **Subobjective 3** can best be explored using qualitative data-collection methods such as in-depth interviews, group interviews with victims, narratives, oral histories, and case studies, as no quantitative method will give you more accurate data on what it means for a victim to live in a house with domestic violence.

4 The reasons for living in the relationship in spite of violence **(subobjective 4)** can be investigated through a number of data-collection methods belonging to both research approaches. You can collect data through one method only or through a number of them.

5 Similarly, "types of service" **(subobjective 5)** can best be studied through an interpretive data-collection approach such as in-depth interviews with social workers and their clients alike.

6 The "profile of consumers" **(subobjective 6)** may be answered by using traditional quantitative data-collection methods such as mailed survey questionnaires or highly structured interview schedules.

## USING BOTH APPROACHES IN A SINGLE STUDY

**G**iven the seemingly contradictory philosophical beliefs associated with the two research approaches (quantitative and qualitative), it's difficult to imagine how they could exist together in a single mixed-methods research study. Thus, many research studies use only one approach. The reason may, in part, relate to philosophy, but practical considerations of cost, time, and resources are also major factors.

If you're using a quantitative approach, for example, you could still ask research participants a few open-ended questions to more fully explain their experiences. In this instance, your quantitative research report would contain some pieces of qualitative data to help bring meaning to the study's quantitative findings (see box 7.2 on page 157).

Let's say you want to conduct a qualitative research study to examine your research question about discrimination within the public social service system. Surely you would want to identify how many research participants were included, as well as important defining characteristics such as their average age, the number who had difficulty accessing social services, or the number who were satisfied with the services they received. While it's possible to incorporate qualitative research activities into a quantitative study (and quantitative research activities into a qualitative one), the dominant approach you select must be guided by your purpose for conducting the study in the first place.

> It's not unusual to see quantitative data used within a qualitative study or qualitative data in a quantitative one.

## WHAT DO YOU REALLY WANT TO KNOW?

As mentioned previously, both research approaches have their advantages and disadvantages, and both shine in different phases within the research method. Which approach you select for a particular study depends not on whether you are a positivist or an interpretivist but on what particular research question your study is trying to answer. Are you looking for descriptions or explanations? If the former, a qualitative study will be spot on; if the latter, a quantitative one will do the trick.

Human nature being what it is, we are always looking, in the end, for explanations. We want to know not only what reality is like but also what its interconnections are and what we can do to change it to make our lives more comfortable and safer. However, first things first: Description comes before explanation. Before you can know whether poverty is related to child abuse, for example, you must be able to describe both poverty and child abuse as fully as possible. Similarly, if you want to know whether low self-esteem in women contributes to spousal abuse, you must know what self-esteem is and what constitutes abuse.

By now, because you are a social worker interested in people and not numbers, you may be ready to throw the whole quantitative research approach out the window. But let's be sure that you don't throw out the baby with the bathwater. Social work values dictate that you must make room for different approaches to knowledge development, different opinions, and differing views on what reality really is. Believe us, the two different approaches each have value in their own way, depending on what kind of data (quantitative and/or qualitative) you hope to gain from a particular research study.

### Example

Suppose you believe that cesarean operations are being conducted too often and unnecessarily for the convenience of obstetricians rather than for the benefit of mothers and their babies. To confirm or refute this hunch (it has yet to be proven), you would need data on the number of cesarean births in a particular time frame, and on how many of them were justified on the basis of medical need. Numbers would be required—quantitative data.

The questions about how many and how often could not be answered solely by descriptions of Ms. Smith's individual experiences. On the other hand, Ms. Smith's experiences would certainly lend richness to the part of your study that asks how far the hospital's services take the well-being of mothers into account.

Many of the best research studies use quantitative and qualitative methods within the same study (the topic of chapter 10). It's important to remember that the former provides the necessary numerical data while the latter provides the human depth that allows for a richer understanding of the numbers in their particular context.

Sometimes, therefore, depending on the research question (assumption) to be answered, Ms. Smith will be seen as no more than a number. At other times, her individuality will be of paramount importance. If she is seen as a number, her role will be passive. She will be one of a large number of persons. On the other hand, if she is seen as an individual, her part in the research study will be far more active. It's her reality that you are now exploring. She will be front and center in a research study that is driven by her and not the researcher. Even the language will change. She is no longer a subject—or possibly an object—but a full and equal participant, along with the researcher.

Box 7.2 on the following page provides an interesting example of how one researcher asked both open- and closed-ended questions in a mail survey. The closed-ended questions could be considered quantitative, while the open-ended could be considered qualitative.

> Ultimately, all research studies are about the pursuit of knowledge, but what kind of knowledge you are after is totally up to you—the social work researcher.

> Which research approach you select for a particular study depends not on whether you are a positivist or an interpretivist but on what particular research question your study is trying to answer.

## Evaluating a Research Study

As we know, there are three general types of research studies, or approaches to knowledge development: quantitative, qualitative, and mixed-methods. The first two (i.e., quantitative, qualitative) have their own respective evaluative criteria. The third one (i.e., mixed-methods), uses the evaluative criteria for the first two since this research approach is simply a combination of the quantitative approach and the qualitative approach.

| Box 7.2 | Example: A Basic Mixed-Methods Research Approach |
| --- | --- |

**Qualitative analysis seeks** to capture the richness of people's experiences in their own terms. Understanding and meaning emerge from in-depth analysis of detailed descriptions and verbatim quotations. In the following example, one nurse's responses to open- and closed-ended questions on a survey illustrate what is meant by depth, detail, and meaning. The first question was from a closed-ended question on a survey questionnaire.

**Quantitative closed-ended question:**
Accountability, as practiced in our primary health care system, creates an undesirable atmosphere of high anxiety among nurses. Check one below:

  √ **1** Strongly agree
  **2** Agree
  **3** Disagree
  **4** Strongly disagree

As you can see above one nurse marked "strongly agree" to the above question. Now compare this response (1) to her response to the following open-ended question.

**Qualitative open-ended question:**
Please add any personal comments you'd like to make about any part of the primary health care system's accountability approach.

**Her response:**

"Fear" is the word for "accountability" as applied in our system. Accountability is a political ploy to maintain power and control us. The disappointment in our system is incredible. You wouldn't believe the new layers of administration that have been created just to keep this system going. Come down and visit us in hell sometime.

These two responses illustrate one kind of difference that can exist between qualitative data derived from responses to open-ended questions and quantitative measurement. Quantitative measures are succinct and easily aggregated for analysis; they are systematic, standardized, and easily presented in a short space.

By contrast, qualitative responses are longer and more detailed; analysis is difficult because the responses are neither systematic nor standardized. The open-ended response permits us to understand the world as seen by the respondent.

Direct quotations are a basic source of raw data in interpretive studies. They reveal the respondent's level of emotion, thoughts, experiences, and basic perceptions.

It's important to keep in mind that the purposes and functions of qualitative and quantitative data on questionnaires are different, yet complementary. The statistics from standardized items make summaries, comparisons, and generalizations quite easy and precise, whereas the narrative comments from open-ended questions are typically meant to provide a forum for explanations, meanings, and new ideas.

## USE THE APPENDIXES

Appendix A lists numerous questions you can ask (when you put on your "critical thinking" hat) for each step of the quantitative research process, and Appendix B lists questions about each phase of the qualitative research process.

More specifically, you can find numerous questions in Appendix A that you can ask to determine the overall credibility of *quantitative* studies (questions 1–275 on pages 474–494) and Appendix B for *qualitative* ones (questions 276–460 on pages 495–510). You can ask the questions contained in both appendixes for mixed-methods studies.

### LET'S GET REACQUAINTED

This is the perfect time for you to become reacquainted with how to use the first three appendixes at the end of this book (i.e., Appendixes A–C on pages 474–522).

- First, read over the overall structure of the appendixes and the directions on how to use them on pages 468–473.
- Second, glance over the potential questions you can ask about any information you come across from:
  — Reading *quantitative* research studies (Appendix A)
  — Reading *qualitative* research studies (Appendix B)
  — Reading *mixed-methods* research studies (Appendixes A and B)
  — Finding information on the *Internet* (Appendix C)

> Many of the questions we can ask about quantitative studies can also be asked for qualitative ones as well. And vice versa.

## CHAPTER RECAP

- The scientific method of inquiry contains three research complementary research approaches.
- The positivist research approach tries to rule out uncertainty within any given research study.
- The interpretive research approach takes the position that "reality" is defined by the research participants' interpretations of their own realities. In sum, the subjective

reality is studied via the qualitative research approach rather than the objective one studied by the quantitative approach.

- A mixed-methods research approach integrates both quantitative and qualitative data in a single study. It capitalizes on the advantages that the quantitative and qualitative research approaches bring to the research enterprise.

## REVIEW EXERCISES

1  Before you entered your social work program and before you read this chapter, how did you think the quantitative research approach contributed to our profession's knowledge base? Discuss fully.

2  Discuss why the quantitative research approach is useful to knowledge generation. Discuss in detail using a social work example to illustrate your points.

3  In your own words, describe the quantitative research process by using one common social work example throughout your discussion.

4  What is the positivistic way of thinking? Discuss in detail. Provide a social work example to illustrate your points.

5  Discuss why the quantitative research approach places such a heavy emphasis on *the measurability of variables* within research studies. Discuss in detail using a social work example to illustrate your points.

6  Discuss why the quantitative research approach places such a heavy emphasis on *objectivity* within research studies. Discuss in detail using a social work example to illustrate your points.

7   Discuss why the quantitative research approach places such a heavy emphasis on *trying to reduce uncertainty* within research studies. Discuss in detail using a social work example to illustrate your points.

8   Discuss why the quantitative research approach places such a heavy emphasis on the *duplication of research studies.* Discuss in detail using a social work example to illustrate your points.

9   Discuss the qualitative (interpretive) way of thinking. Now discuss the quantitative (positivistic) way of thinking. Compare and contrast the two ways of thinking using one common social work example throughout your discussion.

10  What kind of data do positivistic research studies produce? What kind of data do interpretive research studies produce? Provide specific social work examples for each research approach.

11  How many realities do positivistic researchers believe to exist? How many realities do interpretive researchers believe to exist? Compare and contrast their differential perceptions of realities. Use as many social work examples that you can think of to illustrate your points.

12  Discuss the differential roles that research participants play within quantitative and qualitative research studies. Provide examples to illustrate your points.

13  Discuss the differences between *data* and *information.* Use a social work example throughout your discussion.

14  Discuss the term "value awareness" in reference to quantitative and qualitative studies. Provide social work examples to illustrate your points.

15  List, discuss, and provide social work examples of the commonalities in all qualitative research studies.

16  List, discuss, and provide specific social work examples of all the phases within the qualitative research approach.

17  Provide one common social work example when comparing both research approaches in reference to their *philosophical differences.*

18  Provide one common social work example when comparing both research approaches in reference to their *differential perceptions of reality.*

19  Provide one common social work example when comparing both research approaches in reference to their *differential perceptions on ways of knowing.*

20  Provide one common social work example when comparing both research approaches in reference to their *differential value bases.*

21  Provide one common social work example when comparing both research approaches in reference to their *applications to social work practice.*

22  List, discuss, and provide specific social work examples of the two research approaches in reference to their *similarities.*

23  Discuss in detail how you would go about combining both research approaches in a single social work research study.

# 8

CHAPTER

## 2015 EPAS COMPETENCIES

| COMPETENCY 1 | Demonstrate Ethical and Professional Behavior |
|---|---|

You will learn that in order to be a successful evidence-based practitioner you have an ethical obligation to integrate three research roles into your daily practice activities as discussed in Chapter 3: (1) research consumer, (2) research partner—either as a co-researcher or research participant, and (3) creator and disseminator of research (or knowledge).

This entire chapter pertains to these three professional roles because an ethical and professional evidence-based social work practitioner must understand and appreciate the advantages and disadvantages that are embedded within all three research approaches to knowledge development that produce social work practice recommendations: quantitative (this chapter), qualitative (Chapter 9), and mixed-methods (Chapter 10).

| COMPETENCY 4 | Engage in Practice-Informed Research and Research-Informed Practice |
|---|---|

Competency 4 also pertains to the entire chapter because you have to:

1   Evaluate the overall value of the practice recommendations that a quantitative (positivistic) research study puts forward by assessing how closely the study followed the quantitative research approach that was used to formulate the study's findings and practice recommendations (**research consumer**—research-informed practice);

2   Participate in a research study—either as a co-researcher or research participant (**research partner**—practice-informed research). See 1 above and 3 below; and

3   Understand and appreciate the advantages and disadvantages of using the quantitative research approach to knowledge building before you actually do a quantitative research study (**creator and disseminator of research**—practice-informed research).

You'll also need to utilize evidence-based practice recommendations whenever possible; that is, you need to integrate (1) the best available research-based evidence with (2) your clinical expertise and (3) your client's values.

All of the above implies you'll need to know how to assess the overall rigor of a quantitatively based research study that produced its quantitative research-based evidence (see Appendix A). In short, you need to ask and then answer a simple question: How seriously should I take the findings of any specific quantitatively oriented research study given how well the study followed the positivist way of thinking as discussed in the previous chapter?

| COMPETENCY 9 | Evaluate Practice with Individuals, Families, Groups, Organizations, & Communities |
|---|---|

See Competencies 1 and 4.

# The Quantitative Research Approach

| | | |
|---|---|---|
| CHAPTERS 1 & 3 | Step 1. | Understanding the Research Process |
| CHAPTER 2 | Step 2. | Formulating Research Questions |
| CHAPTER 4 APPENDIXES A–C | Step 3. | Reviewing the Literature Evaluating the Literature |
| CHAPTERS 5 & 6 | Step 4. | Being Aware of Ethical and Cultural Issues |
| CHAPTERS 7–10 | Step 5. | Selecting a Research Approach |
| CHAPTERS 11 & 12 | Step 6. | Specifying How Variables Are Measured |
| CHAPTER 13 | Step 7. | Selecting a Sample |
| CHAPTERS 14 & 15 | Step 8. | Selecting a Research Design |
| CHAPTERS 16 & 17 | Step 9. | Selecting a Data-Collection Method |
| CHAPTERS 18 & 19 | Step 10. | Analyzing the Data |
| CHAPTERS 20 & 21 | Step 11. | Writing the Research Report |

# The Quantitative Research Approach

"At this point in our quantitative analysis, something hit the fan, but our School's *Code of Conduct* prevents me from talking about it."

STEPS OF THE RESEARCH APPROACH
STEP 1: IDENTIFYING THE RESEARCH PROBLEM
STEP 2: SELECTING SPECIFIC VARIABLES
    Substep 2a: What Have Others Found?
    Substep 2b: Refining the Problem Area
    Substep 2c: Developing Concepts
        *Concepts*
    Substep 2d: Identifying Variables
    Substep 2e: Defining Attributes of Variables
    Substep 2f: Defining Variables
        *No Independent or Dependent Variables*
    Substep 2g: Constructing a Hypothesis
        *Nondirectional Hypotheses*
        *Directional Hypotheses*
    Substep 2h: Evaluating the Hypothesis
        *Relevance*
        *Completeness*
        *Specificity*
        *Potential for Testing*
        *Ethically and Culturally Sensitive*
STEP 3: DESIGNING THE STUDY
    Substep 3a: Measuring Variables
    Substep 3b: Sample and Research Design
    Substep 3c: Ethical and Cultural Issues

STEP 4: COLLECTING THE DATA
STEP 5: ANALYZING THE DATA
    Descriptive Statistics
    Inferential Statistics
STEP 6: INTERPRETING THE FINDINGS
    Substep 6a: Comparing Results
    Substep 6b: Study's Limitations
STEP 7: DISSEMINATING THE STUDY'S FINDINGS
AN EXTENDED EXAMPLE
    What's the Problem?
    Formulating Initial Impressions
    Determining What Others Have Found
    Refining the General Problem Area
    Measuring the Variables
    Selecting a Sample
    Addressing Ethical and Cultural Issues
    Collecting the Data
    Analyzing the Data
    Interpreting the Data
    Comparing Results
    Specifying the Study's Limitations
    Disseminating the Study's Results
EVALUATING QUANTITATIVE RESEARCH STUDIES
    Use Appendix A
CHAPTER RECAP
REVIEW EXERCISES

As you know, the previous chapter discussed the underlying philosophies of three complementary research approaches embedded within the scientific method of inquiry: quantitative, qualitative, and mixed-methods. However, it did not present the specific processes that researchers go through when they actually perform their respective studies. The process of actually doing a research study varies dramatically among the three research approaches.

Thus, building on Chapter 7, this chapter briefly presents the general process, in a step-by-step format, of actually doing a research study using the quantitative research approach. Thus, it's important for you to have a sound understanding of the fundamental concepts in Chapter 7 before reading this chapter.

## STEPS OF THE QUANTITATIVE RESEARCH APPROACH

We now turn our attention to the seven general sequential steps (in a more-or-less straightforward manner) that all quantitative studies follow, as illustrated in Figure 7.1 on page 145. The most important thing to remember at this point is that all the steps in Figure 7.1 are highly intertwined to various degrees and it's difficult, if not impossible, to describe a single step in isolation from the remaining six steps. However, for the sake of simplicity, we'll describe each step in a sequential manner.

These steps yield a very useful format for obtaining knowledge in our profession. The quantitative research approach is a tried and tested method of scientific inquiry. In a nutshell, most of the critical decisions to be made in a quantitative research study occur before the study is ever started. This means that the researcher is well aware (or should be aware!) of all the study's limitations before the study actually begins. It's possible, therefore, for a researcher to decide that a quantitative study has simply way too many limitations and to conclude that it should not be performed. Regardless of whether a proposed study is ever carried out, the process always begins with choosing a research topic and focusing the research question (Chapter 2).

## STEP 1: IDENTIFYING THE RESEARCH PROBLEM

As can be seen in Figure 7.1 on page 145, the first step of the quantitative approach to knowledge development is to identify a general problem area to study and then to refine this general area into a research question that can be answered or a hypothesis that can be tested. Quantitative studies are usually deductive processes; that is, they usually begin with a broad and general query about a general social problem then pare it down to a specific research question or hypothesis. For instance, your general research problem may have started out with a curiosity about racial discrimination within public social service agencies. Your general problem area could be simply as:

**General problem area**
Racial discrimination within public social service agencies

## STEP 2: SELECTING SPECIFIC VARIABLES

**Y**ou may have noticed through your professional practice as a medical social worker in a local hospital, for example, that many of the patients within your hospital are from ethnic minority backgrounds who have the following three characteristics (or variables, if you will):

1   High unemployment rates
2   A large proportion of their members living under the poverty level
3   Low levels of educational attainment

You believe that these three conditions alone should increase the likelihood that they will use the hospital's social service department where you work. Conversely, and at the same time, you have also observed that there are more ethnic majorities than minorities who are seen in your hospital's social service department. Where the research study actually takes place is called the *research setting*. So your research setting for this study is the hospital where you're employed.

Your personal observations may then lead you to question whether discrimination against ethnic minorities exists in terms of their access to your hospital's social service department. You can easily test the possibility of such a relationship by using the quantitative research approach. As should be evident by now, Steps 1 and 2 are highly intertwined and comingled, and they usually take place at the same time. Step 2 within the quantitative research process has eight substeps:

**Substep 2a**   Determining what others have found
**Substep 2b**   Refining the general problem area
**Substep 2c**   Developing concepts
**Substep 2d**   Identifying variables within concepts
**Substep 2e**   Defining attributes of variables
**Substep 2f**   Defining independent and dependent variables
**Substep 2g**   Constructing a hypothesis
**Substep 2h**   Evaluating the hypothesis

## SUBSTEP 2A: WHAT HAVE OTHERS FOUND?

The next phase in focusing your research question is visiting the library and using the Internet to review the literature related to your two concepts:

• Racial discrimination within social services (Concept 1)
• Access to social service (Concept 2)

You will want to read the literature related to your two main concepts within the general research question: racial discrimination within social service agencies and access to them. You will want to learn about how various theories explain both of your main concepts in order to arrive at a meaningful research question. It may be, for example, that many ethnic minority cultures are unlikely to ask strangers for help with life's personal difficulties.

## SUBSTEP 2B: REFINING THE GENERAL PROBLEM AREA

Furthermore, you may learn that most social service programs are organized using bureaucratic structures, which require potential clients to talk to several strangers (e.g., telephone receptionist, waiting-room clerk, intake worker) before they are able to access social services.

Given that you know, via the literature, that ethnic minorities do not like talking with strangers about their personal problems, and that social services are set up for people to deal with a series of strangers, you could develop a very simple quantitative research question:

**Quantitative research question**
Do patients who come from ethnic minority backgrounds have difficulty accessing my hospital's social service department?

## SUBSTEP 2C: DEVELOPING CONCEPTS

You have made the general broad general problem area of racial discrimination more specific by narrowing it down to a person's ethnicity. At this point, you have yet to refine your second concept in your research question, access to your hospital's social services. This will be done later on. For now, let's review the concept of concepts.

### CONCEPTS

What are concepts anyway? When you speak of a client's ethnic background, for example, you have in mind the concept of ethnicity. When you use the word ethnicity, you are referring to the underlying idea that certain groups of people can be differentiated from other groups in terms of physical characteristics, customs, beliefs, language, and so on.

Take a female patient in your hospital, for example, who has just been referred to your social service department. She is a patient in the hospital, she is a woman, and she is now also your client. If she's married, she's a wife. If she has children, she's a mother. She may be a homeowner, a committee member, an Asian, and a Catholic. She may even be hostile, demanding, or compassionate.

> Concepts are nothing more than ideas.

All of these characteristics are concepts. They are simply ideas that all members of a society share—to a greater or lesser degree, of course. Some concepts are perceived the same way by all of us. On the other hand, some concepts give rise to huge disagreements. The concept of being a mother, for example, involves the concept of children and, specifically, the concept of having given birth to a child. Today, however, most people would agree that giving birth to a child is only one way of defining a mother.

The idea of motherhood in Western society involves more than simply giving birth. Also involved in motherhood are the concepts of loving the child, caring for the child's physical needs, offering the child emotional support, advocating for the child with others, accepting legal and financial responsibility for the child, and being there for the child in all circumstances and at all times. Some of us could easily argue that a woman who does all of these things is a mother, whether she has given birth or not.

Others would say that the biological mother is the only real mother, even if she abandoned her child at birth. Like many other qualities of interest to social workers, ethnicity is a highly complex concept with many possible dimensions. Intelligence is another such concept, as are alienation, morale, conformity, and a host of others.

## SUBSTEP 2D: IDENTIFYING VARIABLES

You can now break down your global concept, the ethnicity of patients who seek out your hospital's social service department, into a variable by breaking down ethnicity into different ethnic groups. Some patients will belong to one ethnic group, some to another, some to a third, and so on. In other words, these people vary with respect to which ethnic group they belong to. Any concept that can vary, logically enough, is called a *variable*, so your variable's name is ethnic group.

## SUBSTEP 2E: DEFINING ATTRIBUTES OF VARIABLES

You now have gone from your general concept of ethnicity to a variable, ethnic group. Finally, you need to think about which particular ethnic groups will be useful for your study. Perhaps you know that Asians are patients within your hospital, as are Caucasians, Latinxs, African Americans, and Native Americans. This gives you five attributes for your ethnic group variable:

**Attributes for ethnic group variable**
1  Asian
2  Caucasian
3  Latinx
4  African American
5  Native American

During your quantitative study you will ask all of the hospital's patients which one of these five ethnic groups they belong to; or perhaps these data will be recorded on the hospital's intake forms, and you will not need to ask them at all.

In any case, the resulting data will be in the form of numbers or percentages for each attribute. You will have succeeded in measuring the variable ethnic group by describing it in terms of five attributes. You will note that these five categories only provide one possible description. You could also have included Pacific Islanders, for example, if there were any receiving medical treatment in your hospital, and then you would have had six attributes of your ethnic group variable instead of only five.

**Attributes for ethnic group variable**
1  Asian
2  Caucasian
3  Latinx
4  African American
5  Native American
6  Pacific Islanders

If you were afraid that not all clients receiving medical treatment would fit into one of your six categories, then you could include a seventh miscellaneous category, other, to be sure you had accounted for everyone.

**Attributes for ethnic group variable**

1  Asian

2  Caucasian

3  Latinx

4  African American

5  Native American

6  Pacific Islanders

7  Other

By reviewing the literature and your knowledge of your social service unit, you have more or less devised a direction for your study in relation to your ethnicity concept. From the general problem area of racial discrimination, you have come up with a concept (ethnicity), a variable (ethnic group), and seven attributes for your variable as illustrated below.

**General Problem Area:** Racial discrimination
**Concept:** Ethnicity
**Variable:** Ethnic group
**Attributes:** Asian
Caucasian
Latinx
African American
Native American
Pacific Islander
Others

As you know, ethnicity is not the only concept of interest in your study. There is also access to social work services, which is the idea that some people, or groups of people, are able to access social work services more readily than other people or groups. You might think of access simply in terms of how many of the patients receiving medical treatment within your hospital actually saw a social worker. Clients will vary with respect to whether they saw a social worker, so you have the variable, saw social worker, and two attributes of that variable:

**Saw a social worker?**
Yes, the client saw a social worker.
No, the client did not see a social worker.

You could, for example, ask each patient upon leaving the hospital a very simple question:

**Question**
Did you see a social worker while you were in the hospital?

1  Yes

2  No

If you wish to explore access in more depth, you might be interested in the factors affecting access. For example, perhaps your review of the literature has led you to believe that some ethnic groups tend to receive fewer referrals to social work services than other groups. If this is the case in your hospital, clients will vary with respect to whether they received a referral, and you immediately have a second variable—referral—and two attributes of that variable:

**Was the patient referred?**
Yes, the patient was referred.
No, the patient was not referred.

Once again, this variable can take the form of a very simple question:

**Question**
When you were a patient within the hospital, were you at any time referred to the hospital's social service department?

**1** Yes

**2** No

However, there is more to accessing hospital social work services than just being referred. Perhaps, according to the literature, certain ethnic groups are more likely to follow up on a referral than other groups because of cultural beliefs around the appropriateness of asking non-family members for help. In that case, you have a third variable, follow-up of referral, with two attributes of its own:

**Did the client follow-up on the referral?**
Yes, the client followed up.
No, the client did not follow up.

This also can be put into a question form:

**Question**
If you were referred to social work services while you were a patient in the hospital, did you follow up on the referral and actually see a social worker?

**1** Yes

**2** No

In addition, those who do try to follow up on referrals may meet circumstances within the referral process that are more intimidating for some than for others. Perhaps they are obliged to fill out a large number of forms or tell their stories to many unfamiliar people before they actually succeed in getting an appointment with a social worker. If this is the case, they vary with respect to how intimidating they find the process, which gives you a fourth variable, feelings of intimidation around the referral process. The attributes here are not so immediately apparent, but you might decide on just three:

**Feelings of intimidation**
- Not at all intimidated
- Somewhat intimidated
- Very intimidated

This also can be put into the form of a simple question that you would ask all patients who were referred to social services:

**Simple research question**
How intimidated were you when you were referred to the social service department?

By reviewing the literature and your knowledge of your hospital's social service department, you have more or less devised a direction for your study in relation to your access concept. You have come up with a concept, four variables, and attributes for each one of the four variables.

---

**Concept:** Access to social work services

  **First Variable:** Saw social worker?
        *Attributes:* Yes
                     No
  **Second Variable:** Referral?
        *Attributes:* Yes
                     No
  **Third Variable:** Follow-up of referral?
        *Attributes:* Yes
                     No
  **Fourth Variable:** Feeling of intimidation surrounding the referral process
        *Attributes:* Not at all intimidated
                     Somewhat intimidated
                     Very intimidated

---

# SUBSTEP 2F: DEFINING VARIABLES

A simple quantitative research study may choose to focus on the relationship between only two variables, which is called a bivariate relationship. The study tries to answer, in general terms: Does variable $X$ affect variable $Y$? Or, how does variable $X$ affect variable $Y$? This would be a great time for you to review Figure 2.3 on page 48.

If one variable affects the other, the variable that does the affecting is called an independent variable, symbolized by $X$. The variable that is affected is called the dependent variable, symbolized by $Y$. If enough is known about the topic, and you have a good idea of what the effect will be, the question may be phrased, If $X$ occurs, will $Y$ result? If variable $X$ affects variable $Y$, whatever happens to $Y$ will depend on $X$.

## NO INDEPENDENT OR DEPENDENT VARIABLES

Some quantitative research studies are not concerned with the effect that one variable might have on another. Perhaps it's not yet known whether two variables are even associated, and it's far too soon to postulate what the relationship between them might be. For example, your study might try to find the answer to a simple question:

**Question**
How intimidated were you when you were referred to the social service department?

1  Not at all intimidated

2  Somewhat intimidated

3  Very intimidated

In the above simple question, there is no independent variable, nor is there a dependent variable. There is only one variable: the degree of intimidation felt by one group of people, members of the ethnic minority. You could even include members of the ethnic majority as well and ask this question:

**Simple research question**
How intimidated do ALL patients feel when they are referred to my hospital's social service department?

## Substep 2g: Constructing a Hypothesis

There are many types of hypotheses, but we will only briefly discuss two:

1  Nondirectional
2  Directional

### Nondirectional Hypotheses

A nondirectional hypothesis (also called a two-tailed hypothesis) is simply a statement that says you expect to find a relationship between two or more variables. You're not willing, however, to stick your neck out as to the specific relationship between them. A nondirectional hypothesis for each one of your access variables could be, for example:

- **Nondirectional Research Hypothesis 1:** *Saw a Social Worker*
  Ethnic minorities and ethnic majorities see hospital social workers differently.

- **Nondirectional Research Hypothesis 2:** *Referral*
  Ethnic minorities and ethnic majorities are referred to the hospital's social service department differentially.

- **Nondirectional Research Hypothesis 3:** *Follow-up*
  Ethnic minorities and ethnic majorities vary to the degree they follow up on referrals.

- **Nondirectional Research Hypothesis 4:** *Intimidation*
  Ethnic minorities and ethnic majorities differ in terms of how intimidated they were about the referral process.

### Directional Hypotheses

Unlike a nondirectional hypothesis, a directional hypothesis (also called a one-tailed hypothesis) specifically indicates the predicted direction of the relationship between two variables. The direction stated is based on an existing body of knowledge related to the research question. You may have found out through the literature (in addition to your own observations), for example, that you have enough evidence to suggest the following directional research hypotheses:

> Hypotheses can be either nondirectional or directional.

- **Directional Research Hypothesis 1:** *Saw a Social Worker*
  Ethnic majorities see hospital social workers more often than ethnic minorities.

- **Directional Research Hypothesis 2:** *Referral*
  Ethnic majorities are referred to the hospital's social service department more often than ethnic minorities.

- **Directional Research Hypothesis 3:** *Follow-up*
  Ethnic majorities follow up with social service referrals more often than ethnic minorities.

- **Directional Research Hypothesis 4:** *Intimidation*
  Ethnic minorities are more intimidated by the referral process than ethnic majorities.

As you shall see in this book, many research questions have at least one independent variable and one dependent variable. You could easily design your quantitative study to have one independent variable, ethnicity (i.e., ethnic minority or ethnic majority), and one dependent variable, difficulty in accessing social services (i.e., yes or no). You could easily organize your variables in this way because you are expecting that a person's ethnicity is somehow related to his/her difficulty in accessing social services.

It would be absurd to say the opposite—where the degree of difficulty that people have in accessing social services somehow influences their ethnicities. You could write your directional hypothesis as follows:

**Directional hypothesis**
Ethnic minorities have more difficulty than ethnic majorities in accessing my hospital's social service department.

Having set out your hypothesis in this way, you can plainly see that your research design will compare two groups of folks (ethnic minorities and ethnic majorities) in terms of whether or not (yes or no) each group had difficulty accessing your hospital's social service department. Your research design is the blueprint for the study. It's a basic guide to deciding how, where, and when data will be collected.

## SUBSTEP 2H: EVALUATING THE HYPOTHESIS

You must now evaluate your hypothesis. Our discussion on how to evaluate hypotheses has been adapted and modified from Rick Grinnell and Margaret Williams (1990), Margaret Williams, Leslie Tutty, and Rick Grinnell (1995), and Margaret Williams, Yvonne Unrau, and Rick Grinnell (1998). Hypotheses have to contain five ingredients; that is, they must be:

1 Relevant
2 Complete
3 Specific
4 Testable
5 Ethically and culturally sensitive

### RELEVANCE

It's hardly necessary to stress that a useful hypothesis is one that contributes to the profession's knowledge base. Nevertheless, some social work problem areas are so complex that people may become sidetracked while reading the professional literature and end up developing very interesting hypotheses that are totally unrelated to the original problem area they had wanted to investigate.

They needlessly run down a bunch of rabbit holes. The relevancy criterion is a reminder that the hypothesis must be directly related to the research question, which in turn must be directly related to the study's general problem area.

### COMPLETENESS

A hypothesis should be a complete statement that expresses your intended meaning in its entirety. The reader should not be left with the impression that some word or phrase is missing, such as:

**An incomplete hypothesis**
Moral values are declining.

Other examples would include a whole range of comparative statements without a reference point. The statement "Males are more aggressive," for example, may be assumed to mean "Men are more aggressive than women," but someone investigating the social life of animals may have meant "Male humans are more aggressive than male gorillas."

### SPECIFICITY

A hypothesis must be unambiguous. The reader should be able to understand what each variable contained in the hypothesis means and what relationship, if any, is hypothesized to exist between them. Consider, for example, this hypothesis:

**A poorly worded hypothesis**
Bad timed family therapy affects success.

"Badly timed family therapy" may mean that therapy is offered too soon or too late for the family to benefit; or that the social worker or family are late for therapy sessions; or that sessions are too long or too short to be effective. Similarly, "success" may mean that the family's problems are resolved as determined by objective measurement, or it may mean that the family or the social worker is satisfied with the therapy, or any combination of these.

With regard to the relationship between the two variables, the reader may assume that you are hypothesizing a negative correlation; that is, the more badly timed the therapy, the less success will be achieved. On the other hand, perhaps you are only hypothesizing an association, that bad timing will invariably coexist with lack of success. Be that as it may, the reader should not be left to guess at what you mean by a hypothesis. If you are trying to be both complete and specific, you may hypothesize, for example:

**A properly worded hypothesis**
Family therapy that is undertaken after the male perpetrator has accepted responsibility for the sexual abuse of his child is more likely to succeed in reuniting the family than family therapy undertaken before the male perpetrator has accepted responsibility for the sexual abuse.

This hypothesis is complete and specific. It leaves the reader in no doubt as to what you mean, but it's also somewhat wordy and clumsy. One of the difficulties in writing a good hypothesis is that specific statements need more words than ambiguous statements.

### POTENTIAL FOR TESTING

The fourth criterion for judging whether a hypothesis is good and useful is the ease with which its truth can be verified. Some statements cannot be verified at all with currently available measurement techniques. "Telepathic communication exists between identical twins" is one such statement. A hypothesis of sufficient importance will often generate new data-gathering techniques, which will enable it to be eventually tested. Nevertheless, as a rule it's best to limit hypotheses to statements that can be tested immediately by currently available measurement methods.

### ETHICALLY AND CULTURALLY SENSITIVE

Well, if we have to explain this criterion you don't belong in social work. Read Chapter 5 on ethics and Chapter 6 on cultural competence to review all of the ethical and cultural issues that must be dealt with in a research study—especially when it comes to formulating research questions and hypotheses.

## STEP 3: DESIGNING THE STUDY

**A**fter all of the necessary work has been done in relation to formulating your research question and/or hypothesis, you need to state how your study is going to unfold; that is, you now need to describe how you are going to measure your variables and select your research sample. Like Step 2, Step 3 also has substeps:

**Substep 3a** Measuring variables

**Substep 3b** Deciding on a sample

**Substep 3c** Addressing ethical and cultural issues

## SUBSTEP 3A: MEASURING VARIABLES

All of your variables must be able to be objectively measured. This means that you must precisely record the variable's frequency, duration, and/or magnitude (intensity). Think about your ethnic minority variable for a minute. As noted earlier, you could simply operationalize this variable into two categories, ethnic minority and ethnic majorities:

### Question
Are you a member of an ethnic minority?

1 Yes

2 No

Here you are simply measuring the presence (ethnic minority) or absence (ethnic majority) of a trait for each research participant within your study. You also need to measure the variable of difficulty in accessing the hospital's social service department. One again, you could have measured this variable in a number of ways. You are measuring it by asking each person a simple question:

### Question
Did you have difficulty in accessing our hospital's social service department?

1 Yes

2 No

## SUBSTEP 3B: SAMPLE AND RESEARCH DESIGN

Sampling is nothing more than selecting units (e.g., people, organizations) from a specific population of interest so that by studying the sample you can generalize your results back to the population from which the sample was drawn. You will be analyzing the data from your sample to determine if your research question has been answered or your hypothesis has been confirmed.

How you go about selecting your sample, administering the measuring instruments, and analyzing your data is loosely referred to as your general research design. Much more will be said about sampling in Chapter 13 and research designs in Chapters 14 and 15.

## SUBSTEP 3C: ETHICAL AND CULTURAL ISSUES

It goes without saying that you must review all the ethical and cultural issues in every step of your proposed research study before you collect one speck of data. The main two questions you need to ask yourself at this point are:

1 Is my proposed research study ethical (chapter 5)?

2 Is my proposed research study culturally sensitive (chapter 6)?

## STEP 4: COLLECTING THE DATA

**O**nly **after you decide** that your study is ethical and culturally sensitive can you start to collect your data. Data collection is where the rubber hits the road. The data you collect must reflect a condition in the real world and should not be biased by the person collecting the data in any way.

In your quantitative study, the research participants produce the data—not you, the researcher. That is, you only record the data that each participant individually provides (probably through a questionnaire of some type) for both of your variables:

- "Ethnic minority" or "ethnic majority" for the ethnicity variable
- "Yes" or "No" for the access to social service variable

Your data-collection procedures must be able to be duplicated by others. In other words, they must be sufficiently clear and straightforward that other researchers could use them in their research studies. Data collection is a critical step in the research process because it's the link between theory and practice. Your research study always begins with an idea that is molded by a conceptual framework, which uses preexisting knowledge about your study's problem area.

Once your research question has been refined to a researchable level, data are sought from a selected source(s) and gathered using a data-collection method. The data collected are then used to support or supplant your original study's conceptions about the research problem under investigation.

## STEP 5: ANALYZING THE DATA

Once you have collected your data via the previous step, you need to analyze them. You asked your research participants to fill out a simple two-question questionnaire that only asked two questions:

**Question 1**
Are you a member of an ethnic minority?

1  Yes

2  No

**Question 2**
Did you have difficulty in accessing our hospital's social service department?

1  Yes

2  No

There are two major types of quantitative data analysis:

1  Descriptive statistics
2  Inferential statistics

## DESCRIPTIVE STATISTICS

As presented in Chapter 18, descriptive statistics describe your study's sample or population. Consider your ethnicity variable for a moment. You can easily describe your research participants in relation to their ethnicity by stating how many of them fell into each attribute of the variable. Suppose, for example, that 40 percent of your sample is in the ethnic minority category and the remaining 60 percent are in the ethnic majority category as shown:

**Attributes**
Ethnic minority . . . 40%
Ethnic majority . . . 60%

These two percentages will give you a picture of what your sample looks like in relation to ethnicity. A different picture could be produced where 10 percent of your sample are members of ethnic minorities and 90 percent are not:

**Attributes**
Ethnic minority . . . 10%
Ethnic majority . . . 90%

The above describes only one variable—ethnicity. A more detailed picture is given when data for two variables are displayed at the same time (e.g., table 8.1). Suppose, for example, that 70 percent of your research participants who are members of ethnic minorities reported that they had difficulty in accessing your hospital's social services, compared with 20 percent of those who are in the ethnic majority (see table 8.1 below).

**Table 8.1**
Difficulty in Accessing Social Services

|  | Having Difficulty? | |
| --- | --- | --- |
| Ethnicity | Yes | No |
| Ethnic Minority | 70% | 30% |
| Ethnic Majority | 20% | 80% |

Other descriptive information about your research participants could include variables such as average age, percentages of males and females, average income, and so on. Much more will be said about descriptive statistics in Chapter 18 when we discuss how to analyze quantitative data (data that are in the form of numbers).

## INFERENTIAL STATISTICS

Inferential statistics determine the probability that a relationship between the two variables within your sample also exists within the population from which it was drawn. Suppose in your quantitative study, for example, you find a statistically significant relationship between your research participant's ethnicity and whether they accessed social services within your hospital setting.

The use of inferential statistics will permit you to say whether or not the relationship detected in your study's sample exists in the larger population from which it was drawn. Much more will also be said about inferential statistics in Chapter 18.

## STEP 6: INTERPRETING THE FINDINGS

Once your data have been analyzed and put into a visual display, they need to be interpreted; that is, what do they mean—in words? You could come up with the following simple interpretation after looking at Table 8.1 above:

Members of ethnic minorities had more difficulty in accessing social services than members of ethnic majorities.

## SUBSTEP 6A: COMPARING RESULTS

Your findings now need to be compared with what other studies have found. This is the time to review the literature once again, as discussed in Chapter 4. At this point, you need to state how your study's findings are either consistent with or inconsistent with other findings from similar studies.

## SUBSTEP 6B: STUDY'S LIMITATIONS

At this point, you need to state the limitations of your study. You will need to state how well your study addressed all the threats to internal and external validities, as discussed in Chapter 15.

## STEP 7: DISSEMINATING THE STUDY'S FINDINGS

**Q**uantitative findings are easily summarized in tables, figures, and graphs. When data are disseminated to laypeople, we usually rely on straightforward graphs and charts to illustrate our findings. As discussed in Chapter 20, presentations of statistical findings are typically reserved for professional journals.

## AN EXTENDED EXAMPLE

**L**et's forget about racial discrimination and access to social services within your hospital for a moment and focus on poverty, domestic violence, substance abuse, and homelessness.

## WHAT'S THE PROBLEM?

Let's pretend for a moment that you're a social worker in a large social service agency. Agency intake data from the past three years reveal that many of your clients experience similar social issues (see Figure 3.2 on page 68). More specifically, most clients seeking services from your agency regularly present with one or more of the following four problems:

1  Poverty
2  Domestic violence
3  Substance abuse
4  Homelessness

Your agency's executive director establishes a "Practice Informed by Research" Committee that is charged with the following mandate:

**Mandate**
To design a research study involving agency clientele so that workers at the agency will be better informed about the complex relationship between the issues of poverty, domestic violence, substance abuse, and homelessness

You are asked to chair this committee. Gladly, you accept and begin leading your committee through the remaining steps of the research process, as outlined in Figure 7.1 on page 145.

## FORMULATING INITIAL IMPRESSIONS

As committee chair, your first step is to invite open discussion with your committee members about what they "know" about each of the four presenting problems, or issues, and the relationship between them.

Drawing upon the task-group facilitation skills you learned in one of your social work practice classes, you help your committee members tease out the source(s) of their collective wisdom (or knowledge) as a group.

As a group you discuss possible relationships among the presenting problems and try to determine whether your answers are based on authority, tradition, experience, intuition, or the scientific method. During these discussions, the committee members learn some very important things from previous research studies, such as (1) how much of their present knowledge is based on empirical knowledge versus other ways of knowing; (2) the biases, values, or beliefs that are active among committee members; and (3) how findings derived from the scientific method on inquiry can be used to expand everyone's knowledge base. Six possible questions you could formulate are as follows:

1   Is poverty related to domestic violence?
2   Is poverty related to substance abuse?
3   Is poverty related to homelessness?
4   Is domestic violence related to substance abuse?
5   Is domestic violence related to homelessness?
6   Is substance abuse related to homelessness?

## DETERMINING WHAT OTHERS HAVE FOUND

Given your superb skills as a group facilitator, you have energized your committee members and stimulated their curiosity such that they are eager to read the latest research about poverty, domestic violence, substance abuse, and homelessness. Each committee member accepts a task to search the literature for articles and information about the relationship between one or more of the four presenting problems of interest.

Committee members search a variety of sources such as professional journals, credible websites, and books. Using quality criteria to evaluate the evidence of information gathered, the committee synthesizes the knowledge gathered from these empirical sources. If so desired, the committee might endeavor to systematically assess the literature gathered through meta-analyses. Below are two general questions that you need to address in relation to your problem area:

• What does the available literature have to say about poverty, domestic violence, substance abuse, and homelessness?

• Has it been established that any two or more of these variables are, in fact, related? And if so, what is the relationship between or among them?

With a synthesis of the literature gathered, your committee will be in an excellent position to make an informed statement about up-to-date knowledge on the relationship between poverty, domestic violence, substance abuse, and homelessness.

## REFINING THE GENERAL PROBLEM AREA

By this point, the excitement of your committee members has waned. As it turns out, the task of reviewing the literature has been more onerous than anticipated because the number of research studies investigating poverty, domestic violence, substance abuse, and homelessness is overwhelming. For example, when searching for studies on domestic violence, committee members had to define "partner" in domestic violence and decide whether the research studies to be reviewed would include gay and lesbian partners as well as heterosexual partners. Moreover, applying criteria to evaluate individual studies was not as straightforward as initially thought.

But your committee has trudged through and found relevant empirical articles. To recharge the committee and keep the momentum of the research process going, you work with committee members to set priorities for the remainder of your work together. In short, you need to decide what research question(s)—exploratory, descriptive, or explanatory—will be the focus of your investigation. You also need to decide which research design is best suited to investigating the proposed research question.

The committee now decides to focus on the descriptive relationship between only two presenting problem areas—domestic violence and substance abuse. One of the many oversimplified examples from the preceding four highly interrelated variables (i.e., poverty, domestic violence, substance abuse, homelessness) might be:

**Hypothesis: Relationship between two variables**
Clients with substance abuse problems will also have domestic violence issues.

## MEASURING THE VARIABLES

You need now to review with your committee members the work you have accomplished in the previous steps. Planning thus far has largely been a conceptual exercise. However, when you start to define and decide how to measure your variables, you soon realize that the tasks become much more specific. With respect to measurement, committee members must develop a way to measure the two presenting problems (i.e., substance abuse and domestic violence) that will be studied and find measuring instruments for each variable.

Find out how other researchers measured their variables. If you feel that the variables were measured properly in previous studies, then you can use the same method to measure your variables, too. There is no need to reinvent the wheel if the previous measurements are valid and reliable. Your committee believes that the previous studies measured the two variables well, so you decide also to use them in your study. Thus you decide that your two variables will be measured as follows:

1   Substance abuse: Substance Abuse Questionnaire (SAQ)
2   Domestic violence: Domestic Violence Inventory (DVI)

## SELECTING A SAMPLE

With a clear research hypothesis (i.e., Clients with substance abuse problems will also have domestic violence issues), a solid understanding of other research studies, and the selection of measuring instruments for key variables, your next step for the committee is to decide on the sampling procedures that will be used in the study. At this point, research and practice knowledge come together to help you ascertain which parameters for the sample will be most meaningful.

For example, it turns out that intake data show that most (but not all) clients presenting with either substance abuse or domestic violence problems at intake report that they have been living together for more than one year. The intake data show that only a handful of coupled clients are in new relationships of less than one year. Consequently, this characteristic of agency clients becomes a criterion to define the population, and consequently the sample, to be studied.

Once all of the sampling criteria are established, the committee must decide which particular sampling method to use. The aim is to select a sample that is representative (e.g., similar in age, race, marital status, and service history) of all clients who fit the eligibility criteria. Much more will be said about sampling in Chapter 13. After reviewing the literature and evaluating all of the logistics in relation to administering the measuring instruments, the committee members decide to administer them as follows:

**Protocol for administering the measuring instruments to a sample**
The SAQ and DVI will be administered to all partners living together for more than one year who are receiving social services from XYZ agency from July 1, 2022 to June 30, 2023. Both measuring instruments will be administered by the intake worker during the client's second visit to the agency.

## ADDRESSING ETHICAL AND CULTURAL ISSUES

As an ethical social work practitioner who adheres to the NASW *Code of Ethics*, you are aware that not one speck of data for the study will be collected until proper procedures have been developed and independently reviewed. After reading Chapters 5 and 6 of this text and Section 5 of the NASW *Code of Ethics*, the committee gets to work on developing proper consent forms and research protocols as well as obtaining all necessary ethics approvals. Remember you need to reread Chapters 5 and 6 and be sure to:

- Write the research participant consent form.
- Obtain written permission from your agency
- Obtain written approvals from appropriate institutional review boards (IRBs)

## COLLECTING THE DATA

At this point in the quantitative research process your study should be ethically and culturally sound. As discussed in Chapter 5, you can only collect data after you have obtained written consent from your research participants. Data collection is a step that indicates the study is underway.

There are many different methods of data collection available, and each has particular advantages and disadvantages. Continuing with our example, data collection involves administering the SAQ and DVI instruments to sampled partners who have been living together for more than one year.

Once the study is underway, the protocols established for data collection should be carried out precisely so as to avoid errors. Moreover, data-collection procedures should not be changed. If changes are necessary, then they must be approved by the ethical oversight bodies involved before those changes are implemented. Your committee's focus at this point is only to monitor that the study is being carried out as planned and to use research principles to troubleshoot any problems that arise.

## ANALYZING THE DATA

Gathering and analyzing your data is an exciting process because this is when you and your committee will get the answer to your hypothesis. Your committee members ensure that the data are properly entered into an appropriate computer program and analyzed. Chapter 18 discusses quantitative data analysis in detail. Your quantitative data analysis could be as simple as the following:

**Data analysis**
- There was a total of 200 couples in the study; 150 had domestic violence issues, and 50 did not.

- Of the 150 couples who had domestic violence issues, 85 percent of them had at least one partner also experiencing substance abuse issues.

## INTERPRETING THE DATA

Getting an answer to your hypothesis and deciding on the usefulness of the answer are two separate steps. The committee will go beyond the reported "facts," as stated above, and make a conclusive statement such as:

### Conclusion from the data analysis
Substance abuse and domestic violence are co-occurring problems for most clients served by the agency. Thus, social work practitioners must be skilled in treating both presenting problems.

## COMPARING RESULTS

As committee chair, you know that every research study is only a single piece in the puzzle of knowledge development. Consequently, you ask the committee to consider the findings of your study in the context of the other research studies that you reviewed, as well as any new studies published while your study was being done.

By contrasting your findings with what others have found, your committee builds on the existing knowledge base. Simply put, your findings need to be compared with what others have found. For example,

### Comparing your study's findings with findings from other studies
- The findings from this study are consistent with the findings from other studies; that is, domestic violence and substance abuse issues are highly related to one another.
- This study adds new knowledge by finding this relationship for couples that have been living together for more than one year.

## SPECIFYING THE STUDY'S LIMITATIONS

No research study is perfect, and that includes yours. Many study limitations are predetermined by the particular research design that was used. For example, threats to internal and external validity are limitations commonly discussed in research reports and journal articles (chapter 15).

Acknowledging your study's limitations can be a humbling experience. While you may be better informed at the conclusion of your study, completing one research study is not enough to alleviate your clients' struggles and suffering. The limitation section of your research report could read:

### Limitations of your study
- The limitations of this descriptive research design do not permit any inference of causation. We will never know if substance abuse causes domestic violence, or if domestic violence causes substance abuse.
- Also, we will never know how poverty and homelessness play a role in domestic violence and substance abuse since these two variables were not included in the study.

## DISSEMINATING THE STUDY'S RESULTS

A final, important step in the research process is sharing the new knowledge learned in your study. In the academic world, dissemination most often refers to publication of the study in a peer-reviewed journal. While some practitioners also publish in peer-reviewed journals, dissemination in the practice world more commonly refers to sharing findings at conferences or local meetings.

The idea of dissemination is to make your study's results available to others who are working in the same area—whether as practitioners, researchers, policymakers, or educators. As committee chair you want to share your study's results with others in your agency. The knowledge gained might be used to develop new procedures in the agency (e.g., intake, training, or referrals). Whatever the route of dissemination, the aim is to complete your research study with the highest level of integrity so that your results will be most useful to others.

Even with all the limitations of your study's research design, some data are better than none; that is, no matter how many threats to internal and external validity exist (chapter 15), as long as the study's procedures and limitations are clearly spelled out in the final report, your study's findings will be useful to others.

## EVALUATING QUANTITATIVE RESEARCH STUDIES

**A**ssessing the overall credibility and usefulness of a quantitative research study can be a daunting task at the best of times. Nevertheless, you can ask a series of questions contained in Appendix A. Many of the terms covered in the questions will be new to you and will be explained in forthcoming chapters. At this point in the book all we want you to do is glance over the questions contained in Appendix A.

### USE APPENDIX A

How to evaluate the overall creditability of a quantitative research study is totally up to you—and only you. You are the one who must ask and answer the questions in Appendix A (pages 474–494). More important, you need to address two extremely difficult tasks:

> Many of the questions we can ask about the overall integrity of quantitative studies can also be asked for qualitative ones as well. And vice versa.

1    You must have a rationale for why you're asking each question in the first place. Appendix A only lists potential questions you can ask. Can you guess why each one was listed and what importance your answer to each question has on your overall evaluation of the research study?

2    You also must have some kind of idea of what you're going to do with your answer to each question. For example, question 124 on page 483 asks, "Are the measuring instruments valid?" Let's say your answer was "no". What are you going to do with your answer? That is, how are you going to use it in your overall evaluation of the study's creditability? Now what about if your answer was "yes"?

Simply put: You need to evaluate the overall creditability and usefulness of all quantitative research studies you come across given the principles discussed in all of the chapters within this book.

## CHAPTER RECAP

- All the steps within the quantitative research approach are highly intertwined with one another.
- Concepts are nothing more than ideas.
- All variables have attributes.
- Attributes are nothing more than value labels we put on variables.

- Independent variables are what causes the dependent variables to change.
- Dependent variables are affected by independent variables.
- Some research studies have no independent and dependent variables.
- Hypotheses are cause-effect relationships

- between and among variables.
- Hypotheses can be evaluated in terms for their relevance, completeness, specificity, testability, in addition to their ethical and cultural sensitively.

- A hypothesis can be directional or nondirectional.
- Quantitative research studies usually use descriptive and/or inferential statistics.

## REVIEW EXERCISES

1   In your own words, describe the quantitative research process by using one common social work example throughout your discussion.

2   What are *concepts*? Provide a few social work examples of them.

3   What are *variables*? Provide a few social work examples of them.

4   What are the main differences between concepts and variables? Provide social work examples to illustrate your points.

5   What are *attributes* of variables? Provide social work examples to illustrate your points.

6   What are *independent variables*? What are *dependent variables*? What are the main differences between them? Provide social work examples to illustrate your points.

7   What are nondirectional hypotheses? Provide a few social work examples.

8   What are *directional hypotheses*? Provide a few social work examples.

9   What are the differences between nondirectional and directional hypotheses? Provide a common example in your answer.

### The quantitative approach and the researcher

10   **Scenario 1:** Make an argument that to be a competent social work researcher *you need to know* the fundamental principles of the quantitative (positivistic) research approach in addition to its advantages and disadvantages. Provide clear and explicit research-related social work examples to illustrate your main points.

11   **Scenario 2:** Make an argument that *you do not need to know* the fundamental principles of the quantitative (positivistic) research approach in addition to its advantages and disadvantages to be a competent social work researcher. Provide explicit research-related social work examples to illustrate your main points.

12   **Time to choose**: Which one of the previous two scenarios (question 10 or 11) do you feel is more consistent with the

place of research in social work? Why? Provide relevant social work examples to illustrate your main points.

### The quantitative approach and the practitioner

13   **Scenario 1:** Make an argument that to be an effective evidence-based social work practitioner *you need to know* the fundamental principles of the quantitative (positivistic) research approach in addition to its advantages and disadvantages. Provide clear and explicit practice-related social work examples to illustrate your main points.

14   **Scenario 2:** Make an argument that *you do not need to know* the fundamental principles of the quantitative (positivistic) research approach in addition to its advantages and disadvantages whatsoever to be an effective evidence-based social work practitioner. Provide clear and explicit practice-related social work examples to illustrate your main points.

15   **Time to choose:** Which one of the above two scenarios (question 13 or 14) do you feel is more consistent with the concept of the contemporary evidence-based social work practice process as illustrated on pages 46–51? Why? Provide relevant social work examples to illustrate your main points.

### Time to put on your critical thinking hat

16   Discuss the similarities and differences of your responses between questions 10 through 12 and between questions 13 through 15.

17   Locate a published quantitatively oriented social work research article that contains a social work problem area or population that you're interested in. We suggest you locate a quantitatively oriented research study in Bruce Thyer's journal *Research on Social Work Practice* (Sage Publications). Hands down, this is the best journal to find good quantitatively oriented social work research studies. Use your newfound article when discussing the exercises that follow in addition to Figure 7.1 on page 145.

**Use the above article (question 17) in answering the following questions (questions 18–24)**

**18** **Step 1** (pages 163–164 and chapter 2): Discuss how the author identified the general problem area (Step 1 of the quantitative research approach). Do you have a clear understanding of the study's problem area? Could the author have been clearer? Justify your response by citing specific examples within the article's problem area that could have been clearer.

**19** **Step 2** (pages 164–172): Describe in your own words how the author probably followed the eight substeps in Step 2 of the quantitative research approach. Due to journal space limitations, most authors do not describe the process they used within each of the eight substeps. Nevertheless, all researchers who do quantitative studies have to go through each substep in "one way or another."

Describe what you believe this "one way or another" was for each one of the eight substeps; that is, what do you think was going through the author's mind when addressing each substep? What specific questions within this step do you think the author should have asked—and answered—for the study to be successful?

**20** **Step 3** (pages 172–173): Hypothetically describe how the author could have addressed the three substeps in Step 3. What specific questions within this step do you think the author should have asked—and answered—for the study to be successful?

**21** **Step 4** (pages 173–174 and chapters 15 and 17). Once again, get inside the author's head and discuss what she must have been thinking about when deciding on a data collection method for the study (What specific questions within this step do you think the author should have asked—and answered—for the study to be successful?

**22** **Step 5** (pages 174–175 and chapter 18): You guessed it—it's time to do the same task as above only in relation to data analysis.

**23** **Step 6** (pages 175–176): Yup, once again, but this time pay particular attention to the how the author compared the results of her study with other studies.

**24** **Step 7** (page 176 and chapter 20): Nothing to do here since the author published the study you found at the beginning of this exercise—which is Step 7 of the quantitative research approach, dissemination of findings.

**Quantitative research and your professional development**

**25** Review the three social work research-related roles you can take when you graduate—CSWE Competency 1 at the beginning of this chapter on page 160 (also discussed in chapter 3 on pages 63–67). Thoroughly discuss how you feel this chapter will help you to perform one or more research-related roles when you graduate. Which one of the three roles do you believe this chapter helped you with the most? Why? Discuss in detail and provide an example to illustrate your main points.

**26** Review CSWE Competency 4 at the beginning of this chapter on page 160. Thoroughly discuss how you feel this chapter will help you to become a practice-informed researcher and a research-informed practitioner. Discuss in detail and provide an example to illustrate your main points.

**27** Review the evidence-based practice process as discussed in Chapter 3. Thoroughly discuss how this chapter helps you to develop the skills you'll need for implementing one or more steps of the evidence-based practice process as outlined in Box 3.2 on pages 70–71.

**Moving ahead by looking back**

**28** At this point in your research methods course, how comfortable are you with discussing the place of research in social work with your field instructor, with your practice instructor, with your research instructor, with your supervisor at work, with the director of your social work program, or with your classmates? Discuss in detail.

| COMPETENCY 1 | Demonstrate Ethical and Professional Behavior |
|---|---|

You will learn that in order to be a successful evidence-based practitioner you have an ethical obligation to integrate three research roles into your daily practice activities as discussed in Chapter 3: (1) research consumer, (2) research partner—either as a co-researcher or research participant, and (3) creator and disseminator of research (or knowledge).

This entire chapter pertains to these three professional roles because an ethical and professional evidence-based social work practitioner must understand and appreciate the advantages and disadvantages that are embedded within all three research approaches to knowledge development that produce social work practice recommendations: quantitative (Chapter 8), qualitative (this chapter), and mixed-methods (Chapter 10).

| COMPETENCY 4 | Engage in Practice-Informed Research and Research-Informed Practice |
|---|---|

Competency 4 also pertains to the entire chapter because you have to:

1  Evaluate the overall value of the practice recommendations that a qualitative (interpretive) research study puts forward by evaluating the kinds of qualitative evidence that it used to formulate its findings and practice recommendations (**research consumer**—research-informed practice);

2  Participate in a research study—either as a co-researcher or research participant (**research partner**—practice-informed research). See 1 above and 3 below; and

3  Understand and appreciate the advantages and disadvantages of using the qualitative research approach to knowledge building before you actually do a qualitative research study (**creator and disseminator of research**—practice-informed research).

You'll also need to utilize evidence-based practice recommendations whenever possible; that is, you need to integrate (1) the best available research-based evidence with (2) your clinical expertise and (3) your client's values.

All of the above implies you'll need to know how to assess the overall rigor of a qualitatively based research study that produced its qualitative research-based evidence. In short, you need to ask and then answer a simple question: How seriously should I take the findings of any specific qualitatively oriented research study given how well the study followed the interpretive way of thinking as thoroughly discussed in Chapter 7?

| COMPETENCY 9 | Evaluate Practice with Individuals, Families, Groups, Organizations, & Communities |
|---|---|

See Competencies 1 and 4.

# The Qualitative Research Approach

CHAPTERS 1 & 3        Step 1.  Understanding the Research Process

CHAPTER 2             Step 2.  Formulating Research Questions

CHAPTER 4            Step 3.  Reviewing the Literature
APPENDIXES A–C               Evaluating the Literature

CHAPTERS 5 & 6        Step 4.  Being Aware of Ethical and Cultural Issues

CHAPTERS 7–10        Step 5.  Selecting a Research Approach

CHAPTERS 11 & 12     Step 6.  Specifying How Variables Are Measured

CHAPTER 13           Step 7.  Selecting a Sample

CHAPTERS 14 & 15     Step 8.  Selecting a Research Design

CHAPTERS 16 & 17     Step 9.  Selecting a Data-Collection Method

CHAPTERS 18 & 19     Step 10.  Analyzing the Data

CHAPTERS 20 & 21     Step 11.  Writing the Research Report

# The Qualitative Research Approach

"Yes! I know you feel that the F in your qualitative research methods course stands for Fantastic, but in my quantifiable world, it's a big fat Zero."

QUANTITATIVE VERSES QUALITATIVE APPROACHES
PHASES OF THE QUALITATIVE RESEARCH APPROACH
    Phases 1 & 2: Problem Identification and Question Formulation
    Phase 3a: Designing the Research Study
    Phase 3b: Collecting the Data
    Phases 3c & 3d: Analyzing and Interpreting Data
        *Numbers versus Words*
        *Data ≠ Information*
    Phases 4 & 5: Presentation and Dissemination of Findings
COMPARING RESEARCH APPROACHES
ADVANTAGES AND DISADVANTAGES
EVALUATING QUALITATIVE RESEARCH STUDIES
    Use Appendix B
CHAPTER RECAP
REVIEW EXERCISES

As you know, **Chapter 7** discussed the underlying philosophies of three complementary research approaches embedded within the scientific method of inquiry: quantitative, qualitative, and mixed-methods. However, it did not present the processes that researchers go through when they actually carry out their respective studies. The process of actually doing a research study varies dramatically among the three research approaches.

Thus, building upon Chapter 7, this chapter briefly presents the general process in a step-by-step format of actually doing a research study using the qualitative research approach. Thus, it's important for you to have a sound understanding of the fundamental concepts in Chapters 7 and 8 before reading this chapter.

## QUANTITATIVE VERSUS QUALITATIVE APPROACHES

L**ike quantitative researchers,** qualitative researchers make a major commitment in terms of time, money, and resources when they undertake research studies. As can be seen in Figure 7.1 on page 145, a quantitative study has basic sequential steps that must be followed to produce useful quantitative data.

On the other hand, as can be seen in Figure 7.2 on page 149, a qualitative study does not have these specific steps—the activities are more phases than steps, as many of the phases highly interact with one another as the study progresses from one phase to the next. Look at how Phases 3a through 3d interact between and among one another. In short, they all are done at the same time. See the bold arrows between the dashed phases that show how Phases 3a–3d highly interact with one another.

> The qualitative research approach is akin to exploring a social problem maze that has multiple entry points and paths.

One of the major differences between the two research approaches is how they utilize the literature. In a quantitative study, the literature is utilized the most within the first three steps of the research process. In a qualitative study, the literature is heavily utilized in all of the phases.

You have no way of knowing whether the maze will lead you to a place of importance or not, but you enter into it out of your own curiosity and, perhaps, even conviction. You enter the maze without a map or a guide; you have only yourself to rely on and your notebook to record important events, observations, conversations, and impressions along the way.

You will begin your journey of qualitative inquiry by stepping into one entrance and forging ahead. You move cautiously forward, using all of your senses in an effort to pinpoint your location and what surrounds you at any one time. You may enter into dead-end rooms within the maze and have to backtrack. You may also encounter paths that you did not think possible. In some cases, you may even find a secret passageway that links you to a completely different maze.

## PHASES OF THE QUALITATIVE RESEARCH APPROACH

**Q**ualitative studies are generally inductive and require you to reason in such a way that you move from a part to a whole or from a particular instance to a general conclusion (see figure 1.2 on page 20). Let's return to the research problem introduced in the last chapter—racial discrimination within the social services. You begin the qualitative research process, once again, from your observations and/or hunches—ethnic minorities have the highest incidence of unemployment, poverty, and low education, but more Caucasians than ethnic minorities seek assistance from social services.

### PHASES 1 & 2: PROBLEM IDENTIFICATION AND QUESTION FORMULATION

You can focus your qualitative research question by identifying the key concepts in your question. These key concepts set the parameters of your research study—they represent the outside boundaries of your maze. As in the quantitative research approach, you would want to review the literature related to your key concepts, but your literature review would have a very different purpose.

Rather than pinpointing exact variables to study, you review the literature to see how your key concepts have been generally described and defined by previous researchers. You might learn whether your maze will have rounded or perpendicular corners, or whether it will have multiple levels.

The knowledge you glean from the literature search assists you with ways of thinking that you hope will help you move through the maze and arrive at a meaningful understanding of the problem it represents. However, you must also be prepared to abandon what you think you know and accept new experiences as you proceed. Let's revisit your research question:

**Research question**
Do ethnic minorities have difficulty in accessing social services?

In your literature review, you would want to focus on definitions and theories related to discrimination within the social services. In the quantitative research approach, you reviewed the literature to search for meaningful variables that could be measured. In the qualitative approach, however, you do not want to rely on the literature to define your key variables. Rather, you will rely upon the qualitative research process itself to identify key variables and how they relate to one another. Remember, the identification and refinement of these variables will be coming from your research participants.

On rare occasions, hypotheses can be used in a qualitative research study. They can focus your research question even further. A hypothesis in a qualitative study is less likely to be outright accepted or rejected, as is the case in a quantitative study. Rather, it's a working hypothesis and is refined over time as new data are collected.

Your hypothesis is changed throughout the qualitative research process based on the reasoning of the researcher, not on any statistical test. All of this leads us to ask the question, "What do qualitative researchers actually do when they carry out a research study?"

One of the major differences between the quantitative and qualitative research approaches is how they utilize the literature.

W. Lawrence Neuman and Karen Robson (2018) have outlined ten activities that a qualitative researcher engages in when carrying out a study:

1  Observes ordinary events and activities as they happen in natural settings, in addition to any unusual occurrences.

2  Is directly involved with the people being studied and personally experiences the process of daily social life in the field.

3  Acquires an insider's point of view while maintaining the analytic perspective or distance of an outsider.

4  Uses a variety of techniques and social skills in a flexible manner as the situation demands.

5  Produces data in the form of extensive written notes, as well as diagrams, maps, or pictures to provide detailed descriptions.

6  Sees events holistically (e.g., as a whole unit, not in pieces) and individually in their social context.

7  Understands and develops empathy for members in a field setting, and does not just record "cold" objective facts.

8  Notices both explicit and tacit aspects of culture.

9  Observes ongoing social processes without upsetting, disrupting, or imposing an outside point of view.

10  Is capable of coping with high levels of personal stress, uncertainty, ethical dilemmas, and ambiguity.

## PHASE 3A: DESIGNING THE RESEARCH STUDY

You can enter into a qualitative research study with general research questions or working hypotheses, but you are far less concerned about homing in on specific variables. Because qualitative research studies are inductive processes, you do not want to constrain yourself with preconceived ideas about how your concepts or variables will relate to one another.

> A qualitative study is aimed at obtaining an in-depth understanding of a few cases rather than a general understanding of many cases or people.

Thus, while you will have a list of key concepts, and perhaps loosely defined variables, you want to remain open to the possibilities of how they are defined by your research participants and any relationships that your research participants may draw. In short, your research participants will refine the variables as your study progresses.

Thus, more often than not, the number of research participants in a qualitative study is much smaller than in a quantitative one. As discussed in Chapter 13, you will probably want to use a purposeful sampling strategy to select your research participants. This process selects the "best-fitting" people to provide data for your study.

The qualitative research approach is about studying a social phenomenon within its natural context. As such, the *case study* is a major qualitative research design. A case can be *a* person, *a* group, *a* community, *an* organization, or *an* event. You can study many different types of social phenomena within any one of these cases. Any case study design can be guided by different qualitative research methods.

## PHASE 3B: COLLECTING THE DATA

Qualitative researchers are the principal instruments of data collection. This means that data collected are somehow "processed" through the person collecting them. Interviewing, for example, is a common data-collection method that produces text data (see chapter 16 on data collection). Data collection in the interview is interactive, so you can check out your understanding and interpretation of your participants' responses as you go along. To collect meaningful text data, you want to be immersed into the context or setting of the study.

You want to have some understanding, for example, of what it's like to be a client of a social service agency before you talk to clients about their experiences of discrimination, if any, within the social services. If you do not have a grasp of the setting in which you are about to participate, then you run the risk of misinterpreting what your research participants tell you.

Given that your general research question evolves in a qualitative study, the data collection process is particularly vulnerable to the biases of the data collector. There are three principles to guide you in your data collection efforts:

- **Make every effort to be aware of your own biases.** In fact, your own notes on reactions and biases to what you are studying will be used as sources of data later on, when you interpret the data (Chapter 19).
- **Data collection is a two-way street.** The research participants tell you their stories, and you tell them your understanding or interpretation of their stories. It's a process of checks and balances.
- **Qualitative data collection typically involves multiple data sources and multiple data-collection methods.** In your study, you may see clients, line-level social workers, and supervisors as potential data sources. You may collect data from each of these groups using interviews, observation, and existing documentation (data-collection methods).

> The qualitative research approach is about studying a social phenomenon within its natural context.

## PHASES 3C & 3D: ANALYZING AND INTERPRETING DATA

Collecting, analyzing, and interpreting qualitative data are highly intermingled. Let's say that, in your first round of data collection, you interview a number of ethnic minority clients about their perceptions of racial discrimination in the social services. Suppose they consistently tell you that to be a client of social services, they must give up many of their cultural values. You could then develop more specific research questions for a second round of interviews in an effort to gain a deeper understanding of the relationship between cultural values and being a social service client.

Overall, the process of analyzing qualitative data is an iterative one. This means that you must read and reread the volumes of data that you have collected. You will look for patterns and themes that help to capture how your research participants are experiencing the problem you are studying.

You want to explain meaning according to the beliefs and experiences of those who provided the data. The aim is for you to "walk the walk" and "talk the talk" of your research participants and not to impose "outside" meaning to the data they provided. Much more will be said about analyzing and interpreting qualitative data in Chapter 19.

> The ultimate goal is to interpret data in a way that reveals the true expressions of your research participants.

### NUMBERS VERSUS WORDS

The qualitative approach to knowledge development says that the only real way to find out about the subjective reality of our research participants is to ask them, and the answer will come back in words, not in numbers. More often than not, qualitative research approaches produce qualitative data in the form of text. Quantitative research methods produce quantitative data in the form of numbers.

### DATA ≠ INFORMATION

Let's pause for a moment to discuss what is meant by *data*. The word "data" is plural; the singular is "datum" (from the Latin dare, "to give"). A datum is thus something that is given, either from a quantitative observation and/or measurement or from a qualitative discussion with Ms. Smith about her experiences in giving birth at her home.

A number of observations and/or measurements with the quantitative approach, or a number of discussions with the qualitative approach constitute data. Data are not the same thing as information, although the two words are often used interchangeably. The most important thing to remember at this point is that both approaches to the research method produce data; they simply produce different kinds of data.

Information is something you hope to get from the data once you have analyzed them—whether they are numbers or words. You might, for example, collect data about the home-birthing experiences of a number of women, and your analysis might reveal commonalties between them: perhaps all the women felt that their partners had played a more meaningful role in the birthing process at home than would have been possible in a hospital setting: numbers or words.

> Information is something you hope to get from the data once you have analyzed them—whether they are numbers or words.

The enhanced role of the partner is information that you, as the researcher, have derived from the interview data. In other words, data are pieces of evidence in the form of words (qualitative data) or numbers (quantitative data) that you put together to give you information—which is what the scientific research method is all about.

So, in a nutshell, information is how you interpret the data. For example, if it's 86 degrees Fahrenheit outside, this is a fact measured by a thermometer. Someone who lives in Arizona may interpret this fact by saying it's "mild," while someone in Alaska may say it's "very hot." The interpretation of facts depends on one's individual reality. Information is nothing more than the subjective interpretation of objective facts.

## PHASES 4 & 5: PRESENTATION AND DISSEMINATION OF FINDINGS

Qualitative research reports are generally lengthier than quantitative ones. This is because it's not possible to strip the context of a qualitative study and present only its findings. The knowledge gained from a qualitative endeavor is nested within the context from which it was derived. Furthermore, text data are more awkward and clumsy to summarize than numerical data.

Unlike quantitative studies, you cannot rely on a simple figure or table to indicate a finding. Instead, you display text, usually in the form of quotes or summary notes, to support your conclusions. Much more will be said about the presentation and dissemination of the findings derived from qualitative research studies in Chapters 19 and 21.

## COMPARING RESEARCH APPROACHES

**B**y comparing the philosophical underpinnings of quantitative and qualitative research approaches you can more fully appreciate their important differences. Each approach offers you a unique method of studying a social work–related problem and the same research problem can be studied using either approach.

Suppose for a moment that you are interested in a broad social problem such as racial discrimination. In particular, let's say you are interested in studying the social problem of racial discrimination within public social service programs. Let's now look at the major differences, via their philosophical concepts, between the two approaches and see how a general research problem, racial discrimination, could be studied under both approaches.

Table 7.2, on page 152 compares how the two different research approaches could be used to examine the identical general problem area—racial discrimination within the public social service system. So far, we have been focusing on the differences between the two research approaches, but they also have many similarities. First, they both use careful and diligent research processes in an effort to discover and interpret knowledge. They both are guided by systematic procedures and orderly plans.

Second, both research approaches can be used to study any particular social problem. The quantitative approach is more effective than the qualitative approach in reaching a specific and precise understanding of one aspect (or part) of an already well-defined social problem. The quantitative approach seeks to answer research questions that ask about quantity, such as:

- Are women more depressed than men?
- Does the use of child sexual abuse investigation teams reduce the number of times an alleged victim is questioned by professionals?
- Is the degree of aggression related to the severity of crimes committed among inmates?

A qualitative research approach, on the other hand, aims to answer research questions that provide you with a more comprehensive understanding of a social problem from an intensive study of a few people. This approach is usually conducted within the context of the research participants' natural environments (Rubin & Babbie, 2017). Research questions for which the qualitative research approach would be appropriate might include:

- How do women experience depression as compared with men?
- How do professionals on child sexual abuse investigation teams work together to make decisions?
- How do federal inmates describe their own aggression in relation to the crimes they have committed?

As you will see throughout this book, both approaches can be used to study the same social problem—with different research questions, of course. Whichever approach is used clearly has an impact on the type of findings produced to answer a research question or to test a hypothesis.

## ADVANTAGES AND DISADVANTAGES

According to the Writing Center at Colorado State University (2019), the qualitative research approach has several advantages and disadvantages.

### Advantages
- It accounts for the complexity of group behaviors.
- It reveals interrelationships among multifaceted dimensions of group interactions.
- It provides context for behaviors.
- It reveals qualities of group experience in a way that other forms of research cannot.
- It helps determine questions and types of follow-up research.
- It reveals descriptions of behaviors in context by stepping outside the group.
- It allows qualitative researchers to identify recurring patterns of behavior that participants may be unable to recognize.

Qualitative research expands the range of knowledge and understanding of the world beyond ourselves. It often helps us see why something is the way it is, rather than just presenting a phenomenon. For instance, a quantitative study may find that students who are taught composition using a process method receive higher grades on papers than students taught using a product method. However, a qualitative study of composition instructors could reveal why many of them still use the product method even though they are aware of the benefits of the process method.

### Disadvantages

- Researcher bias can bias the design of a study.
- Researcher bias can enter into data collection.
- Sources or research participants may not all be equally credible.
- Some research participants may be previously influenced and affect the outcome of the study.
- Background information may be missing.
- The study group may not be representative of the larger population.
- The analysis of observations can be biased.
- Any group that is studied is altered to some degree by the very presence of the researcher. Therefore, any data collected are somewhat skewed.
- It takes time to build trust with research participants that facilitates full and honest self-representation. Short-term observational studies are at a particular disadvantage where trust building is concerned.
- The quality of the data alone is problematic. Ethnographic research is time-consuming, potentially expensive, and requires a well-trained researcher.
- Too few data can lead to false assumptions about behavior patterns. Conversely, a large quantity of data may not be effectively processed.
- The data collector's first impressions can bias data collection.
- Narrative inquiries do not lend themselves well to replicability and generalizability.
- Narrative inquiries are considered unreliable by experimentalists. However, ethnographies can be assessed and compared for certain variables to yield testable explanations; this is as close as ethnographic research gets to being empirical in nature.
- Qualitative research is neither prescriptive nor definite. While it provides significant data about groups or cultures and prompts new research questions, narrative studies do not attempt to answer questions, nor are they predictive of future behaviors.

## EVALUATING QUALITATIVE RESEARCH STUDIES

**A**ssessing the overall credibility and usefulness of a qualitative research study can be a daunting task at the best of times. Nevertheless, you can ask a series of questions in four general areas: (1) creditability, (2) transferability, (3) dependability, and (4) confirmability. Many of the terms covered in these areas will be new to you and will be explained when we discuss qualitative data analysis (chapter 19) qualitative report writing (chapter 21), and the criteria used in the evaluation of qualitative research studies (appendix B).

At this point in the book all we want you to do is glance over the four evaluative areas mentioned above so you can get a flavor of how qualitative research studies strive to be just as "objective and rigorous" as quantitative ones. The most overarching concept we need to consider when considering qualitative rigor is trustworthiness.

Trustworthiness ensures the quality of the study's findings and increases the reader's confidence in them. This requires that there be logical connections among the various

Many of the questions we can ask about the overall credibility of qualitative studies can also be asked for quantitative ones as well. And vice versa.

phases in the research process from the purpose of the study through to the analyses and interpretation (see figure 7.2 on page 149). The four highly overlapping components of a study's trustworthiness are:

1  **Credibility** is related to the "true" picture of the phenomenon being studied (See questions 405–419 on pages 504–505 in appendix B).

2  **Transferability** is related to whether the findings can be transferred to other situations. Transferability is ensured through adequate descriptions of the study's sample and setting in which the study took place (See questions 420–433 on pages 505–507 in appendix B).

3  **Dependability** relates to the consistency between the data and the findings (See questions 434–435 on page 507 in appendix B).

4  **Confirmability** involves the strategies used to limit bias in the research study, specifically the neutrality of the data not the researcher (See question 436 on page 507 in appendix B—note that there are a number of questions imbedded within this one question).

## USE APPENDIX B

How to evaluate the overall trustworthiness of a qualitative research study is totally up to you—and only you. You are the one who must ask and answer the questions in Appendix B (pages 495–510). More importantly, you need to address two extremely difficult tasks:

1  You must have a rationale for why you're asking each question in the first place. Appendix B only lists a few of the potential questions you can ask. Can you guess why each one was listed and what importance your answer to each question has on your overall evaluation of the research study?

2  You also must have some kind of idea of what you're going to do with your answer to each question. For example, question 385 on page 503 asks, "Are strategies used to improve dependability?" Let's say your answer was "no". What are you going to do with your answer? That is, how are you going to use it in your overall evaluation of the study's trustworthiness? Now what about if your answer was "yes"?

> Two people can assess the same research study and come up with two different opinions in respect to its overall trustworthiness.

---

## CHAPTER RECAP

- The qualitative research approach complements the quantitative research approach.

- The qualitative research approach has phases where the quantitative research approach has steps.

- The qualitative research approach usually analyzes words, diagrams, illustrations, pictures, and stories.

- Valid and reliable data are facts.

- Information is how we interpret the facts.

- The qualitative research approach usually utilizes the literature more than the quantitative research approach.

- In a quantitative study, the literature is utilized the most within the first three steps of the research process. In a qualitative study, the literature is heavily utilized in all of the phases.

---

## REVIEW EXERCISES

1  Discuss the qualitative (this chapter) way of thinking. Now discuss the quantitative (chapter 8) way of thinking. Compare and contrast the two ways of thinking using one common social work example.

2  What kind of data do positivistic research studies produce? What kind of data do interpretive research studies produce?

Provide specific social work examples for each research approach.

3 How many realities do positivistic researchers believe to exist? How many realities do interpretive researchers believe to exist? Compare and contrast their differential perceptions of realities. Use as many social work examples that you can think of to illustrate your points.

4 Discuss the differential roles that research participants play within quantitative and qualitative research studies. Provide examples to illustrate your points.

5 Discuss the differences between *data* and *information*. Use a social work example throughout your discussion.

6 Discuss the commonalities in all qualitative research studies.

7 List, discuss, and provide specific social work examples of all the phases within the qualitative research approach.

**Critical Thinking—Application—Integration Exercises**

8 Locate a published qualitatively oriented social work research article that contains a social work problem area or population that you're interested in. We suggest you locate a qualitatively oriented research study in Karen Staller and Karen Broadhurst's journal *Qualitative Social Work* (Sage Publications). Hands down, this is the best journal to find good qualitative social work research studies. Use your newfound article when discussing exercises 9–13 in addition to all the preceding chapters in this book.

9 **Phases 1 and 2** (pages 188–189): Using the book's content when discussing this phase in relation to *problem identification and question formulation*, list and discuss the specific questions you think the author should have asked—and answered—for the study to be successful.

10 **Phase 3a** (page 189): Using the book's content when discussing this phase in relation to *designing the research study*, list and then discuss the specific questions you think the author should have asked—and answered—for the study to be successful.

11 **Phase 3b** (pages 189–190 and chapters 16–17): Using the book's content when discussing this phase in relation to *collecting data*, list and discuss the specific

questions you think the author should have asked—and answered—for the study to be successful.

12 **Phase 3c and 3d** (pages 190–191 and chapter 19): Using the book's content when discussing this phase in relation to *analyzing and interpreting qualitative data*, list and discuss the specific questions you think the author should have asked—and answered—for the study to be successful.

13 **Phases 4 and 5** (page 191 and chapter 21): Using the book's content when discussing this phase in relation to *disseminating the study's findings*, list and discuss the specific questions you think the author should have asked—and answered—for the study to be successfully published.

**Qualitative research and your professional development**

14 Review the three social work research-related roles you can take when you graduate—CSWE Competency 4 at the beginning of this chapter on page 184 (also discussed in Chapter 3 on pages 63–67). Thoroughly discuss how you feel this chapter will help you to perform one or more research-related roles when you graduate. Which one of the three roles do you believe this chapter helped you with the most? Why? Discuss in detail and provide an example to illustrate your main points.

15 Review the evidence-based practice process as illustrated on pages 68–72. Thoroughly discuss how this chapter helps you to develop the skills you'll need for implementing one or more steps of the evidence-based practice process. Discuss which step(s) you feel this chapter will help you with the most. Why? Be very specific and use relevant social work examples to illustrate your main points throughout your discussion.

**Moving ahead by looking back**

16 At this point in your research methods course, how comfortable are you with discussing the place of research in social work with your field instructor, with your practice instructor, with your research instructor, with your supervisor at work, with the director of your social work program, or with your classmates.

## 2015 EPAS COMPETENCIES

| COMPETENCY 1 | Demonstrate Ethical and Professional Behavior |
| --- | --- |

You will learn that in order to be a successful evidence-based practitioner you have an ethical obligation to integrate three research roles into your daily practice activities as discussed in Chapter 3: (1) research consumer, (2) research partner—either as a co-researcher or research participant, and (3) creator and disseminator of research (or knowledge).

This entire chapter pertains to these three professional roles because an ethical and professional evidence-based social work practitioner must understand and appreciate the advantages and disadvantages that are embedded within all three research approaches to knowledge development that produce social work practice recommendations: quantitative (Chapter 8), qualitative (Chapter 9), and mixed-methods (this chapter).

| COMPETENCY 4 | Engage in Practice-Informed Research and Research-Informed Practice |
| --- | --- |

Competency 4 also pertains to the entire chapter because you have to:

1  Evaluate the overall value of the practice recommendations that a mixed-method research study puts forward by evaluating the kinds of mixed-method evidence that it used to formulate its findings and practice recommendations (**research consumer**—research-informed practice);

2  Participate in a research study—either as a co-researcher or research participant (**research partner**—practice-informed research). See 1 above and 3 below; and

3  Understand and appreciate the advantages and disadvantages of using the mixed-methods research approach to knowledge building before you actually do a mixed-methods research study (**creator and disseminator of research**—practice-informed research).

You'll also need to utilize evidence-based practice recommendations whenever possible; that is, you need to integrate (1) the best available research-based evidence with (2) your clinical expertise and (3) your client's values

All of the above implies you'll need to know how to assess the overall rigor of a mixed-methods research study that produced its mixed-methods research-based evidence (see Appendixes A and B). In short, you need to ask and then answer a simple question: How seriously should I take the findings of any specific mixed-methods research study given how well the study followed the positivist and interpretive ways of knowing, as discussed in Chapter 7?

| COMPETENCY 9 | Evaluate Practice with Individuals, Families, Groups, Organizations, & Communities |
| --- | --- |

See Competencies 1 and 4.

# The Mixed-Methods Research Approach

| | | |
|---|---|---|
| CHAPTERS 1 & 3 | Step 1. | Understanding the Research Process |
| CHAPTER 2 | Step 2. | Formulating Research Questions |
| CHAPTER 4 APPENDIXES A–C | Step 3. | Reviewing the Literature Evaluating the Literature |
| CHAPTERS 5 & 6 | Step 4. | Being Aware of Ethical and Cultural Issues |
| CHAPTERS 7–10 | Step 5. | Selecting a Research Approach |
| CHAPTERS 11 & 12 | Step 6. | Specifying How Variables Are Measured |
| CHAPTER 13 | Step 7. | Selecting a Sample |
| CHAPTERS 14 & 15 | Step 8. | Selecting a Research Design |
| CHAPTERS 16 & 17 | Step 9. | Selecting a Data-Collection Method |
| CHAPTERS 18 & 19 | Step 10. | Analyzing the Data |
| CHAPTERS 20 & 21 | Step 11. | Writing the Research Report |

# The Mixed-Methods Research Approach

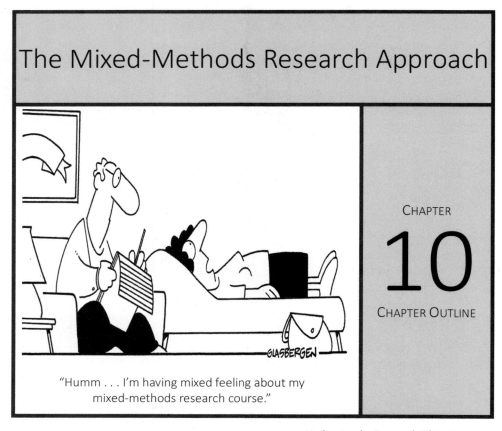

"Humm . . . I'm having mixed feeling about my mixed-methods research course."

POPULARITY OF THE APPROACH
    An Intuitive Research Method
    An Accessible Approach to Scientific Inquiry
RESEARCH PROBLEMS AND MIXED METHODS
    One Data Source May Be Insufficient
        *Example*
    Explain a Study's Initial Results
        *Example*
    Generalize Exploratory Findings
        *Example*
    Enhance a Study
        *Example*
    Employ a Theoretical Stance
        *Example*

    Understand a Research Objective
        *Example*
ADVANTAGES
CHALLENGES
    Skills of the Researcher
        *Quantitative Skills*
        *Qualitative Skills*
        *Solid Grounding in Mixed-Methods Research*
    Time and Resources
CONVINCING OTHERS
FINDING MIXED-METHODS RESEARCH STUDIES
CHAPTER RECAP
REVIEW EXERCISES

As you know, Chapter 7 discussed the underlying philosophies of three complementary research approaches embedded within the scientific method of inquiry: quantitative, qualitative, and mixed-methods. However, it did not present the processes that researchers go through when they actually carry out their respective studies. The process of actually doing a research study varies dramatically among the three research approaches.

Thus, building upon the previous three chapters, this chapter presents numerous examples of how the mixed-methods research approach utilizes both quantitative and qualitative data within a single research study. Thus, it's important for you to have a sound understanding of the fundamental concepts contained in the previous two chapters (i.e., chapter 8 on quantitative research and chapter 9 on qualitative research) before reading further.

As presented in Table 7.1 on pages 142–144, the scientific method contains three types of research approaches to answer our research questions or to test our hypotheses—the quantitative approach (sometimes called *positivistic*) and the qualitative approach (sometimes called *interpretive*).

With a little forethought you can easily combine both research approaches into a single study. When this is done the third research approach is called the *mixed-methods research approach*. Mixed-methods research studies involve carefully integrating both the quantitative and qualitative approaches into a single study.

## POPULARITY OF THE APPROACH

**Why are researchers** drawn to the mixed-methods research approach? Its popularity can be easily documented through journal articles, conference proceedings, books, and the formation of special interest groups (Creswell, 2010; Plano Clark, 2010). The mixed-methods research approach has been called:

- The "third methodological movement" following the developments of the first quantitative (positivistic) and then qualitative (interpretive) research approach (Tashakkori & Teddlie, 2003, 5),
- The "third research paradigm" (Johnson & Onwuegbuzie, 2004, 15), and
- "A new star in the social science sky" (Mayring, 2007, 1).

## AN INTUITIVE RESEARCH METHOD

Why does this approach merit such superlatives? One answer is that it's an intuitive way of doing a research study that we use in our everyday lives. Consider for a moment *An Inconvenient Truth* (2006), the award-winning documentary on global warming featuring the former U.S. Vice President and Nobel Prize winner Al Gore.

In Gore's documentary, he narrated both the statistical trends (quantitative) and the stories (qualitative) of his personal journey related to the changing climate and global warming. His documentary brings together both quantitative data (derived from the positivistic point of view) and qualitative data (derived from the interpretive point of view) to tell a single story.

Also, listen closely to CNN's broadcast reports about President Trump's asinine tweets, immigration, hurricanes, tornadoes, Russia, China, North Korea, global warming, tidal waves, forest fires, gun laws, voting rights, budget hearings, or financial bailouts. The "trends" uncovered using quantitative data-collection techniques (e.g., standard measuring instruments such as thermometers for global warming topics) are supported by the individual stories collected using qualitative techniques (e.g., qualitative interviews, subjective observations).

Or listen to commentators at sporting events. There's often a play-by-play commentator who describes the somewhat linear unfolding of the game (a positivistic perspective, if you will) and then the additional commentary by the "color" announcer who tells us about the individual stories and highlights of the personnel on the playing field (from an interpretive point of view, if you will). Again, both quantitative and qualitative data come together in these broadcasts.

In these instances, we see mixed-methods thinking in ways that Jennifer Greene (2007) called the "multiple ways of seeing and hearing." These multiple ways are visible in everyday life, and the mixed-methods research approach becomes a natural outlet for many, but not all, research studies.

## AN ACCESSIBLE APPROACH TO SCIENTIFIC INQUIRY

But other factors also contribute to the ever-growing interest in mixed-methods research. We now fully recognize it as an accessible approach to the scientific inquiry process (see figure 1.1 on page 18). Many researchers have research questions (or problems) that can best be answered using mixed-methods approaches, and they see the value of using them (as well as the challenges they pose).

Understanding the nature of the mixed-methods research approach is an important first step to actually using it in a research study. Thus, this chapter reviews several preliminary considerations necessary before you can design a mixed-methods study. We are assuming you have mastered the content in the previous three chapters.

## RESEARCH PROBLEMS AND MIXED METHODS

**W**hen preparing a research study employing the mixed-methods approach, we need to provide a justification for its use. Not all research questions justify the use of a mixed-methods approach, just as not all situations justify the use of either the quantitative or the qualitative approach.

There might be times, however, when the qualitative approach is indeed the best approach to use, such as when we wish to explore a problem, honor the voices of our research participants, map the complexity of the situation, or convey multiple perspectives from our research participants. At other times, the quantitative research approach might be best, because we may seek to understand the relationship among variables or to determine if one group performs better on an outcome variable than another group.

We suggest that you formulate a good meaningful research question first, and then and only then, proceed to select the research approach that best answers the research question. Never the other way around; that is, selecting a research approach first and then formulating a research question that can be answered by your predetermined research approach. Think of it this way: Research questions precede research approaches.

For example, we may find that a mailed survey best fits a quantitative approach because of the need to understand the views of a large number of participants within an entire population. An experiment may also work best when we need to determine whether a treatment works better than a control condition. Likewise, ethnography may best fit a qualitative approach because of the need to understand how culture-sharing groups work. What situations, then, warrant an approach that thoughtfully and systematically combines quantitative and qualitative research methodologies—a mixed-methods inquiry? Research problems suited for mixed-methods approaches are those in which:

1   One data source may be insufficient.

2   Results need to be explained.

3   Exploratory findings need to be generalized.

4   A second method is needed to enhance a primary method.

5   A theoretical stance needs to be employed.

6   An overall research objective can be best addressed with multiple phases or projects.

## ONE DATA SOURCE MAY BE INSUFFICIENT

Qualitative data can provide a detailed understanding of a problem while quantitative data can provide a more general understanding of a problem. This qualitative understanding arises out of studying a few individuals and exploring their perspectives in great depth whereas the quantitative understanding arises from examining a large number of people and assessing responses to a few variables. The limitations of one approach can be offset by the strengths of the other, and the combination of quantitative and qualitative data can provide a more complete understanding of the research problem than either approach by itself.

There are several ways in which one data source (who generated the data) may be inadequate. One type of data may not tell the complete story, or we may lack confidence in the ability of one type of data to fully answer the research question. The results from the quantitative and qualitative data may be contradictory, which could not be known by collecting only one type of data. Further, the type of evidence gathered from one level in an organization might differ from evidence obtained from other levels. These are all situations in which using only one approach to address the research problem would be insufficient. A mixed-methods design best fits this kind of scenario.

### EXAMPLE

When John Knodel and Chanpen Saengtienchai (2005) studied the role that older-aged parents play in the care and support of adult sons and daughters with HIV and AIDS and AIDS orphans in Thailand, they collected both quantitative survey data and qualitative open-ended interview data. They explained that they used both forms of data to understand the problem because quantitative data alone would be inadequate:

> The issues [in the interviews] covered were similar to the AIDS parents survey, but the conversational nature of the interview and the fact it allowed open-ended

responses provided parents the opportunity to elaborate on the issues and the circumstances affecting them. (670)

## EXPLAIN A STUDY'S INITIAL RESULTS

Sometimes the results of a study may provide an incomplete understanding of a research problem and further explanation is needed. In this case, a mixed-methods study is used with the second database helping to explain the first database. A typical situation is when the meaning of quantitative results requires an explanation. Quantitative results can easily provide general explanations for the relationships among variables, but the more detailed understanding of what the statistical tests or effect sizes actually mean is lacking. Qualitative data and results can help build that understanding.

### EXAMPLE

Stevan Weine and colleagues (2005) conducted a mixed-methods study investigating family factors and processes involved in Bosnian refugees participating in multiple-family support and education groups in Chicago. The first quantitative phase of their study addressed the factors that predicted engagement in the groups, while the second qualitative phase consisted of interviews with family members to assess the family processes involved in engagement as multiple-family groups. The researchers' rationale for using a mixed-methods design to study this situation was as follows:

> Quantitative analysis addressed the factors that predicted engagement. In order to better understand the processes by which families experience engagement, we conducted a qualitative content analysis to gain additional insight. (560)

## GENERALIZE EXPLORATORY FINDINGS

In some research projects, the investigators may not know the questions that need to be asked, the variables that need to be measured, and the theories that may guide the study. These unknowns may be due to the specific remote population being studied (e.g., Native Americans in Alaska) or the novelty of the research topic. In these situations, it's best to explore qualitatively to learn what questions, variables, theories, and so forth need to be studied and then follow up with a quantitative study to generalize and test what was learned from the exploration. A mixed-methods project is ideal in these situations. In a nutshell, we can easily begin a study with a qualitative phase in order to explore and then follow up with a quantitative phase to test whether the qualitative results generalize.

### EXAMPLE

Jean Kutner and colleagues (1999) studied issues important to terminally ill patients. Their study began with qualitative data generated via one-on-one interviews, and this information was used to develop a quantitative measuring instrument that was administered to a second sample of terminally ill patients to test whether the identified issues varied by demographic characteristics:

> The use of initial open-ended interviews to explore the important issues allowed us to formulate relevant questions and discover what were truly concerns to this population. (1350)

## ENHANCE A STUDY

In some situations, a second research approach can be added to the study to provide an enhanced understanding of some phase of the research project. For example, we can enhance a quantitative design (e.g., experiment, correlational study) by adding qualitative data or by adding quantitative data to a qualitative design (e.g., grounded theory, case study). In both of these cases, a second approach is embedded, or nested, within a primary approach. The embedding of qualitative data within a quantitative study is typical.

### EXAMPLE

Jenny Donovan and colleagues (2002) conducted an experimental trial comparing the outcomes for three groups of men with prostate cancer who were receiving different treatment procedures. They began their study, however, with a qualitative component in which they interviewed the men to determine how best to recruit them into the study (e.g., how best to organize and present the information) because all the men had received abnormal results and sought the best treatment. Toward the end of their article they reflected on the value of this preliminary, smaller, qualitative component used to design procedures for recruiting individuals to the study:

> We showed that the integration of qualitative research methods allowed us to understand the recruitment process and elucidate the changes necessary to the content and delivery of information to maximize recruitment and ensure effective and efficient conduct of the study. (768)

## EMPLOY A THEORETICAL STANCE

A situation may exist in which a theoretical perspective provides a framework for the need to gather both quantitative and qualitative data in a mixed-methods study. The data might be gathered at the same time or in a sequence, with one form of data building on the other. The theoretical perspective could seek to bring about change or simply provide a lens through which the entire study might be viewed.

### EXAMPLE

Christopher Fries (2009) conducted a study using Bourdieu's reflexive sociology ("the interplay of objective social structure with subjective agency in social behavior," 327) as a theoretical lens for gathering both quantitative and qualitative data in the use of complementary and alternative medicine. He gathered survey and interview data in the first phase, analyzed statistical population health data in the second phase, and analyzed interview data in the third phase. Fries concluded that:

> This study has presented a case study from the sociology of alternative medicine to show how reflexive sociology might provide a theoretical basis for mixed-methods research oriented toward understanding the interplay of structure and agency in social behavior. (345)

## UNDERSTAND A RESEARCH OBJECTIVE

In research projects that span several years and have many components, such as program evaluation studies and multiyear health investigations, we may need to connect several studies to reach an overall objective. These studies may involve projects that gather both quantitative and qualitative data simultaneously or sequentially. These types of studies are called multiphase or multiproject mixed-methods studies and often involve teams of researchers working together over many phases of the project.

### EXAMPLE

Genevieve Ames and colleagues (2009) conducted a multiphase study of the drinking patterns of young U.S. Navy recruits during their first three years of military service. They conducted a study over a five-year period and gathered data to develop a measuring instrument in one phase, to modify their model in another phase, and to analyze their data through a final phase. The researchers presented a figure depicting the phases of their study over the five years and introduced the implementation sequence in this way:

The complexity of the resulting research design, consisting of both longitudinal survey data collection with a highly mobile population coupled with qualitative interviewing in diverse settings, required the formation of a methodologically diverse research team and a clear delineation of the temporal sequence by which qualitative and quantitative findings would be used to inform and enrich one another. (130)

The preceding scenarios illustrate situations in which the mixed-methods approach fits the problems under study. They also begin to lay the groundwork for understanding the designs of mixed-methods approaches and the reasons the authors cite for undertaking them. Although in each example we cite only a single reason for using the mixed-methods approach, many authors cite multiple reasons, and we recommend that aspiring (and experienced) researchers begin to take note of the rationales that authors provide for using mixed-methods approaches.

# ADVANTAGES

Understanding the nature of the mixed-methods research approach involves more than knowing its definition and when it should be used. We also need to know the advantages of using it so that we can convince others of its value.

Mixed-methods research provides strengths that offset the weaknesses of both the quantitative and qualitative approaches. This has been the historical argument for mixed-methods research for more than thirty years (e.g., Jick, 1979). One might argue that the quantitative approach is weak in understanding the context or setting in which people talk, and the voices of research participants are not directly heard in a quantitative study. Further, quantitative researchers remain in the background, and their biases and interpretations are seldom discussed.

The qualitative research approach makes up for these weaknesses, but it is seen as deficient because of the personal interpretations made by the researchers and the ensuing bias that is generated, and the difficulty in generalizing findings to a large group because of the limited number of participants studied. The quantitative approach does not have these weaknesses. Thus, the strengths of one approach make up for the weaknesses of the other.

Mixed-methods research provides more evidence for studying a research problem than either the quantitative or the qualitative approach alone. Researchers are able to use all the data-collection tools available rather than only the strategies typically associated with either the positivistic (quantitative) or the interpretive (qualitative) research traditions. In a nutshell, mixed-methods approaches help answer questions that cannot be answered solely by the quantitative or the qualitative approach alone.

For example, "Do participant views from interviews and from standardized measuring instruments converge or diverge?" is a mixed-methods question. Others would be, "In what ways do qualitative interviews explain the quantitative results of a study?" (using qualitative data to explain the quantitative results) and "How can a treatment be adapted to work with a particular sample in an experiment?" (exploring qualitatively before an experiment begins). To answer these questions, neither a quantitative nor a qualitative approach by itself would provide a satisfactory answer. Mixed-methods provides a bridge between the quantitative and qualitative research approaches.

We are social, behavioral, and human sciences researchers first, and divisions between quantitative and qualitative research only serve to narrow the approaches and the opportunities for collaboration. The mixed-methods approach encourages the use of multiple worldviews or paradigms (i.e., beliefs, values) rather than those typically associated with either the positivistic tradition or the interpretive tradition.

It also encourages us to think about a paradigm that might encompass all of the quantitative and qualitative approaches, such as pragmatism. Mixed-methods approaches are practical in the sense that researchers are free to use all methods possible to address various research problems.

They are also practical because individuals tend to solve problems using both numbers and words, combine inductive and deductive thinking, and employ skills in observing people as well as recording behavior. It's natural, then, for individuals to employ mixed-methods approaches as preferred modes for understanding the real social world.

## CHALLENGES

The **mixed-methods research approach** is not the answer for every researcher or for every research situation or problem. Some studies are best done using either quantitative or qualitative methods alone. The mixed-methods approach requires certain skills, time, and resources for extensive data collection and analysis. Researchers may need to explain why they used a mixed-methods design so that our scholarly community will accept the study. There are two major issues that need to be addressed before doing a mixed-methods research study:

1  Skills of the researcher
2  Time and resources

### SKILLS OF THE RESEARCHER

The mixed-methods research approach is realistic for a research study if the researcher has the requisite skills. We strongly recommend that researchers first gain experience with both the quantitative approach (chapters 7 and 8) and the qualitative approach (chapters 7 and 9) separately before undertaking a mixed-methods study. At a minimum, we should be acquainted with both quantitative and qualitative data collection (chapters 16 and 17) and analysis (chapters 18 and 19) procedures. Given the preceding discussion mixed-methods researchers have to have the following three skills:

1  Quantitative research skills
2  Qualitative skills research skills
3  Solid grounding in mixed-methods research

#### QUANTITATIVE SKILLS

Mixed-methods researchers should be familiar with common methods of collecting quantitative data, such as using standardized measurement instruments and closed-ended attitudinal scales. You will need an awareness of the logic of hypothesis testing and the ability to use and interpret statistical analyses, including common descriptive and inferential procedures available in statistical software packages. Finally, you will need to understand essential issues of rigor in quantitative research studies, including reliability, validity, experimental control, and generalizability. Quantitative data analysis is discussed in-depth in Chapter 18.

#### QUALITATIVE SKILLS

A similar set of qualitative research skills is necessary. You should be able to identify the central phenomenon of your study; to pose qualitative, meaning-oriented research questions; and to consider research participants as the experts. You should be familiar with common methods of collecting qualitative data, such as semistructured interviews using open-ended questions (chapter 16) and qualitative observations.

You'll also need basic skills in analyzing qualitative text data, including coding text and developing themes and descriptions based on these codes, and should be acquainted with various qualitative data-analysis software packages. Finally, it's important that you understand essential issues of persuasiveness in qualitative research, including credibility, trustworthiness, and common validation strategies. Qualitative data analysis is discussed in depth in Chapter 19.

### SOLID GROUNDING IN MIXED-METHODS RESEARCH

Finally, those undertaking this approach to answer a research question should have a solid grounding in mixed-methods research. This requires reading the literature on mixed-methods that has accumulated since the late 1980s and noting the best procedures and the latest techniques for conducting a good inquiry. It may also mean taking courses in mixed-methods research, which are beginning to appear both online and in residence on many campuses. It may mean apprenticing with someone familiar with doing mixed-methods studies who can provide an understanding of the skills involved in conducting this form of scientific inquiry.

## TIME AND RESOURCES

Even when you have these basic quantitative and qualitative research skills, you should ask yourself if a mixed-methods approach is feasible, given your time frame and resources. These are important issues to consider early in the planning stage. Your study may require extensive time, resources, and effort. You'll need to consider the following questions:

1. Is there sufficient time to collect and analyze two different types of data?
2. Are there sufficient resources to collect and analyze both types of data?
3. Do I have the skills to complete this study?

In answering these questions, you'll need to consider how long it will take to gain approval for your study, to gain access to your research participants, and to complete the data collection and analysis. You will also need to keep in mind that qualitative data collection and analysis often require more time than that needed for quantitative data. The length of time required for a mixed-methods study also depends on whether your study will be using a one-phase, two-phase, or multiphase design. You'll also need to think about the expenses that will be part of your study. These expenses may include, for example, printing costs for measuring instruments, recording and transcription costs for interviews, cost for data analyses, and costs for software programs.

Because of the increased demands associated with mixed-methods designs, you should consider working in a team. Teams bring together individuals with diverse methodological and content expertise and involve more personnel in the mixed-methods project. Working within a team setting, however, can be challenging and can easily increase the costs associated with your research project.

In addition, individuals with the necessary skills need to be located, and team leaders need to create and maintain a successful collaboration among all team members. However, the diversity of a team may be a strength because the members will represent different specialties and content areas.

## CONVINCING OTHERS

**M**ixed-methods research studies are relatively new in terms of the methodologies available to social work researchers. As such, others may not be convinced of or understand the value of their use. Some may see it as a "new" approach. Others may feel that they do not have time to learn this new approach, and some may object to the use of mixed methods on philosophical grounds regarding the mixing of different philosophical positions (see table 7.2 on pages 142–144). Still others might be so entrenched in their own methods and approaches to research that they might not be open to the possibility of there being another approach to knowledge generation.

One way to help convince others of the utility of the mixed-methods approach is to locate exemplary mixed-methods studies in the literature on a topic or in a content area and share these studies with others in an effort to educate them. These studies can be selected from prestigious journals with national and international reputations.

## FINDING MIXED-METHODS RESEARCH STUDIES

**H**ow do you find these mixed-methods studies? They can be difficult to locate in the literature because only recently have researchers begun to use the term "mixed-methods" in their titles or in their articles. Also, some disciplines may use different terms for naming this research approach. Based on our extensive work with the literature, we have developed a short list of terms that you can use to search for mixed-methods studies within electronic databases and journal archives. These four terms are:

1  mixed method* (where * is a wildcard that will allow hits for "mixed method," "mixed methods," and "mixed methodology")
2  quantitative AND qualitative
3  multimethod
4  survey AND interview

Note that the second search term uses the logic operator AND (i.e., quantitative AND qualitative). This requires that both words appear in the document so it will satisfy the search criteria. If you find too many articles try limiting your search so that the terms must appear within the abstract or restricting it to recent years. If not enough articles result, try searching for combinations of common data-collection techniques, such as "survey AND interview."

By using these strategies, you may locate a few good examples of mixed-methods studies that illustrate the core characteristics introduced in this chapter. Sharing these examples with stakeholders can be helpful when convincing them of the utility and feasibility of a mixed-methods approach.

## CHAPTER RECAP

- A mixed-methods research study is an intuitive research method.

- Mixed-methods research studies are very popular among social work researchers.

- Research problems suited for mixed-methods research approaches are those in which one data source may be insufficient, results need to be explained, exploratory findings need to be generalized, a second method is needed to enhance a primary method, a theoretical stance needs to be employed, or an overall research objective can be best addressed with multiple phases or projects.

- Mixed-methods research provides strengths that offset the weaknesses of both the quantitative and qualitative approaches. Mixed-methods research provides more evidence for studying a research problem than either the quantitative or the qualitative approach alone.

- Mixed-methods provides a bridge across the sometimes adversarial divide between quantitative and qualitative researchers.

- Mixed-methods approaches are practical in the sense that researchers are free to use all methods possible to address various research problems.

- Mixed-methods research studies are far more expensive than quantitative and qualitative ones because they use both approaches in a single study.

- Mixed-methods research studies require researchers to know how to do quantitative and qualitative studies.

## REVIEW EXERCISES

1   Discuss the *qualitative* (interpretive) way of thinking. Discuss the *quantitative* (positivistic) way of thinking. Discuss the rationale of why a research study—if at all possible—should contain both research approaches in a single research study. Use one common social work example throughout your discussion to illustrate your main points.

2   There are six situations for which a mixed-methods research approach is better to use than only a quantitative research approach or only a qualitative research approach. List all six and provide a hypothetical social work example in relation to how a mixed-methods research approach is better suited for each type of study than using either only a quantitative approach or only a qualitative approach.

3   Doing a mixed-methods research study requires specific skills, time, and resources. List and thoroughly discuss each one.

Provide a social work example of each in your discussion.

4   Discuss why the mixed-methods research approach is an "accessible approach" to scientific inquiry. Provide as many social work examples as you can to illustrate your main points.

5   Discuss why it is not advisable to select one of the three research approaches *before* formulating your research question.

6   With the above question in mind, discuss why you need to formulate your research question before you select a research approach to answer it. Provide as many social work examples as you can to illustrate your main points.

7   With respect to the above question, list the specific skills you would need to do a quantitative study, a qualitative study, and a mixed-methods study. Do you have them? If not, how will you get them?

# PART III

# MEASURING VARIABLES

**CHAPTER 11:** Measurement  **210**

**CHAPTER 12:** Measuring Instruments  **234**

## 2015 EPAS COMPETENCIES

| COMPETENCY 1 | Demonstrate Ethical and Professional Behavior |
| --- | --- |

You will learn that in order to be a successful evidence-based practitioner you have an ethical obligation to integrate three research roles into your daily practice activities as discussed in Chapter 3: (1) research consumer, (2) research partner—either as a co-researcher or research participant, and (3) creator and disseminator of research (or knowledge).

This entire chapter pertains to these three professional roles when it comes to the process of determining the validity and reliability of measuring instruments that are used not only within social work practice settings (research consumer) but also in research situations (research partner and creator and disseminator of research).

| COMPETENCY 4 | Engage in Practice-Informed Research and Research-Informed Practice |
| --- | --- |

Competency 4 also pertains to the entire chapter because you have to:

1   Evaluate the criteria the authors of research studies used in relation to the selection of their measuring instruments. You'll also need to know the advantages, the disadvantages, and the specific criteria that apply to evaluating measuring instruments (**research consumer**—research-informed practice);

2   Participate in a research study—either as a co-researcher or research participant (**research partner**—practice-informed research). See 1 above and 3 below; and

3   Know how to determine the validity and reliability of measuring instruments that will measure the variables in your research study (**creator and disseminator of research**—practice-informed research).

You also need to utilize evidence-based practice recommendations whenever possible; that is, you need to integrate (1) the best available research-based evidence with (2) your clinical expertise and (3) your client's values.

All of the above implies you'll need to know how to assess the overall strengths and limitations of the measuring instrument(s) used in a research study that produced its research-based evidence. In short, you need to ask and then answer a simple question: How seriously should I take the findings of any specific research study given the reliability and validity of the measuring instrument(s) the study utilized?

| COMPETENCY 9 | Evaluate Practice with Individuals, Families, Groups, Organizations, & Communities |
| --- | --- |

See Competencies 1 and 4.

# Measurement

| | | |
|---|---|---|
| CHAPTERS 1 & 3 | Step 1. | Understanding the Research Process |
| CHAPTER 2 | Step 2. | Formulating Research Questions |
| CHAPTER 4<br>APPENDIXES A–C | Step 3. | Reviewing the Literature<br>Evaluating the Literature |
| CHAPTERS 5 & 6 | Step 4. | Being Aware of Ethical and Cultural Issues |
| CHAPTERS 7–10 | Step 5. | Selecting a Research Approach |
| CHAPTERS 11 & 12 | Step 6. | Specifying How Variables Are Measured |
| CHAPTER 13 | Step 7. | Selecting a Sample |
| CHAPTERS 14 & 15 | Step 8. | Selecting a Research Design |
| CHAPTERS 16 & 17 | Step 9. | Selecting a Data-Collection Method |
| CHAPTERS 18 & 19 | Step 10. | Analyzing the Data |
| CHAPTERS 20 & 21 | Step 11. | Writing the Research Report |

# Measurement

"Yes, we finally agree on something! All of your course grades are the same which means you're extremely reliable. Reliable, yes—valid, no."

LEVELS OF MEASUREMENT
    Nominal Measurement
    Ordinal Measurement
    Interval Measurement
    Ratio Measurement
DESCRIBING VARIABLES BY MEASURING THEM
    Correspondence
    Standardization
    Quantification
    Duplication
CRITERIA FOR SELECTING AN INSTRUMENT
    Utility
    Sensitivity to Small Changes
    Nonreactivity
    Reliability
        *Test-Retest Method*
        *Alternate-Form Method*
        *Split-Half Method*
        *Observer Reliability*

Validity
    *Content Validity*
    *Criterion Validity*
        Concurrent
        Predictive
    *Face Validity*
    *Construct Validity*
RELIABILITY AND VALIDITY REVISITED
MEASUREMENT ERRORS
    Constant Errors
    Random Errors
IMPROVING VALIDITY AND RELIABILITY
EVALUATING THE MEASUREMENT OF VARIABLES
    Use Appendix A
CHAPTER RECAP
REVIEW EXERCISES

THE MEASUREMENT OF VARIABLES is the cornerstone of all social work positivistic research studies. Shining and formidable measuring instruments may come to mind, measuring things to several decimal places. The less scientifically inclined might merely picture rulers, but, in any case, measurement for most of us means reducing something to numbers. As we know, these "somethings" are called variables, and all variables can take on different measurement levels.

## LEVELS OF MEASUREMENT

**O**ur discussion of measurement levels has been adapted and modified from Margaret Williams, Leslie Tutty, and Rick Grinnell (1995). As we know from Chapter 8, the characteristics that describe a variable are known as its attributes. The variable gender, for example, can have two attributes—male and female—because gender in humans can generally be thought of as only containing two attributes: male and female.

However, our current and evolving notion of gender is changing drastically where male and female have been expanded to include many more attributes than the traditional two. In fact, Facebook now allows users to self-identify as something other than either male or female. It has fifty-six different categories for gender—not just the customary two.

The variable ethnicity has a number of possible attributes: African American, Native American, Asian, Latinx American, and Caucasian are just five examples of the many attributes of the variable ethnicity. A point to note here is that the attributes of gender differ in kind from one another—male is different from female—and, in the same way, the attributes of ethnicity are also different from one another.

Now consider the variable income. Income can only be described in terms of amounts of money: $15,000 per year, $288.46 per week, and so forth. In whatever terms a person's income is actually described, it still comes down to a number. Because every number has its own category, as we mentioned before, the variable income can generate as many categories as there are numbers, up to the number covering the research participant who earns the most.

These numbers are all attributes of income, and they are all different, but they are not different in kind, as male and female are, or Native American and Latinx; they are only different in quantity. In other words, the attributes of income differ in that they represent

> All variables have to be measured in some form or another.

more or less of the same thing whereas the attributes of gender differ in that they represent different kinds of things. Income will, therefore, be measured in a different way from gender. When we want to measure income, for example, we will be looking for categories (attributes) that are *lower* or *higher* than each other; on the other hand, when we measure gender, we will be looking for categories (attributes) that *are different in kind* from each other.

Mathematically, there is not much we can do with categories that are different in kind. We cannot subtract Latinxs from Caucasians, for example, whereas we can quite easily subtract one person's annual income from another and come up with a meaningful difference. As far as mathematical computations are concerned, we are obliged to work at a lower level of complexity when we measure variables like ethnicity than when we measure variables like income.

Depending on the nature of their attributes, all variables can be measured at one (or more) of four measurement levels:

1  Nominal
2  Ordinal
3  Interval
4  Ratio

## Nominal Measurement

Nominal measurement is the lowest level of measurement and is used to measure variables whose attributes are different in kind. As we have seen, gender is one variable measured at a nominal level, and ethnicity is another. *Place of birth* is a third, because "born in California," for example, is different from "born in Chicago," and we cannot add "born in California" to "born in Chicago," or subtract them or divide them, or do anything statistically interesting with them at all.

## Ordinal Measurement

Ordinal measurement is a higher level of measurement than nominal and is used to measure those variables whose attributes can be rank ordered: for example, socioeconomic status, sexism, racism, client satisfaction, and the like. If we intend to measure client satisfaction, we must first develop a list of all the possible attributes of client satisfaction; that is, we must think of all the possible categories into which answers about client satisfaction might be placed.

Some clients will be *very satisfied*—one category, at the high end of the satisfaction continuum; some will be *not at all satisfied*—a separate category, at the low end of the continuum; and others will be *generally satisfied, moderately satisfied,* or *somewhat satisfied*—three more categories, at differing points on the continuum, as illustrated:

1  Not at all satisfied
2  Somewhat satisfied
3  Moderately satisfied
4  Generally satisfied
5  Very satisfied

The above is a 5-point scale with a brief description of the degree of satisfaction represented by a number (i.e., 1, 2, 3, 4, 5). Of course, we may choose to express the anchors in different words, substituting *extremely satisfied* for *very satisfied*, or *fairly satisfied* for *generally satisfied*. We may select a 3-point scale instead, limiting the choices to *very satisfied, moderately satisfied,* and *not at all satisfied*; or we may even use a 10-point scale if we believe that our respondents will be able to rate their satisfaction with that degree of accuracy.

Whichever particular method is selected, some sort of scale is the only measurement option available because there is no other way to categorize client satisfaction except in terms of more satisfaction or less satisfaction. As we did with nominal measurement, we might assign numbers to each of the points on the scale. If we used the 5-point scale as illustrated on the previous page, we might assign:

- **5** to very satisfied
- **4** to generally satisfied
- **3** to moderately satisfied
- **2** to somewhat satisfied
- **1** to not at all satisfied

Here, the numbers do have some mathematical meaning. Five (very satisfied) is in fact better than 4 (generally satisfied), 4 is better than 3, 3 is better than 2, and 2 is better than 1. The numbers, however, say nothing about *how much better* any category is than any other. We cannot assume that the difference in satisfaction between *very* and *generally* is the same as the difference between *generally* and *moderately*.

In short, we cannot assume that the intervals between the anchored points on the scale are all the same length. Most definitely, we cannot assume that a client who rates a service at 4 (generally satisfied) is twice as satisfied as a client who rates the service at 2 (somewhat satisfied). In fact, we cannot attempt any mathematical manipulation at all. We cannot add the numbers 1, 2, 3, 4, and 5, nor can we subtract, multiply, or divide them. As its name might suggest, all we can know from ordinal measurement is the order of the categories.

## INTERVAL MEASUREMENT

Some variables, such as client satisfaction, have attributes that can be rank-ordered—from *very satisfied* to *not at all satisfied*, as we have just discussed. As we saw, however, these attributes cannot be assumed to be the same distance apart if they are placed on a scale; and, in any case, the distance they are apart has no real meaning. No one can measure the distance between *very satisfied* and *moderately satisfied*; we only know that the one is better than the other.

Conversely, for some variables, the distance, or interval, separating their attributes does have meaning, and these variables can be measured at the interval level. An example in physical science would is the Fahrenheit or Celsius temperature scales. The difference between 80 degrees and 90 degrees is the same as the difference between 40 and 50 degrees. Eighty degrees is not twice as hot as 40 degrees; nor does zero degrees mean no heat at all.

In social work, interval measures are most commonly used in connection with standardized measuring instruments, as presented in Chapter 12. When we look at a standardized intelligence test, for example, we can say that the difference between IQ scores of 100 and 110 is the same as the difference between IQ scores of 95 and 105, based on the scores obtained by the many thousands of people who have taken the test over the years.

## RATIO MEASUREMENT

The highest level of measurement, ratio measurement, is used to measure variables whose attributes are based on a true zero point. It may not be possible to have zero intelligence, but it's certainly possible to have zero children or zero money. Whenever a question about a particular variable might elicit the answer "none" or "never", that variable can be measured at the ratio level.

The question "How many times have you seen your social worker"? might be answered "Never". Other variables commonly measured at the ratio level include length of residence in a given place, age, number of times married, number of organizations belonged to, number of antisocial behaviors, number of case reviews, number of training sessions, number of supervisory meetings, and so forth. With a ratio level of measurement, we can meaningfully interpret the comparison between two scores.

A person who is 40 years of age, for example, is twice as old as a person who is 20 and half as old as a person who is 80. Children aged 2 and 5, respectively, are the same distance apart as children aged 6 and 9. Data resulting from ratio measurement can be added, subtracted, multiplied, and divided. Averages can be calculated, and other statistical analyses can be performed.

It's useful to note that although some variables can be measured at a higher level, they may not need to be. The variable income, for example, can be measured at a ratio level because it's possible to have a zero income, but, for the purposes of a particular study, we may not need to know the actual incomes of our research participants, only the range within which their incomes fall.

A person who is asked how much he or she earns may be reluctant to give a figure ("mind your own business" is a perfectly legitimate response) but may not object to checking one of a number of income categories, choosing, for example, between:

1   less than $5,000 per year
2   $5,001 to $15,000 per year
3   $15,001 to $25,000 per year
4   $25,001 to $35,000 per year
5   more than $35,000 per year

Categorizing income in this way reduces the measurement from the ratio level to the ordinal level. It will now be possible to know only that a person checking Category 1 earns less than a person checking Category 2, and so on. We will not know how much less or more one person earns than another, and we will not be able to perform statistical tasks such as calculating average incomes, but we will be able to say, for example, that 50 percent of our sample falls into Category 1, 30 percent into Category 2, 15 percent into Category 3, and 5 percent into Category 4. If we are conducting a study to see how many people fall in each income range, this may be all we need to know.

In the same way, we might not want to know the actual ages of our sample, only the range in which they fall. For some studies, it might be enough to measure age at a nominal level—to inquire, for example, whether people were born during the Depression, or whether they were born before or after 1990. When studying variables that can be measured at any level, the measurement level chosen depends on what kind of data are needed, and this in turn is determined by why the data are needed, which in turn is determined by our research question.

## DESCRIBING VARIABLES BY MEASURING THEM

**T**he purpose of measuring a variable is to describe it as completely and accurately as possible. Often, the most complete and accurate possible description of a variable involves not only numbers but also words. When doing any research study we need to describe our variables as accurately as possible for four reasons:

1  Correspondence
2  Standardization
3  Quantification
4  Duplication

## CORRESPONDENCE

Correspondence means making a link between what we measure and/or observe and the theories we have developed to explain what we have measured and/or observed. For example, the concept of attachment theory can easily explain the different behaviors (variables) of small children when they are separated from—or reunited with—their mothers.

Measuring and recording children's behaviors in this context provide a link between the abstract and the concrete—between attachment (an unspecific and nonmeasurable concept) and its indicators, or variables, such as a child's behaviors (a more specific and more measurable variable).

## STANDARDIZATION

Like concepts, a single variable can at times mean different things to different people, even when using the same words. "Self-esteem", for example, can mean different things to different people. However, the perceptions linked to self-esteem (that is, the empirical indicators of self-esteem) may be drawn together in the form of a measuring instrument, as they are in Hudson's *Index of Self-Esteem* (see figure 11.1 on the following page).

> Variables can be complex, and the more complex they are the more likely it is that people will interpret the exact same variable in different ways.

You may or may not agree that all of the twenty-five items, or questions, contained in Hudson's *Index of Self-Esteem* together reflect what you mean by self-esteem—but at least you know what Hudson meant, and so does everyone else who is using his measuring instrument. By constructing this instrument, Hudson has standardized a complex variable so that everyone using his instrument will mean the same thing by the variable and measure it in the same way. Moreover, if two or more different researchers use his instrument with the same research participants, they ought to get approximately the same results. The use of the word "approximately" here means that we must allow for a bit of error—something discussed at the end of this chapter.

## QUANTIFICATION

Quantification means nothing more than defining the level of a variable in terms of a single number, or score. The use of Hudson's *Index of Self-Esteem*, for example, results in a single number, or score, obtained by following the scoring instructions. Reducing a complex variable such as self-esteem to a single number has disadvantages in that the richness of the variable can never be completely captured in this way.

However, it also has advantages in that numbers can be used in statistics to search for meaningful relationships between one variable and another. For example, you might hypothesize that there is a relationship between two variables: self-esteem and marital satisfaction. Hudson has *quantified* self-esteem, allowing the self-esteem of any research participant to be represented by a single number. He has also done this for the variable of marital satisfaction and other variables as well. Because the variables have been broken down to numbers, you can use statistical methods (discussed in chapter 18) to see whether the relationship you hypothesized actually does exist.

## DUPLICATION

In the physical sciences, experiments are routinely duplicated. For example, if you put a test-tube containing 25 ounces of a solution into an oven to see what is left when the liquid evaporates, you may use five test-tubes containing 25 ounces each, not just one.

Then, you will have five identical samples of solution evaporated at the same time under the same conditions, and you will be much more certain of your results than if you had just evaporated one sample. The word *duplication* means doing the same thing more than once at the same time.

---

Name:_____              Today's Date:_____

This questionnaire is designed to measure how you see yourself. It is not a test, so there are no right or wrong answers. Please answer each item as carefully and as accurately as you can by placing a number beside each item as follows:

        1 = None of the time
        2 = Very rarely
        3 = A little of the time
        4 = Some of the time
        5 = A good part of the time
        6 = Most of the time
        7 = All of the time

1. ____ I feel that people would not like me if they really knew me well.
2. ____ I feel that others get along much better than I do.
3. ____ I feel that I am a beautiful person.
4. ____ When I am with others I feel they are glad I am with them.
5. ____ I feel that people really like to talk with me.
6. ____ I feel that I am a very competent person.
7. ____ I think I make a good impression on others.
8. ____ I feel that I need more self-confidence.
9. ____ When I am with strangers I am very nervous.
10. ____ I think that I am a dull person.
11. ____ I feel ugly.
12. ____ I feel that others have more fun than I do.
13. ____ I feel that I bore people.
14. ____ I think my friends find me interesting.
15. ____ I think I have a good sense of humor.
16. ____ I feel very self-conscious when I am with strangers.
17. ____ I feel that if I could be more like other people I would have it made.
18. ____ I feel that people have a good time when they are with me.
19. ____ I feel like a wallflower when I go out.
20. ____ I feel I get pushed around more than others.
21. ____ I think I am a rather nice person.
22. ____ I feel that people really like me very much.
23. ____ I feel that I am a likeable person.
24. ____ I am afraid I will appear foolish to others.
25. ____ My friends think very highly of me.

3, 4, 5, 6, 7, 14, 15, 18, 21, 22, 23, 25

---

**Figure 11.1**

Hudson's *Index of Self-Esteem*

In our profession, we can rarely duplicate research studies for a number of reasons. With that said, other researchers should be able to confirm the first researcher's results by duplicating the same thing again later on, as much as is practically possible under the same conditions. This duplication process increases certainty, and it's only possible if the variables being studied have been standardized and quantified.

For example, you could duplicate another researcher's work on attachment only if you measured attachment in the same way. If you used different child behaviors to indicate attachment and you assigned different values to mean, say, "weak attachment" or "strong attachment", you may have done a useful study, but it would not be a duplicate of the first.

## CRITERIA FOR SELECTING AN INSTRUMENT

**N**ow that you know why you need to measure variables, let's go on to look at how you measure them in the first place. To measure a variable, you need a measuring instrument to measure it with—much more about this topic is in the next chapter. Most of the measuring instruments used in social work are paper and pencil instruments like Figure 11.1 on the previous page.

Many other people besides Hudson have come up with ways of measuring self-esteem, and if you want to measure self-esteem in your study, you will have to choose between the various measuring instruments that are available. The same embarrassment of riches applies to most of the other variables you might want to measure. Remember that a variable is something that varies between research participants. Participants will vary, for example, with respect to their levels of self-esteem. What you need are some criteria to help you decide which instrument is best for measuring a particular variable in any given particular situation. There are five criteria that will help you to do this:

1 Utility
2 Sensitivity to small changes
3 Nonreactivity
4 Reliability
5 Validity

## UTILITY

In order to complete Hudson's *Index of Self-Esteem* (i.e., figure 11.1 on the previous page) for example, a research participant must preferably be able to read. Even if you, as the researcher, read the items to the participants, they must be able to relate a number between 1 and 7 (where 1 = none of the time, and 7 = all of the time) to each of the twenty-five items, or questions.

Further, they must know what a "wallflower" is before they can answer item 19. If the research participants in your study cannot do this for a variety of reasons, then no matter how wonderful Hudson's *Index of Self-Esteem* might be in other respects, it's not useful to you in your particular study.

Hudson's *Index of Self-Esteem* may take only a few minutes to complete, but other instruments can take far longer. The *Minnesota Multiphase Personality Inventory* (the *MMPI*), for example, can take three hours or more to complete, and some people may not have the attention span or the motivation to complete the task. In sum, a measuring instrument is not useful if your research participants are unable or unwilling to complete it for whatever reasons. If they do complete it, however, you then have to score it.

The simple measuring instrument contained in Figure 11.1 is relatively quick and simple to score, but other instruments are far more complex and time consuming. Usually, the simple instruments—quick to complete and easy to score—are less accurate than the more demanding instruments, and you will have to decide how far you are prepared to sacrifice accuracy for utility.

The main consideration here is what you are going to do with the measurements once you have obtained them. If you are doing an assessment that might affect a client's life in terms of treatment intervention, referral, placement, and so on, accuracy is paramount, and you will need the most accurate instrument (probably the longest and most complex) that the client can tolerate.

On the other hand, if you are doing an exploratory or descriptive research study where the result will be a tentative suggestion that some variable may be related to another, a little inaccuracy in measurement is not the end of the world, and utility might be more important.

## SENSITIVITY TO SMALL CHANGES

Suppose that one of your practice objectives with your 8-year-old client Johnny is to help him stop wetting his bed during the night. One obvious indicator of the variable—bedwetting—is a wet bed. Thus, you hastily decide that you will measure Johnny's bedwetting behavior by having his mother tell you when Johnny has—or has not—wet his bed during the week. That is, did he or did he not wet his bed at least once during the week?

However, if Johnny has reduced the number of his bedwetting incidents from five per week to only once per week, you will not know whether your intervention was working well because just the one bedwetting incident per week was enough to officially count as "wetting the bed". In other words, the way you chose to measure Johnny's bedwetting behavior was sensitive to the large difference between wetting and not wetting in a given week, but insensitive to the smaller difference between wetting once and wetting more than once in a given week.

In order to be able to congratulate Johnny on small improvements, and of course to track his progress over time, you will have to devise a more sensitive measuring instrument, such as one that measures the *number of times* Johnny wets his bed per week. Often, an instrument that is more sensitive will also be less convenient to use, and you will have to balance sensitivity against utility.

## NONREACTIVITY

A *reactive* measuring instrument is nothing more than an instrument that changes the behavior or feeling of a person that it was supposed to measure. For instance, you might have decided, in the example of Johnny, to use a device that rings a loud bell every time Johnny has a bedwetting accident.

His mother would then leap from sleep, make a check mark on the form you had provided, and fall back into a tormented doze. This would be a sensitive measure—though intrusive and thus less useful. However, it might also cause Johnny to reduce his bedwetting behavior, in accordance with behavior theory.

Clinically, this would be a good thing—unless he develops a bell phobia—but it's important to make a clear distinction between an *instrument* that is designed to *measure* a behavior and an *intervention* that is designed to *change* it. If the bell wakes up Johnny so that he can go to the bathroom and thus finally eliminate his bedwetting behavior, the bell is a wonderful intervention. It's not a good measuring instrument, however, as it has changed the very behavior it was supposed to measure. A change in behavior resulting from the use of a measuring instrument is known as a *reactive effect*.

A *nonreactive* measuring instrument is one that has no effect on the variable being measured.

If you want to know, for example, whether a particular intervention is effective in raising self-esteem in girls who have been sexually abused, you will need to be sure that any measured increase in self-esteem is due to the intervention and not to the measuring instrument you happen to be using. If you fail to make a distinction between the measuring instrument and the intervention, you will end up with no clear idea at all about what is causing what.

Sometimes, you might be tempted to use a measuring instrument as a clinical tool. If your client responded to Hudson's *Index of Self-Esteem* item 13 (figure 11.1) that she felt she was boring people all of the time, you might want to discuss with her the particular conversational gambits she feels are so boring in order to help her change them. This is perfectly legitimate so long as you realize that, by so doing, you have turned a measuring instrument into part of an intervention.

## RELIABILITY

A good measuring instrument is reliable in that it gives the same score over and over again provided that the measurement is made under the same conditions and nothing about the research participant has changed. A reliable measuring instrument is obviously necessary because, if you are trying to track the increase in a client's self-esteem, for example, you need to be sure that the changes you see over time are due to changes in the client, not to inaccuracies in the measuring instrument.

Researchers are responsible for ensuring that the measuring instruments they use are reliable. Hence, it's worth looking briefly at the four main methods used to establish the reliability of a measuring instrument:

1 Test-retest method
2 Alternate-form method
3 Split-half method
4 Observer reliability

### TEST-RETEST METHOD

The test-retest method of establishing reliability involves administering the same measuring instrument to the same group of people on two separate occasions. The two sets of results are then compared to see how similar they are; that is, how well they correlate. We will discuss correlation more fully in Chapter 18. For now, it's enough to say that correlation in this context can range from 0 to 1, where 0 means no correlation at all between the two sets of scores and 1 means a perfect correlation.

Generally, a correlation of 0.8 means that the instrument is reasonably reliable and 0.9 is very good. Note that there is a heading RELIABILITY in Figure 11.1a on the following page, which means that Hudson's *Index of Self-Esteem* has "excellent stability with a two-hour test-retest correlation of 0.92". The "two-hour" bit means, of course, that the two administrations of the instrument took place two hours apart.

The problem with completing the same instrument twice is that the answers given on the first occasion may affect the answers given on the second. This is known as a *testing effect*. For example, Ms. Smith might remember what she wrote the first time and write something different just to enliven the proceedings. She may be less anxious, or more bored or irritated the second time, just because there was a first time, and these states might affect her answers.

Obviously, the greater the testing effects, the less reliable the instrument. Moreover, the closer together the tests, the more likely testing effects become because Ms. Smith is more likely to remember the first occasion. Hence, if the instrument is reliable over an

**AUTHOR:** Walter W. Hudson

**PURPOSE:** To measure problems with self-esteem.

**DESCRIPTION:** The *ISE* is a 25-item scale designed to measure the degree, severity, or magnitude of a problem the client has with self-esteem. Self-esteem is considered as the evaluative component of self-concept. The *ISE* is written in very simple language, is easily administered, and is easily scored. Because problems with self-esteem are often central to social and psychological difficulties, this instrument has a wide range of utility for a number of clinical problems.

    The *ISE* has a cutting score of 30 (+ or −5), with scores above 30 indicating the respondent has a clinically significant problem and scores below 30 indicating the individual has no such problem. Another advantage of the ISE is that it is one of nine scales of *The Clinical Measurement* Package (Hudson, 1982), all of which are administered and scored the same way.

**NORMS:** This scale was derived from tests of 1,745 respondents, including single and married individuals, clinical and nonclinical populations, college students and nonstudents. Respondents included Caucasians, Japanese, and Chinese Americans, and a smaller number of members of other ethnic groups. Not recommended for use with children under the age of 12.

**SCORING:** For a detailed description on how to score the ISE, see: Bloom, Fischer, and Orme (2009) or go to: www.walmyr.com.

**RELIABILITY:** The *ISE* has a mean alpha of .93, indicating excellent internal consistency, and an excellent (low) S.E.M. of 3.70. The *ISE* also has excellent stability with a two-hour test-retest correlation of .92.

**VALIDITY:** The *ISE* has good known-groups validity, significantly distinguishing between clients judged by clinicians to have problems in the area of self-esteem and those known not to. Further, the *ISE* has very good construct validity, correlating well with a range of other measures with which it should correlate highly, e.g., depression, happiness, sense of identity, and scores on the *Generalized Contentment Scale* (depression).

**PRIMARY REFERENCE:** Hudson, W. W. (1982). *The clinical measurement package: A field manual.* Chicago: Dorsey.

**Figure 11.1a**

Basic Information about Hudson's *Index of Self-Esteem*

interval of two hours and you want to administer it to your study participants on occasions a day or a month apart, it should be even more reliable with respect to testing effects. People may change their answers on a second occasion for reasons other than testing effects: they are having a good day or a bad day; or they have a cold; or there is a loud pneumatic drill just outside the window.

However, a word of caution is in order. Sometimes clients complete the same measuring instrument every few weeks for a year or more as a way of monitoring their progress over time. The more often an instrument is completed, the more likely it is to generate testing effects. Hence, social service programs that use instruments in this way need to be sure that the instruments they use are still reliable under the conditions in which they are to be used.

## ALTERNATE-FORM METHOD

The second method of establishing the reliability of a measuring instrument is the alternate-form method. As the same suggests, an alternate form of an instrument is a second instrument that is as similar as possible to the original except that the wording of the items contained in the second instrument has changed. Administering the original form and then the alternate form reduces testing effects because the respondent is less likely to base the second set of answers on the first.

However, it's time-consuming to develop different but equivalent instruments, and they must still be tested for reliability using the test-retest method, both together as a pair and separately as two distinct instruments.

### SPLIT-HALF METHOD

The split-half method involves splitting one instrument in half so that it becomes two shorter instruments. Usually, all the even-numbered items, or questions, are used to make one instrument while the odd-numbered items make up the other. The point of doing this is to ensure that the original instrument is internally consistent; that is, it's homogeneous, or the same all the way through, with no longer or more difficult items appearing at the beginning or the end.

When the two halves are compared using the test-retest method, they should ideally yield the same score. If they did give the same score when one half was administered to a respondent on one occasion and the second half to the same respondent on a different occasion, they would have a perfect correlation of 1. Again, a correlation of 0.8 is thought to be good and a correlation of 0.9 very good. Figure 11.1a, under the RELIABILITY section, shows that Hudson's *Index of Self-Esteem* has an internal consistency of 0.93.

### OBSERVER RELIABILITY (RELIABILITY OF THE PROCESS)

Sometimes, behaviors are measured by observing how often they occur, or how long they last, or how severe they are. The results are then recorded on a straightforward, simple form. Nevertheless, this is not as easy as it sounds because the behavior, or variable, being measured must first be very carefully defined and people observing the same behavior may have different opinions as to how severe the behavior was, or how long it lasted, or whether it occurred at all.

The level of agreement or correlation between trained observers thus provides a way of establishing the reliability of the process used to measure the behavior. Once we have established the reliability of the process, we can use the same method to assess the reliability of other observers as part of their training. The level of agreement between observers is known as *inter-rater reliability*.

| Box 11.1 | A Summary of the Major Types of Reliability |
|---|---|

| | |
|---|---|
| **TEST-RETEST METHOD** | Does an individual respond to a measuring instrument in the same general way when the instrument is administered twice? |
| **ALTERNATE-FORMS METHOD** | When two forms of an instrument that are equivalent in their degree of validity are given to the same individual, is there a strong convergence in how that person responds? |
| **SPLIT-HALF METHOD** | Are the scores on one half of the measuring instrument similar to those obtained on the other half? |
| **OBSERVER RELIABILITY** | Is there an agreement between the observers who are measuring the same variable? |

# VALIDITY

A measuring instrument is valid if it measures what it's supposed to measure—and measures it accurately. If you want to measure the variable assertiveness, for example, you don't want to mistakenly measure aggression instead. There are several kinds of validity—in fact, we should really refer to the *validities* of an instrument—and we will look at the following four:

1 Content validity
2 Criterion validity
3 Face validity
4 Construct validity

## CONTENT VALIDITY

Think for a moment about the variable self-esteem. In order to measure it accurately, you must first know what it is; that is, you must identify all the indicators (questions contained in the measuring instrument) that make up self-esteem, such as feeling that people like you, feeling that you are competent, and so on—and on and on and on . . . It's probably impossible to identify all the indicators that contribute to self-esteem.

It's even less likely that everyone (or even most people) will agree with all the indicators identified by someone else. Arguments may arise over whether "feeling worthless," for example, is really an indicator of low self-esteem or whether it has more to do with depression, which is a separate variable altogether. Furthermore, even if agreement could be reached, a measuring instrument like Hudson's *Index of Self-Esteem* would have to include at least one item, or question, for every agreed-upon indicator. If just one was missed—for example, "sense of humor"—then the instrument would not be accurately measuring self-esteem.

Because it did not include all the possible content, or indicators, related to self-esteem, it would not be content valid. Hudson's *Index of Self-Esteem,* then, is not perfectly content valid because it's not possible to cover every indicator related to self-esteem in just twenty-five items. Longer instruments have a better chance of being content valid (perhaps one could do it in twenty-five pages of items), but, in general, perfect content validity cannot be achieved in any measuring instrument of a practical length.

Content validity is a matter of "more or less" rather than "yes or no", and moreover it is strictly a matter of opinion. For example, experts differ about the degree to which various instruments are content valid. It's therefore necessary to find some way of validating an instrument to determine how well it is, in fact, accurately measuring what it's supposed to measure. One such way is through a determination of the instrument's criterion validity.

## CRITERION VALIDITY

An instrument has criterion validity if it gives the same result as a second instrument that is designed to measure the same variable. A client might complete Hudson's *Index of Self-Esteem,* for example, and achieve a score indicating high self-esteem. If the same client then completes a second instrument also designed to measure self-esteem and again achieves a good score, it's very likely that both instruments are, in fact, measuring self-esteem. Not only do they have good criterion validity in that they compare well with each other, but probably each instrument also has good content validity.

If the same client does not achieve similar scores on the two instruments, however, then neither of them are criterion valid; probably one is not content valid, and both will have to be compared with a third instrument to resolve the difficulty. There are two categories of criterion validity:

1 Concurrent validity

2 Predictive validity

**CONCURRENT VALIDITY.** Concurrent validity mainly deals with the *present*. For example, suppose you have an instrument—say, a reading test—designed to distinguish between children who need remedial reading services and children who do not. To validate the measuring instrument, you ask the classroom teacher which children she thinks need remedial reading services. If the teacher and your instrument both come up with the same list of children, your instrument has criterion validity. If not, you will need to find another comparison: a different reading test or the opinion of another teacher.

In short, concurrent validity refers to the ability of a measuring instrument to predict accurately an individual's current status. An example of an instrument with concurrent validity is a psychopathology scale that is capable of distinguishing between adolescents who are currently in need of psychiatric treatment and those who are not.

**PREDICTIVE VALIDITY.** Predictive validity deals with the *future*. Perhaps you have an instrument (say a set of criteria) designed to predict which students will achieve high grades in their social work programs. If the students your instrument identified had indeed achieved high grades by the end of their BSW programs and the others had not, your instrument would have predictive validity.

In sum, concurrent and predictive validity are concerned with prediction, and both make use of some external criterion that is purportedly a valid and reliable measure of the variable being studied. What differentiates the two is time. Once again, concurrent validity predicts *current* performance or status, and predictive validity predicts *future* performance or status.

The major concern of criterion validity, however, is not whether an instrument is valid for concurrent or future discriminations. Rather, the concern is with the use of a second measure as an independent criterion to check the validity of the first measure.

### FACE VALIDITY

Face validity, in fact, has nothing to do with what an instrument actually measures but only with what it *appears* to measure to the one who is completing it. Strictly speaking, it's not a form of validity. For example, suppose that you are taking a course on social work administration. You have a lazy instructor who has taken your final exam from a course he taught for business students last semester. The exam, in fact, quite adequately tests your knowledge of administration theory, but it does not seem relevant to you because the language it uses relates to the business world not to social work situations.

You might not do very well on this exam because, although it has content validity (it adequately tests your knowledge), it does not have face validity (an appearance of relevance to the respondent). The moral here is that a measuring instrument should not only be content valid, to the greatest extent possible, but also should appear content valid to the person who completes it.

### CONSTRUCT VALIDITY

What sets construct validity apart from content and criterion validity is its preoccupation with theory, explanatory constructs, and the testing of hypothesized relationships between and among variables. Construct validity is very difficult to understand because it involves determining the degree to which an instrument successfully measures a theoretical concept. The difficulty derives in part from the abstract nature of concepts.

As you know, a concept is a characteristic or trait that does not exist as an isolated, observable dimension of behavior. It cannot be seen, felt, or heard, and it cannot be measured directly—its existence must be inferred from the evidence at hand. Thus, the concept "hostility" may be inferred from observations of presumably hostile or aggressive acts; the concept "anxiety" may be inferred from test scores, galvanic skin responses, observations of anxious behaviors, and so on. Other typical concepts of concern to us are motivation, social class, delinquency, prejudice, and organizational conflict.

Construct validity is evaluated by determining the degree to which certain explanatory concepts account for variance, or individual differences, in the scores of an instrument. Put another way, it's concerned with the meaning of the instrument—that is, what it is measuring, and how and why it operates the way it does. To assess the construct validity of the Rorschach inkblot test, for example, we would try to determine the factors, or concepts, that account for differences in responses on the test. Attempts might be made to determine whether the test measures emotional stability, sociability, or self-control and whether it also measures aggressiveness. The question would be: What proportion of the total test variance is accounted for by the concepts of emotional stability, sociability, self-control, and aggressiveness?

With construct validity, there is usually more interest in the property, or concept, being measured than in the instrument itself. Thus, it involves validation not only of the instrument but also of the theory underlying it. To establish construct validity, the meaning of the concept must be understood, and the propositions the theory makes about the relationships between this and other concepts must be identified.

We try to discover what predictions can be made on the basis of these propositions and whether the measurements obtained from the instrument will be consistent with those predictions. If the predictions are not supported, there is no clear-cut guide as to whether the shortcoming is in the instrument or in the theory.

Suppose a study is conducted to test the hypothesis that self-referred clients are more likely to have favorable attitudes toward treatment than those who come to the agency on some other basis. If the findings do not support the predicted relationship between self-referral and attitude toward treatment, should it be concluded that the measure is not valid or that the hypothesis is incorrect?

> Predictive validity denotes an instrument's ability to predict future performance or status from present performance or status. An instrument has predictive validity if it can distinguish between individuals who will *differ at some point in the future.*

| Box 11.2 | A Summary of the Major Types of Validity |
|---|---|
| **CONTENT VALIDITY** | Does the measuring instrument adequately measure the major dimensions of the variable under consideration? |
| **(FACE VALIDITY)** | Does the measuring instrument *appear* to measure the subject matter under consideration? (Not really a form of validity.) |
| **CRITERION VALIDITY** | Does the individual's measuring instrument score predict the probable behavior on a second variable (criterion-related measure)? |
| **CONSTRUCT VALIDITY** | Does the measuring instrument appear to measure the general construct (element) it purports to measure? |

In such a situation, the concept of attitude toward treatment and the network of propositions that led to this prediction should be reexamined. Then the concept might be refined with more detailed hypotheses about its relationship to other concepts, and changes might be made in the instrument. Construct validation makes use of data from a variety of sources. It is a painstaking building process much like theory construction—an attempt to ferret out the dimensions that an instrument is tapping and thereby to validate the theory underlying the instrument.

## RELIABILITY AND VALIDITY REVISITED

**B**efore we leave reliability and validity, we should say something about the relationship between them. If an instrument is not reliable, it cannot be valid. That is, if the same person completes it a number of times under the same conditions and it gives different results each time, it cannot be measuring anything accurately. However, if an instrument is reliable, that does not necessarily mean it's valid. It could be reliably and consistently measuring something other than what it's supposed to measure, in the same way that people can be reliably late or watches can be reliably slow.

The relationship between validity and reliability can be illustrated with a simple analogy. Suppose that you are firing five rounds from a rifle at three different targets, as illustrated in Figure 11.2 on the following page:

- In **Figure 11.2a,** the bullet holes are scattered, representing a measuring instrument that is neither reliable nor valid.
- In **Figure 11.2b,** you have adjusted your sights, and now all the bullet holes are in the same place but not in the center as you intended. This represents a measuring instrument that is reliable but not valid.
- In **Figure 11.2c,** all the shots have hit the bull's eye: the instrument is both reliable and valid.

## MEASUREMENT ERRORS

**N**o matter how good the reliability and validity of a measuring instrument, no measurement is entirely without error. You can make two errors when you measure variables. Your measurements can contain:

1 Constant errors
2 Random errors

### CONSTANT ERRORS

Constant errors, as the name suggests, are those errors that stay constant throughout the research study. They stay constant because they come from an unvarying source. That source may be the measuring instruments used, the research participants, or the researchers themselves. Because we have already spent some time discussing the limitations of measuring instruments, we will focus this discussion on errors caused by the researchers and their research participants.

Research participants, with all the best will in the world, may still have personal styles that lead to error in research results. If they are being interviewed, for example, they may exhibit acquiescence (a tendency to agree with everything the researcher says, no matter what it is), or social desirability (a tendency to say anything that they think makes them look good), or deviation (a tendency to seek unusual responses).

> Constant errors are those errors that stay constant throughout the research study.

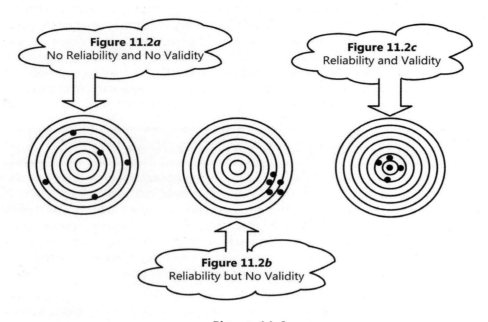

**Figure 11.2**

Targets Illustrating the Validity/Reliability Relationship

If they are filling out a self-administered instrument, such as Hudson's *Index of Self-Esteem,* they may show error of central tendency, always choosing the number in the middle and avoiding commitment to either of the ends. Moreover, they have personal characteristics with respect to gender, age, ethnic background, and knowledge of the English language that remain constant throughout the study and may affect their answers.

Researchers also have personal styles and characteristics. Interviewers can affect the answers they receive by the way they ask the questions, by the way they dress, by their accent, mannerisms, gender, age, ethnic background, or even by their hairstyles. According to Gerald Bostwick and Nancy Kyte (2018), observers who are watching and rating participants' behaviors can commit various sins in a constant fashion, for example:

1  **Contrast error**—to rate others as opposite to oneself with respect to a particular characteristic.

2  **Halo effect**—to think that a participant is altogether wonderful or terrible because of one good or bad trait. Or to think that the trait being observed must be good or bad because the participant is altogether wonderful or terrible.

3  **Error of leniency**—to always give a good report.

4  **Error of severity**—to always give a bad report.

5  **Error of central tendency**—observers, like participants, can choose always to stay comfortably in the middle of a rating scale and avoid both ends.

Because these errors are constant throughout the study, they are sometimes recognized, and steps can be taken to deal with them. A different interviewer or observer might be found, for example, or allowances might be made for a particular participant's characteristics or style.

## RANDOM ERRORS

Random errors that are not constant are difficult to find and make allowances for. Random errors spring out of the dark, wreak temporary havoc, and go back into hiding. It has been suggested that eventually they cancel each other out, and indeed they might. They might not as well, but there is little researchers can do about them except to be aware that they exist. According to Gerald Bostwick and Nancy Kyte (2018) there are three types of random error:

1 **Transient qualities of the research participant**—things such as fatigue or boredom, or any temporary personal state that will affect the participant's responses.

2 **Situational factors**—the weather, the pneumatic drill outside the window, or anything else in the environment that will affect the participant's responses.

3 **Administrative factors**—anything relating to the way the instrument is administered, or the interview conducted, or the observation made. These include transient qualities of the researcher (or whoever collects the data) as well as accidents like reading out the wrong set of instructions.

---

| Box 11.3 | Toward Culturally Sensitive Measurement |

### Instrument Bias

Researchers have debated measurement issues with racial/ethnic minorities for decades. Prominent among the debates has been the issue of testing the intelligence of ethnic minority children. Some researchers have argued that scores on standardized intelligence tests are underestimates of these children's actual abilities. The primary concern pertains to the standardization of the measuring instruments themselves.

It has been suggested that the samples used to standardize the instruments did not include enough ethnic minority children to provide the valid interpretation of the instruments' scores when they were used with ethnic minority children. Also, to do well on intelligence tests, ethnic minority children must demonstrate proficiency with the European American culture.

On the other hand, there is no such requirement for European American children to demonstrate proficiency with ethnic minority cultures. By default, the European American culture is deemed "superior" to the ethnic minority culture.

### Measurement Sensitivity

The lack of sensitivity of measuring instruments with ethnic minority populations has been well documented. However, these instruments continue to be used with populations for which they were not designed. The question of validity is apparent. As we know from this chapter, validity addresses the extent to which a measuring instrument achieves what it claims to measure.

In many cases, we have no means to determine the validity of measuring instruments or procedures with ethnic minorities because ethnic minorities were not included in the development of instruments or procedures. Nevertheless, researchers have attempted to interpret results using culturally insensitive instruments. This undoubtedly has led to the misrepresentation and misunderstanding of ethnic minorities.

### Importance of Variables Measured

Of equal concern to the quality of measurement is whether or not the variables being measured are similarly important to all cultures and ethnic groups. The assumption that all groups value variables equally is another potential misuse of measurement and could assert the superiority of one group's values and beliefs over those of another. For example, when spirituality, a variable, is studied, it may be of greater importance for Native Americans than for other groups.

For a group who values spirituality, attainment of material possessions may be of lesser importance than spirituality. We know that there are often competing values in research. Thus, we need to study those variables that are important to each group—not only important to the researcher—and attempt to further our understanding of the importance placed on their valued beliefs and lifestyles.

### Language

Language also creates measurement issues. Some ethnic minorities lack facility with the English language, yet they are assessed with measuring instruments that assume English is their primary language. There have been some efforts to translate measuring instruments into other languages, but few studies have been conducted regarding the equivalency of the translations from the original instruments to the newly translated ones. The results of translated versions may be different from those with the English versions.

Translators and interpreters also have been used to bridge the language barriers with ethnic minority populations. Some suggest that the presence of interpreters and translators influences the participants' responses. The extent to which interpreters and influence the research participants' responses remains a contentious issue.

### Observations

Qualitative studies using observational data collection methods are subject to misinterpretation as well. In observing nonverbal communication such as body language, for example, a researcher can easily misinterpret research participants' behaviors. In some Native American cultures, for example, a subordinate making direct eye contact with a person in authority would be deemed disrespectful. But in European American culture, direct eye contact indicates respect. In this case, unfamiliarity with the culture could easily lead a researcher to incorrectly interpret the eye-contact behavior.

In short, measuring instruments and procedures remain problematic with research studies that focus on ethnic minorities. The validity of studies using instruments insensitive to ethnic minorities has created erroneous and conflicting reports. Refinement of the instruments (and their protocols) is necessary to improve the understanding of ethnic minorities with respect to their own values, beliefs, and behaviors.

## IMPROVING VALIDITY AND RELIABILITY

**W**hen a measuring instrument does not achieve acceptable levels of validity and reliability—that is, when much error occurs—researchers often attempt to redesign the instrument so that it's more valid and reliable. Below are techniques for improving a measuring instrument's reliability and validity (Hilton, Fawson, Sullivan, & DeJong, 2019):

1  **Be clearer on what you are measuring.** Often, validity and reliability are compromised because the researcher is not sufficiently clear and precise about the nature of the variables being measured and their possible indicators. Rethinking the variables helps in revising the instrument to make it more valid.

2  **Provide better training for those who will apply the measuring instruments.** This is especially useful when a measuring instrument is used to assess research participants' feelings or attitudes. Previous research studies show that people who apply an instrument can be intentionally and unintentionally biased, and thus intentionally and/or unintentionally produce error.

3  **Obtain the research participants' personal reactions about the measuring instrument.** Those under study may have some insight regarding why the verbal reports, observations, or archival reports are not producing accurate measures of their behaviors, feelings, or knowledge levels. They may, for example, comment that the wording of questions is ambiguous or that members of their subculture interpret some words differently than the researcher intended.

4 **Obtain higher measurement levels of a variable.** This does not guarantee greater validity and reliability, but a higher level of measurement can produce a more reliable measuring instrument in some cases. So when the researcher has some options in terms of how to measure a variable, it's worth considering a higher level of measurement (e.g., nominal to ordinal, ordinal to interval).

5 **Use more indicators of a variable.** This also does not guarantee enhanced reliability and validity, but a summated measuring instrument that has many questions, or items, can produce a more valid measure than one with fewer items. Thus, the more items, the higher the reliability and validity.

6 **Conduct an item-by-item assessment.** If the measuring instrument consists of a number of questions, or items, perhaps only one or two of them are the problem. Deleting them may improve the instrument's validity and reliability.

## EVALUATING THE MEASUREMENT OF VARIABLES

**M**ost published quantitatively-oriented research studies measure variables of some kind or another. Thus, it's important to assess the overall validity and reliability of the measuring instruments that were used to measure the variables—the very topic of this chapter. Quantitatively-oriented research studies are only as good as the measuring instruments they utilized—nonvalid and/or nonreliable measurements can easily produce nonvalid and/or nonreliable research findings.

### USE APPENDIX A

There are a few highly interweaved and non-mutually exclusive questions you can ask when you begin to evaluate the overall validly and reliability of a study's measuring instruments. Appendix A contains numerous questions you can ask (when you put on your "critical thinking" hat) about potential measurement issues. More specifically, you can ask a number of "measurement-type" questions (i.e., questions 117–141 on pages 483–484 in appendix A).

How to evaluate the overall validity and reliability of the measurements used in a research study is totally up to you—and only you. You're the one who must ask and answer the questions. More important, you need to address two extremely difficult critical thinking tasks:

1 You must have a rationale for why you're asking each question in the first place. You just can't ask questions without knowing why you're asking them. Appendix A only lists potential questions you can ask. Can you guess why each one was listed and what importance your answer to each question has for your overall evaluation of the research study?

2 You also must have some kind of idea of what you're going to do with your answer to each question. For example, question 122 on page 483 asks, "Does the author discuss the overall validity of the measuring instruments used in the study?" Let's say your answer was "no". What are you going to do with your answer? That is, how are you going to use it in your overall evaluation of the study's measurements? Now what about if your answer was "yes"?

> Two people can assess the same study in reference to the overall validity and reliability of the measurements used within a research study and come up with two different conclusions.

## CHAPTER RECAP

- The measurement of variables is the cornerstone of all social work positivistic research studies.

- The purpose of measuring a variable is to describe it as completely and accurately as possible.

- The characteristics that describe a variable are known as its attributes.

- Depending on the nature of their attributes, all variables can be measured at one (or more) of four measurement levels: nominal, ordinal, interval, and ratio.

- Measuring instruments can be evaluated by five criteria: utility, sensitivity to small changes, nonreactivity, reliability, and validity.

- The *test-retest method* of reliability asks the question, Does an individual respond to a measuring instrument in the same general way when the instrument is administered twice?

- The *alternate-forms method* of reliability is when two forms of an instrument that are equivalent in their degree of validity are given to the same individual and asks the question: Is there a strong convergence in how that person responds?

- The *split-half method* of reliability asks the question: Are the scores on one half of the measuring instrument similar to those obtained on the other half?

- *Observer reliability* asks the question: Is there an agreement between the observers who are measuring the same variable?

- *Content validity* asks the question: Does the measuring instrument adequately measure the major dimensions of the variable under consideration?

- *Face validity* asks the question: Does the measuring instrument appear to measure the subject matter under consideration?

- *Criterion validity* asks the question: Does the individual's measuring instrument score predict the probable behavior on a second variable (criterion-related measure)?

- *Construct validity* asks the question: Does the measuring instrument appear to measure the general construct (element) it purports to measure.

## REVIEW EXERCISES

1   Before you entered your social work program, and before you read this chapter, how knowledgeable were you about measurement validity and reliability?

2   The measurement of variables has four basic functions. List each function and then discuss why each one is important for social work researchers and practitioners to know. Provide social work examples throughout your discussion to illustrate your main points.

3   What is *measurement validity*? What is measurement reliability? Discuss the main differences between the two concepts and provide examples throughout your discussion to illustrate your main points.

4   In your own words describe *content validity* and provide social work examples throughout your discussion to illustrate your main points.

5   In your own words describe *face validity* and provide social work examples throughout your discussion to illustrate your main points.

6   In your own words describe *criterion validity* and provide social work examples throughout your discussion to illustrate your main points.

7   In your own words describe *concurrent* and *predictive validity* and provide social work examples throughout your discussion to illustrate your main points.

8   In your own words describe *construct validity* and provide social work examples throughout your discussion to illustrate your main points.

9   In your own words describe *convergent-discriminant validation* and provide social work examples throughout your discussion to illustrate your main points.

10   In reference to the reliability of a measuring instrument, discuss the concept of *stability*. Provide social work examples throughout your discussion to illustrate your main points.

11   In reference to the reliability of a measuring instrument, discuss the concept of *equivalence*. Provide social work examples throughout your discussion to illustrate your main points.

12   In reference to the reliability of a measuring instrument, discuss the concept of *homogeneity*. Provide social work examples throughout your discussion to illustrate your main points.

13   In reference to the reliability of a measuring instrument, describe the *test-retest method* and provide social work examples throughout your discussion to illustrate your main points.

14   In reference to the reliability of a measuring instrument, describe the *effects of testing* and provide social work examples throughout your discussion.

15 In reference to the reliability of a measuring instrument, describe the *alternate-forms method* and provide social work examples throughout your discussion to illustrate your main points.

16 In reference to the reliability of a measuring instrument, describe the *split-half method* and provide social work examples throughout your discussion to illustrate your main points.

17 What is measurement error? Why is it important to know? Provide social work examples throughout your discussion to illustrate your main points.

18 In reference to measurement error, describe *constant errors* and provide social work examples throughout your discussion to illustrate your main points.

19 In reference to measurement error, describe *random errors* and provide social work examples throughout your discussion to illustrate your main points.

20 List and discuss each one of the three measurement errors that can occur due to the personal styles of respondents. Provide social work examples throughout your discussion to illustrate your main points.

21 List and discuss each one of the five measurement errors that can occur due to the reactions of observers. Provide social work examples throughout your discussion to illustrate your main points.

**Measurement and the practitioner**

22 **Scenario 1:** Make an argument that to be an effective evidence-based social work **practitioner** *you need to know* how to assess the reliability and validity of measuring instruments that are used in social work research studies. Provide a clear and explicit practice-related social work example to illustrate your main points.

23 **Scenario 2:** Make an argument that *you do not need to know* how to assess the validity and reliability of measuring instruments that are used in social work research studies to be an effective evidence-based **practitioner**. Provide a clear and explicit practice-related social work example to illustrate your main points.

24 **Time to Choose:** Which one of the preceding two scenarios (22 or 23 ) do you feel is more consistent with the concept of the contemporary evidence-based social work practice process as

illustrated on pages 68–72? Why? Provide relevant social work examples to illustrate your main points.

**Measurement and the researcher**

25 **Scenario 1:** Make an argument that to be a competent social work **researcher** *you need to know* how to assess the reliability and validity of measuring instruments. Provide a clear and explicit research-related social work example to illustrate your main points.

26 **Scenario 2:** Make an argument that *you do not need to know* how to assess the reliability and validity of measuring instruments to be a competent social work **researcher**. Provide a clear and explicit research-related social work example to illustrate your main points.

27 **Time to Choose:** Which one of the above two scenarios (25 or 26) do you feel is more consistent with the place of research in social work? Why? Provide relevant social work examples to illustrate your main points.

**Application of validity and reliability**

28 Locate a published quantitative social work-related journal article that utilized a measuring instrument of some kind. We suggest you locate a quantitatively oriented research study in Bruce Thyer's journal *Research on Social Work Practice* (Sage Publications). Hands down, this is the best journal to find good quantitatively oriented social work research studies.

29 What is the name of the measuring instrument used, and what variable did it measure?

30 Did the author of the study provide information on the instrument's reliability and validity? If so, what types of reliability and validity were reported?

31 Did the author mention anything about the instrument's cultural sensitivity (Chapter 6)? If so, what was discussed?

32 Do you feel the measuring instrument really measures the variable it purports to measure? If so, why? If not, why not?

**Moving ahead by looking back**

33 At this point in your research methods course, how comfortable are you with discussing the place of research in social work with your field instructor, with your practice instructor, with your research instructor, with your supervisor at work, with the director of your social work program, or with your classmates? Discuss in detail.

# 12

## 2015 EPAS COMPETENCIES

| COMPETENCY 1 | Demonstrate Ethical and Professional Behavior |
|---|---|

You will learn that in order to be a successful evidence-based practitioner you have an ethical obligation to integrate three research roles into your daily practice activities as discussed in Chapter 3: (1) research consumer, (2) research partner—either as a co-researcher or research participant, and (3) creator and disseminator of research (or knowledge).

This entire chapter pertains to these three professional roles when it comes to selecting, implementing, and evaluating the various measuring instruments that are used in social work practice (research consumer) and research studies (research partner and creator and disseminator of research).

| COMPETENCY 4 | Engage in Practice-Informed Research and Research-Informed Practice |
|---|---|

Competency 4 also pertains to the entire chapter because you have to:

1   Evaluate the author's rationale for why a specific measuring instrument(s) was used to measure the variables within the research study. You'll also need to know the advantages, the disadvantages, and the specific criteria that apply to evaluating measuring instruments—especially standardized measuring instruments (**research consumer**—research-informed practice);

2   Participate in a research study—either as a co-researcher or research participant (**research partner**—practice-informed research). See 1 above and 3 below; and

3   Know how to find, evaluate, and select appropriate measuring instruments to measure the variables in your research study (**creator and disseminator of research**—practice-informed research).

You also need to utilize evidence-based practice recommendations whenever possible; that is, you need to integrate (1) the best available research-based evidence with (2) your clinical expertise and (3) your client's values.

All of the above implies you'll need to know how to assess the strengths and limitations of the various measuring instruments (and methods of their use) that were used in a research study that produced its research-based evidence. In short, you need to ask and then answer a simple question: How seriously should I take the findings of any specific research study given the degree of reliability and validity of the study's measuring instrument(s)?

| COMPETENCY 9 | Evaluate Practice with Individuals, Families, Groups, Organizations, & Communities |
|---|---|

You will learn that to determine your practice effectiveness, you will need to know how to select appropriate instruments to measure the outcomes (evaluation) of your practices with your various client systems. See Competencies 1 and 4.

# Measuring Instruments

| CHAPTERS 1 & 3 | Step 1. | Understanding the Research Process |
| CHAPTER 2 | Step 2. | Formulating Research Questions |
| CHAPTER 4 APPENDIXES A–C | Step 3. | Reviewing the Literature Evaluating the Literature |
| CHAPTERS 5 & 6 | Step 4. | Being Aware of Ethical and Cultural Issues |
| CHAPTERS 7–10 | Step 5. | Selecting a Research Approach |
| CHAPTERS 11 & 12 | Step 6. | Specifying How Variables Are Measured |
| CHAPTER 13 | Step 7. | Selecting a Sample |
| CHAPTERS 14 & 15 | Step 8. | Selecting a Research Design |
| CHAPTERS 16 & 17 | Step 9. | Selecting a Data-Collection Method |
| CHAPTERS 18 & 19 | Step 10. | Analyzing the Data |
| CHAPTERS 20 & 21 | Step 11. | Writing the Research Report |

# Measuring Instruments

"If our measuring instruments collected valid and reliable data let's go with those results. If all we have are uninformed and biased opinions, let's go with mine."

QUESTIONS TO ASK BEFORE MEASURING

*Why* Do We Want to Make the Measurement?

*What* Do We Want to Measure?

*Who* Will Make the Measurement?

*What* Format Do We Require?

*Where* Will the Measurement Be Made?

*When* Will the Measurement Be Made?

TYPES OF MEASURING INSTRUMENTS

Journals or Diaries

Logs

Inventories

Checklists

Summative Instruments

STANDARDIZED MEASURING INSTRUMENTS

Advantages and Disadvantages

Locating Measuring Instruments

*Commercial or Professional Publishers*

*Professional Books and Journals*

EVALUATING MEASURING INSTRUMENTS

CHAPTER RECAP

REVIEW QUESTIONS

**As we know** from the previous chapters in this book, on a very general level, variables refine concepts, and attributes refine variables. For example, the concept "ethnicity" can be refined more specifically in terms of the existence of ethnic groups. "Ethnic group" is a variable because research participants will vary with respect to which ethnic group they belong to.

"Ethnic group" can be refined further via its attributes. The ethnic groups that people can belong to—Asian, Caucasian, Latinx, and so on—constitute the attributes (or value labels, if you will) of the variable "ethnic group." All of this refinement stuff boils down to measurement, as pure and simple as that. As we saw in the last chapter, we need to measure the variables in our research study. One easy way to measure them is through measuring instruments that are as valid and reliable as possible. Before we select a measuring instrument to measure them, however, we need to ask ourselves a few basic questions.

## QUESTIONS TO ASK BEFORE MEASURING

**W**hat we want is some method of selecting from the huge array of measuring instruments that exist. There are six questions we can ask ourselves to help us make our choice. When we have answered them, we will be able to distinguish the kind of instrument we need from the kind we do not need; hopefully, this will eliminate a large number of all those instruments lying in wait in the library and on the Internet. The questions are:

1 *Why* do we want to make the measurement?
2 *What* do we want to measure?
3 *Who* will make the measurement?
4 *What* format do we require?
5 *Where* will the measurement be made?
6 *When* will the measurement be made?

Let's take an extremely simple and offbeat example to illustrate how the use of measuring instruments can be used. Let's say we want to know whether there is a relationship between the two variables: *depression* and *sleep patterns.*

## WHY DO WE WANT TO MAKE THE MEASUREMENT?

The first question is *Why* do we want to make the measurement? At first glance, this does not seem too difficult to answer. We just want to measure depression and sleep patterns with some type of measuring instruments—one for depression and one for sleep patterns—in order to study the relationship between the two variables, if any. But things are not quite as simple as they appear. You just cannot select an instrument in a willy-nilly fashion. The selection of a measuring instrument must be rationally made.

The point of making this selection is to discover how accurate we need the instrument to be. If our measurement is going to affect someone's life, for example, it has to be as accurate as we can possibly make it. We might be doing an assessment that will be used in making decisions about treatment interventions, referrals, placements, and so forth. On the other hand, if our measurement will not affect anyone's life directly, we can afford to be a little less rigid in our requirements. How much less rigid depends on what we are doing.

If this is to be a beginning research study (e.g., exploratory) in a relatively unexplored field, the result will only be a tentative suggestion that some variable is possibly related to some other variable—for instance, sleep patterns are related to depression. A little inaccuracy in measurement in this case is not the end of the world.

When a little more is known in our subject area (e.g., descriptive, explanatory), we might be able to formulate and test a more specific hypothesis; for example, depressed people spend less time in delta-wave NREM sleep than nondepressed people. In this case, we obviously should be able to measure sleep patterns accurately enough to distinguish between delta-wave NREM sleep and other kinds of sleep.

All in all, how accurate our measurement needs to be depends on our purpose. Because we are only doing a beginning study, we can afford to be relatively inaccurate. In general, the higher our research question is on the knowledge level continuum (figure 2.3 on page 48), the more accurate our measurements of our variables need to be.

In short, measuring instruments that measure the variables within causality-comparative interaction questions (the highest level of research questions) need to be more accurate than instruments that are used to measure existence questions (the lowest level of research questions). We have now answered the first question: Why do we want to make the measurement?

## WHAT DO WE WANT TO MEASURE?

The second question is *What* do we want to measure? We know the answer to that one also: We simply want to measure two variables, depression and sleep patterns. But here again, it's not as simple as it may seem. Not only are measuring instruments more accurate or less accurate, they can be wideband or narrowband. Wideband instruments measure a broad trait or characteristic. A trait is pretty much the same thing as a characteristic, and it means some aspect of character such as bravery, gaiety, or depression.

Logically enough, narrowband instruments measure just a particular aspect of a particular trait. A narrowband instrument, for example, might tell us how depressed Uncle Fred feels about his daughter moving to Moose Jaw, but it will not give us an overall picture of Uncle Fred's depression. Thus, a wideband instrument will give an overall picture of Uncle Fred's depression, but it will not tell us how he feels about his daughter moving to Moose Jaw.

In our particular study, we are not interested too much in how Uncle Fred feels about his daughter moving to Moose Jaw. If he's one of our research participants, we just want to know about his overall depression level so that we can relate it to his sleep patterns.

We need a wideband instrument then, which does not have to be absolutely smack-on 100% accurate.

## *WHO* WILL MAKE THE MEASUREMENT?

The third question asks, *Who* will make the measurement? We will—that seems obvious enough. However, it's not always social workers who complete the measuring instruments. More often than not, our research participants complete them. In our study, it will be the people who participate in our study who will fill out the instrument to measure their depression levels. Sometimes family members complete the measuring instruments, or teachers, specially trained outside observers, or the staff members in an institution.

The point is that different kinds of people require different kinds of measuring instruments. An instrument that could be completed easily and accurately by a trained social worker might prove too difficult for Uncle Fred, who has arthritis and cataracts and a reading level of around the fourth grade. In our simple research study, we will have to be sure the instrument we finally select is easy for our research participants to understand. So far, then, to measure the depression levels of our research participants, we need a wideband instrument, easy to complete, and not necessarily smack-on accurate.

## *WHAT* FORMAT DO WE REQUIRE?

The fourth question is *What* format do we require? A format is the way our questions will look on the page. They may appear as:

- **A simple inventory, such as:**

  List below the things that make you feel depressed.

  1

  2

  3

  4

  5

- **Or a checklist, such as:**

  Check below all the things that you sometimes feel.

  \_\_\_\_\_ My mother gets on my nerves

  \_\_\_\_\_ My father does not understand me

  \_\_\_\_\_ I do not get along very well with my sister

  \_\_\_\_\_ I think I hate my family sometimes

- **Or a scale, such as:**

  How satisfied are you with your life? (Circle one number below.)

  1 Very unsatisfied

  2 Somewhat satisfied

  3 Satisfied

  4 More than satisfied

  5 Very satisfied

More often than not, measuring instruments contain a number of items, or questions, that when totaled yield more accurate results than just asking one question. These measuring instruments are called *summative instruments* and will be discussed more thoroughly later in this chapter.

After careful thought, we decide that a wideband, easy-to-complete, not-smack-on-accurate summative scale would do the job. However, we have not finished yet. Instruments may be unidimensional or multidimensional. A unidimensional instrument only measures one variable—for example, self-esteem (e.g., figure 11.1 on page 218).

By contrast, a multidimensional instrument measures a number of variables at the same time. A multidimensional instrument is nothing more than a number of unidimensional instruments stuck together. Most often these are called *subscales*. For example, Figure 12.1 on the following page is a multidimensional instrument that contains three subscales, or three unidimensional instruments:

1   Relevance of received social services (items 1–11)
2   The extent to which the services reduced the problem (items 12–21)
3   The extent to which services enhanced the client's self-esteem and contributed to a sense of power and integrity (items 22–34)

Because our study is rather simplistic, we only need two unidimensional instruments—one for depression and one for sleep patterns.

## *WHERE* WILL THE MEASUREMENT BE MADE?

The fifth question asks, *Where* will the measurement be made? Well, probably in our good friend's sleep laboratory. At first glance, it may seem that it does not matter where the measurement is made, but in fact it matters a great deal. For example, we might have a child who throws temper tantrums mostly in school. In this case, measurements dealing with temper tantrums should obviously be made at school.

We can see that an instrument that is to be completed in a railway station might differ from an instrument that is to be used in the comparative serenity of our office. It should be shorter, say, and simpler, and possibly printed on paper that glows in the dark so that if it gets torn out of our hands, we can chase after it more easily. We decide that our research participants will probably be equally depressed everywhere, more or less, and that the measurements will take place in our friend's sleep laboratory.

## *WHEN* WILL THE MEASUREMENT BE MADE?

Our last question is, *When* will the measurement be made? We'll probably use it sometime in August, if it all goes well. But no, the month of the year is not what is meant by *when*. *When* refers to the time or times during the study when a measurement is made.

As will be seen in Chapters 14 and 15, there are certain research designs in which we measure a client's problem, do something to change the problem, and then measure the problem again to see if we have changed it. This involves two measurements, the first and second measurements of the problem. In research jargon, we represent these measurements as *O*s (*O* stands for *Observation*). Whatever we do to change the problem—usually a social work intervention—is represented by *X*.

In short, in research designs we represent the dependent variables by *O*s, and the independent variables by *X*s. If our research design is such that we make an initial measurement of the dependent variable ($O_1$), introduce an independent variable ($X$), and then measure the same dependent variable again ($O_2$), our design would look like: $O_1 \, X \, O_2$.

## SOCIAL SERVICE SATISFACTION SCALE

Using the scale from one to five described below, please indicate at the left of each item the number that comes closest to how you feel.

1 Strongly agree

2 Agree

3 Undecided

4 Disagree

5 Strongly disagree

1. ___ The social worker took my problems very seriously.
2. ___ If I had been the worker, I would have dealt with my problems in the same way.
3. ___ The worker I had could never understand anyone like me.
4. ___ Overall the agency has been very helpful to me.
5. ___ If friends of mine had similar problems I would tell them to go to the agency.
6. ___ The social worker asks a lot of embarrassing questions.
7. ___ I can always count on the worker to help if I'm in trouble.
8. ___ The agency will help me as much as it can.
9. ___ I don't think the agency has the power to really help me.
10. ___ The social worker tries hard but usually isn't too helpful.
11. ___ The problem the agency helped me with is one of the most important in my life.
12. ___ Things have gotten better since I've been going to the agency.
13. ___ Since I've been using the agency my life is more messed up than ever.
14. ___ The agency is always available when I need it.
15. ___ I got from the agency exactly what I wanted.
16. ___ The social worker loves to talk but won't really do anything for me.
17. ___ Sometimes I just tell the social worker what I think she wants to hear.
18. ___ The social worker is usually in a hurry when I see her.
19. ___ No one should have any trouble getting some help from this agency.
20. ___ The worker sometimes says things I don't understand.
21. ___ The social worker is always explaining things carefully.
22. ___ I never looked forward to my visits to the agency.
23. ___ I hope I'll never have to go back to the agency for help.
24. ___ Every time I talk to my worker I feel relieved.
25. ___ I can tell the social worker the truth without worrying.
26. ___ I usually feel nervous when I talk to my worker.
27. ___ The social worker is always looking for lies in what I tell her.
28. ___ It takes a lot of courage to go to the agency.
29. ___ When I enter the agency I feel very small and insignificant.
30. ___ The agency is very demanding.
31. ___ The social worker will sometimes lie to me.
32. ___ Generally the social worker is an honest person.
33. ___ I have the feeling that the worker talks to other people about me.
34. ___ I always feel well treated when I leave the agency.

**Figure 12.1**

Reid-Gundlach *Social Service Satisfaction Scale*

# TYPES OF MEASURING INSTRUMENTS

**T**he type of measuring instrument you choose to measure your variables within your research study depends on your research situation—the question you are asking, the kind of data you need, the research participants you have selected, and the time and money you have available. Every measuring instrument you consider must be evaluated in terms of the five criteria discussed in the previous chapter; that is, it must be useful, sensitive, nonreactive, reliable, and valid. In general, there are many different types of measuring instruments. We will only discuss five:

1   Journals or diaries
2   Logs
3   Inventories
4   Checklists
5   Summative instruments

## JOURNALS OR DIARIES

Journals or diaries are a useful means of data collection when you are undertaking an interpretive study. They are usually not used as data collection methods within positivistic studies. Perhaps in your interpretive study you are asking the question "What are women's experiences of home birth?" and you want your research participants to keep a record of their experiences from early pregnancy to after delivery.

With respect to the five criteria mentioned in the previous chapter, a journal is valid in this context to the extent that it completely and accurately describes the relevant experiences and omits the irrelevant ones. This can only be achieved if the women keeping them have reasonable language skills, can stick pretty much to the point (will they include a three-page description their cats or their geraniums?), and are willing to complete their journals on a regular basis.

A word is in order here about retrospective data—that is, data based on someone's memory of what occurred in the past. There is some truth to the idea that we invent our memories. At least, we might embellish or distort them, and a description is much more liable to be accurate if it's written immediately after the event it describes rather than days or weeks later.

The journal is reliable insofar as the same experience evokes the same written response. Over time, women may tire of describing again an experience almost identical to the one they had last week, and they may omit it (affecting validity), or change it a little to make it more interesting (again affecting validity), or try to write it in a different way (affecting reliability).

Utility very much depends on whether the woman likes to write and is prepared to continue with what may become an onerous task. Another aspect of utility relates to your own role as researcher. Will you have the time required to go through each journal and perform the kind of qualitative analysis as outlined in Chapter 19?

Sensitivity has to do with the amount of detail included in the journal. To some degree, this reflects completeness and is a validity issue, but small changes in women's experiences as the pregnancy progresses cannot be tracked unless the experiences are each described in some detail.

Journals are usually very reactive. Indeed, they are often used as therapeutic tools simply because the act of writing encourages the writer to reflect on what has been written, thus achieving deeper insights that may lead to behavior and/or affective changes.

Reactivity is not desirable in a measuring instrument. On the other hand, an interpretive study seeks to uncover not just the experiences themselves but the meaning attached to them by the research participants, and meaning may emerge more clearly if the participants are encouraged to reflect. Researchers themselves always keep journals while conducting interpretive studies. Journal keeping by the researcher is discussed in Chapter 19 on qualitative data analyses.

## LOGS

You have probably used logs in your field placement, so we will not discuss their use in depth. When used in research situations, they are nothing more than a structured kind of journal, where the research participant is asked to record in note form the events related to particular experiences or behaviors.

Each note usually includes headings: the event itself, when and where the event happened, and who was there. A log may be more valid than a journal in that the headings prompt the participant to include only relevant information with no discursive wanderings into cats or geraniums.

The log may be more reliable than a journal because it's more likely that a similar experience will be recorded in a similar way. It may be more useful because it takes less time for the participant to complete and less time for the researcher to analyze. It's usually less sensitive to small changes because it includes less detail, and it may be somewhat less reactive depending on the extent to which it leads to reflection and change.

## INVENTORIES

An inventory is a list made by the research participants. For example, the following is an inventory designed to measure depression:

**List below the things that make you feel depressed.**

1

2

3

This is valid to the degree that the list is complete, and sensitive in that the addition or omission of items over time is indicative of change. It's useful if the participant is prepared to complete it carefully and truthfully, and it's probably fairly reactive in that it provokes thought. Inventories are commonly used in interpretive studies.

## CHECKLISTS

A checklist is a list prepared by the researcher. For example, a checklist designed to measure depression would include more items than shown but would follow this format:

**Check below all the things that you have felt during the past week.**

\_\_\_\_\_　A wish to be alone

\_\_\_\_\_　Sadness

\_\_\_\_\_　Powerlessness

\_\_\_\_\_　Anxiety

With respect to the five evaluative criteria presented in the previous chapter, the same considerations apply to a checklist as to an inventory except that content validity may be compromised if the researcher does not include all the possibilities that are relevant to the participant in the context of the study.

## SUMMATIVE INSTRUMENTS

On a general level, inventories and checklists ask for yes or no answers. In other words, they are dichotomous in that research participants can only respond in one of two ways: yes, this occurred, or no, this did not occur. Summative measuring instruments provide a greater range of responses, usually asking how frequently or to what degree a particular item, or question, applies. For example, the depression checklist shown on the previous page may be presented in the form of a summated instrument, as follows:

**Indicate how often you have experienced the following feelings by circling the appropriate number:**

|                | Never | Rarely | Sometimes | Often |
|----------------|-------|--------|-----------|-------|
| Being alone    | 1     | 2      | 3         | 4     |
| Sadness        | 1     | 2      | 3         | 4     |
| Powerlessness  | 1     | 2      | 3         | 4     |
| Anxious        | 1     | 2      | 3         | 4     |

The words "never" and "often" are known as anchors and serve to describe the meanings attached to their respective values. Participants circle a number for each item, and the scores are summed, or totaled. With only the four items shown (an actual depression scale would contain many more), the lowest possible score is 4, and the highest possible score is 16.

This instrument is an example of a summative instrument. A summative measuring instrument is any instrument that allows the researcher to derive a sum or total score from a number of items, or questions. Most, but not all, summated measuring instruments are usually designed so that low scores indicate a low level of the variable being measured (depression, in this case) and high scores indicate a high level. Figure 11.1 on page 218 and figure 12.1 on page 241 are two excellent examples of summative instruments.

When doing a positivistic study, summative measuring instruments should be used whenever possible as they are more valid and reliable than the other four types. However, you must always take into account your research question or hypothesis and from this question or hypothesis determine what type of instrument will be the best one to measure your variables.

## STANDARDIZED MEASURING INSTRUMENTS

**S**tandardized measuring instruments are used widely in social work because they have usually been extensively tested and they come complete with information on the results of that testing. Figure 11.1 (page 218), via Figure 11.1a (page 222), is an excellent example of a summative standardized measuring instrument in that it provides information about itself in six areas:

1  Purpose
2  Description
3  Norms
4  Scoring
5  Reliability (see chapter 11)
6  Validity (see chapter 11)

*Purpose* is a simple statement of what the instrument is designed to measure. *Description* provides particular features of the instrument, including its length and often its clinical cutting score. The clinical cutting score is different for every instrument (if it has one, that is) and is the score that differentiates the respondents with a clinically significant problem from the respondents with no such problem. In Hudson's *Index of Self-Esteem* (figure 11.1 on page 218), for example, people who score above 30 (±5 for error) have a clinically significant problem with self-esteem, and people who score less than 30 do not.

The section on *norms* tells you who the instrument was validated on. The *Index of Self-Esteem,* for example (see NORMS in figure 11.1a on page 222), was tested on 1,745 respondents, including single and married individuals, clinical and nonclinical populations, college students and nonstudents, Caucasians, Japanese and Chinese Americans, and a smaller number of other ethnic groups.

It's important to know this because people with different characteristics tend to respond differently to the sort of items contained in Hudson's *Index of Self-Esteem.* For instance, a woman from a culture that values modesty might be unwilling to answer that she feels she is a beautiful person all of the time (item 3). She might not know what a wallflower is (item 19), and she might be very eager to assert that she feels self-conscious with strangers (item 16) because she thinks that women ought to feel that way.

It's therefore very important to use any measuring instrument only with people who have the same characteristics as the people who participated in the development of the instrument. As another example, instruments used with children must have been developed using children.

*Scoring* gives instructions about how to score the instrument. Reliability and validity were already discussed in the previous chapter. Summated standardized instruments are usually reliable, valid, sensitive, and nonreactive. It's therefore very tempting to believe that they must be useful, whatever the research situation. More often than not, they are useful—provided that what the instrument measures and what the researcher wants to measure are the same thing.

If you want to measure family coping, for example, and come across a wonderful standardized instrument designed to measure family cohesion, you must resist the temptation to convince yourself that family cohesion is what you really wanted to measure in the first place. Just remember that the variable you wish to measure selects the instrument, the instrument doesn't select the variable.

## ADVANTAGES AND DISADVANTAGES

Like everything in life, there are advantages and disadvantages to standardized measuring instruments. Judy Krysik (2018) briefly lists them as follows:

**Advantages**
1 Standardized instruments are readily available and easy to access.
2 The development work has already been done.
3 They have established reliability and validity estimates.
4 Norms may be available for comparison.
5 Most are easy to complete and score.
6 In many instances, they are available free of charge.
7 They may be available in different languages.
8 They specify age range and reading level.
9 Time required for administration has been determined.

**Disadvantages**

1  The norms may not apply to the target population.
2  The language may be difficult.
3  The tone might not fit with the philosophy of the program, for example, deficit based versus strength based.
4  The target population may not understand the translation.
5  The scoring procedure may be overly complex.
6  The instrument may not be affordable.
7  Special qualifications or training might be required for use.
8  The instrument may be too long or time consuming to administer.

# LOCATING MEASURING INSTRUMENTS

Once you decide that you want to measure a variable through the use of a standardized instrument, the next consideration is to find it. Two sources for locating instruments are:

1  Commercial or professional publishers
2  Professional books and journals

## COMMERCIAL OR PROFESSIONAL PUBLISHERS

Numerous commercial and professional publishing companies specialize in the production and sale of standardized measuring instruments for use in the social services. They can be easily found on the Internet. The cost of instruments purchased from a publisher varies considerably, depending on the instrument, the number of copies needed, and the publisher.

The instruments generally are well developed, and their psychometric properties are supported by the results of several research studies. Often manuals that include the normative data for the instrument accompany them. As well, publishers are expected to comply with professional standards such as those established by the American Psychological Association. These standards apply to claims made about the instrument's rationale, development, psychometric properties, administration, and interpretation of results.

Standards for the use of some instruments have been developed to protect the interests of clients. Consequently, purchasers of instruments may be required to have certain qualifications, such as possession of an advanced degree in a relevant field. A few publishers require membership in particular professional organizations. Most publishers will, however, accept an order from a social work student if a qualified person, such as an instructor, who will supervise the use of the instrument, cosigns it.

## PROFESSIONAL BOOKS AND JOURNALS

Standardized measuring instruments are most commonly described in human service journals. The instruments usually are supported by evidence of their validity and reliability, although they often require cross-validation and normative data from more representative samples and subsamples. More often than not, however, the complete instrument cannot be seen in the articles that describe them. However, they usually contain a few items that can be found within the actual instrument.

Locating instruments in journals or books is not easy. Of the two most common methods, computer searches of databanks and manual searches of the literature, the former is faster, unbelievably more thorough, and easier to use. Unfortunately, financial support for the development of comprehensive databanks has been limited and intermittent.

Another disadvantage is that many articles on instruments are not referenced with the appropriate indicators for computer retrieval. These limitations are being overcome by the changing technology of computers and information retrieval systems.

Several services now allow for a complex breakdown of measurement need. Databanks that include references from over 1,300 journals, updated monthly, are now available from a division of Psychological Abstracts Information Services and from Bibliographic Retrieval Services.

Nevertheless, most social workers will probably rely on manual searches of references such as Psychological Abstracts. Although the reference indexes will be the same as those in the databanks accessible by computer, the literature search can be supplemented with appropriate seminal (original) reference volumes.

## EVALUATING MEASURING INSTRUMENTS

**M**any published quantitatively-oriented research studies measure variables with standardized measuring instruments—the very topic of this chapter. Thus, it's important to assess their overall credibility.

There are a few highly interweaved and non-mutually exclusive questions you can ask when you begin to evaluate the overall creditability of standardized measuring instruments. Appendix A contains numerous questions you can ask (when you put on your "critical thinking" hat) about potential issues that can arise when using standardized measurements. More specifically, you can ask a number of "standardized measurement-type" questions (i.e., questions 142–159 on pages 484–485 in appendix A).

How to evaluate the overall creditability of the measurements used in a research study is totally up to you—and only you. You're the one who must ask and answer the questions. More important, you need to address two extremely difficult tasks:

> Two people can assess the same standardized measuring instrument that was used within a research study and come up with two different conclusions.

1 You must have a rationale for why you're asking each question in the first place. You just can't ask questions without knowing why you're asking them. Appendix A only lists potential questions you can ask. Can you guess why each one was listed and what importance your answer to each question has on your overall evaluation of the research study?

2 You also must have some kind of idea of what you're going to do with your answer to each question. For example, question 152 on page 485 asks, "Are the measuring instrument appropriate lengths?" Let's say your answer was "no". What are you going to do with your answer? That is, how are you going to use it in your overall evaluation of the study's measurements? Now what about if your answer was "yes"?

## CHAPTER RECAP

- There are six questions you need to ask and answer before selecting a measuring instrument.

- There are five basic types of measuring instruments.

- Whenever possible, it's always best to use standardized measuring instruments rather than designing your own.

- You can locate standardized measuring instruments through commercial publishers in addition to books and journals.

## REVIEW QUESTIONS

1   Before you entered your social work program, and before you read this chapter, how knowledgeable were you about the various types of standardized measuring instruments? Discuss in detail.

2   In your own words describe measuring instruments. What's so "standardized" about them anyway? Provide social work examples throughout your discussion to illustrate your main points.

3   List and discuss the main advantages of using standardized measuring instruments in social work research and practice. Provide social work examples throughout your discussion to illustrate your main points.

4   What are *journals or diaries*? How can they be used in social work research and practice? Provide social work examples throughout your discussion to illustrate your main points.

5   What are *logs*? How can they be used in social work research and practice? Provide social work examples throughout your discussion to illustrate your main points.

6   What are *inventories*? How can they be used in social work research and practice? Provide social work examples throughout your discussion to illustrate your main points.

7   What are *checklists*? How can they be used in social work research and practice? Provide social work examples throughout your discussion to illustrate your main points.

8   What are *summative instruments*? How can they be used in social work research and practice? Provide social work examples throughout your discussion to illustrate your main points.

9   When selecting an instrument to measure a variable of some kind, you need to ask and answer six questions. List each question and discuss why the answer is important for you to know either as a social work researcher or as a social work practitioner. Provide social work examples throughout your discussion to illustrate your main points.

10   When choosing a standardized measuring instrument from the hundreds that exist, you need to ask and answer four questions. List each question and discuss why the answer is important for you to know either as a social work researcher or as a social work practitioner. Provide social work examples throughout your discussion to illustrate your main points.

11   What are *nonstandardized* measuring instruments? In what research or practice situations would it be appropriate to use them? Provide social work examples throughout your discussion to illustrate your main points.

12   List and then discuss each one of the nine advantages of using standardized measuring instruments either in research situations or practice situations. Provide social work examples throughout your discussion to illustrate your main points.

13   List and then discuss each one of the eight disadvantages of using standardized measuring instruments either in research situations or practice situations. Provide social work examples throughout your discussion to illustrate your main points.

14   List the six questions that need to be answered before selecting a measuring instrument.

- Now pretend you're going to find a measuring instrument that measures the interviewing skills of social work students. Answer each of the six questions in relation to finding such an instrument, keeping in mind who is going to complete the instrument— which is probably you.

- Could your field instructor also fill it out? Why or why not?

- How about your instructor who taught you interviewing skills?

- How about your clients that you saw in your field placement?

# PART IV

# SAMPLING AND RESEARCH DESIGNS

CHAPTER 13: Sampling   250

CHAPTER 14: Single-Subject Designs   268

CHAPTER 15: Group Designs   292

# 2015 EPAS COMPETENCIES

| COMPETENCY 1 | Demonstrate Ethical and Professional Behavior |
|---|---|

You will learn that in order to be a successful evidence-based practitioner you have an ethical obligation to integrate three research roles into your daily practice activities as discussed in Chapter 3: (1) research consumer, (2) research partner—either as a co-researcher or research participant, and (3) creator and disseminator of research (or knowledge).

This entire chapter pertains to these three professional research-related roles when it comes to selecting, implementing, and evaluating the various sampling methods that can be used in social work research studies.

| COMPETENCY 4 | Engage in Practice-Informed Research and Research-Informed Practice |
|---|---|

Competency 4 also pertains to the entire chapter because you have to:

1   Evaluate the appropriateness of the sampling method(s) utilized in a published research study (**research consumer**—research-informed practice);

2   Participate in a research study—either as a co-researcher or research participant (**research partner**—practice-informed research). See 1 above and 3 below; and

3   Know the advantages and disadvantages of the various sampling methods, in addition to knowing how to implement them, when you actually conduct a research study (**creator and disseminator of research**—practice-informed research).

You also need to utilize evidence-based practice recommendations whenever possible; that is, you need to integrate (1) the best available research-based evidence with (2) your clinical expertise and (3) your client's values.

All of the above implies you'll need to know how to assess the strengths and limitations of the various sampling methods that were used in a research study that produced its research-based evidence. In short, you need to ask and then answer a simple question: How seriously should I take the findings of any specific research study given the appropriateness of the study's sampling method?

| COMPETENCY 9 | Evaluate Practice with Individuals, Families, Groups, Organizations, & Communities |
|---|---|

You will learn that to design an evaluation of any kind, you will need to choose appropriate sampling methods to evaluate a single client system (Chapter 14) or an entire social service program (Chapter 15). See Competencies 1 and 4.

# Sampling

| | | |
|---|---|---|
| CHAPTERS 1 & 3 | Step 1. | Understanding the Research Process |
| CHAPTER 2 | Step 2. | Formulating Research Questions |
| CHAPTER 4 APPENDIXES A–C | Step 3. | Reviewing the Literature Evaluating the Literature |
| CHAPTERS 5 & 6 | Step 4. | Being Aware of Ethical and Cultural Issues |
| CHAPTERS 7–10 | Step 5. | Selecting a Research Approach |
| CHAPTERS 11 & 12 | Step 6. | Specifying How Variables Are Measured |
| CHAPTER 13 | Step 7. | Selecting a Sample |
| CHAPTERS 14 & 15 | Step 8. | Selecting a Research Design |
| CHAPTERS 16 & 17 | Step 9. | Selecting a Data-Collection Method |
| CHAPTERS 18 & 19 | Step 10. | Analyzing the Data |
| CHAPTERS 20 & 21 | Step 11. | Writing the Research Report |

# Sampling

"Darn it! Our last sample didn't give us the results we needed so we're going to find a more cooperative one."

POPULATIONS AND SAMPLING FRAMES
    Sampling Frames
SAMPLING PROCEDURES
    Probability Sampling
        *Simple Random Sampling*
        *Systematic Random Sampling*
        *Stratified Random Sampling*
        *Cluster Random Sampling*
    Nonprobability Sampling
        *Availability Sampling*
        *Purposive Sampling*
        *Quota Sampling*
        *Snowball Sampling*
SAMPLE SIZE
    Lessons about Sample Quality
ADVANTAGES AND DISADVANTAGES
EVALUATING RESEARCH SETTINGS AND SAMPLES
    Research Settings
    Use the Appendixes
    Samples
CHAPTER RECAP
REVIEW EXERCISES

THE LAST CHAPTER BRIEFLY DISCUSSED measuring instruments—how to select them, where to find them, and how to evaluate them. This chapter discusses who will complete them. In short, we discuss how to select the actual people, or research participants, you will administer the measuring instruments to.

Let's continue with the previous example we used in the last chapter where we are trying to discover whether there is a relationship between two variables—*depression* and *sleep patterns*. At this point, it's obviously necessary to find a few people so we can measure their depression levels (variable 1) and sleep patterns (variable 2).

One way of doing this is to phone our trusty social worker friend, Ken, who works with people who are depressed and ask if he will please find us some clients, or research participants, who do not mind sleeping in a laboratory once a week with wires attached to their heads. "Certainly," says Ken crisply. "How many do you want?" "Er . . ." we say, "how many have ya got?".

"Oh, lots," says Ken with cheer. "Now, do you want them young or old, male or female, rich or poor, acute or chronic, severely or mildly depressed . . . ?" He adds, "Oh, and by the way, all of them are refugees from Outer Ganglinshan." We decide that we need to think about this some more. Suppose that the sleep patterns of Outer Ganglinshanians who are depressed are different from the sleep patterns of Bostonians who are depressed.

Suppose even further that men who are depressed have different sleep patterns from women who are depressed, or adolescents who are depressed from seniors who are depressed, or Anabaptists who are depressed from Theosophists who are depressed. The list of possibilities is endless.

One solution, of course, would be to assemble all the people who are depressed in the Western Hemisphere in the hope that Anabaptists and Theosophists and so forth are properly represented. This leaves out the Eastern Hemisphere, but we have to eliminate something because our sleep laboratory has only ten beds. There is another difficulty, too. Not only are we restricted to ten sleeping people, but also on our limited budget we will be hard pressed to pay them bus fare from their homes to our laboratory.

This being the case, we have to forget about the Western Hemisphere and concentrate on the area served by the city transit, within which there are probably very few Anabaptists who are depressed and no Theosophists at all to speak of. How are we going to select

> *Sampling theory* is the logic of using methods to ensure that a sample drawn from a population are similar in all relevant characteristics.

ten people from this small area and still be fair to the Theosophist population? The answer is simple: We do this through the use of creating populations and sampling frames.

## POPULATIONS AND SAMPLING FRAMES

A population is the totality of persons or objects with which our research study is concerned. If, for example, we are interested in all the people who are depressed in the Western Hemisphere, then our population is all the people who are depressed in the Western Hemisphere. If we decide to restrict our study to all the people who are depressed in the area served by city transit, then our population is all the people who are depressed in the area served by city transit. Simple as that.

However we decide to define our population, the results of our study will apply only to that population from which our sample was drawn. Thus, we cannot do our study on folks within the confines of city transit and then apply the results to the whole of the Western Hemisphere.

### SAMPLING FRAMES

When our population has been clearly identified, the next step is to make a list of all the people (or other units such as case files) included in that population. Such a list is called a *sampling frame.* For example, if our population of interest is all the people who are depressed in the area served by city transit, then we must create a list, or sampling frame, of all the people who are depressed in the area served by city transit. Obtaining a sampling frame is often one of the hardest parts of doing any research study.

We probably will not be able to generate a list of all the people who are depressed in the area served by city transit because there is not a single person or social service program that knows all of them. It might be better to restrict our study to all the depressed people treated by Ken—or some other source of people who are depressed who will provide us with a list.

Suppose, then, that we have decided to restrict our study to all the people who are depressed treated by Ken. We may think that "all the people who are depressed treated by Ken" is a reasonable definition of our population. But a population has to be defined exactly. "All the people who are depressed treated by Ken" is possibly not very exact, especially when we consider that Ken has been treating them for over twenty years.

The ones treated eighteen and nineteen years ago have doubtless disappeared by now over the far horizon; indeed, the fates of those treated a mere year ago might be equally veiled in mystery. Perhaps we should redefine our population as "all the people who are depressed treated by Ken over the last three months," or better yet as "all the people who are depressed treated by Ken from January 1 to March 31."

> A population is the totality of persons (or units) with which your research study is concerned.

> A sampling frame is a specific list of persons (or units) that you're interested in within your population.

## SAMPLING PROCEDURES

If you can make a three-month list of all the people who are depressed and treated by Ken from January 1 to March 31, you not only have selected your population but your sampling frame as well. The next thing is to select folks from your sampling frame to include in your research study. This process is called *sampling,* and the people (or other units such as case files) picked from a sampling frame make up a sample. There are two basic ways of selecting samples from sampling frames.

1   **Probability sampling** is a procedure in which all the persons, events, or objects in the sampling frame have a *known* probability of being included in the sample.

2  **Nonprobability sampling** is a procedure in which all the persons, events, or objects in the sampling frame have an *unknown* probability of being included in the sample.

# PROBABILITY SAMPLING

The first main category of sampling procedures is probability sampling. This method of sampling is used more often in positivistic studies than in interpretive ones. A probability sample is one in which all the people (or units in the sampling frame) have the same known probability of being selected for the sample. By probability, we mean chance, such as the probability of winning a lottery. The selection is based on some form of random procedure of which there are four main types.

1  **Simple random sampling** is a procedure in which members of a sampling frame are selected one at a time, without a chance of being selected again, until the desired sample size is obtained.

2  **Systematic random sampling** is a procedure in which every person at a designated interval in a specific sampling frame is selected to be included in a research study's sample.

3  **Stratified random sampling** is a procedure in which a sampling frame is divided into two or more strata to be sampled separately, using simple random or systematic random sampling techniques.

4  **Cluster random sampling** is a procedure in which the sampling frame is divided into groups (or clusters); the groups, rather than the individuals, are selected for inclusion in the sample.

## SIMPLE RANDOM SAMPLING

The first type of probability sampling is simple random sampling. Suppose that there are 100 names in our sampling frame; that is, Ken has seen 100 different clients who were depressed from January 1 to March 31.

We assign each one of these clients a number; the first one on the list will be 001, the second 002, and so on until 100 is reached. Then we take a book of random numbers, open the book at random, and pick a digit on the page also at random. The first half page of such a table is shown in Table 13.1 on the following page.

Suppose the digit we happen to pick is 1, the second digit in the number in the sixth row from the bottom in the second column from the left. (That whole number is **81864** and is highlighted in **bold**.) The two digits immediately to the right of 1 are 8 and 6; thus, we have 186. We take three digits in total because 100, the highest number on our sampling frame, has three digits. The number 186 is more than 100, so we ignore it.

Going down the column, 954 is also more than 100, so we ignore it also. The next one, 021, is less than 100, so we can say that we have selected number 021 on our sampling frame to take part in our study. After 072 and 045 there are no more numbers less than 100 in the second column (middle three digits), so we go to the third column (middle three digits). Here we discover seven more people (i.e., 016, 094, 096, 049, 031, 057, 022).

We go down the columns and pick out numbers until it occurs to us that we do not really know how many numbers should be selected. Our sleep laboratory has accommodation for ten, but then if we do a different ten each night of the week, that is seventy people. With Sundays off, to keep us sane, we have sixty. If we keep union hours, we are looking at closer to thirty-five. There has to be a better way than union hours to figure out our sample size. So, before looking at sample size, we should examine three more probability sampling procedures.

---

The two sampling procedures are methods of selecting members from the sampling frame for inclusion in your research study.

### Table 13.1
Partial Page of a Random Numbers Table

| | | | | | | | |
|---|---|---|---|---|---|---|---|
| 02584 | 75844 | 50162 | 44269 | 76402 | 33228 | 96152 | 76777 |
| 66791 | 44653 | 90947 | 61934 | 79627 | 81621 | 74744 | 98758 |
| 44306 | 88222 | 30967 | 57776 | 90533 | 01276 | 30525 | 66914 |
| 01471 | 15131 | 38577 | 03362 | 54825 | 27705 | 60680 | 97083 |
| 65995 | 81864 | 19184 | 61585 | 19111 | 08641 | 47653 | 27267 |
| 45567 | 79547 | 89025 | 70767 | 25307 | 33151 | 00375 | 17564 |
| 27340 | 30215 | 28376 | 47390 | 11039 | 39458 | 67489 | 48547 |
| 02584 | 75844 | 56012 | 44269 | 76402 | 33228 | 96152 | 76777 |
| 66791 | 44653 | 90497 | 61934 | 79627 | 81621 | 74744 | 98758 |
| 44306 | 80722 | 30317 | 57776 | 90533 | 01276 | 30525 | 66914 |
| 65995 | **81864** | 19184 | 61585 | 19131 | 08641 | 47653 | 27267 |
| 45567 | 79547 | 89025 | 70767 | 25307 | 33151 | 00375 | 17564 |
| 27340 | 30215 | 23456 | 47390 | 11039 | 39458 | 67489 | 48547 |
| 02471 | 10721 | 30577 | 03362 | 54825 | 27705 | 60680 | 97083 |
| 60791 | 40453 | 90227 | 61934 | 79627 | 81621 | 74744 | 98758 |
| 43316 | 87212 | 36967 | 57576 | 90533 | 01276 | 30525 | 66914 |

## SYSTEMATIC RANDOM SAMPLING

The second type of probability sampling is systematic random sampling. Here, the size of our sampling frame is divided by the desired sample size to give us our sampling interval. To state it more simply, if we only want half the sampling frame to be in our sample, we select every other person. If only a third of the sampling frame is needed to be in our sample, we pick every third person; for a quarter, every fourth person; for a fifth, every fifth person; and so on.

The problem with this approach is that we need to know the exact size of our sampling frame in order to do it. We will not really know what our sample size ought to be until later in this chapter. At this point, we can only make a guess. Let's assume that we will work at our sleep lab every weeknight. Ten sleepers every night for five nights gives us a sample size of five nights times ten sleepers which equals fifty.

The idea of a sampling interval can be expressed mathematically in the following way. Suppose that the size of our sampling frame is 100 and we have set our sample size—the number of people taking part in our study—at fifty. Then, dividing the former by the latter (100/50 = 2) provides the size of the sampling interval, which in this case is two.

If our sample was only going to be one-fourth of the size of our sampling frame (instead of one-half), our sampling interval would be four instead of two. We might start at the fourth person on our sampling frame and pick out, as well, the eighth, twelfth, sixteenth persons, and so on. The problem with this method is that everyone does not have the same chance of being selected. If we are selecting every other person, starting with the second person, we select the fourth, sixth, and so on. But this means that the third and the fifth never get a chance to be chosen. This procedure introduces a potential bias that calls for caution.

**Table 13.2**

Stratified Random Sample Example (sampling frame = 100 people)

| Category | Number | 1/10 Proportionate Sample | Number and (Disproportionate Sampling Fractions) for a Sample of 1 per Category |
|---|---|---|---|
| Jews | 40 | 4.0 | 1 (1/40) |
| Christians | 19 | 1.9 | 1 (1/19) |
| Muslims | 10 | 1.0 | 1 (1/10) |
| Buddhists | 10 | 1.0 | 1 (1/10 |
| Hindus | 10 | 1.0 | 1 (1/10) |
| Sikhs | 10 | 1.0 | 1 (1/10) |
| Theosophists | 1 | .1 | 1 (1) |
| Totals . . . | 100 | 10.0 | 7 |

Suppose, for example, we have applied for a credit card and the credit card company examines our bank account every thirtieth day. Suppose, further, that the thirtieth day falls regularly on the day after we have paid this month's rent and on the day before we receive last month's paycheck. In other words, our bank account, while miserable at all times, is particularly low every thirtieth day. This is hardly fair because we never get a chance to show the company how rich we are on days other than the thirtieth.

If we do not have to worry about this sort of bias, then a systematic sample is largely the same as a simple random sample. The selection is just a bit easier because we do not have to bother with random numbers as presented in Table 13.1 on the previous page.

### STRATIFIED RANDOM SAMPLING

The third type of probability sampling is stratified random sampling. If, for example, our study of depression and sleeping patterns is also concerned with religious affiliation, we can look at our sampling frame and count how many of them are Christians, Jews, Muslims, Buddhists, Hindus, Theosophists, and so forth. Suppose that, in our population of 100, we found forty Jews, nineteen Christians, ten Muslims, ten Buddhists, ten Hindus, ten Sikhs, and one lone Theosophist.

Now we can sample our religious categories, or strata, either proportionally or disproportionally. If we sample our sampling frame proportionally, we will choose, say, one-tenth of each category to make up our sample; that is, we will randomly select four Jews, 1.9 Christians, one Muslim, one Buddhist, one Hindu, one Sikh, and 0.1 of a Theosophist. This comprises a total sample of ten, as illustrated in Table 13.2 above.

However; the 1.9 Christians and 0.1 of a Theosophist present a difficulty. In this case, it is necessary to sample disproportionately. For example, it may be preferable to choose one member of each religious affiliation for a total sample of seven. In this case, the sampling fraction is not the same for each category; it is 1/40 for Jews, 1/19 for Christians, 1/10 for Muslims, Buddhists, Hindus, and Sikhs, and 1 for Theosophists. A total sample of only seven is not a good idea for reasons that will be discussed shortly.

Our sampling frame is divided into religious categories only if we believe that religious affiliation will affect either depression or sleep patterns—that is, if we really believe that Buddhists who are depressed have different sleep patterns than Muslims who are depressed, everything else being equal.

However, we must admit that we do not believe this. There is nothing in the literature or our past experience to indicate anything of the sort. And anyway, our friend's clients who are depressed, from whom our sample will be drawn, will not include anything so interesting as Buddhists and Muslims. Probably the best we can hope for is a few odd sects and the town atheist.

This method, though, could be used to look at the sleep patterns of different age groups. Our sampling frame could be divided quite sensibly into eight categories: those aged 10 to 20, 21 to 30, and 31 to 40 years, and so on until we reach 81 to 90 years. We might then sample proportionately by randomly selecting one-tenth of the people in each category. Or we might sample disproportionately by selecting, say, six people from each category, regardless of the number of people in the category. It might be preferable to sample disproportionately, for example, because there are a small number of people in the 71 to 80 and 81 to 90 categories, but it is our belief that advanced age significantly affects sleep patterns. Therefore, we want to include in our sample more than the one or two elderly people who would be included if we took one-tenth of each category.

Categorizing people in terms of age is fairly straightforward. They have only one age, and they usually know what it is. Other types of categories, though, are more complex. Psychological labels, for instance, can be uncertain such that people fall into more than one category and the categories themselves are not homogeneous; that is, the categories are not made up of people who are all alike.

There's no point in using stratified random sampling unless the categories are both homogeneous and different from each other. In theory, the more homogeneous the categories are, the fewer people will be needed from each category to make up our sample. Suppose, for example, we had invented robots that were designed to perform various tasks. Those robots designed to be electricians were all identical, and so were all the plumbers, doctors, lawyers, and so forth. Of course, each kind of robot was different from every other kind.

If we then wanted to make some comparison between all lawyer and all doctor robots, we would only need one of each because same-kind robots are all the same; or, in other words, the robot categories are completely homogeneous. People categories are never completely homogeneous, but the more homogeneous they are, the fewer we need from each category to make comparisons.

The fewer we need, the less our study will cost. However, we must take care not to spend the money we save in this manner on the process of categorization. If people already are in categories, as they might be in a hospital, very good. If they are easy to categorize—say, by age—that's very good, too. If they are not already categorized and are difficult to categorize, it might be more appropriate to use another sampling method.

There is one more point to be considered. The more variables we are looking at, the harder it is to create homogeneous strata. It is easy enough, for example, to categorize people as Buddhists or Hindus, or as aged between 21 and 30 or 31 and 40. It is not nearly so easy if they have to be, say, between 21 and 30 and Buddhist.

## CLUSTER RANDOM SAMPLING

The fourth type of probability sampling is cluster random sampling. This is useful if there is a difficulty in creating a sampling frame. Suppose, for a moment, we want to survey all the people in the area served by city transit (the population) to see whether they are satisfied with the transit system. We do not have a list of every person in this specific population, so we can't construct a sampling frame. There is a list, however, of all the communities in the city served by the transit system, and we can use this list as an alternative sampling frame.

First, we randomly select a community, or cluster, and survey every person living there. We will be certain of what this community thinks about the transit system because we talked to every member of it. But there is still the possibility that this community, in which there are a large number of families with children, has a different opinion from that of a second community, which consists largely of senior citizens.

Perhaps we ought to survey the second community as well. Then there is a third community inhabited largely by penniless writers, artists, and social work students who might have yet a different opinion. Each community is reasonably homogeneous; that is, the people within each individual community are very much like each other. But the communities themselves are totally unlike; that is, they are heterogeneous with respect to each other.

One of the problems here is that we may not be able to afford to survey everyone in the three clusters. But we could compromise. Perhaps we could survey not every street in each cluster but only some streets taken at random—and not every house on our chosen streets, but only some houses, also taken at random. This way, we survey more clusters but fewer people in each cluster.

The only difficulty here is that, because we are not surveying everyone in the community, we might happen to select people who do not give us a true picture of that community. In a community of people with small children, for example, we might randomly select a couple who do not have children and do not intend to, and whose home was demolished, moreover, to make way for the transit line. Such untypical people introduce an error into our results that is due to our sampling procedure and is therefore called *sampling error.*

We will now turn our attention to the second, and last, category of sampling procedures—nonprobability sampling.

## NONPROBABILITY SAMPLING

In nonprobability sampling, not all the people in the sampling frame have the same probability of being included in the sample, and for each one of them the probability of inclusion is unknown. This form of sampling is often used in qualitative (or interpretive) studies where their purpose is just to collect as much valid and reliable data as possible. There are four types of nonprobability sampling procedures.

1   **Availability sampling** is a procedure that relies on the closest and most available research participants to constitute a sample. Sometimes it's called *convenience* sampling or *accidental* sampling.

2   **Purposive sampling** is a procedure in which research participants with particular characteristics are purposely selected for inclusion in a research study; also known as *judgmental* or *theoretical* sampling.

3   **Quota sampling** is a procedure in which the relevant characteristics of the sampling frame are identified, the proportion of these characteristics in the sampling frame is determined, and research participants are selected from each category until the predetermined proportion (quota) has been achieved.

4   **Snowball sampling** is a procedure in which individuals selected for inclusion in a sample are asked to identify other individuals who might be included; useful to locate people with divergent points of view.

### AVAILABILITY SAMPLING

The first type of nonprobability sampling is availability sampling. It is also called *accidental sampling* and *convenience sampling*. It's the simplest of the four nonprobability sampling procedures. As its name suggests, it involves selecting for our sample the first people or units who make themselves available to us. We might survey people, for example, who pass us in a shopping mall. Or we might base our study on the caseload of a particular social worker.

Or we might just seize upon the first fifty of Ken's clients who are depressed who agree to sleep in our lab with wires attached to their heads. In fact, Ken himself was selected by availability—he was a friend of ours, and he was available. There was nothing random about selecting Ken whatsoever. This procedure is not very scientific to say the least, but it is very practical indeed.

### PURPOSIVE SAMPLING

The second type of nonprobability sampling is purposive sampling. This type is used when we want to purposely choose a particular sample. For example, if we are testing a questionnaire that must be comprehensible to less well-educated people while not offending the intelligence of better-educated people, we might present it both to doctoral candidates and to people who left school cheerfully as soon as they could.

In other words, we purposely choose the doctoral candidates and the happy school leavers to be in our two subsamples. There is nothing random about it. In the same way, if we know from previous studies that there is more family violence in the city than in the country, we might restrict our sample to those families who live in cities. Purposive sampling is very useful in qualitative (or interpretive) research studies.

### QUOTA SAMPLING

The third type of nonprobability sampling is quota sampling. In this type of sampling, we decide, on the basis of theory, that we should include in our sample so many of a certain type of person. Suppose we wanted to relate the sleep patterns of people who are depressed to body weight and age.

We might decide to look at extremes; for example, obese and young, nonobese and young, obese and old, and nonobese and old. This gives us four categories (i.e., *A, B, C,* and *D*) as illustrated in Table 13.3 below.

We might want, for example, fifteen people in each category, or for some reason we might need more elderly people than young. In this case, we may decide on ten people in each of categories *A* and *B* and twenty people in each of categories *C* and *D*.

Whatever quotas we decide on, we only have to find enough people to fill them who satisfy the two conditions of weight and age. We might discover all the obese people at a weight loss clinic, for example, or all the young, nonobese ones at a support group for anorexics. It doesn't matter where or how we find them so long as we do.

**Table 13.3**

Quota Sampling Matrix of Body Weight by Age

| Age | Body Weight | |
| --- | --- | --- |
| | Obese | Nonobese |
| Young | Category *A* Obese / Young | Category *B* Nonobese / Young |
| Old | Category *C* Obese / Old | Category *D* Nonobese / Old |

## SNOWBALL SAMPLING

The fourth, and final, type of nonprobability sampling is snowball sampling. If a follow-up study is to be conducted on a self-help group that broke up two years ago, for example, we might find one member of the group and ask that member to help us locate other members. The other members will then find other members and so on until the whole group has been located.

The process is a bit like telling one person a secret, with strict instructions not to tell it to anyone else. Like purposive sampling, snowball sampling is commonly used in qualitative research studies as discussed in Chapters 7–10.

| Box 13.1 | Toward Cultural Sensitivity and Sampling |
| --- | --- |

**Sampling—how we select people to participate in research studies**—has been and remains problematic in culturally based studies. In some cases, it is very difficult to define the population to be studied, let alone draw a representative sample from the population. For example, sexual orientation remains ill defined, thereby rendering studies with this population somewhat limited. Given the limited precision with which we define groups, convenience sampling (studying those who are available) is prominent in cultural and ethnic research. Convenience samples can be problematic for a variety of reasons.

It is certain that convenience samples will be biased. For example, the literature on African Americans is focused primarily upon poor and disadvantaged individuals and families. Many poor and disadvantaged African Americans appear at public agencies to seek some type of assistance. While seeking assistance, they may participate in research studies or provide data that then are used to make inferences about all African Americans in general.

However, are we certain that data collected from poor and disadvantaged African Americans are applicable to African Americans who are not similarly disadvantaged? Probably not. Nevertheless, generalizations based upon skewed samples have been made with respect to all African Americans.

A similar predicament exists in terms of sexual orientation. The emergence of AIDS and HIV has brought much attention to gays. Sexual activity and other behaviors associated with contracting and transmitting the HIV were scrutinized. Some researchers concluded that some gays have many sexual partners and use illicit substances. This may be true for some, but not all.

Recent efforts by gays to gain legal recognition of same-sex unions and marriages suggest that some gays prefer long-term relationships over casual sexual encounters. Overgeneralizations, based upon research samples of gays with AIDS and their substance-abuse behaviors, have hindered understanding of gays and their relationships.

Research studies that have focused on women's issues are also subject to sampling errors. As mentioned previously, research samples composed of single mothers in poverty have been used to make generalizations for all women. Convenience samples drawn from women living under poverty conditions are insufficient when addressing the needs of women who may not be in poverty.

It's nearly impossible to replicate a research study that uses a convenience sample. As we know, one of the benchmarks of the scientific method is its ability to replicate research studies. Research studies that use convenience samples, however, are susceptible to local and geographic influences. The extent of the generalization of their findings is compromised because of the susceptibility to regional influences.

While convenience samples may be better than no samples at all, recognition of the limitations of convenience samples must be observed when interpreting a study's findings. The dangers of overgeneralizations made from samples that are too small or inadequate can have far-reaching negative consequences for the populations being studied.

In a perfect world (and where would that be?), probabilistic sampling techniques are preferable to nonprobabilistic ones. Inadequate definitions of specific population parameters (or the sampling frame) of minority and ethnic populations increase the difficulty associated with adequate sample selections. Sampling remains an area requiring further refinement if we are to improve research efforts with women and with ethnic and cultural groups.

## SAMPLE SIZE

**B**efore our sample can be selected, we obviously have to decide on how many people are needed to take part in our study; in other words, we have to decide on our sample size. The correct sample size depends on both our population and the research question. If we are dealing with a limited population, for example, such as the victims of some rare disease, we might include the whole population in our study. Then we would not take a sample. Usually, however, the population is large enough that we do need to take a sample, with the general rule being the larger the sample, the better.

As far as a minimal sample size is concerned, experts differ. Some say that a sample of 30 will allow us to perform basic statistical procedures, while others would advise a minimum sample size of 100. In fact, sample size depends on how homogeneous our population is with respect to the variables we are studying.

Recalling all those categories of robot doctors, lawyers, and so forth we considered a while back, if our population of robot doctors is all the same—that is, 100 percent homogeneous—we only need one robot doctor in our sample. On the other hand, if the factory messed up and our robot doctors have emerged with a wide range of medical skills, we will need a large sample to tell us anything about the medical skills of the entire robot doctor population. In this case, of course, medical skill is the variable we are studying.

Sample size must also be considered in relation to the number of categories required. If the sample size is too small, there may be only one or two people in a particular category—for example, 1.9 Christians and 0.1 of a Theosophist. This should be anticipated and the sample size adjusted. The situation can also be handled using the disproportionate stratified random sampling procedure. This procedure is the one where we selected one person from each religious category, thus neatly avoiding our 1.9 Christians and 0.1 of a Theosophist.

There are many formulas available for calculating sample size, but they are complicated and difficult to use. Usually, a sample size of one-tenth of the population is considered sufficient to provide reasonable control over sampling error. The same one-tenth convention also applies to categories of the population; we can include one-tenth of each category in our sample.

Now that you know that more confidence can be placed in the generalizability of statistics from larger samples when compared to smaller ones, you may be eager to work with random samples that are as large as possible. Unfortunately, researchers often cannot afford to sample a very large number of cases. They therefore try to determine during the design phase of their studies how large a sample they must have to achieve their purposes. They have to consider the degree of confidence desired, the homogeneity of the population, the complexity of the analysis they plan, and the expected strength of the relationships they will measure. Russell Schutt (2008) presents four pointers when it comes to selecting sample sizes:

1 The less sampling error desired, the larger the sample size must be.

2 Samples of more homogeneous populations can be smaller than samples of more diverse populations. Stratified sampling uses prior information on the population to create more homogeneous population strata from which the sample can be selected, so the sample can be smaller than if simple random sampling were used.

3 If the only analysis planned for a survey sample is to describe the population in terms of a few variables, a smaller sample is required than if a more complex analysis involving sample subgroups is planned.

4 When the researchers will be testing hypotheses and expect to find very strong relationships between and among the variables, they will need smaller samples to detect these relationships than if they expect weaker relationships.

Researchers can make more precise estimates of the sample size required through a method termed *statistical power analysis*—a statistical/research design technique that is way beyond the scope of this book. Statistical power analysis requires a good advance estimate of the strength of the hypothesized relationship in the population. In addition, the math is complicated, so it helps to have some background in mathematics or to consult a statistician.

You can obtain some general guidance about sample sizes from the current practices of social scientists. For professional studies of the national population in which only a simple description is desired, professional social science studies typically have used a sample size of between 1,000 and 1,500, with up to 2,500 being included if detailed analyses are planned. Studies of local or regional populations often sample only a few hundred people, in part because these studies lack sufficient funding to draw larger samples. Of course, the sampling error in these smaller studies is considerably larger than in a typical national study (Schutt, 2008).

## LESSONS ABOUT SAMPLE QUALITY

Rafael Engle and Russell Schutt (2016) provide four points that are implicit in the evaluation of samples:

1 **We can't evaluate the quality of a sample if we don't know what population it is supposed to represent.** If the population is unspecified because the researchers were never clear about just what population they were trying to sample, then we can safely conclude that the sample itself is no good.

2 **We can't evaluate the quality of a sample if we don't know how the cases in the sample were selected from the population.** If the method was specified, we then need to know whether cases were selected in a systematic fashion or on the basis of chance. In any case, we know that a haphazard method of sampling (e.g., availability sampling) undermines the generalizability of the findings.

3 **Sample quality is determined by the sample actually obtained, not just by the sampling method itself.** If many of the people selected for our sample are nonrespondents or people (or other entities) who do not participate in the study although they have been selected for the sample, the quality of our sample is undermined—even if we chose the sample in the best possible way.

4 **We need to be aware that even researchers who obtain very good samples may talk about the implications of their findings for some other groups that are larger than or just different from the population they actually sampled.** For example, findings from a representative sample of students in one university often are discussed as if they tell us about all university students in general. And maybe they do; we just don't know.

> Sampling error is the degree of difference that can be expected between the sample and the population from which it was drawn; that is, it's a mistake in a research study's results that is due to sampling procedures.

## ADVANTAGES AND DISADVANTAGES

**T**homas Black (1999), via Table 13.4 below, provides us with a brief list of the advantages and disadvantages of the various sampling techniques that can be used in all kinds of social work research studies.

### Table 13.4
#### Advantages and Disadvantages of Various Sampling Methods

| Method | Description | Advantages | Disadvantages |
|---|---|---|---|
| Simple random | Random sample from whole population | Highly representative if all research participants participate; the ideal | Not possible without complete list of population members; potentially uneconomical to achieve; can be disruptive to isolate members from a group; time-scale may be too long, data/sample could change |
| Stratified random | Random sample from identifiable groups (strata), subgroups, etc. | Can ensure that specific groups are represented, even proportionally, in the sample(s) (e.g., by gender), by selecting individuals from strata list | More complex, requires greater effort than simple random; strata must be carefully defined |
| Cluster | Random samples of successive clusters of research participants (e.g., by institution) until small groups are chosen as units | Possible to select randomly when no single list of population members exists, but local lists do; data collected on groups may avoid introduction of confounding by isolating members | Clusters in a level must be equivalent and some natural ones are not for essential characteristics (e.g., geographic: numbers equal, but unemployment rates differ) |
| Availability (accidental) (convenience) | Either asking for volunteers, or the consequence of not all those selected finally participating, or a set of research participants who just happen to be available | Inexpensive way of ensuring sufficient number of research participants in a study | Can be highly unrepresentative |

| Method | Description | Advantages | Disadvantages |
|---|---|---|---|
| Purposive (judgmental) (theoretical) | Hand-pick research participants on the basis of specific characteristics | Ensures balance of group sizes when multiple groups are to be selected | Samples are not easily defensible as being representative of populations due to potential subjectivity of the researcher |
| Quota | Select research participants as they come to fill a quota by characteristics proportional to populations | Ensures selection of adequate numbers of research participants with appropriate characteristics | Not possible to prove that the sample is representative of designated population |
| Stage | Combination of cluster (randomly selecting clusters) and random or stratified random sampling of individuals | Can make up probability sample by random at stages and within groups; possible to select random sample when population lists are very localized | Complex, combines limitations of cluster and stratified random sampling |
| Snowball | Research participants with desired traits or characteristics give names of further appropriate research participants | Possible to include members of groups where no lists or identifiable clusters even exist (e.g., drug abusers, criminals) | No way of knowing whether the sample is representative of the population from which it was drawn |

# EVALUATING RESEARCH SETTINGS AND SAMPLES

## RESEARCH SETTINGS

When you read a research report of some kind you need to ask a few questions about the setting in which the study was housed. All research studies take place in research settings. It's critical that an author describes the setting in as much detail as possible in order to enhance study's external validity (see chapter 15).

There are a few highly interweaved and non-mutually exclusive questions you can ask when you begin to evaluate the quality of the author's description of the research setting. Appendix A lists of questions you can ask about research settings that were used in quantitative research studies and Appendix B for qualitative research studies. More specifically,

1 For *quantitative* research studies (Appendix A), you can ask questions 160–164 found on pages 485–486.

2 For *qualitative* research studies (Appendix B), you can ask questions 437–439 found on page 507.

## Samples

All research studies take place in research settings and they all use some type of sample (or population). Thus, it's important to assess the quality and suitability of the sample used within any given research study. Appendix A lists of questions you can ask about samples that were used in quantitative research studies and Appendix B for qualitative research studies. More specifically,

1  For *quantitative* research studies (Appendix A), you can ask questions 165–174 found on pages 486–487.

2  For *qualitative* research studies (Appendix B), you can ask questions 440–447 found on page 508.

How to evaluate the overall creditability of a research setting and sample selection used in a research study is totally up to you—and only you. You're the one who must ask and answer the questions. More important, you need to address two extremely difficult tasks:

1  You must have a rationale for why you're asking each question in the first place. You just can't ask questions without knowing why you're asking them. Appendixes A and B only list potential questions you can ask. Can you guess why each one was listed and what importance your answer to each question has for your overall evaluation of the research study?

2  You also must have some kind of idea of what you're going to do with your answer to each question. For example, question 166 on page 486 asks, "Does the author describe the inclusion and exclusion criteria that was used to select the sampling frame?" Let's say your answer was "no". What are you going to do with your answer? That is, how are you going to use it in your overall evaluation of the study's setting and sample? Now what about if your answer was "yes"?

> All research studies take place in research settings and they all use some type of population and/or sample.

> Many of the questions we can ask about a quantitative research study's population, sample, and research setting can also be asked for qualitative studies ones as well. And vice versa.

## Chapter Recap

- Sampling procedures can be divided into either probability or nonprobability methods.

- There are four types of probability sampling procedures. Each has advantages and disadvantages.

- There are four types of nonprobability sampling procedures. Each has advantages and disadvantages.

## Review Exercises

1  In your own words discuss the concepts of *populations* and *sampling frames*. Provide a single social work example throughout your discussion.

2  List and then discuss the two *sampling procedures.* Provide as many social work examples as you can to illustrate your main points for each procedure.

3  List and then discuss the four *probability sampling* methods. Provide as many social work examples as you can to illustrate your main points for each sampling method.

4  List and then discuss the four *nonprobability sampling* methods. Provide

as many social work examples as you can to illustrate your main points for each sampling method.

5  Discuss the concept of *sample size*. Provide a social work example throughout your discussion.

6  Take a look at Table 13.4 on pages 264–265. From this table, and in your own words, discuss the advantages and disadvantages of each of the eight types of sampling methods. Provide a social work example that highlights your main points for each method.

7 Pretend for a moment that you want to do a *quantitative* research study (chapter 8) that will assess the teaching effectiveness of the instructors who teach in your social work program.

- What's your population?
- What's your sampling frame?
- What sampling method(s) are you going to use for selecting instructors from your sampling frame?
- List and then discuss the advantages and disadvantages of the sampling method(s) you selected.

8 Pretend for a moment that you want to do a *qualitative* research study (chapter 9) that will assess the teaching effectiveness of the instructors who teach in your social work program.

- What's your population?
- What's your sampling frame?
- What sampling method(s) are you going to use for selecting instructors from your sampling frame?
- List and then discuss the advantages and disadvantages of the sampling method(s) you selected.

9 With the preceding two questions in mind (i.e., 7 and 8), discuss in detail how the two separate studies could be combined into one mixed-methods study (chapter 10), paying particular attention to the different sampling methods you are going to use—for the *quantitative* component and the *qualitative* component.

10 Review the three social work research-related roles you can take when you graduate—CSWE Competency 1 at the beginning of this chapter on page 250. This concept is also discussed in Chapter 3 on pages 63–67. Thoroughly discuss how you feel this chapter will help you to perform one or more research-related roles when you graduate. Which one of the three roles do you believe this chapter helped you with the most? Why? Discuss in detail and provide an example to illustrate your main points.

11 Review CSWE Competency 4 at the beginning of this chapter on page 250. Thoroughly discuss how you feel this chapter will help you to become a practice-informed researcher and a research-informed practitioner. Discuss in detail and provide an example to illustrate your main points.

12 Review the evidence-based practice process as illustrated on pages 68–72. Thoroughly discuss how this chapter helps you to develop the skills you'll need for implementing one or more steps of the evidence-based practice process. Discuss which step(s) you feel this chapter will help you with the most. Why? Be very specific and use relevant social work examples to illustrate your main points throughout your discussion.

13 Locate a published quantitative social work-related journal article of your choice. Be sure the study used a sampling method that this chapter describes. We suggest you locate a quantitatively oriented research study in Bruce Thyer's journal *Research on Social Work Practice* (Sage Publications). Hands down, this is the best journal to find good quantitatively oriented social work research studies.

- What was the study's population?
- What was the study's sampling frame—data source?
- What was the study's sampling method(s) for each data source (e.g., research participants, client files, databanks)?
- Would you have used a different sampling method to collect the data to answer the study's research question? If so, what method would you have used, and why?

14 With your knowledge of the various sampling methods that research studies can use, thoroughly discuss how you will use the material contained within this chapter when you begin to evaluate the appropriateness of a research study.

**Moving ahead by looking back**

15 At this point in your research methods course, how comfortable are you with discussing the place of research in social work with your field instructor, with your practice instructor, with your research instructor, with your supervisor at work, with the director of your social work program, or with your classmates? Discuss in detail.

# 14

CHAPTER

# 2015 EPAS COMPETENCIES

| COMPETENCY 1 | Demonstrate Ethical and Professional Behavior |
|---|---|

You will learn that in order to be a successful evidence-based practitioner you have an ethical obligation to integrate three research roles into your daily practice activities as discussed in Chapter 3: (1) research consumer, (2) research partner—either as a co-researcher or research participant, and (3) creator and disseminator of research (or knowledge).

This entire chapter pertains to these three professional research-related roles when it comes to selecting, implementing, and evaluating the various single-subject designs that can be used in social work research and practice situations.

| COMPETENCY 4 | Engage in Practice-Informed Research and Research-Informed Practice |
|---|---|

Competency 4 also pertains to the entire chapter because you have to:

1  Evaluate the appropriateness of the single-subject designs that were utilized in a published research study (**research consumer**—research-informed practice);

2  Participate in a single-subject research study either as a co-researcher or research participant (**research partner**—practice-informed research). See 1 above and 3 below; and

3  Know how to select and implement a single-subject design when you actually do a research study (**creator and disseminator of research**—practice-informed research).

You also need to utilize evidence-based practice recommendations whenever possible; that is, you need to integrate (1) the best available research-based evidence with (2) your clinical expertise and (3) your client's values.

All of the above implies you'll need to know how to assess the advantages and disadvantages of the single-subject design that was used in a research study that produced its research-based evidence. In short, you need to ask and then answer a simple question: How seriously should I take the findings of any specific single-subject research study given the specific design and data source(s) the study used?

| COMPETENCY 9 | Evaluate Practice with Individuals, Families, Groups, Organizations, & Communities |
|---|---|

You will learn that you can easily evaluate the effectiveness of your day-to-day practice activities by using single-subject designs, whether your client is an individual, a family, a group, an organization, or a community. This competency pertains to the entire chapter. See Competencies 1 and 4.

# Single-Subject Designs

| | | |
|---|---|---|
| CHAPTERS 1 & 3 | Step 1. | Understanding the Research Process |
| CHAPTER 2 | Step 2. | Formulating Research Questions |
| CHAPTER 4 APPENDIXES A–C | Step 3. | Reviewing the Literature Evaluating the Literature |
| CHAPTERS 5 & 6 | Step 4. | Being Aware of Ethical and Cultural Issues |
| CHAPTERS 7–10 | Step 5. | Selecting a Research Approach |
| CHAPTERS 11 & 12 | Step 6. | Specifying How Variables Are Measured |
| CHAPTER 13 | Step 7. | Selecting a Sample |
| CHAPTERS 14 & 15 | Step 8. | Selecting a Research Design |
| CHAPTERS 16 & 17 | Step 9. | Selecting a Data-Collection Method |
| CHAPTERS 18 & 19 | Step 10. | Analyzing the Data |
| CHAPTERS 20 & 21 | Step 11. | Writing the Research Report |

# Single-Subject Designs

"No, *ABBA* is not a single-subject research design. It's a Swedish pop musical group that was formed in Stockholm in 1972."

CHAPTER

# 14

CHAPTER OUTLINE

WHAT ARE SINGLE-SUBJECT DESIGNS?

THE RESEARCH PROCESS

UNIT OF ANALYSIS

REQUIREMENTS

   Setting Measurable Client Objectives

      Target Problems

   Selecting Outcome Measures

   Graphically Displaying the Data

EXPLORATORY DESIGNS

   *A* Design

   *B* Design

   $BB_1$ Design

   *BC* Design

DESCRIPTIVE DESIGNS

   *AB* Design

   *ABC* and *ABCD* Designs

EXPLANATORY DESIGNS

   Reversal Designs

      *ABA* and *ABAB* Designs

      *BAB* Design

      *BCBC* Design

   Multiple-Baseline Designs

      *More Than One Case*

      *More Than One Setting*

      *More Than One Problem*

RETROSPECTIVE BASELINES

CHAPTER RECAP

REVIEW EXERCISES

THE PREVIOUS CHAPTER DISCUSSED how we can select research participants for our research studies. This chapter is a logical extension in that we now discuss simple research designs that will include our selected research participants. The simplest type of research design—the topic of this chapter—is commonly referred to as a *single-subject design*. These are also called *single-case designs*, *single-system designs*, N = 1, *case-level designs*, *single-case experimentations*, and *idiographic research*.

## WHAT ARE SINGLE-SUBJECT DESIGNS?

**O**n a very general level, single-subject designs are more "practice oriented" than group-level designs (discussed in the next chapter). That is, they are used more by social work "practitioners" than by social work "researchers."

Single-subject designs provide data about how well a treatment intervention is working so that alternative or complementary interventive strategies can be adopted if necessary. They can also indicate when a client's problem has been resolved. Single-subject designs are used to monitor client progress up to, and sometimes beyond, the point of termination.

They can also be used to evaluate the effectiveness of a social service program as a whole by aggregating or compiling the results obtained by numerous social workers serving their individual clients within the program. A family social service program might be evaluated, for example, by combining family outcomes from a number of families who have been seen by different social workers who work within the program.

According to Martin Bloom, Joel Fischer, and John Orme (2009), the advantages of single-subject designs are as follows:

- They can be built into every social worker's practice with each and every case/situation without disruption of practice.

- They provide the tools for evaluating the effectiveness of our practice with each client, group, or system with which we work.

- They focus on individual clients or systems. If there is any variation in effect from one client or system to another, single-subject designs will be able to pick it up.

> A *case* is a basic unit of social work practice, whether it be *an* individual, *a* couple, *a* family, *an* agency, *a* community, *a* county, *a* state, or *a* country.

- They provide a continuous record of changes in the target problem over the entire course of intervention, not just pre- and posttest.

- They are practice-based and practitioner-oriented. Single-subject designs provide continuous assessment and outcome data to practitioners so that they can monitor progress and make changes in the nature of the intervention program if so indicated. Unlike traditional group designs—and the intervention programs they are used to evaluate—which ordinarily cannot be changed once the study has begun, single-subject designs are flexible; the worker can change the intervention and the design depending on the needs of the case.

- They can be used to test hypotheses or ideas regarding the relationship between specific intervention procedures and client changes, ruling out some alternative explanations and allowing an inference regarding causality: Was the intervention program responsible for the change in the target problem?

- They can be used to help the worker assess the case/situation, leading to selection of a more appropriate program of intervention by clarifying what seem to be the relevant factors involved in the problem.

- They essentially are theory-free; that is, they can be applied to the practice of any practitioner regardless of the worker's theoretical orientation or approach to practice.

- They are relatively easy to use and understand. They can be applied within the same time frame the social worker is currently using in seeing clients or others. In fact, the use of single-subject designs can actually enhance the worker's efficiency by saving time and energy in trying to record and evaluate the social worker's practice.

- They avoid the problem of outside researchers coming into an agency and imposing a study on the social workers. Single-subject designs are established and conducted by practitioners for their benefit and for the benefit of the client/systems.

- They provide a model for demonstrating our accountability to ourselves, our clients and consumers, our funding sources, and our communities. Systematic, consistent use of single-subject designs allows practitioners and agencies to collect a body of data about the effectiveness of practice that provides more or less objective information about the success of our practice.

# THE RESEARCH PROCESS

Any research design—positivistic and interpretive alike—is nothing more than a plan for conducting the entire research study from beginning to end. They all try to answer the following basic questions:

1  When, and over what period of time, should the research study be conducted?
2  What variables need to be selected and then measured?
3  How should the variables be measured?
4  What other variables need to be accounted for or controlled?
5  From whom should the data be collected (data sources)?
6  When and where should the data be collected?
7  How should the data be collected?
8  How should the data be analyzed?
9  How should the results of the study be disseminated?

As you should know by now, these questions are highly commingled and are directly related to the research question we are trying to answer or the hypothesis we are testing. If you are exploring the concept of bereavement, for example, you will collect data from bereaved people and perhaps involved social workers, and you may also need to measure variables related to bereavement, such as grief, anger, depression, and levels of coping.

You might need to measure these variables over a period of months or years, and the way you measure them will suggest appropriate methods of how you will analyze your data. Decisions about how best to accomplish these steps depend on how much we already know about the bereavement process; that is, where your bereavement research questions fall on the knowledge level continuum as presented in Chapter 2.

## UNIT OF ANALYSIS

**S**ingle-subject designs are used to fulfill the major purpose of social work practice: to improve the situation of a client system—*an* individual client, *a* couple, *a* family, *a* group, *an* organization, or *a* community. Any of these client configurations can be studied with a single-subject design. In short, they are used to study one individual or one group intensively, as opposed to studies that use two or more groups of research participants.

> A *unit of analysis* is a specific research participant (person, object, or event) or the sample or population relevant to the research question; the persons or things being studied.

Some single-subject designs are conducted to study one individual or case, some to study groups of people (including families, organizations, and communities), and some to study social artifacts (such things as birth practices or divorces). The individual, group, or artifact being studied is called the *unit of analysis*.

If you are exploring the advantages and disadvantages of home birth, for example, you might be asking questions of women who have experienced home birth, but the thing you are studying—the unit of analysis—is the social artifact: home birth. Conversely, if you are a social work practitioner studying the impact of home birth on a particular client, the unit of analysis is the client or individual; and if you are studying the impact on a group of women, the unit of analysis is the group of women.

## REQUIREMENTS

**T**he following discussion on the requirements of single-subject designs has been adapted and modified from three sources: Rick Grinnell and Margaret Williams (1990); Margaret Williams, Leslie Tutty, and Rick Grinnell (1995); and Margaret Williams, Yvonne Unrau, and Rick Grinnell (1998). In order to carry out a single-subject design:

> Single-subject designs collect data about a single-client system—an individual, couple, group, organization, or community—in order to evaluate the outcome of an intervention for the client system.

1  The client's problem must be clearly identified.

2  The desired objective to be achieved must be decided upon.

3  The intervention that is most likely to eliminate the client's problem must be selected.

4  The intervention must be implemented.

5  The client's progress must be continually monitored to see whether the client's problem has been resolved or at least reduced.

If practitioners are careful to organize, measure, and record what they do, via the above five points, single-subject designs will naturally take shape in the clients' files, and the results can be used to guide future interventive efforts. Only three things are required when doing a single-subject design:

1   Setting measurable client objectives

2   Selecting valid and reliable outcome measures

3   Graphically displaying the resulting data

## Setting Measurable Client Objectives

One of the first tasks a social worker does when initially seeing a client is to establish the purpose of why they are together. Why has the client approached the worker? Or, in many nonvoluntary situations such as in probation and parole or child abuse situations, why has the worker approached the client? The two need to formulate objectives for their mutual working relationship.

### Target Problems

Client target problems are feelings, knowledge levels, or behaviors that need to be changed. Many times clients do not have just one target problem—they have many (see Scenario 1.2 on page 12 for example). They sometimes have a number of interrelated problems; even when there is only one that is more important than the rest, they may not know what it is. Nevertheless, they may be quite clear about the desired outcome of their involvement with social work services.

They may want to "fix" their lives so that "Johnny listens when I ask him to do something". or "My partner pays more attention to me", or "I feel better about myself at work". Unfortunately, many clients express their desired target problems in vague, ambiguous terms, possibly because they do not know themselves exactly what they want to change; they only know that something should be different. If a worker can establish (with the guidance of the client) what should be changed, why it should be changed, how it should be changed, and to what degree it should be changed, the solution to the problem will not be far away.

**Clearly Stating the Target Problem.** Consider Heather, for example, who wants her partner Ben to pay more attention to her. Heather may mean sexual attention, in which case the couple's sexual relations may be the target problem. On the other hand, Heather may mean that she and Ben do not socialize enough with friends, or that Ben brings work home from the office too often or has hobbies she does not share, or any of a host of things.

Establishing clearly what the desired change would look like is the first step in developing the target problem. Without this, the worker and client could wander around forever through the problem maze, never knowing what, if anything, needs to be solved. Desired change cannot occur if no one knows what change is desired. It is, therefore, very important that the target problem to be solved be precisely stated as early as possible in the client–social worker relationship.

Continuing with the example of Heather and Ben, and after a great deal of exploration, the worker agrees that Heather and Ben have many target problems to work on, such as improving their child-discipline strategies, improving their budgeting skills, improving their communication skills, and many other issues that, when dealt with, can lead to a successful marriage. For now, however, they agree to work on one target problem: increasing the amount of time they spend together with friends. Heather may say that she wishes she and Ben could visit friends together more often. The target problem has now become a little more specific: it has narrowed from "increasing the amount of time they spend together with friends" to "Heather and Ben visiting friends more often". "Visiting friends more often with Ben," however, is still an ambiguous phrase. It may mean once a month or every night, and the achievement of the target problem's solution cannot be known until the meaning of "more often" has been clarified.

> A specific, measurable, client-desired outcome objective is known as a *client target problem.*

If Heather agrees that she would be happy to visit friends with Ben once a week, the ambiguous objective may be restated as a specific, measurable objective—"to visit friends with Ben once a week". The social worker may discover later that "friends" is also an ambiguous term. Heather may have meant "her friends", but Ben may have meant "his friends", and the social worker may have imagined that "the friends" were mutual.

The disagreement about who is to be regarded as a friend may not become evident until the worker has monitored their progress for a month or so and found that no improvement was occurring. In some cases, poor progress may be due to the selection of an inappropriate interventive strategy. In other cases, it may mean that the target problem itself is not as specific, complete, and clear as it should be. Before deciding that the interventive strategy needs to be changed, it is always necessary to clarify with the client exactly what it is that specifically needs to be achieved.

> Target problems are what social workers seek to solve with their clients.

## SELECTING OUTCOME MEASURES

A target problem must be measurable with valid and reliable measuring instruments as discussed in Chapters 11 and 12. Can Heather and Ben, who wanted to visit friends more often, be trusted to report truthfully on whether the friends were visited? Suppose she says they were not visited and he says they were? Social workers must always be very conscious of what measurement methods are both available and feasible when formulating a target problem with a client.

> An *outcome measure* is the dependent variable in a single-subject design. It's what the social worker hopes to change such as feelings, behaviors, and knowledge levels.

It may be quite possible for the social worker to telephone the friends and ask if they were visited; but if the worker is not prepared to get involved with Heather's and Ben's friends, this measurement method will not be feasible. If this is the case, and if Heather and/or Ben cannot be trusted to report accurately and truthfully, there is little point in setting the target problem.

Heather and Ben's target problem can be easily observed and measured. However, quite often a client's target problem involves feelings, attitudes, knowledge levels, or events that are known only to the client and cannot be easily observed and/or measured.

Consider Bob, a client who comes to a social worker because he is depressed. The worker's efforts may be simply to lessen his target problem, depression, but how will the worker and/or Bob know when his depression has been alleviated or reduced?

Perhaps he will say that he feels better, or his partner may say that Bob cries less, or the worker may note that he spends less time in therapy staring at his feet. All these are indicators that his depression is lessening, but they are not very valid and reliable indicators. What is needed is a more "scientific method" of measuring depression. Fortunately, a number of paper-and-pencil standardized measuring instruments have been developed that can be filled out by the client in a relatively short period of time, can be easily scored, and can provide a fairly accurate picture of the client's condition.

One such widely used instrument that measures depression is Hudson's *General Contentment Scale* (*GCS*). Because higher scores indicate higher levels of depression, and lower scores indicate lower levels of depression, the target problem in Bob's case would be to reduce his score on the *GCS* to a level at which he can adequately function. People who are not depressed will still not score zero on the *GCS.*

Everyone occasionally feels blue (item 2) or downhearted (item 10). There is a clinical cutting score that differentiates a clinically significant problem level from a non–clinically significant problem level, and it will often be this score that the client aims to achieve.

If the target problem is "to reduce Bob's score on the *GCS* to or below the clinical cutting score of 30", the worker will know not only what the target problem is, but also precisely how Bob's success is to be measured. Usually, client success, sometimes referred to as *client outcome*, can be measured in a variety of ways. Bob's partner, Maria, for example, may be asked to record the frequency of his crying spells, and the target problem here may be to reduce the frequency of these spells to once a week or less.

Again, it would be important to further refine the term "crying spell" so that Maria knows exactly what it was she has to measure. Perhaps "crying spell" could be defined as ten minutes or more of continuous crying, and a gap of at least ten minutes without crying would define the difference between one "spell" and another.

There are now two independent and complementary indicators of Bob's level of depression: the *GCS* as rated by Bob, *and* the number of his ten-minute crying spells per day as rated by Maria. If future scores on both indicators display improvement (that is, they both go down), the worker can be reasonably certain that Bob's depression is lessening and the intervention is effective.

If the two indicators do not agree, however, the worker will need to find out why. Perhaps Bob wishes to appear more depressed than he really is, and this is an area that needs to be explored. Or perhaps Maria is not sufficiently concerned to keep an accurate recording of the number of Bob's ten-minute crying spells per day, and it may be Maria's attitude that has caused Bob's crying in the first place. Accurate measurements made over time can do more than reveal the degree of a client's improvement. They can cast light on the problem itself and suggest new avenues to be explored, possibly resulting in the utilization of different interventive strategies.

Be that as it may, a client's target problem cannot be dealt with until it has been expressed in specific measurable indicators. These indicators cannot be said to be measurable until it has been decided how they will be measured. Specification of the target problem will, therefore, often include mention of an instrument that will be used to measure it. It will also include who is to do the measuring and under what circumstances.

It may be decided, for example, that Bob will rate himself on the *GCS* daily after dinner or once a week on Saturday morning, or that Maria will make a daily record of all crying spells that occurred in the late afternoon after he has returned home from work. The physical record itself is very important, both as an aid to memory and to track Bob's progress. In a single-subject design, progress is usually monitored by displaying the measurements made in the form of graphs.

> *Operational definitions* are explicit specifications of variables in such a way that their measurements are possible.

## GRAPHICALLY DISPLAYING THE DATA

As we know from Chapter 11, the word *measurement* can be simply defined as the process of assigning a number or value to a variable. If the variable, or target problem, being considered is depression as measured by Hudson's *Generalized Contentment Scale* (*GCS*), and if Bob scores, say 62, then 62 is the number assigned to Bob's initial level of depression.

The worker will try to reduce his initial score of 62 to at least 30—the desired minimum score. The worker can then select and implement an intervention and ask Bob to complete the *GCS* again—say, once a week—until the score of 30 has been reached. Bob's depression levels can be plotted over time on a graph such as the ones displayed in this chapter.

## EXPLORATORY DESIGNS

**S**uppose you have a client—Cecilia—whose underlying problem, you believe, is her high social anxiety level. She will be the "subject" in your single-subject design. Before you go ahead with an intervention designed to decrease her social anxiety—an intervention Cecilia doesn't need if your belief is wrong—you will have to answer the simple question, "Does Cecilia really have a clinically significant problem with social anxiety?" In other words, does the "social anxiety problem" you think she has really exist in the first place?

In order to answer this question, you select a measuring instrument to measure her social anxiety level that is valid, reliable, sensitive to change, nonreactive, and useful in this particular situation. Say you choose the *Interaction and Audience Anxiousness Scale* (*IASS*). On this particular measuring instrument, higher scores indicate higher social anxiety levels, and the minimal clinical cutting score is 40. Clinical cutting scores are usually displayed as dashed lines, as can be seen in Figure 14.1. You administer the *IASS* to Cecilia, and she initially scores a 62 as shown in Figure 14.1 below.

Scores above the clinical cutting score indicate a clinically significant problem. You might think "Ah-ha! She has a problem since her score was 22 points higher than the minimum clinical cutting score", and you rush forward with your intervention.

On the other hand, any social work intervention has the potential to harm as well as help (in the same way that any medication does), so you first want to be sure that this is a persisting problem and not just a reflection of Cecilia's high social anxiety today. You might also want to be sure that her high anxiety problem will not go away by itself. Doctors usually do not treat conditions that resolve themselves, given time, and the same is true for social workers.

In order to see if Cecilia meets these three criteria for treatment—first, there really is a problem; second, the problem is persisting; and third, the problem is either stable at an unacceptable level or getting worse—you will need to administer the same measuring instrument two or three times more at intervals of, say, a week. You might then graph your results as shown in Figure 14.1 below. This figure constitutes a baseline measure of Cecilia's social anxiety level over a seven-week period and is a very simple example of an *A* design.

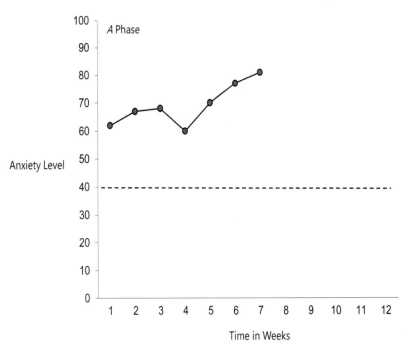

**Figure 14.1**

*A* Design:
Cecilia's Social Anxiety Scores for the First Seven Weeks
(Indicating that an intervention IS warranted)

There are four exploratory designs:

1  *A* design
2  *B* design
3  *BB₁* design
4  *BC* design

## *A* Design

At the risk of sounding a bit ridiculous, we'll note that the *italicized* letter *A* simply desig-
nates "a research study" where the intention is to establish, via measurement, a baseline
for an individual client's problem. Perhaps "research study" is a grandiose term to describe a routine assessment, but the word *research* does mean to look again, and you are
indeed looking again at Cecilia's potential problem in order to see whether her problem
exists in the first place.

Three data points are the minimum number needed to show any kind of trend, and
some experts maintain that you need no less than seven. However, in a clinical situation
the client's need for an intervention is the primary factor, and you will have to use your
professional judgment to decide how long you ought to continue to gather baseline data
before you intervene.

Figure 14.1 on the previous page indicates a worsening problem, needing intervention,
because the scores are generally getting higher as time goes on. Remember, higher scores
mean higher levels of the problem. Had the scores been generally getting lower, the problem would have been improving by itself, and no intervention would be indicated, as illustrated in Figure 14.1a below.

If the scores fell more or less on a horizontal line, intervention would be indicated so
long as the line was above the clinical cutting score (figure 14.1b on the following page)
but not if the line was below it, as illustrated in Figure 14.1c on the following page.

> An *A* phase
> establishes the
> baseline
> measurement of
> the target problem
> before the
> intervention (*B*
> phase) is
> implemented.

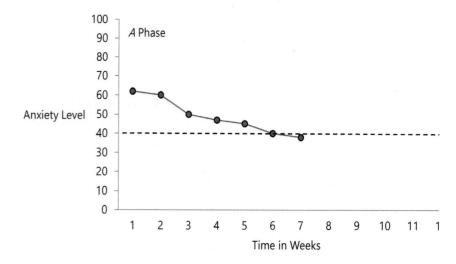

**Figure 14.1a**

*A* Design:
Cecilia's Social Anxiety Scores for the First Seven Weeks
(Indicating that an intervention IS NOT warranted)

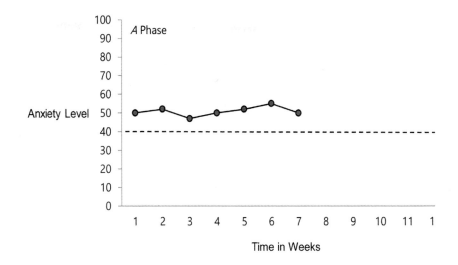

**Figure 14.1b**

*A* Design:
Cecilia's Social Anxiety Scores for the First Seven Weeks
(Indicating that an intervention IS warranted)

## *B* DESIGN

The second type of exploratory single-subject research designs is the *B* design. As we have seen, an *A* design answers the question, "Does the problem exist?" The *A* design also answers another type of exploratory question: "Does the problem exist at different levels over time?" In other words, "Is the problem changing by itself?"

A *B* phase is the intervention, which may, or may not, include simultaneous measurements.

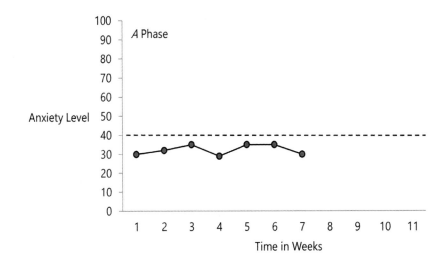

**Figure 14.1c**

*A* Design:
Cecilia's Social Anxiety Scores for the First Seven Weeks
(Indicating that an intervention IS NOT warranted)

A *B* design also addresses the question "Is the problem changing?" but here we want to know whether the problem is changing while an intervention is being applied. Bob is Cecilia's friend and has also come to you complaining that he experiences a great deal of anxiety in social situations.

He is nervous when he speaks to his boss or when he meets people for the first time, and the prospect of giving public presentations at work appalls him. You decide that you will measure Bob's anxiety level using the same standardized measuring instrument as you did with Cecilia (*Interaction and Audience Anxiousness Scale, IASS*). As you know about this particular standardized measuring instrument, higher scores indicate higher social anxiety levels, and the clinical cutting score for the *IASS* is 40.

Bob, like Cecilia, scores 62. This one score is more of a base point rather than a base-line, but you decide that it would be inappropriate to collect baseline data over time in Bob's case as he is experiencing a great deal of discomfort at work, is highly nervous in your presence (you are a stranger, after all), and probably will not be able to bring himself to seek help in the future if he does not receive some kind of intervention now.

You therefore begin your intervention, engaging Bob to the extent that he returns the following week, when you administer the *IASS* again. Now he scores 52. In the third week, he scores 49, as shown in Figure 14.2 below. Figure 14.2 is a simple example of a *B* design, in which you track change in the problem level at the same time as you are intervening. You do not know, from this graph, whether your intervention caused the change you see. Anything else could have caused it.

Perhaps Bob is having a weekly massage to reduce muscle tension, or his boss has been fired, or the public presentation that he was supposed to do has been postponed. Therefore, you cannot use the *B* design to answer explanatory research questions that come quite high on the knowledge continuum (refer to figure 2.3 on page 48).

On the other hand, you might make the clinical decision that it is worth trying a varia-tion on your intervention: You might apply it more frequently by having Bob come twice a week instead of once, or you might apply it more intensively by increasing the amount of time Bob is expected to spend each evening on relaxation exercises. You can graph the changes that occur while you are applying the variation, as shown in Figure 14.3 on the following page.

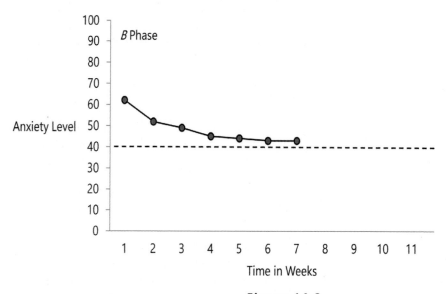

**Figure 14.2**

*B* Design:
Bob's Social Anxiety Scores for the First Seven Weeks

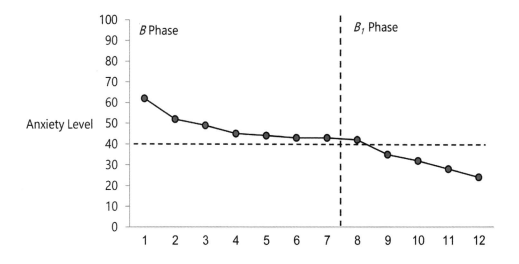

**Figure 14.3**

*BB₁* Design:
Bob's Social Anxiety Scores for the *B* Phase and *B₁* Phase

## *BB₁* DESIGN

Figure 14.2 on the previous page shows that Bob's anxiety level has improved but it has not fallen below the clinical cutting score. Moreover, it does not look as though it will because it has been relatively stable for the last three weeks. It may be that Bob is a naturally anxious person and no intervention, however inspired, will reduce his problem to below clinically significant levels.

Figure 14.3 above shows two phases: the *B* phase and the *B₁* phase, separated by the vertical dotted line that runs between weeks 7 and 8. Week 7 marks the end of your original intervention, designated by the *B* intervention, and all the scores obtained by Bob while you were applying the *B* intervention constitute the *B* phase.

If it seems odd to call the first intervention *B* instead of *A*, remember that *A* has been used already to designate baseline scores. Week 8 marks the beginning of the variation on your original intervention, designated *B₁*, and all the scores obtained by Bob while you were applying the variation constitute the *B₁* phase. The *B* and *B₁* phases together constitute the *BB₁* design.

When you look at the low scores Bob achieved in weeks 9–12, you might be tempted to think, "Hallelujah! My specific intervention did work. All Bob needed was a bit more of it". However, the same considerations apply to the *BB₁* design as apply to the *B* design. You simply cannot be sure that there is any relationship between your intervention and Bob's decreased anxiety, far less that one was the cause of the other.

## *BC* DESIGN

The last exploratory single-subject research design is the *BC* design. Let's go back in time to the point where you decided that it was worth trying a variation on your *B* intervention with Bob. Suppose you had decided instead to try an entirely different intervention, designated as *C* because it is a different intervention, following immediately after *B*.

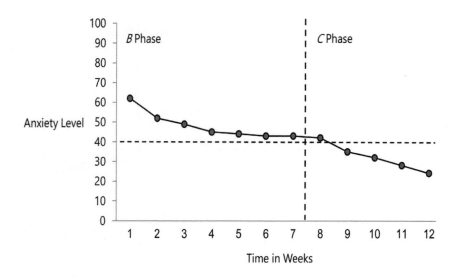

**Figure 14.4**

*BC* Design:
Bob's Social Anxiety Scores for the *B* Phase and *C* Phase

Now you implement the *C* intervention, administering the *IASS* every week, graphing your results, and creating a *C* phase after the *B* phase as shown in Figure 14.4 above. Again, the *B* phase in Figure 14.4 is copied from Figure 14.2, and after the *C* intervention you see that Bob has succeeded in reducing his anxiety level to below the clinical cutting score of 40. Repressing your hallelujahs, you realize that there is still no sure relationship between your intervention and Bob's success. Indeed, the waters are becoming more murky because even if your intervention was in fact related to Bob's success you would still not know whether it was the *C* intervention that did the trick, or a delayed reaction to *B*, or some combination of *B* and *C*.

## DESCRIPTIVE DESIGNS

**There are two kinds** of single-subject research designs that center around answering descriptive research questions:

1  *AB* designs
2  *ABC* and *ABCD* designs

## *AB* DESIGN

An *AB* design is simply an *A*—or baseline phase—followed by a *B* or intervention phase. Returning to Cecilia, let's say she has a problem with low self-esteem and that you have already completed a four-week baseline phase with her, as shown in Figure 14.5 on the following page, and that phase alone answered the two simple exploratory questions: "Does the problem exist?" and "Does the problem exist at different levels over time?" Now you implement a *B* intervention and find, to your pleasure, that Cecilia's self-esteem level approaches the clinical cutting score of 30 and falls below it at weeks 10–12.

What you really want to know, of course, is whether there is any relationship between your *B* intervention and Cecilia's success. You are now in a better position to hypothesize that there is because you know that Cecilia was not doing too well during the four weeks of the baseline phase and began to improve the week after you started your intervention.

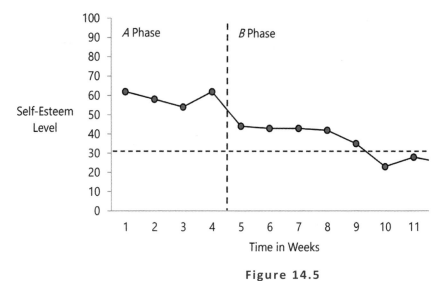

**Figure 14.5**

*AB* Design:
Cecilia's Self-Esteem Scores for the *A* Phase and *B* Phase

*Something* happened in week 5 to set Cecilia on the road to recovery, and it would be very coincidental if that something were not your intervention. However, coincidences do happen, and you cannot be 100 percent certain that your intervention caused the change you see unless you can eliminate all the other coincidental happenings that might have caused it.

Hence, the *AB* design cannot answer explanatory research questions, but the change between the baseline data (getting worse) and the intervention data (getting better) is enough to indicate that there may be some relationship between your intervention and Cecilia's improvement. The moral to the story is to always collect baseline data if you can because social work ethics requires you to be reasonably sure an intervention is effective before you try it again with another client.

## *ABC* AND *ABCD* DESIGNS

As we have discussed, you can always follow a *B* phase with a *C* phase if the *B* intervention did not achieve the desired result. An *A* phase followed by a *B* phase followed by a *C* phase constitutes an *ABC* design, and if there is a *D* intervention as well, you have an *ABCD* design. So long as there is a baseline, you can conclude that there may well be a relationship between the results you see and the interventions you implemented. However, if you have more than one intervention, you will not know which intervention—or combination of interventions—did the trick, and the more interventions you try the murkier the waters become.

Because a single intervention often comprises a package of practice techniques (e.g., active listening plus role play plus relaxation exercises), it is important to write down exactly what you did so that later on you will remember what the *B* or *C* or *D* interventions were.

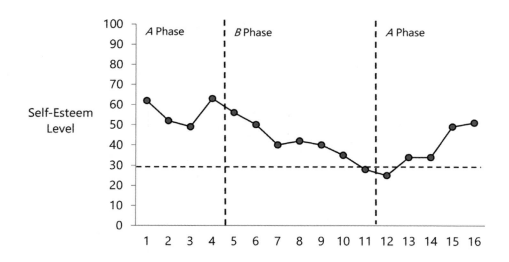

**Figure 14.6**
*ABA* Design:
Cecilia's Self-Esteem Scores

## EXPLANATORY DESIGNS

**A**s we have seen, if you want to show that a particular intervention caused an observed result, you must eliminate everything else that may have caused it; in other words, you must control for intervening variables. There are two types of single-subject designs that can answer causality, or explanatory research questions:

1  Reversal designs
2  Multiple-baseline designs

## REVERSAL DESIGNS

The first type of explanatory single-subject designs are the reversal designs. There are three kinds:

1  *ABA* and *ABAB* designs
2  *BAB* designs
3  *BCBC* designs

### *ABA* AND *ABAB* DESIGNS

Look at Figure 14.6 above which illustrates Cecilia's success in getting her self-esteem score below the clinical cutting score in week 11 of the *B* intervention. In week 12, you decide that you will withdraw your intervention related to Cecilia's self-esteem because she seems to be doing well, but you will continue to monitor her self-esteem levels to ensure that treatment gains are maintained.

Ongoing monitoring of problems that appear to be solved is something of a luxury. Too often our approach is crisis-oriented; follow-up tends to be ignored in the light of other, more pressing problems, and the result may well be a recurrence of the original problem because it had not been solved to the extent that the social worker thought. However, with Cecilia you follow up. In weeks 12 through 16, as shown in Figure 14.6, the score

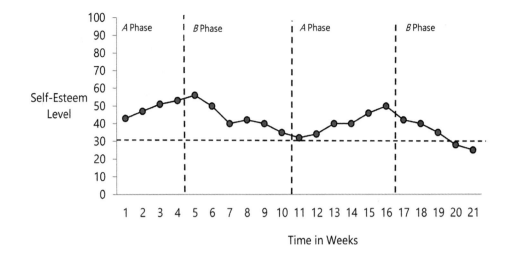

**Figure 14.7**

*ABAB* Design:
Cecilia's Self-Esteem Scores

hovers at the clinical cutting score. Figure 14.6 illustrates an *ABA* design where the client's scores are displayed first without an intervention (the first *A* phase), then with an intervention (the *B* phase), then without an intervention again (the second *A* phase). The scores are not as high in the second *A* phase as they were in the first *A* phase, and this is to be expected because some of the strategies Cecilia learned in the *B* phase should remain with her even though the intervention has stopped.

However, from a research point of view, the very fact that her scores increased again when you stopped the intervention makes it more certain that it was your intervention that caused the improvement you saw in the *B* phase. Cecilia's improvement when the intervention started might have been a coincidence, but it is unlikely that her regression when the intervention stopped was also a coincidence.

Your certainty with respect to causality will be increased even further if you reintroduce the B intervention in week 17 and Cecilia's score begins to drop again as it did in the first *B* phase. Now you have implemented two *AB* designs one after the other with the same client to produce an *ABAB* design. This design is illustrated in Figure 14.7 above. It is sometimes called a *reversal design* or a *withdrawal design*. Causality is established with an *ABAB* design because the same intervention has been shown to work twice with the same client and you have baseline data to show the extent of the problem when there was no intervention.

### *BAB* DESIGN

Let's now return to Bob, with whom you implemented a *B* intervention to reduce his social anxiety as shown in Figure 14.2 on page 280. When Bob's social anxiety level has fallen beneath the clinical cutting score, you might do the same thing with Bob as you did with Cecilia: withdraw the intervention and continue to monitor the problem, creating an *A* phase after the *B* phase. If the problem level worsens during the *A* phase, you intervene again in the same way as you did before, creating a second *B* phase and an overall design of *BAB*.

We have said that causality is established with an *ABAB* design because the same intervention has worked twice with the same client. We cannot say the same for a *BAB* design, however, as we do not really know that our intervention "worked" the first time. Because there was no initial baseline data (no first *A* phase), we cannot know whether the resolution of the problem on the first occasion had anything to do with the intervention.

The problem may have resolved itself or some external event (intervening variable) might have resolved it. Nor can we know the degree to which the problem changed during the first *B* phase (intervention) because there was no baseline data with which to compare the final result.

An indication of the amount of change can be obtained by comparing the first and last scores in the *B* phase, but the first score may have been an unreliable measure of Bob's problem. Bob may have felt less or more anxious that day than usual, and a baseline is necessary to compensate for such day-to-day fluctuations.

Because the effectiveness of the intervention on the first occasion is unknown, there can be no way of knowing whether the intervention was just as effective the second time it was implemented, or less or more effective. All we know is that the problem improved twice, after the same intervention, and this is probably enough to warrant using the intervention again with another client.

### *BCBC* DESIGN

A *BCBC* design, as the name suggests, is a *B* intervention followed by a *C* intervention implemented twice in succession. The point of doing this is to compare the effectiveness of two interventions—*B* and *C*. It is unlikely that a social worker would implement this design with a client because, if the problem improved sufficiently using *B*, you would not need *C*; if you did need *C*, you would hardly return to *B* whether or not *C* appeared to do the trick.

However, if the problem has nothing to do with a client's welfare but is concerned instead with a social work program's organizational efficiency, say, as affected by organizational structure, you might try one structure *B* followed by a different structure *C* and then do the same thing again in order to show that one structure really has proved more effective in increasing efficiency when implemented twice under the same conditions.

## MULTIPLE-BASELINE DESIGNS

The second type of explanatory single-subject designs are the multiple-baseline designs. Multiple-baseline designs are like *ABAB* designs in that the *AB* design is implemented more than once. However, whereas *ABAB* designs apply to one case with one problem in one setting, multiple-baseline designs can be used with:

1   More than one case
2   More than one setting
3   More than one problem

### MORE THAN ONE CASE

Suppose that, instead of Bob with his social anxiety problem, you have three additional clients with anxiety problems: Breanne, Warren, and Alison. All three are residents in the same nursing home. You use the same measuring instrument to measure anxiety (the *IASS*) in all three cases, and you give all three clients the same intervention (*B* phase).

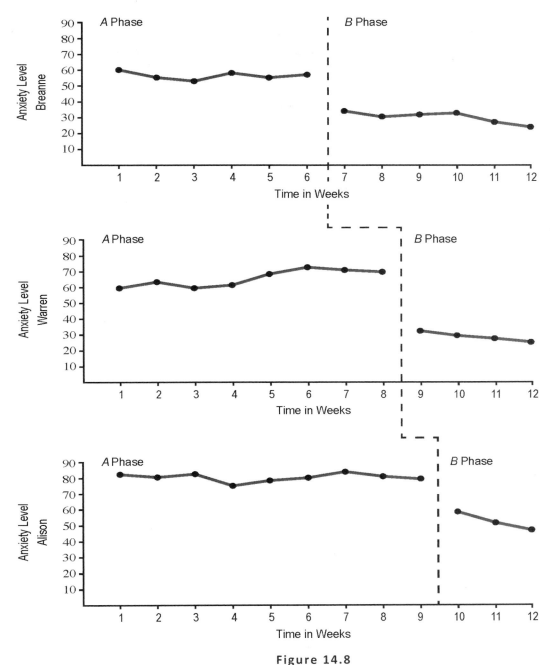

**Figure 14.8**

Multiple-Baseline Design across Clients:
Magnitude of Anxiety Levels for Three Clients

However, you vary the number of weeks over which you collect baseline data (A phase), allowing the baseline phase to last for six weeks in Breanne's case, eight weeks in Warren's case, and nine weeks for Alison. You plot your results as shown in Figure 14.8 as shown above.

Breanne starts to show improvement in week 7, the week you began your intervention. Had that improvement been due to some intervening variable—for example, some anxiety-reducing change in the nursing home's routine—you would expect Warren and Alison to also show improvement.

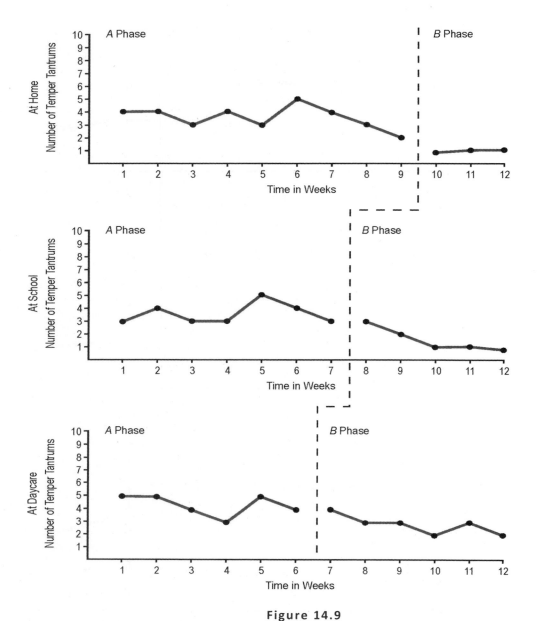

**Figure 14.9**

Multiple-Baseline Design across Settings:
Number of Temper Tantrums for One Client in Three Settings

The fact that their anxiety levels continue to be high indicates that it was your intervention, not some other factor, that caused the improvement in Breanne. Causality is demonstrated again in week 9 when you begin to intervene with Warren, and Warren improves but Alison does not. Your triumph is complete when Alison, given the same intervention, begins to improve in week 10.

In a nutshell, a multiple-baseline design across clients is nothing more than stringing together a series of *AB* single-subject designs that use the same intervention and placing them on one graph. They can have differential baseline periods. This design simply determines whether one intervention will work with more than one client. Simple as that! We now turn our attention to see whether one intervention can work with one client in more than one setting.

## More Than One Setting

Another way to conduct a multiple-baseline study is with one client in a number of settings. Suppose that your objective is to reduce the number of a child's temper tantrums at home, in school, and at the daycare center where the child goes after school. The same intervention (*B* phase) is offered by the parents at home, the teacher in school, and the worker at the daycare center.

They are also responsible for measuring the number of tantrums that occur each day. In our example, the baseline phase continues for different lengths of time in each of the three setting as shown in Figure 14.9 on the previous page. Once again, baselines do not have to be of equal lengths. If the child improves after the intervention begins in all three settings as shown in Figure 14.9, we may conclude that it was the intervention that caused the improvement in all three settings. A multiple-baseline design across settings simply determines whether one intervention will work with one client in multiple settings—in our example, at home, school, and daycare.

## More Than One Problem

A third way to conduct a multiple-baseline study is to use the same intervention to tackle different target problems. Suppose that Joan is having trouble with her daughter, Anita. In addition, Joan is having trouble with her in-laws and with her boss at work. After exploration, a worker may believe that all these troubles stem from her lack of assertiveness. Thus, the intervention would be assertiveness training. Progress with Anita might be measured by the number of times each day she is flagrantly disobedient.

Progress can be measured with Joan's in-laws by the number of times she is able to utter a contrary opinion, and so on. Because the number of occasions on which Joan has an opportunity to be assertive will vary, these figures might best be expressed in percentiles. Figure 14.10 on the following page illustrates an example of a multiple-baseline design that was used to assess the effectiveness of Joan's assertiveness training in three problem areas.

Whether it is a reversal design or a multiple-baseline design, an *ABAB* explanatory design involves establishing a baseline level for the client's target problem. This will not be possible if the need for intervention is acute, and sometimes the very thought of an A-type design will have to be abandoned. It is sometimes possible, however, to construct a retrospective baseline; that is, to determine what the level of the problem was before an intervention is implemented.

## RETROSPECTIVE BASELINES

**The best retrospective baselines** are those that do not depend on the client's memory. If the target problem occurs rarely, memories may be accurate. For example, Tai, a teenager, and his family may remember quite well how many times he ran away from home during the past month. They may not remember nearly so well if the family members were asked how often he behaved defiantly. Depending on the target problem, it may be possible to construct a baseline from archival data—that is, from written records, such as school attendance sheets, probation orders, employment interview forms, and so forth.

Although establishing a baseline usually involves making at least three measurements before implementing an intervention, it is also acceptable to establish a baseline of zero, or no occurrences of a desired event. A target problem, for example, might focus upon the client's reluctance to enter a drug treatment program.

The baseline measurement would then be that the client did not go (zero occurrences), and the desired change would be that the client did go (one occurrence). A social worker

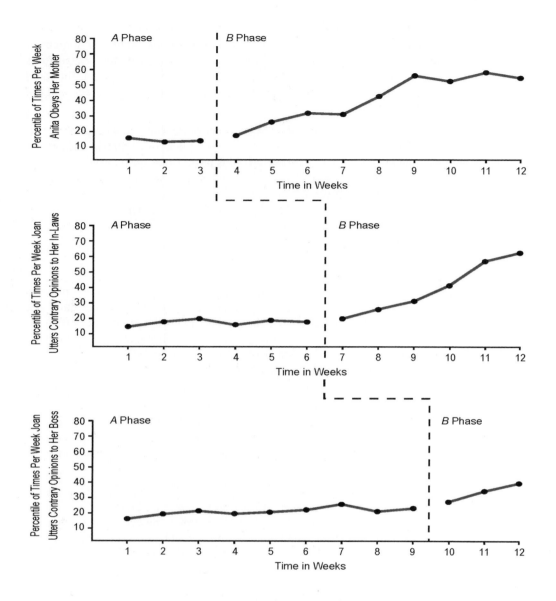

**Figure 14.10**

Multiple-Baseline Design across Client Problems:
Magnitude of Three Client Target Problem Areas for One Client

who has successfully used the same tactics to persuade a number of clients to enter a drug treatment program has conducted a multiple-baseline design across clients. As previously discussed, a usable baseline should show either that the client's problem level is stable or that it is growing worse. Sometimes an A-type design can be used even though the baseline indicates a slight improvement in the target problem. The justification must be that the intervention is expected to lead to an improvement that will exceed the anticipated improvement if the baseline trend continues.

Perhaps a child's temper tantrums are decreasing by one or two a week, for example, but the total number per week is still eighteen to twenty. If a worker thought the tantrums could be reduced to four or five a week, or they could be stopped altogether, the worker would be justified in implementing an intervention even though the client's target problem was improving slowly by itself.

In a similar way, a worker may be able to implement an *A*-type design if the client's baseline is unstable, provided that the intervention is expected to exceed the largest of the baseline fluctuations. Perhaps the child's temper tantrums are fluctuating between twelve and twenty per week in the baseline period, and it is hoped to bring them down to less than ten per week. Nevertheless, there are some occasions when a baseline cannot be established or is not usable, such as when a client's behaviors involve self-injurious ones. Also, sometimes the establishment of a baseline is totally inappropriate.

## CHAPTER RECAP

- Single-subject designs have five requirements.

- A specific, measurable, client-desired outcome objective is known as a client target problem.

- There are four exploratory single-subject designs, two descriptive designs, and two explanatory designs.

- Retrospective baselines can easily be used with single-subject designs.

- Single-subject designs are easy to use in social work practice and research situations alike.

- There are three types of reversal single-subject designs.

- There are three types of multiple-base line single subject designs.

- The individual, group, or artifact being studied is called the *unit of analysis*.

## REVIEW EXERCISES

1   In your own words, list and discuss the advantages of single-subject designs. Provide a single social work example throughout your discussion that illustrates your main points.

2   In your own words, list and then discuss the questions that single-subject designs can answer. Provide a single social work example throughout your discussion that illustrates your main points.

3   What is a *unit of analysis*? Discuss the various units of analysis that single-subject designs can be used for.

4   In your own words, list and discuss the three requirements of using single-subject designs. Provide a single social work example throughout your discussion that illustrates your main points.

5   Discuss the concept of *target problems*. Provide a single social work example throughout your discussion that illustrates your main points.

6   Discuss why single-subject designs need to have valid and reliable measuring instruments. Provide a single social work example throughout your discussion that illustrates your main points.

7   List and then discuss the four exploratory single-subject designs. Provide a social work example throughout your discussion that illustrates your main points.

8   List and then discuss the two descriptive single-subject designs. Provide a social work example throughout your discussion that illustrates your main points for both designs.

9   List and then discuss the two *explanatory* single-subject designs. Provide a social work example throughout your discussion that illustrates your main points for both designs.

10   List and then discuss the three *reversal* single-subject designs. Provide a social work example throughout your discussion that illustrates your main points for each of the three designs.

11   List and then discuss the three *multiple-baseline* designs. Provide a social work example throughout your discussion that illustrates your main points for each of the three designs.

# 15
CHAPTER

## 2015 EPAS COMPETENCIES

| COMPETENCY 1 | Demonstrate Ethical and Professional Behavior |
| --- | --- |

You have an ethical obligation to integrate three research roles into your daily practice activities as discussed in Chapter 3: (1) research consumer, (2) research partner—either as a co-researcher or research participant, and (3) creator and disseminator of research (or knowledge).

This entire chapter pertains to these three professional research-related roles when it comes to knowing the advantages and disadvantages of group research designs that social work researchers can use for quantitative (chapter 8), qualitative (chapter 9), and mixed-methods research studies (chapter 10).

| COMPETENCY 4 | Engage in Practice-Informed Research and Research-Informed Practice |
| --- | --- |

Competency 4 also pertains to the entire chapter because you have to:

1   Evaluate the internal and external validities of the group research design that was utilized in a research study (**research consumer**—research-informed practice);

2   Participate in a research study—either as a co-researcher or research participant (**research partner**—practice-informed research). See 1 above and 3 below; and

3   Know how to select the most appropriate group research design given your research question (or hypothesis) when you actually do a research study (**creator and disseminator of research**—practice-informed research).

You also need to utilize evidence-based practice recommendations whenever possible; that is, you need to integrate (1) the best available research-based evidence with (2) your clinical expertise and (3) your client's values.

All of the above implies you'll need to know how to assess the overall rigor (degree of internal and external validities) of the group research design that a research study used that produced its research-based evidence. In short, you need to ask and then answer a simple question: How seriously should I take the findings of any research study given how well it controlled for the internal and external validities that are inherent within the research design that the study used?

| COMPETENCY 9 | Evaluate Practice with Individuals, Families, Groups, Organizations, & Communities |
| --- | --- |

See Competencies 1 and 4.

# Group Designs

| | | |
|---|---|---|
| CHAPTERS 1 & 3 | Step 1. | Understanding the Research Process |
| CHAPTER 2 | Step 2. | Formulating Research Questions |
| CHAPTER 4<br>APPENDIXES A–C | Step 3. | Reviewing the Literature<br>Evaluating the Literature |
| CHAPTERS 5 & 6 | Step 4. | Being Aware of Ethical and Cultural Issues |
| CHAPTERS 7–10 | Step 5. | Selecting a Research Approach |
| CHAPTERS 11 & 12 | Step 6. | Specifying How Variables Are Measured |
| CHAPTER 13 | Step 7. | Selecting a Sample |
| CHAPTERS 14 & 15 | Step 8. | Selecting a Research Design |
| CHAPTERS 16 & 17 | Step 9. | Selecting a Data-Collection Method |
| CHAPTERS 18 & 19 | Step 10. | Analyzing the Data |
| CHAPTERS 20 & 21 | Step 11. | Writing the Research Report |

# Group Designs

Today's topic: Internal & External Validity

GLASBERG

"I think all that research stuff you're teaching us doesn't have any internal and external validities."

KNOWLEDGE LEVELS
CHARACTERISTICS OF "IDEAL" EXPERIMENTS
    Controlling the Time Order of Variables
    Manipulating the Independent Variable
    Establishing Relationships between Variables
    Controlling Rival Hypotheses
        *Holding Extraneous Variables Constant*
        *Using Correlated Variation*
        *Using Analysis of Covariance*
    Using a Control Group
    Randomly Assigning Participants to Groups
        *Matched-Pairs Method*
CLASSIFYING GROUP RESEARCH DESIGNS
ONE-GROUP DESIGNS
    One-Group Posttest-Only Design
    Cross-Sectional Survey Design
    Longitudinal Designs
        *Trend Studies*
        *Cohort Studies*
        *Panel Studies*
    One-Group Pretest-Posttest Design
INTERNAL VALIDITY
    History
    Maturation
    Testing Effects

Instrumentation Error
Statistical Regression
Differential Selection of Participants
Mortality
Reactive Effects of Research Participants
Interaction Effects
Relations between Groups
    *Diffusion of Treatments*
    *Compensatory Equalization*
    *Compensatory Rivalry*
    *Demoralization*
TWO-GROUP DESIGNS
    Comparison Group Pretest-Posttest Design
    Comparison Group Posttest-Only Design
    Classical Experimental Design
    Randomized Posttest-Only Control Group Design
EXTERNAL VALIDITY
    Selection-Treatment Interaction
    Specificity of Variables
    Multiple-Treatment Interference
    Researcher Bias
EVALUATING RESEARCH DESIGNS
    Use the Appendixes
CHAPTER RECAP
REVIEW EXERCISES

NOW THAT YOU KNOW how to use single-subject designs we turn our attention to the various group-level designs that research studies can take. The two most important factors in determining what group design to use in a specific study are (1) what the research question is, and (2) how much knowledge about the problem area is available.

## KNOWLEDGE LEVELS

If there is already a substantial knowledge base in your problem area, you will be in a position to address very specific research questions, the answers to which could add to the explanation of previously gathered data. If less is known about the problem area, your research questions will have to be of a more general, descriptive nature. If very little is known about the problem area, your questions will have to be even more general, at an exploratory level.

Research knowledge levels are arrayed along a continuum, from exploratory at the lowest end to explanatory at the highest (see figures 2.1 on page 41 and 2.3 on page 48). Because research knowledge levels are viewed this way, the assignment of the level of knowledge accumulated in a problem area prior to a research study and the level that might be attained by the research study are totally arbitrary. There are, however, specific designs that can be used to provide us with knowledge at a certain level.

At the highest level are the explanatory designs, also called *experimental designs* or *"ideal" experiments*. These designs have the largest number of requirements (examined in the following section). They are best used in confirmatory research studies where the area under study is well developed, theories abound, and testable hypotheses can be formulated on the basis of previous work or existing theory. These designs seek to establish causal relationships between the independent and dependent variables.

In the middle range are the descriptive designs, sometimes referred to as *quasi-experimental*. A quasi-experiment resembles an "ideal" experiment in some aspects but lacks at least one of the necessary requirements.

At the lowest level are the exploratory designs, also called *pre-experimental* or *nonexperimental,* which explore only the research question or problem area. These designs do not produce statistically sound data or conclusive results, but they are not intended to.

Their purpose is to build a foundation of general ideas and tentative theories, which can be explored later with more precise and hence more complex research designs and their corresponding data-gathering techniques.

The research designs that allow us to acquire knowledge at each of the three levels are described in a later section of this chapter. Before considering them, however, it's necessary to establish the characteristics that differentiate an "ideal" experiment, which leads to explanatory knowledge, from other studies that lead to the other two lower levels of knowledge (descriptive and exploratory).

## CHARACTERISTICS OF "IDEAL" EXPERIMENTS

An "ideal" experiment is one in which a research study most closely approaches certainty about the relationship between the independent and dependent variables. The purpose of doing an "ideal" experiment is to determine whether it can be concluded from the study's findings that the independent variable is, or is not, the only cause of change in the dependent variable.

As pointed out in previous chapters, some social work research studies have no independent variable. An example would be a study that just wants to find out how many people in a certain community wish to establish a community-based halfway house for people who are addicted to drugs.

The concept of an "ideal" experiment is introduced with the word "ideal" in quotation marks because such an experiment is rarely achieved in social work research situations. On a general level, in order to achieve this high degree of certainty and qualify as an "ideal" experiment, an explanatory research design must meet six conditions:

1   The time order of the independent variable must be established.
2   The independent variable must be manipulated.
3   The relationship between the independent and dependent variables must be established.
4   The research design must control for rival hypotheses.
5   At least one control group should be used.
6   Random assignment procedures (and if possible, random sampling from a sampling frame) must be employed in assigning research participants (or objects) to groups.

## CONTROLLING THE TIME ORDER OF VARIABLES

As you know from Chapter 8, in an "ideal" experiment the independent variable must precede the dependent variable in time. Time order is crucial if our research study is to show that one variable causes another, because something that occurs later cannot be the cause of something that occurred earlier. Suppose we want to study the relationship between adolescent substance abuse and gang-related behavior. After some thought, we formulate a hypothesis:

**Hypothesis**
Adolescent substance abuse causes gang-related behavior.

In this hypothesis, the independent variable is adolescent substance abuse, and the dependent variable is gang-related behavior. The substance abuse must come *before* gang-related behavior because the hypothesis states that adolescent drug use causes gang-related behavior. We could also come up with the following hypothesis, however:

**Hypothesis**
Adolescent gang-related behavior causes substance abuse.

In this hypothesis, adolescent gang-related behavior is the independent variable, and substance abuse is the dependent variable. According to this hypothesis, gang-related behavior must come *before* the substance abuse.

## MANIPULATING THE INDEPENDENT VARIABLE

Manipulation of the independent variable means that we must do something with the independent variable. In the general form of the hypothesis "if *X* occurs, then *Y* will result," the independent variable (*X*) must be manipulated in order to effect a variation in the dependent variable (*Y*). There are essentially three ways in which independent variables can be manipulated:

1 ***X* present versus *X* absent.** If the effectiveness of a specific treatment intervention is being evaluated, an experimental group and a control group could be used. The experimental group would be given the intervention (*X*) and the control group would not (no *X*).

2 **A small amount of *X* versus a larger amount of *X*.** If the effect of treatment time on client outcome is being studied, two experimental groups could be used, one of which would be treated for a longer period of time.

3 ***X* versus something else.** If the effectiveness of two different treatment interventions is being studied, Intervention $X_1$ could be used with Experimental Group 1 and Intervention $X_2$ with Experimental Group 2.

Obviously, certain variables, such as the gender or race of our research participants, cannot be manipulated because they are fixed. They do not vary, so they are called constants, not variables, as was pointed out in Chapter 8. Other constants, such as socioeconomic status or IQ, may vary for research participants over their life spans, but they are fixed quantities at the beginning of the study, probably will not change during the study, and are not subject to alteration by the one doing the study.

Any variable we can alter (such as treatment time) can be considered an independent variable. At least one independent variable must be manipulated in a research study if it's to be considered an "ideal" experiment.

## ESTABLISHING RELATIONSHIPS BETWEEN VARIABLES

The relationship between the independent and the dependent variables must be established in order to infer a cause-and-effect relationship at the explanatory knowledge level. If the independent variable is considered to be the cause of the dependent variable, there must be some pattern in the relationship between these two variables. An example is the hypothesis "The more time clients spend in treatment (independent variable), the better their progress (dependent variable)".

## CONTROLLING RIVAL HYPOTHESES

Rival hypotheses must be identified and eliminated in an "ideal" experiment. The logic of this requirement is extremely important, because this is what makes a cause-and-effect statement possible.

The prime question to ask when trying to identify a rival hypothesis is, "What other extraneous variables might affect the dependent variable?" (What else might affect the client's outcome besides treatment time?) At the risk of sounding redundant, "What else besides *X* might affect *Y*?" Perhaps the client's motivation for treatment, in addition to the time spent in treatment, might affect the client's outcome. If so, motivation for treatment is an extraneous variable that could be used as the independent variable in the rival hypothesis "The higher the clients' motivation for treatment, the better their progress".

Perhaps the social worker's attitude toward the client might have an effect on the client's outcome, or the client might win the state lottery and ascend abruptly from depression to ecstasy. These extraneous variables could potentially be independent variables in other rival hypotheses. They must all be considered and eliminated before it can be said with reasonable certainty that a client's outcome resulted from the length of treatment time and not from any other extraneous variables. Control over rival hypotheses refers to efforts on our part to identify and, if at all possible, to eliminate the extraneous variables in these alternative hypotheses. Of the many ways to deal with rival hypotheses, three of the most frequently used are:

1  Holding extraneous variables constant

2  Using correlated variation

3  Using analysis of covariance

### HOLDING EXTRANEOUS VARIABLES CONSTANT

The most direct way to deal with a rival hypothesis is to keep constant the critical extraneous variables that might affect the dependent variable. As we know, a constant cannot affect—or be affected by—any other variable. If an extraneous variable can be made into a constant, then it cannot affect either the study's real independent variable or the dependent variable.

Let's take an overly simple example to illustrate this point. Suppose a social worker who is providing a treatment intervention called cognitive behavioral therapy (CBT) to anxious clients wants to relate client outcome to length of treatment time. However, a consulting psychiatrist who has them on antidepressant medication is also seeing all her clients.

Because medication may also affect her clients' outcomes (i.e., anxiety levels), it can be considered another independent variable that could be used in a rival hypothesis. However, because her study included her clients who all were taking medication for some time before the treatment intervention began, and who continue to take the same medicine in the same way throughout treatment, then medication can be considered a constant (in this study, anyway).

Any change in the clients' anxiety levels after the CBT intervention will, therefore, be a result of the intervention with the help of the medication. Holding it constant has eliminated the extraneous variable of medication, which might form a rival hypothesis. In short, this study started out with one independent variable, the CBT intervention, then added the variable of medication to it, so the final independent variable = CBT intervention + medication. This is all very well in theory. In reality, however, a client's drug regime is usually controlled by the psychiatrist and may well be altered at any time. Even if the regimen is not altered, the effects of the drugs might not become apparent until the study is underway.

In addition, the client's level of anxiety might be affected by a host of other extraneous variables over which the social worker has no control at all: for example, living arrangements, relationships with other people, the condition of the stock market, the election of an unhinged president, or an unexpected visit from an IRS agent. These kinds of pragmatic difficulties tend to occur frequently in social work practice and research. It's often impossible to identify all rival hypotheses, let alone eliminate them by keeping them constant.

### USING CORRELATED VARIATION

Rival hypotheses can also be controlled with correlated variation of the independent variables. Suppose, for example, that we are concerned that income has an effect on a client's compulsive behavior. The client's income, which in this case is subject to variation due to seasonal employment, is identified as an independent variable. The client's living conditions—a hotel room rented by the week—are then identified as the second independent variable that might well affect the client's level of compulsive behavior.

These two variables, however, are correlated, because living conditions are highly dependent on income. Correlated variation exists if one potential independent variable can be correlated with another; then only one of them has to be dealt with in the research study.

### USING ANALYSIS OF COVARIANCE

In conducting an "ideal" experiment, we must always aim to use two or more groups that are as equivalent as possible on all important variables. Sometimes this goal is not feasible, however. Perhaps we are obliged to use existing groups that are not as equivalent as we would like.

Or perhaps during the course of the study we discover inequivalences between the groups that were not apparent at the beginning. A statistical method called *analysis of covariance* can be used to compensate for these differences. The mathematics of the method are far beyond the scope of this text, but an explanation can be found in most statistics texts.

## USING A CONTROL GROUP

An "ideal" experiment should use at least one control group in addition to the experimental group. The experimental group may receive an intervention that is withheld from the control group, or equivalent groups may receive different interventions or no interventions at all.

A social worker who initiates a treatment intervention is often interested in knowing what would have happened had the intervention not been used or had some different intervention been substituted. Would members of a support group for alcoholics have recovered anyway, without the social worker's efforts? Would they have recovered faster or more completely had family counseling been used instead of the support group approach?

The answer to these questions will never be known if only the support group is studied. But what if another group of alcoholics is included in the research design? In a typical design with a control group, two equivalent groups, 1 and 2, would be formed, and both would be administered the same pretest to determine the initial level of the dependent variable (e.g., degree of alcoholism).

Then an intervention would be initiated with Group 1 but not with Group 2. The group treated—Group 1, or the experimental group—would receive the independent variable (the intervention). The group not treated—Group 2, or the control group—would not receive it. This can be easily diagramed, as illustrated in Figure 15.9 on page 321.

At the conclusion of the intervention, both groups would be given a posttest (the same measure as the pretest). Both the pretest and the posttest consist of the use of some sort of data-gathering procedure, such as a survey or self-report measure, to measure the dependent variable before and after the introduction of the independent variable. There are many types of group research designs, and there are many ways to graphically display them. In general, group designs can be written in symbols.

The $R_a$ in Figure 15.9 (page 321) indicates that the research participants were randomly assigned to each group. The symbol X, which, as usual, stands for the independent variable, indicates that an intervention is to be given to the experimental group after the pretest ($O_1$) and before the posttest ($O_2$). The absence of X for the control group indicates that the intervention is not to be given to the control group. This design is called a classical experimental design because it comes closest to having all the characteristics necessary for an "ideal" experiment.

## RANDOMLY ASSIGNING PARTICIPANTS TO GROUPS

Once a sample frame has been established (see chapter 13), the individuals (or objects or events) in it are randomly assigned to either an experimental or a control group in order to ensure that the two groups are equivalent as much as possible. This procedure is known as random assignment or randomization. In random assignment, the word "equivalent" means equal in terms of the variables that are important to the study, such as the clients' motivation for treatment, or problem severity.

If the effect of treatment time on client outcome is being studied, for example, the research design might use one experimental group that is treated for a comparatively longer time, a second experimental group that is treated for a shorter time, and a control group that is not treated at all.

If we are concerned that the clients' motivation for treatment might also affect their outcomes, the research participants can be assigned so that all the groups are equivalent (on the average) in terms of their motivation for treatment.

The process of random sampling from a population followed by random assignment of the sample to groups can be illustrated as seen in the diagram below. Let's say that the research design calls for a sample size of one-tenth of the population. From a population of 10,000, therefore, a random sampling procedure is used to select a sample of 1,000 individuals.

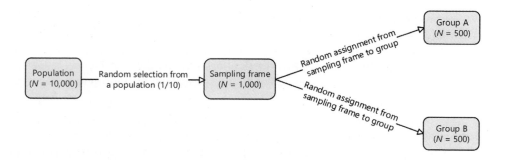

Then random assignment procedures are used to place the sample of 1,000 into two equivalent groups of 500 individuals each. In theory, Group A will be equivalent to Group B, which will be equivalent to the sampling frame, which will be equivalent to the population in respect to all important variables contained within the sample.

### MATCHED-PAIRS METHOD

Another, more deliberate method of assigning research participants or other units to groups, a subset of randomization, involves matching. Suppose a new training program for teaching parenting skills to foster mothers is being evaluated. A standardized measuring instrument that measures parenting skill level (the dependent variable) is administered to ten foster mothers. The scores can range from 100 (excellent parenting skills) to 0 (poor parenting skills).

The ten women would then be matched in pairs according to their parenting skill level; the two most skilled foster mothers would be matched (Pair 1), then the next two (Pair 2), and so on. One person in the first pair would then be randomly assigned to the experimental group and the other placed in the control group.

It doesn't make any difference to which group the first research participant is randomly assigned so long as there is an equal chance that she will go to either the control group or the experimental group. In this example, the first person is randomly chosen to go to the experimental group, as illustrated below:

**Rank Order of Parenting Skills Scores (in parentheses)**

*First Pair*

> (99) Randomly assigned to the experimental group

> (98) Assigned to the control group

*Second Pair*

> (97) Assigned to the control group

> (96) Assigned to the experimental group

*Third Pair*

> (95) Assigned to the experimental group

> (94) Assigned to the control group

*Fourth Pair*

> (93) Assigned to the control group

> (92) Assigned to the experimental group

*Fifth Pair*

> (91) Assigned to the experimental group

> (90) Assigned to the control group

As can be seen, the foster parent with the highest score (99) is randomly assigned to the experimental group, and this person's "match," with a score of 98, is assigned to the control group. This process is reversed with the next matched pair, where the first person is assigned to the control group and the match is assigned to the experimental group.

If the assignment of research participants according to scores is not reversed for every other pair, one group will be higher than the other on the variable being matched. To illustrate this point, suppose the first participant (highest score) in each match is always assigned to the experimental group. The experimental group's average score would be 95 (99 + 97 + 95 + 93 + 91 = 475/5 = 95), and the control group's average score would be 94 (98 + 96 + 94 + 92 + 90 = 470/5 = 94).

If every other matched pair is reversed, however, as in the example, the average scores of the two groups are closer together: 94.6 for the experimental group (99 + 96 + 95 + 92 + 91 = 473/5 = 94.6) and 94.4 for the control group (98 + 97 + 94 + 93 + 90 = 472/5 = 94.4). In short, 94.6 and 94.4 are closer together than 95 and 94 (difference of 1).

## CLASSIFYING GROUP RESEARCH DESIGNS

**G**roup research designs can be classified into as many different types of classification systems as there are folks who are willing to classify them. We are going to classify them into:

1    One-group research designs

2    Two-group research designs

The main difference between the two classifications is that the one-group designs don't compare their research participants with another group; they simply don't have another group of participants to compare to. On the other hand, the two-group designs do just that: they compare one group of research participants with another group—usually to ascertain whether a particular group (experimental group) has more positive outcomes on a dependent variable than the other group (control or comparison group).

Let's begin our discussion with the simplest of all research designs—those that use only one group of research participants.

## ONE-GROUP DESIGNS

**O**ne-group designs measure (1) the participants' success with an intervention (program objective) after they leave a program, and (2) any nonprogram objective at any time. One-group designs are exceptionally useful for providing a framework for gathering data—especially for needs assessments and process evaluations. In fact, two-group designs are rarely used in needs assessments and process evaluations. There are numerous types of one-group research designs, but we present only the four basic ones:

1    One-group posttest-only design (figure 15.1a).

2    Cross-sectional survey design (figure 15.2a).

3    Longitudinal designs:

— Trend studies (figure 15.3a, box 15.1).

— Cohort studies (figure 15.4a, box 15.2).

— Panel studies (figure 15.5a, box 15.3).

4    One-group pretest-posttest design (figure 15.6).

### ONE-GROUP POSTTEST-ONLY DESIGN

The one-group posttest-only design is sometimes called the *one-shot case study* or *cross-sectional case study* design. Suppose in a particular small community there are numerous parents who are abusive toward their children. The city decides to hire a school social worker, Antonia, to implement a social service intervention that is supposed to reduce the number of parents who abuse their children.

She creates a twelve-week child abuse prevention program (the intervention) and offers it to parents who have children in her school who wish to participate on a voluntary basis. A simple research study is then conducted to answer the rather simplistic question, "Did the parents who completed the program stop abusing their children?" The answer to this question will determine the success of her program, or intervention.

There are many different ways in which her program can be evaluated. For now, and to make matters as simple as possible, we are going to evaluate it by simply calculating the percentage of parents who said they stopped abusing their children after they attended the twelve-week program—the program's objective. At the simplest level, the program could be evaluated with a one-group posttest-only design. The basic elements of this design (figure 15.1a on the following page) can be written in symbols such as:

$X$ = Child Abuse Prevention Program, or the intervention

$O$ = First and only measurement of the program objective

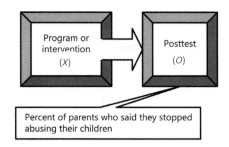

**Figure 15.1a**

One-Group Posttest-Only Design

All that this design provides is a single measure (*O*) of what happens when one group of people is subjected to one intervention or experience (*X*). It's safe to assume that all the members within the program had physically abused their children before they enrolled, because people who do not have this problem would not have enrolled in such a program. Sometimes this design is written as: *X O*.

But even if the value of *O* indicates that some of the parents did stop being violent with their children after the program, it cannot be determined whether they quit solely because of the intervention or because something else may have caused the parents to quit.

Such somethings are called a rival hypotheses, or alternative explanations. Perhaps a law was recently passed that made it mandatory for the police to arrest folks who behave violently toward their children, or perhaps the local television station started to report such incidents on the nightly news, complete with pictures of the abusive parents.

These or other extraneous variables might have been more important in persuading the parents to cease their abusive behavior toward their children than their voluntary participation in Antonia's program. All we will know from this design is the number and percentage of the folks who self-reported that they stopped hurting their children after they successfully completed Antonia's twelve-week program. Figure 15.1b below presents the results from a simple survey question (illustrated below) that Antonia included in a mailed survey that was completed by her past participants.

**Survey question**

Do you continue to abuse your children?

**1** Yes

**2** No

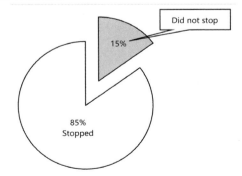

**Figure 15.1b**

Percentage of Parents Who Stopped Physically Abusing
Their Children after Leaving Antonia's Program
(from figure 15.1a)

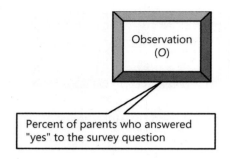

**Figure 15.2a**

Antonia's Cross-Sectional Survey Design

Notice that 85 percent of the parents reported they do not abuse their children after they completed Antonia's program. So Antonia could place the results of her survey question in a simple pie chart such as Figure 15.1b on the previous page. And yes, we are fully aware of the problems with parents self-reporting whether or not they continue to abuse their children, but for now just go along with us. The one-group posttest-only design is also used in process evaluations when it comes to the collection of client satisfaction data.

## CROSS-SECTIONAL SURVEY DESIGN

Let's take another example of a design that does not have an intervention of some kind, called a cross-sectional survey design. In doing a cross-sectional survey we survey only once a cross section of some particular population. In addition to running her child abuse prevention program for abusive parents, Antonia also wants to start a child abuse educational program for all the children in her school.

Before Antonia starts the program, she wants to know what parents think about the idea—kind of like a mini-needs assessment. She may send out questionnaires to all the parents, or she may decide to telephone every second parent, or every fifth or tenth, depending on how much time and money she has. She asks one simple question in her mini-needs assessment survey:

**Survey question**

Do you support our school offering a child abuse educational program that your child could enroll in on a voluntary basis and with your consent?

1   Yes

2   No

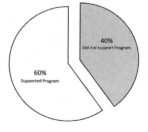

**Figure 15.2b**

Percentage of Parents Who Supported a Voluntary Child
Abuse Educational Program (from figure 15.2a)

The results of her simple survey constitute a single measurement, or observation, of the parents' opinions of her proposed educational program (the one for the children) and may be as shown Figure 15.2a on the previous page.

The symbol *O* in Figure 15.2a represents the entire cross-sectional survey design because such a design involves making only a single observation, or measurement, at one time period. Note that there is no *X*, because there is really no intervention.

Antonia wants only to ascertain the parents' attitudes toward her proposed program—nothing more, nothing less. This type of design is used a lot in needs assessment studies. Data that are derived from such a design can be displayed in a simple pie chart as in Figure 15.2b on the previous page. Notice that 60 percent of the parents supported their children attending a voluntary child abuse educational program.

## LONGITUDINAL DESIGNS

The longitudinal design provides for multiple measurements (*O*s) of the program objective—or some other variable of interest—over time, not just at one point in time. Notice that the two previous designs—the one-group posttest-only design and the cross-sectional survey design—measured a variable only once. In contrast, longitudinal designs measure variables more than one time, thus the name *longitudinal.* They can be broken down into three general types:

1 Trend studies
2 Cohort studies
3 Panel studies

### TREND STUDIES

A trend study takes different samples of people who share a similar characteristic at different points in time. Antonia may want to know whether parents of second-graders at her school are becoming more receptive to the idea of the school offering their children a child abuse prevention education program. Her population of interest is simply the parents who have children in the second grade.

Remember, a trend study samples different groups of people at different points in time from the same population of interest. So, to answer her question, she may survey a sample of the parents of second-graders this year (sample 1), a sample of the parents of the new complement of second-graders next year (sample 2), and so on (sample 3) until she thinks she has sufficient data to answer her question. Each year the parents surveyed will be different, but they will all be parents of second-graders—her population of interest. In this case her research design could be written as,

Where:

$O_1$ = First measurement of a variable in Sample 1 (year 2020)

$O_2$ = Second measurement of the same variable in Sample 2 (year 2021)

$O_3$ = Third measurement of the same variable in Sample 3 (year 2022)

Antonia will be able to determine whether parents, as a group, are becoming more receptive to the idea of introducing child abuse prevention material to their children as early as second grade. In other words, she will be able to measure any attitudinal trend that is, or is not, occurring. The design can be written as shown in Figure 15.3a, and the data from Antonia's study could be displayed in a simple bar graph like Figure 15.3b. Notice that the percentage of parents desiring such a program is going up over time.

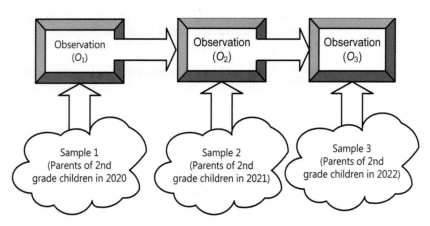

**Figure 15.3a**

Antonia's Trend Study

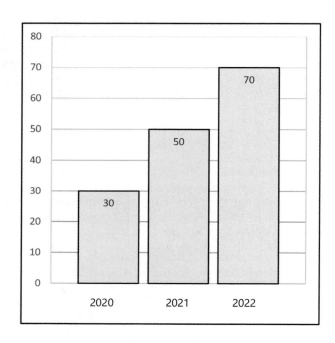

**Figure 15.3b**

Displaying Data for a Trend Study (from figure 15.3a):
Percentage of Parents Who Support a Prevention
Educational Program by Year

| Box 15.1 | Trend Studies in a Nutshell |
|---|---|

**The trend study** is probably the most common longitudinal study among others. A trend study samples different groups of people at different points in time from the same population of interest. For example, trend studies are common around public opinion polls.

Suppose that two months before a year-long gun control campaign, a sample of adults is drawn: 64 percent report that they're in favor of a strict gun control regulation, and 34 percent report that they're not. A year later, a different sample drawn from the same population shows a change: 75 percent report that they're in favor of gun control, and 25 percent report that they're not. This is an example of a trend study.

Trend studies provide information about net changes at an aggregate level. In this example, we know that in the period under consideration the gun control program gained 11 percentage points more support. However, we do not know how many people changed their positions (from con to pro or from pro to con), nor do we know how many stayed with their original choice.

To determine both the gross change and the net change, a panel study would be necessary, as presented in Box 15.3 on page 311.

**Characteristics**

- Data are collected from the population at more than one point in time. (This does not always mean that the same subjects are used to collect data at more than one point in time, but that the subjects are selected from the population for data collection at more than one point in time.)

- There is no experimental manipulation of variables; more specifically, the researcher has no control over the independent variable.

- This kind of study involves data collection only. No intervention is made by the research other than his or her method or tool to collect data.

- In analyzing the data, the researcher draws conclusions and may attempt to find correlations between variables. Therefore, trend studies are uniquely appropriate for assessing change over time and for answering prediction questions because variables are measured at more than one time. However, this method is deficient for answering causal questions because there is no manipulation of an independent variable.

## COHORT STUDIES

A cohort study takes place when research participants have a certain condition and/or receive a particular treatment and are sampled over time. For example, AIDS survivors, sexual abuse survivors, or parents of children can easily be followed over time. Unlike a trend study, which does not follow a particular cohort of individuals over time, a cohort study does just that: It follows a particular cohort of people who have shared a similar experience.

Antonia might select, for example, one particular group of parents who have adopted minority children, and measure their attitudes toward child abuse prevention education in successive years. Again, the design can be written as shown in Figure 15.4a, and the data could be presented in a format in a simple graph such as Figure 15.4b,

Where:

$O_1$ = *First measurement* of a variable for a sample of individuals within a given cohort

$O_2$ = *Second measurement* of the variable for a different sample of individuals within the same cohort 1 year later

$O_3$ = *Third measurement* of the variable for a different sample of individuals within the same cohort 2 years later

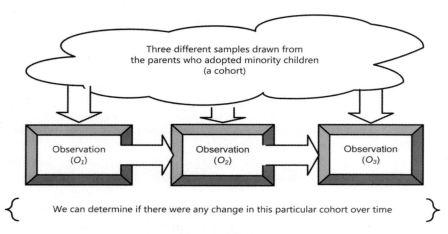

**Figure 15.4a**

Antonia's Cohort Study

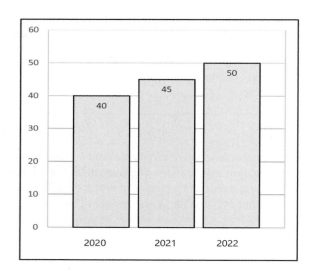

**Figure 15.4b**

Displaying Data for a Cohort Study (from figure 15.4a):
Percentage of Parents with Minority Children Who
Support a Prevention Educational Program by Year

## PANEL STUDIES

In a panel study, the same individuals are followed over a period of time. Antonia might select one random sample of parents, for example, and measure their attitudes toward child abuse prevention education in successive years. Unlike trend and cohort studies, panel studies can reveal both net change and gross change in the program objective for the same individuals. Additionally, panel studies can reveal shifting attitudes and patterns of behavior that might go unnoticed with other research approaches.

For example, Bob is measured once at Time 1, then again at Time 2, and so forth. We would do this for each individual in the study. Again, the design can be illustrated as in Figure 15.5a on page 310, and hypothetical data could be displayed in a simple graph as in Figure 15.5b on page 310.

---

| Box 15.2 | Using Cohort Studies with Two Groups |
|---|---|

**A cohort study** is a study in which research participants who presently have a certain condition and/or receive a particular treatment are followed over time and compared with another group who are not affected by the condition under investigation. For research purposes, a cohort is any group of individuals who are linked in some way or who have experienced the same significant life event within a given period.

There are many kinds of cohorts, including birth (e.g., all those who born between 1970 and 1975), disease, education, employment, family formation, and so on. Any study in which there are measures of some characteristic of one or more cohorts at two or more points in time is a cohort analysis.

In some cases, cohort studies are preferred to randomized experimental designs. For instance, because a randomized controlled study to test the effects of smoking on health would be unethical, a reasonable alternative would be a study that identifies two groups, a group of people who smoke and a group of people who do not, and follows them forward through time to see what health problems they develop.

In general, a cohort analysis attempts to identify cohort effects: Are changes in the dependent variable (health problems in this example) due to aging, or are they present because the sample members belongs to the same cohort (smoking versus nonsmoking)?

In other words, cohort studies are about the life histories of sections of populations and the individuals they comprise. They can tell us what circumstances in early life are associated with the population's characteristics in later life—what encourages the development in particular directions and what appears to impede it. We can study such developmental changes across any stage of life in any life domain: education, employment, housing, family formation, citizenship, or health.

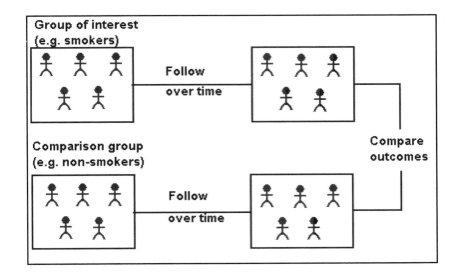

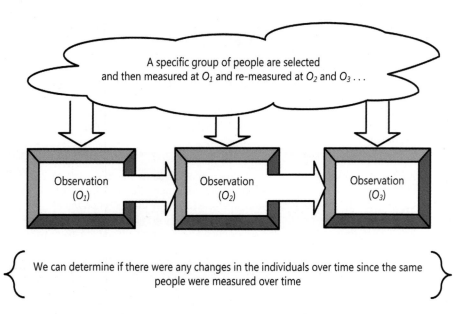

**Figure 15.5a**

Antonia's Panel Study

Figure 15.5b presents the results of the percentages of the same parents who want to have a child abuse prevention education program in their children's school, as measured over a three-year period from 2020 to 2022, where:

$O_1$ = *First measurement* of attitudes toward child abuse prevention education for a sample of individuals (2020)

$O_2$ = *Second measurement* of attitudes toward child abuse prevention education for the same individuals 1 year later (2021)

$O_3$ = *Third measurement* of attitudes toward child abuse prevention education for the same individuals 2 years later (2022)

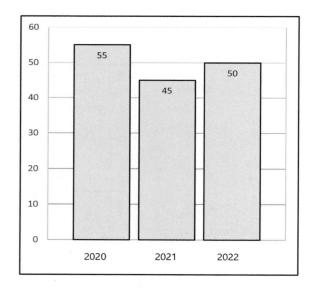

**Figure 15.5b**

Displaying Data for a Panel Study (from figure 15.5a):
Percentage of Parents Who Support a Prevention Educational Program by Year

| Box 15.3 | Panel Studies in a Nutshell |
|---|---|

**Panel studies** measure the same sample of respondents at different points in time. Unlike trend studies, panel studies can reveal both net change and gross change in the dependent variable for the same people. Panel studies can also reveal shifting attitudes and patterns of behavior that might go unnoticed with other research approaches.

Depending on the purpose of the study, researchers can use either a continuous panel (members who report specific attitudes or behavior patterns on a regular basis) or an interval panel (members who agree to complete a certain number of measurement instruments only when the information is needed). In general, panel studies provide data suitable for sophisticated statistical analysis and might enable researchers to predict cause-and-effect relationships.

Panel data are particularly useful in predicting long-term or cumulative effects, which are normally hard to analyze in a one-shot case study (or cross-sectional study). For example, in the early 1980s, the National Broadcasting Company supported a panel study in order to investigate the causal influence of violent TV viewing on aggression among young people. In brief, the methodology in the study involved collecting data on aggression, TV viewing, and a host of sociological variables from children in several metropolitan cities in the United States.

About 1,200 boys participated in the study, and the variables were measured six times for the three-year study period. The researchers sought to determine whether TV viewing at an earlier time added to the predictability of aggression at a later time. After looking at all the results, the investigators concluded that there was no consistent statistically significant relationship between watching violent TV programs and committing later acts of aggression.

## ONE-GROUP PRETEST-POSTTEST DESIGN

The one-group pretest-posttest design is also referred to as a before-and-after design because it includes a pretest of the program objective, and the pretest results are compared with the posttest results. This is the first design we've discussed that uses a pretest of some kind. It's written as shown in Figure 15.6 on the following page and hypothetical data could be displayed as in Table 15.1,

Where:

$O_1$ = First measurement of the program objective

$X$ = Program, or the intervention (see box 15.4 on page 313)

$O_2$ = Second measurement of the program objective

The one-group pretest-posttest design, in which a pretest precedes the introduction of the intervention and a posttest follows it, can be used to determine, on a general level, how the intervention affects a particular group. The design is used often in social work decision-making. The differences between $O_1$ and $O_2$, on which these decisions are based, could be due to many other internal validity factors (to be discussed in the next section) rather than to the intervention.

Let's take another indicator of how Antonia's child abuse prevention program could be evaluated. Besides counting the number of parents who stopped physically abusing their children as the only indicator of her program's success, she could have a second outcome indicator such as a reduction in the parents' risk for abusive and neglectful parenting behaviors.

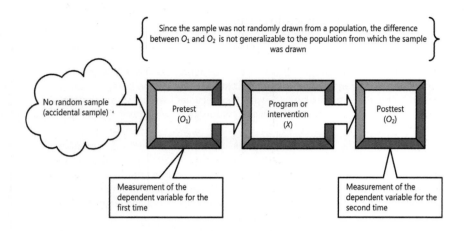

**Figure 15.6**

One-Group Pretest-Posttest Design

**Table 15.1**

Displaying Data for a One-Group Pretest-Posttest Design (from figure 15.6)

|  | Pretest Average $(O_1)$ | Posttest Average $(O_2)$ | Difference Average $(O_2 - O_1)$ |
|---|---|---|---|
| Intervention Group | 50 | 80 | 30 |

An instrument that measures their attitudes toward physical punishment of children could easily measure this program objective. Let's say that Antonia had the parents complete the instrument before participating in the child abuse prevention program ($O_1$) and after completing it ($O_2$). In this example all kinds of things could have happened between $O_1$ and $O_2$ to affect the participants' behaviors and feelings—such as the television station's deciding to publicize the names of parents who are abusive to their children.

Just the experience of taking the pretest could motivate some participants to stop being abusive toward their children. Maturation (the children are growing up and are becoming less difficult to discipline) could also affect the results between the pretest and posttest measurements.

These issues are referred to as alternative explanations and rival hypotheses and can make most of us question the results of just about any outcome evaluation. The easiest way you can control for all this messy stuff is by using two groups of participants, which eliminates many of the threats to internal validity.

## INTERNAL VALIDITY

Internal validity is a term we use to assess the "approximate certainty" about inferences regarding cause-and-effect or causal relationships. Thus, internal validity is predominantly relevant only to the research designs that try to establish causal relationships between the independent and dependent variables. In any causal study we should be able to conclude from our findings that the intervention is, or is not, the only cause of change in the dependent variable, or outcome variable, or program objective.

| Box 15.4 | Treatment: A Variable or a Constant? |
|---|---|

**For instructional purposes,** group designs are displayed using symbols where *X* is the independent variable (treatment) and *O* is the measure of the dependent variable. This presentation is accurate when studies are designed with two or more groups. When one-group designs are used, however, this interpretation does not hold.

In one-group designs, the treatment, or program, cannot truly vary because all research participants have experienced the same event; that is, they all have experienced the program. Without a comparison or control group, treatment is considered a constant because it's a quality shared by all members in the research study. In short, time is the independent variable.

There does not necessarily have to be an independent variable in a study, however; we may just want to measure some variable in a particular population such as the number of people who receive a certain type of social service intervention over a ten-year period. In this situation, there is no independent or dependent variable.

If our explanatory study does not have internal validity, such a conclusion is not possible, and the study's findings can be misleading. Internal validity is concerned with one of the requirements for an "ideal" research study—the control of rival hypotheses, or alternative explanations, which also might be responsible for the change in the dependent variable. In short, the higher the internal validity, the greater the extent to which rival hypotheses (or alternative explanations) can be controlled; the lower the internal validity, the less they can be controlled. We will discuss only ten threats to internal validity, which are:

1  History
2  Maturation
3  Testing effects
4  Instrumentation error
5  Statistical regression
6  Differential selection of research participants
7  Mortality
8  Reactive effects of research participants
9  Interaction effects
10  Relations between experimental and control groups

## HISTORY

The first threat to internal validity, *history,* refers to any outside event, either public or private, that may affect the program objective and that was not taken into account in our design. Many times, it refers to events that occur between the first and second measurement of the program objective (the pretest and the posttest).

If events occur that have the potential to alter the second measurement, there is no way of knowing how much (if any) of the observed change in the program's objective is a function of the intervention and how much is attributable to these events. Suppose, for example, we are investigating the effects of an educational program on racial tolerance. We may decide to measure the program objective (decreasing racial tolerance in the community) before introducing the intervention, the educational program. The educational program is then implemented and is represented by *X*.

Finally, racial tolerance is measured again, after the program has run its course. This final measurement yields a posttest score, represented by $O_2$. As you know, the one-group pretest-posttest study design is presented in Figure 15.6 on page 312. The difference between the values $O_2$ and $O_1$ represents the difference in the degree of racial tolerance in the community before and after the educational program. If the study is internally valid, $O_2 - O_1$ will yield a crude measure of the effect of the educational program on racial tolerance, and this is what we were trying to discover.

Now suppose that before the posttest could be administered, a colossal terrorist attack occurs in the United States, such as the type that occurred in New York on September 11, 2001. It may be fair to say that terrorism can be expected to have a negative effect on racial tolerance, and the posttest scores may, therefore, show a lower level of tolerance than if the terrorist act had not occurred. The effect, $O_2 - O_1$, will now be the combined effects of the educational program and the terrorist act, not the effect of the program alone, as we initially intended.

Terrorism is an extraneous variable that we could not have anticipated and did not control for when we designed the study. Other examples might include an earthquake, an election of a rogue president, illness, divorce, marriage, or a racially divisive incident like the 2012 shooting of Trayvon Martin in Florida—any event, public or private, that could affect the dependent variable, or program objective. Any such variable that is unanticipated and uncontrolled for is an example of history.

However, the effects of history are controlled for with the use of a control group; that is, the control group would theoretically have experienced the act of terrorism exactly like the experimental group. Thus, both groups would have been exposed to the extraneous terrorism variable, and this would make it a constant in the research design.

So whenever a control or comparison group is used in a study, it's usually safe to say that the effects of history have been controlled for (not history itself, of course, as this is reserved for the person up above). The most important thing to remember as a mortal is that you cannot control history—history marches on with or without you. You can however, control for the effects of history by adding a control or comparison group to your research design.

> *History* is a threat to internal validity that refers to events not accounted for in the research designs that may alter the second and subsequent measurements of the dependent variable.

## Maturation

Maturation, the second threat to internal validity, is history's first cousin. It refers to changes, both physical and psychological, that take place in our research participants over time and can affect the dependent variable, or program objective. Suppose that we are evaluating an intervention strategy designed to improve the behavior of adolescents who engage in delinquent behavior. Because the behavior of adolescents changes naturally as they mature, any observed change may have resulted as much from their natural development as from the intervention strategy.

Maturation refers not only to physical or mental growth, however. Over time, people grow older, more or less anxious, more or less bored, and more or less motivated to take part in a study. All these factors and many more can affect the way in which people respond when the program objective is measured a second or third time.

Like history, the effects of maturation can indeed be controlled for with the use of a control or comparison group. Like history, you cannot control maturation; you can only control for the effects of maturation by using control or comparison groups in your research designs.

> *Maturation* is a threat to internal validity that refers to the aging effects or developmental changes that influence the dependent variable.

## TESTING EFFECTS

Testing effects are sometimes referred to as *initial measurement effect.* Thus, the pretests that are the starting point for many research designs are another potential threat to internal validity. One of the most utilized designs involves three steps: (1) measuring some program objective, such as learning behaviors in school or attitudes toward work; (2) initiating a program to change that variable; and then (3) measuring the program objective again at the conclusion of the program. As you know, this design is known as the one-group pretest-posttest design and is illustrated in Figure 15.6 on page 312.

The testing effect is the effect that taking a pretest might have on posttest scores. Suppose that Roberto, a research participant, takes a pretest to measure his initial level of racial tolerance before being exposed to a racial tolerance educational program. He might remember some of the questions on the pretest, think about them later, and change his views on racial issues before taking part in the educational program. After the program, his posttest score will reveal his changed opinions, and we may incorrectly assume that the program was solely responsible, whereas the true cause was his experience with the pretest and the intervention.

*Testing effects* are a threat to internal validity that refers to the principle that taking pretests will affect posttest scores.

Sometimes a pretest induces anxiety in a research participant, so Roberto receives a worse score on the posttest than he should have; or boredom caused by having to respond to the same questions a second time may be a factor. To avoid the testing effect, we may wish to use a design that does not require a pretest.

If a pretest is essential, we then must consider the length of time between the pretest and posttest measurements. A pretest is far more likely to affect the posttest when the time between the two is short. The nature of the pretest is another factor. Measuring instruments that deal with factual matters, such as knowledge levels, may have large testing effects because the questions tend to be more easily recalled.

## INSTRUMENTATION ERROR

The fourth threat to internal validity is instrumentation error. This is simply a list of all the troubles that can afflict the measurement process. The instrument may be unreliable or invalid, as discussed in Chapters 11 and 12. A mechanical instrument, such as an electroencephalogram (*EEG*), may malfunction. Occasionally, the term instrumentation error is used to refer to an observer whose observations are inconsistent or to measuring instruments that are valid and reliable in themselves but have not been administered properly.

*Instrumentation error* is a threat to internal validity that refers to the weaknesses of a measuring instrument itself, such as invalidity, unreliability, improper administration, or mechanical breakdowns.

Administration, with respect to a measuring instrument, means the circumstances under which the measuring instrument is made: where, when, how, and by whom. A mother being asked about her attitudes toward her children, for example, may respond in one way in the social worker's office and in a different way at home while her children are screaming around her feet.

A mother's verbal response may differ from her written response, or she may respond differently in the morning than she would in the evening, or differently alone than she would in a group. These variations in situational responses do not indicate a true change in the feelings, attitudes, or behaviors being measured but are only examples of instrumentation error.

## STATISTICAL REGRESSION

The fifth threat to internal validity, statistical regression, refers to the tendency of extremely low and extremely high scores to regress, or move toward the average score for everyone in the study. Suppose an instructor makes her class take a multiple-choice exam and the average score is 50.

Now suppose that the instructor separates the low scorers from the high scorers and tries to even out the level of the class by giving the low scorers special instruction. To determine whether the special instruction has been effective, the entire class then takes another multiple-choice exam. The result of the exam is that the low scorers (as a group) do better than they did the first time, and the high scorers (as a group) do worse. The instructor believes that this has occurred because the low scorers received special instruction and the high scorers did not.

According to the logic of statistical regression, however, both the average score of the low scorers and the average score of the high scorers would move toward the total average score for both groups (i.e., 50). Even without any special instruction, and still in their state of ignorance, the low scorers (as a group) would be expected to have a higher average score than they did before. Likewise, the high scorers (as a group) would be expected to have a lower average score than they did before.

It would be easy for the research instructor to assume that the low scores had increased because of the special instruction and the high scores had decreased because of the lack of it. This is not necessarily so, however; the instruction may have had nothing to do with it. It may all be due to statistical regression where the high group goes down and the low group goes up.

> *Statistical regression* is a threat to internal validity that refers to the tendency for extreme scores at pretest to become less extreme at posttest.

## DIFFERENTIAL SELECTION OF PARTICIPANTS

The sixth threat to internal validity is differential selection of research participants. To some extent, the participants selected for a study are different from one another to begin with. "Ideal" research designs, however, require random sampling from a population (if at all possible) and random assignment to groups. This ensures that the results of a study will be generalizable to the larger population from which they were drawn (thus addressing threats to external validity, to be discussed later).

This threat, however, is present when we are working with preformed groups or groups that already exist, such as classes of students, self-help groups, or community groups. It's probable those different preformed groups will not be equivalent with respect to relevant variables and that these initial differences will invalidate the results of the posttest.

A child abuse prevention educational program for children in schools might be evaluated by comparing the prevention skills of one group of children who have taken the educational program with the skills of a second group who have not. To make a valid comparison, the two groups must be as similar as possible with respect to age, gender, intelligence, socioeconomic status, and anything else that might affect the acquisition of child abuse prevention skills.

We would have to make every effort to form or select equivalent groups, but the groups are sometimes not as equivalent as might be hoped—especially if we are obliged to work with preformed groups, such as classes of students or community groups. If the two groups were different before the intervention was introduced, there is not much point in comparing them at the end. Accordingly, preformed groups should be avoided whenever possible. If it's not feasible to do this, rigorous pretesting must be done to determine in what ways the groups are (or are not) equivalent and we must compensate for differences by using statistical methods.

> *Differential selection* is a threat to internal validity that refers to the potential lack of equivalency among preformed groups of research participants.

## MORTALITY

The seventh threat to internal validity is mortality, which simply means that research participants may drop out before the end of the study. Their absence will probably have a significant effect on the study's findings because people who drop out are likely to be different in some ways from those participants who stay to the end. People who drop out may be less motivated to participate in the intervention than are people who stay in, for example.

Because dropouts often have such characteristics in common, it cannot be assumed that the attrition occurred in a random manner. If considerably more people drop out of one group than out of the other, the result will be two groups that are no longer equivalent and cannot be usefully compared. We cannot know at the beginning of the study how many people will drop out, but we can watch to see how many do. Mortality is never problematic if dropout rates are 5 percent or less and if the dropout rates are similar for the both groups.

## REACTIVE EFFECTS OF RESEARCH PARTICIPANTS

The eighth threat to internal validity is reactive effects. Changes in the behaviors or feelings of research participants may be caused by their reaction to the novelty of the situation or to the knowledge that they are participating in a study.

The classic example of reactive effects was found in a series of studies carried out at the Hawthorne plant of the Western Electric Company, in Chicago, many years ago. Researchers were investigating the relationship between working conditions and productivity. When they increased the level of lighting in one section of the plant, productivity increased; a further increase in the lighting was followed by an additional increase in productivity. When the lighting was then decreased, however, production levels did not fall accordingly but continued to rise. The conclusion was that the workers were increasing their productivity not because of the lighting level but because of the attention they were receiving as research participants in the study.

The term *Hawthorne effect* is still used to describe any situation in which the research participants' behaviors are influenced not by the intervention but by the knowledge that they are taking part in a research project. Another example of such a reactive effect is the placebo given to patients, which produces beneficial results because the patients believe it is medication.

Ensuring that all participants in a study, in both the experimental and the control groups, appear to be treated equally can control reactive effects. If one group is to be shown an educational film, for example, the other group should also be shown a film—some film carefully chosen to bear no relationship to the variable being investigated. If the study involves a change in the participants' routine, this in itself may be enough to change behavior, and care must be taken to continue the study until novelty has ceased to be a factor.

## INTERACTION EFFECTS

Interaction among the various threats to internal validity can have an effect of its own. Any of the factors already described as threats may interact with one another, but the most common interactive effect involves differential selection and maturation.

Let's say we are studying two preformed groups of clients who are being treated for depression. The intention was for these groups to be equivalent, in terms of both their motivation for treatment and their levels of depression. It turns out that Group A is more generally depressed than Group B, however.

Whereas both groups may grow less motivated over time, it's likely that Group A, whose members were more depressed to begin with, will lose motivation more completely and more quickly than Group B. Nonequivalent preformed groups thus grow even less equivalent over time as a result of the interaction between differential selection and maturation.

---

*Mortality* is a threat to internal validity that refers to the loss of research participants through normal attrition over time in research designs that require pretests and posttests.

*Reactive effects* are a threat to internal validity that refers to a process in which change in the dependent variable is induced by the research procedures themselves.

# RELATIONS BETWEEN GROUPS

The final group of threats to internal validity has to do with the effects that may happen when using two or more groups of research participants. These effects include:

1  Diffusion of treatments
2  Compensatory equalization
3  Compensatory rivalry
4  Demoralization

## DIFFUSION OF TREATMENTS

Diffusion, or imitation, of treatments may occur when members of the experimental and control groups talk to each other about the study. Suppose a study is designed to present a new relaxation exercise to the experimental group and nothing at all to the control group. There is always the possibility that one of the participants in the experimental group will explain the exercise to a friend who happens to be in the control group. The friend explains it to another friend, and so on. This might be beneficial for the control group, but it undermines the study's findings.

## COMPENSATORY EQUALIZATION

Compensatory equalization of treatment occurs when the person doing the study and/or the staff member administering the intervention to the experimental group feels sorry for people in the control group who are not receiving it and attempts to compensate them. A social worker might take a control group member aside and covertly demonstrate the relaxation exercise, for example.

On the other hand, if our study has been ethically designed, there should be no need for guilt on the part of the social worker because some people are not being taught to relax. They can be taught to relax when our study is over as pointed out in Chapter 5 on ethics.

## COMPENSATORY RIVALRY

Compensatory rivalry is an effect that occurs when the control group becomes motivated to compete with the experimental group. For example, a control group in a program to encourage parental involvement in school activities might get wind that something is up and make a determined effort to participate, too, on the basis that "anything they can do, we can do better." There is no direct communication between the groups, as there is in the diffusion of treatment effect, only rumors and suggestions of rumors. However, rumors are often enough to threaten the internal validity of a study.

## DEMORALIZATION

In direct contrast with compensatory rivalry, demoralization refers to feelings of deprivation among the control group that may cause them to give up and drop out of the study, in which case this effect would be referred to as mortality. The people in the control group may also get angry.

Now that you have a sound understanding of internal validity, we turn our attention to two-group designs that have to minimize as many threats to internal validity as possible if they are to support cause-and-effect statements such as "my intervention caused my clients to get better."

> *Interaction effects* are a threat to internal validity that refer to the effects produced by the combination of two or more threats to internal validity.

## TWO-GROUP DESIGNS

**E**xcept for the one-group pretest-posttest design, one-group designs do not intend to determine cause–effect relationships. Thus, they are not concerned with internal validity issues. Two-group designs on the other hand help us produce data for coming a bit closer to proving cause-and-effect relationships; so now internal validity issues come readily into play. There are many two-group designs, but we will discuss only four of them.

1 Comparison group pretest-posttest design (figure 15.7)
2 Comparison group posttest-only design (figure 15.8)
3 Classical experimental design (figure 15.9)
4 Randomized posttest-only control group design (figure 15.10)

## COMPARISON GROUP PRETEST-POSTTEST DESIGN

The comparison group pretest-posttest design simply elaborates on the one-group pretest-posttest design by adding a comparison group. This second group receives both the pretest ($O_1$) and the posttest ($O_2$) at the same time as the experimental group, but it does not receive the intervention. Also, random assignment to groups is never done in this design. This design is written as shown in Figure 15.7 below, and hypothetical data could look like those displayed in Table 15.2 on page 320,

Where:

$O_1$ = First measurement of the program objective

$X$  = The program, or intervention

$O_2$ = Second measurement of the program objective

The experimental and comparison groups formed under this design will probably not be equivalent because members are not randomly assigned to the two groups (notice the 10-point difference at pretest). The pretest scores, however, will indicate the extent of their differences. If the differences are not statistically significant but are still large enough to affect the posttest, the statistical technique of analysis of covariance can be used to compensate for this. So long as the groups are at least somewhat equivalent at pretest, this design controls for nearly all of the threats to internal validity. But because random assignment to groups was not used, many of the external validity threats remain (to be discussed at the end of chapter).

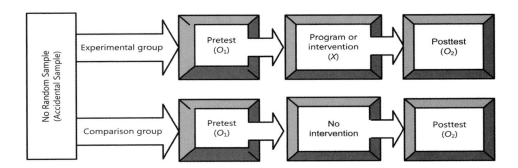

**Figure 15.7**

Comparison Group Pretest-Posttest Design

### Table 15.2

Displaying Data for a Comparison Group Pretest-Posttest Design (from figure 15.7)

| Group | Pretest Average $(O_1)$ | Posttest Average $(O_2)$ | Difference Average $(O_2 - O_1)$ |
|---|---|---|---|
| Intervention Group | 50 | 80 | 30 |
| Comparison Group | 60 | 70 | 10 |
| Difference | | | 20 |

## COMPARISON GROUP POSTTEST-ONLY DESIGN

The comparison group posttest-only design improves on the one-group posttest-only design by introducing a comparison group who do not receive the intervention but are subject to the same posttest as those who do (the intervention or experimental group). The basic elements of the comparison group posttest-only design are as shown in Figure 15.8 below, and hypothetical data could be displayed as in Table 15.3 on page 321, where:

X  = The program, or intervention

$O_1$ = First and only measurement of the program objective

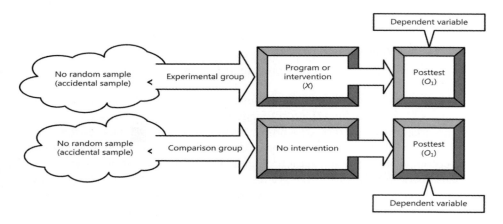

### Figure 15.8

Comparison Group Posttest-Only Design

In Antonia's child abuse prevention program, if the January, April, and August sections are scheduled but the August sessions are canceled for some reason, those who would have been participants in that section could be used as a comparison group. If the values of $O_1$ on the measuring instrument were similar for the experimental and comparison groups, it could be concluded that the program was of little use because those who had experienced it (those who had received X) were not much better or worse off than those who had not.

A problem with drawing this conclusion, however, is that there is no evidence that the groups were equivalent to begin with. Selection, mortality, and the interaction of selection and other threats to internal validity are thus the major difficulties with this design. The use of a comparison group, however, controls for the effects of history, maturation, and testing.

**Table 15.3**

Displaying Data for a Comparison
Group Posttest-Only Design
(from figure 15.8)

| | Posttest Average |
|---|---|
| Intervention Group | 80 |
| Comparison Group | 70 |
| Difference | 10 |

## CLASSICAL EXPERIMENTAL DESIGN

The classical experimental design is the basis for all the experimental designs. It involves an experimental group and a control group, both created by a random assignment method (and, if possible, by random selection from a population). Both groups take a pretest ($O_1$) at the same time, after which the intervention ($X$) is given only to the experimental group; then both groups take the posttest ($O_2$) at the same time.

The classical experimental design is shown in Figure 15.9 below, and the typical way to present the data is displayed in Table 15.4 on page 322. Because the experimental and control groups are randomly assigned, they are equivalent with respect to all important variables. This group equivalence in the design helps control for many of the threats to internal validity because both groups will be affected by them in the same way, where:

$R_a$ = Random assignment to a group

$O_1$ = First measurement of the program objective

$X$ = The program, or intervention

$O_2$ = Second measurement of the program objective

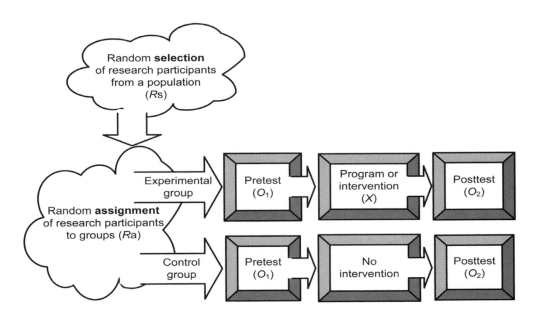

**Figure 15.9**

Classical Experimental Design

**Table 15.4**

Displaying Data for a Classical Experimental Design (from figure 15.9)

| Group | Pretest Average $(O_1)$ | Posttest Average $(O_2)$ | Difference Average $(O_2 - O_1)$ |
|---|---|---|---|
| Intervention | 50 | 80 | 30 |
| Control | 50 | 70 | 20 |
| Difference | | | 10 |

## RANDOMIZED POSTTEST-ONLY CONTROL GROUP DESIGN

The randomized posttest-only control group design is identical to the comparison group posttest-only design, except that the participants are randomly assigned to two groups. This design, therefore, has a control group rather than a comparison group.

This design usually involves only two groups, one experimental and one control. There are no pretests. The experimental group receives the intervention and takes the posttest; the control group only takes the posttest. This design can be written as shown in Figure 15.10 below, and data generated from this design can be presented as in Table 15.5 on page 323.

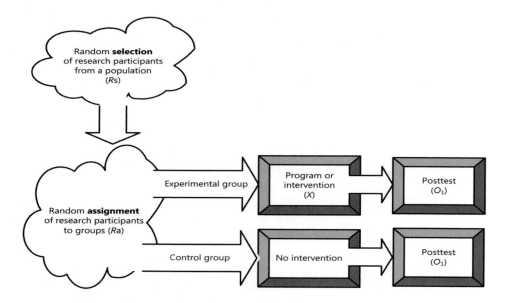

**Figure 15.10**

Randomized Posttest-Only Control Group Design

In addition to measuring change in a group or groups, a pretest also helps to ensure equivalence between the control and the experimental groups. As you know, this design does not have a pretest. The groups have been randomly assigned, as indicated by *R,* and this in itself is theoretically enough to ensure equivalence without the need for a confirmatory pretest.

**Table 15.5**

Displaying Data for a Randomized Posttest-
Only Control Group Design
(from figure 15.10)

| Group | Posttest Average |
|---|---|
| Intervention | 80 |
| Control | 50 |
| Difference | 30 |

The randomized posttest-only control group design is useful in situations where it's not possible to conduct a pretest or where a pretest would be expected to strongly influence the results of the posttest because of the effects of testing. This design also controls for many of the threats to internal validity (previously discussed) and external validity (discussed in the following section).

## EXTERNAL VALIDITY

**E**xternal validity is the degree to which the results of a specific study are generalizable to another population, to another setting, and to another time. There are many threats to external validity, but we will only discuss four of them:

1 Selection-treatment interaction
2 Specificity of variables
3 Multiple-treatment interference
4 Researcher bias

### SELECTION-TREATMENT INTERACTION

The first threat to external validity is selection-treatment interaction. This threat commonly occurs when a design cannot provide for random selection of participants from a population. Suppose we wanted to study the effectiveness of a family service agency staff, for example.

If our research proposal was turned down by fifty agencies before it was accepted by the fifty-first, it's very likely that the accepting agency differs in certain important aspects from the other fifty. It may accept the proposal because its social workers are more highly motivated, more secure, more satisfied with their jobs, or are more interested in the practical application of the study than is an average agency staff member.

As a result, we would be assessing the research participants on the very factors for which they were unwittingly (and by default) selected—motivation, job satisfaction, and so on. The study may be internally valid, but because it will not be possible to generalize the results to other family service agencies it will have little external validity.

### SPECIFICITY OF VARIABLES

Specificity of variables has to do with the fact that a research project conducted with a specific group of people at a specific time and in a specific setting may not always be generalizable to other people at different times and in different settings. For example, a measuring instrument used to measure the social support levels of upper-socioeconomic-level

Caucasian suburban children does not provide an equally accurate measure of social support when it's applied to lower-socioeconomic-level children of racial minorities in the inner city.

## MULTIPLE-TREATMENT INTERFERENCE

The third threat to external validity, multiple-treatment interference, occurs when a research participant is given two or more interventions in succession, so the results of the first intervention may affect the results of the second. A client who attends treatment sessions, for example, may not seem to benefit from one therapeutic technique, so another is tried. In fact, the client may have benefited from the first technique, but the benefit may not become apparent until the second technique has been tried.

As a result, the effects of both techniques become commingled, or the results may be erroneously ascribed to the second technique alone. Because of this threat, interventions should be given separately if possible. If the research design does not allow this, sufficient time should be allowed to elapse between the two interventions in an effort to minimize the possibility of multiple-treatment interference.

In addition, your research participants may be getting help in other places besides the program you are evaluating. They may, for example, being offered help by other caseworkers, probation officers, various self-help groups, hospitals, clinics, friends, clergy, and even their parents in addition to the odd social work practicum student or two. All these other helping sources will affect the results of your study.

## RESEARCHER BIAS

The final threat to external validity is researcher bias. Researchers, like people in general, tend to see what they want to see or expect to see. Unconsciously and without any thought of deceit, they may manipulate a study so that the actual results agree with the anticipated results. A practitioner may favor an intervention so strongly that the study is structured to support it, or the results may be interpreted favorably. The phrase "If I didn't believe it, I wouldn't have seen it" readily comes to mind.

If we know which individuals are in the experimental group and which are in the control group, this knowledge alone might affect the study's results. Students whom an instructor believes to be bright, for example, often are given higher grades than their performance warrants, whereas students believed to be dull are given lower grades. The way to control for researcher bias is to perform a double-blind experiment in which neither the research participants nor the evaluator knows who's in the experimental or control groups. The use of standardized measuring instruments to measure the dependent variables also helps control for researcher bias.

## EVALUATING RESEARCH DESIGNS

**A**ll **quantitative research studies,** whether quantitative, qualitative, or mixed-methods, have research designs. They all have their advantages and disadvantages and the astute researcher uses the best design to answer the study's research question (or to test its hypothesis). Thus, it's crucial to assess the appropriateness and suitability of any research design that was used in any particular study. And to assess a quantitative design's overall credibility, questions need to be asked.

## USE APPENDIX A

There are a few highly interweaved and non-mutually exclusive questions you can ask when you begin to evaluate the quality of a study's research design. Appendix A lists questions you can ask about the design's (1) overall structure, (2) internal validity, and (3) external validity. More specifically:

### Overall Structure and Clarity
- Use Appendix A to ask questions such as those found on pages 488–489 (questions 196–206).

### Internal Validity
- Use Appendix A to ask questions such as those found on pages 487–488 (questions 175–188).

### External Validity
- Use Appendix A to ask questions such as those found on page 488 (questions 189–195).

How to assess the overall creditability of a quantitative research design is totally up to you—and only you. You're the one who must ask and answer the questions. More importantly, you need to address two extremely difficult tasks:

1 You must have a rationale for why you're asking each question in the first place. You just can't ask questions without knowing why you're asking them. Appendix A only list potential questions you can ask. Can you guess why each one was listed and what importance your answer to each question has for your overall evaluation of the research study?

2 You also must have some kind of idea of what you're going to do with your answer to each question. In reference to a quantitative study, for example, question 202 on page 489 asks, "Does the author apply a research design that best addressed the research questions of interest?" Let's say your answer was "no". What are you going to do with your answer? That is, how are you going to use it in your overall evaluation of the study's research design on page 489? Now what about if your answer was "yes"?

> Two people can evaluate a research design that was used within a research study and come up with two different conclusions.

## CHAPTER RECAP

- Research knowledge levels are arrayed along a continuum.
- Research designs can be grouped into two categories.
- Explanatory research design must meet six conditions.
- One-group research designs can be classified into four categories.
- Longitudinal research designs can be classified into three categories.

- Two-group research designs can be classified into four categories.
- There are ten threats to internal validity.
- There are four threats to external validity.
- A "perfect" research design does not exist. They all have their advantages and disadvantages. The most important thing to remember is that a specific research design is chosen to answer a specific research question or to test a hypothesis.

## REVIEW EXERCISES

1 What are *knowledge levels*? Why should we know them? Provide social work examples throughout your discussion.

2 What are "ideal" experiments"? List each of the six conditions necessary for an "ideal" experiment to occur. For each

condition, discuss its underlying premise and provide a social work example throughout your discussion to illustrate your main points.

3 What is the *matched pairs method* of assignment to groups? Provide social work examples throughout your discussion to illustrate your main points.

4 What are *group research designs*? Provide social work examples throughout your discussion to illustrate your main points.

5 What are *one-group research designs*? Provide social work examples throughout your discussion to illustrate your main points.

6 What are *one-group posttest-only designs*? Describe in detail how they work and what they are supposed to accomplish. Provide social work examples throughout your discussion to illustrate your main points.

7 What are *cross-sectional survey designs*? Describe in detail how they work and what they are supposed to accomplish. Provide social work examples throughout your discussion to illustrate your main points.

8 What are *longitudinal designs*? Describe in detail how they work and what they are supposed to accomplish. Provide social work examples throughout your discussion to illustrate your main points.

9 What are *trend studies*? Describe in detail how they work and what they are supposed to accomplish. Provide social work examples throughout your discussion to illustrate your main points.

10 What are *cohort studies*? Describe in detail how they work and what they are supposed to accomplish. Provide social work examples throughout your discussion to illustrate your main points.

11 What are *panel studies*? Describe in detail how they work and what they are supposed to accomplish. Provide social work examples throughout your discussion to illustrate your main points.

12 What are *one-group pretest-posttest designs*? Describe in detail how they work and what they are supposed to accomplish. Provide social work examples throughout your discussion to illustrate your main points.

13 What is *internal validity*? Why do we need to know the internal validity of a research study? Provide social work examples throughout your discussion to illustrate your main points.

14 List the ten threats to a research study's internal validity. Discuss what each threat means to you as a beginning social work researcher. Use social work examples to illustrate your main points.

15 What are *two-group research designs*? Provide examples throughout your discussion to illustrate your main points.

16 What are *comparison group pretest-posttest designs*? Describe in detail how they work and what they are supposed to accomplish. Provide social work examples throughout your discussion to illustrate your main points.

17 What are *comparison group posttest-only designs*? Describe in detail how they work and what they are supposed to accomplish. Provide social work examples throughout your discussion to illustrate your main points.

18 What are *classical experimental designs*? Describe in detail how they work and what they are supposed to accomplish. Provide social work examples throughout your discussion to illustrate your main points.

19 What are *randomized posttest-only control group designs*? Describe in detail how they work and what they are supposed to accomplish. Provide social work examples throughout your discussion to illustrate your main points.

20 With your knowledge of the advantages and disadvantages of the various group research designs that researchers and practitioners alike can use, thoroughly discuss how you will use the material contained within this chapter when you begin to evaluate the appropriateness of any research study's overall internal and external validities. Discuss why you believe each criterion you selected is important for your evaluation of the study's chosen design.

**Group research designs and the researcher**

21 **Scenario 1:** Make an argument that to be a competent social work researcher you *must know* how to select and use group research designs in addition to knowing each design's advantages and disadvantages. Provide clear and explicit research-related social work examples to illustrate your main points.

22 **Scenario 2:** Make an argument that you *do not have to know* how to select and use group research designs in addition to knowing each design's advantages and disadvantages to be a competent social work researcher. Provide clear and explicit

research-related social work examples.

23 **Time to Choose:** Which one of the two preceding scenarios (21 or 22) do you feel is more consistent with the place of research in social work? Why? Provide relevant social work examples to illustrate your main points.

### Group research designs and the practitioner

24 **Scenario 1:** make an argument that to be an effective evidence-based social work practitioner you *must know* how to select and use group research designs to evaluate the effectiveness of your interventions. Provide a clear and explicit practice-related social work example to illustrate your main points.

25 **Scenario 2:** Make an argument that you *do not have to know* how to select and use group research designs to evaluate the effectiveness of your interventions to be an effective evidence-based social work practitioner. Provide clear and explicit practice-related social work examples to illustrate your main points.

26 **Time to Choose:** Which one of the above two scenarios (24 or 25) do you feel is more consistent with the concept of the contemporary evidence-based social work practice process as illustrated on pages 68–72? Why? Provide relevant social work examples to illustrate your main points.

### Application of group research designs

27 Locate a published quantitatively oriented social work journal article that utilized any one of the group research designs presented in this chapter. We suggest you locate a quantitatively oriented research study in Bruce Thyer's journal *Research on Social Work Practice* (Sage Publications). Hands down, this is the best journal to find good quantitatively oriented social work research studies.

- What was the study's sample or population—data source(s)?
- What was the study's dependent variable?
- What was the study's independent variable?
- What was the study's primary data collection method?
- What measuring instrument was used to measure the dependent variable? Was it reliable and valid? If so, how? If not, why not?
- What specific group research design was used in the study?
- What internal and external validity factors did the research design control for? Discuss in detail. Provide specific examples from the research study to illustrate your main points.
- What internal and external validity factors did the research design not control for? Discuss in detail. Provide specific examples from the research study to illustrate your main points.

### Group research designs and your professional development

28 Review the three social work research-related roles you can take when you graduate—CSWE Competency 1 at the beginning of this chapter on page 292. This concept is also discussed in Chapter 1 on pages 63–67. Thoroughly discuss how you feel this chapter will help you to perform one or more research-related roles when you graduate. Which one of the three roles do you believe this chapter helped you with the most? Why? Discuss in detail and provide an example to illustrate your main points.

29 Review CSWE Competency 4 at the beginning of this chapter (page 292). Thoroughly discuss how you feel this chapter will help you to become a practice-informed researcher and a research-informed practitioner. Discuss in detail and provide an example to illustrate your main points.

30 Review the evidence-based practice process as illustrated on pages 68–72. Thoroughly discuss how this chapter helps you to develop the skills you'll need for implementing one or more steps of the evidence-based practice process.

31 Discuss which step(s) you feel this chapter will help you with the most. Why? Be very specific and use relevant social work examples to illustrate your main points throughout your discussion.

**Note:** This exercise should help you to realize that the group research designs that are used in "research studies" are the same that are used in "practice situations." In short, you can use this chapter to help you employ group research designs to evaluate your effectiveness with all of your client systems.

### You're now a researcher

32 Pretend that your school of social work wants to do a research study to determine if the school's curriculum increased the

interviewing skills of its graduating students. Your school's director is putting you in charge of designing a quantitatively oriented group research design to determine if the school is really 100% responsible for increasing the interviewing skills of its student body. (Hint: Notice the word *increased* and the value *100%*.)

- List and then discuss the various group research designs that you could use.

- Select one that you think will be the best to answer your research question. Why did you pick this specific research design? Are you going to randomly assign students to groups? If so, what's the purpose?

- Are you going to use a one-group research design or a two-group design? Why? Justify your position.

- What are the independent and dependent variables?

- What internal and external validates did your selected research design control and not control for?

- What's the unit of analysis?

- What's your population?

- What's your sampling frame?

- Are you going to use standardized measuring instruments? Explain.

- How are you going to collect the data?

- What specific data are you going to collect?

- How are you going to display the data once they have been collected and analyzed?

- Could you use retrospective baseline data? If so, why?

# PART V

# COLLECTING AND ANALYZING DATA

CHAPTER 16: Collecting Data   330

CHAPTER 17: Selecting a Data-Collection Method   366

CHAPTER 18: Analyzing Quantitative Data   382

CHAPTER 19: Analyzing Qualitative Data   404

# 16

## 2015 EPAS COMPETENCIES

| COMPETENCY 1 | Demonstrate Ethical and Professional Behavior |
|---|---|

You will learn that in order to be a successful evidence-based practitioner you have an ethical obligation to integrate three research roles into your daily practice activities as discussed in Chapter 3: (1) research consumer, (2) research partner—either as a co-researcher or research participant, and (3) creator and disseminator of research (or knowledge).

This entire chapter pertains to these three professional research-related roles when it comes to knowing the advantages and disadvantages of the quantitative and qualitative data-gathering methods that social work researchers and practitioners can use.

| COMPETENCY 4 | Engage in Practice-Informed Research and Research-Informed Practice |
|---|---|

Competency 4 also pertains to the entire chapter because you have to:

1   Evaluate the source(s) utilized in a research study (**research consumer**—research-informed practice);

2   Participate in a research study—either as a co-researcher or research participant (**research partner**—practice-informed research). See 1 above and 3 below; and

3   Know how to select the most appropriate data collection method(s) and data source(s) when you actually do a research study (**creator and disseminator of research**—practice-informed research).

You also need to utilize evidence-based practice recommendations whenever possible; that is, you need to integrate (1) the best available research-based evidence with (2) your clinical expertise and (3) your client's values.

All of the above implies you'll need to know how to assess the strengths and limitations of the major data collection method(s) used in a research study that produced its research-based evidence. In short, you need to ask and then answer a simple question: How seriously should I take the findings of any specific research study given the overall suitability of the data collection method(s) and data source(s) the study utilized?

| COMPETENCY 9 | Evaluate Practice with Individuals, Families, Groups, Organizations, & Communities |
|---|---|

See Competencies 1 and 4.

# Collecting Data

| CHAPTERS 1 & 3 | Step 1. | Understanding the Research Process |
| CHAPTER 2 | Step 2. | Formulating Research Questions |
| CHAPTER 4<br>APPENDIXES A–C | Step 3. | Reviewing the Literature<br>Evaluating the Literature |
| CHAPTERS 5 & 6 | Step 4. | Being Aware of Ethical and Cultural Issues |
| CHAPTERS 7–10 | Step 5. | Selecting a Research Approach |
| CHAPTERS 11 & 12 | Step 6. | Specifying How Variables Are Measured |
| CHAPTER 13 | Step 7. | Selecting a Sample |
| CHAPTERS 14 & 15 | Step 8. | Selecting a Research Design |
| CHAPTERS 16 & 17 | Step 9. | Selecting a Data-Collection Method |
| CHAPTERS 18 & 19 | Step 10. | Analyzing the Data |
| CHAPTERS 20 & 21 | Step 11. | Writing the Research Report |

# Collecting Data

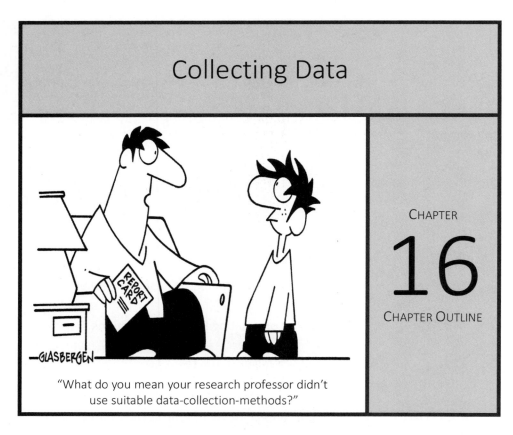

CHAPTER

# 16

CHAPTER OUTLINE

"What do you mean your research professor didn't use suitable data-collection-methods?"

DATA COLLECTION METHODS AND SOURCES
TYPES OF DATA
    Firsthand Data versus Secondhand Data
    Original Data versus Existing Data
    Quantitative Data versus Qualitative Data
QUANTITATIVE DATA-COLLECTION METHODS
    Survey Questionnaires
        *Establishing Data Collection Procedures*
        *Recording Survey Data*
        *Establishing Reliability and Validity*
    Structured Observations
        Establishing Data Collection Procedures
        *Recording Structured Observational Data*
        *Establishing Reliability and Validity*
        *Advantages and Disadvantages*
    Secondary Data
        *Establishing Data Collection Procedures*
        *Recording Secondary Data*
        *Establishing Reliability and Validity*
        *Advantages and Disadvantages*
    Existing Statistics
        *Example of Using Existing Statistics*
        *Establishing Data Collection Procedures*
        *Recording Existing Statistical Data*
        *Establishing Reliability and Validity*
        *Advantages and Disadvantages*

QUALITATIVE DATA-COLLECTION METHODS
    Narrative interviewing
        *Establishing Data Collection Procedures*
        *Recording Narrative Data*
        *Trustworthiness and Truth-Value of Narrative Data*
        *Advantages and Disadvantages*
    Participant Observation
        *Establishing Procedures to Collect Data*
        *Recording Participant Observational Data*
        *Trustworthiness and Truth-Value*
        *Advantages and Disadvantages*
    Secondary Content Data
        *Establishing Procedures*
        *Recording*
        *Establishing the Trustworthiness and Truth-Value*
        *Advantages and Disadvantages*
    Historical Data
        *Establishing Procedures to Collect Data*
        *Recording*
        *Establishing the Trustworthiness and Truth-Value*
        *Advantages and Disadvantages*
    Mixed-Method Data-Collection Methods
EVALUATING A DATA COLLECTION PLAN
    Use the Appendixes
CHAPTER RECAP
REVIEW EXERCISES

DATA COLLECTION IS THE VERY HEARTBEAT of all research studies—positivistic or interpretive alike. Our goal is to collect good data—qualitative data (i.e., words) for interpretive studies and quantitative data (i.e., numbers) for positivistic studies—with a steady rhythm and in a systematic manner. When data collection becomes erratic or stops prematurely, all research studies are in grave danger. With that said, this chapter briefly presents a variety of data collection methods that can produce data for all types of research studies.

## DATA COLLECTION METHODS AND SOURCES

**T**here is a critical distinction between a data collection method and a data source. This distinction must be clearly understood before we collect any data whatsoever:

- **A data collection method** consists of a detailed plan of procedures that aims to gather data for a specific purpose—that is, to answer a research question or to test a hypothesis.

- **A data source** is the person who provides the data. The primary source of data in most social work research studies is people. However, sometimes we use machines (e.g., biofeedback) to monitor change in people's attitudes, knowledge, or behaviors. Rather, more often than not, we tend to collect data about people from the people themselves.

> Any data collection method can tap into a variety of data sources.

Any data *collection method* can tap into a variety of *data sources*. Regardless of the data collection method or the data source, *all* data are eventually collected, analyzed, and interpreted as part of the research process. This chapter discusses the basic data collection methods that commonly produce quantitative data for positivistic studies and qualitative data for interpretive studies. Before we do this, however, we need to understand the various types of data.

## TYPES OF DATA

**W**hat exactly are data? They are recorded units of information that are used as the basis for reasoning, calculation, and discussion (a single unit of data is called a *datum*).

333

## FIRSTHAND DATA VERSUS SECONDHAND DATA

Data collected directly from people can be firsthand or secondhand data.

- **Firsthand data** are obtained from people who are closest to the problem we are studying. Single mothers participating in a parent support group, for example, can easily provide firsthand data to describe their own stresses as single mothers.

- **Secondhand data** may come from people who are indirectly connected to the primary problem (i.e., stress of single mothers) we are studying. A parent support group facilitator, for example, can record secondhand observations of "stress" behaviors displayed by parents in the parent support group. The facilitator can also collect data from family members. Grandparents, for example, can provide data that reflect their perceptions of how "stressed out" their granddaughters may be.

## ORIGINAL DATA VERSUS EXISTING DATA

We can collect original data and/or existing data for our research studies. For example,

- We can collect **original data** (for the first time) during the course of our study to fulfill a specific purpose: to answer our research question or test our hypothesis.

- Unlike original data, we can use **existing data** that have been previously collected and stored, either manually or in a computer, before our study was even begun.

## QUANTITATIVE DATA VERSUS QUALITATIVE DATA

We can distinguish between types of data by the research approach used. For example,

- In a **quantitative study** we can analyze numerical data using mathematical computations and calculations (chapter 18). This chapter presents four of the most common types of quantitative data-gathering methods:

  1  Survey questionnaires
  2  Structured observations
  3  Secondary data
  4  Existing statistics

- On the other hand, a **qualitative study** typically analyzes words or text data (chapter 19). We analyze text data by reading and rereading; our task is to look for common and differentiating characteristics and themes within the words. This chapter presents four types of qualitative data-gathering methods:

  1  Narrative interviewing
  2  Participant observation
  3  Secondary content analysis
  4  Historical content analysis

## QUANTITATIVE DATA-COLLECTION METHODS

The **quantitative research approach** aims to reduce research topics to concepts and clearly defined variables. One of the major steps in a quantitative study is "focusing the question," which requires that we develop operational definitions for all the variables in our study. Let's revisit our two-variable research question that has been used throughout this book:

**Research question**
Do people who come from ethnic minority backgrounds have difficulty in accessing social services?

A quantitative research study requires that we operationally define "ethnicity" and "difficulty in accessing social services" in such a way that we can measure each variable. We could easily measure both of our study's variables using two categories each:

1  **Variable 1: Ethnicity**
   What is your ethnicity? (Circle one category below.)
   - Ethnic minority
   - Ethnic majority
2  **Variable 2: Accessing services**
   Did you have difficulty in accessing any form of social services over the last 12-month period? (Circle one category below.)
   - Yes
   - No

Our two variables (i.e., *ethnicity* and *difficulty in accessing social services*) could be operationally defined in a variety of ways. Let's consider our two-variable research question for the various data-collection methods that are most often associated with producing quantitative data:

1  Survey questionnaires
2  Structured observations
3  Secondary data
4  Existing statistics

## SURVEY QUESTIONNAIRES

Survey research or surveys in themselves are a method for researching social problems. The aim of a survey is to collect data from a population, or a sample of research participants, in order to describe them as a group. One form that a survey can take is a questionnaire, which is a carefully selected set of questions that relate to the variables in our research question.

When data are collected using survey questionnaires, we get our research participants' perceptions about the variable being measured. Think about a survey questionnaire that you have filled out recently—a marketing survey, a consumer satisfaction questionnaire, or a teaching evaluation of your instructor. Your answers reflected your perceptions (yes, you are the data source in this situation) and were probably different from the perceptions of other students (yes, they too are data sources) who answered the same survey.

A survey questionnaire is one data collection method that we can use to collect data in order to answer our two-variable research question. It would have to include items that measure our two variables—*ethnicity* and *difficulty in accessing social services*. We would ask clients within our study to "self-report" what they perceive their ethnicity to be (variable 1) and whether they have experienced difficulty in accessing social services over the last twelve-month period (variable 2).

---

*A single research study can easily incorporate both quantitative and qualitative types of data. In fact, interpretive and positivistic data collection methods can produce complimentary data.*

*The aim of a survey is to collect data from a population, or a sample of research participants, in order to describe them as a group.*

There are two basic types of survey questionnaires. Nonstandardized survey questionnaires are one type. The two questions we posed are a very basic example of a nonstandardized survey questionnaire. The two-question survey is nonstandardized because the items have not been tested for reliability or validity.

We have no way of knowing whether our research participants will respond to our two questions in a uniform way. At best, we can comment on our survey questionnaire's face validity; that is, do its items "look" like they are measuring the variables we are interested in? Nonstandardized questionnaires are often developed when standardized questionnaires are not available or suited to our specific research question.

As you know from Chapters 11 and 12, most standardized survey questionnaires are scientifically constructed to measure one specific variable. Let's say we have searched the library and computer databases for a standardized survey questionnaire that measures our dependent variable, difficulty in accessing social services.

Suppose the closest standardized questionnaire we find is the Reid-Gundlach *Social Service Satisfaction Scale* (*R-GSSSS*), which contains thirty-four items and measures clients' satisfaction with social services they have received (see figure 12.1 on page 241). Clients would read each item and rate how much they agree with each item. A 5-point scale is used:

> There are two basic types of survey questionnaires: nonstandardized and standardized.

1   Strongly agree
2   Agree
3   Undecided
4   Disagree
5   Strongly disagree

The *R-GSSSS* specifically measures satisfaction with social services, a concept that closely relates to our access variable but is not an exact measure of it. In other words, satisfaction with social services is not the same as difficulty in accessing social services, but it could be used as a proxy measure to answer our research question.

Because it is a proxy measure, we would be making a humongous leap to say that the clients who are most dissatisfied with the social services are the same clients that will have the most difficulty in accessing new social services. This is a very huge leap, to say the least.

How we proceed in collecting survey questionnaire data varies depending upon whether we collect them via the mail, telephone interviews, or face-to-face interviews. When a questionnaire is sent through the mail, our research participants must also be provided with sufficient instructions to self-administer the questionnaire. This means that they must have all the necessary instructions to successfully complete the survey questionnaire alone.

When telephone or face-to-face interviews are used, the interviewer is available to assist the research participant with any difficulties in completing the questionnaire. Regardless of how our questionnaires are administered, there are some basic procedures that we can use to increase the likelihood of obtaining accurate and complete data.

## ESTABLISHING DATA COLLECTION PROCEDURES

There are basic procedures that must be considered before any survey questionnaire is administered to potential research participants. First, it's essential that straightforward and simple instructions accompany the questionnaire. Our objective is to have each research participant complete the questionnaire in exactly the same way, which means they must have the same understanding of each question.

Suppose for a moment that we ask one of our two questions posed earlier: "Did you have difficulty in accessing any form of social services over the last 12-month period?" It's clear that we want our research participants to answer our question with respect to the past twelve months and not any other time frame.

A second procedure that must be established is how informed consent will be obtained from the research participants (see chapter 5). This is a task that can be accomplished by writing a cover letter explaining what purpose the research study and questionnaire serves, who the researchers are, that participation is entirely voluntary, how the data will be used, and what steps are taken to guarantee confidentiality. A cover letter is usually sent out with mailed questionnaires, read aloud over the telephone, or presented in face-to-face interviews.

To decrease the likelihood of any misunderstanding, elementary language should be used in the cover letter (the same as in the questionnaire). It may even be possible to have the cover letter (and questionnaire) translated into our participants' native language(s).

In our study, we are asking about ethnicity, which suggests that English could be a second language for many of our research participants. Depending on the geographic area in which we are conducting our study, we may wish to translate our cover letter and questionnaire into the dominant language of the geographic area.

If our survey questionnaire is to be administered over the telephone or face-to-face by an interviewer, training of interviewers will be a necessary third procedure. In the same way that we want research participants to have the same understanding of the questionnaire's items, we want interviewers to handle potential queries in a consistent manner. Interviewers must be trained to ask the questions within our questionnaire in such a way that they do not influence the research participants' answers.

> To save on time and resources, it may be possible to administer survey questionnaires in a group format.

Basically, interviewers should refrain from discussing individual questions with research participants, from varying their tone of voice when asking the questions, and from commenting on the research participants' answers. The interviewer's task is to keep the research participant focused on answering the questions at hand, to answer questions for clarification, and to record the answers.

To save on time and resources, it may be possible to administer survey questionnaires in a group format. This usually means that we meet a group of research participants in their own environment. Suppose, for example, we were specifically interested in the accessibility of social services among Native people. We would need to travel to the reserve, then administer our questionnaire at a central location on the reserve that's convenient for our research participants.

## RECORDING SURVEY DATA

The data we gather from questionnaires usually are in numerical form. Our question that asks whether clients had difficulty accessing any form of social services over the last twelve months will produce a number of "yes" responses and a number of "no" responses. We can add up the total sum of responses for each category and calculate the number of clients who had difficulty accessing social services broken down by ethnicity (i.e., ethnic minority and ethnic majority).

## ESTABLISHING RELIABILITY AND VALIDITY

Reliability and validity are critical to determining the credibility of any data collection instrument. Standardized questionnaires have associated with them values of both. Reliability values tell us how confident we can be in using our questionnaire over two or more time periods, across different people, and across different places. Validity values give us information about how good our questionnaire is at measuring what it purports to measure. The validity value for the *R-GSSSS*, for example, is reasonably high at 0.95 (the highest possible value is 1.0). Reports on the *R-GSSSS* also note that the standardized question-naire is useful for measuring differences in race. Specifically, African Americans and Mex-ican Americans are reported to predictably have lower scores. We can also assess the face validity of the *R-GSSSS* by simply looking at the thirty-four items contained within it (see figure 12.1 on page 241).

A quick glance tells us that the items reflect the "idea" of client satisfaction with social services. When using unstandardized questionnaires, we do not have the luxury of report-ing reliability or validity. In this instance, we must ensure that our questionnaire, at the very least, has face validity.

---

| Box 16.1 | Surveys (Questionnaires) in a Nutshell |
| --- | --- |

**What is a survey (often referred to as a questionnaire)?**
Surveys collect data from a targeted group of people about their opinions, behavior, or knowledge. Common types of surveys are written questionnaires, face-to-face or telephone interviews, focus groups, and electronic (e-mail or website) surveys. Surveys are commonly used with key stakeholders, especially clients and employees, to discover their needs or assess their satisfaction levels.

**When should you use questionnaires for a research study?**
- *When resources are limited and you need data from many people.* You can disseminate questionnaires relatively inexpensively. Your costs will increase if you need to do a lot of follow-up to get a sufficient response rate.

- *To gather data about knowledge, beliefs, attitudes, and behaviors.* Questionnaires are helpful in gathering information that is unique to individuals, such as attitudes or knowledge.

- *When it's important to protect the privacy of participants.* Questionnaires are helpful in maintaining participants' privacy because participants' responses can be anonymous or confidential. This is especially important if you are gathering sensitive information.

**How do you plan and develop a questionnaire?**
- *Define your objectives.* The most critical part of developing your questionnaire is defining what you want from it and how you will use the data to answer your study's questions. By taking the time to define your purpose and objectives you will reduce the likelihood of gathering unusable data.

- *Select the number and type of participants for your questionnaire.* Selecting the type of research participants you want to include is part of determining your objectives. For example, if you need to know if health educators who participated in your training are using the information in their teaching, your participants will be teachers who participated in the training. You should also decide if you should include all possible participants or if a sample will suffice. This will depend on the number of possible participants and the resources you have available.

- *Develop questions that clearly communicate what you want to know.*
  — Use clear and simple wording written at the reading level of your participants.

  — Avoid using abbreviations, jargon, or colloquial phrases.

  — The Question Appraisal System (*QAS-99*) is a method for identifying and fixing communication problems in questionnaires before formal pilot testing (i.e., a preliminary test of your questionnaire to make sure that intended participants understand and respond favorably to it).

- *Decide when to use closed-ended versus open-ended questions.* Closed-ended questions include a list of predetermined answers from which participants can choose. Open-ended questions allow the participant to answer the question in their own words. Closed-ended questions are easier to analyze. Open-ended questions can be useful if you do not know the possible answers to questions or for gathering insightful or unexpected information. However, open-ended questions are more difficult and time-consuming to analyze because you have to categorize and summarize the answers.

- *Include demographic questions.* Questionnaires usually include demographic questions such as sex, race, age, education, and where the participant works or lives. The purpose of these questions is to describe subgroups of respondents. Limit the demographic questions to only those that are important for your analysis. For example, if you do not plan to compare the data by age, do not include age on the questionnaire.

- *Place questions in a logical order that flows well.* Start with less sensitive questions and end with more sensitive questions. Order the questions in a way that makes sense to the participant, such as by topic area.

- *Pilot test the questionnaire.* Testing your questionnaire before you administer it will help you find out if participants will understand the questions, if the questions mean the same thing to all participants, if it provides you with the data you need, and how long it takes to complete. Always pilot test your questionnaire with a small group who are similar to your intended participants.

### How do I get an adequate response rate?

Response rate is the number of participants who responded to your questionnaire divided by the total number of participants you included in your research study. Higher response rates strengthen your study's results. There are several ways you can increase your response rate.

- *Communicate the value of your questionnaire.* Participants will be more likely to complete your questionnaire if they understand its value. Communicate the purpose of the questionnaire, how you plan to use the data, and how the results will help the participants.

- *Follow up.* If the questionnaire is administered by mail or electronically you will need to recontact the participants, perhaps a few times—the more follow-up contacts, the higher the response rate.

- *Provide incentives.* Giving modest financial or other incentives to participants increases the likelihood that they will complete your questionnaire. (see Box 16.1a on the following page.

### Advantages

- Are good for gathering descriptive data.
- Are a relatively inexpensive, quick way to collect large amounts of data from large samples in short amounts of time.
- Are convenient for respondents to complete.
- Can result in more honest responses via anonymity.
- Allow the use of readily available questionnaires.
- Are well suited for answering "What?" "Where?" and "How many" questions.
- Can cover a wide range of topics.
- Can be analyzed using a variety of existing computer software programs.
- Offer a relatively inexpensive way to collect new data.
- Can easily reach a large number of people.
- Provide specific data.
- Collect data efficiently.
- Provide data that can be easily input into a computer.

**Disadvantages**

- May lead to biased reporting from self-report.
- May provide a general picture with data but lack depth.
- Provide limited ability to know whether you are actually measuring what you intend to measure.
- Offer limited ability to discover measurement errors.
- Have limited length and breadth of questions.
- Offer no opportunity to probe or obtain clarification.
- Rely on self-report.
- Rely on participants' ability to recall behaviors and events.
- Have limited capability to measure different kinds of outcomes.
- Are difficult to administer with low-literacy groups.
- May not provide adequate information on context.
- Require research participants to be literate.
- Usually receive a low response rate with surveys.
- Require that research participants have a mailing address or telephone to be reached.
- Are not well suited to answering questions related to "How?" and "Why?"
- Uses simple questions to provide answers to complex research questions.

---

| Box 16.1a | Using Incentives in a Nutshell |

**Why use incentives?**

- Incentives improve questionnaire response rates when you use them in combination with other response boosting strategies such as multiple contacts and user-friendly questionnaires.
- Incentives demonstrate respect and appreciation for participants' time and effort in completing the questionnaire.
- Incentives convey trust that the participant will complete the questionnaire when the incentive is provided before the questionnaire is returned.

**Types of incentives**

The two types of incentives are financial and material. Financial incentives include cash, electronic gift certificates, gift cards, coupons, or financial donations to a charity. Material incentives include non-monetary prizes, gifts, or resources such as books, DVDs, and CDs.

To determine which type of incentive to offer, think about who will be responding to the questionnaire; where participants are geographically located; whether data collection will be conducted in-person, by telephone, mail, or submitted online; and how much time participants will need to complete the questionnaire.

Offering large incentives could be considered coercive by participants who feel obligated to complete the questionnaire because they received a financial or material reward. However, there is no significant difference in response rates between $5 or $20 prepaid incentives. Therefore, we recommend a financial or material incentive ranging in value from $1 to $5 for most mail or online questionnaires. Providing incentives that are low in value (i.e., $1 to $5 in value) is not considered coercive.

> **When to offer incentives**
> You can give incentives to participants either at the beginning of the data collection process (known as prepaid incentives) or immediately following data collection (known as promised incentives). Prepaid incentives have the most significant impact on response rates, especially when they are used with mail questionnaires. Because sending prepaid incentives multiple times does not increase response rates, you should send a prepaid incentive only once.

## STRUCTURED OBSERVATIONS

"Structured observation" is a self-explanatory data collection method. A trained observer records the interaction of others in a specific place over an agreed upon amount of time using specific procedures and measurements. Structured observation aims to observe the natural interactions between and among people that occur either in natural or in artificial settings (Polster & Collins, 2018).

If we want to observe how people of different ethnic backgrounds interact with their social worker, for example, we could set up structured observations at the social worker's offices (natural environment), or we could set up interviews to be observed from behind one-way mirrors (artificial setting). The data collected from structured observation reflect the trained observers' perceptions of the interactions. That is, the observers do not interact with the people they are observing. They simply watch the interactions and record the presence or absence of certain behaviors.

Observers could, for example, count the number of times clients (comparing ethnic minority and ethnic majority groups) mention a barrier or obstacle to accessing a social service, or monitor whether social workers engage in behaviors that specifically assist clients in accessing new services. These observations, of course, would take place during "normal" meetings between social workers and their clients.

Structured observation requires that the variables being measured are specifically defined. We must "micro-define" our variables. In our two-variable research question, for example, we have already operationally defined "ethnic" as having two categories: ethnic minority and non–ethnic minority. In measuring our difficulty in accessing social services variable, we could measure it by the number of social services referred by a social worker in a sixty-minute interview.

We could then compare the results of our difficulty in accessing social services variable across our two ethnicity groups. Would we find that social workers are more or less likely to offer social service referrals to clients who are from an ethnic minority or a non–ethnic minority group?

There are three general types of recording that can be used with structured observation. Observations can be measured for *frequency* (e.g., count a behavior every time it occurs), for *duration* (e.g., how long does the behavior last each time it occurs), and for *magnitude* (e.g., the varying intensity of a behavior such as mild, moderate, or severe). Whether we use frequency, duration, or magnitude (or some combination), depends on the picture we want to develop to answer our research question.

Do we want to describe difficulty in accessing social services by how many times services are offered to clients (frequency), by how much time social workers spend explaining how services can be accessed (duration), or by the degree of sincerity that the workers display when offering service referrals (magnitude)?

When we record the presence or absence of behaviors during an interaction between and among people, our observations can be structured in such a way as to help the observers record the behaviors accurately. Suppose for a moment that social worker interviews with clients take an average of one hour. We could set recording intervals at every minute so that we have sixty recording intervals in one hour. The observers would sit with a stopwatch and record whether the social workers offered any social services to their clients in the first minute, the second minute, and each minute thereafter until the interviews end. Interval recording assists the observers in making continuous observations throughout the interaction. Spot-check recording is another way to schedule observation recordings.

Unlike interval recording which is continuous, spot-check recording is a way to record intermittent observations. It may be possible to observe and record the presence or absence of a behavior for one minute every five minutes, for example.

### ESTABLISHING DATA COLLECTION PROCEDURES

The procedures established for structured observation are firmly decided on before actual observations take place. That is, the observers are specifically trained to watch for the presence or absence of specific behaviors and the recording method is set. The types of data to be recorded are selected (i.e., frequency, duration, or magnitude), and the nature of the recording is decided (i.e., continuous, interval, or spot-check).

Observers and not the persons engaging in the behaviors generally record data. As such, it's essential that observers be trained to "see" behaviors in a reliable way. Imagine that you are one of the observers and your main task is to record magnitude ratings of the degree of sincerity that social workers display when they offer social service referrals. You must decide whether the social workers' gestures are mildly, moderately, or extremely sincere. How would you know to rate a behavior that you observed as *mildly sincere* versus *moderately sincere*? Training of observers requires that all variables be unequivocally clear. Thus, observers are usually trained using mock trials. They are selected for their ability to collect data according to the rules of the research study, not for their unique views or creative observations.

In a nutshell, the observers are an instrument for data collection, and an effort is made to calibrate all instruments of the research study in the same way. To allow for several different observers to view the same situation, we may choose to videotape interactions.

A decision must also be made about who will be the best observers. Should only professionally trained outside observers be selected? This would include people who are completely unfamiliar with the context of the study but are skilled observers. How about indigenous observers—people who are familiar with the nature of the interaction to be observed? In our example, indigenous observers could include people such as other social workers, social work supervisors, other clients, or staff from other social service offices. Who we choose to observe may depend upon availability, expense, or how important we feel it is for the observers to be familiar or unfamiliar with the situation being observed. Measurement that reflects cultural variables, for example, may require indigenous observers.

### RECORDING STRUCTURED OBSERVATIONAL DATA

The recording instrument for structured observation generally takes the form of a grid or checklist. The behaviors being observed and the method of recording are identified. The simplest recording form to construct is one that records frequency. The recording form would simply identify the period of observation and the number of times a specific behavior occurs.

| Observation Period | Frequency |
|---|---|
| 3:00 p.m. to 4:00 p.m. | ✓ ✓ ✓ |

The data collected from structured observation reflect the trained observers' perceptions of the interactions.

Training of observers requires that all variables be unequivocally clear.

For duration recording, it's necessary to add the duration in minutes at each occurrence of the behavior.

| Observation Period | Frequency and (Duration, in minutes) |
|---|---|
| 3:00 p.m. to 4:00 p.m. | 1 (5), 2 (11), 3 (15) |

For magnitude recording, we record the time of occurrence and give a corresponding rating for the behavior. To simplify recording, the magnitude ratings are generally coded by assigning a number to each category.

| Observation Time | Magnitude |
|---|---|
| 3:17 p.m. | 1 |
| 3:25 p.m. | 1 |
| 3:29 p.m. | 2 |

**1** = Mildly sincere
**2** = Moderately sincere
**3** = Extremely sincere

### Establishing Reliability and Validity

As we know from Chapters 11 and 12, validity refers to whether we are measuring what we think we are measuring. In other words, are we really measuring or observing "difficulty in accessing social services"? Validity, in this instance, should make us think about whether our criteria for observation (i.e., how we operationalized our variable) are reasonable representations of the variable.

Reliability, on the other hand, can be assessed in more concrete ways. Once we have established an operational definition for each variable and the procedures for observation and recording, we can test their reliability. A simple method for determining reliability is to use two independent raters who observe the exact same situation.

How well do their recordings match? Do the two observers produce the same frequencies? The same duration periods? The same magnitude ratings? Do they agree 100 percent or only 50 percent? Agreement of 100 percent suggests that the measure is a reliable one, compared to 50 percent, which suggests we should go back to the drawing board to come up with more precise operational definitions for both variables or more exact recording procedures.

### Advantages and Disadvantages

Structured observation helps us to collect precise, valid, and reliable data within complex interactions. We are able to tease out important behaviors that are direct (or indirect) measures of the variable we are interested in. The data produced are objective observations of behaviors and thus are not tainted by our individual self-perceptions.

Think back to the survey questionnaire method of data collection that we discussed at the beginning of this chapter. The data collected using a survey questionnaire reflect the research participants' own perceptions. Structured observation, on the other hand, gives a factual account of what actually took place. It can explain one component of a social interaction with objectivity, precision, and detail.

The major disadvantage of structured observation is the time and resources needed to train skilled observers. Think about the amount of time it would take, for example, to get you and, say, two other observers to agree on what constitutes *mild*, *moderate*, or *extremely* sincere behavior of social workers. Another disadvantage of structured observation is that it's a microscopic approach to dealing with complex social interactions. By

Unlike survey questionnaires or structured observation, collecting secondary data is unobtrusive.

focusing on one or two specific details (variables) of an interaction, we may miss out on many other important aspects of the interactions.

| Box 16.2 | Observations in a Nutshell |
|----------|----------------------------|

**What is observation?**

Observation is a way of gathering data by watching behavior or events or noting physical characteristics in their natural setting. Observations can be overt (everyone knows they are being observed) or covert (no one knows they are being observed, and the observer is concealed). The benefit of covert observation is that people are more likely to behave naturally if they do not know they are being observed. However, you will typically need to conduct overt observations because of ethical problems related to concealing your observation.

Observations can also be either direct or indirect. Direct observation is when you watch interactions, processes, or behaviors as they occur; for example, observing teachers teaching a lesson from a written curriculum to determine whether they are delivering it with fidelity. Indirect observations are when you watch the results of interactions, processes, or behaviors; for example, measuring the amount of plate waste left by students in a school cafeteria to determine whether a new food is acceptable to them.

**When should you use observation for research purposes?**

- *When you are trying to understand an ongoing process or situation.* Through observation you can monitor or watch a process or situation that you're evaluating as it occurs.

- *When you are gathering data on individual behaviors or interactions between people.* Observation allows you to watch peoples' behaviors and interactions directly, or watch for the results of behaviors or interactions.

- *When you need to know about a physical setting.* Seeing the place or environment where something takes place can help increase your understanding of the event, activity, or situation you are evaluating. For example, you can observe whether a classroom or training facility is conducive to learning.

- *When data collection from individuals is not a realistic option.* If respondents are unwilling or unable to provide data through questionnaires or interviews, observation is a method that requires little of the individuals from whom you need data.

**How do you plan for observations?**

- *Determine the focus.* Think about your study's question(s) you want to answer through observation and select a few areas of focus for your data collection. For example, you may want to know how well an HIV curriculum is being implemented in the classroom. Your focus areas might be interactions between students and teachers, and teachers' knowledge, skills, and behaviors.

- *Design a system for data collection.* Once you have focused your research study, think about the specific items for which you want to collect data and then determine how you will collect the information you need. There are three primary ways of collecting observation data. These three methods can be combined to meet your data collection needs.

  — Recording sheets and checklists are the most standardized way of collecting observation data and include both preset questions and responses. These forms are typically used for collecting data that can be easily described in advance (e.g., topics that might be covered in an HIV prevention lesson).

— Observation guides list the interactions, processes, or behaviors to be observed with space to record open-ended narrative data.

— Field notes are the least standardized way of collecting observation data and do not include preset questions or responses. Field notes are open-ended narrative data that can be written or dictated onto a tape recorder.

- *Select the sites.* Select an adequate number of sites to help ensure they are representative of the larger population and will provide an understanding of the situation you are observing.

- *Select the observers.* You may choose to be the only observer or you may want to include others in conducting observations. Stakeholders, other professional staff members, interns and graduate students, and volunteers are potential observers.

- *Train the observers.* It is critical that the observers are well trained in your data collection process to ensure high quality and consistent data. The level of training will vary based on the complexity of the data collection and the individual capabilities of the observers.

- *Time your observations appropriately.* Programs and processes typically follow a sequence of events. It is critical that you schedule your observations so you are observing the components of the activity that will answer your study's questions. This requires advance planning.

### Advantages

- Provides direct information about behavior of individuals and groups.

- Permits researchers to enter into and understand a situation or context.

- Provides good opportunities for identifying unanticipated outcomes.

- Exists in natural, unstructured, and flexible settings.

- Collects data where and when an event or activity is actually occurring.

- Permits objective observations.

- Does not interfere in any way with the group's process when the researcher is hidden from sight.

- Does not rely on people's willingness or ability to provide information.

- Allows you to directly see what people do rather than relying on what people say they did.

### Disadvantages

- Can be expensive and time-consuming compared to other data collection methods.

- Observer presence, if known, can inhibit or change interactions of participants.

- Use of a hidden observer can raise a number of ethical questions.

- Needs highly trained observers, who may also need to be content experts.

- Is susceptible to observer bias.

- May distort data via selective perception of observers.

- May observe atypical behaviors or sets of behaviors.

- Is susceptible to the "testing effect." That is, people usually perform better when they know they are being observed, although indirect observation may decrease this problem.

- Does not increase our understanding of why people behave as they do.

# SECONDARY DATA

When existing data are used to answer a newly developed research question (or to test a hypothesis), the data are considered secondary. In other words, the data are being used for some purpose other than the original one for which they were collected. Unlike survey questionnaires or structured observation mentioned previously, collecting secondary data is unobtrusive.

Because data already exist, it's not necessary to ask people questions (as in survey questionnaires) or to be observed (as in structured observations). Furthermore, secondary data can exist in numerical form (quantitative) or text form (qualitative). Our discussion in this section focuses on existing quantitative data.

Let's go back to our two-variable research question that asks about the relationship between clients' ethnicity and whether they have difficulty in accessing social services. So far, we have discussed data collection methods within a social service context and have focused on the interaction between social workers and their clients. Within a social service program there are many client records that could provide meaningful data to answer our simple research question.

It's likely, for example, that client intake forms collect data about clients' ethnicity. We can be assured that an ethnicity question on an existing client intake form was not thought up to answer our specific research question. Rather, the program likely had other reasons for collecting the data, such as needing to report the percentage of clients who come from an ethnic minority that they have seen in a given fiscal period.

The social service program may also have records that contain data that we could use for our "difficulty in accessing social services" variable. Social workers, for example, may be required to record each service referral made for each client. By reading each client file, we would be able to count the number of service referrals made for each client.

Secondary data can also be accessed from existing databases around the world. Census databases are a common example. With advances in computer technology, databases are becoming easier to access. The Inter-University Consortium for Political and Social Research (ICPSR) is the largest data archive in the world; it holds more than 17,000 files of data from more than 130 countries.

We could use the ICPSR data, for example, to compare the accessibility of social services for clients from different ethnic groups across various countries. Of course, we could only do this if meaningful data already exist within the database to answer our research question.

## Establishing Data Collection Procedures

Given that secondary data already exist, there is no need to collect them. Rather, our focus shifts to evaluating the dataset's worth with respect to answering our research question. The presence of datasets has an important influence on how we formulate our research questions or test our hypotheses. When original data are collected, we design our research study and tailor our data collection procedures to gather the "best" data possible. When data exist, we can only develop a research question that is as good as the data that we have available.

Because secondary data influence how we formulate our research questions, we must firmly settle on a research question before analyzing them. Datasets can have a vertigo effect, leaving us feeling dizzy about the relationships between and among variables contained within them. It may be that we begin with a general research question, such as our two-variable question about ethnicity and difficulty in accessing social services, and move to a more specific hypothesis.

> Secondary data can also be accessed from existing databases around the world.

Suppose our existing dataset contained data about client ethnicity (e.g., Asians, African Americans, Caucasians, Latinx, Native Americans) and data about difficulty in accessing social services (e.g., yes or no). We could return to the literature for studies that might help us formulate a directional (one-tailed) hypothesis.

A directional hypothesis would suggest that one or more of these six ethnic groups would have more (or less) difficulty accessing social services than the remaining groups. If no such literature exists, however, we would pose a nondirectional (two-tailed) hypothesis, which indicates that we have no basis to suggest that one of the six ethnic groups would have more or less difficulty accessing social services than any of the others.

Another influence of an existing data set is on how we operationally define the variables in our study. Our study's variables will have already been operationally defined for us. The definition used to collect the original data will be the definition we use in our study as well.

It's possible to create a new variable by recasting one or more of the original variables in an existing dataset. For instance, suppose we are interested to know whether our clients are parents. Existing program records, however, only list the number of children in each family. We could recast these data by categorizing those clients who have one or more children versus those who have no children, thus creating a two-category variable. Clients with one or more children would be categorized as "parents" versus clients without any children who would be classified as "not parents".

One final consideration for using existing secondary data is that of informed consent. Just because data exist does not mean that we have free rein to use them in future studies. It may be that clients have provided information on intake forms because they believed it was necessary to do so in order to receive services (see chapter 5 on ethics).

### RECORDING SECONDARY DATA

Recording secondary databases is a simple matter because data have already been collected, organized, and checked for accuracy. Our task is to work with them and determine the best possible procedures for data analyses. One feature of existing databases is that they generally include a large number of cases and variables. Thus, some advanced knowledge of statistical software packages is required to extract the variables of interest and conduct the data analyses.

> All databases are not created equal, particularly with respect to their validity and reliability.

### ESTABLISHING RELIABILITY AND VALIDITY

Once our research question is formulated and our variables have been operationally defined, it's important to establish the data set's credibility. We must remember that all datasets are not created equal, particularly with respect to their validity and reliability. Most importantly, we want to check out the data source. If ethnic status is recorded on a social service program's client intake form, for example, we would want to know how the data were obtained.

The data would be considered unreliable and even invalid if the workers simply looked at their clients and checked one of several ethnicity categories. A more reliable and valid procedure would be if they asked their clients what ethnic category they come from and at the same time showed them the categories to be selected. Datasets that are accompanied by clear data collection procedures are generally more valid and reliable than those data-sets that are not.

### ADVANTAGES AND DISADVANTAGES

The advancement of computer technology increases the likelihood that secondary data will be used more often in future social work research studies. It's a reasonably inexpensive way to gather and analyze data to answer a research question or to test a hypothesis.

Given that datasets are developing around the world, researchers can fairly easily compare data sets from different countries and across different time spans. Datasets are at our fingertips, provided that we have a research question or hypothesis to match. One major disadvantage of using an existing dataset is that our research question is limited by the possibilities of the dataset. We must make the best use of the data available to us, with the understanding that the "best" may not be good enough to answer our research question or test our hypothesis.

| Box 16.3 | Secondary Data (Document Review) in a Nutshell |
| --- | --- |

**What are secondary data?**

Secondary data, also called *document reviews*, are ways of collecting data by reviewing existing documents. The documents may be internal to a program or organization (such as records of what components of an asthma management program were implemented in schools) or may be external (such as records of emergency room visits by students served by an asthma management program).

Documents may be hard copy or electronic and may include reports, program logs, performance ratings, funding proposals, meeting minutes, and newsletters.

**When should you use secondary data for a research study?**

- *To gather background information.* Reviewing existing documents helps you understand the history, philosophy, and operation of the program you are evaluating and the organization in which it operates.

- *To determine if implementation of the program reflects program plans.* The review of program documents may reveal a difference between formal statements of program purpose and the actual program implementation. It is important to determine if such a difference exists and to clarify the program intent before moving forward with the study.

- *When you need information to help you develop other data collection tools for your research study.* Reviewing existing documents to better understand the program and organization you are evaluating will help you formulate questions for interviews, questionnaires, or focus groups or develop an observation guide.

- *When you need data to answer* what *and* how many *questions.* Reviewing program documents is useful for answering basic questions related to the number and type of participants, number of program personnel, and program costs.

**How do you plan and conduct a secondary data analysis?**

- *Assess existing documents.* Find out what types of documents exist and determine which ones you think will answer your study's questions.

- *Secure access to the documents you have identified through your assessment.* Certain documents may require the permission of others before being released for review and analysis. You may need to work with legal experts in your agency to understand what limitations you may face and how the experts can help you access documents you will need for your research study.

- *Ensure confidentiality.* Confidentiality is always an important consideration when collecting data for a research study. If you need to review documents that involve confidential data about individuals, develop a system that ensures the confidentiality of individual-level data. Developing these processes and guidelines may also help you in securing access to sensitive or confidential documents.

- *Compile the documents relevant to your research study.* Once you have secured access to the documents you need to answer your research study's questions, compile the documents. It is important that you limit your review to only those documents that answer your questions.

- *Understand how and why the documents were produced.* You will need to talk to the people who know something about the documents you are compiling to better understand the context for which they were developed. This is critical to gathering usable information for your research study.

- *Determine the accuracy of the documents.* Determining the accuracy of the documents may involve comparing the documents that contain similar information, checking the documents against other data you have collected, and speaking with people who were involved in the development of the documents.

- *Summarize the information from documents reviewed.* Create a data collection form to summarize the data gleaned from your document reviews. You may want to include on the form the type of document you are reviewing, a way to reference each document, and information that answers each applicable question. You will use the form to help you compile and analyze your findings.

**Advantages**

- Is available locally.

- Is unobtrusive.

- Reduces problems of memory relating to when, where, and with whom (diaries).

- Provides access to thoughts and feelings that may not otherwise be accessible.

- Can be less threatening to research participants.

- Allows collection and analysis of data on researcher's own schedule.

- Inexpensive when compared to other data-collection methods.

- Grounded in setting and language in which they occur.

- Useful for determining value, interest, positions, political climate, and public attitudes.

- Provides information on historical trends or sequences.

- Provides opportunity for study of trends over time.

- Is a good source of background information.

- Provides a behind-the-scenes look at a program that may not be directly observable.

- May bring up issues not noted by other data-collection methods.

**Disadvantages**

- May provide data that are incomplete, inapplicable, inaccurate, disorganized, unavailable, or out of date.

- May be hampered by quality of data variation among different documents.

- May potentially cause change in participants' behaviors via use of diaries.

- Is not well suited for low-literacy groups.

- Offers no opportunities for clarification of data.

- Could be biased because of selective survival of data.

- Can be time consuming to collect, review, and analyze many documents.

- May be of questionable authenticity.

- May pose challenges in locating suitable documents, or data.

- May be time consuming to analyze, and access may be difficult.

# EXISTING STATISTICS

Existing statistics are a special form of secondary data. They exist in a variety of places. A unique feature of existing statistics is that they exist only in numerical form. We might have statistics, for example, that report 20 percent of clients served by social services were Native, 30 percent were Latinx, and 50 percent were Caucasian.

The following provides an example of how Fran, a clinical director of a private social service agency, used existing statistics for her research question. One difference between existing statistics and secondary data is that statistics summarize data in aggregate form. The following example is from Jackie Sieppert, Steve McMurtry, and Bob McClelland (2011).

### EXAMPLE OF USING EXISTING STATISTICS

Fran is clinical director of a private, nonprofit agency that provides foster care, group-home care, and residential treatment for children in a small city in Arizona. She has noticed that there is a higher number of ethnic minority children in her agency's caseload than would be expected based on the proportion of ethnic minority children in the general population. She decides to do a study of this issue using existing statistics already gathered by various sources as her data collection method.

Fran first talks with the information specialist at the local library, asking for help to conduct a computer search through the library's existing databases. The search reveals a series of reports, titled *Characteristics of Children in Substitute and Adoptive Care*, that were sponsored by the American Public Welfare Association and that provide several years of data reported by states on their populations of children in various kinds of foster and adoptive care.

She also locates an annual publication produced by the Children's Defense Fund, and this provides a variety of background data on the well-being of children in the United States. Next, Fran checks in the library's government documents section. She locates recent census data on the distribution of persons under the age of eighteen across different ethnic groups in her county. Fran now quickly turns to state-level resources, where a quick check of government listings in the telephone book reveals two agencies that appear likely to have relevant data. One is the Foster Care Review Board, which is composed of citizen volunteers who assist juvenile courts by reviewing the progress of children in foster care statewide.

A call to the Board reveals that they produce an annual report that lists a variety of statistics. These include the number of foster children in the state, where they are placed, and how long they have been in care. Fran also learns that the Board's annual reports from previous years contain similar data, thus a visit to the Board's office provides her with the historical data needed to identify trends in the statistics she is using. Finally, she discovers that two years earlier the Board produced a special issue of its annual report that was dedicated to the topic of ethnic minority children in foster care, and this issue offers additional statistics not normally recorded in most annual reports.

Another state agency is the Administration for Children, Youth, and Families, a division of the state's social services department. A call to the division connects her with a staff member who informs her that a special review of foster children was conducted by the agency only a few months before. Data from this review confirm her perception that minority children are overrepresented in foster care in the state, and it provides a range of other data that may be helpful in determining the causes of this problem.

From these sources Fran now has the data she needs to paint a detailed picture of minority foster children at the national and state levels. She also has the ability to examine the problem in terms of both point-in-time circumstances and longitudinal trends, and the latter suggest that the problem of overrepresentation has grown worse. There is also evidence to indicate that the problem is more severe in her state than nationally.

Finally, corollary data on related variables, together with the more intensive work done in the special studies by the Foster Care Review Board and the Administration for Children, Youth, and Families, gives Fran a basis for beginning to understand the causes of the problem and the type of research study that must be done to investigate solutions.

In the same way that secondary data are used for a purpose other than what was originally stated, so it is for existing statistics. With existing statistics, however, we are one step farther removed from the original data. A statistic, for example, can be computed from 3,000 cases or from thirty cases—each produces only a single value.

There are two main types of statistics for us to be concerned with. The first is descriptive statistics, which simply describe the sample or population being studied. Statistics used for descriptive purposes include things like percentages, percentiles, means, standard deviations, medians, ranges, and so on.

The second type of statistics—inferential statistics—includes test statistics such as chisquare, $t$-test, analysis of variance (ANOVA), regression, and correlation. Do not panic—we will give an introductory discussion on statistics in Chapter 18. For now, we need only to know that descriptive statistics tell us about the characteristics of a sample or a population. Inferential statistics tell us about the likelihood of a relationship between and among variables within a population. When using existing statistics as our "data" we proceed in much the same way as when we use secondary data. Both are unobtrusive methods of data collection in that no persons will be asked to provide data about themselves—the data already exist and have been used to calculate a statistic.

### ESTABLISHING DATA COLLECTION PROCEDURES

Using existing statistics in a research study influences our research question (and hypotheses) to a greater degree than when using secondary data. If existing statistics are to assist in developing a research question, then advanced knowledge of statistics is required. We would need to understand the purpose of each statistic, the assumptions behind it, and how it was calculated.

We would not want to gather existing statistics without also collecting information about how the original data (used to calculate our existing statistics) were collected and analyzed. This information is important to assessing the credibility of the statistics that we would use for our research study.

### RECORDING EXISTING STATISTICAL DATA

Recording existing statistics is different from recording secondary data. In the case of secondary data, the data are already in a recorded form. When working with existing statistics, it's usually necessary to extract the statistics from their original sources and reconfigure them in a way that permits us to conduct an appropriate data analysis. It may be, for example, that we need to extract percentage figures from a paragraph within a published article, or mean and standard deviation scores from an already existing table in a research report.

### ESTABLISHING RELIABILITY AND VALIDITY

Checking the reliability and validity of existing statistics requires us to look for a few basic things. First, we want to be sure that the studies or reports from which we are extracting the statistics use comparable conceptual and operational definitions. If we are to compare statistical results about the accessibility of social services to clients who are from different ethnic groups across two different studies, we want to be certain that both studies had similar operational definitions for the two variables that we are interested in.

We can also examine previously conducted studies for their own assessment of their validity and reliability. Were sound procedures used to collect the original data? Were the original data analyzed in an appropriate way? What were the limitations of each study? By asking these types of questions about previous studies, we can get clues as to the credibility of the statistics that we are about to use in our own research study.

## ADVANTAGES AND DISADVANTAGES

The advantages of using existing statistics are many. Given that existing data are used, via the form of statistics, it's a relatively inexpensive approach and is unobtrusive. By using existing statistics, we can push the knowledge envelope of what we already know and ask more complex research questions. The use of existing statistics also provides us with the opportunity to compare the results of several research studies in an empirical way.

One disadvantage of using existing statistics is that we are not provided with data for individual cases. We can only answer research questions and test hypotheses about groups of people. Because data are already presented in a summary (i.e., statistical) form, it's difficult to assess how the data were collected and analyzed. Because the data have been handled by different individuals, there is an increased chance that human error has occurred somewhere along the way.

# QUALITATIVE DATA-COLLECTION METHODS

**A**s we know, all research studies require data—regardless of whether a positivistic or interpretive approach is used. We have already discussed that quantitative data are represented numerically, and qualitative data are usually expressed using words.

A second key difference between these two types of data is that qualitative data are collected to "build" a story or understanding of a concept or variable as compared to quantitative data, which narrows in on a select few variables. A third difference worth noting is that qualitative data are generally "bulkier" than quantitative data. As we will see, a single word, a sentence, or even an entire page of text can represent qualitative data.

The exact point in time when data are collected in the research process is another difference between quantitative and qualitative data. We have stressed that quantitative data collection can only occur once variables have been completely operationally defined—in fact, the reliability and validity of our measurements depend on it. Qualitative data, on the other hand, can be collected during many different steps in the research process. We may collect data near the beginning of our study to help us focus our research question and identify key variables to be explored later on in the research process. Qualitative data collected in later steps in our study can be used to check out any assumptions we may have and any new ideas that emerge (see chapter 9).

When collecting quantitative data, the rules for data collection are tried and tested before collecting any data—procedures can be outlined in a checklist format, where the data collector checks off each procedure as it's completed. For qualitative data, however, explicit procedures of data collection are not necessarily known before the data collection process starts. Rather, the procedures used are documented as they happen.

It's only after data collection is complete that a detailed description of the procedure can be articulated. This is not to say that in qualitative data collection we can willy-nilly change our minds or that anything goes. Research is still research, which means that a systematic approach to inquiry is used. The big difference for interpretive research is that the systematic nature of data collection applies to how we record and monitor the data collection process. Any changes in data collection (e.g., change in questions, research participants, or literature review) are based on data already collected. More will be explained about how qualitative data collection procedures are monitored in Chapter 19. For now, let's return to our research question.

**Research question**
Do ethnic minorities have difficulty in accessing social services?

We have already discussed in the four different methods of collecting quantitative data to answer the above research question. Now we will turn to four data collection methods that are more commonly associated with producing qualitative data to answer the same research question:

1  Narrative interviewing
2  Participant observation
3  Secondary content data
4  Historical data

# NARRATIVE INTERVIEWING

We have seen how interviewing is used to collect quantitative data via survey questionnaires, in which interviewers are trained to ask questions of research participants in a uniform way and interaction between interviewers and their research participants is minimized. Interviewing for qualitative data, on the other hand, has a completely different tone (Tutty, Rothery, & Grinnell, 1996). The aim of narrative interviewing is to have research participants tell stories in their own words. Their stories usually begin when we ask our identified research question. For example, we could begin an interview by saying, "Could you tell me about your experiences as a Native client in terms of accessing social services?"

Qualitative interviewers are not bound by strict rules and procedures. Rather, they make every effort to engage research participants in meaningful discussions. In fact, the purpose is to have research participants tell their own stories in their own ways. The direction the interviews take may deviate from the original research problem being investigated depending on what research participants choose to tell interviewers. Data collected in one research interview can be used to develop or revise further research questions in subsequent research interviews.

The narrative interview is commonly used in case study research where numerous interviews are usually conducted to learn more about a "case," which could be defined as a person, a group of people, an event, or an organization. The narrative interview is also a basic component of other research pursuits, such as feminist research and participatory action research (Gochros, 2018).

### ESTABLISHING DATA COLLECTION PROCEDURES

Data collection and data analysis are intertwined in an interpretive research study. Thus, the steps we take in collecting data from a narrative interview will evolve with our study. Nevertheless, we must be clear about our starting point and the procedures that we will use to "check and balance" the decisions we make along the way. One of the aims of an interpretive research approach is to tell a story about a problem without the cobwebs of existing theories, labels, and interpretations.

As such, we may choose to limit the amount of literature we review before proceeding with data collection. The amount of literature we review is guided by the interpretive research approach we use. A grounded theory approach, for example, suggests that we review some literature at the beginning of our study in order to help frame our research question. We would then review more literature later on, taking direction from the new data that we collect.

It's necessary for us to decide when and how to approach potential research participants before data collection occurs. Think about our simple research question for a moment: Do clients who come from an ethnic minority have difficulty in accessing social services? Who would we interview first? Would we interview someone receiving multiple

> The purpose of narrative interviewing is to have research participants tell their own stories in their own ways.

social services or someone not receiving any? Is there a particular ethnic group that we would want represented in our early interviews?

Remember that the data we collect in our beginning interviews will directly influence how we proceed in later interviews. It's possible for the professional literature, or our expert knowledge, to point us to a particular starting place. Regardless of where we begin, it's critical for us to document our early steps in the data-collection process. The notes we take will be used later on to recall the steps we took, and more importantly why we took them. Let's say, for example, that our interest in our research question stems from the fact that many ethnic minority people we know in our personal lives (not our professional lives) have complained about access to social services. We may choose to begin interviewing with an individual we already know.

On the other hand, we may decide after a cursory review of the literature that most of the existing research on our research problem is based on interviews with people who, in fact, are receiving services. We may then choose to begin interviewing clients who are from an ethnic minority and who are not currently receiving any social services but are named on social service client lists.

We must also establish how the interview will be structured. Interviewing for qualitative data can range from informal casual conversations to more formal guided discussions. An informal interview is unplanned. The interviewer begins, for example, by asking Native clients a general question, such as the one presented earlier: "Could you tell me about your experiences in accessing social services?"

The discussion that would follow would be based on the natural and spontaneous interaction between the interviewer and the research participant. The interviewer has no way of knowing at the outset what direction the interview will take or where it will end. A guided interview, on the other hand, has more structure. The exact amount of structure varies from one guided interview to another. In any case, the interviewer has an interview schedule, which essentially amounts to an outline of questions and/or concepts, to guide the interview with the research participant.

> The data we collect in our beginning interviews will directly influence how we proceed in later interviews.

A loosely structured interview schedule may simply identify key concepts or ideas to include in the interview at the appropriate time. In our study, for example, we might want the interviewer to specifically ask each research participant about language barriers and social isolation, if these concepts do not naturally emerge in the interviews. A highly structured interview schedule would list each question to be asked during the interviews. The interviewer would read the question out to the research participants and record their answers.

### RECORDING NARRATIVE DATA

The most reliable way to record interview data is through the use of audiotape. Videotape is also a possibility, but many people are uncomfortable with being filmed. The audiotape is an excellent record of an interview because it gives us verbatim statements made by our research participants. The tone, pace, and "atmosphere" of the interview can be recalled by simply replaying the tape.

To prepare data for analysis, however, it's necessary to transcribe every word of the interview. As we will see in Chapter 19, the transcription provides text data, which will be read (and reread) and analyzed. Because audio data are transformed into text data, verbatim statements are used. In addition, any pauses, sighs, and gestures are noted in the text. The following is an example of an excerpt of text data based on our question asked earlier.

**Research Participant Number 6:** Being a Native in social services, huh . . . well, it's not so good, the people don't know . . . they don't see the reserve or the kids playing . . . even when they see they don't see. The kids you know, they could have some help, especially the older ones (sighs and pauses for a few seconds). My oldest you know, he's 12 and he goes to school in the city. He comes home and doesn't know what to do. He gets into trouble. Then the social services people come with their briefcases and tell you what to do (voice gets softer). They put in stupid programs and the kids don't want to go you know, they just want to play, get into trouble stuff (laughs) . . .

**Interviewer:** Hmmm. And how would you describe your own experiences with social services?

Because the interviewing approach to data collection is based on the interaction of the interviewer and the research participant, both parts of the discussion are included in the transcript. But data collection and recording do not stop here. The interviewer must also keep notes on the interview to record impressions, thoughts, perspectives, and any data that will shed light on the transcript during analysis. An example of the interviewer's notes from the above excerpt is:

> **September 12 (Research Participant Number 6):** I was feeling somewhat frustrated because the research participant kept talking about his children. I felt compelled to get him to talk about his own experiences but that seemed sooooo much less important to him.

As we will see in Chapter 19, the verbatim transcript and the interviewer's notes are key pieces of data that will be jointly considered when the text data are finally analyzed.

### TRUSTWORTHINESS AND TRUTH-VALUE OF NARRATIVE DATA

Regardless of the type of interview or the data recording strategy that we select, we must have some way to assess the credibility of the data we collect. With quantitative data, we do this by determining the reliability and validity of the data—usually by calculating a numerical value. In contrast, with qualitative data we are less likely to generate numerical values and more likely to document our own personal observations and procedures.

An important question to assess the trustworthiness and truth-value of the text data (and our interpretation of them) is whether we understand what our research participants were telling us from their points of view. Two common ways to check the credibility of interview data are triangulation and member checking. These procedures will be discussed in more detail in Chapter 19.

Briefly, triangulation involves comparing data from multiple perspectives. It may be that we interview several people (i.e., data sources) on one topic, or even that we compare quantitative and qualitative data for the same variable. Member checking simply involves getting feedback from our research participants about our interpretation of what they said.

### ADVANTAGES AND DISADVANTAGES

The major advantage of narrative interviewing is the richness of the data that are generated. Narrative interviewing allows us to remain open to learning new information or new perspectives about old ideas. Because the interviewer is usually the same person who is the researcher, there is a genuine interest expressed in the interviews.

The major disadvantage associated with narrative interviewing is that it's time consuming—very time consuming. Not only does it take time to conduct the interviews, but considerable time also must be allotted for transcribing the text data. Narrative interviews

---

*Interviewing for qualitative data can range from informal casual conversations to more formal guided discussions.*

---

*Regardless of the type of interview or the data recording strategy that we select, we must have some way to assess the credibility of the data we collect.*

produce reams and reams of text, which make it difficult to conduct an analysis. Researchers can tire easily and are subject to imposing their own biases and perspectives on what the research participants say.

## Participant Observation

Participant observation is a way for us to be a part of something and study it at the same time. This method of data collection requires us to establish and maintain ongoing relationships with research participants in the field setting. We not only listen, observe, and record data, but also participate in events and activities as they happen.

Our role in participant observation can be described on a continuum with one end emphasizing the participant role and the other end emphasizing the observer role. An "observer-participant" has the dominant role of observation whereas the "participant-observer" is predominantly a participant. Suppose we were to use participant observation as a data collection method for our study.

An example of an observer-participant is a researcher who joins a group of people, say Natives living on their reserve, for events related to our research study. We may travel with a community social worker, for example, and participate in community meetings on the reserve to discuss access to social services.

An example of a participant-observer could be when a social worker has the dual responsibility of conducting the meeting and observing the interactions of community members. A participant-observer could also be identified within his or her unique community. A Native resident of the reserve, for example, could participate in the meeting as a resident and as an observer. In any case, participant observation always requires that one person assumes a dual role.

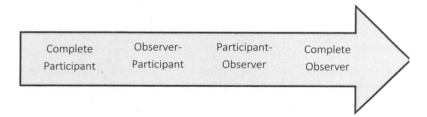

There are four participant observation roles you can take when collecting data for your qualitative study.

For ethical reasons, your role must be made explicit to all persons participating in the research study. Whether the researcher is a social worker or a Native resident of the reserve, he or she must declare his or her dual role before the community meeting (i.e., data collection) gets underway.

### Establishing Procedures to Collect Data

Given the dual role of researchers in participant observation, formulating steps for data collection can be tricky. It's essential for the researcher to keep a balance between "participation" and "observation." Suppose our Native resident who is a participant-observer gets so immersed in the issues of the community meeting that she forgets to look around or ask others questions related to the research study.

Someone who completely participates will not be very effective in noting important details with respect to how other people participated in the meeting. On the other hand, if our Native researcher leans too far into her observation role, others might see her as an outsider and express their views differently than if they believed she had a vested interest within the community.

An important consideration for a participant observation study is how to gain access to the group of people being studied.

An important consideration for a participant observation study is how to gain access to the group of people being studied. Imagine who might be welcomed into a community meeting on a Native reserve and who might be rejected. Chances are that the Native people on a reserve would be more accepting of a Native person, a person known to them, or a person whom they trust as compared to a non-Native person, a stranger, or a person whom they know but do not trust.

In participant observation we would need to understand the culture of the reserve in order to know who to seek permission from. In participant observation, entry and access are a process more analogous to peeling away the layers of an onion than to opening a door. Forming relationships with people is a critical part of data collection.

The more meaningful relationships we can establish, the more meaningful data we will collect. This is not to say, however, that we somehow trade relationship tokens for pieces of information. Rather, research participants should feel a partnership with the researcher that is characterized by mutual interest, reciprocity, trust, and cooperation.

## RECORDING PARTICIPANT OBSERVATIONAL DATA

The data generated from participant observation come from observing, interviewing, using existing documents and artifacts, and reflecting on personal experiences. Below are a few examples.

> **Observation (September 12, 9:30 a.m., Meeting Start Time):** When the social worker announced the purpose of the meeting was to discuss access to social services for people living on the reserve, there was a lot of agreement from a crowd of 42 people. Some cheered, some nodded their heads, and others made comments like, "It's about time."
>
> **Research participant's verbatim comment (September 12, 10:15 a.m.):** "Native people don't use social services because they are not offered on the reserve."
>
> **Existing document:** A report entitled "The Social Service Needs of a Reserve Community" reports that there have been three failed attempts by state social workers to keep a program up and running on the reserve. Worker turnover is identified as the main contributing factor of program failures.
>
> **Researcher's personal note (September 12, 10:44 a.m.):** I feel amazed at the amount of positive energy in the room. I can sense peoples' frustrations (including my own), yet I am in awe of the hopeful and positive outlook everyone has to want to develop something that works for our community. I am proud to be a part of this initiative to improve services in the community.

Overall, participant observers produce "participant observational" data through the use of detailed and rich notes. Several strategies can be used for documenting notes. We can take notes on an ongoing basis, for example, by being careful to observe the time and context for all written entries. A more efficient method, however, would be to carry your trusty smartphone, which gives you the flexibility to state a thought, to record a conversation, and to make summary comments about what you observe and hear. Collecting data on an ongoing basis is preferable because it increases the likelihood of producing accurate notes in addition to remembering key events. In some instances, however, participation in a process prevents us from recording any data, which leaves us to record our notes after the event we are participating in has ended.

## TRUSTWORTHINESS AND TRUTH-VALUE

Given that multiple data sources are possible in participant observation, it's possible to check the credibility of the data through triangulation. By reviewing the four data recording examples on the previous page, we can be reasonably confident that there is agreement about the state of social services on the reserve. The four separate data entries seem to agree that social services on the reserve are inadequate in terms of the community's needs.

The flexibility of participant observation allows us to seek out opportunities to check out our personal assumptions and ideas. After hearing the general response of Native community members at the beginning of the meeting, for example, we may choose to ask related questions to specific individuals. We can also check our perceptions along the way by sharing our own thoughts, asking people to comment on data summaries, or asking people how well they think two data sources fit together.

### ADVANTAGES AND DISADVANTAGES

A major advantage of participant observation is that we can collect multiple sources of data and check the credibility of the data as we go. Because of the participant role, any observations made are grounded within the context in which they were generated. A "complete participant" is more likely to pick up subtle messages, for example, than would be a "complete observer." The disadvantages of participant observation are related to time considerations. As with narrative interviewing, a considerable amount of time must be allotted to data recording and transcription. The researcher also runs the risk of becoming too immersed as a participant or too distant as an observer—both are situations that will compromise the data collected.

## SECONDARY CONTENT DATA

Secondary content data are existing text data. In the same way that existing quantitative data can be used to answer newly developed research questions, so can existing qualitative (or content) data. In this case, the text data were recorded at some other time and for some other purpose than the research question that we have posed. Let's return to our research question—do clients who come from an ethnic minority have difficulty in accessing social services? With the use of content data, we could answer our question using context data that already exist.

It may be, for example, that social workers are mandated to record any discussion they had about barriers to accessing social services for their clients within their client files. Case notes, for example, may read "client does not have reliable transportation" or "client has expressed a strong wish for a worker who has the same ethnic background". These types of comments can be counted and categorized according to meaningful themes. In this instance, we are zeroing in on text data for specific examples of recorded behaviors, much like the microscopic approach of structured observation.

> Content data can be firsthand or secondhand.

We must be aware that content data can be firsthand or secondhand. In our example, firsthand data would be generated when the social workers document their own behaviors in relation to offering services to their clients. When social workers record their own impressions about how their clients respond to offers of services, secondhand data are produced (LeCroy & Solomon, 2001).

### ESTABLISHING PROCEDURES

Content data are restricted to what is available. That is, if sixty-eight client files exist, then we have exactly sixty-eight client files to work from. We do not have the luxury of collecting more data. Like secondary quantitative data, we are in a position only to compile the existing data, not to collect new data.

It's possible, however, that content data are available from several sources. Client journals may be on file, or perhaps the agency recently conducted an open-ended client satisfaction survey, which has handwritten responses to satisfaction-type questions from clients. A major consideration of content data is whether a sufficient amount exists to adequately answer our research question. If there are not enough data, we do not want to spend precious time reading and analyzing them. We must also remember that we are reading and reviewing text data for a purpose that they were not originally intended for.

> Content data exist in text form.

Suppose, for example, you kept a daily journal of your personal experience in your research course. Would you write down the same thoughts if you knew your journal would be private compared with if you were to share your writings with your research instructor? The original intent of writing is essential to remember because it provides the context in which the writing occurred.

Because we are examining confidential client case files, we must establish a coding procedure to ensure that our clients' confidentiality and anonymity are maintained. In fact, it's not at all necessary for us, as researchers, to know the names of the client files we are reading. Given our research question, we need only to have access to those portions of clients' files that contain data about client ethnicity and the difficulty clients have in accessing social services.

### RECORDING

As we know, content data exist in text form. If they exist in handwritten form, it's necessary to type them out into transcript form. It's useful to make several copies of the transcripts to facilitate data analysis. More will be said about transcripts in Chapter 19.

### ESTABLISHING THE TRUSTWORTHINESS AND TRUTH-VALUE

Clearly, firsthand data are more credible than secondhand data when dealing with existing text data. Because the data are secondary, questions of credibility center more around data analysis than data collection. In our example, it may be possible to triangulate data by comparing the files of different workers or by comparing different client files with the same worker. It also may be possible to member check (chapter 19) if workers are available and consent to it.

### ADVANTAGES AND DISADVANTAGES

A major advantage of content data is that they already exist. Thus, time and money are saved in the data-collection process. The task of the researcher is simply to compile data that are readily available and accessible. The disadvantages of content data are that they are limited in scope. The data were recorded for some other purpose and may omit important detail that would be needed to answer our research question.

## HISTORICAL DATA

Historical data are collected in an effort to study the past (Stuart, 2011). Like the participant-observation method to data collection, historical data can come from different data sources. Data collection can be obtrusive, as in the case of interviewing people about past or historical events, or unobtrusive, as in the case when existing documents (primarily content data) are compiled. When our purpose is to study history, however, special cases of content data and interviewing are required. Suppose we recast our research question to ask, "Did clients who come from an ethnic minority have difficulty accessing social services from 1947 to 1965?" Phrased this way, our question directs us to understand what has been rather than what is.

> When collecting historical data, it's important to sort out firsthand data from secondhand data.

In order for us to answer our new research question, we would need to dig up remains from the past that could help us to describe the relationship, if any, between ethnicity and difficulty in accessing social services for our specified time period. We would search for documents such as related reports, memos, letters, transcriptions, client records, and documentaries, all dating back to the time period. Many libraries store this information in their archives.

We could also interview people (e.g., social workers and/or clients) who were part of social services between 1947 and 1965. People from the past might include clients, workers, supervisors, volunteers, funders, or ministers. The purpose of our interviews would be to have people remember the past—that is, to describe factual events from their memories. We are less interested in people's opinions about the past than we are about what "really" happened.

When collecting historical data, it's important to sort out firsthand data from secondhand data. Firsthand data, of course, are more highly valued because the data are less likely to be distorted or altered. Diaries, autobiographies, letters, home videos, photographs, and organizational minutes are all examples of firsthand data. Secondhand data, on the other hand, include documents like biographies, books, and articles.

## ESTABLISHING PROCEDURES TO COLLECT DATA

It's probably more accurate to say that we retrieve historical data than it is to say that we collect it. The data already exist, in long-forgotten written documents, dusty videotapes, or peoples' memories. Our task is to resurface a sufficient amount of data so that we can describe, and sometimes explain, what happened (Stuart, 2011). One of the first considerations for conducting a historical research study is to be sure that the variable being investigated is one that existed in the past.

Suppose, for example, we had a specific interest in the relationship among three variables: client ethnicity, difficulty in accessing social services, and computer technology. More specifically, let us say that we were interested in knowing about the relationship among these three variables, if any, for our specified time period, 1947 to 1965. It would be impossible to determine the relationship among these three variables from a historical perspective because computers were not (or were rarely) used in the social services from 1947 to 1965. Thus, there would be no past to describe or explain—at least not where computers are concerned.

Once we have established that our research question is relevant, we can delineate a list of possible data sources and the types of data that each can produce. The total list of data sources and types must be assessed to determine whether, in fact, sufficient data exist to answer our research question. It's possible, however, that data do exist but they are not accessible. Client records, for example, may be secured. Documents may be out of circulation, thus requiring a researcher to travel to where the data are stored.

### RECORDING

Despite the fact that historical data, in many cases, already exist, it's usually necessary to reproduce the data. When interviews are used, interview notes are recorded and the interviews are transcribed as we have discussed in other interpretive data collection methods. When past documents are used, they ought to be duplicated to create working copies. Original documents should be protected and preserved so that they can be made available to other interested researchers.

### ESTABLISHING THE TRUSTWORTHINESS AND TRUTH-VALUE

Assessing the trustworthiness and truth-value of historical data, in many ways, is the process of data analysis. Do different people recall similar facts? Do independent events from the past tell the same story? Much effort goes into triangulating pieces of data. The more corroboration we have among our data, the stronger our conclusions will be.

When reconstructing the past, our conclusions can only be as good as the data we base them on. Are the data authentic? How much of our data are firsthand compared to secondhand? Do we have sufficient data to describe the entire time period of interest? Perhaps we might have to cut back a few years; or if other data emerge, perhaps we can expand our time period.

### ADVANTAGES AND DISADVANTAGES

Historical data are unique and used for a specific purpose—to describe and explain the past. It's the only way for us to research history. When secondary data are readily available and accessible, the cost is minimized. When interviews are used, they provide us with an opportunity to probe further into the past and our area of interest.

The disadvantages of historical data are that they are not always easily available or accessible. There is also a risk of researcher bias such as when a letter or document is analyzed out of context. The past cannot be reconstructed, for example, if we impose present-day views, standards, and ideas.

## MIXED-METHOD DATA-COLLECTION METHODS

**W**hen investigating human behavior and attitudes, it is most fruitful to use a variety of data collection methods. By using different sources and methods at various points in the research process, you can build on the strength of each type of data collection method and minimize the weaknesses of any single approach. A multimethod data-collection approach can increase both the validity and the reliability of the study's results. As eloquently summed up by Joy Frechtling (2002):

> The range of possible benefits that carefully designed mixed-method designs can yield has been conceptualized by a number of professionals. The validity of your results can be strengthened by using more than one data-collection method to study the same phenomenon. This approach—called triangulation—is most often mentioned as the main advantage of the mixed-methods research approach.
>
> Combining the two methods pays off in improved instrumentation for all data collection methods and in sharpening the researcher's understanding of the study's findings. A typical research design might start out with a qualitative segment such as a focus group discussion alerting the researcher to issues that should be explored in a survey of program participants, followed by the survey, which in turn is followed by in-depth interviews to clarify some of the survey findings.
>
> It should be noted that triangulation, while very powerful when sources agree, can also pose problems when different sources yield different, even contradictory information. There is no formula for resolving such conflicts, and the best advice is to consider disagreements in the context in which they emerge.
>
> But this sequential approach is only one of several that evaluators might find useful. Thus, if an evaluator has identified subgroups of program participants or specific topics for which in-depth information is needed, a limited qualitative data collection can be initiated while a more broad-based survey is in progress.
>
> Mixed methods may also lead researchers to modify or expand the adoption of data collection methods. This can occur when the use of mixed methods uncovers inconsistencies and discrepancies that should alert the researcher to the need for reexamining data collection and analysis procedures. In a nutshell, you should attempt to obtain the most useful data to answer the critical questions about the study and, in so doing, rely on a mixed-methods approach whenever possible. (122)

## EVALUATING A DATA COLLECTION PLAN

**W**hen you read a research report of some kind you need to ask a few questions about how the researcher collected the data. All research studies collect data. The data can be quantitative and/or qualitative. It's critical that an author describes how the data were collected. A study is only as good as the validity and reliability of the data collected (chapters 11 and 12) and how they were collected (this chapter).

### USE THE APPENDIXES

There are a few questions you can ask when you begin to evaluate the quality of a researcher's data-collection method. Appendixes A and B contain a few questions you can ask (when you put on your "critical thinking" hat) about the quality of a data-collection method(s) that was used in a particular research study. More specifically,

1   For *quantitative* research studies (Appendix A) you can ask questions such as those found on pages 489–490 (questions 207–216).

2   For *qualitative* research studies (Appendix B) you can ask questions such as those found on page 503 (questions 380–386).

How to evaluate the overall creditability of a data-collection method that was used in a research study is totally up to you—and only you. You're the one who must ask and answer the questions. More important, you need to address two extremely difficult tasks:

1   You must have a rationale for *why* you're asking each question in the first place. You just can't ask questions without knowing why you're asking them. The appendixes only list potential questions you can ask. Can you guess why each one was listed and what importance your answer to each question has for your overall evaluation of the research study?

2   You also must have some kind of idea of what you're going to do with your answer to each question. For example,

   • In relation to a *quantitative* research study, question 208 on page 489 asks, "Does the author state exactly *where* the data were collected"?

   • In relation to a *qualitative* research study, question 381 on page 503 asks, "Does the author address the issue of subjectivity"?

Let's say your answers to the two preceding questions were "no". What are you going to do with your answers? That is, how are you going to use it in your overall evaluation of the study's data-collection procedures? Now what about if your answer was "yes"?

> Two people can assess the data-collection method that was used in any given research study and come up with two different conclusions.

> Many of the questions we can ask about the data-collection procedures for quantitative studies can also be asked for qualitative ones as well. And vice versa.

## CHAPTER RECAP

• A data collection method consists of a detailed plan of procedures that aims to gather data for a specific purpose—that is, to answer a research question or to test a hypothesis.

• A data source is the person who provides the data.

• The primary source of data in most social work research studies is people.

• Any data collection method can be used with numerous data sources. Firsthand data are obtained from people who are closest to the problem we are studying.

• Secondhand data may come from people who are indirectly connected to the primary problem we are studying.

• We collect original data (for the first time) during the course of our study to fulfill a specific purpose: to answer our research question or test our hypothesis.

- We can use existing data that have been previously collected and stored, either manually or in a computer.

- In a quantitative study we analyze numerical data using mathematical

computations and calculations.

- There are four common types of quantitative data-gathering methods.

- A qualitative study typically analyzes words or text data.

## REVIEW EXERCISES

1  In your own words discuss the differences between a *data-collection method* and a *data source.* Provide a single social work example throughout your discussion.

2  What are *survey questionnaires*? Discuss the advantages and disadvantages of using them as a data-collection method. Provide social work examples throughout your discussion to illustrate your main points.

3  What are *structured observations*? Discuss the advantages and disadvantages of using them as a data-collection method. Provide social work examples throughout your discussion to illustrate your main points.

4  What are *secondary data*? Discuss the advantages and disadvantages of using them as a data-collection method. Provide social work examples throughout your discussion to illustrate your main points.

5  What are *existing statistics*? Discuss the advantages and disadvantages of using them as a data-collection method. Provide social work examples throughout your discussion to illustrate your main points.

6  Pretend for a moment that you want to do a quantitative research study to assess the interviewing skills of your fellow social work students. This would be an excellent time to review Chapters 7–10.

- List and then discuss the various quantitative data-collection methods that you could use.

- What are the advantages and disadvantages of each one? Discuss fully.

- What data would each method produce for your data source(s)? Discuss fully.

7  Pretend that your school of social work wants to do a quantitative research study on determining the competency levels of its graduating students—which includes you, a graduating student.

- List and then discuss the various quantitative data-collection methods that your school could use.

- From a data-source's perspective (you),

what quantitative data-collection method(s) do you think would be best for your school to use with you. Why?

- What data could you provide the school that would be reliable and valid in relation to its research question? Justify your response and use examples to illustrate your main points.

- What qualitative data-collection methods could your school use to supplement its quantitative findings and recommendations?

8  Locate a published quantitative social work–related journal article of your choice. Be sure the author collected quantitative data and the article is reporting the results from a quantitative research study. We suggest you locate a quantitatively oriented research study in Bruce Thyer's journal *Research on Social Work Practice* (Sage Publications). Hands down, this is the best journal to find good quantitatively oriented social work research studies.

- What was the study's data source(s)?

- What quantitative data collection method(s) was used for each data source(s)?

- With your knowledge of the various quantitative data-collection methods that research studies can use, thoroughly discuss how you will use the material contained within this chapter when you begin to evaluate the appropriateness of the research study's quantitative data-collection method(s), and discuss why you believe each criterion you selected is important for your evaluation of the study's chosen method(s).

- Would you have used a different quantitative method to collect the data to answer the study's research question? If so, what method would you have used and why?

9  Pretend for the moment that you wish to do a qualitatively oriented research study

(chapter 9) to determine if MSW-level social workers are "better" at interviewing their clients than BSW-level social workers. You also wish to add a quantitative component (chapter 8) to your study.

- Using what you have learned so far in your research methods course, delineate how you would do your mixed-methods research study (chapter 10), highlighting the specific quantitative data-collection method(s) you have chosen.

- State specifically what the findings of your quantitative component could add to the study's qualitative findings and practice recommendations.

10  In your own words describe qualitative data in detail. Provide social work examples throughout your discussion to illustrate your main points.

11  What is *narrative interviewing*? Discuss in detail how you can use narrative interviewing as a qualitative data-gathering method in social work research situations. Provide social work examples throughout your discussion to illustrate your main points.

12  Discuss how you would record narrative data for a hypothetical social work research study. Provide social work examples throughout your discussion to illustrate your main points.

13  Discuss how you would assess the trustworthiness and truth-value of narrative data. Provide social work examples throughout your discussion to illustrate your main points.

14  Discuss the advantages and disadvantages of using narrative interviewing as a qualitative data-gathering method. Provide social work examples throughout your discussion to illustrate your main points.

15  What is *participant observation*? Discuss in detail how you can use participant observation as a qualitative data-gathering method in social work research situations. Provide social work examples throughout your discussion to illustrate your main points.

16  Discuss how you would record *participant observational data* for a hypothetical social work research study.

17  Discuss how you would assess the trustworthiness and truth-value of *participant observational data*. Provide social work examples throughout your discussion to illustrate your main points.

18  Discuss the advantages and disadvantages of using *participant observational data* as a qualitative data gathering method. Provide social work examples throughout your discussion to illustrate your main points.

19  What *are secondary content data*? Discuss in detail how you can use secondary content data as a qualitative data-gathering method in social work research situations. Provide social work examples throughout your discussion to illustrate your main points.

20  Discuss how you would *record secondary content data* for a hypothetical social work research study. Provide social work examples throughout your discussion to illustrate your main points.

21  Discuss how you would assess the trustworthiness and truth-value of *secondary content data*. Provide social work examples throughout your discussion to illustrate your main points.

22  Discuss the advantages and disadvantages of using *secondary content data* as a qualitative data-gathering method. Provide social work examples throughout your discussion to illustrate your main points.

23  What are *historical data*? Discuss in detail how you can use historical data as a qualitative data-gathering method in social work research situations. Provide social work examples throughout your discussion to illustrate your main points.

24  Discuss how you would record historical data for a hypothetical social work research study. Provide social work examples throughout your discussion to illustrate your main points.

25  Discuss how you would assess the trustworthiness and truth-value of *historical data*. Provide social work examples throughout your discussion to illustrate your main points.

26  Discuss the advantages and disadvantages of using *historical data* as a qualitative data-gathering method. Provide social work examples throughout your discussion to illustrate your main points.

27  Pretend for the moment you're employed as a social worker in your university's student counseling center. A student comes in to your office complaining about his depression. Using this chapter as a guide, describe in detail how you could use some of the qualitative and quantitative data-gathering techniques.

# 17

CHAPTER

## 2015 EPAS COMPETENCIES

| COMPETENCY 1 | Demonstrate Ethical and Professional Behavior |
|---|---|

You will learn that in order to be a successful evidence-based practitioner you have an ethical obligation to integrate three research roles into your daily practice activities as discussed in Chapter 3: (1) research consumer, (2) research partner—either as a co-researcher or research participant, and (3) creator and disseminator of research (or knowledge).

This entire chapter pertains to these three professional research-related roles when it comes to applying eight criteria that must be addressed when selecting and evaluating various data collection method(s) and data source(s) that social work researchers and practitioners can use.

| COMPETENCY 4 | Engage in Practice-Informed Research and Research-Informed Practice |
|---|---|

Competency 4 also pertains to the entire chapter because you have to:

1  Evaluate the appropriateness of the data collection method(s) and data source(s) utilized in a research study (**research consumer**—research-informed practice);

2  Participate in a research study—either as a co-researcher or research participant (**research partner**—practice-informed research). See 1 above and 3 below; and

3  Know how to select the most appropriate data collection method(s) and data source(s) when you actually do a research study (**creator and disseminator of research**—practice-informed research).

You also need to utilize evidence-based practice recommendations whenever possible; that is, you need to integrate (1) the best available research-based evidence with (2) your clinical expertise and (3) your client's values.

All of the above implies you'll need to know how to assess the strengths and limitations of the data collection method(s) and data source(s) used in a research study that produced its research-based evidence. In short, you need to ask and then answer a simple question: How seriously should I take the findings of any specific research study given the overall appropriateness of the data collection method(s) and data source(s) the study utilized?

| COMPETENCY 9 | Evaluate Practice with Individuals, Families, Groups, Organizations, & Communities |
|---|---|

See Competencies 1 and 4.

# 17
CHAPTER

# Selecting a Data-Collection Method

CHAPTERS 1 & 3 — Step 1. Understanding the Research Process

CHAPTER 2 — Step 2. Formulating Research Questions

CHAPTER 4
APPENDIXES A–C — Step 3. Reviewing the Literature
Evaluating the Literature

CHAPTERS 5 & 6 — Step 4. Being Aware of Ethical and Cultural Issues

CHAPTERS 7–10 — Step 5. Selecting a Research Approach

CHAPTERS 11 & 12 — Step 6. Specifying How Variables Are Measured

CHAPTER 13 — Step 7. Selecting a Sample

CHAPTERS 14 & 15 — Step 8. Selecting a Research Design

CHAPTERS 16 & 17 — Step 9. Selecting a Data-Collection Method

CHAPTERS 18 & 19 — Step 10. Analyzing the Data

CHAPTERS 20 & 21 — Step 11. Writing the Research Report

# Selecting a Data-Collection Method

"No need to select different data collection methods to measure my anxiety and depression levels. I only get anxious and depressed when I'm talking to you."

CHAPTER

# 17

CHAPTER OUTLINE

DATA COLLECTION VIA THE RESEARCH PROCESS
    Selecting a Topic and Research Question
    Designing the Study and Collecting Data
    Analyzing and Interpreting the Data
        *Example*
    Presentation and Dissemination of Findings
SELECTING A DATA-COLLECTION METHOD
    Size
    Scope
    Program Participation
    Worker Cooperation
    Intrusion into Research Participants' Lives
    Resources
    Time
    Methods Used in Previous Studies
EXAMPLE: SELECTING A METHOD
TRYING OUT THE METHOD
IMPLEMENTATION AND EVALUATION
    *Implementation*
    *Evaluation*
CHAPTER RECAP
REVIEW EXERCISES

IN THE LAST CHAPTER WE DISCUSSED eight methods of data collection, which were divided by the type of data that each is most likely to produce—quantitative data or qualitative data. This chapter examines the data-collection process from the vantage point of choosing the most appropriate data-collection method and data source for any given research question or hypothesis.

## DATA COLLECTION VIA THE RESEARCH PROCESS

**D**ata collection is a critical step in the research process because it's the link between theory and practice. Our research study always begins with an idea that is molded by a conceptual framework, which uses preexisting knowledge about our study's problem area. Once our research problem and question have been refined to a researchable level, data are sought from a selected source(s) and gathered using a data-collection method. The data collected are then used to support or supplant our original study's conceptions about our research problem under investigation (Unrau, 2011).

The role of data collection in connecting theory and practice is understood when looking at the entire research process. As we have seen in previous chapters of this book, choosing a data-collection method and data source follows the steps of selecting a research topic area, focusing the topic into a research question, and designing the research study. Data collection comes before the steps of analyzing the data and writing the research report. Although data collection is presented in this text as a distinct phase of the research process, in reality it cannot be tackled separately or in isolation.

> One factor that affects how our research question is answered depends upon how we conceptualize and measure the variables within it.

All steps of the research process must be considered if we hope to come up with the best strategy to gather the most relevant, reliable, and valid data to answer a research question or to test a hypothesis. Thus, this chapter discusses the role of data collection in relation to the other steps of the generic research process as outlined in Chapters 7–10.

### SELECTING A TOPIC AND RESEARCH QUESTION

Our specific research question identifies the general problem area and the population to be studied. It tells us what we want to collect data about and alerts us to potential data sources. It does not necessarily specify the exact manner in which our data will be gathered, however. Let's return to our research question:

**Research question**
Do people who come from ethnic minority backgrounds have difficulty in accessing social services?

Our research question identifies a problem area (difficulty in accessing social services for people who are ethnic minorities) and a population (social service clients). It does not state how the question will be answered. We have seen in the last chapter that our research question, in fact, could be answered using various data-collection methods. One factor that affects how our question is answered depends upon how we conceptualize and measure the variables within it. As we know, "accessing social services" could be measured in a variety of ways.

Another factor that affects how a research question is answered (or a hypothesis is tested) is the source of the data—that is, *who* or *what* is providing the data. If we want to get firsthand data about the accessibility of social services, for example, we could target the clients as a potential data source. If such firsthand data sources are not a viable option, secondhand data sources could be sought.

Social workers, for example, can be asked for their perceptions of how accessible social services are to their clients who come from ethnic minorities. In other instances, secondhand data can be gleaned from existing reports (secondary data or content data) written about clients (or client records) that monitor client progress and social worker–client interactions.

By listing all possible data-collection methods and data sources that could provide sound data to answer a research question, we develop a fuller understanding of our initial research problem. It also encourages us to think about our research problem from different perspectives, via the different data sources.

Because social work problems are complex, data collection is strengthened when two or more data sources are used. For example, if social workers (source 1) and clients (source 2) were to each report their perceptions of service accessibility in a similar way, then we could be more confident that the data (from both of these sources) accurately reflect the problem being investigated.

> The research design flows from the research question, which flows from the problem area.

## DESIGNING THE STUDY AND COLLECTING DATA

As we know, the research design flows from the research question, which flows from the problem area. A research design organizes our research question into a framework that sets the parameters and conditions of the study. As mentioned, the research question directs *what* data are collected and *who* data could be collected from. In a positivistic study, the research design refines the *what* question by operationalizing variables and the *who* question by developing a sampling strategy.

In an interpretive study, however, the research design identifies the starting point for data collection and how such procedures will be monitored and recorded along the way. In both research approaches, the research design also dictates (more or less) *when*, *where*, and *how* data will be collected.

The research design outlines how many data collection points our study will have and specifies the data sources. Each discrete data gathering activity constitutes a data-collection point and defines *when* data are to be collected. Thus, using a one-group posttest-only design (i.e., figure 15.1a on page 303), we will collect data only once from a single group of research participants. On the other hand, if a classical experimental design is used (i.e., figure 15.9 on page 321), data will be collected at two separate times with two different groups of research participants—for a total of four discrete data-collection points.

*Where* the data are collected is also important to consider. If our research question is too narrow and begs for a broader issue that encompasses individuals living in various geographic locations, then mailed survey questionnaires would be more feasible than face-to-face interviews. If our research question focuses on a specific population where all research participants live in the same geographic location, it may be possible to use direct observations or individual or group interviews.

Because most social work studies are applied, the setting of our study usually involves clients in their natural environments where there is little control over extraneous variables. If we want to measure the clients' perceptions about their difficulty in accessing social services, for example, do we observe clients in agency waiting rooms, observe how they interact with their social workers, or have them complete a survey questionnaire of some kind? In short, we must always consider which method(s) of data collection will lead to the most valid and reliable data to answer a research question or to test a hypothesis.

The combination of potential data-collection methods and potential data sources is another important consideration. A research study can have one data-collection source and still use multiple data-collection methods. Our program's clients (data source 1) in our study, for example, can fill out a standardized questionnaire that measures their perceptions of how accessible social services are (data-collection method 1) in addition to participating in face-to-face interviews (data-collection method 2). In the same vein, another study can have multiple data sources and one data-collection method. In this case, we can collect data about difficulty in accessing social services through observation recordings by social workers (data source 1), administrators (data source 2), or other citizens (data source 3).

The combination of data-collection methods should not be too taxing on any research participant or any system, such as the social service program itself. That is, data collection should not interfere greatly with the day-to-day activities of the persons providing (or responsible for collecting) the data. In some studies, you can use very simple research designs (e.g., figure 15.2a on page 304). Instead, we can use existing data to answer our research question. Thus, we don't have to bother anyone to supply them for us.

Such is the case when secondary or content data are used. When the data already exist, we put more effort into ensuring that the research question is a good fit with the data at hand. Regardless of what data-collection method is used, once the data are collected, they are subject to analysis and interpretation, the topics that follows.

> We must always consider which method of data collection will lead to the most valid and reliable data to answer a research question or to test a hypothesis.

## ANALYZING AND INTERPRETING THE DATA

Collecting data is a resource-intensive endeavor that can be expensive and time consuming—for both quantitative and qualitative research studies. The truth of this statement is realized in the data analysis step of our research study. Without a great deal of forethought about what data to collect, data can be thrown out because they cannot be organized or analyzed in any meaningful way.

In short, data analyses should always be considered when choosing a data-collection method and data source because the analysis phase must summarize, synthesize, and ultimately organize the data in an effort to have as clear-cut an answer as possible to our research question. When too much (or too little) data are collected, we can easily become bogged down (or stalled) by difficult decisions that could have been avoided with a little forethought.

After thinking through our research problem and research question and selecting a viable data collection and data source, it's worthwhile to list out the details of the type of data that will be produced. Specifically, we must think about how the data will be used in our data analysis. This exercise provides a clearer idea of the type of results we can expect.

Example

The main variable in our research question is difficulty in accessing social services. Suppose the social worker decides to collect data about this variable by giving clients (data source) a brief standardized questionnaire (data-collection method) to measure their perceptions. Many standardized questionnaires contain several subscales that, when combined, give a quantitative measure of a larger concept.

The *GSSSS* introduced in Chapter 12 (figure 12.1 on page 241), for example, is made up of three subscales: (1) relevance, (2) impact, and (3) gratification. Thus, the *GSSSS* has four scores associated with it: (1) a relevance score, (2) an impact score, (3) a gratification score, and (4) a total score—which is a measure of satisfaction. With three separate subscales, we can choose to use any one subscale (one variable), all three subscales (three variables), or a total score (one variable).

Alternatively, if data about difficulty in accessing social services were to be collected using two different data sources such as social worker (data source 1) and client (data source 2) observations, we must think about how the two data sources fit together; that is, will data from the two sources be treated as two separate variables? If so, will one variable be weighted differently in our analysis than the other? Thinking about how the data will be summarized helps us to expose any frivolous data—that is, data that are not suitable to answering our research question.

Besides collecting data about our study's variables, we must also develop a strategy to collect demographic data about the people who participate in our study. Typical demographic variables include age, gender, education level, and family income. However, we must always remember not to collect data that we will not use.

In sum, it's simply unethical to collect data we never intend to use. Demographic data provide a context for our study. Some data-collection methods, such as standardized questionnaires, include these types of data. Often, however, we are responsible for obtaining them as part of the data-collection process.

> Data analyses should always be considered when choosing a data-collection method and data source.

## Presentation and Dissemination of Findings

It's useful to think about our final research report when choosing a data-collection method and data source as it forces us to visualize how our study's findings will ultimately be presented (see chapters 19 and 20). It identifies both who the audience of the study will be and who the people interested in our findings are. Knowing who will read our research report and how it will be disseminated helps us to take more of an objective stance toward our study.

In short, we can take a third-person look at what our study will finally look like. Such objectivity helps us to think about our data-collection method(s) and data source(s) with a critical eye. Will consumers of our research study agree that the clients in fact were the best data-collection source(s)? Were the data-collection method(s) and analysis(es) sound? These are some questions that bring scrutiny to the data-collection process.

> It is unethical for you to collect data that you never intend to use.

## Selecting a Data-Collection Method

**Thinking through the steps** in the research process from the vantage point of collecting data permits us to refine the conceptualization of our study and the place of data collection within it. It also sets the context within which our data will be gathered. Clearly, there are many viable data-collection methods and data sources that can be used to answer any research question. Nevertheless, there are eight practical criteria that ultimately refine the final data-collection method(s) and data source(s) to fit the conditions of any given research study. These are:

1  Size

2  Scope

3  Program participation

4  Worker cooperation

5  Intrusion into the lives of research participants

6  Resources

7  Time

8  Data-collection methods used in previous studies

## SIZE

Yes, size does indeed matter. As with any planning activity, the more people involved, the more complicated the process and the more difficult it is to arrive at a mutual agreement. Decisions about which data-collection method and which data source to use can be stalled when several people, levels, or systems are involved. This is because individuals have different interests and opinions. Imagine if our research question about whether ethnicity is related to difficulty in accessing social services were examined on a larger scale such that all social service programs in the country were included.

The size of our research study reflects just how many people, places, or systems are represented in it.

Our study's complexity is dramatically increased because of such factors as the increased number of programs, clients, funders, government representatives, and social workers involved. The biases within each of these stakeholder groups make it much more difficult to agree upon the best data-collection method(s) and data source(s) for our study.

Our study's sample size is also a consideration. This is particularly true for positivistic studies, which aim to have a sample that is representative of the population of interest. With respect to sample size, this means that we should strive for a reasonable representation of the sampling frame.

When small-scale studies are conducted, such as a program evaluation in one social work program, the total number of people in the sampling frame may be in the hundreds or fewer. Thus, randomly selecting clients poses no real problem. On the other hand, when large-scale studies are conducted, such as when the government chooses to examine a social service program that involves thousands of people, sampling can become more problematic. If our sample is in the hundreds, it's unlikely that we would be able to successfully observe or interview all participants to collect data. Rather, a more efficient manner of data collection—say a mailed survey—may be more appropriate.

## SCOPE

The scope of our research study is the second matter to consider when selecting a data-collection method. If in our research question, for example, we are interested in gathering data on other client-related variables such as language ability, degree of social isolation, and level of assertiveness, then three different aspects of our problem area will be covered.

Scope refers to how much of our problem area will be covered.

In short, we need to consider whether one method of data collection and one data source can be used to collect all the data. It could be that client records, for example, are used to collect data about clients' language abilities, interviews with clients are conducted to collect data about social isolation, and observation methods are used to gather data about clients' assertiveness levels.

## PROGRAM PARTICIPATION

Many social work research efforts are conducted in actual real-life program settings. Program factors that can impact the choice of our data-collection methods and data sources include variables such as the program's clarity in its mandate to serve clients, its philosophical stance toward clients, and its flexibility in client record keeping. For example,

1   If a program is not able to clearly articulate a client service delivery plan, it will be difficult to distinguish between clinical activity and research activity, and to determine when the two overlap.

2   Some programs tend to base themselves on strong beliefs about a client population, which affect who can have access to clients and in what manner. A child sexual abuse investigation program, for example, may be designed specifically to avoid the problem of using multiple interviewers and multiple interviews of children in the investigation of an allegation of sexual abuse. As a result, the program would be hesitant for us to conduct interviews with the children to gather data for research purposes.

3   To save time and energy there is often considerable overlap between program client records and research data collection. The degree of willingness of a program to adapt to new record-keeping techniques will affect how we might go about collecting certain types of data.

> It's essential that we gain the support of program personnel to conduct our study.

## WORKER COOPERATION

On a general level, programs have fewer resources than they need and more clients than they can handle. Such conditions naturally lead their administrators and social workers to place intervention activity as a top priority (versus research activity). When our research study has social workers collecting data as a part of their day-to-day activities, it's highly likely that they will view data collection as additional paperwork and not as a means to expedite decision-making in their work.

Getting the cooperation of social workers within a program is a priority in any research study that relies directly or indirectly on their meaningful participation. They may be asked to schedule additional interviews with families or adjust their intervention plans to ensure that data collection occurs at the optimal time.

Given the fiscal constraints faced by programs, the workers themselves often participate as data collectors. They may end up using new client recording forms or administering questionnaires. Whatever the level of their participation, it's important for us to strive to achieve a maximum level of their cooperation. There are three factors to consider when trying to achieve the maximum cooperation from workers.

> Program workers will be affected by our study whether they are involved in the data collection process or not.

1   **We should make every effort to work effectively and efficiently with the program's staff.** Cooperation is more likely to be achieved when workers participate in the development of our study plan from the beginning. Thus, it's worthwhile to take time to explain the purpose of our study and its intended outcomes at an early stage in the study. Furthermore, administrators and frontline workers alike can provide valuable information about which data-collection method(s) may work best.

2   **We must be sensitive to the workloads of the program's staff.** Data-collection methods and sources should be designed to enhance the work of professionals. Client recording forms, for example, can be designed to provide focus for supervision meetings as well as summarize facts and worker impressions about a case.

3   **A mechanism ought to be set up by which workers receive feedback based on the data they have collected.** When a mechanism for feedback is put in place, for example, workers are more likely to show interest in the data-collection activity. When data are reported back to the program's staff before the

completion of our study, however, we must ensure that the data will not bias later measurements (if any).

## INTRUSION INTO RESEARCH PARTICIPANTS' LIVES

As we know, clients have every right to refuse participation in a research study and cannot be denied services because they are unwilling to participate. It's unethical, for example, when a member of a group-based treatment intervention has not consented to participate in the study but participant observation is used as the data-collection method.

> When clients are used as a data source, client self-determination takes precedence over research activity.

As we know from Chapter 4, this is unethical because group members may end up being observed as part of the group dynamic in the data-collection process even though they refused to give their prior consent. The data-collection method(s) we finally select must be flexible enough to allow our study to continue even with the possibility that some clients will not participate.

Ethnic and cultural consideration must also be given to the type of data-collection method used. One-on-one interviewing with Syrian refugees, for example, may be extremely terrifying for them, given the interrogation they may have experienced in their own country. Moreover, if we, as data collectors, have different ethnic backgrounds than our research participants, it's important to ensure that interpretation of the data (e.g., their behaviors, events, or expressions) are accurate from the clients' perspectives—not our own!

We must also recognize the cultural biases of standardized measuring instruments because most are based on testing with Caucasian groups. The problems here are twofold.

1  We cannot be sure whether the concept that the instrument is measuring is expressed the same way in different cultures. For instance, a standardized self-report instrument that measures family functioning may include an item such as "We have flexible rules in our household that promote individual differences," which would likely be viewed positively by North American cultures but negatively by many Asian cultures.

2  Because most standardized measuring instruments are written in English, research participants must have a good grasp of English to ensure that the data collected from them are valid and reliable. Another consideration comes into play when particular populations have been the subjects of a considerable amount of research study already.

Many aboriginal people living on reserves, for example, have been subjected to government surveys, task force inquiries, independent research projects, and perhaps even to the curiosities of social work students in their practicum settings. When a population has been extensively researched, it's even more important that we consider how the data-collection method will affect those people participating in the study. Has the data-collection method been used previously? If so, what was the nature of the data collected? Could the data be collected using less intrusive methods?

## RESOURCES

There are various costs associated with collecting data in any given research study. Materials and supplies, equipment rental, transportation costs, and training for data collectors are just a few things to consider when choosing a data-collection method. In addition, once the data are collected, additional expenses can arise when the data are entered into a computer or transcribed.

In our example, to ask clients about their perceptions about the difficulty in accessing social services via an open-ended interview may offer rich data, but we take the risk that clients will not fully answer our questions in the time allotted for the interview. On the other hand, having them complete a self-report questionnaire about access to social services is a quicker and less costly way to collect data, but it gives little sense about how well the clients understood the questions being asked of them or whether the data obtained reflect their true perceptions.

## TIME

Time constraints may be self-imposed or externally imposed. Self-imposed time constraints are personal matters we need to consider. Is our research project a part of a thesis or dissertation? What are our personal time commitments?

Externally imposed time restrictions are set by someone other than the person who is doing the study. For instance, our research study may be limited by the fiscal year of a social service program and/or funding source. Other external pressures may be political, such as an administrator who wants research results for a funding proposal or to present at a conference.

## METHODS USED IN PREVIOUS STUDIES

Having reviewed the professional literature on our problem, we need to be well aware of other data-collection methods that have been used in similar studies. We can evaluate earlier studies strengths and weaknesses of their data-collection methods and thereby make a more informed decision as to the best data-collection strategy to use in our specific situation.

Further, we need to look for diversity when evaluating other data-collection approaches; that is, we can triangulate results from separate studies that used different data-collection methods and data sources.

> An efficient data-collection method is one that collects credible data to answer a research question or test a hypothesis while requiring the least amount of time and money.

## EXAMPLE: SELECTING A METHOD

**A**s should be evident by now, choosing a data-collection method and data source for a research study is not a simple task, as illustrated in Table 17.1 on the following page. There are numerous conceptual and practical factors that must be thought through if we hope to arrive at the best possible approach to gathering data. How do we appraise all the factors to be considered in picking the best approach?

Table 17.1 on the following page is an example of a grid that can be used to assist us in making an informed decision about which data-collection method is best. The first section of the grid highlights the eight general criteria for selecting a data-collection method discussed earlier. The bottom section provides five additional criteria that were related to a specific research study we did a few years back. Can you guess what our study was all about just by looking at the five additional criteria we used to select our data-collection method(s)?

The grid can be used as a decision-making tool by subjectively rating how well each data-collection method measures up to the criteria listed in the left column of Table 17.2. We mark a "+" if the data-collection method has a favorable rating and a "−" if it has an unfavorable one. When a particular criterion is neutral, in which case it has no positive or negative effect, then a zero is indicated.

Once each data-collection method has been assessed on all the criteria, we can simply add the number of pluses and minuses to arrive at a plus or minus total for each method. This information can be used to help us make an informed decision about the best data-collection method, given all the issues raised. Based on Table 17.1, where only five data-collection methods are illustrated, the survey was the most appealing for our study.

> Time is always a consideration when our research study has a fixed completion date.

## Table 17.1
Decision-Making Grid for Choosing a Data-Collection Method

| Criteria | Five Selected Data-Collection Methods | | | | |
| --- | --- | --- | --- | --- | --- |
| | Surveys | Structured Observations | Secondary Analyses | Content Analysis | Interviewing |
| **General Criteria** | | | | | |
| 1. Size | + | 0 | + | + | + |
| 2. Scope | + | — | — | — | — |
| 3. Program participation | + | 0 | + | + | — |
| 4. Worker cooperation | + | — | + | + | — |
| 5. Intrusion into clients' lives | — | — | + | + | — |
| 6. Resources | + | — | + | + | 0 |
| 7. Time | + | — | + | + | 0 |
| 8. Previous research | + | 0 | — | — | + |
| **Criteria for Our Specific Study** | | | | | |
| 1. Student availability | + | + | 0 | 0 | + |
| 2. Student reading level | + | 0 | 0 | 0 | 0 |
| 3. School preference | + | — | — | 0 | — |
| 4. School year end | — | — | + | + | — |
| 5. Access to existing records | 0 | 0 | + | + | 0 |
| Totals ... | 8 | — 6 | 5 | 6 | — 3 |

# TRYING OUT THE METHOD

**D**ata collection is a particularly vulnerable time for a research study because it's the point where talk turns into action. So far, all the considerations that have been weighed in the selection of a data-collection method have been in theory. All people involved in our research endeavor have conveyed their suggestions and doubts on the entire process.

Once general agreement has been reached about which data-collection method(s) and data source(s) to use, it's time to test the waters. Trying out a data-collection method can occur informally by simply testing it out with available and willing research participants or, at the very least, with anyone who has not been involved with the planning of the study.

**Table 17.2**

Example of a Data-Collection Plan for Two Variables That Are Measured Three Times

| a | b | c | d | e | f | g |
|---|---|---|---|---|---|---|
| Variable | Indicator | *Who* provides the data | *How* data are gathered | *When* data are gathered | *Where* data are gathered | *Who* collects the data |
| Self-esteem | Rosenberg Self-Esteem Scale | Client | 1. Self-administered<br>2. Self-administered<br>3. Self-administered | 1. Intake<br>2. Exit interview<br>3. 3 months after intervention | 1. Waiting room<br>2. Office<br>3. Client's home | 1. Receptionist<br>2. Social Worker<br>3. Case-aide |
| Social support systems | Perceived Social Support Scale | Client | 1. Self-administered<br>2. Self-administered<br>3. Self-administered | 1. Intake<br>2. Last day of intervention<br>3. 1 month after intervention | 1. Waiting room<br>2. In therapy session<br>3. Group interview in coffee shop | 1. Case-aide<br>2. Research assistant<br>3. Researcher |

**Table 17.3**

Guidelines on How to Complete Table 17.2

---

*a* = This column is where you list specifically what dependent variable(s) you are going to measure.

*b* = This column is where you list specifically how you are going to measure each variable in column a. For example, the indicators for self-esteem and social support can be measured by many different means. In our example, we chose one standardized measuring instrument for each variable: the *Rosenberg Self-Esteem Scale* for our self-esteem variable and the *Scale of Perceived Social Support* for our social support variable.

*c* = This column is where you list specifically who is going to provide the data, via the use of your selected measuring instrument, or indicator (*b*). In a nutshell, this person, called a *data source*, is the one who is going to provide the data for the measuring instrument. Once again, a measuring instrument can be completed by a variety of different data sources.

*d* = This column is where you list specifically how the measuring instrument is going to be administered. Not only can you use a variety of indicators (*b*) to measure a variable (*a*), but you also have a variety of options for how to administer them (*d*). For example, you can read the items or questions on the measuring instrument to your clients, or you can have your clients fill out the instrument themselves. You can also have clients complete them individually with no one around or in group settings such as parks, waiting rooms, and coffee shops.

*e* = This column is where you state the exact time frame in which the measuring instrument is going to be completed. Once again, there are many options available. For example, clients could complete measuring instruments at home on Friday nights before bedtime or at the beginning of your interview.

*f* = This column, which is highly related to the previous column (*e*), is where you list the specific location where the measuring instrument will be completed. For example, you can have your clients complete the *Rosenberg Self-Esteem Scale* in your program's waiting room, at home, or in your office.

*g* = This column is where you list specifically who is going to collect the data via the measuring instrument when it's completed. After the data source (*c*) has provided the data for the measuring instrument (*b*), who's going to collect the completed instrument for analysis? And, more importantly, who is going to collate all the data into a databank for further analyses?

---

The purpose of this trial run is to ensure that those who are going to provide data understand the questions and procedures in the way that they were intended. Table 17.2 illustrates an example of how a simple data-collection plan can be formulated before a study actually begins, and Table 17.3 describes an example of how the specific cells within Table 17.2 can be completed. Both tables then can be followed to guide the data-collection process as your research study gets underway.

Data-collection methods might also be tested more formally, such as when a pilot study is conducted. A *pilot study* involves carrying out all aspects of the data-collection plan on a mini-scale. That is, a small portion of our study's actual sample is selected and run through all steps of the data-collection process.

In a pilot study, we are interested in the process of the data collection as well as the content. In short, we want to know whether our chosen data-collection method produces the expected data. Are there any unanticipated barriers to gathering the desired data? How do research participants respond to our data-collection procedures?

## IMPLEMENTATION AND EVALUATION

**T**he data-collection step of a research study can go smoothly if we act proactively. That is, we should guide and monitor the entire data-collection process according to the procedures and steps that were set out in the planning stage of our study and were tested in the pilot study (see tables 17.2 and 17.3).

## IMPLEMENTATION

The main guiding principle to implementing the selected data-collection method is that a systematic approach to data collection must be used. This means that the steps to gathering data should be methodically detailed so that there is no question about the tasks of the person(s) collecting the data—the data collector(s).

This is true whether using a positivistic or interpretive research approach. As we know, the difference between these two research approaches is that the structure of the data-collection process within an interpretive research study (chapter 9) is documented as the study progresses. By contrast, in a positivistic research study (chapter 8) the data-collection process is decided at the study's outset and provides less flexibility after the study is underway.

It must be clear from the beginning who is responsible for collecting the data. When we take on the task, there is reasonable assurance that the data collection will remain objective and be guided by our research interests. Data collection left to only one person may be a formidable task. We must determine the amount of resources available to decide what data-collection method is most realistic. Regardless of the study size, we must attempt to establish clear roles with those involved in the data-collection process.

> It must be very clear from the beginning who is responsible for collecting the data.

The clearer our research study is articulated, the less difficulty there will be in moving through all the steps of the study. In particular, it is critical to identify who will and will not be involved in the data-collection process. To further avoid mix-ups and complications, specific tasks must be spelled out for all persons involved in our study. Where will the data be stored? Who will collect them? How will the data-collection process be monitored?

Thus, it's important to establish data-collection protocols to avoid problems of biased data. In many social work research studies, frontline social workers are involved in data-collection activities as part of their day-to-day activities. They typically gather intake and referral data, write assessment notes, and even use standardized questionnaires as part of their assessments. Data collection in programs can easily be designed to serve the dual purposes of research and intervention inquiry.

> It's important to establish data-collection protocols to avoid problems of biased data.

As mentioned, everyone in a research study must agree when data will be collected, where, and in what manner. Agreement is more likely to occur when we have fully informed and involved everyone participating in our study (see tables 17.2 and 17.3).

## EVALUATION

The process of selecting a chosen data-collection method is not complete without evaluating it. For *quantitative* research studies, see a few questions you can ask (e.g., questions 207–216) on pages 489–490. For *qualitative* ones, see questions 380–386 on page 503.

Evaluation occurs at two levels. First, the strengths and weaknesses of a data-collection method(s) and data source(s) are evaluated, given the research context in which our study takes place. If, for example, data are gathered by a referring social worker about clients presenting problems, it must be acknowledged that the obtained data offer a limited (or restricted) point of view about the clients' problems. The strength of this approach may be that it was the only means for collecting the data.

A second level of evaluation is monitoring the implementation of the data-collection process itself. When data are gathered using several methods (or several sources), it's beneficial to develop a checklist of what data have been collected for each research participant. Developing a strategy for monitoring the data-collection process is especially important when the data must be collected in a timely fashion.

If pretest data are needed before a client enters a treatment program, for example, the data collection must be complete before admission occurs. Once a client has entered the program, the opportunity to collect pretest data is lost.

> A good strategy for monitoring the implementation of a data-collection method is to keep a journal of the data-collection process.

Another strategy for monitoring evaluation is to keep a journal of the data-collection process. The journal records any questions or queries that arise in the data-collection step. We may find, for example, that several research participants completing a questionnaire have difficulty understanding one particular question.

In addition, sometimes research participants have poor reading skills and require assistance with completion of some self-report standardized questionnaires. Documenting these idiosyncratic incidents accumulates important information by which to comment on our data's validity and reliability (overall credibility).

## CHAPTER RECAP

- There are many data-collection methods that can be used in research studies. They all have advantages and disadvantages.

- There are eight practical criteria you can use for selecting a data-collection method for a particular research study.

## REVIEW EXERCISES

1   What is a *data source*? What is a *data-collection method*? Discuss the differences between a data source and data-collection method. Provide social work examples throughout your discussion to illustrate your main points.

2   Discuss how data are collected and utilized within quantitative research studies, within qualitative research studies, and within mixed-methods research studies. Provide social work examples throughout your discussion to illustrate your main points.

3   First, list all eight criteria that need to be addressed when selecting a data-collection method. Second, for each criterion, discuss how this single criterion can influence the selection of a data-collection method. Provide social work examples throughout your discussion to illustrate your points.

4   What is meant by "trying out the selected data-collection method"? Provide social work examples throughout your discussion to illustrate your main points.

5   Formulate a directional hypothesis (chapter 8) that will be tested by an experimental design (i.e., figure 15.9 on page 321).

- List the various data sources that you can use to test your hypothesis.

- List the various data-collection methods that you can use for each data source.

- Discuss the strengths and limitations of each data source and each data-collection method.

- Which data source(s) and data-collection method(s) are the best ones to use in your study? Why? Defend your position using Tables 17.1 and 17.2 as guides.

6   With Question 5 in mind, create your version of Table 17.2 in relation to your hypothesis, highlighting your selected dependent variable(s) [column *a*] and data source(s) [column *c*]

7   Take a look at Table 17.1 on page 377. What other general criteria do you believe are relevant when it comes to selecting a data-collection method? What are their advantages and disadvantages? Provide a social work example throughout your discussion to illustrate your main points.

# 18

CHAPTER

## 2015 EPAS Competencies

| COMPETENCY 1 | Demonstrate Ethical and Professional Behavior |
| --- | --- |

You will learn that in order to be a successful evidence-based practitioner you have an ethical obligation to integrate three research roles into your daily practice activities as discussed in Chapter 3: (1) research consumer, (2) research partner—either as a co-researcher or research participant, and (3) creator and disseminator of research (or knowledge).

This entire chapter pertains to these three professional research-related roles when it comes to collecting, displaying, and analyzing quantitative data.

| COMPETENCY 4 | Engage in Practice-Informed Research and Research-Informed Practice |
| --- | --- |

Competency 4 also pertains to the entire chapter because you have to:

1   Evaluate the appropriateness of the quantitative data analysis that was utilized in a quantitative research study (**research consumer**—research-informed practice);

2   Participate in a quantitative research study—either as a co-researcher or research participant (**research partner**—practice-informed research). See 1 above and 3 below; and

3   Know how to collect, display, and interpret quantitative data before you actually do a quantitative research study (**creator and disseminator of research**—practice-informed research).

You'll also need to utilize evidence-based practice recommendations whenever possible; that is, you need to integrate (1) the best available research-based evidence with (2) your clinical expertise and (3) your client's values.

All of the above implies you'll need to evaluate the strengths and limitations of the research-based quantitative evidence a study produced. In short, you need to ask and then answer a simple question: How seriously should I take the findings and recommendations of any quantitative research study given the level of rigor the author used in analyzing the quantitative data?

| COMPETENCY 9 | Evaluate Practice with Individuals, Families, Groups, Organizations, & Communities |
| --- | --- |

See Competencies 1 and 4.

# Analyzing Quantitative Data

| | | |
|---|---|---|
| CHAPTERS 1 & 3 | Step 1. | Understanding the Research Process |
| CHAPTER 2 | Step 2. | Formulating Research Questions |
| CHAPTER 4 APPENDIXES A–C | Step 3. | Reviewing the Literature Evaluating the Literature |
| CHAPTERS 5 & 6 | Step 4. | Being Aware of Ethical and Cultural Issues |
| CHAPTERS 7–10 | Step 5. | Selecting a Research Approach |
| CHAPTERS 11 & 12 | Step 6. | Specifying How Variables Are Measured |
| CHAPTER 13 | Step 7. | Selecting a Sample |
| CHAPTERS 14 & 15 | Step 8. | Selecting a Research Design |
| CHAPTERS 16 & 17 | Step 9. | Selecting a Data-Collection Method |
| CHAPTERS 18 & 19 | Step 10. | Analyzing the Data |
| CHAPTERS 20 & 21 | Step 11. | Writing the Research Report |

# Analyzing Quantitative Data

"Oh my! The quantitative data doesn't support our hypothesis. But for some reason I'm very happy with the results."

ENTERING DATA INTO COMPUTERS

DESCRIPTIVE STATISTICS

    Frequency Distributions

    Measures of Central Tendency

        *Mode*

        *Median*

        *Mean*

    Measures of Variability

        *Range*

        *Standard Deviation*

INFERENTIAL STATISTICS

    Statistics That Determine Associations

        *Chi-Square*

        *Correlation*

    Statistics That Determine Differences

        *Dependent t-Tests*

        *Independent t-Tests*

        *Analysis of Variance*

EVALUATING A QUANTITATIVE ANALYSIS

CHAPTER RECAP

REVIEW EXERCISES

CHAPTER

# 18

CHAPTER OUTLINE

AFTER QUANTITATIVE DATA ARE COLLECTED as illustrated in the previous chapter, they need to be analyzed—the purpose of this chapter. To be honest, a thorough understanding of quantitative statistical methods is far beyond the scope of this book and would necessitate more in-depth study, through taking one or more statistics courses. Instead, we briefly describe a select group of basic statistical analytical methods that are used frequently in many quantitative and qualitative social work research studies. Our emphasis is not on providing and calculating formulas, but rather on helping the reader to understand the underlying rationale for their use.

We present two basic groups of statistical procedures. The first group is called *descriptive statistics*; these procedures simply describe and summarize one or more variables for a sample or population. They provide information about only the group included in the study.

The second group is called *inferential statistics*; these procedures determine if we can generalize findings derived from a sample to the population from which the sample was drawn. In other words, knowing what we know about a particular sample, can we infer that the rest of the population is similar to the sample that we have studied?

Before you read farther, we encourage you to reread Chapter 11 on levels of measurement. It's extremely important for you to have a sound understanding of the four levels of measurement before you dive into statistics.

## ENTERING DATA INTO COMPUTERS

The use of computers has revolutionized the analysis of quantitative and qualitative data. Where previous generations of researchers had to rely on hand-cranked adding machines to calculate every small step in a data analysis, today we can enter raw scores into a personal computer and with few complications direct the computer program to execute just about any statistical test imaginable. Seconds later, the results are available.

While the process is truly miraculous, the risk is that, even though we have conducted the correct statistical analysis, we may not understand what the results mean, a factor that will almost certainly affect how we interpret the data. We can code data from all four levels of measurement into a computer for any given data analysis (see chapter 9). The coding of nominal data is perhaps the most complex because we have to create categories that correspond to certain possible responses for a variable.

One type of nominal-level data that is often gathered from research participants is *place of birth*. If, for the purposes of our study, we were interested in whether our research participants were born in either Canada or the United States, we would assign only three categories to *place of birth*:

1  Canada
2  United States
9  Other

The *other* category (9) appears routinely at the end of lists of categories and acts as a catchall to cover any category that may have been omitted.

When entering nominal-level data into a computer, because we do not want to enter *Canada* every time the response on the questionnaire is *Canada*, we may assign it the code number 1 so that all we have to enter is 1. Similarly, the *United States* may be assigned the number 2, and "other" may be assigned the number 9.

These numbers have no mathematical meaning. We are not saying that Canada is better than the United States because it comes first, or that the United States is twice as good as Canada because the number assigned to it is twice as high. We are merely using numbers as a shorthand device to record *qualitative* differences: differences in *kind*, not in *amount*.

Most coding for ordinal-, interval-, and ratio-level data is simply a matter of entering the final score, or number, from the measuring instrument that was used to measure the variable directly into the computer. If a person scored a 45 on a standardized measuring instrument, for example, the number 45 would be entered into the computer. Although almost all data entered into computers are in the form of numbers, we need to know at what level of measurement the data exist so that we can choose the appropriate statistic(s) to describe and compare the variables.

As you know from Chapter 11 about the four different measurement levels, let's turn to the first group of statistics that can be helpful for the analyses of data—descriptive statistics. This would is an excellent time to review Chapter 11 as this chapter assumes you know Chapter 11's content inside and out—and don't forget backwards.

# DESCRIPTIVE STATISTICS

**D**escriptive statistics are commonly used in most quantitative and qualitative research studies. They describe and summarize a variable(s) of interest and portray how that particular variable is distributed in the sample, or population. Before looking at descriptive statistics, however, let's examine a social work research example that will be used throughout this chapter.

Thea Black is a social worker who works in a treatment foster care program. Her program focuses on children who have behavioral problems who are placed with "treatment" foster care parents. These parents are supposed to have parenting skills that will help them provide for the children's special needs.

Thus, Thea's program also teaches parenting skills to these treatment foster care parents. She assumes that newly recruited foster parents are not likely to know much about parenting children who have special needs. Therefore, she believes that they would benefit from a training program that teaches these skills in order to help them deal effectively with the special needs of these children who will soon be living with them.

Thea hopes that her parenting skills training program will increase the knowledge about parental management skills for the parents who attend. She assumes that with such training the foster parents will be in a better position to support and provide clear limits for their foster children.

After offering the training program for several months, Thea became curious about whether the foster care providers who attended the program were, indeed, lacking in knowledge of parental management skills as she first believed (her tentative hypothesis).

> Descriptive statistics describe and summarize a variable and portray how that particular variable is distributed in the sample, or population.

She was fortunate to find a valid and reliable standardized instrument that measures the knowledge of such parenting skills, the *Parenting Skills Scale* (*PSS*). Thea decided to find out for herself how much the newly recruited parents knew about parenting skills—clearly a descriptive research question.

At the beginning of one of her training sessions (before they were exposed to her skills training program), she handed out the *PSS*, asking the twenty individuals in attendance to complete it and also to include data about their gender, years of education, and whether they had ever participated in a parenting skills training program before. All of these variables could be potentially extraneous ones that might influence the level of knowledge of parenting skills of the twenty participants.

For each foster care parent, Thea calculated the *PSS* score, called a *raw score* because it has not been sorted or analyzed in any way. The total score possible on the *PSS* is 100, with higher scores indicating greater knowledge of parenting skills. The scores for the PSS scale, as well as the other data collected from the twenty parents, are listed in Table 18.1 on the following page.

At this point, Thea stopped to consider how she could best utilize the data that she had collected. She had data at three different levels of measurement. At the nominal level, Thea had collected data on gender (3rd column), and whether the parents had any previous parenting skills training (4th column). Each of these variables can be categorized into two responses.

The scores on the *PSS* (2nd column) are ordinal because, although the data are sequenced from highest to lowest, the differences between units cannot be placed on an equally spaced continuum. Nevertheless, many measures in the social sciences are treated as if they are at an interval level, even though equal distances between scale points cannot be proved. This assumption is important because it allows for the use of inferential statistics on such data.

Finally, the data on years of formal education (5th column) that were collected by Thea are clearly at the ratio level of measurement because there are equally distributed points and the scale has an absolute zero.

In sum, it seemed to Thea that the data could be used in at least two ways. First, the data collected about each variable could be described to provide a picture of the characteristics of the group of foster care parents. This would call for descriptive statistics. Second, she might look for relationships between some of the variables about which she had collected data, procedures that would utilize inferential statistics. For now let us begin by looking at how the first type of descriptive statistic can be used with Thea's data set.

On a general level, descriptive statistics can be divided into three subgroups of statistics (Weinbach & Grinnell, 2017):

1  Frequency distributions
2  Measures of central tendency
3  Measures of variability

**Table 18.1**

Data Collection for Four Variables from Foster Care Providers

| Case Number | PSS Score | Gender | Previous Training | Years of Education |
|---|---|---|---|---|
| 01 | 95 | Male | No | 12 |
| 02 | 93 | Female | Yes | 12 |
| 03 | 93 | Male | No | 08 |
| 04 | 93 | Female | No | 12 |
| 05 | 90 | Male | Yes | 12 |
| 06 | 90 | Female | No | 12 |
| 07 | 84 | Male | No | 14 |
| 08 | 84 | Female | No | 18 |
| 09 | 82 | Male | No | 10 |
| 10 | 82 | Female | No | 12 |
| 11 | 80 | Male | No | 12 |
| 12 | 80 | Female | No | 11 |
| 13 | 79 | Male | No | 12 |
| 14 | 79 | Female | Yes | 12 |
| 15 | 79 | Female | No | 16 |
| 16 | 79 | Male | No | 12 |
| 17 | 79 | Female | No | 11 |
| 18 | 72 | Female | No | 14 |
| 19 | 71 | Male | No | 15 |
| 20 | 55 | Female | Yes | 12 |

# FREQUENCY DISTRIBUTIONS

One of the simplest procedures that Thea can employ is to develop a frequency distribution of her data. Constructing a frequency distribution involves counting the occurrences of each value, or category, of the variable and ordering them in some fashion. This *absolute* or *simple frequency distribution* allows us to see quickly how certain values of a variable are distributed in our sample.

The *mode,* or the most commonly occurring score, can be easily spotted in a simple frequency distribution (see table 18.2 on the right). In this example, the mode is 79, a score obtained by five parents on the *PSS* scale. The highest and the lowest scores are also quickly identifiable. The top score was 95, while the foster care parent who performed the least well on the *PSS* scored 55.

**Table 18.2**

Frequency Distribution
(from table 18.1 above)

| PSS Score | Absolute Frequency |
|---|---|
| 95 | 1 |
| 93 | 3 |
| 90 | 2 |
| 84 | 2 |
| 82 | 2 |
| 80 | 2 |
| 79 | 5 |
| 72 | 1 |
| 71 | 1 |
| 55 | 1 |

**Table 18.3**

Cumulative Frequency and Percentage Distribution of Parental Skill
Scores (from table 18.1)

| PSS Score | Absolute | Cumulative | Percentage Distribution |
|-----------|----------|------------|-------------------------|
| 95 | 1 | 1 | 5 |
| 93 | 3 | 4 | 15 |
| 90 | 2 | 6 | 10 |
| 84 | 2 | 8 | 10 |
| 82 | 2 | 10 | 10 |
| 80 | 2 | 12 | 10 |
| 79 | 5 | 17 | 25 |
| 72 | 1 | 18 | 5 |
| 71 | 1 | 19 | 5 |
| 55 | 1 | 20 | 5 |
| Totals . . . | 20 | | 100 |

There are several other ways to present frequency data. A commonly used method that can be easily integrated into a simple frequency distribution table is the *cumulative frequency distribution*, shown in Table 18.3 above.

In Thea's data set, the highest *PSS* score, 95, was obtained by only one individual. The group of individuals who scored 93 or above on the *PSS* measure includes four foster care parents. If we want to know how many scored 80 or above, if we look at the number across from 80 in the cumulative frequency column, we can quickly see that twelve of the parents scored 80 or better.

Other tables use percentages rather than frequencies, sometimes referred to as *percentage distributions*, shown in the far-right column in Table 18.3. Each of these numbers represents the percentage of participants who obtained each *PSS* value. Five individuals, for example, scored 79 on the *PSS*. Since there were a total of 20 foster care parents, five out of the twenty, or one-quarter of the total, obtained a score of 79. This corresponds to 25 percent of the participants.

**Table 18.4**

Grouped Frequency Distribution of Parental Skill Scores
(from table 18.1)

| PSS Score | Absolute | Cumulative | Absolute Percentage |
|-----------|----------|------------|---------------------|
| 90–100 | 6 | 6 | 30 |
| 80–89 | 6 | 12 | 30 |
| 70–79 | 7 | 19 | 35 |
| 60–69 | 0 | 19 | 0 |
| 50–59 | 1 | 20 | 5 |
| Totals . . . | 20 | | 100 |

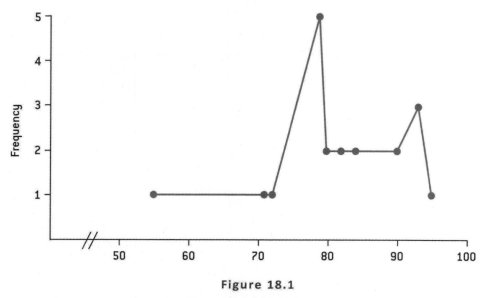

**Figure 18.1**

Frequency Polygon of Parental Scores (from table 18.2)

Finally, *grouped frequency distributions* are used to simplify a table by grouping the variable into equal-sized ranges, as shown in Table 18.4 on the previous page. Both absolute and cumulative frequencies and percentages can also be displayed using this format. Each is calculated in the same way that was previously described for nongrouped data, and the interpretation is identical.

Looking at the absolute frequency column, for example, we can quickly identify the fact that seven of the foster care parents scored in the 70–79 range on the *PSS*. By looking at the cumulative frequency column, we can see that twelve of twenty parents scored 80 or better on the *PSS*. Further, from the absolute percentage column, it's clear that 30 percent of the foster parents scored in the 80–89 range on the parenting skills scale.

Note that each of the other variables in Thea's data set could also be displayed in frequency distributions. Displaying years of education in a frequency distribution, for example, would provide a snapshot of how this variable is distributed in Thea's sample of foster care parents. However, with two category nominal variables, such as gender (male, female) and previous parenting skills training (yes, no), cumulative frequencies become less meaningful, and the data are better described as percentages.

Thea noted that 55 percent of the foster care parents who attended the training workshop were women (obviously the other 45 percent were men) and that 20 percent of the parents had already received some form of parenting skills training (while a further 80 percent had not been trained).

## Measures of Central Tendency

We can also display the values obtained on the *PSS* in the form of a graph. A frequency polygon is one of the simplest ways of charting frequencies. The graph in Figure 18.1 displays the data that we had previously put in Table 18.2. The *PSS* score is plotted in terms of how many of the foster care parents obtained each score. As can be seen from Figure 18.1 above, most of the scores fall between 79 and 93. The one extremely low score of 55 is also quickly noticeable in such a graph because it's so far removed from the rest of the values.

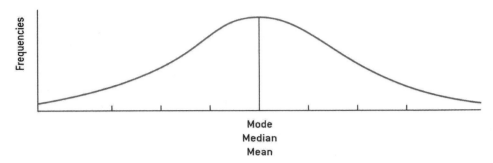

**Figure 18.2**

The Normal Distribution

A frequency polygon allows us to make a quick analysis of how closely the distribution fits the shape of a normal curve. A normal curve, also known as a *bell-shaped distribution* or a *normal distribution,* is a frequency polygon in which the greatest number of responses fall in the middle of the distribution and fewer scores appear at the extremes of either very high or very low scores (see figure 18.2 above).

Many variables in the social sciences are assumed to be distributed in the shape of a normal curve. Low intelligence, for example, is thought to be relatively rare as compared to the number of individuals with average intelligence. On the other end of the continuum, extremely gifted individuals are also relatively uncommon. Of course, not all variables are distributed in the shape of a normal curve. Some are such that a large number of people do very well (as Thea found in her sample of foster care parents and their parenting skill levels). Other variables, such as juggling ability, for example, would be charted showing a fairly substantial number of people performing poorly.

Frequency distributions of still other variables would show that some people do well, and some people do poorly, but not many fall in between. What is important to remember about distributions is that, although all different sorts are possible, most statistical procedures assume that there is a normal distribution of the variable in question in the population.

When looking at how variables are distributed in samples and populations it's common to use measures of *central tendency*, such as,

1  Mode
2  Median
3  Mean

which help us to identify where the typical or the average score can be found. These measures are used so often because not only do they provide a useful summary of the data, they also provide a common denominator for comparing groups to each other.

### MODE

As mentioned earlier, the mode is the score, or value, that occurs the most often—the value with the highest frequency. In Thea's data set of parental skills scores the mode is 79, with five foster care parents obtaining this value. The mode is particularly useful for nominal level data. Knowing what score occurred the most often, however, provides little information about the other scores and how they are distributed in the sample or population.

Because the mode is the least precise of all the measures of central tendency, the median and the mean are better descriptors of ordinal level data and above. We now turn our attention to the second measure of central tendency, the median.

### MEDIAN

The median is the score that divides a distribution into two equal parts or portions. In order to do this, we must rank-order the scores, so at least an ordinal level of measurement is required. In Thea's sample of twenty *PSS* scores, the median would be the score above which the top ten scores lie and below which the bottom ten fall. As can be seen in Table 18.2, the top ten scores finish at 82, and the bottom ten scores start at 80. In this example, the median is 81, since it falls between 82 and 80.

### MEAN

The mean is the most sophisticated measure of central tendency and is useful for interval or ratio levels of measurement. It's also one of the most commonly utilized statistics. A mean is calculated by summing the individual values and dividing by the total number of values. The mean of Thea's sample is $95 + 93 + 93 + 93 + 90 + 90 + ... 72 + 71 + 55/20 = 81.95$. In this example, the obtained mean of 82 (we rounded off for the sake of clarity) is larger than the mode of 79 or the median of 81.

The mean is one of the previously mentioned statistical procedures that assumes that a variable will be distributed normally throughout a population. If this is not an accurate assumption, then the median might be a better descriptor. The mean is also best used with relatively large sample sizes where extreme scores (such as the lowest score of 55 in Thea's sample) have less influence.

## MEASURES OF VARIABILITY

While measures of central tendency provide valuable information about a set of scores, we are also interested in knowing how the scores scatter themselves around the center. A mean does not give a sense of how widely distributed the scores may be. This is provided by measures of variability such as the range and the standard deviation. There are many types of variability. We will only discuss two:

1   Range
2   Standard deviation

### RANGE

The range is the distance between the minimum and the maximum score. The larger the range, the greater the amount of variation of scores in the distribution. The range is calculated by subtracting the lowest score from the highest. In Thea's sample, the range is 40 (95 – 55). The range does not assume equal interval data. It is, like the mean, sensitive to deviant values because it depends on only the two extreme scores.

We could have a group of four scores ranging from 10 to 20: 10, 14, 19, and 20, for example. The range of this sample would be 10 (20 – 10). If one additional score that was substantially different from the first set of four scores was included, this would change the range dramatically. In this example, if a fifth score of 45 was added, the range of the sample would become 35 (45 – 10), a number that would suggest quite a different picture of the variability of the scores.

### STANDARD DEVIATION

The standard deviation is the most utilized indicator of dispersion. It provides a picture of how the scores distribute themselves around the mean. Used in combination with the

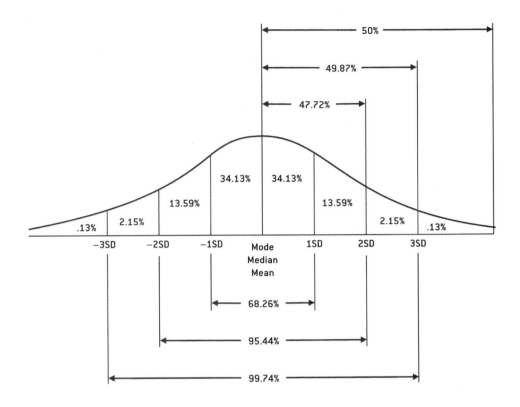

**Figure 18.3**

Proportions of the Normal Curve

mean, the standard deviation provides a great deal of information about the sample or population without our ever needing to see the raw scores. In a normal distribution of scores (as described previously) there are six standard deviations: three below the mean and three above, as is shown in Figure 18.3 above.

In this perfect model we always know that 34.13 percent of the scores of the sample fall within 1 standard deviation above the mean, and another 34.13 percent fall within 1 standard deviation below the mean. Thus, a total of 68.26 percent, or about two-thirds of the scores, is between +1 standard deviation and −1 standard deviation from the mean. This leaves almost one-third of the scores to fall farther away from the mean, with 15.87 percent (50 to 34.13 percent) above +1 standard deviation, and 15.87 percent (50 to 34.13 percent) below 1 standard deviation.

In total, when we look at the proportion of scores that fall between +2 and −2 standard deviations, 95.44 percent of scores can be expected to be found within these parameters. Furthermore, 99.74 percent of the scores fall between +3 standard deviations and −3 standard deviations about the mean. Thus, finding scores that fall beyond 3 standard deviations above and below the mean should be a rare occurrence.

The standard deviation has the advantage, like the mean, of taking all values into consideration in its computation. Also similar to the mean, it's utilized with interval or ratio levels of measurement and assumes a normal distribution of scores.

Several different samples of scores could have the same mean, but the variation around the mean, as provided by the standard deviation, could be quite different, as is shown in Figure 18.4a. Two different distributions could have unequal means and equal standard deviations, as in Figure 18.4b, or unequal means and unequal standard deviations, as in Figure 18.4c.

The standard deviation of the scores of Thea's foster care parents was calculated to be 10. Again, assuming that the variable of knowledge about parenting skills is normally distributed in the population of foster care parents, the results of the *PSS* scores from the sample of parents about whom we are making inferences can be shown in a distribution like Figure 18.5 on the following page.

As can also be seen in Figure 18.5, the score that would include 2 standard deviations, 102, is beyond the total possible score of 100 on the test. This is because the distribution of the scores in Thea's sample of parents does not entirely fit a normal distribution. The one extremely low score of 55 (see table 18.1) obtained by one foster care parent would have affected the mean as well as the standard deviation.

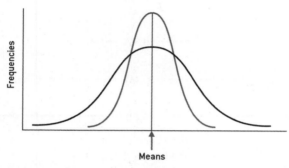

(a) Equal means, unequal standard deviations

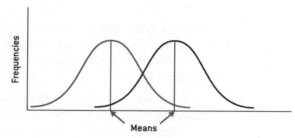

(b) Unequal means, equal standard deviations

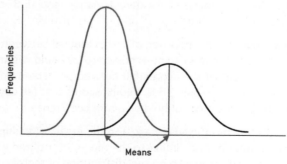

(c) Unequal means, unequal standard deviations

**Figure 18.4**

Variations in the Normal Distribution

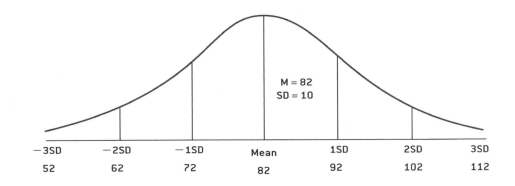

**Figure 18.5**

Distribution of Parental Skills Scores

## INFERENTIAL STATISTICS

The goal of inferential statistical tests is to rule out chance as the explanation for finding either associations between variables or differences between variables in our samples. Because we can rarely study an entire population, we are almost always dealing with samples drawn from that population. The danger is that we might make conclusions about a particular population based on a sample that is uncharacteristic of the population it's supposed to represent.

For example, perhaps the group of foster parents in Thea's training session happened to have an unusually high level of knowledge of parenting skills. If she assumed that all the rest of the foster parents that she might train in the future were as knowledgeable, she would be overestimating their knowledge, a factor that could have a negative impact on the way she conducts her training program.

To counteract the possibility that the sample is uncharacteristic of the general population, statistical tests take a conservative position as to whether we can conclude that there are relationships between the variables within our sample. The guidelines to indicate the likelihood that we have indeed found a relationship or difference that fits the population of interest are called *probability levels.*

The convention in most social science research is that variables are significantly associated or groups are significantly different if we are relatively certain that in nineteen samples out of twenty (or 95 times out of 100) from a particular population, we would find the same relationship. This corresponds to a probability level of .05, written as: $p < .05$.

Probability levels are usually provided along with the results of the statistical test to demonstrate how confident we are that the results actually indicate statistically significant differences. If a probability level is greater than .05 (e.g., .06, .10), this indicates that we did not find a statistically significant difference.

> Inferential statistics try to rule out chance as the explanation for finding either associations between variables or differences between variables in our samples.

### STATISTICS THAT DETERMINE ASSOCIATIONS

There are many statistics that can determine whether there is an association between two variables. We will briefly discuss two:

1  Chi-square

2  Correlation

**Table 18.5**

Frequencies (and Percentages) of Gender by Previous Training
(from table 18.1)

| | Previous Training? | | |
|---|---|---|---|
| Gender | Yes | No | Total |
| Male | 1 (11) | 8 (89) | 9 |
| Female | 3 (27) | 8 (73) | 11 |
| Totals . . . | 4 (20) | 16 (80) | 20 (100) |

## CHI-SQUARE

The chi-square test requires measurements of variables at only the nominal or ordinal level. Thus, it's very useful because much data in social work are gathered at these two levels of measurement. In general, the chi-square test looks at whether specific values of one variable tend to be associated with specific values of another.

In short, we use it to determine whether two variables are related. It cannot be used to determine whether one variable caused another, however. In thinking about the foster care parents who were in her training program, Thea was aware that women are more typically responsible for caring for their own children than men. Even if they are not mothers themselves, they are often in professions such as teaching and social work where they are caretakers.

Thus, she wondered whether there might be a relationship between gender and previous training in parenting skills, such that women were less likely to have taken such training because they already felt confident in their knowledge of parenting skills. As a result, her one-tailed hypothesis was that fewer women than men would have previously taken parenting skills training courses. Thea could examine this possibility with her twenty foster care parents using a chi-square test. In terms of gender, Thea had data from the nine (45 percent) men and eleven (55 percent) women. Of the total group, four (20 percent) had previous training in foster care training, while sixteen (80 percent) had not.

As shown in Table 18.5, the first task was for Thea to count the number of men and women who had previous training and the number of men and women who did not have previous training. She put these data in one of the four categories in Table 18.5. The actual numbers are called *observed frequencies*. It's helpful to transform these raw data into (percentages), making comparisons between categories much easier.

We can, however, still not tell simply by looking at the observed frequencies whether there is a statistically significant relationship between gender (male or female) and previous training (yes or no). To do this, the next step is to look at how much the observed frequencies differ from what we would expect to see if, in fact, if there was no relationship. These are called *expected frequencies*. Without going through all the calculations, the chi-square table would now look like Table 18.6 for Thea's data set.

Because the probability level of the obtained chi-square value in Table 18.6 is greater than .05, Thea did not find any statistical relationship between gender and previous training in parenting skills. Thus, statistically speaking, men were no more likely than women to have received previous training in parenting skills; her research hypothesis was not supported by the data.

**Table 18.6**

Chi-Square Table for Gender by Previous
Training (from table 18.5)

|  | Previous Training? | |
| --- | --- | --- |
| Gender | Yes | No |
| Male | | |
| Observed | 1.0 | 8.0 |
| Expected | 1.8 | 7.2 |
| Female | | |
| Observed | 3.0 | 8.0 |
| Expected | 2.2 | 8.8 |

Note: $\chi^2 = 0.8$; $df = 1$; $p > .05$

## CORRELATION

Tests of correlation investigate the strength of the relationship between two variables. As with the chi-square test, correlation cannot be used to imply causation, only association. Correlation is applicable to data at the interval and ratio levels of measurement. Correlational values are always decimalized numbers, never exceeding ±1.00.

The size of the obtained correlation value indicates the strength of the association, or relationship, between the two variables. The closer a correlation is to zero, the less likely it is that a relationship exists between the two variables. The plus and minus signs indicate the direction of the relationship. Either high positive (close to +1.00) or high negative numbers (close −1.00) signify strong relationships.

In most positive correlations, though, the scores vary similarly, either increasing or decreasing. Thus, as parenting skills increase, so does self-esteem, for example. A negative correlation, in contrast, simply means that as one variable increases the other decreases. An example would be that as parenting skills increase the stresses experienced by foster parents decrease.

Thea may wonder whether there is a relationship between the foster parents' years of education and score on the *PSS* knowledge test. She might reason that the more years of education completed, the more likely the parents would have greater knowledge about parenting skills.

To investigate the one-tailed hypothesis that years of education are positively related to knowledge of parenting skills, Thea can correlate the *PSS* scores with each person's number of years of formal education using one of the most common correlational tests, Pearson's *r*. The obtained correlation between *PSS* score and years of education in this example is $r = -.10$, $p > .05$. It was in the opposite direction of what she predicted. This negative correlation is close to zero, and its probability level is greater than .05. Thus, in Thea's sample, the parents' *PSS* scores are not related to their educational levels.

If the resulting correlation coefficient (*r*) had been positive and statistically significant ($p < .05$), it would have indicated that as the knowledge levels of the parents increased so would their years of formal education. If the correlation coefficient had been statistically significant but negative, this would be interpreted as showing that as years of formal education increased, knowledge scores decreased.

If a correlational analysis is misinterpreted, it's likely to be the case that the researcher implied causation rather than simply identifying an association between the two variables. If Thea were to have found a statistically significant positive correlation between knowledge and education levels and had explained this to mean that the high knowledge scores were a result of higher education levels, she would have interpreted the statistic incorrectly.

## STATISTICS THAT DETERMINE DIFFERENCES

There are three commonly used statistical procedures to determine whether two or more groups are statistically different from one another.

1 Dependent *t*-tests

2 Independent *t*-tests

3 Analysis of variance (ANOVA)

*T*-tests are used with only two groups of scores, whereas ANOVA is used when there are more than two groups. All are characterized by having a dependent variable at the interval or ratio level of measurement, and an independent, or grouping, variable at either the nominal or ordinal level of measurement. Several assumptions underlie the use of both *t*-tests and ANOVA.

First, it's assumed that the dependent variable is normally distributed in the population from which the samples were drawn. Second, it's assumed that the variance of the scores of the dependent variable in the different groups is roughly the same. This assumption is called *homogeneity of variance*. Third, it's assumed that the samples are randomly drawn from the population. Nevertheless, as mentioned in Chapter 15 on group research designs, it's a common occurrence in social work that we can neither randomly select from a population nor randomly assign individuals to either the experimental or the control group. In many cases this is because we are dealing with already preformed groups, such as Thea's foster care parents.

Breaking the assumption of randomization, however, presents a serious drawback to the interpretation of the research findings, which must be noted in the limitations and the interpretations section of the final research report. One possible difficulty that might result from nonrandomization is that the sample may be uncharacteristic of the larger population in some manner.

It's important, therefore, that the results not be used inferentially; that is, the findings must not be generalized to the general population. The design of the research study is thus reduced to a descriptive level, being relevant to only those individuals included in the sample.

### DEPENDENT *T*-TESTS

Dependent *t*-tests are used to compare two groups of scores from the same individuals. The most frequent example in social work research is looking at how a group of individuals change from before they receive a social work intervention (pre) to afterward (post). Thea may have decided that although she knew the knowledge levels of the foster care parents before receiving training was interesting, it did not give her any idea about whether her program helped the parents to improve their skill levels. In other words her research question became: After being involved in the program, did parents know more about parenting skills than before they started? Her hypothesis was that knowledge of parenting skills would improve after participation in her program.

Thea managed to contact all the foster care parents in the original group (group A) one week after they had graduated from the program and asked them to fill out the *PSS*

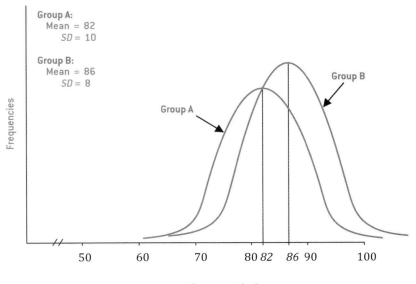

**Figure 18.6**

Frequency Distributions of *PSS* Scores from Two Groups of Foster Care Providers

knowledge questionnaire once again. Because it was the same group of people who were responding twice to the same questionnaire, the dependent *t*-test was appropriate.

Using the same set of scores collected by Thea previously as the pretest, the mean *PSS* was 82, with a standard deviation of 10. The mean score of the foster care parents after they completed the program was calculated as 86, with a standard deviation of 8.

A *t*-value of 3.9 was obtained, significant at the .05 level, indicating that the levels of parenting skills significantly increased after the foster care parents participated in the skills training program. The results suggest that the average parenting skills of this particular group of foster care parents significantly improved (from 82 to 86) after they had participated in Thea's program.

### INDEPENDENT *T*-TESTS

Independent *t*-tests are used for two groups of scores that have no relationship to each other. If Thea had *PSS* scores from one group of foster care parents and then collected more *PSS* scores from a second group of foster care parents, for example, these two groups would be considered independent, and the independent *t*-test would be the appropriate statistical analysis to determine whether there was a statistically significant difference between the means of the two groups' *PSS* scores.

Thea decided to compare the average *PSS* score for the first group of foster care parents (group A) with the average *PSS* score of parents in her next training program (group B). This would allow her to see whether the first group (group A) had been unusually talented or conversely were less well versed in parenting skills than the second group (group B). Her hypothesis was that there would be no differences in the level of knowledge of parenting skills between the two groups.

Because Thea had *PSS* scores from two different groups of participants (groups A and B), the correct statistical test to identify whether there are any statistical differences between the means of the two groups is the independent *t*-test. Let's use the same set of numbers that we previously used in the example of the dependent *t*-test in this analysis, this time considering the posttest *PSS* scores as the scores of the second group of foster care parents.

As can be seen from Figure 18.6, the mean *PSS* of Group A was 82 and the standard deviation was 10. Group B scored an average of 86 on the *PSS*, with a standard deviation of 8. Although the means of the two groups are four points apart, the standard deviations in the distribution of each are fairly large, so there is considerable overlap between the two groups. This would suggest that statistically significant differences will not be found.

The obtained *t*-value to establish whether this four-point difference (86 − 82) between the means for two groups is statistically significant was calculated to be $t = 1.6$ with a $p >$ .05. The two groups were thus not statistically different from one another, and Thea's hypothesis was supported.

Note, however, that Thea's foster care parents were not randomly assigned to each group, thus breaking one of the assumptions of the *t*-test. As discussed earlier, this is a serious limitation to the interpretation of the study's results. We must be especially careful not to generalize the findings beyond the groups included in the study.

Also note that in the previous example, when using the same set of numbers but a dependent *t*-test, we found a statistically significant difference. This is because the dependent *t*-test analysis is more robust than the independent *t*-test, because having the same participant fill out the questionnaire twice, under two different conditions, controls for many extraneous variables, such as individual differences, that could negatively influence an analysis of independent samples.

## ANALYSIS OF VARIANCE

A one-way ANOVA is the extension of an independent *t*-test that uses three or more groups. Each set of scores is from a different group of participants. For example, Thea might use the scores on the *PSS* test from the first group of foster care parents from whom she collected data before they participated in her program, but she might also collect data from a second and a third group of parents before they received the training. The test for significance of an ANOVA is called an *F*-test.

We could actually use an ANOVA procedure on only two groups, and the result would be identical to the *t*-test. Unlike the *t*-test, however, obtaining a significant F-value in a one-way ANOVA does not complete the analysis. Because ANOVA looks at differences between three or more groups, a significant *F*-value only tells us that there is a statistically significant difference among the groups. It does not tell us between which ones. To identify this, we need to do a post hoc test.

A variety is available, such as Duncan's multiple range, Tukey's honestly significant difference test, and Newman-Keuls, and they are provided automatically by most computer statistics programs.  But one caution applies: a post hoc test should be used only after finding a significant *F*-value, because some of the post hoc tests are more sensitive than the *F*-test and so might find significance when the *F*-test does not. Generally, we should use the most conservative test first, in this case the *F*-test.

In the example of Thea's program, let's say that she collected data on a total of three different groups of foster care parents. The first group of foster care parents scored an average of 82 on the *PSS* (standard deviation 10). The second group scored an average of 86 (standard deviation 8), and the mean score of the third group was 88 with a standard deviation of 7.

The obtained *F*-value for the one-way ANOVA is 2.63, with a $p >$ .05. Thus, we must conclude that there are no statistically significant differences between the means of the groups (i.e., 82, 86, and 88). Because the *F*-value was not significant, we would not conduct any post hoc tests. This finding would be interesting to Thea because it suggests that all three groups of foster care parents started out with approximately the same knowledge levels, on average, before receiving training.

## EVALUATING A QUANTITATIVE ANALYSIS

**A**ssessing the overall credibility of a quantitative data analysis can be a daunting task at the best of times. Nevertheless, you can use Appendix A and ask a series of questions about a particular data analysis (e.g., questions 217–238 on pages 490–492).

How to evaluate the overall creditability of a quantitative data analysis is totally up to you—and only you. You are the one who must ask and answer questions. You just don't want to ask questions without knowing why you're asking them. More important, you need to address two extremely difficult tasks:

> Two people can assess the same quantitative data analysis and come up with two different opinions in respect to its overall credibility and usefulness.

1 You must have a rationale for why you're asking each question in the first place. Appendix A only lists potential questions you can ask. Can you guess why each one was listed and what importance your answer to each question has for your overall evaluation of the research study?

2 You also must have some kind of idea of what you're going to do with your answer to each question. For example, question 227 on page 491 asks, "Apart from statistically significant changes, was the clinical significance of any improvements discussed (if applicable)?" Let's say your answer was "no". What are you going to do with your answer? That is, how are you going to use it in your overall evaluation of the study's creditability? Now what about if your answer was "yes"?

## CHAPTER RECAP

- On a simple level there are two types of statistics: descriptive and inferential.

- Descriptive statistics describe and summarize a variable(s) of interest and portray how that particular variable is distributed in the sample or population.

- Inferential statistics try to rule out chance as the explanation for finding either associations between variables or differences between variables in samples drawn from a population.

- Descriptive statistics can be broken down into three categories: frequency distributions, measures of central tendency,

and measures of variability.

- Measures of central tendency contain three groups of statistics: mode, median, and mean.

- Measures of variability contain two groups of statistics: range and standard deviation.

- Inferential statistics can be broken down into two categories: statistics that determine associations (i.e., chi-square, correlation) and statistics that determine differences (i.e., dependent *t*-tests, independent *t*-tests, one-way analysis of variance).

## REVIEW EXERCISES

1 Before you entered your social work program, and before you read this chapter, how knowledgeable were you about the methods of analyzing quantitative data? Discuss fully.

2 What are *quantitative data*? Provide social work examples throughout your discussion to illustrate your main points.

3 What are the four levels of measurement for quantitative data? Provide an example of each and discuss how it can be used in a social work research situation and a social work practice situation.

4 Discuss the purposes of using descriptive statistics to analyze quantitative data. Provide social work examples throughout your discussion to illustrate your main points.

5 What are *frequency distributions*? Provide social work examples throughout your discussion to illustrate your main points.

6 What are *measures of central tendency*? Provide social work examples throughout your discussion to illustrate your main points.

7   What are *modes*? Provide social work examples throughout your discussion to illustrate your main points.

8   What are *medians*? Provide social work examples throughout your discussion to illustrate your main points.

9   What are *means*? Provide social work examples throughout your discussion to illustrate your main points.

10   Locate a quantitatively oriented journal article that used one or more of the three measures of central tendency. Were the statistics meaningful to you? If so, why? If not, why not?

11   What are *measures of variability*? Provide social work examples throughout your discussion to illustrate your main points.

12   What are *ranges*? Provide social work examples throughout your discussion to illustrate your main points.

13   What are *standard deviations*? Provide social work examples throughout your discussion to illustrate your main points.

14   Locate a quantitatively oriented journal article that used standard deviations in its data analysis. Was it meaningful to you? If so, why? If not, why not?

15   Discuss the main purpose of using inferential statistics to analyze quantitative data. Provide social work examples throughout your discussion to illustrate your main points.

16   Discuss how the chi-square test can be used to determine if there is an association between two variables.

17   Locate a quantitatively oriented journal article that used the chi-square test in its data analysis. Was it meaningful to you? If so, why? If not, why not?

18   Discuss how tests of correlation can be used in social work research studies.

19   Discuss how the dependent *t*-test can be used in social work studies.

20   Discuss how the independent *t*-test can be used in social work research studies.

21   What's the main difference between an independent *t*-test and an analysis of variance? Provide social work examples throughout your discussion to illustrate your main points.

22   Discuss how a one-way analysis of variance can be used to determine if there are any significant differences between the means of three or more groups. Provide social work examples throughout your discussion to illustrate your main point.

## 2015 EPAS COMPETENCIES

| COMPETENCY 1 | Demonstrate Ethical and Professional Behavior |
|---|---|

You will learn that in order to be a successful evidence-based practitioner you have an ethical obligation to integrate three research roles into your daily practice activities as discussed in Chapter 3: (1) research consumer, (2) research partner—either as a co-researcher or research participant, and (3) creator and disseminator of research (or knowledge).

This entire chapter pertains to these three professional research-related roles when it comes to collecting, displaying, and analyzing qualitative data.

| COMPETENCY 4 | Engage in Practice-Informed Research and Research-Informed Practice |
|---|---|

Competency 4 also pertains to the entire chapter because you have to:

1  Evaluate the thoroughness of the qualitative data analysis that was used in a qualitative research study (**research consumer**—research-informed practice);

2  Participate in a qualitative research study—either as a co-researcher or research participant (**research partner**—practice-informed research). See 1 above and 3 below; and

3  Know how to collect, display, and interpret qualitative data before you actually do a qualitative research study (**creator and disseminator of research**—practice-informed research).

You'll also need to utilize evidence-based practice recommendations whenever possible; that is, you need to integrate (1) the best available research-based evidence with (2) your clinical expertise and (3) your client's values.

All of the above implies you'll need to evaluate the strengths and limitations of the research-based qualitative evidence the study produced. In short, you need to ask and then answer a simple question: How seriously should I take the findings and recommendations of any qualitative research study given the level of rigor the author used in analyzing the qualitative data?

| COMPETENCY 9 | Evaluate Practice with Individuals, Families, Groups, Organizations, & Communities |
|---|---|

See Competencies 1 and 4.

# Analyzing Qualitative Data

CHAPTERS 1 & 3        Step 1.   Understanding the Research Process

CHAPTER 2             Step 2.   Formulating Research Questions

CHAPTER 4            Step 3.   Reviewing the Literature
APPENDIXES A–C                 Evaluating the Literature

CHAPTERS 5 & 6       Step 4.   Being Aware of Ethical and Cultural Issues

CHAPTERS 7–10        Step 5.   Selecting a Research Approach

CHAPTERS 11 & 12     Step 6.   Specifying How Variables Are Measured

CHAPTER 13           Step 7.   Selecting a Sample

CHAPTERS 14 & 15     Step 8.   Selecting a Research Design

CHAPTERS 16 & 17     Step 9.   Selecting a Data-Collection Method

CHAPTERS 18 & 19     Step 10.  Analyzing the Data

CHAPTERS 20 & 21     Step 11.  Writing the Research Report

# Analyzing Qualitative Data

**CHAPTER**

# 19

CHAPTER OUTLINE

"Now that we have our quantitative data we've got to put some qualitative meaning behind them. Got any ideas?"

PURPOSE OF QUALITATIVE DATA ANALYSIS
  Checking Your Biases at the Door
PHASE 1: PLANNING THE ANALYSIS
  Step 1: Transcribe the Data
    *Task 1a: Select a Computer Program*
    *Task 1b: Transcribe the Data*
  Step 2: Establish Rules for the Analysis
    *Task 2a: Preview the Data*
    *Task 2b: Keep a Journal*
PHASE 2: DOING THE ANALYSIS
  Step 3: Doing First-Level Coding
    *Task 3a: Identify Meaning Units*
    *Task 3b: Create Categories*
    *Task 3c: Assign Codes to Categories*
    *Task 3d: Refine Categories*

  Step 4: Doing Second-Level Coding
    *Task 4a: Comparing Categories*
PHASE 3: LOOKING FOR MEANING
  Step 5: Interpreting Data and Building Theory
    *Task 5a: Conceptual Classifications Systems*
    *Task 5b: Themes or Theory*
  Step 6: Assessing the Results
    *Task 6a: Establish Our Own Credibility*
    *Task 6b: Establish the Dependability of the Data*
    *Task 6c: Establish Our Control of Biases*
EVALUATING YOUR DATA ANALYSIS PLAN
EVALUATING A QUALITATIVE ANALYSIS
CHAPTER RECAP
REVIEW EXERCISES

THE LAST CHAPTER DISCUSSED the methods of analyzing quantitative data that are derived from quantitative research studies. In this chapter, we turn to the analysis of qualitative data that are derived from qualitative research studies—that is, data collected in the form of words (i.e., text data), most often from interviews, open-ended items on questionnaires, or personal logs. Unlike numbers, which are used in quantitative analyses, words give us descriptions or opinions from the unique point of view of the person who spoke or wrote the words.

Like everything else in life, text data have both disadvantages and advantages. The disadvantages are that words tend to be open to different interpretations and cannot be collected from large numbers of people at a time because the process of collection and analysis is much more time consuming than is the case for numerical data. The major advantage is that the material is very rich, containing multiple facets, and may provide us with a deeper understanding of the underlying meaning than would be possible if we just collected numbers (Tutty, Rothery, & Grinnell, 1996).

## PURPOSE OF QUALITATIVE DATA ANALYSIS

Usually, we need the deeper understanding provided by qualitative data when we know very little about the problem or situation we are investigating and are not yet in a position to formulate theories about it for testing. In other words, we are at the exploratory end of the knowledge continuum, seeking to form patterns out of individual experiences so that we can develop more general theories.

The primary purpose of a qualitative data analysis is to sift and sort the masses of words we have collected from our research participants in such a way that we can derive patterns related to our research question—to identify the similarities and differences presented by individuals and the possible links between them.

> Qualitative data analyses analyze the meaning of words (or text data), not numbers.

Suppose for a moment that we are investigating postnatal depression among women. We may be interested in what the symptoms are, how new mothers experience them, and how they feel their depression affects their relationship with their newborns. We may also be interested in whether the women who experience postnatal depression are similar in any way with respect to various characteristics such as age, ethnic background, desire for the baby, partner or family support, socioeconomic status, medical history, and so on.

Indeed, we may have structured our interviews to collect specific data related to these kinds of variables. If we did, then we have already theorized that these characteristics or variables are related to postnatal depression, and we may, even subconsciously, look for patterns in the data that will confirm our theories. There's nothing really evil about this. Researchers are human beings with a normal human tendency to make connections between events on the frailest of evidence, and it's a very rare researcher who starts on a research study with no preconceived notions at all.

## CHECKING YOUR BIASES AT THE DOOR

The important thing is to be aware of our human frailties with respect to drawing unwarranted conclusions, and to organize our data collection and analysis so that these frailties are minimized as far as possible. A look at some of the assumptions underlying qualitative (interpretive) research might help us to accomplish this:

- We're assuming that the goal of interpretive research (chapter 9) is to reach an in-depth understanding of each of our research participants with respect to the research question, including experiences that are unique to them. We will not achieve this goal if we do not allow participants to express their uniqueness during data collection. Neither will we achieve it if we ignore the uniqueness during data analysis because we were hoping to uncover patterns and this is an anomaly that does not quite fit.

- It's also easy to ignore uniqueness if it does not fit with the findings of other researchers. An exploratory topic tends to reveal little in the way of previous research, but there is usually some, and it's tempting to disregard a unique experience if it seems to contravene what others have found.

- Information is always provided in some context. In the case of a research study, the context is the way in which the information was elicited (e.g., the phrasing of a question). In an interview, the context is the relationship between the interviewer and the interviewee.

- Preconceptions on the part of the interviewer tend to elicit responses that fit with the preconceptions. Thus, it's important in analysis not to look at just the response but at the emotional atmosphere surrounding the response and the question that was responded to.

> Unlike numbers, which are used in quantitative analyses, words give us descriptions or opinions from the unique point of view of the person who spoke or wrote the words.

There are three major phases involved in a basic qualitative data analysis. They are:

**Phase 1**  **We must plan how we will do the analysis.** This involves describing exactly how we will transcribe spoken or written data into a usable form and what rules we will use to fit the pieces of data together in a meaningful way.

**Phase 2**  **We must do the analysis that will follow the general rules we set out at the beginning and perhaps revise these rules along the way if we come across some data to which our rules cannot be sensibly applied.** It's important to note though that whatever rules we finally decide on must be applied to all our data. Changing our mind about rules will mean going back over the material we have worked on already; indeed, qualitative analysis is usually a back-and-forth sort of process, involving many re-readings and re-workings as new insights appear and we begin to question our initial theories or assumptions.

**Phase 3**  **We need to draw meaning from our analysis**; that is, to identify relationships between the major themes that have emerged and to build theories around these for testing in the future.

> Your personal biases must always be acknowledged and dealt with when doing a qualitative data analysis.

The remainder of this chapter will describe the three phases of doing a qualitative data analysis briefly mentioned above. We will now turn attention to the first phase—planning the analysis.

# PHASE 1: PLANNING THE ANALYSIS

**T**here are two steps involved in planning a qualitative analysis:

**Step 1** Transcribing the data

**Step 2** Establishing general rules for the analysis

## STEP 1: TRANSCRIBING THE DATA

Transcribing our data itself involves two tasks:

**Task 1a** Deciding what computer program to use (if any)

**Task 1b** Deciding who will transcribe the data

### TASK 1A: DECIDING WHAT COMPUTER PROGRAM TO USE

If responses are written, as in open-ended items on a questionnaire or personal logs, transcription may be a matter of typing the responses, either just for easier reading or with the aim of using a computer program to assist with the analysis. A few researchers, distrustful of computers, prefer to use a traditional cut-and-paste method, physically cutting the manuscript and grouping the cut sections together with other related sections.

A computer need not be used for transcription in this case. A simple outdated type-writer would do, or even legible handwriting. Some researchers trust the computer just sufficiently to allow it to move selected passages together with other selected passages to electronically form a group of related data.

The majority of word-processing programs can accomplish this. An increasing number of researchers, however, use computer programs that have been developed specifically to assist with the analysis of qualitative data. A few familiar names are ETHNOGRAPH, HYPERQUAL, ATLAS.ti, NUD*IST, and NVivo. New programs are always coming onto the market, so it's wise to consult colleagues or computer software companies about which programs might be most helpful for a particular project. It's important to note that no computer program can do the analysis for us. The most it can do is free up time for us to spend on considering the meaning of our data in Phase 3.

### TASK 1B: DECIDING WHO WILL TRANSCRIBE THE DATA

Some researchers are fortunate enough to have a research or administrative assistant to help them in the transcription process. If this is the case, it's necessary to lay down guidelines right at the beginning about how the material should be transcribed. If an interview has been audio recorded or videotaped, for example, the questions should be included in the transcript as well as the answers.

Nonverbal communications such as pauses, laughing or crying, and voice tone should be included in brackets so that the emotional context of the interview is captured as far as possible in the transcript. Those fortunate researchers with assistants are nevertheless well advised to transcribe at least the first few interviews themselves so that assistants can see what ought to be included.

Another concern is how to format the transcript so that it's easy to read and analyze. It's a good idea to leave a margin of at least two inches along the right side so that we can write notes and codes alongside the corresponding text. It's also a good idea to number each line of the transcript so that we can readily identify each segment of data. Computer programs designed to assist in qualitative analysis will automatically do this. For example, suppose we worked in a foster care agency and we were asking foster parents who had resigned from the agency in the past year why they had resigned. A few lines from one of our interviews might be transcribed like this:

1  **Sue (angrily):** His behavior was just too much and nobody from the agency told
2  us that he'd set fires before and was probably going to burn our house down. I
3  suppose they thought that if they'd told us that we wouldn't have taken him but
4  I do feel that we were set up from the beginning (sounding very upset). And when
5  we called the agency, there was only an answering machine and it was a whole
6  day before the social worker called us back.
7  **Interviewer:** That's dreadful.

Reading these lines after the transcript is completed might immediately set us thinking about how foster parents' reasons for resigning could be separated into categories. One category might be the foster child's behavior (much worse than the foster parents had been led to expect).

Or this might be two categories: (1) the child's behavior and (2) the discrepancy between the actual behavior and the expected behavior. Another category might be negative feelings toward the agency, with two subcategories: the feeling of having been set up, and the perceived lack of support in a time of crisis. It might not take long at all for these tentative categories to harden into certainties.

Having read the first six lines from one interview, we now feel we know why foster parents resign, and it only remains to confirm the reasons we have found by picking out similar sentiments from our interviews with other foster parents. Job completed!

Actually, we've barely begun. Since we cannot—and do not wish to—stop our minds from jumping ahead in this fashion, we must find some way to organize our thoughts such that our intuitive leaps do not blind us to different and perhaps contradictory insights yielded by other interviews. There are two techniques that might help us to do this: previewing the data, and keeping a journal. Both these techniques will also help us to establish general rules for our analysis—the second and last step in the planning stage.

## STEP 2: ESTABLISHING RULES FOR THE ANALYSIS

Establishing general rules for the analysis ensures that our efforts are systematic and the same rules are applied to all our data. We use rules to decide how we could fit together pieces of data in a meaningful way and how these groups of data could be categorized and coded (to be discussed shortly).

For example, what criteria or rule do we use to decide whether a child's worsened behavior after a visit with the biological parents should be categorized under "child's behaviors" or under "relationships with biological parents"? Although we clarify and refine the rules throughout the study, by the time we have finished we should have a set of rules that have been consistently applied to every piece of data. We start to think about what rules might apply during the previewing task.

There are two basic tasks that take place when establishing rules for a qualitative data analysis:

**Task 2a**  Previewing the data
**Task 2b**  Keeping a journal

## TASK 2A: PREVIEWING THE DATA

The process of transcription might be ongoing throughout the study, with each interview transcribed as soon as it's completed, or transcription might not begin until all the data have been assembled. Whichever method is used, it's important to read all the transcripts before beginning to formally identify categories.

It's also important to give all the transcripts and all parts of the transcripts the same amount of attention. We may be in peak form at the beginning of the day while reading the first few pages of the first transcript, for example, but by the end of the day and by the end of the third transcript, this initial peak has waned to weary impatience.

We would be better advised to read only for as long as we remain interested in the material. This will obviously mean that the process of previewing the data extends over a longer period; qualitative data analysis takes time—lots and lots of time—in addition to lots of patience.

It's a lengthy process of discovery, whose pace cannot be forced. If we are rereading material, it sometimes helps to read the last third of an interview at moments of high energy instead of the first third. That way, we will not lose valuable insights from later sections of the interview transcript.

## TASK 2B: KEEPING A JOURNAL

Some people love journals, and others hate them, but the interpretive researcher cannot afford to be without one. The journal should be started at the same time as the study is started. It should include notes on the planned method and any changes in the plan, with dates and reasons. For example, perhaps the plan was to interview all the foster parents who had resigned from the agency during the last year, but some of them would not agree to be interviewed.

We may believe that those who agreed differed in some important respects from those who refused. They were more satisfied with the agency perhaps. If this were the case, the data from our more satisfied sample might lead us to faulty conclusions, possibly causing us to place more emphasis on personal reasons for resignation such as failing health or family circumstances, and less on agency-related reasons such as poor information-sharing or support.

Whatever the difficulties we encounter and the assumptions we make, our journal should keep an accurate record of them as we move along in the data analysis. Because the work we do must be open to scrutiny by others, it's essential to keep a record of all our activities and the feelings and reasoning behind them.

When the data-collection stage begins, the journal can be used to record personal reactions to the interview situation. For example, we might feel more personal empathy with one foster parent than with another and be tempted to give more weight to the remarks of the parent with whom we sympathized. An unconscious overreliance on one research participant or one subset of research participants will hopefully reveal itself as we read through our journal entries later during the course of the analysis.

When we begin to categorize and code the data, we can use the journal to keep notes about the process, writing down the general rules, revisions to the rules, and questions or comments with respect to how particular pieces of data might be categorized. Let's now turn our attention to actually analyzing qualitative data.

---

Qualitative researchers use journals that detail the entire research process.

---

Journals are used to record the researcher's personal reactions to interviews.

---

# PHASE 2: DOING THE ANALYSIS

**O**nce all the data have been previewed we can start on coding them. There are two levels of coding:

**Step 3**  *First-level coding,* which deals with the concrete ideas evident in the transcript

**Step 4**  *Second-level coding,* which looks for and interprets the more abstract meanings underlying these concrete ideas

## STEP 3: DOING FIRST-LEVEL CODING

There are four tasks in first-level coding:

**Task 3a**  Identifying meaning units

**Task 3b**  Creating categories

**Task 3c**  Assigning codes to categories

**Task 3d**  Refining and reorganizing categories

### TASK 3A: IDENTIFYING MEANING UNITS

A meaning unit is a piece of data, which we consider to be meaningful by itself. It might be a word, a partial or complete sentence, or a paragraph or more. For example, let's look once again at the interview segment presented earlier on page 410:

1  <u>Sue (angrily): His behavior was just too much and nobody from the agency told</u>
2  *us that he'd set fires before and was probably going to burn our house down. I*
3  *suppose they thought that if they'd told us that we wouldn't have taken him but*
4  **I do feel that we were set up from the beginning (sounding very upset). And when**
5  ***we called the agency, there was only an answering machine and it was a whole***
6  ***day before the social worker called us back.***
7  Interviewer: That's dreadful.

In the above segment we might easily identify four meaning units. The first unit (<u>underlined</u>, line 1) relates to the child's behavior. The second unit (italics, lines 2 and 3) relates to lack of information provided by the agency. The third (**bold**, line 4) relates to feeling set up by the agency. The fourth unit (***bold italics***, lines 5 and 6) relates to poor support on the part of the agency. Of course, different researchers might identify different meaning units or label the same units differently.

For example, lines 4, 5, and 6 might be identified as relating to agency response style rather than poor support and might involve two distinct meaning units, "response method" and "response time." Similarly, the partial sentence in line 2, *"he'd set fires before,"* might be viewed as a separate meaning unit relating to the child's past rather than present behavior.

The first run-through to identify meaning units will always be somewhat tentative and subject to change. If we are not sure whether to break a large meaning unit into smaller ones, it may be preferable to leave it as a whole. We can always break it down later in the analysis, and breaking down large units tends to be easier than combining smaller ones, especially once second-level coding begins.

### TASK 3B: CREATING CATEGORIES

Once we have identified meaning units in the transcript, our next task is to consider which of them fit together into categories. Perhaps we should have a category labeled

> A meaning unit is a piece of data, which we consider to be meaningful all by itself.

"child's behavior" into which we put all meaning units related to the child's behavior, including the second meaning unit identified above, "nobody from the agency told us that he'd set fires before and was probably going to burn our house down."

Or perhaps we should have two categories, "child's present behavior" and "child's past behavior," in which case the second meaning unit might belong in the latter category. Or perhaps we feel that the vital words are "nobody told us," and this second meaning unit really belongs in a different category labeled "provision of information by agency." All other meaning units to do with foster parents being given information by the agency would then belong in this same category even though they had nothing to do with the child's behavior.

Because these kinds of decisions are often difficult to make, it's a good idea to note in our journal how we made the decisions we did and what alternatives we considered at the time. What rules did we use to decide whether a particular meaning unit was similar to—or different from—another meaning unit? How did we define our categories in order to decide whether a group of similar units should be placed in one category or in another?

As we continue to examine new meaning units, we will use these rules to decide whether each new unit is similar to existing units and belongs in an existing category or whether it's different from existing units and needs a new separate category. The number of categories will therefore expand every time we identify meaning units that are different in important ways from those we have already categorized.

Since too many categories will make the final analysis very difficult, we should try to keep the number within manageable limits. This may mean revising our initial rules about how categories are defined and what criteria are used to decide whether meaning units are similar enough to be grouped together. Of course, any change in rules should be noted in our journal, together with the rationale for the change.

The complexity of our categorization scheme also needs to be considered. One meaning unit may, in fact, fall into more than one category, or a group of meaning units may overlap with another group. Large, inclusive categories may consist of a number of smaller, more exclusive subcategories. For example, as we saw, the meaning unit "<u>nobody from the agency told</u> *us that he'd set fires before and was probably going to burn our house down*" has to do both with lack of information provided by the agency and with the child's past behavior.

Sometimes meaning units cannot be clearly placed into any category and fall into the category of "miscellaneous." When we are tired, most everything may seem to be "miscellaneous," but miscellaneous units should make up no more than 10 percent of the total dataset. More than that suggests that there is a problem with the original categorization scheme. The real purpose of a miscellaneous category is to prevent our throwing out meaning units that, at first glance, appear to be irrelevant. Such throwing out is risky because at some point we may decide that our whole categorization scheme needs massive revision and we must start the whole process again from scratch.

### TASK 3C: ASSIGNING CODES TO CATEGORIES

Codes are simply a shorthand form of the category name. They typically take the form of strings of letters and/or symbols. Codes used in *The Ethnograph,* for example, may be up to ten letters long and can also include symbols. Codes are usually displayed in the margins (often the right margin) of the transcribed text.

If we had a category labeled "child's behavior," we might simply code this CB where the C stands for the foster child and the B stands for behavior. If we want to distinguish between past and present behavior, we might use the codes CPASTB and CPRESB, respectively.

---

Qualitative researchers need to keep the number of categories in their analyses to a manageable number.

---

Codes are shorthand forms for labeling categories.

If there is a category relating to the behavior of the foster parents' own children (perhaps this has worsened since the foster child moved in), we might use the codes FPCPASTB and FPCPRESB, respectively, where the FPC stands for the foster parents' child.

In fact, we might make it a rule that codes starting with C, FP, FPC, and A stand for things to do with the foster child, the foster parents, the foster parents' children, and the agency, respectively. Then AINF>FP might mean information provided by the agency to the foster parents, and AINF<FP might mean information provided by the foster parents to the agency.

It's a good idea to keep the codes as short as possible in the beginning because they tend to become longer as the analysis grows more complex. However, there are many different ways to assign codes and so long as the code is clearly related to the category, it doesn't really matter which system is used.

### Task 3d: Refining and Reorganizing Categories

Before moving on from first-level coding, we need to make a final sweep through the data to ensure that our analysis reflects what our research participants have said. We should consider the logic underlying the rules we made for grouping meaning units and defining categories.

We may, for example, be confused about why we created some categories, or feel uncertain about why a particular meaning unit was put into a particular category. We might find that some categories are too complex and need to be split into smaller categories; or some categories are poorly defined; or some of the categories that we expected to emerge from the data are missing altogether.

We might, for example, have expected that some foster parents would resign because of poor health, but there is no category coded FPHEA. Investigation reveals that foster parents did indeed mention their poor health but they always ascribed it to the strain of dealing with the foster child or the foster child's biological parents or the agency.

Hence, the meaning units including poor health have been categorized under "foster child's present behavior (CPRESB)" or "relationships with agency (AREL)" or "relationships with biological parents (BPREL)" and have not been broken down finely enough to isolate poor health as a separate category. We may wish to create such a category, or we may prefer to note its absence in our journal together with other categories that are incomplete or in some way unsatisfactory.

This is a good time to ask a colleague to analyze one or two of our interviews using the rules we have devised. In this way, we can check that the categories themselves and the rules that define them make sense. If our colleague organizes meaning units in a significantly different way, for example, our categorization scheme may need to be substantially revised.

It's probably time to stop first-level coding when all our meaning units fit easily into our current categorization scheme and there are no more units that require the creation of new categories. If interviews are continuing during first-level coding, we will probably find the data becoming repetitive; yielding no new piece of information that cannot be fitted into the present scheme.

Now that we're done first-level coding, it's time to turn our attention to the final step in Phase 2—second level coding.

## Step 4: Doing Second-Level Coding

The next major step in the data analysis process is second-level coding. As noted earlier, this is more abstract and involves interpreting what the first-level categories mean. During first-level coding, we derived meaning units from interviews with individuals, and we derived categories by comparing the meaning units to see which were similar enough to be grouped together.

During second-level coding we will compare the categories themselves to uncover possible relationships between or among them. The point of doing this is to identify themes based on patterns that repeatedly occur among our categories.

### TASK 4A: COMPARING CATEGORIES

A comparison of categories in any interpretive study will probably yield many different types of relationships. Heather Coleman and Yvonne Unrau (2018) have suggested that the following three types of relationships are among those most commonly found:

- **A temporal relationship.** One category may be found to often precede another. For example, foster children whose own parents are abusive might initially behave well because they are happy to be living away from the abuse. Later, however, they may push for a return to their families of origin, and their response to the foster parents may become less positive.

- **A causal relationship.** One category may be perceived to be the cause of another. For example, foster parents may believe that the child's bad behavior after every visit with the biological parent was the cause of their own negative attitudes toward the biological parent. However, it's always risky to assume that one category caused another when, in fact, the opposite may be true. Perhaps the foster parents started off with a negative attitude toward the child's biological parents, the child was more than usually angry about this after visits home, and the child demonstrated rage by behaving badly.

- **One category may be contained within another category.** At this stage of the analysis, we may decide that two categories that we had thought to be separate are in fact linked. For example, foster parents may have said that they were never introduced to the child's biological parents by the agency, and we have categorized this separately from their statement that the agency was not entirely truthful with them about the child's past behavior. Now we realize that these are both examples of lack of information provided to the foster parent by the agency.

Furthermore, foster parents complained that they were not invited to agency meetings in which the child's progress was reviewed. Lack of information and nonattendance at meetings might combine to form a theme related to the agency's attitude toward the foster parents. The theme might be that the agency does not appear to accept the foster parents as equal partners in the task of helping the child.

When we have identified themes based on patterns among our categories, we code these themes in the same way as we coded our categories. If one of our themes is that the agency does not view foster parents as equal partners, for example, we might code this as A<FP-PART. Once themes have been identified and coded, the process of second-level coding is complete.

> A comparison of categories in any qualitative study will probably yield many different types of relationships.

## PHASE 3: LOOKING FOR MEANING

**D**rawing meaning from our data is perhaps the most rewarding step of a qualitative data analysis. It involves two important steps:

Step 5　Interpreting data and building theory

Step 6　Assessing the trustworthiness of the results

## STEP 5: INTERPRETING DATA AND BUILDING THEORY

This step involves two tasks:

**Task 5a**  Developing conceptual classifications systems

**Task 5b**  Presenting themes or theory

### TASK 5A: DEVELOPING CONCEPTUAL CLASSIFICATIONS SYSTEMS

The goal of an interpretive research study is to identify any relationships between the major themes that emerge from the dataset. During first-level coding, we used meaning units to form categories. During second-level coding, we used categories to form themes.

Now we will use themes to build theories. In order to do this, we must understand the interconnections between themes and categories. There are several strategies that might be useful in helping us to identify these connections. Matthew Miles and A. Michael Huberman (1994) have suggested the following strategies for extracting meaning from a qualitative dataset:

- **Draw a cluster diagram.** This form of diagram helps us to think about how themes and categories may or may not be related to one another. Draw and label circles for each theme and arrange them in relation to each other. Some of the circles will overlap, others will stand-alone. The circles of the themes of more importance will be larger, in comparison to themes and categories that are not as relevant to our conclusions. The process of thinking about what weight to give the themes, how they interact, and how important they will be in the final scheme will be valuable in helping us to think about the meaning of our study.

- **Make a matrix.** Matrix displays may be helpful for noting relations between categories or themes. Designing a two-dimensional matrix involves writing a list of categories along the left side of a piece of paper and then another list of categories across the top.

  For example, along the side, we might write categories related to the theme of the degree of partnership between the agency and the foster parents. One such category might be whether the foster parents were invited to agency meetings held to discuss the child's progress. Then, along the top we might write categories related to the theme of foster parents' attitudes toward the agency.

  One category here might be whether foster parents felt their opinions about the child were listened to by the agency. Where two categories intersect on the matrix, we could note with a plus sign (+) those indicators of partnership or lack of partnership that positively affect parents' attitudes. Conversely, we would mark with a minus sign (−) those that seem to have a negative effect. Such a matrix gives us a sense of to what degree and in what ways foster parents' attitudes toward the agency are molded by the agency's view of foster parents as partners.

- **Count the number of times a meaning unit or category appears.** Although numbers are typically associated with quantitative studies, it's acceptable to use numbers in qualitative work in order to document how many of the participants expressed a particular theme. We might be interested, for example, in finding out how many participants experienced specific problems related to lack of agency support. We would write the code names for the foster parents interviewed down the left side of a piece of paper and the list of problems across the top.

  To fill in the chart, we would simply place a check mark beside each foster parent's code name if she or he experienced that particular problem. Numbers will help protect our analysis against bias that occurs when intense but rare examples of problems are presented.

For example, many foster parents may have felt that they were not given sufficient information about the child's past behavior, but only one may have felt that the agency deliberately set her up. Although, we will certainly not discount this foster parent's experience, we might prefer to view it as an extreme example of the results of poor information sharing.

- **Create a metaphor.** Developing metaphors that convey the essence of our findings is another mechanism for extracting meaning. One example of a metaphor concerning battered women is "the cycle of violence," which effectively describes the tension building between couples until the husband beats his wife, followed by a calm, loving phase until the tension builds again.

- **Look for missing links.** If two categories or themes seem to be related but not directly so, it may be that a third variable connects the two.

- **Note contradictory evidence.** It's only natural to want to focus on evidence that supports our ideas. Because of this human tendency, it's particularly important to also identify themes and categories that raise questions about our conclusions. All contradictory evidence must be accounted for when we come to derive theories pertaining to our study area, for example, theories about why foster parents resign.

### TASK 5B: PRESENTING THEMES OR THEORY

Sometimes it's sufficient to conclude an interpretive study merely by describing the major themes that emerged from the data. For example, we may have used the experiences of individual foster parents to derive reasons for resignation common to the majority of foster parents we studied.

When categorized, such reasons might relate to inadequate training; poor support from the agency; failure on the agency's part to treat the foster parents as partners; negative attitudes on the part of the foster parents' friends and extended family; unrealistic expectations on the part of the foster parents with respect to the foster child's progress and behavior; poor relations between the biological and foster parents; the perceived negative influence of the foster child on the foster parents' own children; marital discord attributed to stress; failing health attributed to stress; and so on.

We might think it sufficient in our conclusions to present and describe these categories, together with recommendations for improvement. On the other hand, we might wish to formulate questions to be answered in future studies. What would change if agencies were to view foster parents as partners rather than as clients? If we think we know what would change, we might want to formulate more specific questions. For example,

- Are agencies that view foster parents as partners more likely to provide foster parents with full information regarding the child's background than agencies that do not view foster parents as partners?

Or we might want to reword the above general question to form a hypothesis:

- Agencies that view foster parents as partners are more likely to provide foster parents with full information regarding the child's background than agencies that do not view parents as partners.

In order to arrive at this hypothesis, we have essentially formulated a theory about how two of our concepts are related. We could carry this further by adding other concepts to the chain of relationships and formulating additional hypotheses:

- Foster parents who have full information about the child's background are less likely to have unrealistic expectations about the child's behavior and progress than foster parents who do not have full information about the child's background.

And,

- Foster parents who have unrealistic expectations about the child's behavior and progress are more likely to experience marital discord (due to the fostering process) than foster parents who do not have unrealistic expectations.

Indeed, we might weave all the various woes our study has uncovered into an elaborate pattern of threads, beginning with the agency's reluctance to view foster parents as partners and ending with the foster parents' resignations. In our excitement, we might come to believe that we have solved the entire problem of resigning foster parents. We could naively come up with:

- If agencies would only change their attitudes with respect to foster parents' status and behave in accordance with this change in attitude, then all foster parents would continue to be foster parents until removed by death.

It's at this point that we need to focus on the last stage of our search for meaning: assessing the trustworthiness of our results.

## STEP 6: ASSESSING THE RESULTS

There are major reasons why disgruntled agencies, as well as other actors, may not agree that our results are as trustworthy as we believe. They can be broken into three tasks:

**Task 6a**  Establishing our own creditability

**Task 6b**  Establishing the dependability of the data

**Task 6c**  Establishing our control of biases and preconceptions

### TASK 6A: ESTABLISHING OUR OWN CREDIBILITY

Because an interpretive study depends so much on human judgment, it's necessary to demonstrate that our own personal judgment is to be trusted. Part of this relates to our training and experience. Another important part is the record we made in our journal detailing the procedures we followed, the decisions we made and why we made them, and the thought processes that led to our conclusions. If we can demonstrate that we were qualified to undertake this study and we carried it out meticulously, others are far more likely to take into account our conclusions.

### TASK 6B: ESTABLISHING THE DEPENDABILITY OF THE DATA

If we have been consistent in such things as interview procedures and developing rules for coding, and if we have obtained dependable data through a rigorous, recorded process, then another researcher should be able to follow the same process, make the same decisions, and arrive at essentially the same conclusions. Also, if we ourselves redo part of the analysis at a later date, the outcome should be very similar to that produced in the original analysis. In order to ensure that others and we could duplicate our work, we need to pay attention to the following standard issues:

- **The context of the interviews.** Some data-collection situations yield more credible data than others, and we may choose to weight our interviews accordingly. Some authors claim, for example, that data collected later in the study are more dependable than data collected at the beginning because our interviewing style is likely to be more relaxed and less intrusive. In addition, data obtained firsthand are considered to be more dependable than secondhand data, which are obtained through a third party. Similarly, data offered voluntarily are thought to be stronger than data obtained through intensive questioning, and data obtained from research participants in their natural environments (e.g., home or neighborhood coffee shop) are to be more trusted than data provided by research participants in a foreign or sterile environment (e.g., researcher's office or an interviewing room).

- **Triangulation.** Triangulation is commonly used to establish the trustworthiness of qualitative data. There are several different kinds of triangulation, but the essence of the method lies in a comparison of several perspectives. For example, we might collect data from the agency about what information was provided to foster parents in order to compare the agency's perspective with what foster parents said. With respect to data analysis, we might ask a colleague to use our rules to see if he or she makes the same decisions about meaning units, categories, and themes. The hope is that different perspectives will confirm each other, adding weight to the credibility of our analysis.

- **Member checking.** Obtaining feedback from research participants is particularly unique to interpretive studies. While such feedback should be an ongoing part of the study (e.g., interview transcripts may be presented to research participants for comment), it's particularly useful when our analysis has been completed, our interpretations made, and our conclusions drawn.

Research participants may not agree with our interpretation or conclusions, and may differ among each other. If this is the case, we need to decide whether to exclude the interpretations to which they object, or whether to leave them in, merely recording the dissenting opinions and our position in relation to them.

### TASK 6C: ESTABLISHING OUR CONTROL OF BIASES

Since all human beings inevitably have biases and preconceptions about most everything, one way to demonstrate that we are in control of ours is to list them. Such a list is useful to both ourselves and others when we want to check that our conclusions have emerged from the data rather than from our established beliefs.

Also useful is our journal where we documented our attempts to keep ourselves open to what our research participants had to say. As Heather Coleman and Yvonne Unrau (2018) point out, we may want to consider several points in relation to bias:

- Our personal belief systems may affect our interpretation of the data. Member checking has already been mentioned as a way to safeguard against this.

- We might draw conclusions before the data are analyzed or before we have decided about the trustworthiness of the data collected. Such conclusions tend to set to a cement-like hardness and are likely to persist despite all future indications that they were wrong.

- We might censor, ignore, or dismiss certain parts of the data. This may occur as a result of data overload or because the data contradict an established way of thinking.

- We might make unwarranted or unsupported causal statements based on impressions rather than on solid analysis. Even when our statements are based on solid analysis, it's a good idea to actively hunt for any evidence that might contradict them. If we can demonstrate that we have genuinely searched for (but failed to find) negative evidence, looking for outliers and using extreme cases, our conclusions will be more credible.

- We might be too opinionated and reduce our conclusions to a limited number of choices or alternatives.

- We might unthinkingly give certain people or events more credibility than others.

Perhaps we have relied too much on information that was easily accessible or we have given too much weight to research participants we personally liked. If we detect such a bias, we can interview more people, deliberately searching for atypical events and research participants who differ markedly from those we have already interviewed. Hopefully, these new data will provide a balance with the data originally collected.

Once we have assessed the trustworthiness of our results, it only remains to write the report describing our methods and findings.

## EVALUATING YOUR DATA ANALYSIS PLAN

The best way to actually evaluate the quality of your qualitative data analysis plan is to evaluate your entire research study from the get-go. In short, your data analysis can only be as good as the study's research design that was used to obtain the data in the first place. It's simply impossible to evaluate your study's data analysis plan in total isolation from your study's overall methodology. In this spirit, Jim Raines (2011) has provided a nice list of questions broken down into four generic categories that you should ask yourself before ever embarking on a qualitative research study.

1  **Potential Introduction and Literature Review Issues**
   • Are your philosophical assumptions and values well identified?
   • Are the databases you searched sufficient to the research question you are trying to answer?
   • Is your literature review relevant to both your research problem and population?
   • Is the literature that you reviewed current?
   • Do you use headings and subheadings to organize your ideas?
   • Do you identify any differences in findings from previous research studies?
   • Does your literature review support the purpose of your study?

2  **Potential Research Question, Conceptual Definitions, Rationale, & Ethical Issues**
   • Is your research question crystal clear?
   • Does your research question include all the major concepts that are in your study?
   • Are your conceptual definitions multidimensional?
   • Will your definitions evolve as participants provide their perspectives?
   • Do you have a logical rationale for doing a qualitative study in the first place?
   • Is there a good fit between your research question and your data-collection method?
   • Does your research study demonstrate your value awareness?
   • How do you plan on using informed consent procedures?
   • Does your study advance the common good of your research participants?

3  **Potential Data Collection Procedures and Rigor Issues**
   • Do you explain the reasons for the type of sampling method you will use?
   • How do you plan on reporting your subjectivity?
   • How do you plan on addressing the issue of bias by you and your research participants?

- What strategies are you going to use to improve the credibility of your study's findings?

- What strategies are you going to use to improve the transferability of your study's findings?

- What strategies are you going to use to improve the dependability of your study's findings?

- What strategies are you going to use to improve the confirmability of your study's findings?

**4  Potential Data Analysis Procedures and Discussion Issues**

- What strategies are you going to use to increase the accuracy of your study's transcriptions?

- What is your specific plan for analyzing the data?

- How do you plan on developing categories for first-level coding?

- How to you plan on establishing relationships between categories clarified during second-level coding?

- How to you plan on developing themes and theories within your data analyses?

- How do you plan on addressing your study's limitations from an interpretive perspective?

- How do you plan on integrating your study's results with the previous literature?

- How do you plan on developing implications for social work theory, practice, or policy?

- Do you plan on making recommendations for future research studies?

---

| **Box 19.1** | Qualitative Data Analysis in a Nutshell |
|---|---|

**Qualitative data are information** in non-numeric form. They usually appear in textual or narrative format. For example, focus group notes, open-ended interview or questionnaire responses, and observation notes are all types of qualitative data. Qualitative data analysis is the process of interpreting and understanding the qualitative data that you have collected.

Qualitative data analysis relies heavily on interpretation. During the analysis, you will draw on your own experiences and knowledge of your program to make sense of your data. You will also consider the context of your program to determine how the data fit into the bigger picture. Qualitative data analysis is an iterative process; once you have begun to collect qualitative data, you will begin to review it and use your initial findings to shape how you collect and interpret data in the future.

**How do you plan for qualitative data analysis?**
Because collecting qualitative data is relatively quick and easy, you may feel compelled to collect a large amount. However, be mindful that analysis of qualitative data is time-consuming and labor-intensive. Plan to collect only as much data as your program is able to analyze and use.

It is important to plan ahead when analyzing qualitative data to ensure that it will be meaningful and useful.

1   *Determine your focus.* Consider the research question(s) you want to answer. Keep in mind that these questions will guide the interpretation of your data. Decide how your data will be used to improve your program.

2   *Determine who will analyze the data.* Multiple people should analyze the data to be sure that the interpretation of findings is not biased. Those who conduct the analysis should have ample time and energy to comb through large amounts of text-based data. They should also have enough program knowledge to interpret the findings appropriately. When more than one person analyzes data, everyone must use the same systematic approach for reviewing, organizing, and coding the data.

3   **Obtain the necessary tools you need to analyze your data.** Qualitative data can be analyzed either manually or using a computer software package.

    — Manual analysis involves organizing and labeling your data by hand. You may only need some additional office supplies such as folders and highlighters to store and label your data. This method can be cost effective because of the small amount of extra materials needed. Manual analysis is typically the best method for analyzing your data if you only collect qualitative data periodically and have a manageable amount of data.

    — There are several computer software programs that allow you to organize, label, and search qualitative data by participant, question, or topic area. Computer software programs vary in cost and are often available online for computer download. Keep in mind that computer software programs do not do the analysis for you; they are simply a tool for organizing and searching the data. This method is ideal if you frequently collect qualitative data and have large amounts of data.

### How do you analyze qualitative data?

It is critical that you develop a systematic approach for analyzing your qualitative data. There are four major steps to this process:

1   *Review your data.* Before beginning any analysis, it is important that you understand the data you have collected by reviewing them several times. For example, if your data consist of interview transcripts, read and reread the transcripts until you have a general understanding of the content. As you are reviewing, write notes of your first impressions of the data; these initial responses may be useful later as you interpret your data.

2   *Organize your data.* Qualitative datasets tend to be very lengthy and complex. Once you have reviewed your data and are familiar with what you have, organize your data so that they are more manageable and easier to navigate. This can save you time and energy later. Depending on the evaluation question(s) you want to answer, there are a variety of ways to group your data, including by date, by data collection type (such as focus group vs. interview), or by question asked.

3   *Code your data.* Coding is the process of identifying and labeling themes within your data that correspond with the research questions you want to answer. Themes are common trends or ideas that appear repeatedly throughout the data. You may have to read through your data several times before you identify all of the themes within them.

4   *Interpret your data.* Interpretation involves attaching meaning and significance to your data. Start by making a list of key themes. Revisit your review notes to factor in your initial responses to the data.

    — Review each theme that arose during the coding process, and identify similarities and differences in the responses from participants with differing characteristics.

    — Consider the relationships between themes to determine how they may be connected.

    — Determine what new lessons you have learned from your research study and how those lessons can be applied to future research studies.

**Advantages**

- Is useful for gaining insight and understanding into the process and context.
- Can fill gaps in your study's quantitative data findings.
- Allows you to use your own knowledge and expertise about your intervention and to make sense of your data in addition to adding depth to understanding your program.

**Disadvantages**

- Analysis is very time-consuming and labor-intensive.
- Findings will not likely be generalizable outside the group from which you sampled participants during data collection.
- Reviewer interpretation introduces bias during analysis.
- Findings are subjective and can be interpreted differently by different stakeholders.

## EVALUATING A QUALITATIVE ANALYSIS

Assessing the overall credibility of a qualitative data analysis can be a daunting task at the best of times. Nevertheless, you can ask a series of questions contained in Appendix B on pages 495–510.

Figure 7.2 on page 149 illustrates the four phases of the qualitative research approach to knowledge development. As you know from reading Chapters 7, 9 and 16, Phases 3a–3d within a qualitative research study highly interact with each other. That is, it's totally impossible to assess one particular phase in isolation from the other three.

Thus, in reality, and for all practical purposes, to evaluate the data analysis phase (phase 3c, topic of this chapter) you also need to assess a study's overall research design (phase 3a), and data collection procedures (phase 3b), in addition to how the data were interpreted (phase 3d). This means that you have to also assess the study's: *reliability* (questions 396–404 on page 504), *creditability* (questions 405–419 on pages 504–505), *transferability* (questions 420–433 on pages 505–506), *dependability* (questions 434–435 on page 507), and *confirmability* (question 436 on page 507).

> Two people can assess the same qualitative data analysis and come up with two different opinions in respect to its overall credibility and usefulness.

## CHAPTER RECAP

- Qualitative data analyses analyze words (or text data), not numbers.
- Unlike numbers, which are used in quantitative analyses, words give us descriptions or opinions from the unique point of view of the person who spoke or wrote the words.
- Your personal biases must always be acknowledged and dealt with when doing a qualitative data analysis.
- Qualitative researchers use journals that detail the entire research process.
- A comparison of categories in any qualitative study will probably yield many different types of relationships.
- Journals are used to record the researcher's personal reactions to interviews.
- A meaning unit is a piece of data, which we consider to be meaningful all by itself.
- Qualitative researchers need to keep the number of categories in their analyses to a manageable number.
- Codes are shorthand forms for labeling categories.
- A qualitative data analysis takes a tremendous amount of time and effort.

## REVIEW EXERCISES

1 What are *qualitative data?* Provide social work examples throughout your discussion to illustrate your main points.

2 What is the main difference between *quantitative* data and *qualitative* data? Provide social work examples throughout your discussion to illustrate your main points.

3 In your own words describe what qualitative data analysis is all about. Provide social work examples throughout your discussion to illustrate your points.

4 Phase 1 has two steps (Steps 1 and 2). Describe the overall purpose of both steps using social work examples throughout your discussion.

5 Step 1 requires you to put your qualitative data in transcript form and includes two tasks. Describe each task and use the same social work example throughout your discussion.

6 Step 2 requires you to establish a concrete plan for carrying out your qualitative data analysis and includes two tasks. Describe each task, using your example from the previous question.

7 Phase 2 has two steps (Steps 3 and 4). Describe the overall purpose of both steps

using social work examples throughout your discussion.

8 Step 3 requires you to do first-level coding with your qualitative data. Describe in detail the purpose of first-level coding and provide examples throughout your discussion to illustrate your main points.

9 Step 4 requires you to do second-level coding with your qualitative data. Describe in detail the purpose of second-level coding and provide social work examples throughout your discussion to illustrate your main points.

10 Phase 3 has two steps (Steps 5 and 6). Describe the overall purpose of both steps using social work examples throughout your discussion.

11 Step 5 requires you to interpret your qualitative data. Describe in detail the purpose of qualitative data interpretation and provide social work examples throughout your discussion to illustrate your main points.

12 Step 6 requires you to assess the trustworthiness of your study's results. Why is this necessary? Provide social work examples throughout your discussion to illustrate your main points.

# PART VI

# RESEARCH PROPOSALS AND REPORTS

**CHAPTER 20:** Quantitative Proposals and Reports **426**

**CHAPTER 21:** Qualitative Proposals and Reports **446**

| COMPETENCY 1 | Demonstrate Ethical and Professional Behavior |
|---|---|

You will learn that in order to be a successful evidence-based practitioner you have an ethical obligation to integrate three research roles into your daily practice activities as discussed in Chapter 3: (1) research consumer, (2) research partner—either as a co-researcher or research participant, and (3) creator and disseminator of research (or knowledge).

In reference to numbers 2 and 3 above, this means you need to write quantitative research proposals to advance our profession's knowledge base (practice-informed research) and write reports for possible publication based on your study's results (research-informed practice). This entire chapter is devoted to this topic.

You do not have to have the skills to write quantitative research proposals and reports to be a research consumer.

| COMPETENCY 4 | Engage in Practice-Informed Research and Research-Informed Practice |
|---|---|

Competency 4 also pertains to the entire chapter because you have to:

1  Be competent in writing quantitative research proposals that seek funds to carry out your proposed research studies (**research partner** in addition to **creator and disseminator of research**—practice-informed research);

2  Be competent in writing quantitative research reports based on quantitative research studies (**research partner** in addition to **creator and disseminator of research**—practice-informed research).

| COMPETENCY 9 | Evaluate Practice with Individuals, Families, Groups, Organizations, & Communities |
|---|---|

See Competencies 1 and 4.

# Quantitative Proposals and Reports

| | | |
|---|---|---|
| CHAPTERS 1 & 3 | Step 1. | Understanding the Research Process |
| CHAPTER 2 | Step 2. | Formulating Research Questions |
| CHAPTER 4<br>APPENDIXES A–C | Step 3. | Reviewing the Literature<br>Evaluating the Literature |
| CHAPTERS 5 & 6 | Step 4. | Being Aware of Ethical and Cultural Issues |
| CHAPTERS 7–10 | Step 5. | Selecting a Research Approach |
| CHAPTERS 11 & 12 | Step 6. | Specifying How Variables Are Measured |
| CHAPTER 13 | Step 7. | Selecting a Sample |
| CHAPTERS 14 & 15 | Step 8. | Selecting a Research Design |
| CHAPTERS 16 & 17 | Step 9. | Selecting a Data-Collection Method |
| CHAPTERS 18 & 19 | Step 10. | Analyzing the Data |
| CHAPTERS 20 & 21 | Step 11. | Writing the Research Report |

# Quantitative Proposals and Reports

CHAPTER

# 20

CHAPTER OUTLINE

"I'd like to call it "Research Proposal Lite." Quantitatively speaking, it contains a third fewer required parts but you'd never know it."

WRITING QUANTITATIVE RESEARCH PROPOSALS
    Part 1: Research Topic
    Part 2: Literature Review
    Part 3: Conceptual Framework
    Part 4: Research Question or Hypothesis
    Part 5: Methodology
        *Part 5a: Research Design*
        *Part 5b: Operational Definitions*
        *Part 5c: Population and Sample*
        *Part 5d: Data Collection*
        *Part 5e: Data Analysis*
    Part 6: Limitations
    Part 7: Administration
WRITING QUANTITATIVE RESEARCH REPORTS
    Part 1: Problem
    Part 2: Method
    Part 3: Findings
    Part 4: Discussion
    *Limitations*
CHAPTER RECAP
REVIEW EXERCISES

THIS CHAPTER DISCUSSES both how to write a quantitative (or positivistic) research proposal, which is done before the study begins, and how to write its corresponding research report, which is done after the study is completed. We present them together because a research proposal describes what is *proposed to be done*, while a research report describes what *actually has been done*.

> This chapter assumes you know the contents of Chapters 8, 16, & 18 inside out and backwards. This would be good time to reread these three chapters before reading further.

As will be emphasized throughout the chapter, there is so much overlap between the two that a majority of the material written for a research proposal can be easily used in writing the final research report.

This chapter incorporates most of the contents of the preceding chapters, so it's really a summary of the entire research process (and this book) up to report writing. We will use as an example Lula Wilson, a social work practitioner who works at a local domestic violence shelter. On a very general level, she wants to do a quantitative research study on the problems children experience who have witnessed domestic violence.

## WRITING QUANTITATIVE RESEARCH PROPOSALS

When writing any research proposal, we must always keep in mind the purposes for its development and be aware of politically sensitive research topics (see chapters 5 and 6). These are, primarily, to get permission to do the study and, second, perhaps to obtain some funds with which to do it.

> A majority of the material written for a quantitative research proposal can be easily used in writing the final research report.

There's also a third purpose—to persuade the people who will review the proposal that its author, Lula, is competent to carry out the intended study. Finally, the fourth purpose of a proposal is to force Lula to write down exactly *what* is going to be studied, *why* it's going to be studied, *who's* going to do the study, and *how* it's going to be studied.

In doing this, she may think of aspects of the study that had not occurred to her before. For example, she may look at the first draft of her proposal and realize that some essential details were forgotten—for instance, that the research participants who are going to fill out self-report standardized measuring instruments must be able to read.

The intended readers of the proposal determine how it will be written. It's important to remember that the reviewers will probably have many proposals to evaluate at once. Some proposals will need to be turned down because there will not be sufficient funds, space, or staff time to accept them all. Thus, proposal reviewers are faced with some difficult decisions on which ones to accept and which ones to reject. People who review research proposals often do so on a voluntary basis.

With the preceding in mind, the proposal should be written so that it is easy to read, easy to follow, easy to understand, clearly organized, and brief. It must not ramble or go off into anecdotes about how Lula became interested in the subject in the first place. Rather, Lula's proposal must describe her proposed research study simply, clearly, and concisely. These are very hard tasks and require a lot of rewriting—and we mean a lot of rewriting!

Now that we know the underlying rationale for the proposal, the next step is to consider what content it should include. This depends to some extent on who will be reviewing it. If the proposal is submitted to an academic committee, for example, it will often include more of a literature review and more details of the study's research design than if it is submitted to a local social work funding organization such as United Way. Some funding bodies specify exactly what they want included and in what order; others leave it to the author's discretion.

The simplest and most logical way to write the proposal is in the same order that a research study is conducted. For example, when a research study is done, a general topic area is decided on. This is followed by a literature review in an attempt to narrow the broad research area into more specific research questions or hypotheses.

We will now go back and look at how each step of the quantitative research approach (see figure 7.1 on page 145) leads to the writing of a parallel section in a research proposal. Let's turn to the first task of proposal writing, specifying the research topic.

## PART 1: RESEARCH TOPIC

The first step in beginning any research study is to decide what the study will be about. The first task in writing a proposal, therefore, is to describe, in general terms, what exactly is going to be studied. Lula may describe, for example, her proposed study's general problem area as:

**General problem area**
Problems experienced by children who witness domestic violence

Lula needs to convince the proposal reviewers that the general problem area is a good one to study. This task is accomplished by outlining the significance of Lula's proposed study in three specific social work areas: (1) its practical significance, (2) its theoretical significance, and (3) its social policy significance. Depending on to whom the proposal is submitted, Lula may go into detail about these three areas or describe them briefly.

> Part 1 of a research proposal describes what is going to be studied and why it should be studied.

It may be known, for example, that the funding organization that will review the proposal is mostly interested in improving the effectiveness of individual social workers in their day-to-day practice activities. If this is the case, the reviewers will more likely be interested in the practical significance of Lula's proposed study than its theoretical and/or policy significance. Therefore, Lula's proposal would neither go into detail about how her proposed study might generate new social work theory, nor elaborate on the changes in social policy that might follow directly from the study's results.

Since Lula is going to submit her proposal to the women's emergency shelter where she works, she would be smart in obtaining informal input from her agency's executive director at this stage in writing the proposal. Informal advice at an early stage is astronomically important to proposal writers. In sum, Part 1 of the proposal describes what is going to be studied and why it should be studied.

# PART 2: LITERATURE REVIEW

The second part of a proposal contains the literature review. This is not simply a list of all the books and journal articles that vaguely touch on the general problem area mentioned in Part 1 (i.e., problems experienced by children who witness domestic violence). When a research study is done, it is mainly trying to add another piece to a jigsaw puzzle already begun by other researchers. The purpose of her literature review, then, will be to show how her proposed study fits into "the whole."

The trouble is that it might be a very big whole. There easily could be literally hundreds of articles and books filled with previous research studies on Lula's general topic area. If Lula tries to list every one of these, the reviewers of the proposal, probably her colleagues who work with her at the shelter, will very quickly lose interest and patience somewhere in the middle of Part 2.

Her literature review has to be selective—listing enough material to show that she is thoroughly familiar with her topic area, but not enough to induce stupor in the reviewers. This is a delicate balance. She should include findings from recent research studies along with any classical ones.

On the other side of the coin, another possibility is that previous research studies on Lula's general topic area may be limited. In this case, all available material is included. However, her proposal can also branch out into material that is partially related or describes a parallel topic area.

Lula might find a research article, for example, that claims that children whose parents are contemplating divorce have low social interaction skills. This does not bear directly on the matter of problems children have who witnessed domestic violence (the general problem area previously mentioned). However, since marital separation can be a result of domestic violence, it might be indirectly relevant. In short, a literature review serves four overlapping purposes:

> The literature review has many purposes and is an extremely important component of a research proposal.

1 It shows the reviewers that Lula understands the most current and central issues related to the general topic area that she proposes to study.

2 It points out in what ways her proposed study is the same as, or different from, other similar studies.

3 It describes how the results of her proposed study will contribute to answering her research question.

4 It introduces and conceptually defines all the variables that will be examined throughout the study.

At this stage, Lula does not operationally define her study's variables—that is, in such a way that allows their measurement. They are only abstractly defined. For example, if Lula is going to study the social interaction skills of children who witness domestic violence, her proposal so far introduces only four concepts:

1 Children

2 Domestic violence

3 Children witnessing domestic violence

4 Children's social interaction skills

# PART 3: CONCEPTUAL FRAMEWORK

A conceptual framework takes the variables that have been mentioned in Part 2, illustrates their possible relationship to one another, and discusses why the relationship exists the way Lula proposes they do and not in some other, equally possible way. The author's suppositions might be based on past professional experience. For example, Lula has observed numerous children who accompanied their mothers to women's emergency shelters. She has made subjective observations of these children over the past two years and finally wishes to test out two hunches objectively.

1   Lula believes that children who have witnessed domestic violence seem to have lower social interaction skills than children who have not witnessed domestic violence.

2   Lula believes that of the children who have been a witness to domestic violence, boys seem to have lower social interaction skills than girls.

However, the above two hunches are based on only two-year subjective observations, which need to be objectively tested—the purpose of her study.  As we know, ideally, Lula's hunches should be integrated with existing theory or findings derived from previous research studies. In any case, Lula should discuss these assumptions and the reasons for believing them as the basis for the variables that are included in her proposed study.

> A conceptual framework clearly discusses how the variables in a proposed research study relate to one another.

## PART 4: RESEARCH QUESTION OR HYPOTHESIS

Given the first three parts of Lula's proposal so far, we can easily see that she wants to find out whether children who have witnessed domestic violence have lower social interaction skills than those children who have not witnessed it. And of the children who have witnessed domestic violence, she wants to determine whether boys have lower social interaction skills than girls.

It must be remembered that the two areas her study proposes to explore have been delineated out of her past experiences and have not been formulated on existing theory or previous research findings. From Lula's general problem area, she formulated two related research hypotheses as follows:

**Research hypothesis 1**
Children who have witnessed domestic violence will have lower social interaction skills than children who have not witnessed such abuse.

**Research hypothesis 2**
Of those children who have witnessed domestic violence, boys will have lower social interaction skills than girls.

## PART 5: METHODOLOGY

Part 5 of a research proposal, often commonly called the "methodology" section of a research proposal, contains five highly interdependent subparts:

**Part 5a**   Research design
**Part 5b**   Operational definitions
**Part 5c**   Population and sample
**Part 5d**   Data collection
**Part 5e**   Data analysis

### PART 5A: RESEARCH DESIGN

In relation to Research Hypothesis 1, Lula's study would use the children who accompanied their mothers to the women's emergency shelter. These children would then be broken down into two mutually exclusive groups:

**1** Those children who witnessed domestic violence

**2** Those children who did not witness it

As presented in Chapter 15, a very simple comparison group pretest-posttest research design could be used to test Research Hypothesis 1 (see figure 15.7 on page 319). One group would be those children who witnessed domestic violence, and the second group would be those children who did not witness it. The average social interaction skills between the two groups can then be compared.

In relation to Research Hypothesis 2, within the group of children who have witnessed domestic violence, the children's social interaction skills between the boys and girls can be compared. This simple procedure would test Research Hypothesis 2. Once again, as presented in Chapter 15, a simple comparison group pretest-posttest research design could be used to test Research Hypothesis 2. One group would consist of the boys and the other group would consist of the girls.

In Lula's study, there are two separate mini-research studies running at the same time—Research Hypotheses 1 and 2. All Lula wants to do is to see if there is a relationship between the social interaction skills of children who have and have not witnessed domestic violence (research hypothesis 1). In addition, for those children who have witnessed domestic violence, she wants to see if boys have lower social interaction skills than girls (research hypothesis 2).

> The *research design* section of a research proposal must be clearly linked to the research question to be answered or the hypothesis to be tested.

### PART 5B: OPERATIONAL DEFINITIONS

As mentioned, variables are abstractly and conceptually defined in the conceptual framework part of the proposal (part 3). Part 5b provides operational definitions of them; that is, they must be defined in ways in which they can be measurable. Let's take Lula's first simple research hypothesis, as previously mentioned. In this hypothesis there are four main variables that must be operationalized before Lula's study can begin:

**1** Children

**2** Domestic violence

**3** Children witnessing domestic violence

**4** Children's social interaction skills

Each one of the preceding four variables must be measured in such a way that there is no ambiguity as to what they mean. Let's start off by operationally defining "children."

**VARIABLE 1:** *Children.* For example, what constitutes a child? How old must the child be? Does the child have to be in a certain age range, for example between the ages of 5 and 10? Does the child have to be a biological product of either the mother or the father? Can the child be a stepchild? Can the child be adopted? Does the child have to live full-time at home?

Since Lula's study is extremely basic, she may wish to define a child operationally in such a way that permits the largest number of children to be included in her study. She would, however, turn to the literature to find out how other researchers have operationally defined "children," and she would use this operational definition if it made sense to her.

However, in a simple study such as this one, a child could be operationally defined as "any person who is considered to be a child as determined by the mother." This is a very vague operational definition, at best, but it's more practical than constructing one such as, "a person between the ages of 5 and 17 who has resided full-time with the biological mother for the last 12-month period."

If such a complex operational definition was utilized, Lula would have to provide answers to questions as: Why the ages of 5 to 17, why not 4 to 18? What is the specific reason for this age range? Why must the child live at home full-time, why not part-time? Why must the mother be the biological mother, why not a nonbiological mother? What about biological fathers? Why must the child have had to live at home for the past twelve months, why not two years or four years?

In short, Lula's operational definition of a child must make sense and be based on a rational or theoretical basis. For now, Lula is going to make matters simple: A child in her study will be operationally defined as any child whose mother validates their relationship. This simple operational definition makes the most practical sense to Lula.

**VARIABLE 2:** *Domestic Violence.* Let's now turn to Lula's second variable—domestic violence. What is it? Does the male partner have to shove, push, or threaten his partner? How would a child, as operationally defined above, know when it occurs? Does a husband yelling at his wife imply domestic violence? If so, does it have to last a long time? If it does, what is a long time? Is Lula interested in the frequency, duration, or magnitude of yelling—or all three?

> Operational definitions define how the variables are going to be measured.

A specific operational definition of domestic violence has to be established in order for the study to be of any value. Like most variables, there are as many operational definitions of domestic violence as there are people willing to define it. For now, Lula is going to continue to make her simple study simple by operationally defining domestic violence as "women who say they have been physically abused by their partners." Lula can simply ask each woman who enters the shelter if she believes she has been physically abused by her partner.

The data provided by the women will be "yes" or "no." Lula could have looked at the frequency, duration, or magnitude of such abuse, but for this study the variable is a dichotomous one: Either domestic violence occurred, or it did not occur—as reported by the women. Questions regarding its frequency (how many times it occurred), its duration (how long each episode lasted), and its magnitude (the intensity of each episode) are not asked.

> Operational definitions of all variables must make sense, be realistic, and have a theoretical basis if at all possible.

**VARIABLE 3:** *Children Witnessing Domestic Violence.* The third variable in Lula's hypothesis is the child (or children) who witnesses domestic violence. Now that operational definitions of a "child" and "domestic violence" have been formulated, how will she know that a child has witnessed such an abuse? Each child could be asked directly, or a standardized checklist of possible verbal and physical abuses that a child might have witnessed can be given to the child, who is then asked how many times such abuse has been observed.

Obviously, the child would have to know what constitutes domestic violence to recognize it. In addition, the child would have to be old enough to respond to such requests, and the operational definition that is used for domestic violence must be consistent with the age of the child. For example, the child must be able to communicate to someone that domestic violence has in fact occurred—not to mention the question of whether the child could recognize it in the first place.

In Lula's continuing struggle to keep her study as simple as possible, she operationally defines "a child witnessing domestic violence" by asking the mothers who come to the women's emergency shelter if their child(ren) witnessed the physical abuse.

Lula is interested only in the women who come to the shelter as a result of being physically abused by their partners. Women who come to the shelter for other reasons are not included in her study. It must be kept in mind that Lula's study is focusing only upon physical abuse and not emotional, financial, or mental abuse.

So far, Lula's study is rather simple in terms of operational definitions. Up to this point she is studying mothers who bring their child(ren) with them to one women's emergency shelter. She simply asks the mother if the person(s) with her is her child(ren), which operationally defines "child."

The mother is asked if she believes her partner physically abused her, which defines "domestic violence." The mother is also asked if the child(ren) who is(are) accompanying her to the shelter saw the physical abuse occur, which operationally defines "children witnessing domestic violence."

**VARIABLE 4:** *Children's Social Interaction Skills.* Let's now turn to Lula's fourth and final variable in her hypothesis—the children's social interaction skills. How will they be measured? What constitutes the social interaction skills of a child? They could be measured in a variety of ways through direct observations of parents, social work practitioners, social work researchers, social work practicum students, teachers, neighbors, and even members from the children's peer group.

They could also be measured by standardized measuring instruments such as the ones discussed in Chapters 11 and 12. Lula decides to use one of the many standardized measuring instruments that measure social interaction skills of children, named the *Social Interaction Skills of Children Assessment Instrument (SISOCAI)*. All in all, Part 5b of a proposal provides operational definitions of the variables that were abstractly defined in Part 3. It should be noted that the four variables that have been operationally defined should be defined from the available literature, if appropriate. (This procedure makes a study's results generalizable from one research situation to another.)

However, there might be times when this is not possible. Lula's proposal must specify what data gathering instruments are going to be used, including their validity and reliability, as presented in Chapters 11 and 12.

In summary, let's review how Lula intends to operationally define her key variables:

1  **Child.** Any person who the mother claims is her child.
2  **Domestic Violence.** Asking the mother if her partner physically abused her.
3  **Child Witnessing Domestic Violence.** Asking the mother if the child(ren) who accompanied her to the shelter witnessed the abuse.
4  **Children's Social Interaction Skills.** The *SISOCAI* score for each child in the study.

The first three operational definitions are rather rudimentary, at best. There are many more sophisticated ways of operationally defining them. However, alternative definitions will not be explored; Lula wants to keep her research proposal as uncomplicated as possible because she knows that the shelter does not want a study that would intrude too heavily into its day-to-day operations.

On a very general level, the more complex the operational definitions of variables used in a research study, the more the study will intrude on the research participants' lives—in addition to the agency's day-to-day operations.

## PART 5C: POPULATION AND SAMPLE

This part of the proposal presents a detailed description of who will be studied. Lula's research study will use the children who accompanied their mothers to one women's emergency shelter who wish to voluntarily participate, and whose mothers agree that their children can be included in the study (see chapter 5 on research ethics). Each child will then each go into one of two distinct groups: those who have witnessed domestic violence, and those who have not (according to the mothers, that is).

Lula's study could have used a comparison group of children from the same local community who have never witnessed domestic violence and have never been to a women's emergency shelter. However, Lula chose to use only those children who accompanied their mothers to the shelter where she works. There is no question of random selection from some population, and it's not possible to generalize the study's findings to any general population of children who have and have not witnessed domestic violence. The results of Lula's study will apply only to the children who participated in it.

### PART 5D: DATA COLLECTION

This part presents a detailed account of how the data are going to be collected—that is, the specific data collection method(s) that will be used. As we know, data can be collected using interviews (individual or group), surveys (mail or telephone), direct observations, participant observations, secondary analyses, and content analyses.

Lula is going to collect data on the dependent variable by having her research assistant complete the *SISOCAI* for each identified child during a half-hour interview one day after the mother enters the shelter with her child(ren). Those mothers who do not bring their children with them will not be included in Lula's study. In addition to the children, their mothers are also going to be interviewed to some small degree. Lula will ask each mother if she believes her partner physically assaulted her. These responses will then be used to operationally define "domestic violence."

> All research proposals must clearly state who is going to participate in the research study—that is, who's going to be included in the study's sample.

Each mother will also provide data on whether or not her child(ren) who accompanied her to the shelter saw the abuse occur. The mothers' responses will then operationally define whether or not the child(ren) witnessed domestic violence.

Finally, this section should discuss ethical and cultural issues involved in the data-collection process (chapters 5 and 6). Chapters 16 and 17 in this book present various data-collection methods that can be used in research studies. These chapters should be reread thoroughly before writing Part 5d of a research proposal.

### PART 5E: DATA ANALYSIS

This part describes the way the data will be analyzed, including the statistical procedures to be used, if any. Having clearly specified the research design in Part 5a, this part specifies exactly what statistical test(s) will be used to answer the research questions or test the hypotheses.

The *SISOCAI* produces interval-level data, and a child's social interaction skill score on this particular instrument can range from 0–100, where higher scores mean better social skills than lower scores. Since there are two groups of children who are being used to test both research hypotheses, and the dependent variable (*SISOCAI*) is at the interval-level of measurement, an independent *t*-test would be used to test both research hypotheses.

> All research proposals must clearly state the study's data-collection plan on how data for each variable are to be collected—that is, *who* is going to collect them, and *when and where* will they be collected.

## PART 6: LIMITATIONS

There are limitations in every research study, often due to problems that cannot be eliminated entirely—even though steps can be taken to reduce them. Lula's study is certainly no exception. Limitations inherent in a study might relate to the validity and reliability of the measuring instruments, or to the generalizability of the study's findings. Sometimes the data that were needed could not be collected for some reason. In addition, this part should mention all extraneous variables that have not been controlled for.

For example, Lula may not have been able to control for all the factors that affect the children's social interaction skills. Although she believes that having witnessed domestic violence leads to lower social skills for boys as compared with girls, it may not be possible to collect reliable and valid data about whether the children saw or did not see an abuse occur. In Lula's study, she is going to simply ask the mothers, so in this case she has to take the mothers' word for it.

She could ask the children, however. This would produce another set of limitations in and of itself. For example, it would be difficult for Lula to ascertain whether a child did or did not see a form of domestic violence as perceived by the child. It may be hard for a child to tell what type of abuse occurred.

Also the frequency, duration, and magnitude of a particular form of domestic violence may be hard for the child to recall. All these limitations, and a host of others, must be delineated in this part of the proposal. In addition, asking children if they saw the abuse occur might prove to be a traumatic experience for them.

Some limitations will not be discovered until the study is well underway. However, many problems can be anticipated and these should be included in the proposal, together with the specific steps that are intended to minimize them.

## PART 7: ADMINISTRATION

The final part of a research proposal contains the organization and resources necessary to carry out the study. First, Lula has to find a base of operations (e.g., desk, telephone). She has to think about who is going to take on the overall administrative responsibility for the study. How many individuals will be needed? What should their qualifications be? What will be their responsibilities? To whom are they responsible? What is the chain of command? Finally, Lula has to think about things such as a computer, stationery, telephone, travel, and parking expenses.

When all of the details have been put together, an organizational chart can be produced that shows what will be done, by whom, where, and in what order. The next step is to develop a time frame. By what date should each anticipated step be completed? Optimism about completion dates should be avoided, particularly when it comes to allowing time to analyze the data and writing the final report (to be discussed shortly). Both of these activities always take far longer than anticipated, and it's important that they be properly done—which takes more time than originally planned.

When the organizational chart and time frame have been established, the final step is to prepare a budget. Lula has to figure out how much each aspect of the study—such as office space, the research assistant's time, staff time, and participants' time, if any—will cost.

We have now examined seven parts that should be included when writing a research proposal. Not all proposals are organized in precisely this way; sometimes different headings are used or information is put in a different part of the proposal. For example, in some proposals, previous studies are discussed in the conceptual framework section rather than in the literature review. Much depends on for whom the proposal is being written and on the author's personal writing style.

Most, if not all, of the content that has been used to write the various parts of a research proposal can be used to write the research report. Let's now turn to that discussion.

> All proposed research studies have limitations of some kind such as representative samples, measurement issues, and data-collection and analyses challenges.

## WRITING QUANTITATIVE RESEARCH REPORTS

A **research report** is a way of describing the completed study to other people. The findings can be reported by way of an oral presentation, a book, or a published paper. The report may be addressed solely to colleagues at work or to a worldwide audience. It may be written simply, so that everyone can understand it, or it may be so highly technical that it can only be understood by a few. The most common way of sharing a study's findings with other professionals is to publish a report in a professional journal. Most journal reports run about twenty-five double-spaced, typewritten pages, including figures, tables, and references. As we know, proposals are written with the proposal reviewers in mind. Similarly, a research report is written with its readers in mind.

However, some of the readers who read research reports will want to know the technical details of how the study's results were achieved, and others will only want to know how the study's results are relevant to social work practice, without the inclusion of the technical details. There are a number of ways to deal with this situation.

First, a technical report can be written for those who can understand it, without worrying too much about those who cannot. In addition, a second report can be written that skims over the technical aspects of the study and concentrates mostly on the practical application of the study's findings.

> Two versions of the same study can be written: a technical one and a nontechnical one.

Thus, two versions of the same study can be written: a technical one and a nontechnical one. The thought of writing two reports where one would suffice will not appeal to very many of us, however. Usually, we try to compensate for this by including those technical aspects of the study that are necessary to an understanding of the study's findings. This is essential because readers will not be able to evaluate the study's findings without knowing how they were arrived at. However, life can be made easier for nontechnical audiences by including some explanation of the technical aspects and, in addition, paying close attention to the practical application of the study's results. In this way, we will probably succeed in addressing the needs of both audiences—those who want all the technical details and those who want none.

A report can be organized in many different ways depending on the intended audience and the author's personal style. Often, however, the same common-sense sequence is followed as when the basic problem-solving method was discussed at the beginning of this book. In order to solve a problem, the problem must be specified, ways of solving it must be explored, a solution to solve the problem must be tried, and an evaluation must take place to see if the solution worked.

> All research reports must have some practical, theoretical, or policy significance; that is, they should contribute to social work policy, practice, or education.

In general, this is the way to solve practice and research problems. It's also the order in which a research report is written. First, a research problem is defined. Then, the method used to solve it is discussed. Next, the findings are presented. Finally, the significance of the findings to the social work profession is discussed.

## PART 1: PROBLEM

Probably the best way to begin a research report is to explain simply what the research problem is. Lula might say, for example, that the study's purpose was to ascertain if children who have witnessed domestic violence have lower social interaction skills than children who have not witnessed such abuse.

In addition, the study wanted to find out, of those children who have witnessed domestic violence, if boys have lower social interaction skills than girls. But why would anyone want to know about that? How would the knowledge derived from Lula's study help social workers?

Thinking back to her proposal, this question was asked and answered once before. In the first part of her proposal, when the research topic was set out, the significance of the study was discussed in the areas of practice, theory, and social policy. This material can be used, suitably paraphrased, in Part 1 of the final report. One thing that should be remembered, though, is that a research report written for a journal is not, relatively speaking, very long. A lot of information must be included in less than twenty-five pages, and the author cannot afford to use too much space explaining to readers why this particular study was chosen. Sometimes the significance of the study will be apparent, and there is no room to belabor what is already obvious.

In Part 2 of the proposal, a literature review was done in which Lula's proposed study was compared to other similar studies, highlighting similarities and differences. Also, key variables were conceptually defined. In her final report, she can use both the literature review and her conceptually defined variables that she presented in her proposal. The literature review might have to be cut back if space is at a premium, but the abstract and conceptual definitions of all key variables must be included. In Part 3 of her proposal, she presented a conceptual framework. This can be used in Part 1 of the final report, where Lula must state the relationships between the variables she is studying.

In Part 4 of the research proposal, a research question to be answered or hypothesis to be tested was stated. In the final report, we started out with that, so now we have come full circle. By using the various parts of the proposal for the first part of the research report, we have managed to considerably cut down on our writing time.

In fact, Part 1 of a research report is nothing more than a cut-and-paste job of the first four parts of the research proposal. Actually, if the first four parts of the research proposal were done correctly, there should be very little original writing within Part 1 of a research report.

One of the most important things to remember when writing Part 1 of a report is that the study's findings have to have some form of utilization potential for social workers, or the report would not be worth writing in the first place. More specifically, the report must have some practical, theoretical, or policy significance. Part 1 of a research report tells why the study's findings would be useful to the social work profession. This is mentioned briefly but is picked up later in Part 4.

## PART 2: METHOD

Part 2 of a report contains the method(s) used to answer the research problem. This section usually includes descriptions of the study's research design, a description of the research participants who were a part of the study (study's sample), and a detailed description of the data gathering procedures (who, what, when, how), and presents the operational definition of all variables.

Once again, sections of the original research proposal can be used. For example, in Part 5b of the proposal, key variables were operationally defined; that is, they were defined in a way that would allow them to be measured. When and how the measurements would occur were also presented in Part 5d. This material can be used again in the final report.

Part 5a of the proposal described the study's research design. This section of the proposal was used—about halfway through—to link the parts of the study together into a whole. Since a research design encompasses the entire research process from conceptualizing the problem to disseminating the findings, Lula could take this opportunity to give a brief picture of the entire process. This part presents who would be studied (the research participants, or sample), what data would be gathered, how the data would be gathered, when the data would be gathered, and what would be done with the data once obtained (analysis).

In the final report, there is not a lot of space to provide this information in detail. Instead, a clear description of how the data were obtained from the measuring instruments must be presented. For example, Lula could state in this part of the report that "a research assistant rated each child on the *SISOCAI* during a half-hour interview one day after the mother entered the shelter."

> Research proposals can answer research questions and/or test hypotheses.

Table 20.1

Means and Standard Deviations of Social Interaction Skills of Children Who Did and Did Not Witness Domestic Violence ($N = 80$)

| Witness? | Mean | Standard Deviation | n |
|----------|------|--------------------|---|
| Yes | 45 | 11 | 40 |
| No | 75 | 9 | 40 |
| Average . . . | 60 | | |

## PART 3: FINDINGS

Part 3 of a report presents the study's findings. Unfortunately, Lula's original proposal will not be of much help here because she did not know what she would find when it was written—only what she hoped to find.

One way to begin Part 3 of a report is to prepare whatever figures, tables, or other data displays that are going to be used. For now, let us take Lula's research Hypothesis 1 as an example of how to write up a study's findings.

Let's suppose that there were eighty children who accompanied their mothers to the shelter. All the mothers claimed their partners physically abused them. Lula's research assistant rated the eighty children's social skills via the *SISOCAI,* administered one day after they accompanied their mothers to the shelter. Thus, there are eighty *SISOCAI* scores. What is Lula going to do with all that data?

The goal of tables and figures is to organize the data in such a way that the reader takes them in at a glance and says, "Ah! Well, it's obvious that the children who witnessed domestic violence had lower *SISOCAI* scores than the children who did not see such abuse." As can be seen from Table 20.1 above, the average *SISOCAI* score for all eighty children is 60. These eighty children would then be broken down into two subgroups: those who witnessed domestic violence, and those who did not—according to their mothers, that is.

For the sake of simplicity let us say there were forty children in each subgroup. In the first subgroup, the average *SISOCAI* score for the forty children is 45; in the second subgroup, the average *SISOCAI* score for the forty children is 75. Table 20.1 allows the reader to quickly compare the average *SISOCAI* score for each one of the two subgroups (i.e., yes = 45; no = 75).

The reader can see, at a glance, that there is a 30-point difference between the two average *SISOCAI* scores (75 − 45 = 30). The children who witnessed domestic violence scored an average of 30 points lower on the *SISOCAI* than the children who did not witness domestic violence.

Thus, by glancing at Table 20.1 above, Lula's Research Hypothesis 1 is supported in that the children who witnessed domestic violence had lower social interaction skills than children who had not witnessed it. However, it is still not known from Table 20.1 whether the 30-point difference between the two average *SISOCAI* scores is large enough to be statistically significant. The appropriate statistical procedure for this design is the independent *t*-test, as described in Chapter 18. The results of the *t*-test could also be included under Table 20.1, or they could be described in the findings section:

The result of an independent *t*-test between the *SISOCAI* scores of children who witnessed domestic violence as compared to those children who did not witness it was statistically significant ($t = 3.56$, $df = 78$, $p < .05$). Thus, children who witnessed domestic violence had statistically significantly lower social interaction skills, on the average, than children who did not witness such abuse.

Table 20.2 below presents the study's findings for Lula's second research hypothesis. This table uses the data from the forty children who witnessed domestic violence (from table 20.1). As can be seen from Tables 20.1 and 20.2, the average social skill score for the forty children who witnessed domestic violence is 45.

### Table 20.2

Means and Standard Deviations of Social Interaction Skills of Boys and Girls
Who Witnessed Domestic Violence
(from table 20.1, $N = 40$)

| Gender | Mean | Standard Deviation | $n$ |
|---|---|---|---|
| Boys | 35 | 12 | 20 |
| Girls | 55 | 13 | 20 |
| Average . . . | 45 | | |

Table 20.2 further breaks down these forty children into two subgroups: boys and girls. Out of the forty children who witnessed domestic violence, twenty were boys and twenty were girls. As can be seen from Table 20.2, boys had an average social skill score of 35 as compared with the average score for girls of 55. Thus, the boys scored, on the average, 20 points lower than the girls. So far, Lula's second research hypothesis is supported.

However, it is still not known from Table 20.2 whether the 20-point difference between the two average *SISOCAI* scores is large enough to be statistically significant. The appropriate statistical procedure for this design is the independent *t*-test, as described in Chapter 18. The results of the *t*-test could be included under Table 20.2, or they could be described in the findings section as follows:

The result of an independent *t*-test between the *SISOCAI* scores for boys and girls who witnessed domestic violence was statistically significant ($t = 2.56$, $df = 38$, $p < .05$). Thus, boys had statistically significant lower social interaction skills, on the average, than girls.

Once a table (or figure) is constructed, the next thing that has to be done is to describe in words what it means. Data displays should be self-explanatory if done correctly. It is a waste of precious space to repeat in the text something that is perfectly apparent from a table or figure.

At this point, Lula has to decide whether she is going to go into a lengthy discussion of her findings in this part of the report or whether she is going to reserve the discussion for the next part. Which option is chosen often depends on what there is to discuss. Sometimes it is more sensible to combine the findings with the discussion, pointing out the significance of what has been found as she goes along.

## PART 4: DISCUSSION

The final part of a report presents a discussion of the study's findings. Care should be taken not to merely repeat the study's findings that were already presented in Part 3. It can be tempting to repeat one finding in order to remind the reader about it preliminary to a discussion, and then another finding, and then a third . . . and before we know it, we have written the whole of the findings section all over again and called it a discussion. What's needed here is control and judgment—a delicate balance between not reminding the reader at all and saying everything twice.

On the other hand, Lula might be tempted to ignore her findings altogether, particularly if she did not find what she expected. If the findings did not support her hypothesis, she may have a strong urge to express her viewpoint anyway, using persuasive prose to make up for the lack of objective evidence. This temptation must be resisted at all costs.

The term "discussion" relates to what she found, not to what she thinks she ought to have found or what she might have found under slightly different circumstances. Perhaps she did manage to find a relationship between the variables in both of her hypotheses. However, to her dismay, she may have found that the relationship was the opposite of what she predicted. For example, suppose her data indicated that children who witnessed domestic violence had higher social interaction skills than children who did not witness it (which is the opposite of what she had predicted).

## LIMITATIONS

Lula's unexpected result must be discussed, shedding whatever light on the surprising finding. Any relationship between two variables is worthy of discussion, particularly if they seem atypical or if they are not quite what was anticipated.

A common limitation in social work research has to do with not being able to randomly select research participants from a specific population. Whenever we cannot randomly select research participants the sample cannot be considered to be truly representative of the population in question, and we cannot generalize the study's results back to the population of children who witnessed or did not witness domestic violence in the community. The simplest way to deal with this limitation is to state it directly.

Another major limitation in this study is that we will never know the social interaction skills of children who did not accompany their mothers to the shelter. The social skills of children who stay home may somehow be quite different from those children who accompanied their mothers.

In fact, there are a host of other limitations in this simple study, including the simple fact that, in reference to Research Hypothesis 2, boys who did not see domestic violence may also have lower social interaction skills than girls—this was never tested in Lula's study. Nevertheless, we should also bear in mind the fact that few social work studies are based on truly representative random samples. In Lula's study, however, she still managed to collect some interesting data.

All social work researchers would like to be able to generalize their findings beyond their specific research settings and samples. From a research perspective (not a practice perspective), Lula is not really interested in the specific children in this particular study. She's more interested in children who witness domestic violence in general. Technically, the results of her study cannot be generalized to other populations of children who witness domestic violence, but she can suggest that she might find similar results with other children who accompany their mothers to similar women's shelters. She can recommend further studies into the topic area.

Sometimes we can find support for our suggestions in the results of previous studies that were not conclusive either, but that also managed to produce recommendations. It might even be a good idea to extract these studies from the literature review section in Part 1 of the report and resurrect them in the discussion section.

On occasion, the results of a study will not agree with the results of previous studies. In this case, we should give whatever explanations seem reasonable for the disagreement and make some suggestions whereby the discrepancy can be resolved. Perhaps another research study should be undertaken that would examine the same or different variables. Perhaps, next time, a different research design should be used or the research hypothesis should be reformulated. Perhaps other operational definitions could be used. Suggestions for future studies should always be specific, not just a vague statement to the effect that more research studies need to be done in this area.

In some cases, recommendations can be made for changes in social work programs, interventions, or policies based on the results of a study. These recommendations are usually contained in reports addressed to people who have the power to make the suggested changes. When changes are suggested, the author has to display some knowledge about the policy or program and the possible consequences of implementing the suggested changes.

Finally, a report is concluded with a summary of the study's findings. This is particularly important in longer reports or when a study's findings and discussion sections are lengthy or complex. Sometimes, indeed, people reading a long report read only the summary and a few sections of the study that interests them.

## CHAPTER RECAP

- Research proposals contain statements about what we will do (future tense).

- Research reports contain statements about what we have done (past tense).

- Research proposals can answer research questions and/or test hypotheses.

- A research proposal should be written so that it is easy to read, easy to follow, easy to understand, clearly organized, and brief.

- The simplest and most logical way to write a research proposal is in the same order that a research study is conducted.

- Most, if not all, of the content that has been used to write the various parts of a research proposal can be used to write the final research report.

## REVIEW EXERCISES

1  In your own words, describe what a quantitative research proposal is all about. Use social work examples to illustrate your main points.

2  List and thoroughly discuss the four main purposes of a social work research proposal. Provide a social work example that illustrates each purpose.

3  Online, search for "How to write a research proposal." Locate at least five links on the subject. What are their similarities and differences? Did any of them contain content that this chapter should have included? If so, what content?

4  In groups of four, write a brief four-page research proposal that tests this hypothesis: MSW graduates make better social workers than BSW graduates. Be sure to include all seven components of a research proposal. Hint: You're going to have to operationally define "better" along with "MSW graduates," "BSW graduates," and "social worker."

5  In the same group of four, pretend you actually implemented your proposal (Question 4). Make up fake data that supports your hypothesis. Now use these fake data to write a simple research report that includes all four parts described in this chapter.

6  Discuss how quantitative research proposals utilize all the contents in this book. Provide one simple example from each one of the preceding nineteen chapters that could be included in a research proposal. You should have 19 points in total—one for each chapter.

7  If you currently have a practicum, ask your field instructor for copies of any quantitatively oriented research proposals they may have in their filing cabinets. Select one proposal and critique it using the contents of this chapter—and the entire book for that matter.

**8** Locate a published quantitatively oriented social work research article that contains a social work problem area or population that you're interested in. We suggest you locate a quantitatively oriented research study in Bruce Thyer's journal *Research on Social Work Practice* (Sage Publications). Hands down, this is the best journal to find good quantitatively oriented social work research studies.

- Using the contents of this chapter, write a brief 2-page hypothetical quantitative research proposal that the author could have written for the quantitative research study.

- Compare your quantitative proposal with those generated by your classmates who used the same research study. What did you learn from comparing your proposal with others' proposals?

- Did the research study also contain a "qualitative" component (mixed-methods research as discussed in Chapter 10)? If so, what did it contain? How did this "qualitative" component add more meat to the quantitative findings?

**Note:** You're working backward here. That is, you're reconstructing what a hypothetical quantitatively oriented research proposal could have looked like given the contents of the actual published research study. Remember, research proposals contain statements about what we will do (future tense); research reports contain statements about what we have done (past tense).

## 2015 EPAS COMPETENCIES

| COMPETENCY 1 | Demonstrate Ethical and Professional Behavior |
|---|---|

You will learn that in order to be a successful evidence-based practitioner you have an ethical obligation to integrate three research roles into your daily practice activities as discussed in Chapter 3: (1) research consumer, (2) research partner—either as a co-researcher or research participant, and (3) creator and disseminator of research (or knowledge).

In reference to numbers 2 and 3 above, this means you need to write qualitative research proposals to advance our profession's knowledge base (practice-informed research) and write reports for possible publication based on your study's results (research-informed practice). This entire chapter is devoted to this topic.

You do not have to have the skills to write qualitative research proposals and reports to be a research consumer.

| COMPETENCY 4 | Engage in Practice-Informed Research and Research-Informed Practice |
|---|---|

Competency 4 also pertains to the entire chapter because you have to:

1  Be competent in writing qualitative research proposals that seek funds to carry out your proposed research studies (**research partner** in addition to **creator and disseminator of research**—practice-informed research);

2  Be competent in writing qualitative research reports based on qualitative research studies (**research partner in** addition to **creator and disseminator of research**—practice-informed research).

| COMPETENCY 9 | Evaluate Practice with Individuals, Families, Groups, Organizations, & Communities |
|---|---|

See Competencies 1 and 4.

# Qualitative Proposals and Reports

| | | |
|---|---|---|
| CHAPTERS 1 & 3 | Step 1. | Understanding the Research Process |
| CHAPTER 2 | Step 2. | Formulating Research Questions |
| CHAPTER 4<br>APPENDIXES A–C | Step 3. | Reviewing the Literature<br>Evaluating the Literature |
| CHAPTERS 5 & 6 | Step 4. | Being Aware of Ethical and Cultural Issues |
| CHAPTERS 7–10 | Step 5. | Selecting a Research Approach |
| CHAPTERS 11 & 12 | Step 6. | Specifying How Variables Are Measured |
| CHAPTER 13 | Step 7. | Selecting a Sample |
| CHAPTERS 14 & 15 | Step 8. | Selecting a Research Design |
| CHAPTERS 16 & 17 | Step 9. | Selecting a Data-Collection Method |
| CHAPTERS 18 & 19 | Step 10. | Analyzing the Data |
| CHAPTERS 20 & 21 | Step 11. | Writing the Research Report |

# Qualitative Proposals and Reports

"I think Step 3 is the qualitative part in your mixed-methods research proposal."

CHAPTER

# 21

CHAPTER OUTLINE

WRITING QUALITATIVE RESEARCH PROPOSALS
    Purpose of Writing a Proposal
    Intended Audience
    Content and Writing Style
ORGANIZING THE RESEARCH PROPOSAL
    Part 1: Research Topic
    Part 2: Literature Review
    Part 3: Conceptual Framework
    Part 4: Questions and Hypotheses
    Part 5: Operational Definitions
    Part 6: Research Design
    Part 7: Population and Sample
    Part 8: Data Collection
    Part 9: Data Analysis
    Part 10: Limitations
    Part 11: Administration
WRITING QUALITATIVE RESEARCH REPORTS
    Abstract
    Introduction
    Method
    Analysis and Findings
    Discussion
    References
CHAPTER RECAP
REVIEW EXERCISES

LIKE QUANTITATIVE (POSITIVISTIC) RESEARCH PROPOSALS AND REPORTS presented in the previous chapter, qualitative (interpretive) research proposals and their corresponding reports are also similar to one another. If we explain clearly what we intend to do when we write our proposal, for example, and we actually carry out our study as we originally planned, then writing our research report is largely a matter of changing "we will do" (as in the proposal) to "we did" (as in the report). This is true for everything but describing our study's findings in the research report.

As we will see, there's a good deal of similarity between quantitative and qualitative research proposals and reports. After all, the research process follows a logical progression whether or not it's quantitative or qualitative. We need to know from the very beginning of our research study what we want to study, why we want to study it, what methods we will use to study it, how long our research study will take, and how much it will cost.

In addition, we need to know what data will be collected, from whom, in what way, and how they will be analyzed. For the sake of continuity, this chapter—on qualitative proposals and reports—uses roughly the same format that was used in the last chapter that described quantitative proposals and reports.

We will once again use the same example: Lula Wilson, a social work practitioner, wants to do a qualitative research study on children and their mothers in the women's emergency shelter where she works. Lula did a quantitative proposal in the previous chapter—now she wants to do a qualitative one.

> This chapter assumes you know the contents of Chapters 9, 16, & 19 inside out and backwards. This would be good time to reread these three chapters before reading further.

## WRITING QUALITATIVE RESEARCH PROPOSALS

**B**efore we begin to write the very first word of any research proposal we need to know why we want to write it and who will read it. As we have seen from the last chapter, knowing the purpose and our intended audience helps us to make important decisions about what we should include, in what order, and what writing style to use.

### PURPOSE OF WRITING A PROPOSAL

There are three general highly interrelated purposes for writing a research proposal, no matter what is being proposed:

> Just like in quantitative research proposals, a majority of the material written for qualitative ones can be easily used in writing the final research report.

1   We need to obtain permission to do the study

2   We need to obtain funding for the study

3   We need to write down exactly what we intend to study, why, and how

### RECEIVING PERMISSION

As we know from Chapter 5, obtaining permission to do our study is often a matter of resolving ethical and informed consent issues to the satisfaction of various ethics committees. Most universities and colleges have ethics committees, which decide whether our proposed study is designed in such a way that the interests of its research participants are ethically addressed. Many social services agencies throughout the world have their own ethics committees, which vet all proposed research endeavors that involve their clients and staff.

If Lula is associated in any way with a university, for example, and if her women's emergency shelter has its own ethics committee, she will have to obtain permission from both ethics committees before she can begin her study. Even if no ethics committees are involved, Lula will have to discuss her proposed study with her supervisor, who would probably have to obtain official permission from the shelter's board of directors.

### OBTAINING FUNDS

All research studies require some level of funding. Even if Lula is prepared to do all the work on her own time using her own clients, there will still be direct and indirect costs such as photocopying, travel, phone, faxing, and postage. If Lula wants her shelter to cover these costs, she must include a budget in her proposal and get the budget approved before she begins her study. If it's a larger study, necessitating money from a funding body, then Lula must tailor her research proposal to meet the requirements of the particular funding body to which she is applying.

Most funding bodies have application forms that ask the applicant to supply the study's details under specific headings. Usually, funding bodies also want to know how qualified the particular applicant is to undertake the proposed study. In other words, Lula will have to convince the funding body that she personally has the experience and educational qualifications necessary to obtain meaningful and trustworthy results from her proposed study.

### THINKING CLEARLY

After permission and funding, the third purpose of writing a proposal is to force Lula to clarify her thoughts a bit more. In the process of describing her proposed study in sufficient detail in an attempt to convince others of its importance, Lula may think of aspects of her study that she has not thought of before. She may realize, for example, that she has little experience with interviewing children, and someone who has more experience with interviewing children may be in a better position to interview them.

## INTENDED AUDIENCE

Most research proposals are reviewed by busy people who have a great deal of other work to do and probably a number of proposals to review. Thus, Lula's proposal should be as short as she can possibly make it. It should concisely describe her proposed study, its budget, and time frame in a way that is easy to read, to follow, and to understand. Many proposals have to be rejected because there is insufficient funding or facilities to support them all, and those that are rejected are not necessarily the least worthy in terms of their importance. They are, however, often the least worthy in terms of how well they were organized and written. Lula will therefore be well advised to keep her proposal simple, clear, and brief.

## Content and Writing Style

A proposal's content and writing style will largely depend on who's going to review it. As already noted, some funding bodies stipulate on their application forms what and how much they want included, and in what format and order. If there is no such stipulation, it is simplest and most logical to write the research proposal in the order that the study will be conducted—that is, the order followed in this chapter.

> Just as in quantitative research proposals, authors need to write qualitative ones in the same order that their research studies unfold.

How much to include under what heading depends on the intended audience: A research proposal submitted to an academic committee, for example, often requires more of a literature review than a proposal submitted to a funding organization.

Style similarly depends on the recipient. In most cases, it's safest to write formally, using the third person. As we know, however, qualitative research studies are often more subjective than qualitative ones, their terminology is different, their underlying assumptions are different, and the researcher's own thoughts are an important component.

It may therefore be appropriate to acknowledge the interpretive nature of the study by using a more personal writing style. As will be the case in writing the final research report, the style used depends on the proposal's intended audience and the author's personal judgment.

## Organizing the Research Proposal

**A**s previously noted, if the proposal's recipients have provided no guidance as to how its contents should be organized, it is simplest to present the proposed study in the order in which it would be conducted.

## Part 1: Research Topic

This first section of a research proposal does nothing more than introduce the study to its readers. It examines the nature of the research question being explored and its significance, both to social work in general and to the recipient of the proposal in particular. As with quantitative studies, a qualitative one should have practical significance, theoretical significance, or significance with respect to social policy; or it may touch on all three areas.

> As with quantitative research studies, qualitative ones should have practical significance, theoretical significance, or significance with respect to social policy; or it may touch on all three areas.

The author's task is to explain what research question is being asked and why the answer to this question will be of benefit, paying particular attention to the interests of the proposal's reviewers. Lula may write, for example, about the general topic area in her study as follows:

### General topic area
The problems experienced by children who witness their mothers being physically abused by their fathers

The results of such a study—knowing what these problems are—might generate new social work theory or might lead to changes in social policy. If Lula is going to submit her proposal to the women's emergency shelter where she works, however, her fellow social workers are more likely to be interested in how an understanding of the children's problems might help them to address the children's needs on a very practical level. Lula will therefore emphasize the practical significance of her study.

## Part 2: Literature Review

As with quantitative research studies, there are four purposes in carrying out a literature review for qualitative studies:

1   To assure the reviewers that Lula understands the current issues related to her research topic.

2   To point out ways in which her study is similar to, or different from, other studies that have been previously conducted. Because many qualitative studies deal with topics about which little is known, Lula may not find many studies that have explored children's experiences with respect to their witnessing domestic violence. Such a paucity of information will support Lula's contention that her study needs to be conducted.

3   To fit Lula's study into the jigsaw puzzle of present knowledge. Even if there is little knowledge in the area, there will still be some, and Lula's task is to explain how her study will fit with what is known already and will help to fill the knowledge gaps.

4   To introduce and conceptualize the variables that will be used throughout the study. Lulu's proposal, for example, will include such concepts as children, domestic violence (or partner abuse, marital abuse, wife abuse, whichever term is preferred) and children witnessing domestic violence.

## PART 3: CONCEPTUAL FRAMEWORK

As we know, in quantitative research studies, the conceptual framework identifies the possible relationships between and among concepts to one another. Identifying the ways that concepts might be connected lays the groundwork for developing a research question or research hypothesis. In the last chapter, for example, Lula formulated the research hypothesis as follows:

**Research hypothesis**
Children who have witnessed domestic violence will have lower social interaction skills than children who have not witnessed such violence.

That is, her conceptual framework included the idea that a particular concept—children's social interaction skills—was directly related to another concept—whether the children witnessed the abuse or not.

In qualitative studies, the level of knowledge in the topic area will probably be too low to allow such possible connections between and among concepts to be investigated. Children's poor social interaction skills may indeed be one of the problems experienced by children who witness their mothers being physically abused by their fathers, but Lula does not know that yet. Her research question at this stage is simply, "What problems do these children experience?"

Relationships between and among concepts can still be hypothesized, however, even at an exploratory level, and even if the hypothesized relationships will not be tested during the course of the study. People reading a qualitative study, for example, are usually more interested in where the study took place and whether the influence of the clinical setting (i.e., the shelter) was appropriately acknowledged in the data analysis.

> A conceptual framework identifies the possible relationships between and among concepts to one another.

Lula must therefore take into account the possibility that the problems experienced by the children in her study may have been due to the study's setting (i.e., the shelter) and not so much from their witnessing the abuse. If she conceptualizes this possibility early, she may decide to interview the children's mothers, asking them not only to identify their children's problems but also to describe each problem before and after coming into the shelter. Similarly, she may want to explore the possibility that the children's problems may have been related to the children being abused themselves and not just to their witnessing their mothers being physically abused by their fathers.

## PART 4: QUESTIONS AND HYPOTHESES

A qualitative research study rarely tests a research hypothesis. It's very important, however, that the questions to be answered during the course of a qualitative study be clearly formulated before it begins. Lula could formulate specific research questions, such as:

1 What types of problems do children who have witnessed domestic violence experience?

2 Does the type of abuse witnessed (e.g., hitting, yelling) affect the type of problems experienced by the children?

3 Does the intensity of the abuse—witnessed by the children—affect the problems they experience?

4 Does the frequency (e.g., daily, weekly) of the abuse—witnessed by the children—affect the problems they experience?

5 Does the duration (e.g., over months, years) of the abuse—witnessed by the children—affect the problems they experience?

6 Does the child's gender affect the types of problems they experience?

7 Does the child's age affect the types of problems they experience?

8 Do the child's problems, as perceived by the mother, affect the mother's decision to leave the abusive relationship?

9 Do the child's problems, as perceived by the mother, affect the mother's decision about whether to return to the abusive relationship?

If Lula is going to formulate specific research questions, she will probably need to use a fairly structured interview schedule when she collects interview data from the mothers and their children. On the other hand, she may prefer to formulate just a few more general questions, such as:

1 What types of problems do children who have witnessed domestic violence experience?

2 What effects do these problems have on the children?

> Qualitative research studies rarely test hypotheses.

In this case, she would use an unstructured interview schedule, which would allow the mothers and children to guide the interviews themselves, relating what is important to them in their own way. Lula's decision about whether to formulate specific or general research questions depends on the level of knowledge about the study's topic area.

If enough knowledge is available to enable her to formulate specific research questions, she will probably do that. If not, one of the purposes of her study would be to gain enough knowledge to allow specific research questions to be formulated in the future.

## PART 5: OPERATIONAL DEFINITIONS

As we know, operationally defining a variable in a quantitative (positivistic) research study means defining all variables in such a way that they can be measured. In the last chapter, for example, Lula operationally defined the level of a child's social interaction skills in terms of the child's score derived from a standardized measuring instrument (SISOCAI). The idea behind operationally defining a variable in this way is that both its definition and its measurement are consistent and objective.

Lula did not define "children's social interaction skills" herself (except insofar as she selected the measuring instrument), and she did not ask the children or their mothers what they perceived "children's social interaction skills" to be. Similarly, the measured result for each child (a numerical score) did not depend on anyone's personal perception on how well, or how badly, the child interacted socially with others. Conversely, in qualitative studies, we are not as interested in objectively defining or measuring our concepts as we are when doing quantitative studies. Indeed, we actively encourage our research participants to provide us with their own, subjective definitions because we are trying to understand their problems as they perceive them.

Similarly, we measure the extent, or effect, of a problem in terms of the research participants' subjective viewpoints. Hence, Lula will not have to worry about how to operationally define "a child" or "a child's problem," and she will not have to decide whether "a child witnessing domestic violence" means seeing it, or hearing it, or merely being aware that it's occurring.

Lula might want to collect data about the ages of the children in her study, whether they are the biological children of their mothers, and whether they live full time at home, but none of these data will be used to exclude any child from the study on the grounds that the child is too old or too young, or otherwise does not fit Lula's operational definition of "a child."

Lula does not have an elaborate and complicated operational definition of a child. In her qualitative study, "a child" is simply operationally defined as "any person whom the mother considers to be her child." Similarly, "a problem" is whatever the mother and/or child considers to be problematic. "Domestic violence" is defined as whatever the research participants think it is; and children have "witnessed domestic violence" if they and/or their mothers believe that they have.

It might be as well here to put in a word about measurement. The word "measurement" is often associated with numbers, and hence with positivistic studies. To "measure" something, however, only means to describe it as accurately and completely as possible. If we cannot describe it with numbers, we may still be able to describe it with words, and this qualitative type of measurement is just as valid as a positivistic numerical measurement. Hence, Lula is measuring the problems experienced by children when she encourages the mothers and their children to describe those problems as accurately and completely as they can—in words, not numbers.

In quantitative studies, efforts are made to mitigate the effects of researcher bias through objective measurement. In qualitative studies, however, the use of measurement is to capture the subjective experiences of the research participants. Thus, it's vital for Lula to be aware of the effects of her own feelings upon the research participants she will be interviewing.

Any prior assumptions she has made and any position she might hold must be clearly outlined at the beginning of her study so that the reader of her proposal can evaluate the degree to which her study's potential findings would reflect the research participants' opinions rather than Lula's opinions.

Similarly, it's important to record the interests and possible biases of the organization that is funding the study in addition to the agency where the study actually takes place. Would certain findings be more welcome to the funding body or the agency than other findings? Is the researcher under any pressure to emphasize certain aspects of the study's results to the detriment of other aspects? Again, the reader of a research proposal must be able to evaluate the degree to which the proposed study's auspices would potentially affect the study's findings.

A clear statement of the study's purpose might deflect critics who argue that the proposed study did not fulfill other purposes that the critics, themselves, may perceive as more important. Lula's research study might have a practical purpose, for example, where it would be in tune with the interests of the staff who work within the women's emergency shelter that would provide both funding for the study and access to its clients.

On a general level, most qualitative research studies do not have elaborate and sophisticated operational definitions of the variables they wish to study.

Lula simply wants to know what the children's problems are so that the shelter can better meet the needs of the children and their mothers. She is not overly interested in adding to social work theory or changing social policy, although her study's results may indeed have implications in both of these areas.

She is less likely to be criticized for not placing sufficient emphasis on theory and policy in her discussion if she has clearly stated from the beginning that her proposed study's purpose is to inform day-to-day practice activities within her specific shelter.

## PART 6: RESEARCH DESIGN

We now come to the *how* of the study. This section includes information about what data will be collected, in what way and from whom, and how they will be analyzed. While writing about these matters, there will be many opportunities to address issues related to the study's trustworthiness. Paying attention to four major concerns provides evidence of a study's trustworthiness:

1   **Credibility,** or truth value (*internal validity* in positivistic terms)
2   **Transferability,** or applicability (*external validity* in positivistic terms)
3   **Dependability,** or consistency (*reliability* in positivistic terms)
4   **Confirmability,** or neutrality (*objectivity* in positivistic terms)

> The concept of *transferability* as used in qualitative research studies is like the concept of *external validity* in quantitative ones.

These four concerns are roughly equivalent to the positivistic concepts of internal validity and external validity as outlined in Chapter 15. The first issue related to trustworthiness is credibility (akin to internal validity), which is particularly important and is built on the following five important aspects of all qualitative studies:

1   **Triangulation of data sources**—collecting data about the same thing from a number of different data sources; also engagement with research participants over a long period of time.
2   **Consulting with colleagues**—consulting with them about ethical and legal matters, and about the methods chosen to select the sample of research participants and to collect and analyze the data.
3   **Negative case analysis**—ensuring that information from all data sources is included in the data analysis, even when information from one data source seems to contradict themes or conclusions common to other data sources.
4   **Referential adequacy**—keeping a complete and accurate record of all personal interviews and observations, such as videotapes, audiotapes, case notes, and transcriptions.
5   **Member checks**—asking research participants to provide feedback on the information collected from the researcher and the conclusions drawn by the researcher.

The second issue related to trustworthiness is *transferability* (akin to external validity, or generalizability), which is addressed through a rich description of the study's clinical setting and the research participants. Findings from a qualitative research study are usually not generalized beyond the setting in which the study took place.

The findings may be applicable, however, to similar client populations: women and children in similar women's emergency shelters elsewhere, for example. Readers can only judge to what degree a study's findings may be applicable to their own clientele when the researcher provides a detailed description of the study's research participants in addition to their special needs and circumstances.

The third issue is *dependability* (akin to reliability), which relates to efforts to maintain consistency throughout the study. Were all interviews conducted in the same setting, according to the same format, and recorded in the same way? Were all research participants asked to provide feedback on the data collected, or only some? During data analysis, were rules concerning categorization and coding consistently applied?

Aspects of the study related to credibility, as previously described, may be used to demonstrate dependability as well: for example, referential adequacy, providing evidence of consistent interviewing procedures, and providing evidence that all research participants were asked for their feedback.

The last issue, *confirmability* (akin to objectivity), has to do with Lula's awareness of her own role in influencing the data provided by the research participants and the conclusions she drew from the data. All qualitative researchers should keep journals in which they record their own thoughts and feelings about the study's research participants and about their interviews and observations.

Lula should note in her journal, for example, why she made the decisions she did about methodological matters, such as sampling procedures, and data collection and analysis techniques. While conducting the data analysis, she will record decisions and concerns about organizing and interpreting the data she collected.

These journal entries disclose the degree of impartiality she brought to the entire research process; where she was not impartial, it discloses her awareness, or lack thereof, about her own assumptions and biases. With respect to dependability (discussed previously), it provides a record of how consistent her decision-making was and how consistently she conducted her interviews and analyzed her data.

## PART 7: POPULATION AND SAMPLE

In this part of the proposal, Lula provides only a general description of who her research participants will be, together with a rationale for selecting these and not others. In qualitative studies, there is no attempt to select a random sample. Indeed, the sample often consists of all those persons available to be studied who fit broad criteria. Lula could draw her sample of research participants, for example, from all those women who are residents in her women's emergency shelter at a specific time.

Because Lula's study involves the effects on children who witnessed domestic violence, she will need to exclude from her sample all women who do not have children and all women who say that their children did not witness the abuse. Lula may personally believe that no child whose mother is being abused can remain unaware of that abuse, and the definition of "witnessing" for her may include a child's awareness as well as seeing or hearing.

In addition, it would be interesting to explore conflicting perceptions between the mothers and their children, when the children believe that they have witnessed domestic violence and their mothers believe that they have not. Lula is unlikely, however, to elicit information about the effects of witnessing domestic violence from women who do not believe that their children witnessed it; nor are these women likely to give Lula permission to interview their children on the subject.

Lula may decide to include women who do not have their children with them at the shelter. Whether she does so will depend on a number of factors. First, how many women can she interview, given her own and the women's time constraints? This will depend on how long she expects each interview to take, which, in turn, depends on such factors as the structure and depth of the interview.

> On a general level, qualitative studies mainly use purposive sampling and snowball sampling techniques when it comes to selecting their research participants.

In addition, she must consider the time required for transcribing and analyzing each interview in its entirety. If the number of women who have their children at the shelter is equal to, or larger than, the number of women Lula can reasonably interview, then she will exclude women whose children are not present.

If the number is smaller, she may consider including these women, but that decision as well will depend on a number of factors. Uppermost in the mind of any qualitative researcher is the notion of the study's trustworthiness. As discussed earlier, one way of establishing the trustworthiness of data is to collect data about the same variable from a number of different data sources. Data on the problems experienced by children, for example, may be collected from three data sources:

1   The children themselves

2   Their mothers

3   Shelter staff who have observed the children

Such a triangulation of data sources allows assessment of the trustworthiness of the data obtained from any one given source. If children are not present at the shelter, then data on their problems can be obtained only from their mothers, and there will be no way to check on the "accuracy" of the data they provide.

Another way to establish trustworthiness is to ask each research participant to comment on the data gathered and the conclusions that the researcher drew from the data. Lula might want to submit the transcript of each interview to the research participant concerned to make sure that she has adequately captured what the participant was trying to say. Then she might want to discuss her findings with the other research participants to see if they believe that she has interpreted what they said correctly and has drawn conclusions that seem reasonable to them as well. None of this will be possible if the research participants have left the emergency shelter and disappeared before Lula has transcribed and analyzed her data.

> Ethical and cultural considerations need to be addressed when selecting samples for qualitative research studies.

She might, therefore, want to restrict her sample of women to those who are likely to remain in her shelter for a number of weeks or who will go on to a halfway house or some other traceable address. Of course, if she does this, she will lose data from women whose very transience might affect their children's problems and the way those problems are perceived. Lula must also consider whether to interview the children and, if so, children in what age groups. She may not be skilled in interviewing young children and may feel that children under school age cannot be meaningfully interviewed at all.

If there are enough women in the shelter who have older children present, she may consider restricting her sample of research participants to women whose children are, say, 10 years old or older. She will have to justify selecting age 10 instead of 8 or 12, for example, and she will lose data pertaining to the problems experienced by any excluded children.

With this in mind, she may consider enlisting the assistance of a colleague who is more skilled at eliciting information from younger children—through data collection methods such as drama, art, or play—than she is. But now she has to think about how such interview data would be analyzed and how she would integrate them with the data collected through her own personal interviews with the mothers.

The child's gender may be another consideration. Perhaps Lula has an idea that girls tend to display more internalizing problem behaviors—such as withdrawal and depression—than boys. And Lula may believe that boys tend to display more externalizing behaviors—such as hostility and aggression—than girls. She might therefore want to ensure that her study contains approximately equal numbers of girls and boys.

If she purposefully drew her sample of research participants in this way, she would have to explain that she expected to find more internalizing behaviors in girls and more externalizing behaviors in boys. This would constitute a research hypothesis, which would need to be included in the Questions and Hypotheses section and justified through the literature review. Or perhaps Lula would phrase it as a research question, simply asking whether the gender of the child was related to the type of problem behavior he or she exhibited.

Similarly, Lula might have an idea that the types of problem behaviors exhibited by children depend on their ethnic background. If she were able to conduct only a small number of interviews, for example, she might purposefully select women and children from different ethnic backgrounds to make up her sample of research participants (called *purposive sampling*, see chapter 13). Here again, she would have to justify her choice, including a relevant research question and addressing the matter in the literature review.

Lula thus has a number of factors to consider in deciding whom to include as research participants in her study. The main consideration, however, is always the willingness of the research participant to take part in the study. Like most social work populations, women in emergency shelters are an extremely vulnerable group, and it's vital to ensure that they feel freely able to refuse to participate in the study and know that their refusal will in no way affect the quality of the services they receive.

Similarly, the social workers within Lula's women's emergency shelter must also feel able to refuse and know that their refusal will not affect the terms of their employment. It's quite likely that Lula will not have the luxury of selecting her research participants in terms of the age, gender, or ethnic background of the children.

More probably, Lula will just interview those women who agree to be interviewed and who also give permission for her, or a colleague, to interview their children as well. The children will not be in a position to sign an assent form, as their mothers and the social workers will do, but it's still extremely important to ensure that they understand their rights with respect to refusing to take part in the study or withdrawing from it at any time. (see chapter 5).

## PART 8: DATA COLLECTION

This part of a qualitative research proposal provides a detailed account of how the data are going to be collected, together with a justification for using the data-collection method selected rather than some other method. Lula could use focus groups, for example, rather than unstructured interviews to collect data from the women.

She could decide not to interview children but instead to observe the children's behaviors herself, without involving a colleague or other social workers. If she does involve the shelter's social workers, she might decide just to interview them and ask how they define the children's problem behaviors and what problem behaviors they have observed in the children under study.

On the other hand, she might ask them first to define children's problem behaviors, then to purposefully observe certain children with respect to these behaviors, and finally to report their observations back to her. Whatever she decides, she must first justify her decisions and then clearly describe the methods to be used. She should state, for example, that the abused women, the shelter's workers, and the children aged 10 or over will be interviewed by her, if that is what she has decided to do.

She should also specify where these interviews would take place, how long approximately each is expected to last, and to what degree the content will be guided by an interview schedule. She should also specify the time frame within which all the interviews will be completed and how the interviews will be recorded. Videotaping, audio recording, and taking notes during the interview all have their advantages and disadvantages, which need to be discussed.

If a colleague is to work with the younger children, for example, details of the methods used to elicit interview data from these children must be given. In addition, the colleague's credentials must be included at the beginning of the proposal, since this colleague is now a coresearcher and her experience and qualifications will affect the trustworthiness of the study's findings.

Ethical considerations that were not covered in the discussion about selecting research participants should also be addressed in this section. Should Lula obtain completed consent forms from the mothers and assent forms from their children, for example, before she asks the shelter's social workers to observe the children or to discuss their behaviors with her?

Should she share the social worker's comments with the mothers and their children and tell the social workers beforehand that this is to be done? Should she share data obtained from the children with their mothers or make it clear that such data will not be shared?

Social workers might not be so honest in their comments if they know that the data will be shared, and neither might the children. In addition, children who know they are being observed might not behave as they otherwise would.

These are old dilemmas that always affect data-collection methods, and Lula must specify what dilemmas she may encounter and how she plans to resolve them. It's important as well to state how the mothers, children, and social workers are to be approached, and precisely what they are going to be told about Lula's study and their own part in it. Samples of consent forms (for the mothers) and assent forms (for the children) should be included as two appendixes at the end of the proposal.

Lula's journal is also a form of data. It will include little in the way of data collected from her research participants, but it will include Lula's reactions to these data and a chronology of her study's process. Lula might therefore want to state in her proposal that she will keep a journal to record notes on the decisions she is going to make during every stage of her study, with particular reference to the study's trustworthiness.

## PART 9: DATA ANALYSIS

This part of a qualitative research proposal describes the way the data will be analyzed. There are usually no statistical procedures to be discussed, as there may be in a quantitative study, but there are a number of other matters. As presented in Chapter 19, a decision must be made about whether to use a software computer program to aid in the data analysis and, if so, which one.

Then Lula must decide who will transcribe the interviews and how the transcripts should be formatted. She must establish a plan for her data analysis, including some plan for making journal entries.

She might want to add in her proposal that after she has analyzed the data using first- and second-level coding methods and after she has drawn conclusions, she will assess the trustworthiness of her study's findings. She will do this by documenting what she is going to do to establish credibility, transferability, dependability (consistency), and confirmability (control of biases and preconceptions).

## PART 10: LIMITATIONS

All research studies have limitations. Some might even suggest that one of the main limitations of a qualitative study is that it's not a quantitative one, but this is simply not true.

There are many data-collection methods that can be used in qualitative studies. However, interviewing is probably the most utilized.

Qualitative research studies usually do not try to establish causality between and among variables.

Every study is judged on how well it fulfills its own purpose, and one of the purposes of a qualitative study is usually to understand the experiences of the research participants in depth, including experiences that are unique to them.

The purpose of Lula's study is to gain a better understanding of the problems experienced by children who have witnessed domestic violence, from the different perspectives of the mothers, their children, and the shelter's social workers, so that the needs of these children can be better identified and met.

A discussion of a study's limitations should include only factors that impede the fulfillment of this purpose. Lula's study, for example, is not limited because she did not operationally define the concepts "domestic violence" and "children witnessing domestic violence." Part of her study's purpose is to find out how the mothers and their children themselves define "domestic violence"—that is, to find out what it was that the children in her study actually witnessed, and what they and their mothers think that "witnessing" includes.

From an ideal standpoint, Lula's study is limited with respect to its transferability (generalizability, in positivistic terms). It would have been ideal if she could have constructed a sampling frame of all the children in the world who had witnessed domestic violence, taken a random sample, and interviewed all these children and their mothers in depth.

Quantitative researchers sometimes restrict their studies to manageable samples (research participants) and then generalize from the samples to the populations from which they were drawn. It's a limitation, however, if their samples did not adequately represent their populations, thus restricting the ability to generalize from the samples to their populations.

It's not considered a limitation, however, that interpretive studies do not use larger populations in the first place. Similarly, Lula does not need to apologize for having chosen to work only with those women and their children who were residents in her particular women's emergency shelter at the time she wanted to conduct her study.

On the other hand, some of these women whose children had witnessed domestic violence may have refused to participate, and that would be a limitation to Lula's study. Those women may have felt particularly traumatized by their children's involvement, to the point where they felt unable to discuss it. By losing them, Lula would lose a different and valuable perspective.

Another limitation to Lula's study is that many of the children who have witnessed domestic violence may have been abused themselves. It may be impossible for the mothers and/or children to distinguish between the effects of being abused themselves and the effects of witnessing the abuse.

The only way Lula could deal with this is to divide her population of children who have witnessed abuse into two groups: those who have been abused, according to their mothers, and those who have not.

Of course, it might be argued that witnessing domestic violence constitutes emotional abuse. If Lula subscribes to this view, she might wish to ask the mothers specifically whether their children have been physically or sexually abused, since all the children in her sample will have been emotionally abused according to her own definition.

Nevertheless, in practical terms, Lula can form her two groups of children merely by including a question about physical or sexual abuse during her interviews with them and with their mothers. If Lula identifies this limitation early on while she is conceptualizing her study, she can include the two groups in her study's research design, mentioning the question about domestic violence in the data collection section, and noting, in the data analysis section, that she will accord each group a separate category.

> Generally speaking, qualitative research studies have fewer research participants than those in quantitative ones.

Thus, her study's limitation will have ceased to be a limitation and will have become an integral part of her study. This is one of the purposes of a research design, of course: to identify and address a study's potential limitations so that they can be eliminated or at least alleviated to the greatest possible extent before the study actually starts.

Essentially, what Lula has done in thinking about children who have been abused themselves is to identify a confounding or intervening variable that might interfere with the relationship between their witnessing domestic violence and their experiencing problems, if any, due to witnessing it.

Inevitably, there will be a host of other confounding variables because no one can tell for certain whether children's particular problematic behaviors are due to witnessing domestic violence or to some other factor(s). Lula will be able to conclude only that children who witnessed domestic violence experienced certain problems, not that the problems were caused by witnessing the violence in the first place.

Failure to establish causality, however, is only a limitation if the establishment of causality was one of the purposes of the study. In this case, it was not; indeed, the kind of rigorous research design needed to establish causality is usually inappropriate in a qualitative study.

Lula may find that her sample of children is not diverse enough in terms of age, gender, or ethnic background to allow her to draw conclusions about the effects of these variables on their problem behaviors. Again, this is a study limitation only if she has stated her intention to draw such a conclusion. The major limitation that Lula is likely to encounter in her study is related to the issue of credibility or truth value (internal validity, in positivistic terms).

How will she know whether the mothers and their children were truthful in relating their experiences or whether their remarks were geared more toward pleasing her or making themselves appear more socially desirable? And if their remarks were based on memories of previous abusive behaviors, how far were those memories reliable? These are common dilemmas in both research and clinical interviews. One way to handle them is through triangulation: obtaining data on a variable from more than one data source.

Another way is to constantly reflect on the quality of the data being obtained throughout the interview process and to record the results of these reflections in the researcher's journal. The following are examples of the kinds of questions Lula might ask herself while she is pursuing her reflections:

1   Is the interviewee withholding something? If so, what should I do about it?

2   What impact might my race, age, social status, gender, or beliefs have on my interviewee? What difference might it make that I work at the emergency shelter?

3   Did what the interviewee said ring true—or did she want to please me, or look good, or protect someone else, or save herself embarrassment? Why am I feeling so stressed after this interview? Am I getting the kinds of data that are relevant for my study?

These questions might improve the quality of the data obtained by making Lula more aware of possible sources of error. Even if they do not, Lula will have shown that she has recognized her study's limitations and will take the necessary steps to deal with each limitation.

## PART 11: ADMINISTRATION

The final part of a research proposal deals with the organization and resources necessary to carry out the proposed study. Lula might want to separate her role as a researcher from

> Writing the final research report based off of a qualitative research study takes a tremendous amount of time,

her role as one of the shelter's social workers, for example, by equipping herself with a desk and computer in a room other than that which she usually uses.

If "researcher space" is not a problem, Lula will still need to think about where she should base her operations: where she will write up her notes, analyze her data, and keep the records of her interviews. Then she has to think about administrative responsibilities. Will she take on the overall responsibility for her study herself or will that fall to her supervisor? What will be the responsibilities of her colleague and the shelter's social workers? To whom will they report? What is the chain of command?

When Lula has put together the details of who does what, in what order, and who is responsible to whom, she will be in a position to consider a time frame. How long will each task take and by what date ought it to be completed? It's very easy to underestimate the amount of time needed to analyze qualitative data and to feed the information back to the research participants for their comments (member checking).

It's also easy to underestimate the time needed to write the final report. Neither of these tasks should be skimped, and it's very important to allow adequate time to complete them thoroughly—more time, that is, than the researcher believes will be necessary at the beginning of the qualitative study.

Finally, Lula must consider a budget. If she has to purchase a software computer program to help her analyze her interview data, who will pay for it? Who will cover the costs related to transcribing the data and preparing and disseminating the final report? How much money should she allocate to each of these areas? How much should she ask for overall?

When she has decided on all this, Lula will have completed her research proposal. As discussed, not all proposals are organized in this way, but all essentially contain the information that has been discussed in the preceding sections. This same information can be used to write the final research report.

## WRITING QUALITATIVE RESEARCH REPORTS

As with a positivistic research report, a qualitative one is a way of describing the research study to other people. How it's written and to some degree what it contains depend on the audience it's written for. Lula may want to present her study's findings, for example, only to the board of directors and staff of the women's emergency shelter where she works.

In this case, it will be unnecessary to describe the clinical setting (i.e., the shelter) in detail since the audience is already familiar with it. This very familiarity will also mean that Lula must take extra care to protect the identities of her research participants because personal knowledge of the women and children concerned will make it easier for her audience to identify them.

Lula will probably want to submit a written report—particularly if the shelter funded her study—but she may also want to give an oral presentation. As she imagines herself speaking the words she has written, she may find that she wants to organize the material differently or use a different style than she would if she were preparing a written report. Perhaps she will use less formal language, or include more detail about her own thoughts and feelings, or shorten the direct quotes made by the research participants.

Other possible outlets for her work include books, book chapters, journal articles, and presentations at conferences. Again, depending on the audience, she might write quite simply or she might include a wealth of technical detail, perhaps describing at length the methods she used to categorize and code her interview data.

In order to avoid writing a number of reports on the same study aimed at different audiences, she might choose to include in the main body of the report just sufficient technical detail to establish the study's trustworthiness, while putting additional technical material in appendixes for those readers who are interested. Whatever approach she chooses, it's important to remember that qualitative research studies are based on a different set of assumptions than quantitative ones.

As we know by now, the goal of a qualitative study is to understand the experiences of the study's research participants in depth, and the personal feelings of the researcher cannot be divorced from this understanding. It's therefore often appropriate to report a qualitative study using a more personal style, including both quotes from interviews with the research participants and the researcher's own reflections on the material. The aim is to produce a credible and compelling account that will be taken seriously by the reader.

The material itself can be organized in a number of ways, depending on whether or not it's to be presented in book form or more concisely in the form of a journal article. An article usually contains six parts:

1  An abstract
2  An introduction
3  A discussion of methodology
4  A presentation of the analysis and findings
5  A conclusion, or discussion of the significance of the study's findings
6  A list of references

## ABSTRACT

An abstract is a short statement—often about 200 words—that summarizes the purpose of the study, its methodology, its findings, and its conclusions. Journal readers often decide on the basis of the abstract whether they are sufficiently interested in the topic to want to read further. Thus, the abstract must provide just enough information to enable readers to assess the relevance of the study to their own work. A statement of the study's research question, with enough context to make it meaningful, is usually followed by a brief description of the study's methodology that was used to answer the research question.

Lula might say, for example, that she interviewed eight women and eleven children who were residents in a women's emergency shelter in a small town in Canada, plus three of the shelter's social workers. She might go on to identify the problems experienced by the children who had witnessed domestic violence, stating that these problems were derived from analyses of interview data. Finally, she would outline the implications from the study for social work practice, resulting from a greater understanding of the children's problems.

## INTRODUCTION

The main body of the report begins with the introduction. It describes the what and why components of the study, which Lula has already written about in the first five parts of her research proposal. If she goes back to what she wrote before, she will see that she has already identified her research question and put it into the context of previous work through a literature review. She has discussed why she thinks this question needs to be answered, clarified her own orientation and assumptions, and commented on the interests of the women's emergency shelter or other funding organizations.

In addition, she has identified the variables relevant to her study and placed them within an appropriate framework. In short, she has already gathered the material needed

> Qualitative research studies usually generate longer research reports than quantitative ones.

for her introduction, and all that remains is to ensure that it's written in an appropriate style.

## METHOD

After the what and the why components of the study comes the how. In the methods section, Lula describes how she selected her sample of research participants and how she collected her data. She must provide a justification for why she chose a particular sampling and data collection method(s).

Again, if she looks back at her research proposal, she will see that she has already written about this in Parts 6, 7, and 8: research design, population and sample, and data collection, respectively. As before, she can use this same material, merely ensuring that it's written in a coherent style.

## ANALYSIS AND FINDINGS

Materials on data analysis and findings are often presented together. Descriptive profiles of research participants and direct quotes from their interviews are used to answer the research question being explored. In her proposal, Lula has already written the part on data analysis in her research proposal, which stated what computer programs she was going to use (if any) and what first- and second-level coding methods she proposes to use.

In her research report, however, she would want to identify and provide examples of the meaning units she derived from the first-level coding process. One segment from one of her interviews might have gone as follows:

1   **Pam (sounding upset): The poor kid was never the same after that. The**
2   **first time, you know, it was just a slap on the butt that she might even**
3   **have mistaken for affection, but that second time he slammed me right**
4   **against the wall and he was still hitting my face after I landed. (pause) No**
5   mistaking that one, is there, even for a four-year old? (longer pause) No, well,
6   I guess I'm kidding myself about that first time. She knew all right. *She was*
7   *an outgoing sort of kid before, always out in the yard with friends,* <u>but then</u>
8   <u>she stopped going out, and she'd follow me around, kind of, as if she was</u>
9   <u>afraid to let me out of her sight</u>.

Lula may have identified three meaning units in this data segment. The first (in **bold,** lines 1–4) relates to what might and might not constitute domestic violence in the mind of a 4-year-old child. The second (in *italics,* lines 6 and 7) relates to the child's behavior before witnessing the abuse; and the third (<u>underlined</u>, lines 7–9) relates to the child's behavior after witnessing the abuse. In her report, Lula might want to identify and briefly describe the meaning units she derived from all her interviews, occasionally illustrating a unit with a direct quote to provide context and meaning.

As discussed in Chapter 19, Lula's next task in the analysis is to identify categories, assign each meaning unit to a category, and assign codes to the categories. A description of these categories will also come next in her report. She may have found, for example, that a number of mothers interpreted their child's behavior after witnessing domestic violence as indicative of fear for the mother's safety.

Instead of one large category "child's behavior after witnessing domestic violence," Lula may have chosen instead to create a number of smaller categories reflecting distinct types of behavior. One of these was "after witnessing domestic violence, child demonstrates fear for mother's safety," and Lula coded it as CAWFMSAF, where C stands for "the child," AW stands for "after witnessing domestic violence," and FMSAF stands for "fear for mother's safety."

Depending on the number and depth of the interviews conducted, Lula may have a very large number of meaning units, and may have gone through an intricate process of refining and reorganizing in order to come up with appropriate categories. In a book, there will be room to describe all this, together with Lula's own reflections on the process; but in a journal article, running to perhaps twenty-five pages overall, Lula will have to be selective about what parts of the process she describes and how much detail she provides.

Although meaning units and categories are certainly a major part of Lula's findings, the majority of readers will be more interested in the next part of the analysis: comparing and contrasting the categories to discover the relationships between and among them in order to develop tentative themes or theories. By doing this, Lula may have been able to finally identify the problems most commonly experienced by children who have witnessed domestic violence. She may even have been able to put the children's problems in an order of importance as perceived by the mothers and their children.

In addition, she may have been able to add depth by describing the emotions related to the children's problems: perhaps guilt, on the mother's part, or anger toward the father, or a growing determination not to return to the abusive relationship. These themes will constitute the larger part of Lula's analysis and findings section, and it's to these themes that she will return in her discussion.

## DISCUSSION

This part of the research report presents a discussion of the study's findings. Here, Lula will point out the significance of her study's findings as they relate to the original purpose. If the purpose of her study was to inform practice by enabling the shelter's social workers to better understand the needs of children who have witnessed domestic violence, then Lula must provide a link between the children's problems and their needs resulting from those problems. She must also point out exactly how the shelter's social workers' practice might be informed.

If she has found from her study, for example, that children who witnessed domestic violence tend to experience more fear for their mothers' safety than children who had not witnessed the abuse, then a related need might be to keep the mother always within sight.

Social workers within the shelter who understand this need might be more willing to tolerate children underfoot in the shelter's kitchen, for example, and might be less likely to tell Mary to "give Mom a moment's peace and go and play with Sue." These kinds of connections should be made for each theme that Lula identified in her study.

The final part of a research report often has to do with suggestions for future research studies. During the process of filling knowledge gaps by summarizing the study's findings, Lula will doubtless find other knowledge gaps that she believes ought to be filled. She might frame new research questions relating to these gaps; or she might even feel that she has sufficient knowledge to enable her to formulate research hypotheses for testing in future research studies.

## REFERENCES

Finally, both quantitative and qualitative researchers are expected to provide a list of references that will enable the reader to locate the materials used for documentation within the report. If the manuscript is accepted for publication, the journal will certainly ask for any revisions it considers appropriate with regard to its style. It's important to note that quotes from a study's research participants do not have to be referenced, and adequate steps should always be taken to conceal their identities.

## CHAPTER RECAP

- Research proposals contain statements about what we will do (future tense).

- A proposal's content and writing style will largely depend on who's going to review it.

- Research reports contain statements about what we have done (past tense).

- There are three general purposes for writing a research proposal, no matter what is being proposed: We need to obtain permission to do the study, we need to obtain funding for the

study, and we need to write down exactly what we intend to study, why, and how.

- If the proposal's recipients have provided no guidance as to how its contents should be organized, it is simplest to present the proposed study in the order in which it would be conducted.

- A qualitative research study rarely tests a research hypothesis.

## REVIEW EXERCISES

1   In your own words, describe what a qualitative research proposal is all about. Use social work examples to illustrate your main points.

2   Review the previous chapter, Chapter 20, on writing quantitative research proposals and reports. Discuss the similarities and differences between quantitative research proposals (chapter 20) and qualitative research proposals (this chapter). Use social work examples to illustrate your main points.

3   Review the previous chapter, Chapter 20, on writing quantitative research proposals and reports. Discuss the similarities and differences between quantitative research reports (chapter 20) and qualitative research reports (this chapter). Use social work examples to illustrate your main points.

4   In groups of four, write a brief four-page qualitative research proposal that is geared toward shedding light on social work students' perceptions of their preparedness to enter the social work profession after they graduate.

5   In the same group of four, pretend you actually implemented your proposal (question 4). Make up fake data. Now use these fake data to write a simple qualitative research report.

6   This chapter provided numerous points to consider when evaluating a qualitative research proposal. Discuss whether you believe your research proposal (question 4) adequately addressed each point. If so, how? If not, why not?

7   If you currently have a practicum, ask your field instructor for copies of any qualitative research proposals they might have in their filing cabinets. Select one proposal and critique it using the contents of this chapter—and the entire book, for that matter.

8   Discuss how qualitative research proposals and reports utilize all the contents in this book. Provide one simple example from each one of the preceding twenty chapters that could be included in a qualitative research proposal. You should have 20 points in total—one for each chapter.

# APPENDIXES:
# BECOMING A CRITICAL THINKER
# BY ASKING QUESTIONS

How to Use the Three Appendixes  **468**

**APPENDIX A:**  Evaluating Quantitative Studies  **474**

**APPENDIX B:**  Evaluating Qualitative Studies  **495**

**APPENDIX C:**  Evaluating Internet Resources  **511**

467

# How to Use the Three Appendixes

"Doc, how do I use my three appendixes?"

THE THREE APPENDIXES that follow contain five columns:

- The left-hand column lists a few questions you can ask (and answer) in reference to research findings derived from *quantitative* research studies (Appendix A), *qualitative* research studies (Appendix B), and information found on the *Internet* (Appendix C). For example, in relation to:

  — A *quantitative* research study (Appendix A)—the seventh heading, labeled "7. Ethical Sensitivity" (page 481), includes nine questions (numbers 99–107) you can ask to determine how ethically sensitive the author was toward the study's research participants.

  — A *qualitative* research study (Appendix B)—the tenth heading, labeled "10. Creditability" (pages 504–505), includes sixteen questions (numbers 405–419) you can ask to determine the overall creditability of a qualitative research study.

  — *Internet information* (Appendix C)—the third heading, labeled "3. Accuracy" (pages 517–518), includes nineteen questions (numbers 516–534) you can ask about the accuracy of the website.

- The four right-hand columns (directly under the column labeled "Adequately Addressed") provide you with an opportunity to check whether or not the author provided you with enough information for you to answer each question via simply checking one of four possible options:

| Evaluative Criteria Category | Adequately Addressed | | | |
|---|---|---|---|---|
| | NA | Yes | No | ? |

468

> All headings (or sections) do not have equal weight in their respective importance in determining a study's overall credibility.

Where:

**1**  NA (not applicable)

**2**  Yes

**3**  No

**4**  ? (You don't know)

The last row under all of the headings, or sections, provides you with an opportunity to rate how much you feel the study satisfied each heading via rating it from 1 (low) to 4 (high). Your rating should reflect what you feel the heading should receive after reviewing the appropriate content in this book and answering the questions contained within the heading.

| | Low | | | High |
|---|---|---|---|---|
| Overall Credibility Score for _____ (Derived from Questions XXX–XXX) | 1 | 2 | 3 | 4 |

## QUESTIONS TO HELP GUIDE YOUR ASSESSMENT

**N**ote that each question in the appendixes is a criterion which means you're making a judgment of some kind. And this judgment must be your professional judgment, not just your personal opinions.

It's important to remember that Appendixes A and B are for evaluating quantitative (Appendix A) and qualitative (Appendix B) research studies reported in the form of journal articles/reports. To complement Appendixes A and B, Appendix C is used to evaluate the overall creditability, usefulness, and authenticity of the resources contained within any given website—which may, or may not, contain research articles or reports of some kind.

However, if you download a research article from any website ("official looking" or not) then you need to evaluate the study with the criteria contained in Appendix A (if quantitative), or Appendix B (if qualitative), or Appendixes A and B (if mixed-methods).

In respect to journal articles, it's extremely important to remember that just because an author did not provide information you can use to assess each criterion doesn't mean the study was poorly thought-out and/or executed. There's simply not enough space in journals for an author to address all the criteria contained in the appendixes.

The various questions listed within each category are only there to guide you in your overall evaluation of each section. And, most importantly, they're listed so you can be aware of what you will need to address when you do your own research study after you graduate (the third research role called the "creator and disseminator of knowledge").

### LOOKING FOR A MAGIC ASSESSMENT WAND?

This would be a good time to stop looking for an instant solution! It would be great if our profession had a standardized score card of some kind, but we don't. We don't even have a magic wand or rubric. There's simply not a fairy-tale overall "official-looking" single number or word that determines whether any particular research study was:

- **Creditable or not** (e.g., yes, no). In this case, for example, we could say, "Research Study A was credible, so it was a good study."
- **A number on a numerical continuum** (e.g., 1, 2, 3, 4). In this case, we could say, 'Research Study A scored a 3 on a 4-point scale, so it was a pretty good study."

470          How to Use the Three Appendixes

- **A word on a word continuum** (e.g., poor, average, good, excellent). In this case, we could say, "Research Study A rated poor, so it was poor study."

The questions in Appendixes A and B simply represent a few of the generic, non-mutually exclusive categories that need to be considered when determining the degree of the overall credibility to assign to any research finding or recommendation. And if the finding is indeed credible—from your perspective, that is—what's the yardstick you used to bring you to that conclusion? Your critical-thinking hat needs to be put on at this point. In addition, you should note that some questions are repeated in several sections because they apply to several categories.

## Many Terms and Concepts Will Be Unfamiliar

Don't get your knickers in a knot when you see a word or concept you don't understand. It probably wasn't discussed in this book. Appendixes A and B will more than likely contain numerous concepts you will not be familiar with as this introductory research methods book simply didn't cover them. It's not your fault if you don't know them.

For example, question 17 on page 475 asks you if you know the impact factor of the journal in which an article was published. Chances are that, as of today, you don't have the foggiest clue to what an impact factor is, and it's no big shakes. But we guarantee that you will know what it means before you have completed your first research study and want to submit your research report (manuscript) to a professional social work journal for possible publication.

We have purposely included more sophisticated questions you could ask, and then answer, only after you have taken additional advanced research/evaluation courses and/or have had more experience in designing and executing research studies in the real world.

## Let's Not Get Too Critical

**N**ow the hard part—the extremely hard part. You need to store in the back of your mind exactly why you rated each question as you did. For example, if you rated question 104 on page 481 (i.e., Does the author provide anonymity to the research participants?) as "Yes", then you need to have a clear-cut rationale for why you did so. Same goes for "No". What evidence did the author provide where you could say "Yes" or "No"?

You can't pluck a "Yes" or "No" out of thin air, call it a day, and hope your research instructor doesn't ask why you rated a particular question as you did. You must have a rational for all your evaluative responses to all the questions—even the "not applicable" ones.

Let's now turn our attention to the four possible responses that are available to you when asking the questions contained in the three appendixes.

### NA (Not Applicable)?

You will check "NA" for questions that are simply not applicable, or not relevant, to the research study you're evaluating. For example, if the research participants for a study were social work students like yourself, then the question, "Does the author use appropriate assent forms?" (i.e., question 100 on page 481) would be rated as "NA" because assent forms are simply *not applicable* to this specific population—social work students (see chapter 5 on research ethics, pages 98–99).

## ? (Don't Know)

On the other hand, a researcher may not have discussed how research participants were promised anonymity, but this does not mean they weren't. It more than likely means that there was not enough space in the research report to describe how it was done. So in this case you would check "?" for question 104 on page 481.

## No

You would only check "No" if the author addressed the question, but did it poorly. You will also need to state exactly why you felt the discussion was poorly done and what could have been improved for you to have checked it as "Yes".

## Yes

You would check "Yes" if an author addressed the specific question you're asking and did it well. For example, an author may have discussed how research participants were in fact promised anonymity. In this case you would have to make a judgment on how well it was done. If you believe it was done well then you would check "Yes". If not done well, then you would check "No". Once again, you will need a rationale as to why you checked "Yes" or "No".

# Don't Get Intimidated

At this point, it's extremely important for you not to become overwhelmed and intimidated by the sheer number of potential questions that can be asked about any information or "facts" that you come across. We only provide you with a few questions since you have to know what questions to ask before you can answer them. And yes, that also means you have a responsibility to assess the creditability of facts that were derived from our current "gold standard" of knowing something: facts derived via the scientific method of inquiry—the most objective way of knowing. And now for a little Zen time via Box A below:

| Box A | A Social Work Student's Zen Approach to Becoming a Critical Thinker: *Asking* and *Answering Questions* |
|---|---|

**Life would be grand** if we only did what our fleeting hearts wanted us to do, each moment of the day.

Unfortunately, your laundry, grocery shopping, research papers, homework assignments, difficult conversations, and most importantly, thinking critically about the stuff you read, hear, and see would never get done. The best books would never be written. The best songs never sung. The best movies never seen. All the achievements of humankind would only be imagined, not realized.

Critical thinking takes a lot of time and energy and it's not very chic or a conversation starter to boot. It's a task many students don't want to do since it's much easier to think about the things we want to think about. Reading the chapters in this book and then using the content to ask and answer questions about the credibility of the "facts" we come across is simply not a turn-on. Don't blame you one bit.

So what should you do if you're facing tasks you don't want to do, such as evaluating the overall usefulness of social work practice recommendations that were derived from research studies? Well, you can run, and find distraction. That usually works for a little while, until it causes problems. Or you can find a way to get it done. Below are 10 pointers on how you can get your act together on getting this done:

1　*Meditate on why you need to think critically in the first place.* Instead of easily giving in to distraction, put down your iPhone and sit still for a minute. Why do you need to think critically when you don't want to? Sure, because it's on your to-do list, or because someone else wants you to do it like your social work professors. Or someone's got to do it. But why? What will your increased critical thinking skills help to accomplish anyway? Who are they helping? Dig a lot deeper and find the good that they will create in the world.

　　If you have a part-time job as a dishwasher, for example, you might not think getting dirty dishes clean matters much, but those very dishes are required to serve food, and the food nourishes people and it can make them happy and then they can go out and do something good in the world with a full stomach and smile on their faces. So connect the dishes to the good.

　　Critical thinking skills increase your professional judgments which in turn increase your overall effectiveness as a future social work practitioner. In short, your critical thinking skills will directly help your clients succeed—and this is why you went into social work. So, like connecting dishes to the good, connect critical thinking skills to client success.

2　*Meditate on your fear.* The main thing that's stopping you from thinking critically, such as asking and answering questions about social work research studies, is purely fear. You fear that you will fail or look bad, you fear the discomfort or confusion of the task. So take a moment to look inward and embrace this fear. Everyone feels fear. Feel yours. Accept it as part of you, instead of running from it. It's okay to be afraid.

3　*Let go of your ideal.* If this fear were gone, you could easily do the task of learning how to think critically. So what's causing your fear in the first place? Some ideal you have, some fantasy about life being free of discomfort, confusion, embarrassment, imperfection? That's simply not reality, just a fantasy, and it's getting in your way by causing fear. So let go of the fantasy, the ideal, the expectation. And just embrace reality: learning how to ask and answer questions about what you read, see, and hear, nothing else.

4　*Intention, not results.* You are caught up with the results of the task—what will happen if you do it, what failure might result. So forget about the result—you can't know what it will be anyway. That's in the future. For now, focus on your intention: why are you doing it? If it's to make the life of one of your future clients a tad better, then that's your intention. That intention is true no matter what the result is. Focus on this, not what bad things might or might not happen. You need to have critical thinking skills in order to help your clients. Period. Full stop.

5　*Embrace the suck.* Doing something hard sucks. It's not easy, and often you're confused about how to do it because you haven't done it much before. So what? Hard things suck, but life isn't always peaches and cream with a sprinkle of cinnamon on top. It sucks sometimes, and that's perfectly fine. Embrace all of life, thorns and all. Life would be boring without the suck. So smile, embrace the suck, and get moving.

6　*Do a little, then get up.* If you have to write something, just write a sentence. Then get up, get some water, stretch. Pat yourself on the back for getting started! Now do a little more: write a few more sentences. Get up, take a mental break (don't turn to your iPhone), do a few pushups. Go back, do a bit more. Pretty soon, you're in the flow of it.

7　*Don't let your mind run.* Your mind will want to run. That's okay, that's the nature of minds. They are scared, and they will rationalize turning to distraction, going to what's easy. Watch this happen, don't try to stop the phenomena, but don't give it anywhere to run to. Watch your mind want to run, but don't act. Just watch. It will eventually calm down.

8   *Give yourself constraints.* Everyone tends to rebel against restraints: "I don't want to do this! I want freedom!" Well, unfortunately, having unlimited freedom means unlimited choices, unlimited distractions, and nothing gets done. Simplify by putting restraints on yourself: do only one task at a time. Do just this one task for now. Do it for 10 minutes. Forbid yourself from turning to endless websites or checking Facebook every 5 minutes or doing anything else that you like to do for distraction, until you do those 10 minutes. Ask a friend to hold you accountable—another restraint that often helps.

9   *Find gratitude.* This task might seem hard or sucky at first, but actually there's a lot of great things about it. For example, if you're learning to think critically in a social work course, hey, you're a student! You will someday graduate and have a good job and have money to buy food and shelter! You are grateful for knowing the benefits of thinking critically, to become a better social worker, and to fully appreciate that your clients will be much better off with social workers who have critical thinking skills than workers who do not.

10  *Learn and grow.* By meditating on your intentions and fear, by letting go of ideals and embracing the suck, by giving yourself constraints and finding gratitude ... you're learning about yourself. This task, as mundane or scary as it might seem, is teaching you about you. That's a wonderful thing. So the task of thinking critically is a huge learning opportunity.

## VERY IMPORTANT POINTS TO REMEMBER

More than likely, you will have a bunch of "?" in your overall evaluation of most research studies published as journal articles. As we have said before, this is simply because there's not enough space within the journals for authors to include answers to all the questions that you can ask. The articles would be hundreds of pages long if this was done.

You will also have numerous "NA" since all research studies are never assessed with the same criteria (or questions). For example, if a quantitative research study used a cross-sectional survey design (e.g., figure 15.2a on page 304) then the question "Does the study's research design control for testing effects?" (i.e., number 178 on page 487) would not apply since the criterion is not relevant to this kind of research design—there are no posttests in a cross-sectional survey design. Simple as that.

Two important lessons can be learned from answering the questions contained in the appendixes and they can be broken down into two people-categories: other researchers, and you.

### OTHER RESEARCHERS

Most researchers probably did in fact acknowledge and address each relevant question before they started their research studies but simply did not have enough space in the journal articles to address all of them.

### YOU

Nevertheless, YOU will need to address each relevant question yourself *before* you actually do a research study someday. This process will make your potential study much stronger as you will know in advance what issues (the questions) you need to tackle before you can actually begin to write your research proposal (i.e., chapters 20 and 21).

When it comes to preparing you to do a research study, we have appropriated the British Army's official military adage of "the 7 **P**s": **P**roper **P**lanning and **P**reparation **P**revents **P**iss-**P**oor **P**erformance. Not eloquently stated—but what the heck, it's official, so it must be right.

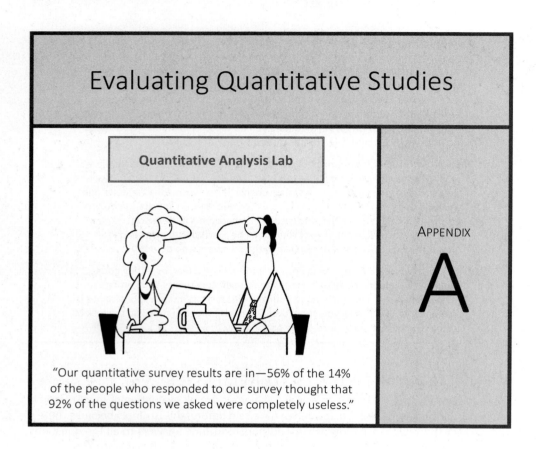

# Evaluating Quantitative Studies

**Quantitative Analysis Lab**

APPENDIX

# A

"Our quantitative survey results are in—56% of the 14% of the people who responded to our survey thought that 92% of the questions we asked were completely useless."

Questions to Consider When Evaluating a
Quantitatively Oriented Research Study

| Title of evidence evaluated: | | | | |
|---|---|---|---|---|
| **1. Author** | \multicolumn{4}{c}{Adequately Addressed} |
| | NA | Yes | No | ? |
| 1  Is the author actually qualified and familiar with the study's topic? | | | | |
| 2  Is the author recognized as an authority on the subject? | | | | |
| 3  Do you know if the author has any financial stake in the statements being made? | | | | |
| 4  Does the author have any known political position? | | | | |
| 5  Is the author affiliated with a college or university? | | | | |

| 1. Author (Continued) | | NA | Yes | No | ? |
|---|---|---|---|---|---|
| 6 | Do you know the authors highest degree obtained? | | | | |
| 7 | Has the author declared any conflict of interest or bias in relation to the subject of the research study? | | | | |
| 8 | Have you Googled the author's name? What comes up? | | | | |
| 9 | Do you know of any additional information about the author that you found on the Internet? | | | | |
| 10 | Do you know where the author is employed, if at all? | | | | |
| 11 | Do you know the author's impact factor (AIF, or h-Index)? | | | | |
| Overall Credibility Score for Author (Derived from questions 1–11) | | Low 1 | 2 | 3 | High 4 |

| 2. Journal and Article | | Adequately Addressed | | | |
|---|---|---|---|---|---|
| | | NA | Yes | No | ? |
| 12 | Is the article published in a reputable peer-reviewed journal? | | | | |
| 13 | Do you know how many years the journal has been in existence (look for the volume number)? | | | | |
| 14 | Do you know when the article was published? | | | | |
| 15 | Do you know the qualifications of the journal's editor (if any)? | | | | |
| 16 | Do you know the qualifications of the journal's editorial board (if any)? | | | | |
| 17 | Do you know the journal's impact factor (JIF)? | | | | |
| 18 | Does the journal have any known biased editorial position? | | | | |
| 19 | Do you know how many times the article been previously cited (and where)? (CINAHL, EMBASE, Google Scholar, Microsoft Academic Search, PsycINFO, Web of Science) | | | | |
| Overall Credibility Score for Journal and Article (Derived from questions 12–19) | | Low 1 | 2 | 3 | High 4 |

| 3. Title | Adequately Addressed | | | |
|---|---|---|---|---|
| | NA | Yes | No | ? |
| 20 Does the title have under 15 words? | | | | |
| 21 Does the title make sense standing alone? | | | | |
| 22 Does the title include the important study variables or theoretical issues? | | | | |
| 23 Does the title refer to the study's sample? | | | | |
| 24 Does the title refer to the study's research setting? | | | | |
| 25 Does the title identify relationships between or among variables? | | | | |
| 26 Does the title identify the dependent variable? | | | | |
| 27 Does the title identify the independent variable? | | | | |
| 28 Is the title extremely clear and not cutesy? | | | | |
| **Overall Credibility Score for Title of Article** (Derived from questions 20–28) | Low            High<br>1    2    3    4 | | | |

| 4. Abstract | Adequately Addressed | | | |
|---|---|---|---|---|
| | NA | Yes | No | ? |
| 29 Is the abstract clear, concise, specific, and to the point? | | | | |
| 30 Is the abstract under 250 words? | | | | |
| 31 Does the abstract use abbreviations that could be unfamiliar to some readers? | | | | |
| 32 Is the abstract accurate in relation to the article's text? | | | | |
| 33 Does the abstract have the usual headings such as, purpose, methods, results, and implications? | | | | |
| 34 Does the abstract use an active voice? | | | | |
| **Overall Credibility Score for Abstract** (Derived from questions 29–34) | Low            High<br>1    2    3    4 | | | |

| 5. Research Question | Adequately Addressed | | | |
|---|---|---|---|---|
| | NA | Yes | No | ? |
| 35  Does the author pose an important research question that can be adequately investigated? | | | | |
| 36  Does the author pose an important research question that can contribute to our profession's knowledge base? | | | | |
| 37  Do the answers to the study's research question have potentially strong implications for social work practice and/or policy, preferably both? | | | | |
| 38  Is the research question based solidly within the profession of social work, including its intellectual history, its core values, the person-in-environment perspective, and its focus on vulnerable populations? | | | | |
| 39  Does the author provide a good argument for the research question's practice significance? | | | | |
| 40  Does the author's research question address clear gaps in the literature? | | | | |
| 41  Are the basic relationships between theoretical concepts stated and tested simply and clearly? You should ask yourself, "Do I really know what is happening in this study?" | | | | |
| 42  Do the author's assumptions between and among variables make sense to you? | | | | |
| 43  Does the author define major concepts and operational definitions that make sense to you? | | | | |
| 44  Does the author provide reasonable assumptions of the relationships between the independent and dependent variables (if any)? | | | | |
| 45  Is the research question researchable and feasible? | | | | |
| 46  Is the research question ethically and culturally sensitive? | | | | |
| 47  Is the research question thought provoking? | | | | |
| 48  Is the research question directly related to the study's overall objectives? | | | | |
| 49  Is the research question short and to the point? | | | | |

| 5. Research Question (Continued) | NA | Yes | No | ? |
|---|---|---|---|---|
| 50  Is the research question unambiguous and straightforward? | | | | |
| 51  Is the research question clearly stated, comprehensive, and did it use common vocabulary? | | | | |
| 52  Is the research question formulated in a manner that will add to the available knowledge of social work practice? | | | | |

| Overall Credibility Score for Research Question (Derived from questions 35–52) | Low 1 | 2 | 3 | High 4 |
|---|---|---|---|---|

| 6. Literature Review | Adequately Addressed | | | |
|---|---|---|---|---|
| | NA | Yes | No | ? |
| 53  Is the study's purpose extremely clear? | | | | |
| 54  Is the research problem identified clearly in the article? | | | | |
| 55  Does the research study have objectives? If so, were they clearly stated? | | | | |
| 56  Does the study have research questions? If so, were they clearly stated? | | | | |
| 57  Does the study have hypotheses? If so, were they clearly stated? | | | | |
| 58  Does the author provide a well-defined research topic and an extremely clear research question or hypothesis? | | | | |
| 59  Does the author distinguish between research, theory, and opinion? | | | | |
| 60  Does the author base the research study on clear chains of inferential reasoning supported and justified by a complete coverage of the relevant literature? | | | | |
| 61  Does the author's review of the literature help you to establish the overall significance of the research study? | | | | |
| 62  Does the author provide you with enough information to convince you that the research study needed to be done? | | | | |

| | 6. Literature Review (Continued) | NA | Yes | No | ? |
|---|---|---|---|---|---|
| 63 | Does the author overlook any key pieces of literature? Answering this would depend on your knowledge of the field. | | | | |
| 64 | Does the literature cited justify the chosen research approach (i.e., quantitative, qualitative, mixed-methods)? | | | | |
| 65 | Does the author incorporate findings from original research studies into the literature review? | | | | |
| 66 | Does the author's assumptions between and among variables make sense to you? | | | | |
| 67 | Does the author define major concepts and operational definitions in a way that makes sense to you? | | | | |
| 68 | Does the author provide reasonable assumptions of the relationships between the independent and dependent variables (if any)? | | | | |
| 69 | Does the author provide conceptual definitions of key terms? | | | | |
| 70 | Does the author indicate the basis for "factual" statements? | | | | |
| 71 | Do the specific research purposes, questions, or hypotheses logically link with one another? | | | | |
| 72 | Is the literature review organized logically? | | | | |
| 73 | Is the literature review directly related to the topic of the research study? | | | | |
| 74 | Is there a balanced review of differing viewpoints or findings? | | | | |
| 75 | Is the literature review one sided, and does it ignore alternative evidence? | | | | |
| 76 | Does the author arrange the literature review by dates of the studies cited? If so, does this make sense to you? | | | | |
| 77 | Does the author arrange the literature review by school of thought/theory? If so, does this make sense to you? | | | | |
| 78 | Does the author arrange the literature review by themes that have emerged from the literature? If so, does this make sense to you? | | | | |

| 6. Literature Review (Continued) | NA | Yes | No | ? |
|---|---|---|---|---|
| 79  Does the author arrange the literature review by research approach? If so, does this make sense to you? | | | | |
| 80  Is the literature review up to date? | | | | |
| 81  Is the literature review convincing? | | | | |
| 82  Is the literature review written critically (giving strengths and weaknesses of previous work)? | | | | |
| 83  Does the author appropriately cite earlier, relevant studies drawn from the professional literature? | | | | |
| 84  Are the parameters of the literature review reasonable? (Why were certain bodies of literature included in the search and others excluded?) | | | | |
| 85  Is primary literature emphasized in the literature review, and secondary literature, if cited, used selectively? | | | | |
| 86  Are most of the literature sources from reputable refereed journals? | | | | |
| 87  Is the cited literature appraised? Or, does the author try to impress readers with a lengthy list of references and no information about their contents? | | | | |
| 88  Are recent developments in the literature emphasized in the literature review? | | | | |
| 89  Are complete bibliographic data provided for each source cited? | | | | |
| 90  Is the literature review sufficiently comprehensive? (Use the "15–10" citation rule to assess its adequacy and comprehensiveness.) | | | | |
| 91  Are the references current, or a combination of current and classic? | | | | |
| 92  Are major research studies discussed in detail and the actual findings cited? | | | | |
| 93  Are the major research studies cited directly related to the author's research problem and methods? | | | | |
| 94  Are the minor research studies cited with similar results (or limitations) summarized as a group? | | | | |
| 95  Is there an adequate analysis (or critique) of the research methodologies of important previous studies so you can determine their overall quality? | | | | |

| 6. Literature Review (Continued) | NA | Yes | No | ? |
|---|---|---|---|---|
| 96 Are previous research studies compared and contrasted and conflicting or inclusive results noted? | | | | |
| 97 For some basic and applied research studies, was the conceptual framework or theory that guided the study explained? | | | | |
| 98 Do you know the P.O.I. of the phenomenon being studied? That is, can you determine the prevalence (P), occurrence (O), and incidence (I) of the phenomenon being studied? | | | | |
| Overall Credibility Score for Literature Review (Derived from questions 53–98) | Low 1 | 2 | 3 | High 4 |

| 7. Ethical Sensitivity | Adequately Addressed | | | |
|---|---|---|---|---|
| | NA | Yes | No | ? |
| 99 Does the author use appropriate consent forms? | | | | |
| 100 Does the author use appropriate assent forms? | | | | |
| 101 Does the author mention the ethical considerations of data collection? | | | | |
| 102 Does the author mention whether IRB approval was obtained or why it was not necessary? | | | | |
| 103 Does the author minimize the risk of harm to the research participants? | | | | |
| 104 Does the author provide anonymity to the research participants? | | | | |
| 105 Does the author provide confidentiality to the research participants? | | | | |
| 106 Does the author avoid deceptive practices? | | | | |
| 107 Does the author provide the research participants with the right to withdraw from the study for any reason whatsoever? | | | | |
| Overall Credibility Score for Ethical Sensitivity (Derived from questions 99–107) | Low 1 | 2 | 3 | High 4 |

| 8. Cultural Sensitivity | Adequately Addressed | | | |
|---|---|---|---|---|
| | NA | Yes | No | ? |
| 108   Does the author address the contextuality of the study—that is, does the author have an understanding of the sociocultural, political, and historical context of where the research participants live? | | | | |
| 109   Does the author address the study's relevance—that is, does the study's research question or hypothesis address meaningful issues faced by the research participants, and Does it serve the interests of improving their lives? | | | | |
| 110   Is the author's communication style appropriate— that is, does the author have an understanding of the preferred communication styles of the research participants and their communities and the subtleties and variations inherent in the language used? | | | | |
| 111   Does the author display an awareness of identity and power differences—that is, was the author aware of researcher–participant power differences, the establishment of credibility, and the development of more horizontal relationships? | | | | |
| 112   Does the author use appropriate disclosure—that is, does the author avoid the use of secrecy and built trust with the research participants? | | | | |
| 113   Is the author aware of reciprocation—that is, does the research study meet mutual goals and objectives of the researcher and the research participants? | | | | |
| 114   Does the author use an empowerment approach to the research process—that is, does the research process contribute to empowering the research participants? | | | | |
| 115   Is the author aware of the concept of time—that is, does the author use a flexible approach within the research process in terms of quantity and quality of time spent with the research participants? | | | | |
| 116   Do you feel the author was respectful to people with other perspectives throughout the study? | | | | |
| Overall Credibility Score for Cultural Sensitivity (Derived from questions 108–116) | Low                High<br>1      2      3      4 | | | |

| 9. Measurement Validity and Reliability | Adequately Addressed | | | |
|---|---|---|---|---|
| | NA | Yes | No | ? |
| 117 Are all outcome measures used in the study specified and referenced, as appropriate? | | | | |
| 118 Does the author state whether the measuring instrument(s) and the measurement process itself, were pilot-tested? | | | | |
| 119 Does the author clearly state what measuring instruments were used, such as checklists, scales, inventories, journals or diaries, logs, or summative scales? | | | | |
| 120 Does the author mention if there were any other materials used during data collection such as, audio/videotapes, reports, manuals, correspondence, or computer records? | | | | |
| 121 Do you feel the measuring instruments were appropriate to the variables being measured given the study's overall purpose? | | | | |
| 122 Does the author discuss the overall validity of the measuring instruments used in the study? | | | | |
| 123 Do you feel the author measured the study's variables appropriately? | | | | |
| 124 Are the measuring instruments valid? | | | | |
| 125 Is the research study internally valid? | | | | |
| 126 Is the research study externally valid? | | | | |
| 127 Is the research study ecologically valid? | | | | |
| 128 Does the author discuss the *content validity* of the measuring instruments? | | | | |
| 129 Does the author discuss the *face validity* of the measuring instruments? | | | | |
| 130 Does the author discuss the *predictive validity* of the measuring instruments? | | | | |
| 131 Does the author discuss the *concurrent validity* of the measuring instruments? | | | | |
| 132 Does the author discuss the *construct validity* of the measuring instruments? | | | | |

| 9. Measurement Validity and Reliability (Continued) | | NA | Yes | No | ? |
|---|---|---|---|---|---|
| 133 | Does the author discuss the overall reliability of the measuring instruments? | | | | |
| 134 | Are the measures used in the study stable? | | | | |
| 135 | Are the measures used in the study internally reliable? | | | | |
| 136 | Does the author discuss the *alternate-forms method* of reliability? | | | | |
| 137 | Does the author discuss the *split-half method* of reliability? | | | | |
| 138 | Does the author discuss *observer reliability*? | | | | |
| 139 | Does the author discuss *constant errors* when it comes to reliability? | | | | |
| 140 | Does the author discuss *random errors* when it comes to reliability? | | | | |
| 141 | Does the author discuss instrumentation bias and measurement sensitivity when measuring variables within minority groups? | | | | |

| Overall Credibility Score for Measurement Validity & Reliability (Derived from questions 117–141) | Low 1 | 2 | 3 | High 4 |
|---|---|---|---|---|

| 10. Standardized Measuring Instruments | Adequately Addressed | | | |
|---|---|---|---|---|
| | NA | Yes | No | ? |
| 142 Is the content domain clearly and specifically defined on the measuring instruments? | | | | |
| 143 Is there a logical procedure for including the items, or questions on the standardized instruments? | | | | |
| 144 Is the measuring instrument's criterion measure reliable and valid? | | | | |
| 145 Is the measuring instrument's theoretical construct clearly and correctly stated? | | | | |
| 146 Does the measuring instrument's scores converge with other relevant measures? | | | | |
| 147 Does the measuring instrument's scores discriminate from irrelevant variables? | | | | |

| 10. Standardized Measuring Instruments (Continued) | NA | Yes | No | ? |
|---|---|---|---|---|
| 148 Were there cross-validation studies conducted with the measuring instruments? | | | | |
| 149 Is there sufficient evidence of the measuring instruments' internal consistencies? | | | | |
| 150 Are there any equivalencies between various forms of the measuring instruments? | | | | |
| 151 Is there stability over a relevant time interval of the measuring instruments? | | | | |
| 152 Are the measuring instruments appropriate lengths? | | | | |
| 153 Is the content of the measuring instruments socially acceptable to the research participants? | | | | |
| 154 Are the measuring instruments feasible to complete? | | | | |
| 155 Are the measuring instruments relatively direct? | | | | |
| 156 Do the measuring instruments have utility? | | | | |
| 157 Are the measuring instruments relatively nonreactive? | | | | |
| 158 Are the measuring instruments sensitive to measuring change? | | | | |
| 159 Are the measuring instruments feasible to score? | | | | |

| Overall Credibility Score for Standardized Measurements (Derived from questions 142–159) | Low 1 | 2 | 3 | High 4 |
|---|---|---|---|---|

| 11. Research Setting | Adequately Addressed | | | |
|---|---|---|---|---|
| | NA | Yes | No | ? |
| 160 Does the author describe the research setting such as a hospital, school, social service agency, public park, client's home, outpatient clinic, inpatient clinic, community center, or library? | | | | |
| 161 Does the author specify *where* the data were collected within the research setting? | | | | |
| 162 Does the author specify *how* data were collected within the research setting? | | | | |

| 11. Research Setting (Continued) | NA | Yes | No | ? |
|---|---|---|---|---|
| 163  Does the author mention the ethical considerations of data collection, including whether IRB approval was obtained or why it was not necessary? | | | | |
| 164  Does the author describe the geography/context in which the research study was conducted? | | | | |

| Overall Credibility Score for Research Setting (Derived from questions 160–164) | Low 1 | 2 | 3 | High 4 |
|---|---|---|---|---|

| 12. Sample | Adequately Addressed | | | |
|---|---|---|---|---|
| | NA | Yes | No | ? |
| 165  Does the author provide a clear description of the sampling method that was used to recruit research participants for the study? That is, what sampling method was used in selecting the sample (e.g., random, stratified random, cluster, stage, purposive, quota, snowball, accidental [or convenience])? | | | | |
| 166  Does the author describe the inclusion and exclusion criteria that was used to select the sampling frame? | | | | |
| 167  Does the author specify the time frame for sample selection? | | | | |
| 168  Given the author's description of the sampling procedures that were used for the study, do you feel you could replicate it if you did a similar study? | | | | |
| 169  Do you know the study's final sample size? | | | | |
| 170  Were salient characteristics (e.g., demographic, clinical, diagnostic) of the study's sample described in clear detail to permit comparisons of this particular sample with those used in prior (and future) studies? | | | | |
| 171  If research participants were assigned to various treatment conditions, is the nature of this assignment process described in sufficient detail to permit replication? That is, if random assignment was employed within the study, is the nature of the randomization process clearly described? Can you replicate it for a similar study? | | | | |
| 172  Is the study's sample representative of a larger population from which it was drawn? | | | | |
| 173  Does the sample present any unique features? | | | | |

| 12. Sample (Continued) | NA | Yes | No | ? |
|---|---|---|---|---|
| 174 Does the author describe the final sample that was used in the study in enough detail so you know what it actually was? | | | | |

| Overall Credibility Score for Sample (Derived from questions 165–174) | Low 1 | 2 | 3 | High 4 |
|---|---|---|---|---|

| 13. Internal Validity | Adequately Addressed | | | |
|---|---|---|---|---|
| | NA | Yes | No | ? |
| 175 Does the author clearly address any alternative explanations for the study's results, apart from the hypothesis that was tested? | | | | |
| 176 Does the study's research design control for the effects of *history*? | | | | |
| 177 Does the study's research design control for the effects of *maturation*? | | | | |
| 178 Does the study's research design control for *testing effects*? | | | | |
| 179 Does the study's research design control for *instrumentation error*? | | | | |
| 180 Does the study's research design control for *statistical regression*? | | | | |
| 181 Does the study's research design control for the *differential selection of research participants*? | | | | |
| 182 Does the study's research design control for the effects of *mortality*? | | | | |
| 183 Does the study's research design control for the *reactive effects of research participants*? | | | | |
| 184 Does the study's research design control for *interaction effects*? | | | | |
| 185 Does the research study's design control for the *diffusion of treatments*? | | | | |
| 186 Does the research study's design control for the effects of *compensatory equalization*? | | | | |
| 187 Does the study's research design control for the effects of *compensatory rivalry*? | | | | |

| 13. Internal Validity (Continued) | NA | Yes | No | ? |
|---|---|---|---|---|
| 188   Does the research study's design control for the effects of *demoralization*? | | | | |

| Overall Credibility Score for Internal Validity (Derived from questions 175–188) | Low 1 | 2 | 3 | High 4 |
|---|---|---|---|---|

| 14. External Validity | Adequately Addressed | | | |
|---|---|---|---|---|
| | NA | Yes | No | ? |
| 189   Does the author provide the necessary information about the research design so it could be reproduced or replicated? | | | | |
| 190   Does the study's research design control for the effects of *researcher bias*? | | | | |
| 191   Does the study's research design control for the effects of *multiple-treatment interference*? | | | | |
| 192   Does the study's research design control for the effects of *specificity of variables*? | | | | |
| 193   Does the study's research design control for the effects of *selection-treatment interaction*? | | | | |
| 194   Is the intervention program (treatment) described in sufficient and extraordinary clear detail to permit replication? If not, does the author provide a source to obtain a treatment manual or a more explicit description of the intervention(s)? | | | | |
| 195   Are measures taken to assess practitioner compliance with intended interventions (called fidelity)? If so, were the interventions carried out as intended? | | | | |

| Overall Credibility Score for External Validity (Derived from questions 189–195) | Low 1 | 2 | 3 | High 4 |
|---|---|---|---|---|

| 15. Research Design | Adequately Addressed | | | |
|---|---|---|---|---|
| | NA | Yes | No | ? |
| 196   Does the author demonstrate why the chosen research design and data-collection method are well suited to the research question? | | | | |
| 197   Does the author provide an extraordinarily clear description of the research design that was used in the study? | | | | |

| 15. Research Design (Continued) | NA | Yes | No | ? |
|---|---|---|---|---|
| 198 Does the author clearly describe the independent variable(s) and dependent variable(s), if any? | | | | |
| 199 Does the author provide crystal clear operational definitions of important variables? | | | | |
| 200 Does the research design limit the influence of confounding variables? | | | | |
| 201 Are pretreatment measures taken of the clients' problems? If so, were the groups of clients assigned to differing experimental conditions roughly equivalent to each other before the treatment? | | | | |
| 202 Does the author apply a research design that best addressed the research questions of interest? | | | | |
| 203 Does the author ensure the study design, methods, and procedures are sufficiently transparent and ensured an independent, balanced, and objective approach to the research study? | | | | |
| 204 Does the author describe the research design in enough detail so it can be reproduced or replicated? | | | | |
| 205 Does the author mention how long it took to complete the entire study? | | | | |
| 206 Does the author use clear language regarding agreement among various assumptions, relationships, hypotheses, measurement devices, data collection procedures, data analyses, and conclusions? | | | | |

| Overall Credibility Score for Research Design (Derived from questions 196–206) | Low | | | High |
|---|---|---|---|---|
| | 1 | 2 | 3 | 4 |

| 16. Data-Collection Plan | Adequately Addressed | | | |
|---|---|---|---|---|
| | NA | Yes | No | ? |
| 207 Does the author state if the data were primary and/or secondary? | | | | |
| 208 Does the author state exactly *where* the data were collected? | | | | |
| 209 Does the author describe *when* the data were collected and by *who*? | | | | |
| 210 Does the author describe exactly *how* the data were collected? | | | | |

| 16. Data Collection Plan (Continued) | NA | Yes | No | ? |
|---|---|---|---|---|
| 211 Is it crystal clear to you who actually provided the data? That is, who was the data source? | | | | |
| 212 Does the author state that the data-collection process was pretested before it was implemented to the full sample or population? Was it pilot-tested? | | | | |
| 213 Does the author state how long it took the data-collectors to collect the data, first by individual case, and then by the entire sample? | | | | |
| 214 Does the author describe the study's data-collection process in enough detail so it could be readily replicated by other researchers? | | | | |
| 215 Does the author abide by research ethics when it comes to data collection? | | | | |
| 216 Does the author describe the data collector's relationship with the research participants? | | | | |

| Overall Credibility Score for Data Collection Plan (Derived from questions 207–216) | Low 1 | 2 | 3 | High 4 |
|---|---|---|---|---|

| 17. Analysis/Results | Adequately Addressed | | | |
|---|---|---|---|---|
| | NA | Yes | No | ? |
| 217 Do the study's findings provide an answer to the author's research question or hypothesis? | | | | |
| 218 If the results were reported in the form of descriptive statistics, is each mean accompanied by a standard deviation? | | | | |
| 219 If inferential statistics were employed, were the data shown to meet the assumptions the tests were based upon (e.g., normal distribution, similar standard deviations, no significant autocorrelation)? | | | | |
| 220 If correlational measures were employed, were the $N$, correlation coefficient, and alpha levels reported? | | | | |
| 221 If a $t$-test or analysis of variance were used, does the report of each such test contain the degrees of freedom, $t$- or $F$-value, and alpha levels? | | | | |
| 222 If a statistically significant result were found, was the proportion of variance explained by this difference reported? | | | | |

| | 17. Analysis/Results (Continued) | NA | Yes | No | ? |
|---|---|---|---|---|---|
| 223 | If multiple statistical tests were performed, were the alpha levels appropriately adjusted to account for the numbers of such tests? | | | | |
| 224 | Does the author include both statistical significance results and effect sizes when possible? | | | | |
| 225 | Are all statistics clear, accurate, and verifiable? | | | | |
| 226 | Could the study's findings be sensitive/changeable depending on the analytical technique used? | | | | |
| 227 | Apart from statistically significant changes, was the clinical significance of any improvements discussed (if applicable)? | | | | |
| 228 | Are the results obtained from the various outcome measures consistent with one another? | | | | |
| 229 | Are the pattern of improvement (or deterioration) clear across all outcome measures? | | | | |
| 230 | Are the study's results written in a way which brings clarity to important issues? | | | | |
| 231 | Does the author attempt to contextualize nonsignificant data in an effort to portray significance? (e.g., discuss findings that had a trend toward significance as if they were significant). | | | | |
| 232 | Are data presented clearly and understandably in tables, graphs, or charts? | | | | |
| 233 | Are the results presented in the form of graphs or tables? If so, are the data comprehensible without recourse to the narrative text? | | | | |
| 234 | Are the titles of the tables, graphs, or charts "stand-alone," meaning you can understand the accompanying table, graph, or chart just by reading the title? | | | | |
| 235 | Are the tables and graphics clear, accurate, and understandable with appropriate labeling of data values, cut points, and thresholds? | | | | |
| 236 | Are there an appropriate number of tables, graphs, or charts? | | | | |
| 237 | Are the tables, graphs, or charts the appropriate lengths? | | | | |

| 17. Analysis/Results (Continued) | NA | Yes | No | ? |
|---|---|---|---|---|
| 238　Does the author state the study's sample size noted both in the title and also within the main column and row headings of the tables, graphs, or charts? | | | | |

| Overall Credibility Score for Data Analysis/Results (Derived from questions 217–238) | Low 1 | 2 | 3 | High 4 |
|---|---|---|---|---|

| 18. Limitations | Adequately Addressed | | | |
|---|---|---|---|---|
| | NA | Yes | No | ? |
| 239　Does the author acknowledge any limitations of the study's research design? | | | | |
| 240　Do you feel that there were study limitations that were not noted by the author? | | | | |
| 241　Does the author mention any potential rival hypotheses that could account for the study's findings? | | | | |
| 242　Does the author acknowledge any threats to internal validity that were not controlled for in the research design? | | | | |
| 243　Does the author acknowledge any threats to external validity that were not controlled for in the research design? | | | | |
| 244　Does the author assess the possible impact of systematic bias that could have occurred during the research process? | | | | |
| 245　Regardless of whether the limitations are cited or not, do you consider them to be major or minor limitations? | | | | |
| 246　Does the author discuss what limitations need attending to in any future research studies of this nature? | | | | |
| 247　Does the author discuss any constant or random errors that could have occurred during the study? | | | | |

| Overall Credibility Score for Limitations (Derived from questions 239–247) | Low 1 | 2 | 3 | High 4 |
|---|---|---|---|---|

| 19. Discussion / Conclusions / Summary | Adequately Addressed | | | |
|---|---|---|---|---|
| | NA | Yes | No | ? |
| 248 Does the author report only conclusions supported by the data? | | | | |
| 249 Are speculations clearly described as such, rather than as facts? | | | | |
| 250 Does the author base any conclusions on faulty logic? | | | | |
| 251 Are suggestions to improve future research studies in the topic area clearly described? | | | | |
| 252 Are the author's conclusions and recommendations both logical and consistent with the study's findings? | | | | |
| 253 Does the author's discussion logically follow the previously presented results? | | | | |
| 254 Does the author use existing *theoretical* literature when discussing the study's findings? | | | | |
| 255 Does the author use existing *research-based* literature when discussing the study's findings? | | | | |
| 256 Does the author present a pro and/or con view, or differing interpretations of the study's results? | | | | |
| 257 Were the study's results expected by the author? | | | | |
| 258 Do you agree with the author's conclusions? (If so, why? If not, why not?) | | | | |
| 259 Does the author's discussion "fit" with the data? Is the discussion logical based on the data and results presented? | | | | |
| 260 Does the author discuss the study's findings in regard to a theoretical framework? | | | | |
| 261 Does the author discuss meaningful implications for social work practice? If so, are they appropriate? | | | | |
| 262 Are the author's key arguments supported by examples from prior research studies or from "life"? | | | | |
| 263 Are the author's key arguments stated and clearly supported? | | | | |

| 19. Discussion/Conclusions/Summary (Continued) | NA | Yes | No | ? |
|---|---|---|---|---|
| 264 Are the author's examples appropriate to the arguments they support? | | | | |
| 265 Does the author use primary research studies to support the arguments? | | | | |
| 266 Does the author use secondary research studies to support the arguments? | | | | |
| 267 Are the cited passages from the literature legitimate support for the author's argument or were they distorted by being quoted out of context? | | | | |
| 268 Does the author consider the study's limitations and/or alternative interpretations of the data analysis? | | | | |
| 269 Are the author's conclusions clearly based on the study's findings? | | | | |
| 270 Apart from statistically significant changes, are the clinical significance of any improvements discussed? | | | | |
| 271 Do you feel the findings of the study can easily be communicated to other professionals without distortion and vagueness? | | | | |
| 272 Do you feel that other social work practitioners can read the research study and derive the same conclusions and practice recommendations? | | | | |
| Overall Credibility Score for Discussion/Conclusions/Summary (Derived from questions 248–272) | Low 1 | 2 | 3 | High 4 |

| 20. References | Adequately Addressed | | | |
|---|---|---|---|---|
| | NA | Yes | No | ? |
| 273 Are the references in APA style? | | | | |
| 274 Are the references up to date? | | | | |
| 275 Are there at least 10 references? | | | | |
| Overall Credibility Score for References (Derived from questions 273–275) | Low 1 | 2 | 3 | High 4 |

Note: Many questions are repeated in several sections because they apply to more than one section.

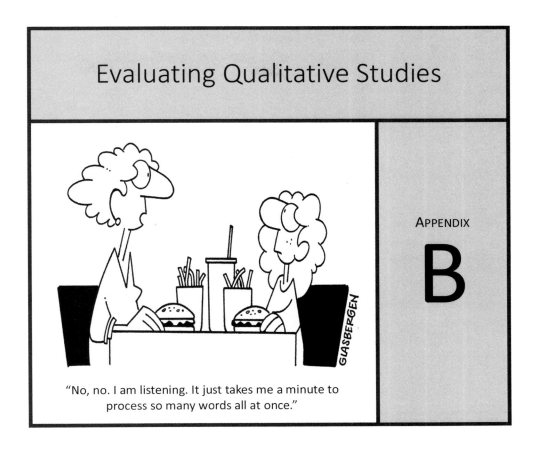

# Evaluating Qualitative Studies

APPENDIX

# B

"No, no. I am listening. It just takes me a minute to process so many words all at once."

## Questions to Consider When Evaluating a Qualitatively-Oriented Research Study

| Title of Evidence Evaluated: | | | | |
|---|---|---|---|---|
| **1. Author** | Adequately Addressed | | | |
| | NA | Yes | No | ? |
| **276** Is the author actually qualified and familiar with the study's topic? | | | | |
| **277** Is the author recognized as an authority on the subject? | | | | |
| **278** Do you know if the author has any financial stake in the statements being made? | | | | |
| **279** Does the author have any known political position? | | | | |

| 1. Author (Continued) | NA | Yes | No | ? |
|---|---|---|---|---|
| **280** Is the author affiliated with a college or university? | | | | |
| **281** Do you know the author's highest degree obtained? | | | | |
| **282** Has the author declared any conflict of interest or bias in relation to the subject of the research study? | | | | |
| **283** Have you Googled the author's name? | | | | |
| **284** Do you know of any additional information about the author that you found on the Internet? | | | | |
| **285** Do you know where the author is employed, if at all? | | | | |
| **286** Do you know the author's impact factor (AIF, or h-Index)? | | | | |

| Overall Credibility Score for Author (Derived from questions 276–286) | Low | | | High |
|---|---|---|---|---|
| | 1 | 2 | 3 | 4 |

| 2. Journal and Article | Adequately Addressed | | | |
|---|---|---|---|---|
| | NA | Yes | No | ? |
| **287** Is the article published in a reputable peer-review journal? | | | | |
| **288** Do you know how many years the journal been in existence (look for volume number)? | | | | |
| **289** Do you know the qualifications of the journal's editor (if any)? | | | | |
| **290** Do you know the qualifications of the journal's editorial board (if any)? | | | | |
| **291** Do you know the journal's impact factor (JIF)? | | | | |
| **292** Do you know if the journal has any known biased editorial position? | | | | |
| **293** Do you know when the article was published? | | | | |
| **294** Do you know how many times the article been previously cited (and where)? (CINAHL, EMBASE, Google Scholar, Microsoft Academic Search, PsycInfo, Web of Science) | | | | |

| Overall Credibility Score for Journal and Article (Derived from questions 287–294) | Low 1 | 2 | 3 | High 4 |
|---|---|---|---|---|

| 3. Title | Adequately Addressed | | | |
|---|---|---|---|---|
| | NA | Yes | No | ? |
| **295** Does the title under 15 words? | | | | |
| **296** Does the title make sense standing alone? | | | | |
| **297** Does the title include the important study variables or theoretical issues? | | | | |
| **298** Does the title refer to the study's sample? | | | | |
| **299** Does the title refer to the study's research setting? | | | | |
| **300** Does the title identify relationships between or among variables? | | | | |
| **301** Does the title identify the independent variable? | | | | |
| **302** Does the title identify the dependent variable? | | | | |
| **303** Is the title extremely clear and not cutesy? | | | | |

| Overall Credibility Score for Title of Article (Derived from questions 295–303) | Low 1 | 2 | 3 | High 4 |
|---|---|---|---|---|

| 4. Abstract | Adequately Addressed | | | |
|---|---|---|---|---|
| | NA | Yes | No | ? |
| **304** Is the abstract clear, concise, specific, and to the point? | | | | |
| **305** Is the abstract under 250 words? | | | | |
| **306** Does the abstract use abbreviations that could be unfamiliar to some readers? | | | | |
| **307** Is the abstract accurate in relation to the article's text? | | | | |
| **308** Does the abstract have the usual headings such as, purpose, methods, results, and implications? | | | | |
| **309** Does the abstract use an active voice? | | | | |

| Overall Credibility Score for Abstract (Derived from questions 304–309) | Low | | | High |
|---|---|---|---|---|
| | 1 | 2 | 3 | 4 |

| 5. Research Question and Literature Review | Adequately Addressed | | | |
|---|---|---|---|---|
| | NA | Yes | No | ? |
| **310** Is the research question crystal clear? | | | | |
| **311** Does the author address any philosophical assumptions prior to doing the study? | | | | |
| **312** Does the author use headings and subheadings to organize ideas? | | | | |
| **313** Does the author identify any differences between and among previous research studies? | | | | |
| **314** Does the literature review support the overall purpose of the study? | | | | |
| **315** Is there evidence the literature was researched iteratively? | | | | |
| **316** Does the research question include all of the major concepts? | | | | |
| **317** Are the conceptual definitions within the research study multidimensional? | | | | |
| **318** Do the definitions evolve as participants provided their perspectives? | | | | |
| **319** Is there a logical rationale for doing a qualitative study rather than a quantitative one? | | | | |
| **320** Is there a good fit between the study's research question and the qualitative research approach that was used to answer the question? | | | | |
| **321** Does the author demonstrate value awareness? | | | | |
| **322** Were informed consent and/or assent procedures adequately described? | | | | |
| **323** Does the author describe how confidentiality or anonymity was kept? | | | | |
| **324** Does the research study advance the common good of its research participants? | | | | |

| 5. Research Question and Literature Review (Continued) | NA | Yes | No | ? |
|---|---|---|---|---|
| **325** Is the purpose of the study extremely clear? | | | | |
| **326** Is the research problem clearly identified in the article? | | | | |
| **327** Does the study have objectives? If so, were they clearly stated? | | | | |
| **328** Does the study have research questions? If so, were they clearly stated? | | | | |
| **329** Does the study have hypotheses (a rarity in qualitative studies)? If so, were they stated? | | | | |
| **330** Does the author provide a well-defined research topic and an extremely clear research question or hypothesis? | | | | |
| **331** Does the author distinguished between research, theory, and opinion? | | | | |
| **332** Does the author base the research study on clear chains of inferential reasoning supported and justified by a complete coverage of the relevant literature? | | | | |
| **333** Does the author's review of the literature help you to establish the overall significance of the research study? | | | | |
| **334** Does the author provide you with enough information to convince you that the research study needed to be done? | | | | |
| **335** Does the author overlook any key pieces of literature? Answering this would depend on your knowledge of the field. | | | | |
| **336** Is the literature cited justify the chosen qualitative research approach. | | | | |
| **337** Does the author incorporate findings from original research studies into the literature review? | | | | |
| **338** Do the author's assumptions between and among variables make sense to you? | | | | |

| 5. Research Question and Literature Review (Continued) | NA | Yes | No | ? |
|---|---|---|---|---|
| 339 Does the author define major concepts and operational definitions in a way that makes sense to you? | | | | |
| 340 Does the author provide reasonable assumptions of the relationships between the independent and dependent variables (if any)? | | | | |
| 341 Does the author provide conceptual definitions of key terms? | | | | |
| 342 Does the author indicate the basis for "factual" statements? | | | | |
| 343 Do the specific research purposes, questions, or hypotheses logically link with one another? | | | | |
| 344 Is the literature review logically organized? | | | | |
| 345 Is the literature review directly related to the topic of the research study? | | | | |
| 346 Is there a balanced review of differing viewpoints or findings? | | | | |
| 347 Is the literature review one sided, and did it ignore alternative evidence? | | | | |
| 348 Does the author arrange the literature review by dates of the studies cited? If so, does this make sense to you? | | | | |
| 349 Does the author arrange the literature review by school of thought/theory? If so, does this make sense to you? | | | | |
| 350 Does the author arrange the literature review by themes that have emerged from the literature? If so, does this make sense to you? | | | | |
| 351 Does the author arrange the literature review by research approach? If so, does this make sense to you? | | | | |
| 352 Is the literature review up to date? | | | | |
| 353 Is the literature review convincing? | | | | |

| 5. Research Question and Literature Review (Continued) | NA | Yes | No | ? |
|---|---|---|---|---|
| 354 Is the literature review written critically (giving strengths and weaknesses of previous work)? | | | | |
| 355 Does the author appropriately cite earlier, relevant studies drawn from the literature? | | | | |
| 356 Are the parameters of the literature review reasonable? (Why were certain bodies of literature included in the search and others excluded?) | | | | |
| 357 Is primary literature emphasized in the literature review, and secondary literature, if cited, used selectively? | | | | |
| 358 Are most of the literature sources from reputable refereed journals? | | | | |
| 359 Is the cited literature appraised? Or did the author try to impress you with a list of references and no information about their contents? | | | | |
| 360 Are recent developments in the literature emphasized in the review? | | | | |
| 361 Are complete bibliographic data provided for each source cited? | | | | |
| 362 Is the literature review sufficiently comprehensive? (Use the "15–10" citation rule to assess its adequacy and comprehensiveness.) | | | | |
| 363 Are the references current, or a combination of current and classic? | | | | |
| 364 Are major studies discussed in detail and the actual findings cited? | | | | |
| 365 Do the reviews of major studies relate explicitly to the author's research problem and methods? | | | | |
| 366 Are minor studies with similar results or limitations summarized as a group? | | | | |
| 367 Is there an adequate analysis or critique of the methodologies of important research studies so you can determine the quality of previous research studies? | | | | |

| 5. Research Question and Literature Review (Continued) | NA | Yes | No | ? |
|---|---|---|---|---|
| 368  Are previous research studies compared and contrasted and conflicting or inclusive results noted? | | | | |
| 369  For some basic and applied studies, is the conceptual framework or theory that guided the study explained? | | | | |
| 370  Do you know the P.O.I. of the phenomenon being studied? That is, can you determine the prevalence (P), occurrence (O), and incidence (I) of the phenomenon being studied? | | | | |

| Overall Credibility Score for Research Question and Literature Review (Derived from questions 310–370) | Low | | | High |
|---|---|---|---|---|
| | 1 | 2 | 3 | 4 |

| 6. Ethical Sensitivity | Adequately Addressed | | | |
|---|---|---|---|---|
| | NA | Yes | No | ? |
| 371  Does the author use appropriate consent forms? | | | | |
| 372  Does the author use appropriate assent forms? | | | | |
| 373  Does the author mention the ethical considerations of data collection? | | | | |
| 374  Does the author mention whether IRB approval was obtained or why it was not necessary? | | | | |
| 375  Does the author minimize the risk of harm to the research participants? | | | | |
| 376  Does the author provide anonymity to the research participants? | | | | |
| 377  Does the author provide confidentiality to the research participants? | | | | |
| 378  Does the author avoid deceptive practices? | | | | |
| 379  Does the author provide the research participants with the right to withdraw from the study for any reason whatsoever? | | | | |

| Overall Credibility Score for Ethical Sensitivity (Derived from questions 371–379) | Low | | | High |
|---|---|---|---|---|
| | 1 | 2 | 3 | 4 |

| 7. Data-Collection Procedures and Rigor | Adequately Addressed | | | |
|---|---|---|---|---|
| | NA | Yes | No | ? |
| 380 Are reasons given for the type of sampling utilized? | | | | |
| 381 Does the author address the issue of subjectivity? | | | | |
| 382 Does the author address the issue of bias by the researchers or respondents? | | | | |
| 383 Are strategies used to improve credibility? | | | | |
| 384 Are strategies used to improve transferability? | | | | |
| 385 Are strategies used to improve dependability? | | | | |
| 386 Are strategies used to improve confirmability? | | | | |
| Overall Credibility Score for Data-Collection Procedures (Derived from questions 380–386) | Low 1 | 2 | 3 | High 4 |

| 8. Data-Analysis Procedures and Discussion | Adequately Addressed | | | |
|---|---|---|---|---|
| | NA | Yes | No | ? |
| 387 Are strategies used to increase the accuracy of transcriptions? | | | | |
| 388 Does the author clearly describe how data were analysed? | | | | |
| 389 Are clear categories developed during first-level coding? | | | | |
| 390 Are relationships between categories clarified during second-level coding? | | | | |
| 391 Are the themes and theories well developed? | | | | |
| 392 Are limitations addressed from an interpretivist perspective? | | | | |
| 393 Are the results integrated with the previous literature? | | | | |
| 394 Are implications for theory, practice, or policy identified? | | | | |

| 8. Data-Analysis Procedures and Discussion (Continued) | NA | Yes | No | ? |
|---|---|---|---|---|
| 395 Are recommendations for future research studies made? | | | | |

| Overall Credibility Score for Data-Analysis Procedures and Discussion (Derived from questions 387–395) | Low 1 | 2 | 3 | High 4 |
|---|---|---|---|---|

| 9. Reliability | Adequately Addressed | | | |
|---|---|---|---|---|
| | NA | Yes | No | ? |
| 396 Is the research question clear, and are the components of the study congruent with them? | | | | |
| 397 Is the author's role and status within the research site explicitly described? | | | | |
| 398 Do the findings show meaningful parallelism across data sources? | | | | |
| 399 Are basic paradigms and analytical constructs clearly specified? | | | | |
| 400 Are data collected across the full range of appropriate settings, times, respondents, and so on suggested by research questions? | | | | |
| 401 If multiple field workers were involved, did they have comparable data-collection protocols? | | | | |
| 402 Are coding checks made, and do they show adequate agreement? | | | | |
| 403 Are data quality checks made? | | | | |
| 404 Do multiple observers' accounts converge in instances, settings, or times when they might be expected to? | | | | |

| Overall Credibility Score for Reliability (Derived from questions 396–404) | Low 1 | 2 | 3 | High 4 |
|---|---|---|---|---|

| 10. Creditability | Adequately Addressed | | | |
|---|---|---|---|---|
| | NA | Yes | No | ? |
| 405 Are the author's descriptions context-rich and meaningful ("thick")? | | | | |

| | 10. Creditability (continued) | NA | Yes | No | ? |
|---|---|---|---|---|---|
| 406 | Does the whole study "ring true." That is, does it seem convincing, makes sense, or enables a "vicarious presence" for the reader? | | | | |
| 407 | Does the triangulation among complementary data-collection methods and data sources produce generally converging conclusions? | | | | |
| 408 | Are the presented data well linked to the categories of prior or emerging theory? | | | | |
| 409 | Are the findings internally coherent? | | | | |
| 410 | Are areas of uncertainty identified? | | | | |
| 411 | Is negative evidence sought? | | | | |
| 412 | Are rival explanations actively considered? | | | | |
| 413 | Are findings replicated in different parts of the database? | | | | |
| 414 | Are the conclusions considered to be accurate by the original informants (research participants)? | | | | |
| 415 | Are any predictions made by the author, and how accurate were they? | | | | |
| 416 | Are descriptions and interpretations of the participants' experiences recognizable? | | | | |
| 417 | Is there a variety of data collection methods used? | | | | |
| 418 | Is a reflective approach used by keeping a journal of reflections, biases or preconceptions, and ideas? | | | | |
| 419 | Is "member checking" used within the study? | | | | |

| Overall Credibility Score for Creditability (Derived from questions 405–419) | Low | | | High |
|---|---|---|---|---|
| | 1 | 2 | 3 | 4 |

| 11. Transferability | Adequately Addressed | | | |
|---|---|---|---|---|
| | NA | Yes | No | ? |
| 420 Does the author discuss possible threats to transferability? | | | | |

| 11. Transferability (continued) | NA | Yes | No | ? |
|---|---|---|---|---|
| **421** Are the characteristics of the original sample of persons, settings, processes, and the like fully described to permit adequate comparisons with other samples? | | | | |
| **422** Is the sampling theoretically diverse enough to encourage broader applicability? | | | | |
| **423** Does the author define the scope and the boundaries of reasonable generalization from the study? | | | | |
| **424** Do the findings include enough thick description for the reader to assess the potential transferability, or appropriateness, for his or her own setting? | | | | |
| **425** Do a range of readers report the findings to be consistent with their experiences? | | | | |
| **426** Are the findings congruent with, connected to, or confirmatory of prior theory? | | | | |
| **427** Are the processes and outcomes described in the Conclusions section of the report generic enough to be applicable in other settings, even those of a different nature? | | | | |
| **428** Are narrative sequences preserved unobscured? | | | | |
| **429** Does the author suggest other settings in which the research findings could be fruitfully tested further? | | | | |
| **430** Have the findings been replicated in other studies to assess their robustness? | | | | |
| **431** Does the author define the scope and the boundaries of reasonable generalization from the study? | | | | |
| **432** Does the author described research participants and the setting in enough detail to allow for comparisons with your population of interest? | | | | |
| **433** Are there concepts developed that might apply to your clients and within their contexts? | | | | |

| Overall Credibility Score for Transferability (Derived from questions 420–433) | Low 1 | 2 | 3 | High 4 |
|---|---|---|---|---|

### 12. Dependability

| | Adequately Addressed | | | |
|---|---|---|---|---|
| | NA | Yes | No | ? |
| **434** Is there a clear explanation of the research process including methods of data collection, and analyses and interpretation often indicated by evidence of an audit trail or peer review? | | | | |
| **435** Does the author provide an audit trail that described the decision points made throughout the entire research process? | | | | |

| Overall Credibility Score for Dependability (Derived from questions 434–435) | Low 1 | 2 | 3 | High 4 |
|---|---|---|---|---|

### 13. Confirmability

| | Adequately Addressed | | | |
|---|---|---|---|---|
| | NA | Yes | No | ? |
| **436** Is the researcher reflective by keeping a journal or asking a colleague to audit the decision points throughout the process and checking with expert colleagues about ideas and interpretation of data, checking with research participants about ideas and interpretation of data, and having a team of researchers? | | | | |

| Overall Credibility Score for Confirmability (Derived from question 436) | Low 1 | 2 | 3 | High 4 |
|---|---|---|---|---|

### 14. Research Setting

| | Adequately Addressed | | | |
|---|---|---|---|---|
| | NA | Yes | No | ? |
| **437** Does the author provide an audit trail that described the decision points made throughout the entire research process? | | | | |
| **438** Does the author specify where the data were collected within the research setting? | | | | |
| **439** Does the author specify how data were collected within the research setting? | | | | |

| Overall Credibility Score for Research Setting (Derived from questions 437–439) | Low 1 | 2 | 3 | High 4 |
|---|---|---|---|---|

| 15. Research Participants (Sample) | Adequately Addressed | | | |
|---|---|---|---|---|
| | NA | Yes | No | ? |
| **440** Does the author provide a clear description of the sampling method that was used to recruit research participants for the study? That is, what sampling method was used in selecting the sample (e.g., random, stratified random, cluster, stage, purposive, quota, snowball, accidental [or convenience])? | | | | |
| **441** Does the author describe the inclusion and exclusion criteria that was used to select the sample? | | | | |
| **442** Does the author specify the time frame for sample selection? | | | | |
| **443** Given the author's description of the sampling procedures that were used for the study, do you feel you could replicate it if you did a similar study? | | | | |
| **444** Do you know the study's sample size? | | | | |
| **445** Are salient characteristics (e.g., demographic, clinical, diagnostic) of the study's sample described in clear detail to permit comparisons of this particular sample with those used in prior (and future) studies? | | | | |
| **446** Does the sample present any unique features? | | | | |
| **447** Does the author describe the final sample that was used in the study in enough detail so you know what it actually was? | | | | |
| Overall Credibility Score for Sample (Derived from questions 440–447) | Low<br>1 | <br>2 | <br>3 | High<br>4 |

| 16. Cultural Sensitivity | Adequately Addressed | | | |
|---|---|---|---|---|
| | NA | Yes | No | ? |
| **448** Did the author address the contextuality of the study? That is, does the author have an understanding of the sociocultural, political, and historical context of where the research participants live? | | | | |

| | | | | | |
|---|---|---|---|---|---|
| 449 | Did the author address the study's relevance? That is, did the study's research question or hypothesis address meaningful issues faced by the research participants and did it serve the interests in improving their lives? | | | | |
| 450 | Is the author's communication style appropriate? That is, does the author understand the preferred communication styles of the research participants and their communities and the subtleties and variations inherent in the language used? | | | | |
| 451 | Does the author display an awareness of identity and power differences? That is, was the author aware of researcher–participant power differences, the establishment of credibility, and the development of more horizontal relationships? | | | | |
| 452 | Does the author use appropriate disclosure? That is, did the author avoid the use of secrecy and built trust with the research participants? | | | | |
| 453 | Is the author aware of reciprocation? That is, did the study meet mutual goals and objectives of the researcher and the research participants? | | | | |
| 454 | Does the author use an empowerment approach to the research process? That is, did the research process contribute to empowering the research participants? | | | | |
| 455 | Is the author aware of the concept of time? That is, did the author use a flexible approach within the research process in terms of quantity and quality of time spent with the research participants? | | | | |
| 456 | Do you feel the author was respectful to people with other perspectives throughout the study? | | | | |
| 457 | Is the author's role and status within the research site explicitly described? | | | | |

| Overall Credibility Score for Cultural Sensitivity (Derived from questions 448–457) | Low | | | High |
|---|---|---|---|---|
| | 1 | 2 | 3 | 4 |

| 17. References | Adequately Addressed | | | |
|---|---|---|---|---|
| | NA | Yes | No | ? |
| 458    Are the references in APA style? | | | | |

| 17. References (Continued) | NA | Yes | No | ? |
|---|---|---|---|---|
| **459**   Are the references up to date? | | | | |
| **460**   Are there at least 10 references? | | | | |
| Overall Credibility Score for References (Derived from questions 458–460) | Low  1 | 2 | 3 | High  4 |

Note: Many questions are repeated in several sections because they apply to more than one section.

# Evaluating Internet Resources

**APPENDIX**

# C

"Diabetes became an epidemic about the same time people started using the Internet. Way too much spam and cookies from the computers!"

PROFESSORS, JOURNALISTS, LIBRARIANS, AND BUSINESS PEOPLE know full well that information is important. But even more important is to know that the information sought after is valid, reliable, authoritative, and pertinent. When information is peer-reviewed, authenticated, and evaluated, you can trust—most of the time, that is—the source is valid and authoritative. But when it isn't, you must assess and evaluate the information you find on the Internet all by yourself.

The Internet, a worldwide, noncommercial, freely accessible network of networks has turned into a humongous source of information with wide coverage and fast access. It's one of the most, if not the most, powerful tool for global communication and exchange of information.

## AVAILABILITY OF INFORMATION

**T**he amount of publicly available information on the Internet is increasing consistently at an unbelievable rate. It has revolutionized the way that people access information and has opened up new possibilities in areas such as digital libraries, education, commerce, entertainment, government, and health care. It has turned into a gigantic digital library, a searchable multibillion-word encyclopedia.

The Internet can be a great resource when doing research on many topics. But putting documents (or pages) on the Internet is easy, inexpensive or free, unregulated, and unmonitored. It's a self-publishing mecca—anyone can publish anything anytime, from anywhere. This means that not everything you find on the Internet is equally valuable or reliable. Information on the Internet exists in large quantities and is continuously being created and revised.

511

This information exists in a large variety of kinds (e.g., facts, opinions, stories, interpretations, statistics) and is created for many purposes (e.g., to inform, to persuade, to sell, to present a viewpoint, and to create or change an attitude or belief). For each of these various kinds and purposes, information exists on many levels of quality or reliability. It ranges from very good to very bad and includes every shade in between. With this wealth and variety of information available, you must proceed with your critical thinking hat on when retrieving these information resources.

Therein lies the rationale for evaluating carefully whatever you find on the Internet. The burden is on you to establish the validity, authorship, timeliness, and integrity of what you find. Documents can easily be copied and falsified—intentionally or accidentally. While searching for information on the Internet people rely on a limited set of search tools, especially general search engines such as Google, not realizing that fewer than 20 percent of all indexable documents are being accessed by Google.

Most pages found on the Internet are self-published or published by small and large businesses with motives to get you to buy something or believe a point of view. Search engines (e.g., Google, Bing, Yahoo, Ask.com, AOL.com, Baidu, Wolframalpha, DuckDuckGo.) and others like them have strengths and weaknesses. A high percentage of non-authoritative content is mixed with quality content, which makes locating relevant information serendipitous at best.

Libraries have always striven to provide the right information to the right user at the right time. In the case of the Internet, there is no controlling authority, subject experts, or review committees. And since there is no competition for space on the Internet, a lot of junk and useless information is being made available by amateur authors at astonishing rates.

Searching for relevant sources on the Internet takes a fair amount of time, a lot of which must be wasted on rejecting irrelevant information. Determining the relevance of sources can often be difficult: It's not always easy to judge the credibility and reliability of the information located from an Internet search. Thus, the purpose of this chapter is to make a few pertinent observations regarding the relevant criteria useful for evaluating the quality of information you run across on the Internet.

## TYPES OF WEBSITES

**G**enerally speaking, there are five different kinds of websites that can be found on the Internet, with varying goals and audiences:

1 **Advocacy Websites.** Advocacy websites are sponsored by organizations (often nonprofits) or individuals attempting to influence public opinion. They often belong to groups who strongly believe in and support a particular cause or issue. Therefore, information found at such sites may be biased. Their Uniform Reference Locator (URL) often ends in .org (for organization).

2 **Business/Marketing Websites.** Business/marketing websites are sponsored by commercial enterprises and are usually trying to promote or sell products. Their URL often ends in .com (for commercial).

3 **Informational Websites.** Informational websites are those whose purpose is to present factual information, and they are often sponsored by educational institutions or government agencies. Such sites are good starting points for scholarly research. Their URL often ends in .edu (for educational) or .gov (for government).

4  **News Websites.** News websites are those whose primary purpose is to provide current information. These are usually "home pages" of news organizations that provide current (and usually not very historical) news coverage. Because the news pages are updated constantly, avoid citing an article from these pages in academic papers as it may be moved to a new URL or be removed entirely from the site. If available, cite the article using the printed version. Their URL usually ends in .com (for commercial).

5  **Personal Websites.** Individuals who may or may not be affiliated with larger institutions can publish personal home pages. Such sites belong to individuals who want to promote themselves and their interests. As anyone can publish on the Internet, avoid using information from such sites unless you can verify the qualifications of the author of the site. Their URL could have a variety of endings, including .com, .edu, or .net (for network access provider).

## WHY EVALUATE INTERNET RESOURCES?

**T**here are **several reasons** why information derived from websites deserves scrutiny and evaluation.

- The amount of information available on the Internet is immense. How likely is it that it will be of a uniformly high quality?

- The fastest growing area of the Internet is the commercial sites. Note the distinction between promotion and real information.

- Many webpages are anonymous in nature. It is often difficult to determine a page's authorship/sponsorship. In such circumstances, a resource must be treated with a degree of skepticism. The information is only useful if it can be otherwise verified. You cannot evaluate what you cannot verify.

- Evidence of accountability (e.g., the author and posting date are provided) can remove much of the uncertainty and mistrust about web-based information.

- There is no quality control on most websites. The editorial input and quality control exercised in the print world are often lacking with online resources. In these circumstances, the author and site information take on extra significance. Other criteria—such as credible and/or authoritative sites that link to a resource—can also play an important part in giving a site credibility. Peer acceptance being evident also can greatly ease the concerns of the site visitor.

- Not all sources are equally valuable or reliable. Critical thinking is required in evaluating Internet resources.

- The value of a resource and its ability to satisfy your information requirements will vary for different audiences.

- It is extremely easy to publish something/anything on the Internet. It is a self-publishing medium. All you need is access to a server.

- Websites tend to come and go with dizzying speed. In addition, the information found on sites can change daily.

- Because Internet resources are rarely static, the task of resource evaluation is more difficult than might otherwise be the case. Any evaluation of a web resource is limited to a particular point in time; an evaluation performed at a different time may lend different results. Thus, the web complements, but does not replace, other sources of information. Using the Internet effectively requires being highly selective in choosing information. The Internet is useful as a tool to aid in your research, but it should not be your only information source.

## A BEGINNING LIST OF EVALUATION CRITERIA

**A** **number of useful criteria** may be used in evaluating Internet-based resources. The questions that follow are to help you to assess the utility of each source for your particular needs. This appendix—like the two previous ones—provides you with a few basic questions you can ask about evaluating what you find on the Internet. It's a starting point. Nothing more. You should not believe it includes all the questions you need to ask, and of course, answer.

The great wealth that the Internet has brought to so much of society is the ability for people to express themselves, find one another, exchange ideas, discover possible peers worldwide they never would have otherwise met, and of course, to see homemade movies about cats doing cute things.

Information everywhere on the Internet exists in large quantities, in a large variety of kinds, and is created for many purposes. With all this wealth and variety of information available, you need to proceed with critical thinking when retrieving these information resources.

In the end, the burden is on you to establish the validity, authorship, timeliness, and integrity of the Internet resources you find. Although the Internet can be a great place to accomplish research on many topics, you must remember that it complements but does not replace other sources. To use the Internet effectively, be highly selective which information you finally chose to use.

## Questions to Consider When Evaluating
## Information from the Internet

| Title of evidence evaluated (source): | | | | |
|---|---|---|---|---|
| **1. Authority/Author** | **Adequately Addressed** | | | |
| | NA | Yes | No | ? |
| **461** Is there an identified author of the website or page? | | | | |
| **462** Does the author list his or her occupation, years of experience, position, education, or other credentials? | | | | |
| **463** Is the author's affiliation clearly indicated? | | | | |
| **464** Does the author belong to an official professional organization of some kind? | | | | |
| **465** If the page is authored by an organization is there additional information about that organization available? | | | | |

| 1. Authority/Author (Continued) | NA | Yes | No | ? |
|---|---|---|---|---|
| 466 Is there contact information, such as an e-mail address, phone, or surface mail available for the author of the document? | | | | |
| 467 Is there a link to additional information about the author (a personal homepage, biography, or curriculum vita) that you can verify? | | | | |
| 468 Is the author an expert in his/her field? | | | | |
| 469 Has the author written articles or books other than webpages? | | | | |
| 470 Has one of your professors ever mentioned this author? | | | | |
| 471 Have you seen the author's name cited in other sources or bibliographies? | | | | |
| 472 Is the website peer-reviewed or edited? | | | | |
| 473 Is the website sponsored by a professional organization and/or association? | | | | |
| 474 Is there a link to a page describing the overall purpose or goal of the sponsoring body? | | | | |
| 475 Is there a statement that the page has the official approval of a sponsoring body? | | | | |
| 476 Is there a way of verifying the legitimacy of the sponsoring body? | | | | |
| 477 Is a phone number and surface mail address given for the organization, in addition to an e-mail address? | | | | |

| Overall Credibility Score for Authority/Author (Derived from questions 461–477) | Low | | | High |
|---|---|---|---|---|
| | 1 | 2 | 3 | 4 |

| 2. Purpose/Coverage | Adequately Addressed | | | |
|---|---|---|---|---|
| | NA | Yes | No | ? |
| 478 Does the content support the purpose of the website? | | | | |
| 479 Is the information geared to a specific audience (e.g., students, scholars, general reader)? | | | | |
| 480 Is the website organized and focused? | | | | |

| 2. Purpose/Coverage (Continued) | NA | Yes | No | ? |
|---|---|---|---|---|
| 481  Are the outside links appropriate for the website? | | | | |
| 482  Do the links go to outside websites rather than its own? | | | | |
| 483  Are there good links to additional coverage? | | | | |
| 484  Is the website intended to explain something? | | | | |
| 485  Is the website intended to explore something? | | | | |
| 486  Is the website intended to persuade you on a particular view? | | | | |
| 487  Is the website intended to entertain you? | | | | |
| 488  Does the website want you to buy something? | | | | |
| 489  Is the website a soapbox for organizations or people? | | | | |
| 490  Does the website describe the intended audience? (a) Students? (b) Professionals? (c) Lay people? (e) Businesses? | | | | |
| 491  Does the website contribute to the social work literature? | | | | |
| 492  It the website's content valuable to you? | | | | |
| 493  Are stereotypes or ethnocentric arguments used? | | | | |
| 494  Are fallacious, misleading, or deceptive arguments used? | | | | |
| 495  Are there links to information sources with other viewpoints? | | | | |
| 496  Is the website a satire, a parody, or a spoof? | | | | |
| 497  Is there advertising on the website? If so, what kind is it? | | | | |
| 498  If there's advertising on the website, can it be differentiated from the informational content? | | | | |
| 499  Does the website cover the subject adequately? | | | | |
| 500  Does the website claim to be selective? | | | | |
| 501  Does the website claim to be comprehensive? | | | | |

| 2. Purpose/Coverage (Continued) | NA | Yes | No | ? |
|---|---|---|---|---|
| **502** Are the website's topics explored in depth? | | | | |
| **503** Does the website provide information with no relevant outside links? | | | | |
| **504** Does the website provide information relevant to your needs? | | | | |
| **505** Can you use the information found on the website? | | | | |
| **506** Do you know the true purpose of the website? | | | | |
| **507** Is the website's scope clearly stated? | | | | |
| **508** Is it clear what topics the website intends to address, and does it succeed in addressing them? | | | | |
| **509** Is there any indication that the website has been completed and is not still under construction? | | | | |
| **510** Are there inexplicable omissions within the website? | | | | |
| **511** Is the audience of the website for experts? | | | | |
| **512** Does the website provide you with the kind and level of information you need? | | | | |
| **513** Is there a fee to access more detailed data? | | | | |
| **514** Is the material presented primary in nature? | | | | |
| **515** Is the material presented secondary in nature? | | | | |

| Overall Credibility Score of Purpose/Coverage (Derived from questions 478–515) | Low 1 | 2 | 3 | High 4 |
|---|---|---|---|---|

| 3. Accuracy | Adequately Addressed | | | |
|---|---|---|---|---|
| | NA | Yes | No | ? |
| **516** Do editors check the information contained on the website? | | | | |
| **517** Are there clues to tell you that the information on the page is really true? | | | | |
| **518** Is the website's information consistent with what you already know to be true? | | | | |
| **519** Does the author explain where the information was obtained? | | | | |

| 3. Accuracy (Continued) | NA | Yes | No | ? |
|---|---|---|---|---|
| **520** Are there any references or bibliographies listed as sources of information? | | | | |
| **521** Can the information be verified elsewhere? Perhaps in print sources? | | | | |
| **522** Is there evidence of potential bias? | | | | |
| **523** Does the author provide both sides of the argument with no evidence of bias? | | | | |
| **524** Does the author have a specific agenda or point of view? | | | | |
| **525** Is it stated who has the ultimate responsibility for the accuracy of the information provided? | | | | |
| **526** Is the author affiliated with a known, respectable institution? | | | | |
| **527** Do statistics and other factual information receive proper references as to their origin? | | | | |
| **528** Does the reading you have already done on the subject make the website's information seem accurate? | | | | |
| **529** Is the website's information comparable to other websites on the same topic? | | | | |
| **530** Does the text follow basic rules of grammar, spelling, and composition? | | | | |
| **531** Is the information free of grammatical, spelling, and other typographical errors? | | | | |
| **532** Is a bibliography list included on the website? | | | | |
| **533** Is the information current? (Check when the work was created because Internet information becomes outdated fairly quickly, like technology news. After determining the date of creation, you need to evaluate whether the work still has value.) | | | | |
| **534** Are there indicators within the website that suggest it is not accurate? (For instance, does the document lack a date or use outdated information? Does it make vague or sweeping generalizations or take a one-sided view that does not acknowledge opposing views or respond to them?) | | | | |

| Overall Credibility Score for Accuracy (Derived from questions 516–534) | Low | | | High |
|---|---|---|---|---|
| | 1 | 2 | 3 | 4 |

| 4. Reasonableness | Adequately Addressed | | | |
|---|---|---|---|---|
| | NA | Yes | No | ? |
| **535** Is the information reasonable? Does it offer a balanced, reasoned argument in a calm, reasoned tone without any attempt to get you emotionally worked up? (Angry, hateful writing often portrays an irrational and unfair attack rather than a reasoned argument.) | | | | |
| **536** Is the information objective? (There is no such thing as pure objectivity, but a good writer should be able to control his/her biases. Be aware that some organizations are naturally not neutral.) | | | | |
| **537** Is the information moderate? (Use your knowledge and experience to ask if the information is really likely, possible, or probable. If a claim being made is surprising or hard to believe, use caution and demand more evidence than you might require for a lesser claim.) | | | | |
| **538** Are there indicators that the information lacks reasonableness? (Does it have an intemperate tone or use language such as "stupid jerks" or "the shrill cries of my extremist opponents"; make claims such as "Thousands of children are murdered every day in the United States"; make sweeping statements such as "This is the most important idea ever conceived!"; or present a conflict of interest such as "Welcome to the Old Stogie Tobacco Company Home Page, to read our report, 'Cigarettes Make You Live Longer,' click here.") | | | | |
| Overall Credibility Score for Reasonableness (Derived from questions 535–538) | Low 1 | 2 | 3 | High 4 |

| 5. Support | Adequately Addressed | | | |
|---|---|---|---|---|
| | NA | Yes | No | ? |
| **539** Is the information comprehensive? | | | | |
| **540** Does the information intentionally leave out important facts? | | | | |
| **541** Are website's sources documented? | | | | |
| **542** Is there collaboration? (Do other sources support this source? This type of confirmation is an important test for truth. Even in areas of judgment or opinion, if an argument is sound, there will probably be a number of people who adhere to it or who are in general agreement with parts of it.) | | | | |

| 5. Support (Continued) | NA | Yes | No | ? |
|---|---|---|---|---|
| **543** Are there indicators of lack of support—are numbers or statistics presented without an identified source? | | | | |

| Overall Credibility Score for Support (Derived from questions 539–543) | Low 1 | 2 | 3 | High 4 |
|---|---|---|---|---|

| 6. Currency | Adequately Addressed | | | |
|---|---|---|---|---|
| | NA | Yes | No | ? |
| **544** Is the information current? | | | | |
| **545** Are there dates on the website's pages? They should indicate: (a) when the page was written. (b) when the page was first placed on the Internet. (c) when the page was last revised. (d) The original copyright date should be posted. (e) If the website or page provides time sensitive information, the frequency of updates should be posted. | | | | |
| **546** Is the page revised regularly? | | | | |
| **547** Are dates of updates of the page stated? | | | | |
| **548** Does the organization or person hosting the website appear to have a commitment to ongoing maintenance and stability of the resource? | | | | |
| **549** If the page was revised, were the changes substantive? | | | | |
| **550** Are all the links active? | | | | |
| **551** Are the links up to date? | | | | |
| **552** Does the website aim to provide current information? | | | | |
| **553** Does the website aim to provide historical information? | | | | |

| Overall Credibility Score for Currency (Derived from questions 544–553) | Low 1 | 2 | 3 | High 4 |
|---|---|---|---|---|

| 7. Objectivity | Adequately Addressed | | | |
|---|---|---|---|---|
| | NA | Yes | No | ? |
| **554** Is the purpose of the website clearly stated? | | | | |
| **555** Is the website based on verifiable facts rather than opinions? | | | | |

| | 7. Objectivity (Continued) | NA | Yes | No | ? |
|---|---|---|---|---|---|
| 556 | Is the website clearly not biased? | | | | |
| 557 | Are there any fallacies in arguments and reasoning? | | | | |
| 558 | Are inflammatory words, or provocative language and phrases, or profanity used in the website? | | | | |
| 559 | Does the author make use of emotional appeals instead of logical arguments as a means to sway the opinion of the audience? | | | | |
| 560 | Is there a commercial or organizational interest associated with the website? | | | | |
| 561 | Are there advertisements on the website? | | | | |
| 562 | Is the website actually an ad disguised as information? | | | | |
| 563 | Is sponsorship of the website acknowledged? | | | | |
| 564 | Is the information provided as a public service? | | | | |
| 565 | Are editorials and opinions clearly identified? | | | | |
| 566 | Are the sources of information clearly stated (whether original or borrowed from elsewhere)? | | | | |

| Overall Credibility Score for Objectivity (Derived from questions 554–566) | Low 1 | 2 | 3 | High 4 |
|---|---|---|---|---|

| 8. Ease of Use and Navigation | Adequately Addressed | | | |
|---|---|---|---|---|
| | NA | Yes | No | ? |
| 567 Is the website laid out clearly and logically with well-organized subsections? | | | | |
| 568 Is the writing style appropriate for the intended audience? | | | | |
| 569 Is the website easy to navigate with clearly labelled Back, Home, Go To, Top icons/links and internal indexing links on lengthy pages? | | | | |
| 570 Does the website load quickly and is readily accessible? | | | | |
| 571 Do the graphics and art serve a function? If so, are they appropriate? | | | | |
| 572 Do all links to remote websites work? | | | | |

| 8. Ease of Use and Navigation (Continued) | NA | Yes | No | ? |
|---|---|---|---|---|
| **573** Is the writing style appropriate for the intended audience? | | | | |
| **574** Does the text follow basic rules of grammar, spelling, and literary composition? | | | | |
| **575** Are the pages on the website easy to read and follow? (Do the backgrounds of the pages interface with their content? Is the color easy on the eyes?) | | | | |
| **576** Is the material presented in an orderly format? | | | | |
| **577** Do the graphics and images add to the presentation of the pages? | | | | |
| **578** Are links appropriate to the topic of each page? | | | | |
| **579** Is there a link at the bottom of the page to go back to the top of the page? | | | | |
| **580** Is there a link on each supporting page to go back to the main page? | | | | |
| **581** Is there a comment link at the bottom of the main page? | | | | |
| **582** Do you need special software to view the information contained on the website? If you don't have the software, how much information are you missing? | | | | |
| **583** Is there a fee to obtain information on the website? | | | | |

| Overall Credibility Score for Ease of Use and Navigation (Derived from questions 567–583) | Low | | | High |
|---|---|---|---|---|
| | 1 | 2 | 3 | 4 |

Note: Many questions are repeated in several sections because they apply to more than one section.

# Glossary

"No, no. A glossary is nothing more than a bunch of opinions expressed as truths in alphabetical order."

**A phase:** In case-level evaluation designs, the phase (*A* phase) in which the baseline measurement of the target problem is established before the intervention (*B* phase) is implemented.

**A priori:** Latin for "from what comes before." Typically, conclusions drawn from self-evident or deductive propositions that a researcher decides to make before collecting the data or examining the results.

**Abstract:** A brief summary of the important parts of a research study.

**Abstracting indexing services:** Providers of specialized reference tools that make it possible to find information quickly and easily, usually through subject headings and/or author approaches.

**Abstracts:** Reference materials consisting of citations and brief descriptive summaries from positivist and interpretive research studies.

**Accountability:** A system of responsibility in which program administrators account for all program activities by answering to the demands of a program's stakeholders and by justifying the program's expenditures to the satisfaction of its stakeholders; taking personal responsibility for one's conduct.

**Accounts:** In an interview, an account is a representation of a situation. Successful analysis depends on treating what the participants say as subjective accounts that the researcher must interpret, rather than factual reports than can be simply accepted at face value.

**Accreditation:** A process in which an accrediting body determines whether an institution or organization meets certain standards developed by the body.

**Acculturation difficulty:** A problem stemming from an inability to appropriately adapt to a different culture or environment.

**Achieved status:** Social status and prestige of an individual acquired as a result of individual accomplishments.

**Action research:** Action research is a research approach that **occurs** when researchers design a field experiment, collect the data, and feed it back to the activists (i.e., participants) both as feedback and as a way of modeling the next stage of the experiment. "Action" refers to the process of identifying issues relevant to a teaching or social situation; "research" refers to the processes of systematically collecting, documenting, and analyzing data. Data can be numerical as well as textual. In the field of applied linguistics, action research is often used by teachers when they investigate their own classrooms.

**Adverse event (AE):** A medically undesirable event occurring in a research subject, such as an abnormal sign, symptom, or worsening of a disease or injury. A serious adverse event (SAE) results in death, hospitalization (or increased hospital stay), persistent disability, birth defect, or any other outcome that seriously jeopardizes the subject's health. AEs that are also unanticipated problems should be reported promptly to institutional review boards and other appropriate officials.

**Aggregate:** Any collection of individuals who do not interact with one another.

**Aggregate-level data:** Derived from micro-level data, aggregate-level data are grouped so that the characteristics of individual units of analysis are no longer identifiable; for example, the variable "gross national income" is an aggregation of data about individual incomes.

**Aggregated case-level evaluation designs:** The collection of a number of case-level evaluations to determine the degree to which a program objective has been met.

**Aggregated statistics:** Information, written as numbers, about whole groups, not individuals in the groups.

**Alternate-forms method:** A method for establishing reliability of a measuring instrument by administering, in succession, equivalent forms of the same instrument to the same group of research participants.

**Alternative hypothesis:** See Rival hypothesis.

**Amendment:** A change to a human subjects research protocol approved by an institutional review board or the board's chair (if the change is minor).

**Analysis:** The breakdown of something that is complex into smaller parts in such a way that leads to a better understanding of the whole.

**Analysis of variance:** A statistical technique for determining the statistical significance of differences among means; used with two or more groups.

**Analytical memos:** Notes made by the researcher in reference to interpretive data that raise questions or make comments about meaning units and categories identified in a transcript.

**Analytic generalization:** The type of generalizability associated with case studies and used as working hypotheses to test practice principles. The research findings of case studies are not assumed to fit another case, no matter how apparently similar; rather, research findings are tested to see if they do in fact fit.

**Analytic induction:** Use of constant comparison specifically in developing hypotheses, which are then tested in further data collection and analysis.

**Analytic memos:** Notes made by the researcher in reference to interpretive data that raise questions or make comments about meaning units and categories identified in a transcript.

**Analytic strategies:** The choices in statistical procedures made by the investigators based on their values or what they consider important in a study.

**Analyzing:** Evaluating data to reach a conclusion about a research study.

**Anecdotal evidence:** What people say about something, which is not provable.

**Annotated bibliography:** A list of sources that gives the publication information and a short description—or annotation—for each source. Each annotation is generally three to seven sentences long. In some bibliographies, the annotation merely describes the content and scope of the source; in others, the annotation also evaluates the source's reliability, currency, and relevance to a researcher's purpose.

**Annual report:** A detailed account or statement describing a program's processes and results over a given year, usually produced at the end of a fiscal year.

**Anonymity:** Research studies that are designed so that no one, not even the person doing the study, knows which research participant gave what response (not be confused with confidentiality).

**ANOVA:** See analysis of variance.

**Antecedent variable:** A variable that precedes the introduction of one or more dependent variables.

**Antiquarianism:** An interest in past events without reference to their importance or significance for the present; the reverse of presentism.

**Applied research approach:** A search for practical and applied research results that can be used in actual social work practice situations; complementary to the pure research approach.

**Area probability sampling:** A form of cluster sampling that uses a three-stage process to provide the means to carry out a research study when no comprehensive list of the population can be compiled.

**Assent:** A subject's affirmative agreement to participate in a research study. Assent may take place when the subject does not have the capacity to provide informed consent (e.g., the subject is a child or mentally disabled) but has the capacity to meaningfully assent.

**Assessment:** A test or other way of measuring something, such as a person's mental health or goals or needs; often the first test in a series of tests, or a test given before treatment starts.

**Assessment rubric:** A rubric for assessment, usually in the form of a matrix or grid; a tool used to interpret and grade a piece of work against criteria and standards. Rubrics are sometimes called "criteria sheets," "grading schemes," or "scoring guides."

**Assessment-related case study:** A type of case study that generates knowledge about specific clients and their situations; focuses on the perspectives of the study's participants.

**Assimilation:** A process of consistent integration whereby members of an ethnocultural group, typically immigrants or other minority groups, are "absorbed" into an established larger community.

**Association (statistical):** A measure of whether and how closely certain values (numbers, amounts) in a study go up or down at the same time.

**Astrology:** The study of the movements and relative positions of celestial objects as a means of divining information about human affairs and terrestrial events.

**Attribute:** A specific value (or label) for a variable.

**Attrition:** The dropout rate among people who are being studied. People may quit because they want to, or they may not be able to stay in the study group (because of illness, lack of time, moving to another city, etc.), or they may not fit into the study anymore (if they get a job or marry, for example, in a study about single people who are not working).

**Audit:** A formal review of research records, policies, activities, personnel, or facilities to ensure compliance with ethical or legal standards or institutional policies. Audits may be conducted regularly, at random, or for-cause (i.e., in response to a problem).

**Audit trail:** The documentation of critical steps in an interpretive research study that allows for an independent reviewer to examine and verify the steps in the research process and the conclusions of the research study.

**Author:** A person who makes a significant contribution to a creative work. Many journal guidelines define an author as someone who makes a significant contribution to (1) research conception and design, (2) data acquisition, or (3) data analysis or interpretation, and who drafts or critically reads the paper and approves the final manuscript.

**Authority:** The reliance on authority figures to tell us what is true; one of the five ways of knowing.

**Authorship, ghost:** Failing to list someone as an author on a work even though they have made a significant contribution to it.

**Authorship, honorary:** Receiving authorship credit when one has not made a significant contribution to the work.

**Autonomy:** The capacity for self-governance—the ability to make reasonable decisions; a moral principle barring interference with autonomous decision-making. See decision-making capacity.

**Availability sampling:** See convenience sampling.

**Axes:** Straight horizontal and vertical lines in a graph upon which values of a measurement or the corresponding frequencies are plotted.

**B phase:** In case-level evaluation designs, the intervention phase, which may or may not include simultaneous measurements.

**Back-translation:** The process of translating an original document into a second language, then having an independent translator conduct a subsequent translation of the first translation back into the language of origin; the second translation is then compared with the original document for equivalency.

**Bad apples theory:** The idea that most research misconduct is committed by individuals who are morally corrupt or psychologically ill. This idea can be contrasted with the view that social, financial, institutional, and cultural factors play a major role in causing research misconduct.

**Bar graph:** A drawing that uses bars for various groupings. The height of the bar shows how many things or people are in that grouping.

**Baseline:** A period of time, usually three or four data collection periods, in which the level of the client's target problem is measured while no intervention is carried out; designated as the A phase in single-system designs (case-level designs).

**Baseline analysis:** An analysis of data collected before a treatment or intervention is applied.

**Belief system:** A way in which a culture collectively constructs a model or framework for how it thinks about something. A religion is a particular kind of belief system.

**Beliefs and intuition:** Two highly related ways of obtaining knowledge; together they form one of the five ways of knowing.

**Bell curve:** See normal frequency distribution curve.

**Belmont Report:** A report issued by the U.S. National Commission for the Protection of Human Subjects in Biomedical and Behavioral Research in 1979 that has had a significant influence over human subjects research ethics, regulation, and policy. The report provided a conceptual foundation for the Common Rule and articulated three principles of ethics: respect for persons, beneficence, and justice.

**Benchmark:** A standard, test, or point of reference (often a number).

**Beneficence:** Refraining from maltreatment and maximizing potential benefits to research participants while minimizing potential harm; the ethical obligation to do good and avoid causing harm; the ethical obligation to do good and avoid causing harm. See also Belmont Report.

**Benefit:** A desirable outcome or state of affairs, such as medical treatment, clinically useful information, or self-esteem. In the oversight of human subjects research, money is usually not treated as a benefit.

**Between research methods approach:** Triangulation by using different research methods available in both the interpretive and the positivist research approaches in a single research study.

**Bias:** Something that may lead a researcher to wrong conclusions, such as mistakes or problems in how the study is planned or how the information is gathered or looked at. If two different interviewers had different styles that caused people with the same thoughts to give different answers but the answers were all put together in one pool, there would be a bias. It is impossible to conduct completely bias-free research.

**Biased sample:** A sample unintentionally selected in such a way that some members of the population are more likely than others to be picked for sample membership.

**Biculturalism:** The simultaneous identification with two cultures when an individual feels equally at home in both cultures and feels emotional attachment with both cultures.

**Bimodal distribution:** A range of scores that has two most frequent scores instead of one.

**Binomial effect size display (BESD):** A technique for interpreting the r value in a meta-analysis by converting it into a 2 × 2 table displaying magnitude of effect.

**Bioethics:** The study of ethical, social, or legal issues arising in biomedicine and biomedical research.

**Biography:** Tells the story of one individual's life, often suggesting what the person's influence was on social, political, or intellectual developments of the times.

**Bivariate analysis:** The study of how two variables are related.

**Boundedness:** A term used in a case study to refer to the parameters of a case. These could include the individual or entity, such as a school, under investigation and the setting in which social action takes place.

**Case:** The basic unit of social work practice, whether it be an individual, a couple, a family, an agency, a community, a county, a state, or a country.

**Case study:** An in-depth study of a case or cases (a "case" can be a program, an event, an activity, an individual), studied over time, using multiple sources of information (e.g., observations, documents, archival data, interviews). Can be exploratory, explanatory, or descriptive, or a combination of these.

**Case-level evaluation designs:** Designs in which data are collected about a single-client system—an individual, group, or community—in order to evaluate the outcome of an intervention for the client system; a form of appraisal that monitors change for individual clients; also called single-system research designs.

**Caste system:** Hereditary system of stratification. Hierarchical social status is ascribed at birth and often dictated by religion or other social norms.

**Categorical variable:** A piece of information that can be put in a single category instead of being given a number: for example, the information about whether a person owns a car or about whether the person belongs to a certain race can be put in the category of "yes" or the category of "no."

**Categories:** Groupings of related meaning units that are given one name; used to organize, summarize, and interpret qualitative data. Categories in an interpretive study can change throughout the data-analysis process, and the number of categories in a given study depends upon the breadth and depth the researcher aims for in the analysis.

**Category:** In an interpretive data analysis, an aggregate of meaning units that share a common feature.

**Category saturation:** The point in a qualitative data analysis when all identified meaning units fit easily into the existing categorization scheme and no new categories emerge; the point at which first-level coding ends.

**CATI:** See computer-assisted telephone interviewing.

**Causality:** A relationship of cause and effect; the effect will invariably occur when the cause is present.

**Causal relationship:** A relationship between two variables for which we can state that the presence or absence of one variable determines the presence or absence of the other variable; a relationship of cause and effect; the effect will invariably occur when the cause is present.

**CD-ROM sources:** Computerized retrieval systems that allow searching for indexes and abstracts stored on compact computer discs (CDs).

**Ceiling effects:** A term used to describe what happens when a group of subjects in a study have scores that are close to or at the upper limit (ceiling) of a variable. For example, the majority of subjects score 100% correct because the task is too easy.

**Censorship:** Taking steps to prevent or deter the public communication of information or ideas. In science, censorship may involve prohibiting the publication of research or allowing publication only in redacted form (with some information removed).

**Census data:** Data from the survey of an entire population, in contrast to a survey of a sample.

**Chi-square:** A statistical significance test that is appropriate when the data are in the form of frequency counts.

**Citation:** A brief identification of a reference that includes name of author(s), title, source, page numbers, and year of publication.

**Citation amnesia:** Failing to cite important work in the field in a paper, book, or presentation.

**Classic experimental design:** An explanatory research design with randomly assigned experimental and control groups in which the dependent variable is measured before and after the treatment (the independent variable) for both groups, but only the experimental group receives the treatment (the dependent variable).

**Classification:** A way of putting facts, things, people, and so on into groups based on something they have in common.

**Classifications of research questions:** Questions that can be classified into seven categories: existence, composition, relationship, descriptive-comparative, causality, causality-comparative, and causality-comparative interaction.

**Classified research:** Research that the government keeps secret to protect national security. Access to classified research is granted to individuals with the appropriate security clearance on a need-to-know basis.

**Client system:** An individual client, a couple, a family, a group, an organization, or a community that can be studied with case- and program-level evaluation designs and with positivist and interpretive research approaches.

**Clinical investigator:** A researcher involved in conducting a clinical trial.

**Clinical trial:** An experiment designed to test the safety or efficacy of a type of therapy (such as a drug).

**Clinical trial, active controlled:** A clinical trial in which the control group receives a treatment known to be effective. The goal of the trial is to compare different treatments.

**Clinical trial, placebo controlled:** A clinical trial in which the control group receives a placebo. The goal of the trial is to compare a treatment to a placebo.

**Clinical trial, registration:** Providing information about a clinical trial in a public registry. Most journals and funding agencies require that clinical trials be registered. Registration information includes the name of the trial, the sponsor, study design and methods, population, inclusion/exclusion criteria, and outcome measures.

**Clinical utility:** The clinical usefulness of information, for example, for making decisions concerning diagnosis, prevention, or treatment.

**Closed-ended questions:** Items in a measuring instrument that require respondents to select one of several response categories provided; also known as fixed-alternative questions.

**Cluster analysis:** A study that puts people or things into a small number of separate groups, so that there will be as much likeness within each group and as much difference among the groups as possible.

**Cluster diagram:** An illustration of a conceptual classification scheme in which the researcher draws and labels circles for each theme that emerges from the data; the circles are organized in a way to depict the relationships between themes.

**Cluster sampling:** A multistage probability sampling procedure in which the population is divided into groups (or clusters); the groups, rather than the individuals, are selected for inclusion in the sample.

**Code:** The label assigned to a category or theme in a qualitative data analysis; shortened versions of the actual category or theme label; used as markers in a qualitative data analysis; usually no longer than eight characters in length and can use a combination of letters, symbols, and numbers.

**Codebook:** A device used to organize qualitative data by applying labels and descriptions that draw distinctions between different parts of the data that have been collected.

**Coding:** Coding is one aspect of data analysis. When researchers code, they are trying to make sense of the data by systematically looking through it, clustering or grouping together similar ideas, phenomena, people, or events, and labeling them. Coding helps researchers find similar patterns and connections across the data. It helps researchers get to know the data better and to organize their thinking, and it also makes storage and retrieval of data easier.

**Coding frame:** A specific framework that delineates what data are to be coded and how they are to be coded in order to prepare them for analyses.

**Coding sheets:** In a literature review, a sheet used to record for each research study the complete reference, research design, measuring instrument(s), population and sample, outcomes, and other significant features of the study.

**Coercion:** Using force, threats, or intimidation to make a person comply with a demand.

**Cohort study:** A longitudinal survey design that uses successive random samples to monitor how the characteristics of a specific group of people, who share certain characteristics or experiences (cohorts), change over time.

**Collaboration agreement:** An agreement between two or more collaborating research groups concerning the conduct of research. The agreement may address the roles and responsibilities of the scientists, access to data, authorship, and intellectual property.

**Collaterals:** Professionals or staff members who serve as indigenous observers in the data collection process.

**Collective biographies:** Studies of the characteristics of groups of people who lived during a past period and had some major factor in common.

**Collectivist culture:** Societies that stress interdependence and seek the welfare and survival of the group above that of the individual; collectivist cultures are characterized by a readiness to be influenced by others, preference for conformity, and cooperation in relationships.

**Commercialization:** The process of developing and marketing commercial products (e.g., drugs, medical devices, or other technologies) from research. See also copyright, intellectual property.

**Common law:** A body of law based on judicial decisions and rulings.

**Common Rule:** The U.S. Department of Health and Human Services regulations (45 CFR 46) for protecting human subjects, which has been adopted by 17 federal agencies. The Common Rule includes subparts with additional protections for children, neonates, pregnant women and fetuses, and prisoners.

**Community review:** A process for involving a community in the review of research conducted on members of the community. Some research studies include community advisory boards as a way of involving the community.

**Comparability:** A measure of whether things can really be compared in a way that is fair and helpful. For example, oranges and grapefruits, because they are both citrus fruits, would have comparability in a study of vitamin C content, but oranges and sausages would not.

**Comparative rating scale:** A rating scale in which respondents are asked to compare an individual person, concept, or situation with others.

**Comparative research design:** The study of more than one event, group, or society to isolate explanatory factors. There are two basic strategies in comparative research: (1) the study of elements that differ in many ways but that have some major factor in common, and (2) the study of elements that are highly similar but different in some important aspect, such as modern industrialized nations that have different health insurance systems.

**Comparison group:** A nonexperimental group to which research participants have not been randomly assigned for purposes of comparison with the experimental group. Not to be confused with control group.

**Comparison group posttest-only design:** A descriptive research design with two groups, experimental and comparison, in which the dependent variable is measured once for both groups, and only the experimental group receives the treatment (the independent variable).

**Comparison group pretest-posttest design:** A descriptive research design with two groups, experimental and comparison, in which the dependent variable is measured before and after the treatment for both groups, but only the experimental group receives the treatment.

**Compensation:** Attempts by researchers to compensate for the lack of treatment for control group members by administering it to them; a threat to internal validity.

**Compensatory rivalry:** Motivation of control group members to compete with experimental group members; a threat to internal validity.

**Competence:** The legal right to make decisions for one's self. Adults are considered to be legally competent until they are adjudicated incompetent by a court.

**Completeness:** One of the four criteria for evaluating research hypotheses.

**Complete observer:** A term describing one of four possible research roles on a continuum of participant observation research; the complete observer acts simply as an observer and does not participate in the events at hand.

**Complete participant:** The complete participant's research role, at the far end of the continuum from the complete observer in participant observation research, is characterized by total involvement.

**Compliance:** In research, complying with laws, institutional policies and ethical guidelines related to research.

**Composite index:** A combination of scores made of distinct factors or fundamental dimensions.

**Comprehensive qualitative review:** A nonstatistical synthesis of representative research studies relevant to a research problem, question, or hypothesis.

**Computational formulas:** A mathematical equation, of a fact or other logical relation, that helps to convey the conceptual basis of statistical tests.

**Computer-assisted telephone interviewing (CATI):** A method of interviewing people over the phone; CATI uses a computer to choose the interviewees and to ask questions and record answers as well as to keep track of information.

**Computerized retrieval systems:** Systems in which abstracts, indexes, and subject bibliographies are incorporated in computerized databases to facilitate information retrieval.

**Concept mapping:** Grouping ideas or results based on how alike they are and showing the groups in picture form.

**Concept:** An understanding, an idea, or a mental image; a way of viewing and categorizing objects, processes, relations, and events.

**Conceptual classification system:** The strategy for conceiving how units of qualitative data relate to each other; the method used to depict patterns that emerge from the various coding levels in qualitative data.

**Conceptual framework:** A frame of reference that serves to guide a research study and is developed from theories, findings from a variety of other research studies, and the author's personal experiences and values.

**Conceptual validity:** See construct validity.

**Conceptualization:** The process of selecting the specific concepts to include in positivist and interpretive research studies.

**Conclusion:** A summary of the key points and a statement of opinion or decisions reached about the research study.

**Concurrent validity:** A form of criterion validity that is concerned with the ability of a measuring instrument to predict accurately an individual's status by comparing concurrent ratings (or scores) on one or more measuring instruments.

**Conduct:** Action or behavior. For example, conducting research involves performing actions related to research, such as designing experiments, collecting data, analyzing data, and so on.

**Confidence interval:** Quantifies the uncertainty in measurement. It is usually reported as a 95% CI, which is the range of values within which it can be 95% certain that the true value for the whole population lies.

**Confidentiality:** The obligation to keep some types of information confidential or secret; the researcher knows how a particular participant responded and has agreed not to divulge the information to anyone else; not to be confused with anonymity.

**Confirmability:** A concept that researchers should fully explain or disclose the data that they are basing their interpretations on, or at least make those data available. Confirmability can be improved by maintaining precise data records and keeping all data for additional scrutiny.

**Conflict of interest (COI):** A situation in which a person has a financial, personal, political, or other interest that is likely to bias his or her judgment or decision making concerning the performance of his or her ethical or legal obligations or duties.

**Conflict of interest, apparent or perceived:** A situation in which a person has a financial, personal, political, or other interest that is not likely to bias his or her judgment or decision-making concerning the performance of his or her ethical or legal obligation or duties but which may appear to an outside observer to bias his or her judgement or decision-making.

**Conflict of interest, institutional:** A situation in which an institution (such as a university) has financial, political, or other interests that are likely to bias institutional decision-making concerning the performance of institutional ethical or legal duties.

**Conflict of interest, management:** Strategies for minimizing the adverse impacts of a conflict of interest, such as disclosure, oversight, or recusal/prohibition.

**Confounding factors:** The inability to tell between the separate impacts of two or more factors on a single outcome. For example, one may find it difficult to tell between the separate impacts of genetics and environmental factors on depression.

**Confounding variable:** A variable operating in a specific situation in such a way that its effects cannot be separated; the

effects of an extraneous variable thus confound the interpretation of a research study's findings.

**Consent:** See informed consent.

**Consequentialism:** An approach to ethics, such as utilitarianism, that emphasizes maximizing good over bad consequences resulting from actions or policies.

**Consistency:** Holding steadfast to the same principles and procedures in the qualitative data-analysis process.

**Constant:** A concept that does not vary and does not change; a characteristic that has the same value for all research participants or events in a research study.

**Constant comparative method:** A method of data analysis from grounded theory in which the researcher constantly compares new data to data already placed in existing categories, to help develop and define that category and decide if a new category should be created.

**Constant error:** Systematic error in measurement; error due to factors that consistently or systematically affect the variable being measured and that are concerned with the relatively stable qualities of respondents to a measuring instrument.

**Constant variable:** A variable that is not changed during the research study.

**Construct:** A general idea that tries to explain something; for example, social status is a construct.

**Constructivism:** A belief that that there is no universally agreed upon reality or universal "truth." Rather, meaning is socially constructed by individuals interacting with their world. Through that interaction, each individual creates his or her own unique understandings of the world. As a result, there are multiple constructions and interpretations of reality, so multiple 'truths' exist. These interpretations change, depending upon time and circumstances, so reality is not universal but person, context, and time bound.

**Construct validity:** The degree to which a measuring instrument successfully measures a theoretical construct; the degree to which explanatory concepts account for variance in the scores of an instrument; also referred to as conceptual validity in meta-analyses.

**Content analysis:** A form of analysis that usually counts and reports the frequency of concepts/words/ behaviors held within the data. The researcher develops brief descriptions of the themes or meanings, called codes. Similar codes may at a later stage in the analysis be grouped together to form categories.

**Content validity:** The extent to which the content of a measuring instrument reflects the concept that is being measured and in fact measures that concept and not another.

**Contextual detail:** The particulars of the environment in which the case (or unit of analysis) is embedded; provides a basis for understanding and interpreting case study data and results.

**Continuing review:** In human subjects research, subsequent review of a study after it has been approved by an institutional review board. Continuing review usually happens on an annual basis.

**Continuous variable:** Something that has an unlimited number of possible values; for example, height, weight, and age are all continuous because a person's height, weight, or age could be measured in smaller and smaller fractions between the numbers of the whole inches, pounds, or years.

**Contradictory evidence:** Identifying themes and categories that raise questions about the conclusions reached at the end of qualitative data analysis; outliers or extreme cases that are inconsistent or contradict the conclusions drawn from qualitative data; also called negative evidence.

**Contributing partner:** A social work role in which the social worker joins forces with others who perform various roles in positivist and interpretive research studies.

**Control group:** A group of randomly assigned research participants in a research study who do not receive the experimental treatment and are used for comparison purposes; not to be confused with comparison group.

**Control variable:** A variable, other than the independent variable(s) of primary interest, whose effects we can determine; an intervening variable that has been controlled for in the study's research design.

**Convenience sampling:** A nonprobability sampling procedure that relies on the closest and most available research participants to constitute a sample.

**Convergent validity:** The degree to which different measures of a construct yield similar results, or converge.

**Copyright:** A right, granted by a government, that prohibits unauthorized copying, performance, or alteration of creative works. Copyright laws include a fair use exemption that allows limited, unauthorized uses for noncommercial purposes.

**Correction (or errata):** Fixing a minor problem with a published paper. A minor problem is one that does not impact the reliability or integrity of the data or results. Journals publish correction notices and identify corrected papers in electronic databases to alert the scientific community to problems with the paper. See also retraction.

**Correlated variables:** Variables whose values are associated; values of one variable tend to be associated in a systematic way with values in the others.

**Correlation:** A measure of how well two or more variables change together.

**Correlation coefficient:** A decimal number between 0.00 and ±1.00 that indicates the degree to which two variables are related.

**Cost-benefit analysis:** An analytical procedure that not only determines the costs of the program itself but also considers the monetary benefits of the program's effects.

**Cost-effectiveness analysis:** An analytical procedure that assesses the costs of the program itself; the monetary benefits of the program's effects are not assessed.

**Council on Social Work Education (CSWE):** The official educational organization that sets minimum curriculum standards for bachelor of social work (BSW) and master of social work (MSW) programs throughout the United States.

**Covariance:** When changes in one variable are accompanied by changes in another variable. For example, if a person takes a vocabulary test and a reading comprehension test, changes in scores on one test might be accompanied with changes in scores on the other test.

**Covariate:** A variable that may affect the relationship between two variables of interest, but is not of intrinsic interest itself. The researcher may choose to control for or statistically reduce the effect of a covariate.

**Cover letter:** A letter to respondents or research participants that is written under the official letterhead of the sponsoring organization and describes the research study and its purpose.

**Credibility:** A concept that researchers should maximize the accuracy of how they define concepts and how they characterize the people they are investigating—with a particular focus on how the various participants feel about the interpretations the researcher makes. Credibility can be enhanced by using prolonged engagement, careful observation, triangulation, peer debriefing, negative case analysis, and member checks.

**Criterion validity:** The degree to which the scores obtained on a measuring instrument are comparable with scores from an external criterion believed to measure the same concept.

**Criterion variable:** The variable whose values are predicted from measurements of the predictor variable.

**Critical ethnography:** A type of ethnography that examines cultural systems of power, prestige, privilege, and authority in society. Critical ethnographers study marginalized groups from different classes, races, and genders to advocate the needs of these participants.

**Critical thinking:** Understanding the meaning of a statement, judging ambiguity, judging whether an inductive conclusion is warranted, and judging whether statements made by authorities are acceptable; sometimes called directional thinking.

**Cronbach's alpha:** A number showing whether all the items on a scale or test are related and pulling in the same direction.

**Cross-comparability:** The degree in which similarities and differences in the characteristics of research participants from different groups can be assessed.

**Cross-cultural:** An interaction between individuals from different cultures. The term cross-cultural is generally used to describe comparative studies of cultures. Intercultural is also used for the same meaning.

**Cross-cultural awareness:** Develops from cross-cultural knowledge as the learner understands and appreciates the deeper functioning of a culture.

**Cross-cultural communication:** A field of study that looks at how people from differing cultural backgrounds try to communicate; also referred to as intercultural communication.

**Cross-cultural communication skills:** Refers to the ability to recognize cultural differences and similarities when dealing with someone from another culture and also the ability to recognize features of one's own behavior that are affected by culture.

**Cross-cultural comparisons:** Research studies that include culture as a major variable; studies that compare two or more diverse cultural groups.

**Cross-cultural competence:** The final stage of cross-cultural learning that signals the individual's ability to work effectively across cultures.

**Cross-cultural knowledge:** Refers to a surface level familiarization with cultural characteristics, values, beliefs and behaviors. It is vital to basic cross-cultural understanding and without it cross-cultural competence cannot develop.

**Cross-cultural method (comparative method):** A way of studying different cultural groups to see how they are the same and how they are different.

**Cross-cultural sensitivity:** Refers to an individual's ability to read into situations, contexts, and behaviors that are culturally rooted; consequently the individual is able to react to them suitably.

**Crossover participants:** A type of intervention assignment in which participants may receive different interventions during the life of the study.

**Crossover study design:** The administration of two or more experimental therapies, one after the other, in a specified or random order to the same group of people.

**Cross-sectional research design:** A survey research design in which data are collected to indicate characteristics of a sample or population at a particular moment in time.

**Cross-sectional study:** Research studies that compare people at one time only. Cause and effect cannot be determined in this type of study.

**Cross-tabulation table:** A simple table showing the joint frequency distribution of two or more nominal-level variables.

**Cross-validation:** A method used to prove the validity of a test by administering it a second time on a new selected group from the same population.

**Cultural alienation:** The process of devaluing or abandoning one's own culture or cultural background in favor of another.

**Cultural boundaries:** Those invisible lines that divide territories, cultures, traditions, practices, and worldviews.

**Cultural competency:** The ability to respond respectfully and effectively to people of all cultures, classes, ethnic backgrounds, and religions in a manner that recognizes and values cultural differences and similarities.

**Cultural components:** Attributes that vary from culture to culture, including religion, language, architecture, cuisine, technology, music, dance, sports, medicine, dress, gender roles, laws, education, government, agriculture, economy, grooming, values, work ethic, etiquette, courtship, recreation, and gestures.

**Cultural construct:** The idea that the characteristics people attribute to social categories such as gender, illness, death, status of women, and status of men are culturally defined.

**Cultural convergence:** An idea that increased communication among the peoples of the world via the Internet will lead to the differences among national cultures becoming smaller over time, eventually resulting in the formation of a single global culture.

**Cultural diversity:** Differences (e.g., in race, language, or religion) in one community, organization, or nation.

**Cultural encapsulation:** The assumption that differences between groups represent some deficit or pathology.

**Cultural identity:** The identity of a group or culture, or of individuals as belonging to a group or culture that affects their view of themselves. People who feel they belong to the same culture share a common set of norms.

**Culturally equivalent:** Similarity in the meaning of a construct between two cultures.

**Cultural relativity:** The belief that human thought and action can be judged only from the perspective of the culture out of which they have grown.

**Cultural sensitivity:** A necessary component of cultural competence, meaning that we make an effort to be aware of the potential and actual cultural factors that affect our interactions with others.

**Cultural traits:** Distinguishing features of a culture such as language, dress, religion, values, and an emphasis on family; these traits are shared throughout that culture.

**Cultural values:** The individual's desirable or preferred way of acting or knowing.

**Culture:** The shared values, norms, traditions, customs, arts, history, folklore, and institutions of a group of people.

**Culture of integrity:** The idea that the institutional culture plays a key role in preventing research misconduct and promoting research integrity. Strategies to promote a culture of integrity include education and mentoring in the responsible conduct of research; research policy development; institutional support for research ethics oversight, consultation, and curriculum development; and ethical leadership.

**Cumulative frequency distribution:** A graphic depiction of how many times groups of scores appear in a sample.

**Cut-and-paste method:** A method of analyzing qualitative data whereby the researcher cuts segments of the transcript and sorts these cuttings into relevant groupings; it can be done manually or with computer assistance.

**Data:** Numbers, words, or scores, or other information generated by positivist and interpretive research studies. The word data is plural.

**Data analysis:** A systematic process of working with the data to provide an understanding of the research participant's experiences. While there are several methods of qualitative analysis that can be used, the aim is always to provide an understanding through the researcher's interpretation of the data.

**Data and safety monitoring board (DSMB):** A committee that monitors data from human subjects research to protect participants from harm and promote their welfare. DSMBs may recommend to an institutional review board that a study be stopped or altered.

**Data archive:** A place where many data sets are stored and from which data can be accessed.

**Data auditing:** See audit.

**Database:** A collection of information organized for retrieval. In libraries, databases usually contain references to sources retrievable by a variety of means. Databases may contain bibliographic citations, descriptive abstracts, full-text documents, or a combination.

**Data coding:** Translating data from one language or format into another, usually to make it readable for a computer.

**Data collection:** The gathering of information through surveys, tests, interviews, experiments, library records, and so on.

**Data-collection method:** Procedures specifying techniques to be employed, measuring instruments to be used, and activities to be conducted in implementing a positivist or interpretive research study.

**Data imputation:** The use of statistical methods to fill in or replace missing or lost data. Imputation is not considered to be fabrication if it is done honestly and appropriately.

**Data management:** Practices and policies related to recording, storing, auditing, archiving, analyzing, interpreting, sharing, and publishing data.

**Data matrix:** A table where the variable name is entered at the tops of the columns that will contain the data for that variable, and the case records are entered across the rows.

**Data outlier:** A data point that is more than two standards deviations from the mean. Removal of outliers without articulating a legitimate reason may constitute data, falsification.

**Data processing:** Recording, storing, calling up, and analyzing information with a computer program.

**Data repository:** A centralized data storage system containing the data collected from different research sites.

**Data saturation:** As researchers collect data and simultaneously create categories through data analysis, they will get to a point at which these categories are "saturated"—no new information adds to their understanding of the category.

**Data set:** A collection of related data items, such as the answers given by respondents to all the questions in a survey.

**Data source:** The provider of the data, whether it be primary (the original source) or secondary (an intermediary between the research participant and the researcher analyzing the data).

**Data use agreement (DUA):** An agreement between institutions for the sharing and use of research data.

**Datum:** Singular of data.

**Debriefing:** Involves explaining the true purpose of the research study to the participants after the study is completed, along with why the deception was necessary in the first place.

**Deception:** In human subjects research, using methods to deceive the participants about the goals and nature of a study or the methods, tests, interventions, or procedures used in the study; occurs as the result of researchers providing false or incomplete information to research participants for the purpose of misleading them. Should be used with extreme caution.

**Deception and consent:** Universal ethical concerns about the rights of participants to be informed honestly and openly, and not to be coerced into participating in a study.

**Decision-making capacity (DMC):** The ability to make sound decisions. DMC is often situational and comes in degrees; for example, a person may be able to order food from a menu but not be able to make a decision concerning complex medical treatment. Factors that can compromise DMC include mental illness or disability, extreme emotional stress, drugs, age, or serious physical illness. DMC is not the same as legal competence: a demented adult may be legally competent but lack DMC.

**Deduction:** A conclusion about a specific case(s) based on the assumption that it shares a characteristic with an entire class of similar cases.

**Deductive thinking:** A way of reasoning that works from the more general to the more specific. It begins with a general theory, which generates predictions about specific phenomena. These theories can be tested empirically by seeing if the predictions are true. The opposite is inductive thinking.

**Degrees of freedom (df):** The number of values/amounts that are free to vary in one calculation. Degrees of freedom are used in the formulas that test hypotheses statistically.

**De-identified data or samples:** Data or biological samples that have been stripped of information, such as name or medical record number, that personally identifies individuals.

**Demand needs:** When needs are defined by only those individuals who indicate that they feel or perceive the need themselves.

**Demographic data:** Vital and social facts that describe a sample or a population.

**Demography:** The study of a group of people, including its size, how old different members are, what sex and race different members belong to, how many people are married, how many years they went to school, and so on.

**Demoralization:** Feelings of deprivation among control group members that may cause them to drop out of a research study; a threat to internal validity.

**Deontology:** An approach to ethics, such as Kantianism, that emphasizes adherence to rules or principles of conduct.

**Dependability:** An emphasis on the need for researchers to account for the ever-changing context and shifting conditions within which research occurs; the soundness of both the steps taken in a qualitative data analysis and the conclusions reached. In their published accounts, the researcher should describe the changes that occur in the setting and how these changes affected the way the researcher approached the study.

**Dependent events:** Events that influence the probability of each other occurring.

**Dependent t-test:** A statistical test that assesses whether the means of two related groups are statistically different from each other.

**Dependent variable:** A variable dependent on, or caused by, another variable; an outcome variable that is not manipulated directly but is measured to determine whether the independent variable has had an effect.

**Derived scores:** Raw scores of research participants or groups converted in such a way that meaningful comparisons with other individuals or groups are possible.

**Descriptive research:** Research studies undertaken to increase precision in the definition of knowledge in a problem area where less is known than at the explanatory level; situated in the middle of the knowledge continuum.

**Descriptive statistics:** Methods used for summarizing and describing data in a clear and precise manner.

**Design bias:** Any effect that systematically distorts the outcome of a research study so that the study's results are not representative of the phenomenon under investigation.

**Determinism:** A contention in positivist research studies that only an event that is true over time and place and that will occur independent of beliefs about it (a predetermined event) permits the generalization of a study's findings; one of the four main limitations of the positivist research approach.

**Deterministic causation:** When a particular effect appears, the associated cause is always present; no other variables influence the relationship between cause and effect; the link between an independent variable that brings about the occurrence of the dependent variable every time.

**Diary studies:** First-person or third-person case studies in which individuals keep a reflective journal using introspection and/or retrospection.

**Dichotomous variable:** A variable that can take on only one of two values.

**Differential scale:** A questionnaire-type scale in which respondents are asked to consider questions representing different positions along a continuum and to select those with which they agree.

**Differential selection:** A potential lack of equivalency among preformed groups of research participants; a threat to internal validity.

**Diffusion of treatments:** Problems that may occur when experimental and control group members talk to each other about a research study; a threat to internal validity.

***d* index:** A measure of effect size in a meta-analysis.

**Direct observation:** An obtrusive data-collection method in which the focus is entirely on the behaviors of a group, or persons, being observed.

**Direct observation notes:** The first level of field notes, usually chronologically organized, containing a detailed description of what was seen and heard and potentially also including summary notes made after an interview.

**Directional hypothesis:** See one-tailed hypotheses.

**Directional test:** See one-tailed hypotheses.

**Direct relationship:** A relationship between two variables such that high values of one variable are found with high values of the second variable.

**Discourse analysis:** The linguistic analysis of naturally occurring connected speech or written discourse. It is also concerned with language use in social contexts, and in particular with interaction or dialogue between speakers.

**Discrete variables:** Separate values or groupings, with no possible values (numbers, measurements) between them. The only choices are separate categories; for example, "male" and "female" are discrete variables.

**Discriminant validity:** The degree to which a construct can be empirically differentiated or discriminated from other constructs.

**Discrimination:** Treating people differently based on irrelevant characteristics, such as skin color, ethnicity, or gender.

**Disinformation:** False information that is intended to mislead, especially propaganda issued by a government organization to a rival power or the media.

**Distractors:** Any questions or events that divert attention from what is being tested. Usually, items in a questionnaire to keep subjects from understanding what's being tested.

**Distribution:** The measure of how often something is found in the group being studied; also the range of those measures.

**Divergent validity:** The extent to which a measuring instrument differs from other instruments that measure unrelated constructs.

**Diversity:** The understanding that each individual is unique, and the recognition of individual differences along the dimensions of race, ethnicity, gender, sexual orientation, socioeconomic status, age, physical abilities, religious beliefs, political beliefs, or other ideologies.

**Domain:** An area or topic or focus of a research study.

**Dominant culture:** Usually the one "dominant" culture in each area that forms the basis for defining that culture.

This is determined by power and control in cultural institutions (church, government, education, mass media, and monetary systems.

**Double-barreled question:** A question in a measuring instrument that contains two questions in one, usually joined by an and or an or.

**Double-blinding:** Processes used to prevent human research subjects and researchers from discovering who is receiving an experimental treatment vs. a placebo. Double-blinding is used to control for the placebo effect.

**Dropout:** A person who was being studied but couldn't keep on with the study or didn't want to continue.

**Dual use research:** Research that can be readily used for beneficial or harmful purposes.

**Dummy variable:** A piece of information that has only one of only two possible values.

**Duplicate publication:** Republishing the same paper or data without proper acknowledgment.

**Duration recording:** A method of data collection that includes direct observation of the target problem and recording of the length of time each occurrence lasts within a specified observation period.

**Ecological fallacy:** A mistake based on believing that what is true for a group must also be true for each individual in the group.

**Edge coding:** Adding a series of blank lines on the right side of the response category in a measuring instrument to aid in processing the data.

**Effectiveness:** The measure of how well something does what it is supposed to do for a certain group of people under normal conditions.

**Effect size:** A measurement of the strength of a relationship between two variables. In meta-analysis, the most widely used measure of the dependent variable—the effect size statistic provides a measure of the magnitude of the relationship found between the variables of interest and allows for the computation of summary statistics that apply to the analysis of all the studies considered as a whole.

**Efficacy study:** A study comparing an experimental group (who receive the treatment) to a control group (who do not receive the treatment).

**Egocentric thinking:** Results from the unfortunate fact that humans do not naturally consider the rights and needs of others.

**Elaboration:** A way of studying or thinking about other causes that may also change an effect, instead of looking at only one cause.

**Eligibility criteria:** The detailed rules for what kind of people a researcher will let into a certain study. For example, being over age 60 and having a diagnosis of anxiety disorder could be the eligibility criteria for a study about how a new medication works for elderly, anxious people.

**Embedded design:** A mixed-methods design in which the researcher collects and analyzes quantitative and qualitative data within a traditional quantitative or qualitative design to enhance the overall design in some way.

**Emergency research:** In human subjects research, research that is conducted when a subject who cannot provide informed consent faces a life-threatening illness that requires immediate treatment and has no available legally authorized representative to provide consent. The Food and Drug Administration has developed special rules for emergency research involving products that it regulates.

**Emergent mixed-methods designs:** Designs where the use of mixed methods arises due to issues that develop while conducting the research.

**Emerging themes:** Concepts (explanatory ideas) that are identified from the data in the first stages of analysis and given a label or code that describes them. Concepts that are closely linked in meaning can be formed into categories, and categories that have similar meanings can be brought together into a theme. The term emerging themes refers to the development or "emergence" of themes from the data, and this overall method of analysis is referred to as thematic analysis.

**Empirical:** Knowledge derived from the five ways of knowing.

**Empirical method:** A kind of research that is based on believing that all real facts must come through the senses or a practical experiment, not just through reasoning. A conclusion must be proven by facts (results that can be measured, like blood pressure or body weight) rather than just "following" or "making sense."

**Enculturation:** A process whereby an established culture teaches an individual its accepted norms and values by establishing a context of boundaries and correctness that dictates what is and is not permissible within that society's framework.

**Equipoise:** Research studies that randomize their research participants to different treatment groups, which should be conducted only if there is a true uncertainty about which of the treatment alternatives is most likely to benefit them; also called the uncertainty principle.

**Equivalency data:** When there is more than one group (e.g., control and experimental) in a study, the researcher must ensure that both groups are equally represented by using equivalency data to avoid discrepancies (e.g., an equal number of females in both groups).

**Error:** An unintended adverse outcome; a mistake.

**Error of central tendency:** A measurement error due to the tendency of observers to rate respondents in the middle of a variable's value range, rather than consistently too high or too low.

**Error of measurement:** See measurement error.

**Ethical dilemma:** A situation in which two or more potential actions appear to be equally justifiable from an ethical point of view. That is, one must choose between the lesser of two evils or the greater of two goods.

**Ethical reasoning:** Making a decision in response to a moral dilemma based a careful and thorough assessment of the different options in light of the facts and circumstances and ethical considerations.

**Ethical relativism:** The view that ethical standards are relative to a particular culture, society, or historical period. (When in Rome, do as the Romans do.)

**Ethical theory:** A set of statements that attempts to unify, systematize, and explain our moral experience—our intuitions or judgments about right and wrong, good and bad, and so on.

**Ethical universalism:** The view that the same standards of ethics apply to all people at all times.

**Ethics, applied:** The study of ethics in specific situations, professions, or institutions; for example, medical ethics and research ethics.

**Ethics in research:** Positivist and interpretive data that are collected and analyzed with careful attention to their accuracy, fidelity to logic, and respect for the feelings and rights of the research participants; one of the four main criteria for evaluating research problem areas and formulating research questions out of the problem areas.

**Ethics, meta:** The study of the meaning, truth, and justification of ethical statements.

**Ethics, normative versus descriptive:** Normative ethics studies the standards of conduct and methods of reasoning that people ought to follow. Descriptive ethics studies the standards of conduct and reasoning processes that people in fact follow. Normative ethics seeks to prescribe and evaluate conduct, whereas descriptive ethics seeks to describe and explain conduct. Disciplines such as philosophy and religious studies take a normative approach to ethics, whereas sociology, anthropology, psychology, neuroscience, and evolutionary biology take a descriptive approach.

**Ethnic group:** A group characterized by cultural similarities (shared among members of that group) and differences (between that group and others).

**Ethnicity:** A term that implies a common ancestry and cultural heritage and encompasses customs, values, beliefs, and behaviors.

**Ethnocentricity:** Assumptions about normal behavior that are based on one's own cultural framework without taking cultural relativity into account; the failure to acknowledge alternative worldviews; a belief in the superiority of one's own ethnic group; seeing the world through the lenses of one's own people or culture so that one's own culture always looks best and becomes the pattern everyone else should fit into.

**Ethnograph:** A computer program designed for qualitative data analyses.

**Ethnographic:** A form of content analysis used to document and explain the communication of meaning as well as to verify theoretical relationships; any of several methods of describing social or cultural life based on direct, systematic observation, such as becoming a participant in a social system.

**Ethnography:** A qualitative research methodology that enables a detailed description and interpretation of a cultural or social group to be generated. Data collection is primarily through participant observation or through one-to-one interviews. The importance of gathering data on context is stressed, as only in this way can an understanding of social processes and the behavior that comes from them be developed.

**Ethnomethodology:** A research method that focuses on the commonsense understanding of social life held by ordinary people (the ethos), usually as discovered through participant observation. Often the observer's own methods of making sense of the situation become the object of investigation.

**Evaluation:** A form of appraisal using valid and reliable research methods. There are numerous types of evaluations geared to produce data that in turn produce information that helps in the decision-making process. Data from evaluations are used to develop quality programs and services.

**Evaluative research designs:** Case- and program-level research designs that apply various research designs and data-collection methods to find out whether an intervention (or treatment) worked at the case level and whether a social work program worked at the program level.

**Evidence-based guidelines:** Sometimes referred to as practice guidelines, systematically compiled and organized statements of empirically tested knowledge and procedures that help social workers select and implement interventions that are most effective and appropriate for attaining the desired outcomes.

**Evidence-based practice:** A process in which practitioners integrate information about client needs and values with knowledge of research findings on effective interventions.

**Evidence hierarchies:** Hierarchies that are commonly used for ranking interventions or evidence-based practices.

**Exclusion criteria:** The basis for excluding subjects from the sample who do not meet the basic parameters for participation within the study because they do not have a certain characteristic or trait.

**Exculpatory language:** Language in an informed consent form, contract, or other document intended to excuse a party from legal liability.

**Exempt research:** Human subjects research that is exempted from review by an institutional review board. Some types of exempt research include research on existing human samples or data in which the researcher cannot readily identify individuals and anonymous surveys of individuals.

**Existing documents:** Physical records left over from the past.

**Existing statistics:** Previously calculated numerical summaries of data that exist in the public domain.

**Expected outcome:** The effects and unique contributions attributed to an intervention or specific treatment that the investigator expects to find.

**Expedited review:** In human subjects research, review of a study by the chair of an institutional review board (or designee) instead of by the full board. Expedited review may be conducted on new studies that pose minimal risks to subjects, for continuing review in which a study is no longer recruiting subjects, or on amendments to approved studies that make only minor changes.

**Experience:** Learning what is true through personal past experiences; one of the five ways of knowing.

**Experiment:** A research study in which we have control over the levels of the independent variable and over the assignment of research participants, or objects, to different experimental conditions; an organized process used to test hypotheses.

**Experimental designs:** (1) Explanatory research designs or "ideal experiments." (2) Case-level research designs that examine the question, "Did the client system improve because of social work intervention?"

**Experimental group:** In an experimental research design, the group of research participants exposed to the manipulation of the independent variable; also referred to as a treatment group.

**Explanatory research:** "Ideal" research studies undertaken to infer cause-and-effect and directional relationships in areas where a number of substantial research findings are already in place; situated at the top end of the knowledge continuum.

**Explanatory research questions:** Questions formulated to infer cause-and-effect and directional relationships in areas where a number of substantial research findings are already in place; situated at the top end of the knowledge continuum.

**Exploitation:** Taking unfair advantage of someone else.

**Exploratory analysis:** A type of analysis that is used to understand an observable fact or event when there are no assumptions or expectations about the outcomes.

**Exploratory research:** Research studies undertaken to gather data in areas of inquiry where very little is already known; situated at the lowest end of the knowledge continuum. See nonexperimental design.

**Expression of concern:** In a scholarly journal, a published statement that a paper has come under suspicion for wrongdoing or is being investigated for possible research misconduct.

**External evaluation:** An evaluation that is conducted by someone who does not have any connection with the program; usually an evaluation that is requested by the agency's funding sources. This type of evaluation complements an in-house evaluation.

**External validity:** The extent to which the findings of a research study can be generalized outside the specific research situation.

**Extraneous data:** Data that are not relevant to the specific question or area being analyzed.

**Extraneous variables:** See rival hypothesis.

**Fabrication:** Making up data or results.

**Face-to-face interview:** A meeting to ask and answer questions in person, not over the phone or by mail or e-mail.

**Face validity:** The degree to which a measurement has self-evident meaning and measures what it appears to measure.

**Fact:** A statement that can be proven true.

**Factor analysis:** A type of study used to find the underlying causes and characteristics of something. The general purpose of this test is to take the information in a large number of "variables" and to link it with a smaller number of "factors" or causes.

**Fake news:** A type of yellow journalism or propaganda that consists of deliberate disinformation or hoaxes spread via traditional print and broadcast news media or online social media; fabricated information that mimics news media content in form but not in organizational process or intent. The false information is often caused by reporters paying sources for stories, an unethical practice called checkbook journalism. The news then often reverberates as misinformation via social media and occasionally finds its way to the mainstream media as well.

**Falsification:** Changing, omitting, or manipulating data or results deceptively; or deceptive manipulation of research materials or experiments.

**Feasibility:** One of the four main criteria for evaluating research problem areas and formulating research questions out of the problem areas.

**Feasibility study:** A first, small study to see whether a larger study will be possible and to see what problems the larger study might have; also called a pilot study.

**Feedback:** When data and information are returned to the persons who originally provided or collected them; used for informed decision making at the case and program levels; a basic principle underlying the design of evaluations.

**Fidelity:** The observance of the actual treatment delivery to the set of rules originally developed. Fidelity assessment considers to what degree the program was implemented as planned. Alternatively referred to as "treatment integrity."

**Field notes:** Detailed notes written or recorded while observing in the research setting, or made during or after interviewing research participants. Some researchers also include their own personal ideas in their field notes, while others put them in analytic memos.

**Field research:** Research conducted in a real-life setting, not in a laboratory. The researcher neither creates nor manipulates anything within the study, only observes it.

**Field-tested:** The pilot of an instrument or research method in conditions equivalent to those that will be encountered in the research study.

**Fieldwork:** Refers to the research activity of collecting data through observation (and other means) in the "field," the designated research setting or settings.

**File drawer problem:** (1) In literature searches or reviews, the difficulty in locating studies that have not been published or are not easily retrievable. (2) In meta-analyses, errors in effect size due to reliance on published articles showing statistical significance.

**First-hand data:** Data obtained from people who directly experience the problem being studied.

**First-level coding:** A process of identifying meaning units in a transcript, organizing the meaning units into categories, and assigning names to the categories.

**Flexibility:** The degree to which the design and procedures of a research study can be changed to adapt to contextual demands of the research setting.

**Floor effects:** A term used to describe what happens when a group of subjects in a study have scores that are close to or at the lower limit (floor) of a variable. For example, the majority of subjects score very poorly because the task is too difficult.

**Focus group interview:** Used to elicit the views of a group (usually around 6 to 10 individuals) who have common experiences or interests. They are brought together with the purpose of discussing a particular subject, under the guidance of a facilitator.

**Follow-up:** Contact with a person being studied, made after the first stage of the study, to see if there have been changes since then, and to see how long changes last. The term can also mean the length of time a person is studied, or the length of time between stages in the study.

**Formative evaluation:** A type of evaluation that focuses on obtaining data that are helpful in planning the program and in improving its implementation and performance.

**Framework:** A method of qualitative data analysis involving five key stages: familiarization, identifying a thematic framework, indexing, charting, and mapping and interpretation.

**Fraud:** Knowingly misrepresenting the truth or concealing a material (or relevant) fact to induce someone to make a decision to his or her detriment. Some forms of research misconduct may also qualify as fraud. A person who commits fraud may face civil or criminal legal liability.

**Freedom of Information Act (FOIA):** A law enacted in the United States and other countries that allows the public to obtain access to government documents, including documents related to government-funded scientific research such as data, protocols, and e-mails. Several types of documents are exempt from FOIA requests, including classified research and confidential information pertaining to human subjects research.

**Frequency distributions:** A mathematical function showing the number of instances in which a variable takes each of its possible values.

**Frequency polygons:** Graphical devices for understanding the shapes of distributions.

**Frequency recording:** A method of data collection by direct observations in which each occurrence of the target problem is recorded during a specified observation period.

**F-test:** A statistical test (also known as analysis of variance) used to compare two or more groups for statistically significant differences between/among them.

**Fugitive data:** Informal information found outside regular publishing channels.

**Gaining access:** A term used in interpretive research studies to describe the process of engagement and relationship development between the researcher and the research participants.

**Gatekeeper:** A person whose permission or approval is necessary for a researcher to gain access to a research site or setting.

**Generalizable explanation evaluation model:** An evaluation model whose proponents believe that many solutions are possible for any one social problem and that the effects of programs will differ under different conditions.

**Generalizing results:** Extending or applying the findings of a research study to individuals or situations not directly involved in the original research study; the ability to extend or apply the findings of a research study to subjects or situations that were not directly investigated.

**Goal Attainment Scale (GAS):** A modified measurement scale used to evaluate case or program outcomes.

**Good clinical practices (GCPs):** Rules and procedures for conducting clinical trials safely and rigorously.

**Good record-keeping practices (GRKPs):** Rules and procedures for keeping research records. Records should be thorough, accurate, complete, organized, signed and dated, and backed up.

**Government documents:** Documents issued by local, state, and federal governments; they include reports of legislative committee hearings and investigations, studies commissioned by legislative commissions and executive agencies, statistical compilations such as the census, the regular and special reports of executive agencies, and much more.

**Grand tour questions:** Queries in which research participants are asked to provide wide-ranging background information; mainly used in interpretive research studies.

**Graph:** A diagram that shows the relationship between two variables.

**Graphic rating scale:** A rating scale that describes an attribute on a continuum from one extreme to the other, with points of the continuum ordered in equal intervals and then assigned values.

**Grounded theory:** A qualitative research methodology with systematic guides for the collection and analysis of data that aims to generate a theory that is "grounded in" or formed from the data and is based on inductive reasoning. This contrasts with other approaches that stop at the point of describing the participants' experiences. The researcher uses qualitative data collection methods like interviews to collect information until data saturation is reached, then groups ideas together into categories using the constant comparison method to develop a context-specific or "substantive" theory.

**Group evaluation designs:** Evaluation designs that are conducted with groups of cases for the purpose of assessing to what degree program objectives have been achieved.

**Group research designs:** Research designs conducted with two or more groups of cases, or research participants, for the purpose of answering research questions or testing hypotheses.

**Guideline:** A nonbinding recommendation for conduct.

**Halo effect:** A measurement error due to the tendency of an observer to be influenced by a favorable trait of a research participant.

**Harassment:** Repeatedly annoying, bothering, or intimidating research participants.

**Hawthorne effect:** Effects on research participants' behaviors or attitudes attributable to their knowledge that they are taking part in a research study; a reactive effect; a threat to external validity.

**Helsinki Declaration:** Ethical guidelines for conducting medical research involving human subjects research adopted by the World Medical Association.

**Heterogeneity of respondents:** The extent to which a research participant differs from other research participants.

**Heuristic:** A theory used to stimulate creative thought and scientific activity.

**Historical data:** Collected in an effort to study the past.

**Historical research:** The process by which we study the past; a method of inquiry that attempts to explain past events based on surviving artifacts.

**History in research design:** The possibility that events not accounted for in a research design may alter the second and subsequent measurements of the dependent variable; a threat to internal validity.

**Homogeneity of respondents:** The extent to which a research participant is similar to other research participants.

**Honesty:** The ethical obligation to tell the truth and avoid deceiving others. In science, some types of dishonesty include data fabrication or falsification, and plagiarism; a key ingredient of a social work researcher and practitioner.

**Human subjects protections:** Rules and laws to make sure the people being studied in a research project are treated fairly.

**Human subjects research:** Research involving the collection, storage, or use of private data or biological samples from living individuals by means of interactions, interventions, surveys, or other research methods or procedures.

**Hypothesis:** A prediction of whether the independent variable will have an effect on the dependent variable or a prediction of the nature of the effect; an educated guess that explains why or how something occurs; a theory-based prediction of the expected results of a research study; a tentative explanation that a relationship between or among variables exists.

**Hypothetico-deductive method:** A hypothesis-testing approach that a hypothesis is derived on the deductions based from a theory.

**Ideographic research:** Research studies that focus on unique individuals or situations.

**Incidental finding:** Information inadvertently discovered during medical treatment or research that was not intentionally sought. For example, if a research subject receives an MRI as part of a brain-imaging study and the researcher notices an area in the fontal cortex that appears to be a tumor, this information would be an incidental finding.

**Independence or independently:** When one factor does not exert influence on another. For example, what one study participant does should not influence what another participant does. They make decisions independently. Independence is critical for a meaningful statistical analysis.

**Independent *t*-test:** A statistical test used to determine whether there is a statistically significant difference between the means of two independent samples.

**Independent variable:** A variable that is not dependent on another variable but is believed to cause or determine changes in the dependent variable; an antecedent variable that is directly manipulated to assess its effect on the dependent variable.

**Index:** A group of individual measures that, when combined, are meant to indicate some more general characteristic.

**Indigenous observers:** People who are naturally a part of the research participants' environment and who perform the data-collection function; includes relevant others (e.g., family members, peers) and collaterals (e.g., social workers, staff members).

**Indirect measures:** A substitute variable, or a collection of representative variables, used when there is no direct measurement of the variable of interest; also called a proxy variable.

**Individualism:** In individualistic cultures, such as the mainstream North American culture, people work toward individual goals and achievement.

**Individualized research results:** In human subjects research, results pertaining to a specific individual in a study, such as the subject's pulse, blood pressure, or the results of laboratory tests (e.g., blood sugar levels, blood cell counts, genetic or genomic variants). Individualized results may include intended findings or incidental findings. There is an ongoing ethical controversy concerning whether, when, and how individualized research results should be shared with human subjects. Some argue that individualized results should be returned if they are based on accurate and reliable tests and have clinical utility because inaccurate, unreliable, or uncertain results may be harmful. Others claim that the principle of autonomy implies that subjects should be able to decide whether to receive their results.

**Induction (an inductive process):** Logical thought process in which generalizations are developed from specific observations: reasoning moves from the particular to the general.

**Inductive reasoning:** A method of reasoning whereby a conclusion is reached by building on specific observations of events, things, or processes to make inferences or more general statements; applied to data collection and research results to make generalizations to see if they fit a theory.

**Inductive thinking:** Working from the specific to the more general; taking specific observations or instances, noting patterns, then extrapolating from them to create general conclusions or a general theory. The opposite is deductive thinking.

**Infer:** To predict something based on what is true about a smaller group of people or about parts of the larger whole; building a larger idea or conclusion from blocks of smaller examples.

**Inference:** A logical explanation or conclusion based on observations and/or facts.

**Inferential statistics:** Using a random sample of data taken from a population to describe and make inferences about the population from which the sample was drawn.

**Inferring:** The process of making an inference, an interpretation based on observations and prior knowledge.

**Informant:** A person from within the cultural group being studied who provides the researcher with "insider" information.

**Information:** Something you hope to get from the data once you have analyzed them.

**Information anxiety:** A feeling attributable to a lack of understanding of information, being overwhelmed by the amount of information to be accessed and understood, or not knowing whether certain information exists.

**Informed consent:** Based on the principles of beneficence and respect for persons, the process of ensuring that participants understand their role in a study, agree to participate voluntarily, and can withdraw from the study at any time without prejudice.

**Informed consent, blanket (general):** A provision in an informed consent document that gives general permission to researchers to use the subject's data or samples for various purposes and share them with other researchers.

**Informed consent, documentation:** A record (such as a form) used to document the process of consent. Research regulations require that consent be documented; however, an institutional review board may decide to waive documentation of consent if the research is minimal risk and (1) the principle risk of the study is breach of confidentiality and the only record linking the subject to the study is the consent form or (2) the research involves procedures that normally do not require written consent outside of the research context.

**Informed consent, specific:** A provision in an informed consent document that requires researchers to obtain specific permission from the subject before using samples or data for purposes other than those that are part of the study or sharing them with other researchers.

**Informed consent, tiered:** Provisions in an informed consent document that give the subject various options concerning the use and sharing of samples or data. Options may include blanket consent, specific consent, and other choices.

**Informed consent, waiver:** In human subjects research, the decision by an institutional review board to waive (or set aside) some or all of the informed consent requirements. Waivers are not usually granted unless they are necessary to conduct the research and pose minimal risks to the subjects.

**In-house evaluation:** An evaluation that is conducted by someone who works within a program; usually an evaluation for the purpose of promoting better client services; also known as an internal evaluation. This type of evaluation complements an external evaluation.

**Institutional review board (IRB):** A committee responsible for reviewing and overseeing human subjects research; boards set up by institutions to protect research participants and to ensure that ethical issues are recognized and responded to in a study's research design. An IRB may also be called a research ethics committee (REC) or research ethics board (REB). IRBs usually include members from different backgrounds and disciplines.

**Instrumentation:** Weaknesses of a measuring instrument, such as invalidity, unreliability, improper administration, or mechanical breakdowns; a threat to internal validity.

**Intellectual property:** Legally recognized property pertaining to the products of intellectual activity, such as creative works or inventions. Forms of intellectual property include copyrights on creative works and patents on inventions.

**Interaction effects:** Effects produced by the combination of two or more threats to internal validity.

**Internal consistency:** The extent to which the scores on two comparable halves of the same measuring instrument are similar; inter-item consistency.

**Internal validity:** The extent to which it can be demonstrated that the independent variable within a research study is the only cause of change in the dependent variable; overall soundness of the experimental procedures and measuring instruments.

**Internet:** A global system of interconnected computer networks that use the Internet protocol suite (TCP/IP) to link devices worldwide.

**Internet café approach:** An approach to assessing research findings in an effort to help one become a better critical thinker.

**Interobserver reliability:** The stability or consistency of observations made by two or more observers at one point in time.

**Interpretation:** The researcher's explanation of why participants behave or think in the way that they do. In qualitative research, this is usually based on the data, and is developed through inductive thinking.

**Interpretative:** Exploration of the human experiential interpretation of any observed phenomena, enabling researchers to gain a better understanding of the underlying processes that may influence behavior.

**Interpretive analysis:** Analysis emphasizing the role of the researcher as an interpreter of the data, and the self-reflective nature of qualitative research.

**Interpretive notes:** Notes on the researcher's interpretations of events that are kept separate from the record of the facts noted as direct observations.

**Interpretive research approach:** Research studies that focus on the facts of nature as they occur under natural conditions and emphasize qualitative description and generalization; a process of discovery sensitive to holistic and ecological issues; a research approach that is complementary to the positivist research approach.

**Interquartile range:** A measure of statistical dispersion being equal to the difference between the third and first quartiles.

**Interrater reliability:** The degree to which two or more independent observers, coders, or judges produce consistent results.

**Interrupted time-series design:** An explanatory research design in which there is only one group of research participants and the dependent variable is measured repeatedly before and after treatment; used in case and program evaluation designs.

**Interval level of measurement:** The level of measurement with an arbitrarily chosen zero point that classifies its values on an equally spaced continuum.

**Interval recording:** A method of data collection that involves a continuous direct observation of an individual during specified observation periods divided into equal time intervals.

**Intervening variable:** See Rival hypothesis.

**Intervention:** A planned change, such as a new therapy or a new medication; or the act of making this change.

**Interview data:** Isolated facts that are gathered when research participants respond to carefully constructed research questions; data in the form of words, recorded by transcription.

**Interview guide:** Also known as an interview schedule, a list of topics and questions that the researcher writes before an interview. It helps the researcher prepare for the interview, ensuring that all the important areas of interest are being considered, and it can also guide the interview itself.

**Interviewing:** A conversation with a purpose.

**Interview protocol:** A form used in qualitative research to collect qualitative data. On the form are questions to be asked during an interview and space for recording data gathered during the interview. This protocol also provides space to record essential data such as the time, day, and place of the interview.

**Interview schedule:** A measuring instrument used to collect data in face-to-face and telephone interviews.

**Intraobserver reliability:** The stability of observations made by a single observer at several points in time.

**Intrusion into lives of research participants:** The understanding that specific data-collection methods can have negative consequences for research participants; a criterion for selecting a data-collection method.

**Inview:** Involves a detailed and careful reading of the subject matter, ensuring that one understands the concepts and follows the author's argument.

**Itemized rating scales:** A measuring instrument that presents a series of statements that respondents or observers rank in different positions on a specific attribute.

**Iteration (an iterative process):** Relates to the process of repeatedly returning to the source of the data to ensure that the understandings are truly coming from the data. In practice this means a constant process of collecting data, carrying out a preliminary analysis, and using that to guide the next piece of data collection then continuing this pattern until the data collection is complete.

**Journal:** A type of periodical usually sold by subscription and containing articles written for specialized or scholarly audiences. Alternatively, a written record of the process of an interpretive research study. Journal entries are made on an ongoing basis throughout the study and include study procedures as well as the researcher's reactions to emerging issues and concerns during the data-analysis process.

**Justice:** (1) Fair treatment of people. (2) An ethical principle that obligates one to treat people fairly. Distributive justice refers to allocating benefits and harms fairly; procedural justice refers to using fair processes to make decisions that affect people; formal justice refers to treating similar cases in the same way. In human subjects research, the principle of justice implies that subjects should be selected equitably. See also Belmont Report.

**Key informants:** A subpopulation of research participants who seem to know much more about "the situation" than other research participants.

**Knowledge base:** A body of knowledge and skills specific to a certain discipline.

**Knowledge creator and disseminator:** A social work role in which the social worker actually carries out and disseminates the results of a positivist and/or interpretive research study to generate knowledge for our profession.

**Knowledge-level continuum:** The range of knowledge levels, from exploratory to descriptive to explanatory, at which all research questions can be answered.

**Law:** A rule enforced by the coercive power of the government. Laws may include statutes drafted by legislative bodies (such as Congress), regulations developed and implemented by government agencies, and legal precedents established by courts (i.e., common law).

**Legal authorized representative (LAR):** A person, such as a guardian, parent of a minor child, health care agent, or close relative, who is legally authorized to make decisions for another person when they cannot make decisions for themselves. LARs may also be called surrogate decision-makers. See competence, decision-making capacity.

**Latent content:** In a content analysis, the true meaning, depth, or intensity of a variable or concept under study.

**Levels of measurement:** The degree to which characteristics of a data set can be modeled mathematically; the higher the level of measurement, the more statistical methods that are applicable.

**Lifelong learning:** A process where we continue to learn new and exciting stuff throughout our entire life span.

**Likert Scale:** A scale to show how a person feels about something. It usually includes a range of possible answers, from "strongly agree" to "strongly disagree," which each have a number. The total score is found by adding all these numbers.

**Limited review:** An existing literature synthesis that summarizes in narrative form the findings and implications of a few research studies.

**Linear relationship:** A relationship between two variables that are directly related.

**Literature review:** An article or paper describing published research on a particular topic. The purpose of a literature review (sometimes called a review article) is to select the most important publications on the topic, sort them into categories, and comment on them to provide a quick overview of leading scholarship in that area. Published articles often include a literature review section to place their research in the context of other work in the field.

**Literature search:** Scanning books and journals for basic, up-to-date research articles on studies relevant to a research question or hypothesis; should be sufficiently thorough to maximize the chance of including all relevant sources.

**Logical consistency:** The requirement that all the steps within a positivist research study must be logically related to one another.

**Logical positivism:** A philosophy of science holding that the scientific method of inquiry is the only source of certain knowledge; in research, focuses on testing hypotheses deduced from theory.

**Logistics:** In evaluation, refers to getting research participants to do what they are supposed to do, getting research instruments distributed and returned; in general, activities that ensure that the procedural tasks of a research or evaluation study are carried out.

**Longitudinal case study:** An exploratory research design in which there is only one group of research participants and the dependent variable is measured more than once.

**Longitudinal data:** Data collected over time from a variable or group of subjects.

**Longitudinal research design:** A survey research design in which a measuring instrument is administered to a sample of research participants repeatedly over time; used to detect dynamic processes such as opinion change.

**Magnitude recording:** A direct-observation method of soliciting and recording data on the amount, level, or degree of the target problem during each occurrence.

**Mail survey:** A questionnaire mailed to people or groups who fill out the form and mail it back to the researcher.

**Management Information System (MIS):** A way of storing, accessing, and managing data in electronic form.

**Manifest content:** Content of a communication that is obvious and clearly evident.

**Matching:** A random assignment technique that assigns research participants to two or more groups so that the experimental and control groups are approximately equivalent in terms of pretest scores or other characteristics, or so that all differences except the experimental condition are eliminated.

**Matrix of categories:** A method of displaying relationships among themes in analyzing case study data that shows whether changes in categories or degrees along one dimension are associated with changes in the categories of another dimension.

**Maturation:** Unplanned change in research participants due to mental, physical, or other processes operating over time; a threat to internal validity.

**Mean:** The sum of the scores in a distribution divided by the number of scores in the distribution.

**Meaning units:** In a qualitative data analysis, a discrete segment of a transcript that can stand alone as a single idea; can consist of a single word, a partial or complete sentence, a paragraph, or more; used as the basic building blocks for developing categories.

**Measurement:** The assignment of labels or numerals to the properties or attributes of observations, events, or objects according to specific rules.

**Measurement error:** Any variation in measurement that cannot be attributed to the variable being measured; variability in responses produced by individual differences and other extraneous variables.

**Measures of central tendency:** A central or typical value for a probability distribution; the most common measures of central tendency are the mean, median, and mode.

**Measuring instrument:** Any instrument used to measure a variable.

**Media embargo:** A policy, adopted by some journals, that allows journalists to have access to a scientific paper before publication provided they agree not to publicly disclose the contents of the paper until it is published. Some journals will refuse to publish papers that have already appeared in the media.

**Media myths:** The content of television shows, movies, and newspaper and magazine articles.

**Median:** The midpoint or number in a distribution having 50% of the scores above it and 50% of the scores below it.

**Member checking:** A process of obtaining feedback and comments from research participants on interpretations and conclusions made from the qualitative data they provided; asking research participants to confirm or refute the conclusions made.

**Mentor:** Someone who provides education, training, guidance, critical feedback, or emotional support to a student. In science, a mentor may be the student's advisor but need not be.

**Merging:** A mixing strategy in which quantitative and qualitative results are brought together through a combined analysis.

**Meta-analysis:** A statistical technique that integrates the results of several independent randomized controlled trials that are similar enough statistically that the results can be combined and analyzed as if they were one study.

**Methodology:** The procedures and rules that detail how a single research study is conducted.

**Micro-level data:** Data derived from individual units of analysis, whether these data sources are individuals, families, or corporations; for example, age and years of formal schooling are two variables requiring micro-level data.

**Minimal risk:** A risk that is not greater than the risk of routine medical or psychological tests or exams or the risk ordinarily encountered in daily life activities.

**Minority group:** A group that occupies a subordinate position in a society. Minorities may be separated by physical or cultural traits disapproved of by the dominant group and as a result often experience discrimination.

**Misconduct:** See research misconduct.

**Misinformation:** False or inaccurate information, especially that which is deliberately intended to deceive.

**Mismanagement of funds:** Spending research funds wastefully or illegally; for example, using grant funds allocated for equipment to pay for travel to a conference. Some types of mismanagement may also constitute fraud or embezzlement.

**Missing data:** Data not available for a research participant about whom other data are available, such as when a respondent fails to answer one of the questions in a survey.

**Missing links:** When two categories or themes seem to be related but not directly so, it may be that a third variable connects the two.

**Mixed-methods case study:** Variant of the embedded design in which the researcher collects both qualitative and quantitative data within a case study.

**Mixed-methods research questions:** Questions in a mixed-methods study that address the mixing or integration of quantitative and qualitative data.

**Mixed research model:** A model combining aspects of interpretive and positivist research approaches within all (or many) of the methodological steps contained within a single research study.

**Mode:** Most frequent score in a distribution.

**Monitoring approach to evaluation:** Evaluation that aims to provide ongoing feedback so that a program can be improved while it is still under way; it contributes to the continuous development and improvement of a human service program; this approach complements the project approach to evaluation.

**Monochronic:** In monochronic cultures people try to sequence actions on the "one thing at a time" principle. Interpersonal relations are subordinate to time schedules and deadlines.

**Morality:** See ethics.

**Mortality:** Loss of research participants through normal attrition over time in an experimental design that requires retesting; a threat to internal validity.

**Multiculturalism:** A belief or policy that endorses the principle of cultural diversity of different cultural and ethnic groups so that they retain distinctive cultural identities.

**Multicultural research:** Representation of diverse cultural factors in the subjects of study; such diversity variables may include religion, race, ethnicity, language preference, and gender.

**Multigroup posttest-only design:** An exploratory research design in which there is more than one group of research participants and the dependent variable is measured only once for each group.

**Multiple-baseline design:** A case-level evaluation design with more than one baseline period and intervention phase, which allows causal inferences to be made regarding the relationship between a treatment intervention and its effect on clients' target problems and which helps control for extraneous variables. See interrupted time-series design.

**Multiple-group design:** An experimental research design with one control group and several experimental groups.

**Multiple-treatment interference:** Effects of the results of a first treatment on the results of second and subsequent treatments; a threat to external validity.

**Multistage probability sampling:** Probability sampling procedures used when a comprehensive list of the population does not exist and it is not possible to construct one.

**Multivariate:** (1) A relationship involving two or more variables. (2) A hypothesis stating an assertion about two or more variables and how they relate to one another.

**Multivariate analysis:** A statistical analysis of the relationship among three or more variables.

**$N$:** A measure of how many people or things in a group were studied by the researcher; followed by an equal sign and a number, such as $N = 45$.

**Narrative inquiry:** A qualitative research approach that employs a variety of data collection methods, particularly interviews, to elicit, document, and analyze life experiences as they are recounted by the individuals who live them.

**Narrative interviewing:** Research participants tell stories in their own words.

**Narrowband measuring instrument:** Measuring instruments that focus on a single variable or a few variables.

**National Association of Social Workers (NASW):** A professional organization of social workers in the United States; provides guidance, research, up-to-date information, advocacy, and other resources for its members and for social workers in general.

**Nationality:** Refers to country of origin.

**Naturalist:** A person who studies the facts of nature as they occur under natural conditions.

**Natural settings:** Refers to the ordinary, everyday worlds of participants—where they live, work, and study. These natural settings include such places as homes and workplaces, staffrooms, classrooms and self-access centers, and online chat rooms. These settings are complex, dynamic, and multifaceted.

**Nazi research on human subjects:** Heinous experiments conducted on concentration camp prisoners, without their consent, during World War II. Many of the subjects died or received painful and disabling injuries. Experiments included wounding prisoners to study healing, infecting prisoners with diseases to test vaccines, and subjecting prisoners to electrical currents, radiation, and extremes of temperature or pressure.

**Needs assessment:** Program-level evaluation activities that aim to assess the feasibility for establishing or continuing a particular social service program; an evaluation that aims to assess the need for a human service by verifying that a social problem exists within a specific client population to an extent that warrants services.

**Negative case sampling:** Purposefully selecting research participants based on the fact that they have different characteristics than previous cases.

**Negligence:** A failure to follow the standard of care that results in harm to a person or organization. In science, research that is sloppy, careless, or poorly planned or executed may be considered negligent.

**Nominal level of measurement:** The level of measurement that classifies variables by assigning names or categories that are mutually exclusive and exhaustive.

**Noncompliance:** The failure to comply with research regulations, institutional policies, or ethical standards. Serious or continuing noncompliance in human subjects research should be promptly reported to the institutional review board and other authorities. See compliance.

**Nondirectional test:** See two-tailed hypotheses.

**Nonexperimental design:** A research design at the exploratory, or lowest, level of the knowledge continuum; also called pre-experimental.

**Nonlinear relationship:** A relationship between two variables that are not directly related to each other.

**Nonoccurrence data:** In the structured-observation method of data collection, a recording of only those time intervals in which the target problem did not occur.

**Nonparametric tests:** Refers to statistical tests of hypotheses about population probability distributions, but not about specific parameters of the distributions.

**Nonprobability sampling:** Sampling procedures in which all of the persons, events, or objects in the sampling frame have an unknown, and usually different, probability of being included in a sample.

**Nonreactive:** Methods of research that do not allow the research participants to know that they are being studied; thus, they do not alter their responses for the benefit of the researcher.

**Nonresponse:** The rate of nonresponse in survey research is calculated by dividing the total number of respondents by the total number in the sample, minus any units verified as ineligible.

**Nonresponse bias:** A research fault based on the people who didn't agree to be studied, although they were chosen. People who didn't agree may have been different in other important ways from people who did, so the study's results might be true for only part of the chosen group.

**Nonsampling errors:** Errors in a research study's results that are not due to the sampling procedures.

**Norm:** In measurement, an average or set group standard of achievement that can be used to interpret individual scores; normative data describing statistical properties of a measuring instrument such as mean and standard deviation.

**Normal distribution:** An arrangement of a data set in which most values cluster in the middle of the range and the rest taper off symmetrically toward either extreme.

**Normal frequency distribution curve:** A bell-shaped curve of values (amounts, numbers, scores) in which the average, the midpoint, and the most frequent score are all the same.

**Normalization group:** The population sample to which a measuring instrument under development is administered to establish norms; also called the norm group.

**Normative needs:** When needs are defined by comparing the objective living conditions of a target population with what society—or, at least, that segment of society concerned with helping the target population—deems acceptable or desirable from a humanitarian standpoint.

**Null hypothesis:** A statement concerning one or more parameters that is subjected to a statistical test; a statement that there is no relationship between the two variables of interest.

**Numbers:** The basic data unit of analysis used in positivist research studies.

**Nuremberg Code:** The first international ethics code for human subjects research, adopted by the Nuremberg Council during the war crimes tribunals in 1947. The code was used as a basis for convicting Nazi physicians and scientists for war crimes related to their experiments on concentration camp prisoners.

**Objective inclusion scales:** A set of items in a questionnaire designed to measure objective and impartial information about the participant (e.g., "How often do you feel sad?").

**Objective measures:** Any measure that is based on fact rather than opinion.

**Objectivity:** (1) The tendency for the results of scientific research to be free from bias. (2) An ethical and epistemological principle instructing one to take steps to minimize or control for bias.

**Objectivity:** A research stance in which a study is carried out and its data are examined and interpreted without distortion by personal feelings or biases.

**Observation:** A strategy for data collection, involving the process of watching participants directly in the natural setting.

Observation can be participative (i.e., taking part in the activity) or nonparticipative (the researcher watches from the outside)

**Observational research:** A type of research design in which there's no interaction between the researcher and the research participants.

**Observer:** One of four roles on a continuum of participation in participant observation research; the level of involvement of the observer participant is lower than of the complete participant and higher than of the participant observer.

**Observer (or Hawthorne) effect:** The tendency for individuals to change their behavior when they know they are being observed. Some social science experiments use deception to control for the observer effect.

**Obtrusive data-collection methods:** Direct data-collection methods that can influence the variables under study or the responses of research participants; data-collection methods that produce reactive effects.

**Occurrence data:** In the structured-observation method of data collection, a recording of the first occurrence of the target problem during each time interval.

**Office of Human Research Protections (OHRP):** A federal agency that oversees human subjects research funded by the Department of Health and Human Services, including research funded by the National Institutes of Health. OHRP publishes guidance documents for interpreting the Common Rule, sponsors educational activities, and takes steps to ensure compliance with federal regulations, including auditing research and issuing letters to institutions concerning noncompliance.

**Office of Research Integrity (ORI):** A U.S. federal agency that oversees the integrity of research funded by the Public Health Service, including research funded by the National Institutes of Health. ORI sponsors research and education on research integrity and reviews reports of research misconduct inquiries and investigations from institutions.

**One-group posttest-only design:** An exploratory research design in which the dependent variable is measured only once.

**One-group pretest-posttest design:** A descriptive research design in which the dependent variable is measured twice—before and after treatment.

**One-stage probability sampling:** Probability sampling procedures in which the selection of a sample that is drawn from a specific population is completed in a single process.

**One-tailed hypotheses:** Statements that predict specific relationships between independent and dependent variables.

**One-way analysis of variance:** An extension of the independent group t-test when there are more than two groups.

**Online sources:** Computerized literary retrieval systems that provide printouts of indexes and abstracts.

**Open-ended questions:** Questions that let people answer in their own words instead of having to choose from set answers like "a" or "b" or "true" or "false"; questions in which the response categories are not specified or detailed.

**Open interviews:** Interviews that develop naturally, rather than being guided by a preprepared interview guide or list of questions. They are also known as "open-ended," "in-depth," or "unstructured" interviews.

**Openness:** The ethical obligation to share the results of scientific research, including data and methods.

**Operational definition:** Explicit specification of a variable in such a way that its measurement is possible.

**Operationalization:** The process of developing operational definitions of the variables that are contained within the concepts of a positivist and/or interpretive research study.

**Opinion:** Expresses someone's belief, feeling, view, idea, or judgment about something or someone; statements that cannot be validated.

**Ordinal level of measurement:** The level of measurement that classifies variables by rank-ordering them from high to low or from most to least.

**Ordinal scale:** A ranking of values (amounts, numbers, scores) from greatest to least, lowest to highest, first to last, but by a category instead of a number.

**Outcome:** The effect of the manipulation of the independent variable on the dependent variable; the end product of a treatment intervention; the way something, often a treatment or a program or a study, turns out; the effect it has on people; or the record or measure of the effects.

**Outcome-oriented case study:** A type of case study that investigates whether client outcomes were in fact achieved.

**Outcome variables:** Variables that are used to measure the overall impact of the study.

**Outliers:** Abnormal values in the data that are unusually large or unusually small compared to the others.

**Outside observers:** Trained observers who are not a part of the research participants' environment and who are brought in to record data.

**Overview:** One slightly engages with the literature.

**Paired observations:** An observation involving two variables, where the intent is to examine the relationship between them.

**Panel research study:** A longitudinal survey design in which the same group of research participants (the panel) is followed over time by surveying them on successive occasions.

**Parametric tests:** Statistical methods for estimating parameters or testing hypotheses about population parameters.

**Participant observation:** An obtrusive data-collection method in which the researcher, or the observer, participates in the life of those being observed; both an obtrusive data-collection method and a research approach, this method is characterized by the one doing the study undertaking roles that involve establishing and maintaining ongoing relationships with research participants who are often in the field settings, and observing and participating with the research participants over time.

**Participant observer:** One of four roles on a continuum of participation in participant observation research; the level of involvement of the participant observer is higher than of the complete observer and lower than of the observer participant.

**Participants:** People in a research study. They are also called respondents (particularly when data are collected using interviews or questionnaires); in the quantitative research approach, they are often referred to as "subjects."

**Participatory action research (PAR):** A type of study in which a researcher becomes a member of the group being studied and finds out information by doing what the group is doing.

**Paternalism:** Restricting a person's decision-making for their own good. In soft paternalism, one restricts the choices made by someone who has a compromised ability to make decisions (see decision-making capacity). In hard paternalism, one restricts the choices made by someone who is fully autonomous (see autonomy).

**Peer review:** Part of the publication process for scholarly publications in which a group of experts examines a document to determine whether it is worthy of publication. Journals and other publications use a peer review process—usually arranged so that reviewers do not know who the author of the document is—to assess articles for quality and relevance. See also refereed publication.

**Peer review, double-blind:** A peer review process in which neither the authors nor the reviewers are told each other's identities.

**Peer review, open:** A peer review process in which the authors and reviewers are told each other's identities.

**Peer review, single-blind:** A peer review process, used by most scientific journals, in which the reviewers are told the identities of the authors but not vice versa.

**Percentage:** A part of a whole, when the whole is divided in hundredths.

**Percentile:** A number showing how many cases, out of every hundred, fall below the point (score, amount) in question.

**Periodical:** A publication issued at regular intervals. Periodicals may be magazines, journals, newspapers, or newsletters. See also serial.

**Periodical index:** A list of all the articles that have been published in a magazine, journal, newspaper, newsletter, or a set of periodicals. Many periodical indexes have been converted to online databases, though many online versions are limited to recent decades.

**Permanent product recording:** A method of data collection in which the occurrence of the target problem is determined by observing the permanent product or record of the target problem.

**Phenomenology:** An approach that allows the meaning of having experienced the phenomenon under investigation to be described, as opposed to a description of what the experience was. This approach allows the reader to have a better understanding of what it was like to have experienced a particular phenomenon.

**Phenomenon:** Any observable fact or event that occurs.

**Pie chart:** A drawing of a circle that is divided into pieces like a pie. Each piece shows how much of the whole is taken up by that group, thing, or process.

**Pilot study:** Administration of a measuring instrument to a group of people who will not be included in the study to determine any difficulties the research participants may have in answering questions and the general impression given by the instrument; sometimes called a pretest.

**Placebo:** A biologically or chemically inactive substance or intervention given to a research subject that is used to control for the placebo effect.

**Placebo effect:** A person's psychosomatic response to the belief that they are receiving an effective treatment. Researchers may also be susceptible to the placebo effect if they treat subjects differently who they believe are receiving effective treatment. See also double-blinding.

**Placebo treatment:** A fake treatment that should have no effect, outside of the power of suggestion.

**Plagiarism:** The unattributed use of a source of information that is not considered common knowledge. In general, the following acts are considered plagiarism: (1) failing to cite quotations or borrowed ideas, (2) failing to enclose borrowed language in quotation marks, (3) failing to put summaries or paraphrases in your own words, and (4) submitting someone else's work as your own.

**Plot:** A way of summarizing data and to illustrate the major characteristics of the distribution of the data in a convenient form.

**Plural society:** A society that combines ethnic contrasts and economic interdependence of the ethnic groups.

**Poll:** A survey that asks people questions about certain issues, topics, or candidates, either face to face, by mail, by phone, or by computer.

**Pooling:** Term used to describe the act of combining data from more than one group of subjects or combining scores from different variables to produce a single score.

**Population:** An entire set, or universe, of people, objects, or events of concern to a research study, from which a sample is drawn.

**Positivism:** See positivist research approach.

**Positivist research approach:** A research approach to discover relationships and facts that are generalizable; research that is "independent" of subjective beliefs, feelings, wishes, and values; a research approach that is complementary to the interpretive research approach.

**Posttest:** Measurement of the dependent variable after the introduction of the independent variable.

**Potential for testing:** One of the four criteria for evaluating research hypotheses.

**Power:** The odds that you will observe a treatment effect when it occurs.

**Practitioner/researcher:** A social worker who guides practice through the use of research findings; collects data throughout an intervention using research methods, skills, and tools; and disseminates practice findings.

**Pragmatists:** Researchers who believe that both interpretive and positivist research approaches can be integrated in a single research study.

**Precautionary principle (PP):** An approach to decision-making that holds we should take reasonable measures to prevent, minimize, or mitigate harms that are plausible and serious. Some countries have used the PP to make decisions concerning environmental protection or technology development. See also risk/benefit analysis, risk management.

**Predicting:** The process of forecasting what will happen in the future based on past experience or evidence.

**Predictive validity:** A form of criterion validity that is concerned with the ability of a measuring instrument to predict future performance or status on the basis of present performance or status.

**Predictor variable:** The variable that, it is believed, allows us to improve our ability to predict values of the criterion variable.

**Preexposure:** Tasks to be carried out in advance of a research study to sensitize the researcher to the culture of interest; these tasks may include participation in cultural experiences, intercultural sharing, case studies, ethnic literature reviews, value statement exercises, and so on.

**Preliminary plan for data analysis:** A strategy for analyzing qualitative data that is outlined in the beginning stages of an interpretive research study. The plan has two general steps: (1) previewing the data and (2) outlining what to record in the researcher's journal.

**Preponderance of evidence:** In the law, a standard of proof in which a claim is proven if the evidence shows that it is more likely true than false (i.e., probability >50%). Preponderance of evidence is the legal standard generally used in research misconduct cases. This standard is much lower than the standard used in criminal cases (i.e., proof beyond reasonable doubt).

**Pre-post testing:** Giving the same test before treatment and just after treatment.

**Presentism:** Applying current thinking and concepts to interpretations of past events or intentions; the reverse of antiquarianism.

**Pretest:** (1) Measurement of the dependent variable before the introduction of the independent variable. (2) Administration of a measuring instrument to a group of people who will not be included in the study to determine difficulties the research participants may have in answering questions and the general impression given by the instrument; also called a pilot study.

**Pretest-treatment interaction:** Effects that a pretest has on the responses of research participants to the introduction of the independent variable or the experimental treatment; a threat to external validity.

**Preview:** One does a broad and superficial sweep of the literature.

**Previous research:** Research studies that have already been completed and published and that provide information about data-collection methods used to investigate research questions that are similar to our own; a criterion for selecting a data-collection method.

**Primary data:** Data in their original form, as collected from the research participants. A primary data source is one that puts as few intermediaries as possible between the production and the study of the data.

**Primary language:** The preferred language of the research participants.

**Primary reference source:** A report of a research study by the person who conducted the study, usually an article in a professional journal.

**Primary source:** An original source, such as a speech, a diary, a novel, a legislative bill, a laboratory study, a field research report, or an eyewitness account. While not necessarily more reliable than a secondary source, a primary source has the advantage of being closely related to the information it conveys and as such is often considered essential for research, particularly in history. In the sciences, reports of new research written by the scientists who conducted it are considered primary sources.

**Principal investigator (PI):** The main person running a research study.

**Privacy:** A state of being free from unwanted intrusion into one's personal space, private information, or personal affairs. See also confidentiality.

**Probability sampling:** Sampling procedures in which every member of the designated population has a known probability of being selected for the sample.

**Problem area:** In social work research, a general expressed difficulty about which something researchable is unknown; not to be confused with research question.

**Problem-solving process:** A generic method with specified phases for solving problems; sometimes called the scientific method.

**Procedure:** A list that describes all the steps taken during a research study. The list should provide enough detail for any person to be able to repeat the study exactly the same way, like a recipe in a cookbook.

**Process measure:** A measure of things that matter during actual treatment. These might include whether the client had easy access to services or whether the client was involved in treatment planning.

**Process-oriented case study:** A type of case study that illuminates the micro-steps of intervention that lead to client outcomes; describes how programs and interventions work and gives insight into the "black box" of intervention.

**Professional journal:** A journal containing scholarly articles addressed to a particular professional audience such as doctors, lawyers, teachers, engineers, or accountants. Professional journals differ from trade publications, which usually do not include in-depth research articles.

**Professional judgments:** A conscious process whereby facts, as far as they are known, are supplemented with the knowledge derived from all five ways of knowing to form the basis for rational decisions.

**Professional standards:** Rules for making judgments about evaluation activity that are established by a group of persons who have advanced education and usually have the same occupation.

**Program:** An organized set of political, administrative, and clinical activities that function to fulfill some social purpose.

**Program development:** The constant effort to improve program services to better achieve outcomes; a basic principle underlying the design of evaluations.

**Program efficiency:** Assessment of a program's outcome in relation to the costs of obtaining the outcome.

**Program evaluation:** A form of appraisal, using valid and reliable research methods, that examines the processes or outcomes of an organization that exists to fulfill some social purpose.

**Program goal:** A statement defining the intent of a program that cannot be directly evaluated; it can, however, be evaluated indirectly by the program's objectives, which are derived from the program goal; not to be confused with program objectives.

**Program-level evaluation:** A form of appraisal that monitors change for groups of clients and organizational performance.

**Program objectives:** A statement that clearly and exactly specifies the expected change, or intended result, for individuals receiving program services; qualities of well-chosen objectives are meaningfulness, specificity, measurability, and directionality; not to be confused with program goal.

**Program participation:** The philosophy and structure of a program that will support or supplant the successful implementation of a research study within an existing social service program; a criterion for selecting a data-collection method.

**Program process:** The coordination of administrative and clinical activities that are designed to achieve a program's goal.

**Program results:** A report on how effective a program is at meeting its stated objectives.

**Project approach to evaluation:** Evaluation that aims to assess a completed or finished program. This approach complements the monitoring approach.

**Propensity scores:** Measure of an individual's predicted probability of being a program participant given his/her observed characteristics.

**Proprietary research:** Research that a private company owns and keeps secret.

**Protocol:** A set of steps, methods, or procedures for performing an activity, such as a scientific experiment.

**Protocol, deviation:** A departure from a protocol. In human subjects research, serious or continuing deviations from approved protocols should be promptly reported to the institutional review board.

**Proxy:** An indirect measure of a variable that a researcher wants to study; often used when the variable of inquiry is difficult to measure or observe directly.

**Psychometrics:** Psychological tests that are standardized (formal, set); for example, an IQ test.

**Publication:** The public dissemination of information. In science, publication may occur in journals or books, in print or electronically. Abstracts presented at scientific meetings are generally considered to be a form of publication.

**Publication bias:** Bias related to the tendency publish or not publish certain types of research. For example, some studies have documented a bias toward publishing positive results.

**Pure research approach:** A search for theoretical results that can be used to develop theory and expand our profession's knowledge bases; complementary to the applied research approach.

**Purists:** Researchers who believe that interpretive and positivist research approaches should never be mixed.

**Purpose statement:** A declaration of words that clearly describes a research study's intent.

**Purposive sampling:** A nonprobability sampling procedure in which research participants with particular characteristics are purposely selected for inclusion in a research sample; also known as judgmental or theoretical sampling.

*P*-value: The way in which statistical significance is reported (i.e., $p < .05$ means that there is a less than 5% chance that the results of a study are due to random chance).

Qualitative data: Data that measure a quality or kind. When referring to variables, qualitative is another term for categorical or nominal variable values; when speaking of kinds of research, qualitative refers to studies of subjects that are hard to quantify.

Qualitative data analysis: Process that involves coding the data set, dividing the text into small units (phrases, sentences, or paragraphs), assigning a label to each unit, and then grouping the codes into themes.

Qualitative methods: Methods used in research studies involving detailed, verbal descriptions of characteristics, cases, and settings. Qualitative research typically uses observation, interviewing, and document review to examine the quality, meaning, and context of people's answers.

Qualitative observation: An observation using descriptive words.

Qualitative research: In qualitative research, researchers try to understand participants' experiences with the central phenomenon (the focus of the study) in a natural setting, using research approaches such as ethnography or case study. Instead of numbers, researchers collect words (text, such as interviews or observation notes), and images (pictures or audiovisual footage) about the phenomenon of the study. As much as possible without preconceived hypotheses or ideas, they analyze the data for common patterns (themes) in order to allow multiple interpretations of participants' individual experiences.

Qualitative research questions: Research questions that can be answered by gathering and analyzing data in forms such as words or diagrams.

Qualitative validity: Assessing whether the information obtained through qualitative data collection is accurate through such strategies as member checking, triangulation of evidence, searching for disconfirming evidence, and asking others to examine the data.

Quality control/quality assurance: Processes for planning, conducting, monitoring, overseeing, and auditing an activity (such as research) to ensure that it meets appropriate standards of quality.

Quantification: In measurement, the reduction of data to numerical form in order to analyze them by way of mathematical or statistical techniques.

Quantitative data: Data that measure a quantity or amount.

Quantitative data analysis: Process that involves analyzing the data based on the type of questions or hypotheses and using the appropriate statistical test to address the questions or hypotheses.

Quantitative observation: An observation that deals with a number or amount.

Quantitative research: A research approach in which numeric data are collected and statistically analyzed in an objective and unbiased manner.

Quantitative research questions: Research questions that can be answered by gathering and analyzing numerical data.

Quasi-experiment: A research design at the descriptive level of the knowledge continuum that resembles an "ideal" experiment but does not allow for random selection or assignment of research participants to groups and often does not control for rival hypotheses.

Questionable research practices (QRPs): Research practices that are regarded by many as unethical but are not considered to be research misconduct. Duplicate publication and honorary authorship are considered by many to be QRPs.

Questionnaire-type scale: A type of measuring instrument in which multiple responses are usually combined to form a single overall score for a respondent.

Quota sampling: A nonprobability sampling procedure in which the relevant characteristics of the sample are identified, the proportion of these characteristics in the population is determined, and research participants are selected from each category until the predetermined proportion (quota) has been achieved.

**Race:** A variable based on physical attributes that can be subdivided into the Caucasoid, Negroid, and Mongoloid races.

**Racism:** Theories, attitudes, and practices that display dislike or antagonism toward people seen as belonging to particular ethnic groups. Social or political significance is attached to culturally constructed ideas of difference.

**Random assignment:** The process of assigning individuals to experimental or control groups so that the groups are equivalent; also referred to as randomization.

**Random error:** Variable error in measurement; error due to unknown or uncontrolled factors that affect the variable being measured and the process of measurement in an inconsistent fashion.

**Randomization:** A process for randomly assigning subjects to different treatment groups in a clinical trial or other biomedical experiment.

**Randomized controlled trial (RCT):** An experiment, such as a clinical trial, in which subjects are randomly assigned to receive an experimental intervention or a control; considered the gold standard for evaluating the effectiveness of different treatments or interventions.

**Randomized cross-sectional survey design:** A descriptive research design in which there is only one group, the dependent variable is measured only once, the research participants are randomly selected from the population, and there is no independent variable.

**Randomized longitudinal survey design:** A descriptive research design in which there is only one group, the dependent variable is measured more than once, and research participants are randomly selected from the population before each treatment.

**Randomized one-group posttest-only design:** A descriptive research design in which there is only one group, the dependent variable is measured only once, and the research participants are randomly selected from the population.

**Randomized posttest-only control group design:** An explanatory research design in which there are two or more randomly assigned groups, the control group does not receive treatment, and the experimental groups receive different treatments.

**Random numbers table:** A computer-generated or published table of numbers in which each number has an equal chance of appearing in each position in the table.

**Random sampling:** An unbiased selection process conducted so that all members of a population have an equal chance of being selected to participate in a research study.

**Range:** The distance between the minimum and the maximum score in any given data set.

**Rank-order scale:** A comparative rating scale in which the rater is asked to rank specific individuals in relation to one another on some characteristic.

**Rating scale:** A type of measuring instrument in which responses are rated on a continuum or in an ordered set of categories, with numerical values assigned to each point or category.

**Ratio level of measurement:** The level of measurement that has a nonarbitrary, fixed zero point and classifies the values of a variable on an equally spaced continuum.

**Raw scores:** Scores derived from administration of a measuring instrument to research participants or groups.

**Reactive effect:** (1) An effect on outcome measures due to the research participants' awareness that they are being observed or interviewed; a threat to external and internal validity. (2) Alteration of the variables being measured or the respondents' performance on the measuring instrument due to administration of the instrument.

**Reactivity:** The belief that things being observed or measured are affected by the fact that they are being observed or measured; one of the four main limitations of the positivist research approach.

**Reassessment:** A step in a qualitative data analysis in which the researcher interrupts the data-analysis process to reaffirm the rules used to decide which meaning units are placed within different categories.

**Recoding:** Developing and applying new variable value labels to a variable that has previously been coded. Usually, recoding is done to make variables from one or more data sets comparable.

**Reductionism:** In the positivist research approach, the operationalization of concepts by reducing them to common measurable variables; one of the four main limitations of the positivist research approach.

**Refereed publication:** A publication for which every submission is screened through a peer review process. Refereed publications are considered authoritative because experts have reviewed the material in advance of publication to determine its quality. See also peer review.

**Reference:** (1) A source used in research and mentioned by a researcher in a paper or article. (2) In libraries, a part of the library's collection that includes encyclopedias, handbooks, directories, and other publications that provide useful overviews, common practices, and facts. (Note: Reference may also indicate a desk or counter where librarians provide assistance to researchers.)

**Reflexive:** Being "reflexive" means critically thinking about the research process and your role in it.

**Reflexivity:** The open acknowledgement by the researcher of the central role they play in the research process. A reflexive approach considers and makes explicit the effect the researcher may have had on the research findings.

**Relevancy:** One of the four main criteria for evaluating research problem areas and formulating research questions out of the problem areas.

**Reliability:** (1) The degree of accuracy, precision, or consistency in results of a measuring instrument, including the ability to produce the same results when the same variable is measured more than once or repeated applications of the same test on the same individual produce the same measurement. (2) The degree to which individual differences on scores

or in data are due either to true differences or to errors in measurement.

**Reliance agreement:** An agreement between two institutions in which one institution agrees to oversee human subjects research for the other institution for a particular study or group of studies.

**Remuneration:** In human subjects research, providing financial compensation to subjects.

**Replication:** Repetition of the same research procedures by a second researcher for the purpose of determining whether earlier results can be confirmed.

**Reproducibility:** The ability for an independent researcher to achieve the same results of an experiment, test, or study under the same conditions. A research paper should include information necessary for other scientists to reproduce the results. Reproducibility is not the same as repeatability, in which researchers repeat their own experiments to verify the results. Reproducibility is one of the hallmarks of good science.

**Request for proposals (RFP):** An announcement that a grant or other funding is available.

**Research:** A systematic attempt to develop new knowledge.

**Researchability:** The extent to which a research problem is in fact researchable and the problem can be resolved through the consideration of data derived from a research study; one of the four main criteria for evaluating research problem areas and formulating research questions out of the problem areas.

**Research approach:** A tradition such as narrative inquiry, case study, ethnography, phenomenology, grounded theory, or action research that employs generally accepted research methods.

**Research attitude:** A way that we view the world; an attitude that highly values craftsmanship, with pride in creativity, high-quality standards, and hard work.

**Research compliance:** See compliance.

**Research consumer:** A social work role reflecting the ethical obligation to base interventions on the most up-to-date research knowledge available.

**Research design:** The entire plan of a positivist and/or interpretive research study from problem conceptualization to the dissemination of findings.

**Researcher bias:** The tendency of researchers to find the results they expect to find; a threat to external validity.

**Research findings:** Findings derived from research studies that used the scientific method of inquiry; the most objective way of knowing; one of the five ways of knowing.

**Research hypothesis:** A statement about a study's research question that predicts the existence of a particular relationship between the independent and dependent variables; can be used in both the positivist and interpretive approaches to research.

**Research institution:** An institution, such as a university or government or private laboratory, that is involved in conducting research.

**Research integrity:** Following ethical standards in the conduct of research.

**Research integrity official (RIO):** An administrator at a research institution who is responsible for responding to reports of suspected research misconduct.

**Research misconduct:** Intentional, knowing, or reckless behavior in research that is widely viewed as highly unethical and often illegal. Most definitions define research misconduct as fabrication or falsification of data or plagiarism; some include other behaviors in the definition such as interfering with a misconduct investigation, significant violations of human research regulations, or serious deviations from commonly accepted practices. Honest errors and scientific disputes are not regarded as misconduct.

**Research misconduct, inquiry versus investigation:** If suspected research misconduct is reported at an institution, the research integrity official may appoint an inquiry committee to determine whether there is sufficient evidence to conduct an investigation. If the committee determines that there is sufficient evidence, an investigative committee will be appointed to gather evidence and interview witnesses. The investigative committee will determine whether there is sufficient evidence to prove misconduct and make a recommendation concerning adjudication of the case to the research integrity official.

**Research participants:** Those participating in research studies; sometimes called research subjects.

**Research question:** A clear statement in the form of a question of the specific issue that a researcher wishes to answer in order to address a research problem. A specific research question that is formulated directly out of the general research problem area; answered by the interpretive and/or positivist research approach; not to be confused with problem area.

**Research sponsor:** An organization, such as a government agency or private company, that funds research.

**Research subject (also called research participant):** A living individual who is the subject of an experiment or study involving the collection of the individual's private data or biological samples. See also human subjects research.

**Resources:** The costs associated with collecting data in any given research study; includes materials and supplies, equipment rental, transportation, training staff, and staff time; a criterion for selecting a data-collection method.

**Respect for persons:** A moral principle, with roots in Kantian philosophy, that holds that we should respect the choices of autonomous decision-makers (see autonomy, decision-making capacity) and that we should protect the interests of those who have diminished autonomy (see vulnerable subject). See also Belmont Report.

**Respondent validation:** Refers to seeking the participants' views of the initial interpretations of the data. The aim is not to ensure that the researcher agrees about the meaning of the data but that the researcher has the opportunity to incorporate the participants' responses into the analysis.

**Response categories:** Possible responses assigned to each question in a standardized measuring instrument, with a lower value generally indicating a low level of the variable being measured and a larger value indicating a higher level.

**Response rate:** The total number of responses obtained from potential research participants to a measuring instrument divided by the total number of responses requested, usually expressed in the form of a percentage.

**Response set:** Personal style; the tendency of research participants to respond to a measuring instrument in a particular way, regardless of the questions asked, or the tendency of observers or interviewers to react in certain ways; a source of constant error.

**Responsible conduct of research (RCR):** Following ethical and scientific standards and legal and institutional rules in the conduct of research. See also ethics, research integrity.

**Retraction:** Withdrawing or removing a published paper from the research record because the data or results have subsequently been found to be unreliable or because the paper involves research misconduct. Journals publish retraction notices and identify retracted papers in electronic databases to alert the scientific community to problems with the paper. See correction.

**Review of the literature:** (1) A search of the professional literature to provide background knowledge of what has already been examined or tested in a specific problem area. (2) Use of any information source, such as a computerized database, to locate existing data or information on a research problem, question, or hypothesis.

**Right:** A legal or moral entitlement. Rights generally imply duties or obligations. For example, if A has a right not be killed, then B has a duty not to kill A.

**Risk:** The product of the probability and magnitude (or severity) of a potential harm.

**Risk/benefit analysis:** A process for determining an acceptable level of risk, given the potential benefits of an activity or technology. See also risk minimization, precautionary principle.

**Risk minimization:** In human subjects research, the ethical and legal principle that the risks to the research participants

should be minimized using appropriate methods, procedures, or other safety measures.

**Risks, reasonable:** In human subjects research, the ethical and legal principle that the risks to the subjects should be reasonable in relation to the benefits to the subjects or society. See risk/benefit analysis, social value.

**Rival hypothesis:** A hypothesis that is a plausible alternative to the research hypothesis and might explain the results as well or better; a hypothesis involving extraneous or intervening variables other than the independent variable in the research hypothesis; also referred to as an alternative hypothesis.

**Rules of correspondence:** A characteristic of measurement stipulating that numerals or symbols are assigned to properties of individuals, objects, or events according to specified rules.

**Salami science:** Dividing a scientific project into the smallest papers that can be published (least publishable unit) to maximize the total publications from the project. See questionable research practices.

**Sample:** A subset of a population of individuals, objects, or events chosen to participate in or to be considered in a research study.

**Sampling error:** (1) The degree of difference that can be expected between the sample and the population from which it was drawn. (2) A mistake in a research study's results that is due to sampling procedures.

**Sampling frame:** A listing of units (people, objects, or events) in a population from which a sample is drawn.

**Sampling plan:** A method of selecting members of a population for inclusion in a research study, using procedures that make it possible to draw inferences about the population from the sample statistics.

**Sampling theory:** The logic of using methods to ensure that a sample and a population are similar in all relevant characteristics.

**Saturation:** The point at which no further themes are generated when data from more participants are included in the analysis. The sampling process can be considered to be complete at this point.

**Scale:** A measuring instrument composed of several items that are logically or empirically structured to measure a construct.

**Scattergram:** A graphic representation of the relationship between two interval- or ratio-level variables.

**Science:** Knowledge that has been obtained and tested through use of positivist and interpretive research studies.

**Scientific community:** A group that shares the same general norms for both research activity and acceptance of scientific findings and explanations.

**Scientific determinism:** See determinism.

**Scientific method:** A generic method with specified steps for solving problems; the principles and procedures used in the systematic pursuit of knowledge.

**Scientific (or academic) freedom:** The institutional and government obligation to refrain from interfering in the conduct or publication of research, or the teaching and discussion of scientific ideas. See censorship.

**Scientific validity (or rigor):** Processes, procedures, and methods used to ensure that a study is well designed to test a hypothesis or theory.

**Scope of a study:** The extent to which a problem area is covered in a single research study; a criterion for selecting a data-collection method.

**Score:** A numerical value assigned to an observation; also called data.

**Search statement:** A statement developed by the researcher before a literature search that contains terms that can be combined to elicit specific data.

**Secondary analysis:** An unobtrusive data-collection method in which available data that predate the formulation of a research study are used to answer the research question or test the hypothesis.

**Secondary content data:** Existing text data.

**Secondary data:** The term refers to data that were collected for other studies. For the first researcher they are primary data, but for the second researcher they are secondary data.

**Secondary data sources:** A data source that provides nonoriginal, secondhand data.

**Secondary source:** A source that comments on, analyzes, or otherwise relies on primary sources. An article in a newspaper that reports on a scientific discovery or a book that analyzes a writer's work is a secondary source. See also primary source.

**Secondhand data:** Data obtained from people who are indirectly connected to the problem being studied.

**Selection-treatment interaction:** The relationship between the manner of selecting research participants and their response to the independent variable; a threat to external validity.

**Self-administered questionnaire (self-report):** A set of written questions that the person being studied fills out and returns to the researcher.

**Self-anchored scales:** A rating scale in which research participants rate themselves on a continuum of values, according to their own referents for each point.

**Self-awareness:** A psychological state in which individuals focus their attention on and evaluate different aspects of their self-concepts.

**Self-deception:** In science, deceiving one's self in the conduct of research. Self-deception is a form of bias that may be intentional or unintentional (subconscious).

**Self-disclosure:** Shared communication about oneself, including one's behaviors, beliefs, and attitudes.

**Self-regulation:** Regulation of an activity by individuals involved in that activity as opposed to regulation by the government. See also law.

**Self-selection:** A way of choosing the people for a study by letting them set themselves apart from a larger group in some way; for example, by responding to a questionnaire or by going to a program.

**Semantic differential scale:** A modified measurement scale in which research participants rate their perceptions of the variable under study along three dimensions—evaluation, potency, and activity.

**Sequential triangulation:** When two distinct and separate phases of a research study are conducted and the results of the first phase are considered essential for planning the second phase; research questions in phase 1 are answered before research questions in phase 2 are formulated.

**Service recipients:** People who use human services—individuals, couples, families, groups, organizations, and communities; also known as clients or consumers; a stakeholder group in evaluation.

**Setting:** A place where the research study is carried out. "Place" here refers to more than just the physical location—it also includes the people, artifacts, language used, and intangible aspects (like beliefs) of that location.

**Sharing:** A key ingredient of a social work researcher and practitioner.

**Significance:** A mathematical test of whether a study's results could be caused by chance or whether they really show what they seem to show.

**Simple random sampling:** A one-stage probability sampling procedure in which members of a population are selected one at a time, without a chance of being selected again, until the desired sample size is obtained.

**Simultaneous triangulation:** When the results of a positivist and interpretive research question are answered at the same time; results to the interpretive research questions, for example, are reported separately and do not necessarily relate to, or confirm, the results from the positivist phase.

**Situationalists:** Researchers who assert that certain research approaches (interpretive or positivist) are appropriate for specific situations.

**Situation-specific variable:** A variable that may be observable only in certain environments and under certain circumstances, or with particular people.

**Size of a study:** The number of people, places, or systems that are included in a single research study; a criterion for selecting a data-collection method.

**Skeptic:** A key ingredient of a social work researcher and practitioner.

**Snowball sampling:** A nonprobability sampling procedure in which individuals selected for inclusion in a sample are asked to identify other individuals from the population who might be included; useful to locate people with divergent points of view.

**Social desirability:** (1) A response set in which research participants tend to answer questions in a way that they perceive as giving favorable impressions of themselves. (2) The inclination of data providers to report data that present a socially desirable impression of themselves or their reference groups; also referred to as "impression management."

**Socially acceptable response:** Bias in an answer that comes from research participants trying to answer questions as they think a "good" person should, rather than in a way that reveals what they actually believe or feel.

**Social problems:** Problems social work researchers wish to solve. The problems must be changeable.

**Social responsibility:** In science, the obligation to avoid harmful societal consequences from one's research and to promote good ones.

**Social value:** (1) The social benefits expected to be gained from a scientific study, such as new knowledge or the development of a medical treatment or other technology. (2) The ethical principle that human subjects research should be expected to yield valuable results for society.

**Social work research:** A systematic and objective inquiry that utilizes the scientific method of inquiry to solve human problems and creates new knowledge that is generally applicable to the social work profession.

**Sociocentric thinking:** Results when people do not understand the degree to which they have uncritically internalized the dominant prejudices of their society or culture.

**Socioeconomic variables:** Any one of several measures of social rank, usually including income, education, and occupational prestige; the combined measure indicates socioeconomic status (SES).

**Solomon four-group design:** An explanatory research design with four randomly assigned groups, two experimental and two control; the dependent variable is measured before and after treatment for one experimental and one control group, but only after treatment for the other two groups, and only experimental groups receive the treatment.

**Special populations:** Groups of people who cannot be studied in the same way and by the same rules as other groups for some reason.

**Specificity:** One of the four criteria for evaluating research hypotheses.

**Split-half method:** A method for establishing the reliability of a measuring instrument by dividing it into comparable halves and comparing the scores between the two halves.

**Split-half reliability:** A measure of how well the different parts of a measuring instrument are working together; found by comparing half the items with the other half (for example, the odd-numbered items with the even-numbered items).

**Spot-check recording:** A method of data collection that involves direct observation of the target problem at specified intervals rather than on a continuous basis.

**Stakeholder:** A person or group of people having a direct or indirect interest in the results of an evaluation.

**Stakeholder service evaluation model:** According to proponents of this evaluation model, program evaluations will be more likely to be used—and thus have a greater impact on social problems—when they are tailored to the needs of stakeholders. In this model, the purpose of program evaluation is not to generalize findings to other sites but rather to restrict the evaluation effort to a particular program.

**Standard deviation:** Provides a picture of how the scores distribute themselves around the mean.

**Standardized measuring instrument:** A professionally developed measuring instrument that provides for uniform administration and scoring and generates normative data against which later results can be evaluated.

**Standard operating procedures (SOPs):** Rules and procedures for performing an activity, such as conducting or reviewing research.

**Statistical significance:** A measure of the degree that an observed result (such as relationship between two variables) is due to chance. Statistical significance is usually expressed as a p value. A p value of 0.05, for example, means that the observed result will probably occur as a result of chance only 5% of the time.

**Statistics:** The branch of mathematics concerned with the collection and analysis of data using statistical techniques.

**Stereotypes:** Generalizations or assumptions that people make about the characteristics of all members of a group based on an inaccurate image about what people in that group are like.

**Stratification:** A way of ordering individual people within a social system. The different rungs of the ladder depend on, for example, income, education, work, or power. The term can also mean ranking anything on different levels, by group or category.

**Stratified random sampling:** A one-stage probability sampling procedure in which a population is divided into two or more strata to be sampled separately, using simple random or systematic random sampling techniques.

**Structured interview schedule:** A complete list of questions to be asked and spaces for recording the answers. The interview schedule is used by interviewers when questioning respondents.

**Structured observation:** A data-collection method in which people are observed in their natural environments using specified methods and measurement procedures. See direct observation.

**Study blind policy:** Guidelines designed to limit or prohibit access of data by unauthorized users in a study.

**Subject selection:** Rules for including/excluding human subjects in research. Subject selection should be equitable; that is, subjects should be included or excluded for legitimate scientific or ethical reasons. For example, a clinical trial might exclude subjects who do not have the disease under investigation or are too sick to take part in the study safely. See risk minimization, justice.

**Subjective inclusion scales:** A set of items in a questionnaire designed to measure personal impressions or feeling about a subject. An example of a question might be, "How do you feel about other people?"

**Subjective measures:** Any measure that is based on the researcher's feelings or intuitions about the topic being studied.

**Subscale:** A component of a scale that measures some part or aspect of a major construct; also composed of several items that are logically or empirically structured.

**Summated scale:** A questionnaire-type scale in which research participants are asked to indicate the degree of their agreement or disagreement with a series of questions.

**Summative evaluation:** A type of evaluation that examines the ultimate success of a program and assists with decisions about whether a program should be continued or chosen in the first place among program options.

**Summative measuring instrument:** A type of measuring instrument in which multiple responses are usually combined to form a single overall score for a respondent; also called a questionnaire-type scale.

**Surrogate decision-maker:** See legal authorized representative.

**Survey research:** A data-collection method that uses survey-type instruments to obtain opinions or answers from a population or sample of research participants in order to describe or study them as a group.

**Synthesis:** Undertaking the search for meaning in our sources of information at every step of the research process; combining parts such as data, concepts, and theories to arrive at a higher level of understanding.

**Systematic error:** Measurement error that is consistent, not random.

**Systematic random sampling:** A one-stage probability sampling procedure in which every person at a designated interval in a specific population is selected to be included in a research study's sample.

**Systematic:** Methodical; used to refer to how the steps of a research study are arranged.

**Systematic review:** A comprehensive review of a body of data, or a series of studies, that uses explicit methods to locate primary studies representing the gold standard of evidence (i.e., randomized controlled trials), appraise them, and then summarize them according to a standard methodology.

**Target population:** The group about whom a researcher wants to draw conclusions; another term for a population about whom one aims to make inferences.

**Target problem:** (1) In case-level evaluation designs, the problem social workers seek to solve for their clients. (2) A measurable behavior, feeling, or cognition that is either a problem in itself or symptomatic of some other problem.

**Temporal research design:** A research study that includes time as a major variable. The purpose of this design is to investigate change in the distribution of a variable or in relationships among variables over time. There are three types of temporal research designs: cohort, panel, and trend.

**Temporal stability:** Consistency of responses to a measuring instrument over time; reliability of an instrument across forms and across administrations.

**Testability:** The ability to test a hypothesis or theory. Scientific hypotheses and theories should be testable.

**Testing effect:** The effect that taking a pretest might have on posttest scores; a threat to internal validity.

**Test-retest reliability:** Reliability of a measuring instrument established through repeated administration to the same group of individuals.

**Thematic notes:** In observational research, a record of emerging ideas, hypotheses, theories, and conjectures. They provide a place for the researcher to speculate and identify themes, link ideas and events, and articulate thoughts as they emerge in the field setting.

**Theme:** In a qualitative data analysis, a concept or idea that describes a single category or a grouping of categories; an abstract interpretation of qualitative data.

**Theoretical framework:** A frame of reference that serves to guide a research study and is developed from theories, findings from a variety of other studies, and the researcher's personal experiences.

**Theoretical sampling:** A procedure in grounded theory for selecting participants on the basis of whether or not they will contribute to the development of the theory.

**Theory:** A reasoned set of propositions, derived from and supported by established data, that serves to explain a group of phenomena; a conjectural explanation that may or may not be supported by data generated from interpretive and positivist research studies.

**Therapeutic misconception:** The tendency for human subjects in clinical research to believe that the study is designed to benefit them personally; the tendency for the subjects of clinical research to overestimate the benefits of research and underestimate the risks.

**Thick description:** Refers to the rich, vivid descriptions and interpretations that researchers create as they collect data. It encompasses the circumstances, meanings, intentions, strategies, and motivations that characterize the participants, research setting, and events. Thick description helps researchers paint a meticulous picture for the reader.

**Thought units:** In discourse analysis, thought units are segments of the transcribed text that reflect a particular thought or idea.

**Three Rs:** Ethical guidelines for protecting animal welfare in research, including reduction (reducing the number of animals used in research), replacement (replacing higher species with lower ones, or replacing animals with cells or computer models), and refinement (refining research methods to minimize pain and suffering).

**Time orientation:** An important cultural factor that considers whether one is more focused on the future, the present, or the past. For instance, individuals who are "present oriented" would not be as preoccupied with advance planning as those who are "future oriented."

**Time-series design:** See interrupted time-series design.

**Tools:** Ways of testing or measuring, such as questionnaires or rating scales.

**Tradition:** Traditional cultural beliefs that we accept without question as true; one of the five ways of knowing.

**Transcribing data:** A process of converting verbal data to written data for analysis.

**Transcript:** An electronic, written, printed, or typed copy of interview data or any other written material that have been gathered for an interpretive research study.

**Transferability:** Refers to the degree to which the results of qualitative research can be generalized or transferred to other contexts or settings. That decision is made by the reader; the qualitative researcher can enhance transferability by thoroughly describing the research setting using thick description, and clearly stating the assumptions that were central to the research study.

**Transition statements:** Sentences used to indicate a change in direction or focus of questions in a measuring instrument.

**Transparency:** In science, openly disclosing information that concerned parties would want to know, such as financial interests or methodological assumptions. See also conflict of interest, management.

**Treatment group:** See experimental group.

**Trend study:** A longitudinal study design in which data from surveys carried out at periodic intervals on samples drawn from a particular population are used to reveal trends over time.

**Trials:** Repetition of a research study, or parts of it. Increasing the number of times a research study is repeated allows for averaging of data and "better" analysis.

**Triangulation:** The idea of combining different research methods in all steps associated with a single research study; assumes that any bias inherent in one particular method will be neutralized when used in conjunction with other research methods; seeks convergence of a study's results, often using more than one research method and source of data to study the same phenomenon and to enhance validity. There are several types of triangulation, but the essence of the term is that multiple perspectives are compared. It can involve multiple data sources or multiple data analyzers; the hope is that the different perspectives will confirm each other, adding weight to the credibility and dependability of qualitative data analysis.

**Triangulation design:** A mixed methods design in which quantitative and qualitative data are collected and analyzed concurrently and then compared to understand the research problem more completely.

**Triangulation of analysts:** Using multiple data analysts to code a single segment of a transcript and comparing the amount of agreement between them; a method used to verify coding of qualitative data.

**Trustworthiness:** Refers to standards for judging the quality and usefulness of qualitative research studies, which are composed of criteria for methodologically.

**T-test:** A statistical test of the difference between two group "means."

**Tuskegee Syphilis Study:** A study, sponsored by the U.S. Department of Health, Education, and Welfare, conducted in Tuskegee, Alabama, from 1932 to 1972, which involved observing the progression of untreated syphilis in African American men. The men were not told they were in a research study; they thought they were getting treatment for "bad blood." Researchers also steered them away from clinics where they could receive penicillin when it became available as a treatment for syphilis in the 1940s.

**Two-phase research model:** A model combining interpretive and positivist research approaches in a single study where each approach is conducted as a separate and distinct phase of the study.

**Two-tailed hypotheses:** Statements that do not predict specific relationships between independent and dependent variables.

**Type I error:** A mistake based on saying there is a difference when there is not.

**Type II error:** A mistake based on saying there isn't a difference when there is.

**Typology:** A system that groups information into different types.

**Unanticipated problem (UP):** An unexpected problem that occurs in human subjects research. Serious UPs that are related to research and suggest a greater risk of harm to subjects or others should be promptly reported to institutional review boards and other authorities.

**Undue influence:** Taking advantage of someone's vulnerability to convince them to make a decision.

**Unit of analysis:** A specific research participant (person, object, or event) or the sample or population relevant to the research question; the persons or things being studied; what size or number is being counted as separate within a larger group in a study. Units of analysis in research are often persons but may be groups, political parties, newspaper editorials, unions, hospitals, or schools. A particular unit of analysis from which data are gathered is called a case.

**Univariate:** A hypothesis or research design involving a single variable.

**Universe:** See population.

**Unobtrusive methods:** Data-collection methods that do not influence the variable under study or the responses of research participants; methods that avoid reactive effects.

**Unstructured interviews:** A series of questions that allow flexibility for both the research participant and the interviewer to make changes during the process.

**Utilitarianism:** An ethical theory that holds that the right thing to do is to produce the greatest balance of good/bad consequences for the greatest number of people. Act utilitarians focus on good resulting from particular actions; rule utilitarians focus on happiness resulting from following rules. Utilitarians may equate the good with happiness, satisfaction of preferences, or some other desirable outcomes. See also consequentialism, ethical theory.

**Validity:** (1) The extent to which a measuring instrument measures the variable it is supposed to measure and measures it accurately. (2) The degree to which an instrument is able to do what it is intended to do, in terms of both experimental procedures and measuring instruments (internal validity) and generalizability of results (external validity). (3) The degree to which scores on a measuring instrument correlate with measures of performance on some other criterion.

**Value:** Something that is worth having or desiring, such as happiness, knowledge, justice, or virtue.

**Value awareness:** A key ingredient of a social work researcher and practitioner.

**Value, instrumental:** Something that is valuable for the sake of achieving something else; for example, a visit to the dentist is valuable for dental health.

**Value, intrinsic:** Something that is valuable for its own sake, such as happiness, human life.

**Value, scale of:** The idea that some things can be ranked on a scale of moral value. For example, one might hold that human beings are more valuable than other sentient animals, sentient animals are more valuable than nonsentient animals, and so on. Some defenders of animal experimentation argue that harming animals in research to benefit human beings can be justified because human beings are more valuable than animals.

**Value (statistical):** An amount written in numbers, not in words or pictures.

**Variable:** A concept with characteristics that can take on different values.

**Verbatim recording:** Recording interview data word for word and including significant gestures, pauses, and expressions of persons in the interview.

**Virtue:** A morally good or desirable character trait, such as honesty, courage, compassion, modesty, and fairness.

**Virtue ethics:** An ethical theory that emphasizes developing virtue as opposed to following rules or maximizing good/bad consequences.

**Visual diagram:** A graphical representation of the research procedures used in a mixed methods study.

**Voluntariness:** The ability to make a free (uncoerced) choice.

**Vulnerable subject:** A research subject who has an increased susceptibility to harm or exploitation due to his or her compromised ability to make decisions or advocate for his/her interests or dependency. Vulnerability may be based on age, mental disability, institutionalization, language barriers, socioeconomic deprivation, or other factors. See decision-making capacity, informed consent.

**Whistleblower:** A person who reports suspected illegal or unethical activity, such as research misconduct or noncompliance with human subjects or animal regulations. Various laws and institutional policies protect whistleblowers from retaliation.

**Wideband measuring instrument:** An instrument that measures more than one variable.

**Within-methods research approach:** Triangulation by using different research methods available in either the interpretive or the positivist research approaches in a single research study.

**Words:** The basic data unit of analysis used in interpretive research studies.

**Worker cooperation:** The actions and attitudes of program personnel when carrying out a research study within an existing social service program; a criterion for selecting a data-collection method.

**Working hypothesis:** An assertion about a relationship between two or more variables that may not be true but is plausible and worth examining.

# Credits

"I've got to give credit where credit is due.
I didn't do it. Bobbie did."

METHODOLOGICAL CONTENT has been adapted and modified from: Grinnell, R. M., Jr., Williams, M., & Unrau, Y. A. (2018). *Research methods for social workers: An Introduction* (12th ed. and all previous editions). Kalamazoo, MI: Pair Bond Publications LLC.

CARTOONS: © Randy Glasbergen, Inc. Permission to modify original cartoon captions granted by Karen and Christie Glasbergen, Glasbergen Cartoon Service, Inc.

Boxes: 1.1: From *Calgary Herald,* "Another kidnap bid has parents nervous," September 6, 1991, p. 1. Used with permission; 1.2: Adapted and modified from: Skills You Need. (2019, July 1). *Critical thinking skills.* Retrieved from: https://www.skillsyouneed.com/personal-skills.html; 2.1: From *Calgary Herald,* "Show ignores Native stereotype," September 6, 1991, Section B, p. 6. Used with permission; 2.2: Adapted and modified from: Manuel, J. I., Fang, L., Bellamy, J. L., Bledsoe, S. E., (2018). Evaluating existing evidence. In R. M. Grinnell, Jr., & Y. A. Unrau (Eds.). *Social work research and evaluation: Foundations of evidence-based practice* (11th ed., pp. 229–247). New York: Oxford University Press; 2.3, 3.1, 6.4: Adapted and modified from: Bassham, G., Irwin, W., Nardone, H., & Wallace, J. M. (2011). *Critical thinking: A student's introduction* (4th ed.). New York: McGraw-Hill. 4.1: Adapted and modified from: William M. K. Trochim, *Research Methods Knowledge Base.* Retrieved July 22, 2010 at: www.socialresearch methods.net. 4.2: Adapted and modified from: Nosich, G. M. (2009). *Learning to think things through: A guide to critical thinking across the curriculum.* Upper Saddle River, NJ: Pearson/Prentice Hall. 6.1 & 6.3: Adapted and modified from: McKinney, R. (2018). Research with minority and disadvantaged groups. In R. M. Grinnell, Jr., & Y. A. Unrau (Eds.). *Social work research and evaluation: Foundations of evidence-based practice* (11th ed., pp. 163–192). New York: Oxford University Press. 6.2 & 6.4: Adapted and modified from: Paul, R., & Elder, L. (2016). *Critical thinking: Concepts & tools* (7th. ed.). Tomales, CA: Foundation for Critical Thinking. 7.1 & Table 7.1: Adopted and modified from: Kumar, R. (2014). *Research methodology: A step-by-step guide for beginners* (4th ed.). Thousand Oaks, CA: Sage. 7.2: Adapted and modified from: Silverman, D. (2010). *Qualitative research* (3rd ed.). Thousand Oaks, CA: Sage. 11.1 & 11.2: Adapted and modified from: Kyte, N. S., & Bostwick, G. J., Jr. (1981). Measurement. In R. M. Grinnell, Jr. (Ed.), *Social work research and evaluation.* Itasca, IL: F. E. Peacock. Used with permission; 11.3 & 13.1: Adapted and modified from: McKinney, R. (2011). Research with minority and disadvantaged groups. In R. M. Grinnell, Jr., & Y. A. Unrau (Eds.). *Social work research and evaluation: Foundations of evidence-based practice* (10th ed.). New York: Oxford University Press. Used with permission; 15.1–15.3: Adapted and modified from: *Web Center for Social Research Methods.* (2017, July 22). Retrieved from: www.socialresearch methods.net; 16.1: Adapted and modified from: Centers for Disease Control and Prevention (November 2008). *Data collection methods for program evaluation: Questionnaires.* Atlanta: Author. Used with permission; 16.1a: Adapted and modified from: Centers for Disease Control and Prevention (July 2010). *Using incentives to boost response rates.* Atlanta: Author. Used with permission; 16.2: Adapted and modified from: Centers for Disease Control and Prevention (January 2009). *Data collection methods for program evaluation: Interviews.* Atlanta: Author. Used with permission; 16.3: Adapted and modified from: Centers for Disease Control and Prevention (July 2008). *Data collection methods for program evaluation: Focus Groups.* Atlanta: Author. Used with permission; 16.4: Adapted and modified from: Centers for Disease Control and Prevention (December 2008). *Data collection methods for program evaluation: Observation.* Atlanta: Author. Used with permission; 16.5: Adapted and modified from: Centers for Disease Control and Prevention (January 2009). *Data collection methods for program evaluation: Document Review.* Atlanta: Author. Used with permission; 19.1: Adapted and modified from: Centers for Disease Control and Prevention (April 2009). *Analyzing qualitative data for evaluation.* Atlanta: Author. Used with permission; and Box A: Adapted and modified from Leo Babautta, *10 ways to do what you don't want to do.* (2019, June 1). Retrieved from https://zenhabits.net/unwanted

FIGURES: 3.1: From: Duehn, W. D. (1985). Practice and research. In R. M. Grinnell, Jr. (Ed.), *Social work research and evaluation* (2nd ed.). Itasca, IL: F. E. Peacock. Used with permission; 11.1 & 11.1a: From: Walter W. Hudson. Copyright © 1993 by WALMYR Publishing Company. Used with permission; 12.1: From: Reid, P. N., & Gundlach, J. H. (1983). A scale for the measurement of consumer satisfaction with social services, *Journal of Social Service Research, 7,* 37–54. Used with permission; 14.8–14.10 (and related text): From: Polster, R., & Lynch, M. (1981).

Single-subject designs. In R. M. Grinnell, Jr. (Ed.), *Social work research and evaluation.* Itasca: IL: F. E. Peacock Publishers. Used with permission; 18.3 & 18.4: From: Beless, D. W. (1981). Univariate analysis. In R. M. Grinnell, Jr. (Ed.), *Social work research and evaluation.* Itasca, IL: F. E. Peacock Publishers. Used with permission;

CHAPTERS: 4: By Vivienne Bozalek and Nelleke Bak; 5: By Andre Ivanoff and Betty Blythe; 6: By Carol Ing; 10: Adapted and modified from: Creswell, J. W., & Plano Clark, V. L. (2007). *Designing and conducting mixed-methods research.* Thousand Oaks, CA: Sage. Reprinted with permission; 18 & 20: Adapted and modified from: Williams, M., Tutty, L. M., & Grinnell, R. M., Jr. (1995). *Research in social work: An introduction* (2nd ed.). Itasca, IL: F.E. Peacock. Used with permission;

APPENDIXES: A & B: Adapted and modified from: Black, T. R. (2001). *Understanding social science research: An introduction* (2nd ed.). Thousand Oaks, CA: Sage; Bonaccorsi, A. (2018). *The evaluation of research in social sciences and humanities: Lessons from the Italian experience.* New York: Springer; Carr, S., & Bostock, L. (2015). Appraising the quality of evidence. In M. Webber (Ed.). *Applying research evidence in social work practice* (pp. 44–58). London: Palgrave Macmillan; Evans, T. (2015). Using evidence to inform decision-making. In M. Webber (Ed.). *Applying research evidence in social work practice* (pp. 77–90). London: Palgrave Macmillan; Fischer, J. (1981). A framework for evaluating empirical research reports. In R. M. Grinnell, Jr. (Ed.). *Social work research and evaluation* (pp. 569–589). Itasca, IL: F. E. Peacock; Hart, V. (2015). Using research evidence in practice: A view from the ground. In M. Webber (Ed.). *Applying research evidence in social work practice* (pp. 91–107). London: Palgrave Macmillan; Grinnell, R. M., Jr., & Unrau, Y. A. (2013). *Social work research proposals: A workbook.* Kalamazoo, MI: Pair Bond Publications; Harris, S. R. (2014). *How to critique journal articles in the social sciences.* Thousand Oaks, CA: Sage; Holosko, M. J. (2005). *A primer for critiquing social research: A student guide.* Belmont, CA: Thomson Nelson, Brooks/Cole; Holosko, M. J. (2006). A suggested authors' checklist for submitting manuscripts to *Research on Social Work Practice. Research on Social Work Practice, 16,* 449–454; Holosko, M. J. (2018). Evaluating quantitative studies. In R. M. Grinnell, Jr., & Y. A. Unrau. (Eds.). *Social work research and evaluation: Foundations of evidence-based practice* (11th ed., pp. 573–596). New York: Oxford University Press; Litz, C. A., & Zayas, L. E. (2018). Evaluating qualitative studies. In R.

M. Grinnell, Jr., & Y. A. Unrau. (Eds.). *Social work research and evaluation: Foundations of evidence-based practice* (11th ed., pp. 597–611). New York: Oxford University Press; Lomand, T. C. (2012). *Social science research: A cross section of journal articles for discussion & evaluation* (7th ed.). New York: Routledge; National Association of Social Workers. (2005). *Perspectives: Peer review & publication standards in social work journals:* The Miami statement. *Social Work Research, 29,* 119–121; Pyrczak, F. (2016). *Evaluating research in academic journals: A practical guide to realistic education* (6th ed.). Los Angeles, CA: Pyrczak Publications; Ross, P. D. S. (2015). Locating evidence for practice. In M. Webber (Ed.). *Applying research evidence in social work practice* (pp. 22–43). London: Palgrave Macmillan; Stern, P. C. (1979). *Evaluating social science research.* New York: Oxford University Press; Thyer, B. A. (1991). Guidelines for evaluating outcome studies on social work practice. *Research on Social Work Practice, 1,* 76–91; Thyer, B. A. (1994). *Successful publishing in scholarly journals.*

Thousand Oaks, CA: Sage; Webber, M., & Carr, S. (2015). Applying research evidence in social work practice: Seeing beyond paradigms. In M. Webber (Ed.). *Applying research evidence in social work practice* (pp. 3–21). London: Palgrave Macmillan; and The Writing Center. (2018). *Checklist for analyzing research material.* Chapel Hill, NC: University of North Carolina. Appendix C: Adapted and modified from: Singh, R., Singh, R. K., & Srivastava, A. K. (2005 December). *Untangling the web: Evaluating internet resources.* Paper presented at the 25th annual conference of the Indian Association of Special Libraries and Information Centers, Chennai India. Used with permission.

GLOSSARY: See previous entries in Grinnell, R. M., Jr., Williams, M., & Unrau, Y. A. (2018). *Research methods for social workers: An introduction* (12th ed. and all previous editions). Kalamazoo, MI: Pair Bond Publications, LLC; and Shamoo A. E., & Resnik D. B. (2015). *Responsible conduct of research* (3rd ed.). New York: Oxford University Press.

# References and Further Readings

"Paperback books are very interesting but I find they will never replace hardcover books—they make very poor doorstops."

Ames, G. M., Duke, M. R., Moore, R. S., & Cunradi, C. B. (2009). The impact of occupational culture on drinking behavior of young adults in the U.S. Navy. *Journal of Mixed Methods Research, 3,* 129–150.

Bassham, G., Irwin, W., Nardone, H., & Wallace, J. M. (2011). *Critical thinking: A student's introduction* (4th ed.). New York: McGraw-Hill.

Bigby, M. (1998). Evidence-based medicine in a nutshell. *Archives of Dermatology, 134,* 1609–1618.

Black, T. R. (1999). Doing quantitative research in the social sciences: An integrated approach to research design, measurement, and statistics. Thousand Oaks, CA: Sage.

Black, T. R. (2001). *Understanding social science research: An introduction* (2nd ed.). Thousand Oaks, CA: Sage.

Bloom, M., Fischer, J., & Orme, J. (2009). *Evaluating practice: Guidelines for the accountable professional* (6th ed.). Englewood Cliffs, NJ: Prentice-Hall.

Bonaccorsi, A. (2018). *The evaluation of research in social sciences and humanities: Lessons from the Italian experience.* New York: Springer.

Bostwick, G. J., Jr., & Kyte, N. S. (2018). Measurement. In R. M. Grinnell, Jr., & Y. A. Unrau (Eds.), *Social work research and evaluation: Foundations of evidence-based practice* (11th ed., pp. 275–295). New York: Oxford University Press.

Brett, J. A., Heimendinger, J., Boender, C., Morin, C., & Marshall, J. A. (2002). *Using ethnography to improve intervention design. American Journal of Health Promotion, 16*(6), 331–340.

Bronson, D. E. (2009). Critically appraising studies for evidence-based practice. In A. R. Roberts (Ed.), *Social workers' desk reference* (2nd ed., pp. 1137–1141). New York: Oxford University Press.

Caelli, K., Ray, L., & Mill, J. (2003). Clear as mud: Toward greater clarity in generic qualitative research. *International Journal of Qualitative Methods, 2*(2), Article 1. Retrieved from http://www.ualberta.ca/~iiqm/backissues /pdf/caellietal.pdf.

Carr, S., & Bostock, L. (2015). Appraising the quality of evidence. In M. Webber (Ed.), *Applying research evidence in social work practice* (pp. 44–58). London: Palgrave Macmillan.

Classen, S., Lopez, D. D. S., Winter, S., Awadz, K. D., Ferree, N., & Garvan, C. W. (2007). Population-based health promotion perspective for older driver safety: Conceptual framework to intervention plan. *Clinical Intervention in Aging, 2,* 677–693.

Coleman, H., & Unrau, Y. (2018). Qualitative data analysis. In R. M. Grinnell, Jr., & Y. A. Unrau (Eds.), *Social work research and evaluation: Foundations of evidence-based practice* (11th ed., pp. 549–570). New York: Oxford University Press.

Colorado State University's Writing Center (2019).https://writingcenter.colostate.edu.

Cooper, H., & Hedges, L. V. (1994). *The handbook of research synthesis.* New York: Russell Sage Foundation.

Cooper, J., Calloway-Thomas, C., & Simonds, C. J. (2007). Non-verbal communication. In P. J. Cooper, C. Calloway-Thomas, & C. J. Simonds (Eds.), *Intercultural communication: A text with readings* (pp. 132–142). Boston: Pearson.

Corcoran, J., & Littell, J. H. (2009). Meta-analysis and evidence-based practice. In A. R. Roberts (Ed.), *Social workers' desk reference* (2nd ed., pp. 1149–1152). New York: Oxford University Press.

Corcoran, K., & Hozack, N. (2010). Locating assessment instruments. In B. Thyer (Ed.), *The handbook of social work research methods* (2nd ed.). Thousand Oaks, CA: Sage.

Corcoran, K., & Roberts, A. R. (Eds.). (2015). *Social workers' desk reference* (3rd ed.). New York: Oxford University Press.

Council on Social Work Education (2015). *Baccalaureate and masters curriculum policy statements.* Alexandria, VA: Author.

Creswell, J. W. (2010). *Designing and conducting mixed-methods research* (2nd ed.). Thousand Oaks, CA: Sage.

Creswell, J. W., & Miller, D. L. (2000). Determining validity in qualitative inquiry. *Theory into Practice, 39,* 124–130.

Creswell, J. W., & Plano Clark, V. L. (2017). *Designing and conducting mixed methods research* (3rd ed.). Thousand Oaks, CA: Sage.

Davies, D., & Dodd, J. (2002). Qualitative research and the question of rigor. *Qualitative Health Research, 12,* 279–289.

Denzin, N. K. (1989). *Interpretive interactionism* (2nd ed.). Thousand Oaks, CA: Sage.

Devers, K. J. (1999). How will we know "good" qualitative research when we see it? Beginning the dialogue in health services research. *Health Services Research, 34,* 1153–1188.

Donovan, J., Mills, N., Smith, M., Brindle, L., Jacoby, A., Peters, T., et al. (2002). Improving design and conduct of randomized trials by embedding them in qualitative research: ProectT (Prostate Testing for Cancer and Treatment) study. *British Medical Journal, 325,* 766–769.

Doyle, C. (1901/1955). *A treasury of Sherlock Holmes.* Garden City, NY: Hanover House.

Drisko, J. W. (1997). Strengthening qualitative studies and reports: Standards to promote academic integrity. *Journal of Social Work Education, 33,* 185–197.

Duehn, W. D. (1985). Practice and research. In R. M. Grinnell, Jr. (Ed.), *Social work research and evaluation* (2nd ed., pp. 19–48). Itasca, IL: F. E. Peacock.

Engel, R., & Schutt, K. (2016). *The practice of research in social work* (4th ed.). Thousand Oaks, CA: Sage.

Evans, T. (2015). Using evidence to inform decision-making. In M. Webber (Ed.), *Applying research evidence in social work practice* (pp. 77–90). London: Palgrave Macmillan.

Farmer, J., & Knapp, D. (2008). Interpretation programs at a historic preservation site: A mixed methods study of long-term impact. *Journal of Mixed Methods Research, 2,* 340–361.

Fischer, J. (1981). A framework for evaluating empirical research reports. In R. M. Grinnell, Jr. (Ed.), *Social work research and evaluation* (pp. 569–589). Itasca, IL: F. E. Peacock.

Fischer, J., & Corcoran, K. (2007). *Measures for clinical practice* (3rd ed.). Volume 1: Couples, families, and children. Volume 2:

Adults. New York: Oxford University Press.

Frankel, R. (1999). Standards of qualitative research. In B. Crabtree & W. Miller (Eds.), *Doing qualitative research* (2nd ed., pp. 333–346). Thousand Oaks, CA: Sage.

Frechtling, J. (2002). *The 2002 user friendly handbook for project evaluation.* Alexandra, VA: National Science Foundation.

Friedmann, B. (2007). *The research tool kit: Putting it all together* (2nd ed.). Belmont, CA: Wadsworth.

Fries, C. J. (2009). Bourdieu's reflexive sociology as a theoretical basis for mixed methods research: An application to complementary and alternative medicine. *Journal of Mixed Methods Research, 3,* 326–348.

Gambrill, E. (2003). Evidence-based practice: Sea change or emperor's new clothes. *Journal of Social Work Education, 39,* 3–23.

Gambrill, E. (2006). Evidence-based practice and policy: Choices ahead. *Research on Social Work Practice, 16,* 338–357.

Gambrill, E. (2009). Integrating information from diverse sources in evidence-based practice. In A. R. Roberts (Ed.), *Social workers' desk reference* (2nd ed., pp. 1120–1126). New York: Oxford University Press.

Gambrill, E. (2019). *Critical thinking and the process of evidence-based practice.* New York: Oxford University Press.

Gambrill, E., & Gibbs, L. (2009). Developing well-structured questions for evidence-informed practice. In A. R. Roberts (Ed.), *Social workers' desk reference* (2nd ed., pp. 1120–1126). New York: Oxford University Press.

Geertz, C. (1975). *The interpretation of cultures: Selected essays.* London: Hutchinson.

Gochros, H. L. (2018). Qualitative interviewing. In R. M. Grinnell, Jr., & Y. A. Unrau (Eds.), *Social work research and evaluation: Foundations of evidence-based practice* (11th ed.). New York: Oxford University Press.

Greene, J. C. (2007). *Mixed methods in social inquiry.* San Francisco: Jossey-Bass.

Greene, J. C., Caracelli, V. J., & Graham, W. F. (1989). Toward a conceptual framework for mixed-method evaluation designs. *Educational Evaluation and Policy Analysis, 11*(3), 255–274.

Grinnell, F. (1992). *The scientific attitude* (2nd ed.). Boulder, CO: Westview Press.

Grinnell, R. M., Jr. (1981). Becoming a knowledge-based social worker. In R. M. Grinnell, Jr. (Ed.), *Social work research and evaluation* (pp. 1–8). Itasca, IL: F. E. Peacock.

Grinnell, R. M., Jr. (1985). Becoming a practitioner/researcher. In R. M. Grinnell, Jr. (Ed.), *Social work research and evaluation* (5th ed., pp. 3–24). Itasca, IL: F. E. Peacock.

Grinnell, R. M., Jr. (1993). Group research designs. In R. M. Grinnell, Jr. (Ed.), *Social work research and evaluation* (4th ed., pp. 118–153). Itasca, IL: F. E. Peacock.

Grinnell, R. M., Jr. (1995). The generation of knowledge. In R. M. Grinnell, Jr. (Ed.), *Social work research and evaluation* (2nd ed., pp. 1–15). Itasca, IL: F. E. Peacock.

Grinnell, R. M., Jr. (1997a). The generation of knowledge. In R. M. Grinnell, Jr. (Ed.), *Social work research and evaluation: Quantitative and qualitative approaches* (5th ed., pp. 3–24). Itasca, IL: F. E. Peacock.

Grinnell, R. M., Jr. (1997b). Preface. In R. M. Grinnell, Jr. (Ed.), *Social work research and evaluation: Quantitative and qualitative approaches* (5th ed., pp. xvii–xxvi). Itasca, IL: F. E. Peacock.

Grinnell, R. M., Jr., Rothery, M., & Thomlison, R. J. (1993). Research in social work. In R. M. Grinnell, Jr. (Ed.), *Social work research and evaluation* (4th ed., pp. 2–16). Itasca, IL: F. E. Peacock.

Grinnell, R. M., Jr., & Siegel, D. H. (1988). The place of research in social work. In R. M. Grinnell, Jr. (Ed.), *Social work research and evaluation* (3rd ed., pp. 9–24). Itasca, IL: F. E. Peacock.

Grinnell, R. M., Jr., & Stothers, M. (1988). Research designs. In R. M. Grinnell, Jr. (Ed.), *Social work research and evaluation* (3rd ed., pp. 199–239). Itasca, IL: F. E. Peacock.

Grinnell, R. M., Jr., & Unrau, Y. A. (2013). *Social work research proposals: A workbook.* Kalamazoo, MI: Pair Bond Publications.

Grinnell, R. M., Jr., & Unrau, Y. A. (Eds.). (2018). *Social work research and evaluation: Foundations of evidence-based practice* (11th ed.). New York: Oxford University Press.

Grinnell, R. M., Jr., & Williams, M. (1990). *Research in social work: A primer.* Itasca, IL: F. E. Peacock.

Grinnell, R. M., Jr., Williams, M., & Tutty, L. M. (1997). Case-level evaluation. In R. M. Grinnell, Jr. (Ed.), *Social work research and evaluation: Quantitative and qualitative approaches* (5th ed., pp. 529–559). Itasca, IL: F. E. Peacock.

Grinnell, R. M., Jr., Williams, M., & Unrau, Y. A. (2018a). *Research methods for social workers* (12th ed.). Kalamazoo, MI: Pair Bond Publications.

Grinnell, R. M., Jr., Williams, M., & Unrau, Y. A. (2018b). Why study research? In R. M. Grinnell, Jr., & Y. A. Unrau (Eds.), *Social work research and evaluation: Foundations of evidence-based practice* (11th ed., pp. 2–36). New York: Oxford University Press.

Hall, E. T. (1983). *The dance of life: Other dimensions of time.* New York: Doubleday.

Harris, P. R., & Moran, T. (1996). *Managing cultural differences: Leadership strategies for a new world business* (4th ed.). London: Gulf.

Harris, R. (2018, October 15). *Evaluating Internet research sources.* VirtualSalt. Retrieved from https://www.virtualsalt.com/evalu8it.htm

Harris, S. R. (2014). *How to critique journal articles in the social sciences.* Thousand Oaks, CA: Sage.

Hart, V. (2015). Using research evidence in practice: A view from the ground. In M. Webber (Ed.), *Applying research evidence in social work practice* (pp. 91–107). London: Palgrave Macmillan.

Heidegger, M. (1927/1962). *Being and Time.* San Francisco, CA: Harper. (Original work published 1927).

Higgins, J. P. T., & Green, S. (Eds.). (2005). *Cochrane handbook for systematic reviews of interventions* 4.2.5 [updated May 2005]. In The Cochrane Library, Issue 3. Chichester, UK: Wiley.

Hilton, T. P., Fawson, P. R., Sullivan, T. J., & DeJong, C. R. (2019). *Applied social research: A tool for the human services* (10th ed.). New York: Springer.

Holden, G., & Barker (2018). Should social workers be engaged in these practices? *Journal of Evidence-Informed Social Work, 15*(1), 1–13.

Holosko, M. J. (2005). *A primer for critiquing social research: A student guide.* Belmont, CA: Thomson Nelson, Brooks/Cole.

Holosko, M. J. (2006). A suggested authors' checklist for submitting manuscripts to Research on Social Work Practice. *Research on Social Work Practice, 16,* 449–454.

Holosko, M. J. (2018). Evaluating quantitative studies. In R. M. Grinnell, Jr., & Y. A. Unrau (Eds.), *Social work research and evaluation: Foundations of evidence-based practice* (11th ed., pp. 573–596). New York: Oxford University Press.

Horsburgh, D. (2003). Evaluation of qualitative research. *Journal of Clinical Nursing, 12,* 307–312.

Howard, M. O., Perron, B. E., Vaughn, M. G. (2009). Practice-guidelines and evidence-based practice. In A. R. Roberts (Ed.), *Social workers' desk reference* (2nd ed., pp. 1157–1162). New York: Oxford University Press.

Hudson, W. W. (1982). *The clinical measurement package: A field manual.* Chicago: Dorsey.

Igo, L. B., Kiewra, K. A., & Bruning, R. (2008). Individual differences and intervention flaws: A sequential explanatory study of college students' copy-and-paste note taking. *Journal of Mixed Methods Research, 2,* 149–168.

Ivanoff, A., & Blythe, B. (2018). Research ethics. In R. M. Grinnell, Jr., & Y. A. Unrau (Eds.), *Social work research and evaluation: Foundations of evidence-based practice* (11th ed.). New York: Oxford University Press.

Jadad, A. (1998). *Randomized controlled trials: A user's guide.* London: BMJ Publishing.

Jadad, A. R., Haynes, R. B., Hunt, D., & Browman, G. P. (2000). The Internet and evidence-based decision-making: A needed synergy for efficient knowledge management in health care. *Canadian Medical Association Journal, 162,* 362–365.

Jick, T. D. (1979). Mixing qualitative and quantitative methods: Triangulation in action. *Administrative Science Quarterly, 24,* 602–611.

Johnson, R. B., & Onwuegbuzie, A. J. (2004). Mixed methods research: A research paradigm whose time has come. *Educational Researcher, 33*(7), 14–26.

Jordan, C., Franklin, C., & Corcoran, K. (2018). Standardized measuring instruments. In R. M. Grinnell, Jr., & Y. Unrau (Eds.), *Social work research and evaluation: Foundations of evidence-based practice* (11th ed.). New York: Oxford University Press.

Knodel, J., & Saengtienchai, C. (2005). Older-aged parents: The final safety net for adult sons and daughters with AIDS in Thailand. *Journal of Family Issues, 26,* 665–698.

Koyama, T. (1992). Japan: *A handbook in intercultural communication.* Sydney: National Center for English Language and Teaching and Research.

Krysik, J. (2018). *Research for effective social work practice* (4th ed.). New York: Routledge.

Krysik, J., & Grinnell, R. M., Jr. (1997). Quantitative approaches to the generation of knowledge. In R. M. Grinnell, Jr., & Y. A. Unrau (Eds.), *Social work research and evaluation: Quantitative and qualitative approaches* (5th ed., pp. 67–105). Itasca, IL: F. E. Peacock.

Kumar, R. (1994). *Research methodology: A step-by-step guide for beginners.* White Plains, NY: Longman.

Kutner, J. S., Steiner J. F., Corbett, K. K., Jahnigen, D. W, & Barton, P. L. (1999). Information needs in terminal illness. *Social Science and Medicine, 48,* 1341–1352.

Lazer, D. M., Baum, M. A., Benkler, Y., Berinsky, A. J., Greenhill, K. M., Menczer F., et al. (2018). The science of fake news. *Science, 359,* 1094–1096.

LeCroy, C. W., & Solomon, G. (2001). Content analysis. In R. M. Grinnell, Jr. (Ed.), *Social*

work research and evaluation: Quantitative and qualitative approaches (6th ed., pp. 367–381). Itasca, IL: F. E. Peacock.

Lewis, R. D. (1997). *When cultures collide: Managing successfully across cultures.* London: Nicholas Brealey.

Lilienfeld, S. O., Lynn, S. J., Ruscio, J., & Beyerstein, B. L. (2010). *50 Great myths of popular psychology.* West Sussex, UK: Wiley-Blackwell.

Lincoln, Y. S. (2001). Varieties of validity: Quality in qualitative research. In J. C. Smart & W. G. Tierney (Eds.), *Higher education: Handbook of theory and research* (Vol. 16, pp. 25–72). New York: Agathon Press.

Lincoln, Y. S., & Guba, E. G. (1985). *Naturalistic inquiry.* Thousand Oaks, CA: Sage.

Littell, J. H., & Corcoran, J. (2009). Systematic reviews and evidence-based practice. In A. R. Roberts (Ed.), *Social workers' desk reference* (2nd ed., pp. 1152–1156). New York: Oxford University Press.

Lietz, C. A., Lacasse, J. R., Hayes, M., & Cheung, J. (2013*). How services facilitate the process of mental health recovery: A qualitative examination of service experiences of people diagnosed with Serious Mental Illness* (SMI). Unpublished paper.

Lietz, C. A., Langer, C., & Furman, R. (2006). Establishing trustworthiness in social work research: Implications from a study regarding spirituality. *Qualitative Social Work, 5,* 441–458.

Litz, C. A., & Zayas, L. E. (2018). Evaluating qualitative studies. In R. M. Grinnell, Jr., & Y. A. Unrau (Eds.), *Social work research and evaluation: Foundations of evidence-based practice* (11th ed., pp. 597–611). New York: Oxford University Press.

Lomand, T. C. (2012). *Social science research: A cross section of journal articles for discussion and evaluation* (7th ed.). New York: Routledge.

Lucas, L. (2017). Chapter 7: *Critical thinking and evaluating information.* In EDUC 1300: Effective Learning Strategies. Lumen Learning/Austin Community College. Retrieved from https://courses.lumenlearning.com/austinccclearningframeworks/chapter/chapter-

7-critical-thinking-and-evaluating-information.

Main, T. (1998). How to think about homelessness: Balancing structural and individual causes. *Journal of Social Distress and the Homeless, 7,* 41–54.

Mak, L., & Marshall, S. K. (2004). Perceived mattering in young adults' romantic relationships. *Journal of Social and Personal Relationships, 24,* 469–486.

Manuel, J. I., Fang, L., Bellamy, J. L., Bledsoe, S. E., (2018). Evaluating existing evidence. In R. M. Grinnell, Jr., & Y. A. Unrau (Eds.), *Social work research and evaluation: Foundations of evidence-based practice* (11th ed., pp. 229–247). New York: Oxford University Press.

Maschi, T., & Youdin, R. (2012). *Social worker as researcher: Integrating research with advocacy.* Boston: Pearson.

Mayring, P. (2007). Introduction: Arguments for mixed methodology. In P. Mayring, G. L. Huber, L. Gurtler, & M. Kiegelmann (Eds.), *Mixed methodology in psychological research* (pp. 1–4). Rotterdam/Taipei: Sense Publishers.

McMahon, S. (2007). Understanding community-specific rape myths: Exploring student athlete culture. *Affilia, 22,* 357–370.

Miles, M. B., & Huberman, A. M. (1994). *Qualitative data analysis:* An expanded sourcebook. Thousand Oaks, CA: Sage.

Montgomery, P., & Mayo-Wilson, E. (2009). Randomized controlled trials and evidence-based practice. In A. R. Roberts (Ed.), *Social workers' desk reference* (2nd ed., pp. 1142–1148). New York: Oxford University Press.

Morrow, S. (2007). Qualitative research in counseling psychology: Conceptual foundations. *Counseling Psychologist, 35,* 209–235.

Mullen, E. J., Bellamy, J. L., & Bledsoe, S. E. (2018). Evidence-based practice. In R. M. Grinnell, Jr., & Y. A. Unrau (Eds.), *Social work research and evaluation: Foundations of evidence-based practice* (11th ed., pp. 248–272). New York: Oxford University Press.

Mullins, J., Cheung, J., & Lietz, C. A. (2012). Family preservation services: Incorporating the voice of families into service implementation. *Child and Family Social Work, 17,* 265–274.

National Association of Social Workers. (2005). Perspectives: Peer review & publication standards in social work journals: The Miami Statement. *Social Work Research, 29,* 119–121.

National Association of Social Workers. (2017). *Code of ethics.* Silver Spring, MD: Author.

Neuman, L. W. (2012*). Basics of social research: Qualitative and quantitate approaches* (3rd ed.). Boston: Pearson.

Neuman, L. W., & Robson, K. (2018). *Basics of social research: Qualitative and quantitative approaches* (4th ed.). Don Mills, Ontario: Pearson Canada.

Nosich, G. M. (2009). *Learning to think things through: A guide to critical thinking across the curriculum* (3rd ed.) Upper Saddle River, NJ: Pearson.

Padgett, D. K. (2008). *Qualitative methods in social work research: Challenges and rewards.* Thousand Oaks, CA: Sage.

Paul, R., & Elder, L. (2016). *Critical thinking: Concepts and tools* (7th ed.). Tomales, CA: Foundation for Critical Thinking.

Petticrew, M., & Roberts, H. (2003). Evidence, hierarchies, and typologies: Horses for courses. *Journal of Epidemiology of Community Health, 57,* 527–529.

Plano Clark, V. L. (2005). *Cross-disciplinary analysis of the use of mixed methods in physics education research, counseling psychology, and primary care.* Doctoral dissertation, University of Nebraska at Lincoln, 2005. Dissertation Abstracts International, 66, 02A.

Plano Clark, V. L. (2010). The adoption and practice of mixed methods: U.S. trends in federally funded health-related research. *Qualitative Inquiry, 16,* 428–440.

Plano Clark, V. L., & Badiee, M. (2010). Research questions in mixed methods research. In A. Tashakkori & C. Teddlie (Eds.), *SAGE Handbook of mixed methods in social & behavioral research* (2nd ed.). Thousand Oaks, CA: Sage.

Plano Clark, V. L., & Creswell, J. W. (2010). *Understanding research: A consumer's guide.* Upper Saddle River, NJ: Pearson Education.

Plano Clark, V. L., & Galt, K. (2009, April). *Using a mixed methods approach to strengthen instrument development and validation.* Paper presented at the annual meeting of the American Pharmacists Association, San Antonio, TX.

Plano Clark, V. L., Huddleston-Casas, C. A., Churchill, S. L., Green, D. O., & Garrett, A. L. (2008). Mixed methods approaches in family science research. *Journal of Family Issues, 29,* 1543–1566.

Plano Clark, V. L., & Wang, S. C. (2010). Adapting mixed methods research to multicultural counseling. In J. G. Ponterotto, J. M. Casas, L. A. Suzuki, & C. M. Alexander (Eds.), *Handbook of multicultural counseling* (3rd ed., pp. 427–438). Thousand Oaks, CA: Sage.

Polster, R. A., & Collins, D. (2018). Structured observation. In R. M. Grinnell, Jr., & Y. A. Unrau (Eds.), *Social work research and evaluation: Foundations of evidence-based practice* (11th ed.). New York: Oxford University Press.

Porter, R. E., & Samovar, L. A. (2006). Understanding intercultural communication: An overview. In L. A. Samovar, R. E. Porter, & E. R. McDaniel (Eds.), *Intercultural communication: A reader* (11th ed., pp. 6–16). Belmont, CA: Wadsworth.

Punch, K. F. (2014). *Introduction to research methods in education* (2nd ed.). Thousand Oaks, CA: Sage.

Pyrczak, F. (2016). *Evaluating research in academic journals: A practical guide to realistic education* (6th ed.). Los Angeles, CA: Pyrczak Publications.

Raines, J. C. (2011). Evaluating qualitative research studies. In R. M. Grinnell, Jr., & Y. A. Unrau (Eds.), *Social work research and evaluation: Foundations of evidence-based practice* (9th ed., pp. 488–503). New York: Oxford University Press.

Raines, J. C., & Massat, C. (2004). Getting published: A guide for the aspiring practitioner. *School Social Work Journal, 29,* 1–17.

Reid, W. J., & Smith, A. D. (1989). *Research in social work* (2nd ed.). New York: Columbia University Press.

Resnick, D., B. (2015, December 28). *What is ethics in research and why is it important?* Retrieved from https://www.niehs.nih.gov/research/resources/bioethics/whatis/index.cfm

Rosen, A. (2003). Evidence-based social work practice: Challenges and promise. *Social Work Research, 27,* 197–208.

Rosen, A., & Proctor, E. K. (2003). Practice guidelines and the challenge of effective practice. In A. Rosen & E. K. Proctor (Eds.), *Developing practice guidelines for social work intervention* (pp. 1–14). New York: Columbia University Press.

Ross, P. D. S. (2015). Locating evidence for practice. In M. Webber (Ed.), *Applying research evidence in social work practice* (pp. 22–43). London: Palgrave Macmillan.

Royse, D., Thyer, B., & Padgett, D. (2009). *Program evaluation: An introduction.* Belmont, CA: Wadsworth.

Rubin, A., & Babbie, E. (2017). *Research methods for social work* (9th ed.). New York: Cengage.

Rubin, A., & Parrish, D. (2009). Locating credible studies for evidence-based practice. In A. R. Roberts (Ed.), *Social workers' desk reference* (2nd ed., pp. 1127–1136). New York: Oxford University Press.

Russell, B. (1950). *An outline of intellectual rubbish. In Unpopular essays.* New York: Simon & Schuster.

Ryan, G. W., & Bernard, H. R. (2006). Techniques to identify themes. *Field Methods, 15,* 85–109.

Sackett, D. L., Rosenberg, W. M. C., Muir Gray, J. A., Haynes, R. B., & Richardson, W. S. (1996). Evidence-based medicine: What it is and what it isn't: It's about integrating individual clinical expertise and the best external evidence. *British Medical Journal, 31,* 71–72.

Sackett, D. L., Straus, S. E., Richardson, W. S., Rosenberg, W., & Haynes, R. B. (2000). *Evidence based medicine: How to practice and teach EBM* (2nd ed.). New York: Churchill Living.

Samovar, L. A., Porter, R. E., & Stefani, L. A. (1998). *Communication between cultures.* Belmont, CA: Wadsworth.

Sandelowski, M. (1986). The problem of rigor in qualitative research. *Advances in Nursing Science, 8,* 27–37.

Sayre, K. (2002). *Guidelines and best practices for culturally-competent evaluations.* Denver, CO: Colorado Trust.

Schutt, R. (2008). *Investigating the social world: The process and practice of research* (6th ed.). Thousand Oaks, CA: Pine Forge Press.

Shenton, A. (2004). Strategies for ensuring trustworthiness in qualitative research projects. *Education for Information, 22,* 63–75.

Sieppert, J. D., McMurtry, S. L., & McClelland, R. W. (2011). Utilizing existing statistics. In R. M. Grinnell, Jr., & Y. A. Unrau (Eds.), *Social work research and evaluation: Foundations of evidence-based practice* (9th ed., pp. 389–401). New York: Oxford University Press.

Silverman, D. (1997). The logics of qualitative research. In G. Miller & R. Dingwall (Eds.), *Context and method in qualitative research* (pp. 12–25). London: Sage.

Smith, G. (2018, September 15). Revealed: *The 17 characteristics of critical thinkers.* English @ High School. Retrieved from https://englishathighschool.com/2018/01/31/revealed-the-17-characteristics-of-critical-thinkers.

Stern, P. C. (1979). *Evaluating social science research.* New York: Oxford University Press.

Straus, S. E., Richardson, W. S., Glasziou, P., & Haynes, R. B. (2005*). Evidence-based medicine: How to practice and teach EBM* (3rd ed.). New York: Elsevier/Churchill Livingstone.

Strauss, A., & Corbin, J. (1998). *Basics of qualitative research: Techniques and procedures for developing grounded theory.* Thousand Oaks, CA: Sage.

Strunk, W., Jr., & E. B. White (1979). *The elements of style* (3rd ed.). New York: Macmillan.

Stuart, P. (2011). Historical research. In R. M. Grinnell, Jr., & Y. A. Unrau (Eds.), *Social work research and evaluation: Foundations of evidence-based practice* (9th ed., pp. 402–412). New York: Oxford University Press.

Studylib, (2019). https://studylib.net/Press

Tashakkori, A., & Creswell, J. W. (2007). Exploring the nature of research questions in mixed methods research [Editorial]. *Journal of Mixed Methods Research, 1*(3), 207–211.

Tashakkori, A., & Teddlie, C. (1998). *Mixed methodology: Combining qualitative and quantitative approaches.* Thousand Oaks, CA: Sage.

Tashakkori, A., & Teddlie, C. (Eds.). (2003). *Handbook of mixed methods in social and behavioral research.* Thousand Oaks, CA: Sage.

Tashiro, J. (2002). Exploring health promoting lifestyle behaviors of Japanese college women: Perceptions, practices, and issues. *Health Care for Women International, 23,* 59-70.

Thomas, D. C., & Inkson, K. (2009). *Cultural intelligence: Living and working globally* (2nd ed.). San Francisco: Berrett-Koehler.

Thyer, B. A. (1991). Guidelines for evaluating outcome studies on social work practice. *Research on Social Work Practice, 1,* 76–91.

Thyer, B. A. (1994). *Successful publishing in scholarly journals.* Thousand Oaks, CA: Sage.

Thyer, B. A., & Myers, L. L. (2007). *A social worker's guide to evaluating practice outcomes.* Alexandria VA: Council on Social Work Education.

Thyer, B. A., & Myers, L. L. (2009). *N* = 1 experiments and their role in evidence-based practice. In A. R. Roberts (Ed.), *Social workers' desk reference* (2nd ed., pp. 1176–1182). New York: Oxford University Press.

Thyer B. A., & Myers, L. L. (2010). Cultural diversity and social work practice: An evidenced-based approach. In B. A. Thyer, J. S. Wodarski, L. Myers, & D. F. Harrison (Eds.), *Human diversity and social work practice: An evidenced-based approach* (3rd ed., pp. 3–28). Springfield, IL: Charles C. Thomas.

Thyer, B. A, & Pignotti, M. G. (2015). *Science and pseudoscience in social work practice.* New York: Springer.

Tilbury, C., Osmond, J., & Scott, T. (2010). Teaching critical thinking in social work education: A literature review. *Advances in Social Work and Welfare Education, 11,* 31–50.

Tutty, L. M., Grinnell, R. M., & Williams, M. (1997). Research problems and questions. In R. M. Grinnell, Jr. (Ed.), *Social work research and evaluation: Quantitative and qualitative approaches* (5th ed., pp. 49–66). Itasca, IL: F. E. Peacock.

Tutty, L. M., Rothery, M. L., & Grinnell, R. M., Jr. (Eds.). (1996). *Qualitative research for social workers: Phases, steps, and tasks.* Boston: Allyn & Bacon.

Unrau, Y. A. (2011). Selecting a data collection method and data source. In R. M. Grinnell, Jr., & Y. A. Unrau (Eds.), *Social work research and evaluation: Foundations of evidence-based practice* (9th ed., pp. 413–426). New York: Oxford University Press.

Webber, M., & Carr, S. (2015). Applying research evidence in social work practice: Seeing beyond paradigms. In M. Webber (Ed.), Applying research evidence in social work *practice* (pp. 3–21). London: Palgrave Macmillan.

Weinbach, R. W., & Grinnell, R. M., Jr. (2017). *Statistics for social workers* (9th ed.). New York: Pearson.

Weine, S., Knafi, K., Feetham, S., Kulauzovic, Y, Klebic, A., Sclove, S., et al. (2005). A mixed methods study of refugee families engaging in multiple-family groups. *Family Relations, 54,* 558–568.

Williams, M., Grinnell, R. M., Jr., & Tutty, L. M. (1997). Research contexts. In R. M. Grinnell, Jr. (Ed.), *Social work research and evaluation: Quantitative and*

qualitative approaches (5th ed., pp. 25–45). Itasca, IL: F. E. Peacock.

Williams, M., Tutty, L. M., & Grinnell, R. M., Jr. (1995). *Research in social work: An introduction* (2nd ed.). Itasca, IL: F. E. Peacock.

Williams, M., Unrau, Y. A., & Grinnell, R. M., Jr. (1998). *Introduction to social work research* (3rd ed.). Itasca, IL: F. E. Peacock.

Wodarski, J. S., & Hopson, L. M. (2012). *Research methods for evidence-based practice.* Thousand Oaks, CA: Sage.

Wodarski, J. S., & Hopson, L. M. (2014). Issues for evidence-based practitioners. In R. M. Grinnell, Jr., & Y. A. Unrau (Eds.), *Social work research and evaluation: Foundations of evidence-based practice* (10th ed., pp. 218–231). New York: Oxford University Press.

The Writing Center. (2018). *Checklist for analyzing research material.* Chapel Hill, NC: University of North Carolina.

Yegidis, B. L., Weinbach, R. W., & Myers, L. L. (2018). *Research methods for social workers* (8th ed.). New York: Pearson.

Zayas, L. E., McMillen, J. C., Lee, M. Y., & Books, S. J. (2011). Challenges to quality assurance and improvement efforts in behavioral health organizations: A qualitative assessment. *Administration and Policy in Mental Health and Mental Health Services Research, 40,* 190–198.

# Index

"You asked me how many professors it takes to make a book index? The answer is three but they all get co-authored publications out of it."

*A* designs, 278–279
*AB* designs, 282–283
*ABA* and *ABAB* designs, 284–285
*ABC* and *ABCD* designs, 283
Absolute certainty, 19
Accountability, 2–29, 33–34
Adapting research processes, 133
Adapting research studies, 132
Alternate-form method of reliability, 222–223
Analysis of covariance, 299
Analysis of variance, 400
Analyzing data, 179–180, 190, 371–372
Anonymity of research participants, 99
Applied research, 10–11
Assent forms, 98–99
Assessing the trustworthiness of a study's results, 418–420
Assigning codes to categories, 413–414
Assuming, 19
Assumptions, unwarranted, 130–131
Attitudes of researchers, 62
Authority, as a way of knowing, 12–14
Availability sampling, 259–260
Awareness of researcher's values, 61

*B* designs, 279–280
*BAB* designs, 285–286

*BB₁* designs, 281
*BC* designs, 281–282
*BCBC* designs, 286
Beliefs and intuition, as a way of knowing, 15–16
Beneficence, 106
Bribery, 97–98

Café, Internet, 62
Causality research questions, 49
Causality-comparative interaction questions, 50
Causality-comparative research questions, 49–50
Changing realities, 150
Checklists, 243
Chi-square, 396
Classical experimental design, 321
Client objectives, setting measurable, 274–275
Clients as research participants, 95–96
Clinical experience and reports from experts or committees, 47
Cluster random sampling 258–259
Cohort study, 307–308
Collecting data, 173–174, 189–190, 330–364
Comparison group posttest-only design, 320
Comparison group pretest-posttest design, 319
Compensatory equalization, 318
Compensatory rivalry, 318
Completeness, 64
Composition of research questions, 49

Concepts, developing, 165–166
Concurrent validity, 225
Confidentiality of research participants, 99
Constant measurement errors, 227–228
Construct validity, 225–226
Consumer of research findings, 64–65
Content validity, 224
Contract errors, 228
Contributing partner, 65–66
Control groups, using, 299–300
Correlated variation, using, 299
Correlation, 397–398
Correspondence, 217
Council on Social Work Education, 6
Creating categories, 412
Creating causal relationships, 415
Creating metaphors, 417
Creating temporal relationships, 415
Creator and disseminator of research, 65
Credible evidence, 13–14
Criteria for research questions, 50–53
Criterion validity, 224–225
Critical thinking activities, 23–24
Critical thinking:
    definitions of, 21–22
    process, 23
    skills, 21
Cross-cultural research, concepts of, 120–121
Cross-sectional survey research design, 304–305
Cultural awareness, 109, 122–123, 130–131:
    definition of, 119
Cultural competence, definition of, 119
Cultural issues in research, 102
Cultural knowledge, definition of, 119
Cultural sensitivity, definition of, 119
Culturally competent research, 116–136
Culturally competent researchers, 129–134
Culture, impact of, 121–122
Culture, knowledge of, 131–132

Data analysis, ethical, 109
Data collection method, definition of, 333
Data collection plan, evaluation of, 361–362
Data collection, 108–109, 173–174, 179, 330–364
Data entry into a computer, 385–386
Data interpretation, 180
Data sources, 201, 333
Data vs information, 190
Data-collection method, selection of, 372–376
Data:
    ethical collection of, 108
    orientation to, 126
    types of, 333–324

Debriefing, 107–108
Deception, 97–98. 106–106
Decision making, 127
Demoralization, 318

Dependent *t*-test, 398–399
Dependent variables, 169–171
Description, purpose of research, 8
Descriptive research studies, 42
Descriptive single-subject designs, 282–284
Descriptive statistics, 174–175, 386–394
Descriptive-comparative research questions, 49
Diaries, 242
Differential selection of research participants,
    as a threat to internal validity, 316
Diffusion of treatments, 318
Displaying data, 276
Dissemination of research findings, 372
Domestic violence, understanding, 154–155
Drawing cluster diagrams, 416
Duplication, 147–148, 217–218

Egocentric thinking, 125
Enculturation, 123
Equipoise, 106
Error of central tendency, 228
Error:
    of leniency, 228
    of severity, 228
Establishing one's creditability, 418
Establishing our control of biases, 419–420
Ethical and cultural considerations of research
    questions, 38
Ethical and cultural issues, addressing, 179
Ethical and professional behavior, 6
Ethical concerns, professional, 16
Ethics and cultural issues in research, 173
Ethics, research, 94–115
Ethnocentrism, 122–123
Evaluate practice with individuals, families,
    groups, organizations, and communities, 6
Evaluation, purpose of research, 8–9
Evidence, credible, 13–14
Evidence-based:
    guidelines, 4546
    hierarchy, 44–47
    practice, 58–75
    process of, 70–71
    steps of, 68–70
Existence research questions, 47–48
Existing data, 334
Existing statistics, 349–352
Experience, as a way of knowing, 15
Experimental research, 46
Explanation, purpose of research, 8
Explanatory research studies, 42–44
Explanatory single-subject designs, 284–289
Exploration, purpose of research, 8
Exploratory research studies, 41–42
Exploratory single-subject designs, 275–282
External validity, 323–324
Extraneous variables, holding constant, 298

Face validity, 225
Fairness, 64

Firsthand data, 334
Frequency distributions, 388–390
Funding requirements, 113, 115

Gaps in the literature, identifying, 82
General problem area, refinement of, 165
Generalizability of research findings, 202
Graphically displaying data, 276
Group research designs, 292–328

Halo effect, 228
Historical data, 359–361
History, as a threat to internal validity, 313–314
Honesty, 62
Hudson's *Index of Self-Esteem,* 218
Hypotheses:
    construction of, 170–171
    directional, 170
    evaluation of, 171–173
    nondirectional, 170

Ideal experiments, characteristics of, 296–301
Identification of opposing views, 83
Identifying meaning units, 412
Independent *t*-test, 399
Independent variables, 169–171
Independent variables, manipulation of, 297
Individualism, 127
Inferential statistics, 175, 395–400
Information vs data, 190
Informed consent:
    elements of, 98
    obtainment of, 96–99
Instrumentation bias, 229
Instrumentation error, as a threat to Internal
    validity, 315
Interaction effects, as a threat to internal
    validity, 317
Intercultural communication skills, 123–124,
    131
Internal validity, 312–318
Internet Café, 62
Interpreting data, 371–372:
    building theory, 416–418
    research findings, 175–176
Interpretive way of thinking, 149–153
Interval measurement, 215
Inventories, 243
Inviews, 85–86

Journals, 242
Journals, keeping, 410
Justifying decisions already made, 112

Knowledge base, expanding of our, 82
Knowledge levels, 295–296

Levels of measurement, 213–216
Lifelong learning, 72–73
Limitations of research studies, 176

Literature reviews, 76–91:
    criteria of, 89
    definition of, 79–80
    evaluation of, 90
    logic of, 81
    organization of, 87–89
    tips, 80–81
Logical correctness, 64
Logs, 243
Longitudinal research design, 305–311
Looking for missing links, 417

Macro-level culture, 121
Making matrixes, 416
Matched-pairs method of random assignment,
    300–301
Maturation, as a threat to internal validity, 314
Mean, 392
Meaningful research products, 133–143
Measurability, striving toward, 146
Measurement errors, 227–230
Measurement, 210–233:
    of variables, 102, 176
    levels of, 213–216
    sensitivity, 229
Measures of central tendency, 390–392
Measures of variability, 392–394
Measuring instruments, 234–248:
    selection of, 219–227
Measuring observations, 18
Median, 392
Member checking, 419
Micro-level culture, 121
Mixed-methods data collection methods, 361
Mixed-methods research approach, 153–155,
    198–208:
    advantages of, 204–205
    disadvantages of, 205–206
    example of, 157
    research studies, 140–141
Mode, 391–392
Moral and ethical obligations, 16–17
Mortality, as a threat to internal validity, 316–
    317
Multiple-baseline designs, 286–289
Multiple-treatment interference, 324
Myths, 13–14

Narrative interviewing, 353–365
National Association of Social Workers, 7
Nominal measurement, 214
Nonexperimental research, 47
Nonprobability sampling, 259–262:
    definition of, 255
Nonreactivity of measuring instruments, 220–
    221
Nonverbal communication, 124
Noticing contradictory evidence, 417
Numbers vs words, 190

Objectivity, striving toward, 147
Observations, 18
Observer reliability, 223
Observing and/or measuring, 19
One-group posttest-only research design, 302–304
One-group pretest-posttest design, 311–312
One-group research designs, 302–312
Ordinal measurement, 214–215
Original data, 334
Outcome measures, selection of, 275–276
Overviews, 85

Pace of life, 128
Panel study, 308–311
Participant observation, 355–358
Political and social considerations of research questions, 38–39
Populations, defining, 254
Positivistic way of thinking, 146–148
Practice-informed research and research informed practice, 6
Presenting themes or theory, 417–418
Previewing qualitative data, 410
Previews, 85
Probability sampling, definition of, 254
Problem identification and question formulation, 188–189
Professional ethical concerns, 16
Professional judgments, forming, 20–29
Public relations, safeguarding, 112
Pure research, 9–10
Purposive sampling, 260

Qualitative data analysis, 406–424
Qualitative data collection plan, assessing, 420–421
Qualitative data, 334
Qualitative research approach, 149–153, 186–195:
    advantages of, 192–193
    commonalities of all, 151
    disadvantages of, 193
    evaluation of, 193–194
    studies, 40, 141
Quantification, 217
Quantitative data analysis, 174, 382–402
Quantitative data, 334
Quantitative research approach, 145–148, 160–183:
    research studies, 40, 141
    steps within, 163–176
Quasi-experimental research, 46
Quota sampling, 260

Random assignment to groups, 300
Random errors, 228–229
Randomized posttest-only control group design, 322
Range, 392

Ratio measurement, 215–216
Reacher bias, 324
Reactive effects of research participants, as a threat to internal validity, 317
Reality, 150
Refining and reorganizing categories, 414
Reid-Gundlach *Social Service Satisfaction Scale*, 241
Relations between groups, as a threat to internal validity, 318
Relationship research questions, 49
Relationships between variables, 297
Reliability of measuring instruments, 221–223
Research approaches:
    comparison of, 191–192
    selection of, 142–144
Research consumer, 64–65
Research creator and disseminator of research, 65
Research design and data collection, 370–371
Research designs:
    ethical, 105–106
    group, 292–328
    single-subject, 270–291
Research ethics, 94–115
Research findings:
    sharing of, 62
    use of, 17
Research participants, ethical recruitment of, 104
Research problems, identification of, 163–164
Research project, contextualizing of, 82–83
Research proposals:
    writing qualitative, 449–462
    writing quantitative, 426–437
Research questions:
    clarity of, 51
    classifications of, 47–50
    ethical, 100
    ethical and culturally sensitivity of, 53
    factors affecting, 34–39
    feasibility of, 52
    formulating, 33–55
    precision of, 51
    relevancy of, 52
    researchability of, 52
Research reports:
    ethical, 110–111
    writing qualitative, 462–465
    writing quantitative, 437–443
Research results:
    dissemination of, 180–181
    misuse of, 112–113
Research roles, 63–67:
    integration of, 66–67
Research settings, 265
Research studies, pure, 9–10
Research study, designing of, 189
Research teams, working with, 120
Research vs practice, 67

Research:
    applied, 10–11
    definition of, 72
    pure, 9–10
    purpose of, 8–9
Researchers:
    attitudes, 62
    value systems of, 37–38, 151
Retrospective baselines, 289–291
Reversal designs, 284–286
Revising, 20
Rival hypotheses, controlling for, 297–298
Roles of researchers, 63–67

Sample, 103–104, 173:
    quality, 263
    selection of, 176
    size, 262–263
Sampling, 250–267
Sampling frames, 254
Scientific method of inquiry, 138–159
Scientific method, process of, 17–20
Searching for information, 83–84
Secondary content data, 358–359
Secondary data, 345–349
Secondhand data, 334
Selection-treatment interaction, 323
Sensitivity of measuring instruments, 220
Sharing research findings, 62
Simple random sampling, 255
Single-subject designs, 268–291:
    definition of, 271–272
    requirements of, 272–276
Snowball sampling, 261
Sociocentric thinking, 125–126
Specificity of variables, 323–324
Split-half method of reliability, 223
Staff performances, 114
Stakeholders, working with, 120, 132
Standard deviation, 392–394
Standardization, 217
Standardized measuring instruments, 244–247:
    advantages of, 245
    disadvantages of, 246
    evaluation of, 247
    locating, 246
Standardized procedures, striving toward, 148
Statistical regression, as a threat to internal
    validity, 315–316

Storing and managing information, 84
Stratified random sampling, 257

Structured observations, 341–345
Subjects vs research participants, 150
Summative instruments, 244
Survey questionnaires, 335–341
Systematic random sampling, 256–257
Systematic reviews and meta analyses, 45

Target problems, 274–275
Test-retest method of reliability, 221–222
Testing effects, as a threat to internal validity,
    315
Testing, 19–20
Theoretical frameworks, 86
Theoretical stances, 203
Thinking:
    egocentric, 125
    interpretatively, 149–153
    logically, completely, and fairly, 63
    positivistically, 146–147
    sociocentric, 125–126
Time-order of variables, controlling for, 296–297
Tradition, 128:
    as a way of knowing, 14–15
Transcribing qualitative data, 409
Trend study, 305–307
Triangulation, 419
Two-group research designs, 319–324

Uncertainty principle, 106
Unit of analysis, 273
Utility of measuring instruments, 219–220

Validity of measuring instruments, 224–227
Variables:
    attributes of, 164–169
    dependent, 169–171
    describing, 216–219
    identification of, 166
    independent, 169–171
    selection of, 164–172
Verbal communication, 124

Ways of knowing, 11–17
Words vs numbers, 190